Structured Programming in Turbo Pascal

Structured Programming in Turbo Pascal

SECOND EDITION

L. Wayne Horn

Pensacola Junior College

Prentice Hall
Englewood Cliffs, New Jersey 07632

Library of Congress Cataloging-in-Publication

Horn, Lister Wayne.
Structured programming in Turbo Pascal / L. Wayne Horn. –– 2nd ed.
  p.   cm.
Includes bibliographical references and index.
ISBN 0-13-311721-9 (paper)
  1. Pascal (Computer program language)   2. Turbo Pascal (Computer file)   3. Structured programming.   I. Title.
QA76.73.P2H67   1994
005.265––dc20   94-35625
                                                          CIP

Editorial director: Dave Riccardi
Managing editor: Linda Behrens
Editor-in-chief/Acquisitions editor: Marcia Horton
Editorial/production supervision: Jennifer Wenzel
Copy editor: Brian Baker

Cover design: Rosemarie Votta
Cover photo: McCormick/The Stock Market
Manufacturing buyer: Lori Bulwin
Editorial assistant: Dolores Mars
Supplements editor: Alice Dworkin

©1995, 1990 by Prentice-Hall, Inc.
A Simon & Schuster Company
Englewood Cliffs, New Jersey 07632

The author and publisher of this book have used their best efforts in preparing this book. These efforts include the development, research, and testing of the theories and programs to determine their effectiveness. The author and publisher make no warranty of any kind, expressed or implied, with regard to these programs or the documentation contained in this book. The author and publisher shall not be liable in any event for incidental or consequential damages in connection with, or arising out of, the furnishing, performance, or use of these programs.

Printed in the United States of America

10 9 8 7 6 5 4 3 2 1

ISBN 0-13-311721-9

Prentice-Hall International (UK) Limited, *London*
Prentice-Hall of Australia Pty. Limited, *Sydney*
Prentice-Hall Canada Inc., *Toronto*
Prentice-Hall Hispanoamericana, S.A., *Mexico*
Prentice-Hall of India Private Limited, *New Delhi*
Prentice-Hall of Japan, Inc., *Tokyo*
Simon & Schuster Asia Pte. Ltd., *Singapore*
Editora Prentice-Hall do Brasil, Ltda., *Rio de Janeiro*

TRADEMARK INFORMATION

Apple, Apple II, AppleIIe, and ProDos are registered trademarks of Apple Computer, Inc.

IBM, IBM PC, and IBM Personal System /2 are registered trademarks of International Business Machines Corporation.

CP/M is a registered trademark of Digital Research, Inc.

Intel is a registered trademark of Intel Corporation.

WordStar is a registered trademark of MicroPro International Corporation.

Turbo Pascal is a registered trademark of Borland International, Inc.

MS-DOS is a registered trademark of Microsoft Corporation.

Motorola 6502 is probably a trademark of Motorola Corporation.

Z80 is probably a trademark of Zilog Corporation.

Contents

6 Control Structures: Iteration *263*

7 Data Types *331*

8 String Data and Functions *381*

Preface

This text presents concepts of structured programming in the context of Turbo Pascal. There is a continuing emphasis on problem solving and principles of program design and testing. The book is suitable for use with later versions (6.0 and beyond), as well as earlier versions (5.0 and 5.5), of Turbo Pascal. All of the material required for a first course in computer science is covered, and additional material can be used for enrichment if desired.

NEW FEATURES IN THIS EDITION

New Chapter on Graphics

This is a major new chapter on using the Graph Unit in Turbo Pascal to create graphics screens involving text, lines, ellipses, and so forth. Case studies in this chapter include graphing a function and creating presentation graphics (a bar graph and a pie chart).

New Chapter on Units

Not only does the text cover using the Turbo Pascal-supplied units (including System, Printer, Crt, Dos, and Graph), but it also covers techniques students can use to create their own units. Case studies in this chapter include the creation of a unit containing statistical functions and presentation graphics tools.

New Chapter on Objects

The concepts of object-oriented programming are explored in the context of the Turbo Pascal object data type. Concepts of encapsulation, inheritance, and polymorphism are explained, as is the Turbo Pascal implementation of these ideas. The case study in this chapter is an implementation of an abstract data type.

Turbo Pascal 7.0

All examples and programs in the book have been revised and tested using Turbo Pascal 7.0. Material on Turbo Pascal 5.0 and 5.5 has been retained (in Appendix E) for use in schools that have not upgraded to one of the newer versions of Turbo Pascal.

Syntax Diagrams

In addition to the syntax descriptions used in the previous edition, this edition includes a full complement of syntax diagrams (Appendix C).

System-related Exercises

Appendix H contains descriptions of three separate systems, together with related programming assignments suitable for use with each chapter of the text. These assignments can be used by instructors who wish to have students work on a single project throughout the course, rather than write programs for several different problem areas.

Early Introduction of Text Files

This edition includes an introduction to Text files in Chapter 3. Subsequent chapters revisit the topic and expand on it as appropriate. Each later chapter contains exercises that are file oriented, as well as exercises that require interactive data entry.

Other New Material

Material on preconditions and postconditions related to procedures and loops has been added. A detailed explanation of the pitfalls encountered in using global identifiers is included. The material on value versus variable parameters is expanded and includes several new examples that clarify the difference between the two types of parameters. A new section on using the Dos unit is included.

OTHER FEATURES

Logical Organization

The text is divided into 15 chapters of approximately equal length. Each chapter has a major theme that ties its content together. For example, the three major iteration statements are grouped together in one chapter, making it easier for the student to grasp the similarities and differences among the statements and to make an informed choice among them. Another chapter gathers together related ideas about data types into one coordinated presentation. Not only does this method of organizing the material make the subject easier to teach and learn, but it also makes it easier to use the book as a reference, since related topics are grouped together.

Emphasis on Problem Solving

The text includes numerous case studies that are consistently presented in terms of an analysis of the problem; a design of the procedure required to solve the problem (presented in the form of pseudocode); the completed solution, including the program; a structure diagram where appropriate; and a sample execution of the program. Problem solving is one of the most troublesome areas in teaching programming; students need repeated reinforcement of basic systematic problem-solving techniques that they can apply in their own work.

Emphasis on Program Documentation and Readability

In program examples presented in the text, pseudocode from the program design is incorporated into the Pascal program in the form of comments, and careful attention is given to consistent formatting of source code. Students are encouraged to incorporate similar practices into their own programs to enhance readability and to make programs self-documenting.

Emphasis on Top-Down Program Design

Top-down program design at the pseudocode level is used consistently in descriptions of problem analysis and the derivation of complete program designs. The purpose of this practice is to reinforce its power continually and to encourage students to use it as a matter of habit in their own problem solving.

Emphasis on Program Debugging and Testing

Many chapters have separate sections devoted to program debugging and testing. A separate appendix is included covering the integrated debugging facility of Turbo Pascal, Version 7.0. This emphasis will help students do a more thorough job of debugging and testing programs—a very important part of the programmer's task that students often fail to perform adequately.

Presentation of Standard as well as Turbo Pascal

Differences between ANSI standard and Turbo Pascal are presented at appropriate points in the text. Where appropriate, technical details of the Turbo Pascal implementation are discussed. This will help students make effective use of Turbo Pascal, as well as prepare them to use other versions if the need arises.

Early Introduction of Procedures

The concept of procedures (without parameter lists) is presented very early in the text (Chapter 3). The use of procedures and functions to break a program into appropriately sized and related modules is a recurring theme throughout the rest of the book. This encourages students to begin using procedures almost from the start and contributes to better program design. Such an early exposure to procedures makes the later more rigorous presentation of procedures with parameter lists in Chapter 5 much more comprehensible and effective.

Effective Use of Structure Diagrams and Data-Flow Diagrams

Structure diagrams are introduced at the same time as the introduction of procedures as a method for designing and documenting a program. When procedures with parameters are introduced, the structure diagrams are converted to data-flow diagrams showing the passing parameters among program modules. These diagrams make it easier for students to visualize abstract relationships.

Wide Selection of Subject Matter for Examples and Exercises

Case studies and exercises are carefully chosen to include a representative sample of general-interest, business, mathematical, and scientific subject areas. There should be a sufficient number of examples and exercises in each chapter to keep the interest of students with a wide variety of backgrounds and ability levels. (Over 150 exercises are contained in the text.)

Integration of Text and Software

The text includes a student software supplement containing the source programs for over 120 examples presented in the text. (This is approximately twice as many examples as in the first edition.) The text includes numerous "Time Out" exercises that often direct the student to test and/or make modifications to programs contained on the disk. This makes it possible for the student to try out new ideas and concepts in the context of a working program, without having to write a complete program just to test one new statement or concept. Such an approach makes effective use of the computer as a teaching tool and is especially appropriate when students have ready access to computers in the classroom, in the lab, or at home.

Complete Learning Aids Incorporated into the Text

In addition to the "Time Out" exercises, which are placed at regular intervals in the body of the text, each chapter includes review questions that can be used as the basis for class discussion or homework and programming exercises. The programming exercises are drawn from a variety of areas and are chosen to enable the student to practice the concepts contained in the chapter. A comprehensive glossary is also included. In the text, terms printed in bold are included in the glossary.

Comprehensive Instructor's Manual is Available

For each chapter in the text, the instructor's manual contains a chapter overview, learning objectives, answers to review questions, test questions in multiple-choice format, and an overview of programming exercises. Software that accompanies the instructor's manual includes the source code for solutions to all exercises. Masters for overhead transparencies round out the instructor's materials. A computerized test-generation system is also available.

The author wishes to thank Marcia Horton of Prentice Hall, who believed in this project and enabled it to be completed. Thanks are also extended to Hamid R. Arabnia of the University of Georgia; William J. Joel; Peter M. Schleppenbach of Los Angeles Pierce College; Michael Olan of the University of Wisconsin-La Crosse; Richard S. Schultz of Miramar College; Charlene Wagstaff of San Jacinto College; and Bruce Sisko of Belleville Area College.

Program Directory

---

[1]Contained on disk but not reproduced in text.

1

Introduction to Computers and Programming

Welcome to the world of computers! This book will help you understand what computers are, what they can do, and, perhaps most importantly, how you can use a computer to solve problems. You will find that the computer is a very valuable tool for a virtually unlimited number of tasks, but, like any powerful tool, it requires some effort to learn how to use the tool effectively. You will learn by reading, by analyzing examples provided in the book and on the accompanying disk, and, most of all, by experimenting with solutions of your own. If you approach the computer as a new "toy"—a very powerful and interesting toy—and begin the process of "playing" with that toy early on, you should master the subject painlessly; indeed, most people actively enjoy the process.

In this first chapter you learn basic concepts about computers and their use. You will be able to solve certain simple but interesting problems using the programming language Pascal. Once basic concepts are mastered, you will devote the remainder of your study to techniques for solving problems and the details of Pascal.

1.1   COMPUTER HARDWARE

The computer is an electronic device that is capable of processing data—numbers and ideas expressed in symbolic form. A variety of operations can be performed on data to transform them into a more useful form. Operations such as calculation, summarization, sorting, storing, retrieving, and reproducing are performed by the computer under the control of a **program**—a set of instructions specifying exactly what the machine is to do and the order in which the operations are to be performed. The fact that computers are programmable accounts for a great deal of their utility and power. The same machine can solve an almost infinite variety of problems if a program designed to solve the problem at hand is available. The practical usefulness of the computer results from its speed. A computer can execute program instructions at the rate of several million instructions per second—millions of times faster than a human could do the same task.

The physical components of computers—the keyboard, video monitor, disk drives, circuit boards, and so forth—are called hardware. **Computer hardware** should be carefully distinguished from the programs that make the computer work, which are called **computer software**. Computers come in a wide variety of shapes and sizes, but all share the same basic components. A computer may be visualized as being composed of the five **basic units** shown in Figure 1.1.

The **input unit** is designed to transfer data from the outside world into the computer. Input may be numeric (e.g., the amount of a purchase or a person's birth date) or alphabetic (e.g., a description of an item that is purchased or the name of a person). In either case, the input unit translates the data into binary code (a series of 1's and 0's) suitable for processing by the computer. Input into most small computers is provided by a keyboard similar to a typewriter and a small pointing device called a mouse. Touching a key on the keyboard transmits a character or command to the system. Moving the mouse and/or pressing one of the buttons on the mouse (called "clicking")

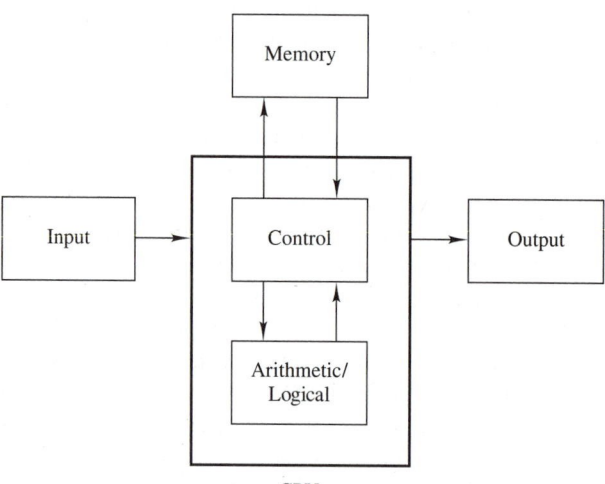

Figure 1.1 Basic units of a computer.

can also be used to enter a command into or communicate other types of information to the computer.

The **output unit** is designed to transfer data that have been processed by the computer to some useful external form. The cathode-ray tube (CRT) screen and the printer are examples of output devices found on most computers. Both of these devices receive signals in binary form (called digital signals—a series of 1's and 0's) and translate them to meaningful symbols on the screen or the paper. Output displayed on the screen is often called *soft copy* to distinguish it from the more permanent document produced by the printer, which is called *hard copy*.

The **memory unit** is designed to store programs and data during the time that a computer is solving a problem. Memory is divided into addressable locations; each location in memory is capable of being accessed by the specification of its address. In the actual machine, each address is a number; however, we are able to assign symbolic names (descriptive words) to memory locations when we write programs in Pascal. Moreover, memory is randomly accessible—that is, each memory location can be read from or written to with equal speed. Memory locations are used interchangeably to store program instructions and data, depending on the needs of the particular problem. This characteristic of computers makes them very flexible; the concept is attributed to the mathematician John von Neumann.

The **arithmetic/logical unit** is used to carry out arithmetic operations (add, subtract, multiply, and divide) and logical operations such as the comparison of two data items. This unit acts as the calculator for the computing system by performing required tasks on data passed to it from memory.

The **control unit** is used to execute program instructions. Once a program has been loaded into a computer's memory (a separate step in the process of using the computer to solve a problem), the control unit executes the program one instruction at a time. Program instructions may call for input, produce output, perform computations, describe comparisons to be made, or call for the next instruction in the program to be taken from somewhere other than the next sequential location. (Instructions of the latter type are called *branching instructions*; they give the computer the ability to select among alternative actions and the ability to repeat a series of instructions.) In any case, the control unit copies the instruction from memory and executes the instruction by signaling the appropriate unit and passing required data to it. When the instruction has been successfully completed, the control unit fetches the next instruction and repeats the process. This action is automatic; once a program has been placed in memory and the command to begin execution has been given, the computer user has nothing more to do than to supply data as needed by the program. At the conclusion of the program, a special "halt" instruction causes the computer to stop and wait for another task.

As shown in Figure 1.1, the control and arithmetic/logical units are usually referred to collectively as the **central processing unit** (CPU). The smallest CPUs can be made up of a single microchip and hence are called **microprocessors.** Two of the most popular families of microprocessors are the Intel 8086 (and its relatives the 80286, 80386, and 80486), which are used by IBM and many other manufacturers, and the Motorola 68000 family, which is used in Apple Macintosh computers. Computers such as the IBM Value Point, IBM PS/2, and Apple Macintosh are called **microcomputers**, or personal computers. They are the most popular type of computer today because of their ability to perform a great many useful functions at a relatively low cost.

Microcomputers are most often single-user systems; that is, they are dedicated to a single person's problem-solving activities. Somewhat larger systems are called minicomputers; these systems allow several users to be connected to a single, somewhat more powerful CPU, which has the capability of supporting faster input and output devices. Minicomputers are often found in scientific laboratories and in some schools. Still more powerful systems are called mainframes. They support a larger number of users, who are often located at great distance from the CPU. Telecommunications networks are used to communicate with the central computer. Mainframes are used by large businesses, governmental agencies, and most colleges and universities.

Microcomputers are made up of several components, as shown in Figure 1.2. A keyboard is used to type in commands to the system and to supply data to programs. Some systems have a mouse pointing device attached. A CRT screen (which may be monochrome or have color capabilities) is used to echo what is typed at the keyboard and as a basic output device for information not needed in permanent form. The screen will have some type of visible cursor—a symbol that shows where the next data to be displayed on the screen will appear (see Figure 1.3). Most systems have a printer attached. Most printers have the capability of printing alphanumeric data (letters and numbers) and also graphic data (pictures). The system unit houses the CPU and memory. Memory is measured in bytes; one byte can store one character. The memory units on current microcomputers are capable of storing at least 1,000,000 characters, and most have memories of 4,000,000 characters or more. Two commonly used terms describing memory are *kilobyte* (abbreviated K), which is 1,024 bytes, and *megabyte* (abbreviated M), which is 1,240,000 bytes. The system unit also contains a power transformer to reduce the voltage of power from the ordinary 110–120 volts to the much lower voltages required by electronic devices and the circuits used to communicate between the CPU and the other devices in the system.

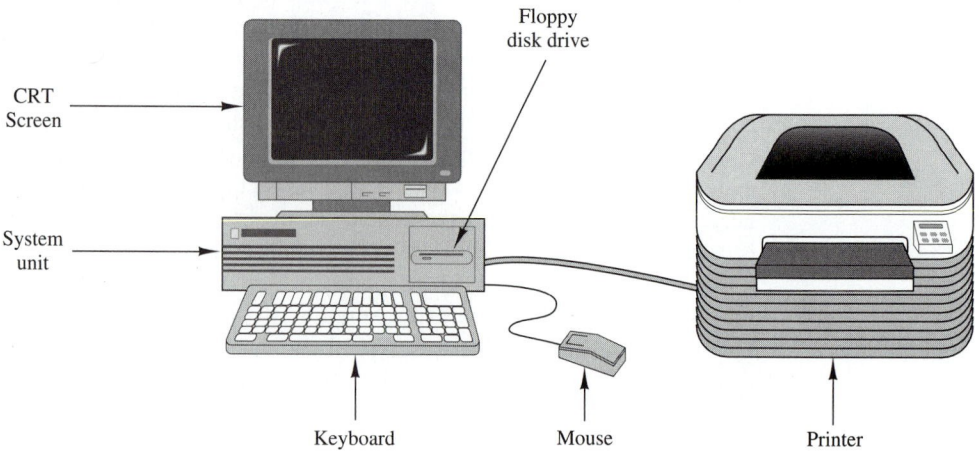

Figure 1.2 Components of a microcomputer system.

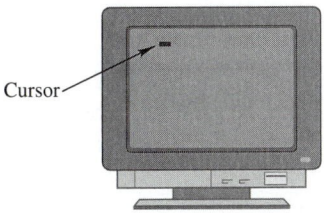

Cursor

Figure 1.3 Typical screen with cursor.

A very important component of any microcomputer system, which has been mentioned only in passing up to now, is the **disk drive**. This device is used to read information from and write information on **floppy disks**. A **disk** is classified as **secondary memory** because it is accessed through the input/output units, as contrasted with the main memory, which is connected directly to the CPU. Disks are used for long-term storage of programs and data. They are removable and, if cared for properly, are almost permanent. Disks are nonvolatile; that is, they do not require a constant power source to retain their content, because a magnetic recording medium is used and data is stored on the disk as tiny spots of magnetic flux representing 1's or 0's. (By contrast, main memory is volatile, requiring constant power. If a computer is turned off, the content of its main memory is erased, but the content of the secondary memory—the disk—is not harmed.) One of the basic tasks that must be carried out when you use a computer is to save the content of main memory on secondary storage for later use. Fortunately, this is easy to do because a command to carry out such a function is usually readily available.

A floppy disk is a circular piece of mylar (a type of plastic) that has been coated with iron oxide. Data is read from and written onto the disk by a small electromagnet called a read/write head, which is inside the disk drive. The disk is encased in a sleeve with an opening that is used to give the read/write head access to the disk. The circular hole in the center of the disk is used by the disk drive to rotate the disk past the read/write head, thereby giving the head access to all parts of the disk. Information is recorded on the disk in a series of concentric circular tracks. The read/write head is moved by the disk drive to read or write information on different tracks. Typical capacities for floppy disks are 720 K and 1.4 M, depending on the type of disk and the type of disk drive installed.

A basic unit of storage for data is the file. Files contain related data in much the same way that a file folder in an office contains related items. A file may contain data regarding the employees of a company, the items in an inventory, observations of an experiment, a letter to someone, a program to solve a problem, and so forth. Files are accessed by name. The name usually is helpful in deciding what is in the file. For example, Turbo Pascal is usually in a file called Turbo. The disk contains a directory of all the files on it so that the system can retrieve data from files as needed.

Because of the way they are constructed, floppy disks are somewhat fragile. The user should take care to store disks at moderate temperatures, away from any source of magnetism. The exposed surface of a disk should never be touched, and the disk should never be exposed to dust or moisture. Inexpensive carrying cases for disks are available and are highly advised. With proper care, a floppy disk is a very satisfactory and inexpensive form of storage.

All current microcomputer models have an alternative type of disk drive called a **hard disk**. Like a floppy disk, a hard disk is a form of secondary storage, but the capacity of a hard disk is much larger than that of a floppy disk. Hard disks typically can store from 80,000,000 to 250,000,000 characters of data or more. Most software packages, including recent versions of Turbo Pascal,[1] require a hard disk.

1.2   COMPUTER SOFTWARE

Computer hardware is completely useless without software—programs that enable the computer to work. There are three major classifications of software: system software, application software, and program-development software. **System software** is used to perform routine management functions required by all computer users. Tasks such as loading programs, managing the content of disks, and handling error conditions are performed by system software. **Application software** is used to perform more specific tasks related to the requirements of individual problems. For example, word-processing software makes it easy to store, revise, and print documents such as letters and reports. **Program-development software** is used to help in the task of writing and testing programs. This software is used to develop both application and system software. Numerous programming languages—including Basic, Fortran, COBOL, Ada, C, and, of course, Pascal—are available and widely used. Languages differ from one another in capabilities and intended usage. This section is devoted to application software; succeeding sections contain more detail on system software and program-development software.

It is useful to subdivide application software into two categories: application packages and custom-designed programs. An application package is software designed to solve a general class of problems, with the user providing details of the specific problem he or she wishes to solve. Examples for application packages include word processors designed to facilitate the creation of documents; spreadsheets, which enable the manipulation of data in two-dimensional tables; data-base management systems, which facilitate the storage and retrieval of data; graphics systems, which perform the task of creating graphic images; communications packages and network software, which handle the details of communications between multiple systems; and a variety of specific packages designed for accounting, entertainment, investment, education, music, and so forth. Custom-designed software is software written to the exact specification of a user's problem. The type of problem at hand will often dictate the type of application software that is most appropriate. Many times, custom-designed software is much easier to use than application package software, which requires more effort on the part of the user to learn its various commands and capabilities. It is sometimes more cost effective to purchase an application package to solve a problem than to write a custom program, because of the time and effort involved in the design and creation of custom programs. On the other hand, the limitations imposed by application packages may make it impossible to solve a particular problem

---

[1]The software development system itself requires a hard disk but programs developed with Turbo Pascal usually are small enough to be placed on a floppy disk if desired.

with a package. Some problems are sufficiently unique to preclude the use of a package. Sometimes also, the use of package software is too cumbersome and time consuming or requires more expertise than the intended user has. In these cases, it is advantageous to develop custom-designed software. The primary focus of this text is the development of custom-designed programs using the programming language Pascal.

1.3   OPERATING SYSTEMS

Another term for system software is **operating system**. As the name implies, this software facilitates the task of operating the computer. An operating system is the user's basic means of communicating with the computer and is what allows him or her to perform useful work with the computer. An operating system is almost always supplied by the manufacturer of a microcomputer. It consists of a number of programs needed to perform various fundamental operations.

The operating system is usually installed on the hard disk in its own directory. In order to make use of the computer, the user merely has to turn on the power to the system unit and monitor. The operating system is loaded into memory from the hard drive automatically (a process called "booting" the system)[2].

Once the system is on and the operating system is fully operational, the user can enter commands into the operating system as desired. The operating system will interpret each command and carry out the desired operation. Tasks that can be carried out with the operating system include the following, among others:

1. **Load a program and begin execution.** The system will copy a program from disk into memory and begin execution of the program at an appropriate instruction.

2. **Format a disk.** This operation is required to prepare a new disk for use. The system verifies that the disk is error free and creates the nucleus of a directory on the disk so that files can be stored on it. Sometimes a portion of the operating system is also placed on the new disk as a part of this operation.

3. **Copy some or all of one disk to another.** This is necessary to create a backup copy of software or to give software to another user. *Caution*: Some software is copyrighted. This means that it can be copied for backup purposes only; it cannot be legally copied and distributed to other users. Turbo Pascal is such a software package. Other software may be copy protected in such a way that the operating system copy function cannot copy the software at all.

4. **Obtain a listing of files contained on a disk.** This enables a user to determine what files are available on a disk and, usually, certain information about each file, such as its size and type.

5. **Delete files from a disk.** Deleting files removes files no longer needed and frees up space on the disk.

---

[2]The term "booting" is derived from the early days of computing, when the user was required to enter a short program called a "bootstrap program" manually into the memory of the machine as the first step in loading the operating system.

6. **Rename a file.** This enables the user to change the name of a file on a disk.
7. **Set the time and/or date.** Most systems have a built-in clock and calendar, which can be manipulated by the user.

Unfortunately, there is no industrywide standard for operating systems. Each computer has one or more operating systems designed for the unique characteristics of that computer. IBM microcomputers use an operating system called PC DOS (personal computer disk-operating system). Other computers that are essentially equivalent to the IBM microcomputers (called clones or compatibles in the industry) use MS DOS (Microsoft disk-operating system). PC DOS and MS DOS are nearly identical insofar as the user is concerned.

MS DOS and PC DOS have undergone numerous revisions over the years. Versions 4.0 and later of the operating system feature an interface called DOSSHELL that enables the user to perform some activities by selecting among alternatives presented in a menu format. Despite improvements in DOS, it has yet to incorporate a graphical user interface (GUI)—a system popularized by the Apple Macintosh. In a GUI, the user can perform many actions by pointing to a picture called an icon and selecting an action by clicking a button on the mouse. A package called Microsoft Windows has made this interface available to users of IBM microcomputers or clones. Borland has introduced another version of Turbo Pascal for the Windows environment; Turbo Pascal 5.0, 5.5, 6.0, and 7.0 are all intended to be run as DOS applications, since they make no use of the added facilities provided by Microsoft Windows.

1.4   DATA PROCESSING CONCEPTS

The terms *data* and *information* are frequently used in connection with computers. Sometimes they are used as synonyms, but it is actually useful to make a distinction between the two. We may think of data as a collection of symbols that record some event that has occurred. People have always found it useful to record their thoughts in symbols—be they pictographs painted on the side of a cave, cuneiform characters etched on a clay tablet, or characters written on a piece of paper. These symbols are data out of which meaning can be derived. The meaning associated with data is information. The process of deriving meaning from data may be as simple as pronouncing the words represented by grouped letters, or it may be much more complex.

An example will help clarify the relationship between data and information. Consider the United States census. First, data is collected. (Workers place symbols on printed forms.) Then, after all of the forms are collected and analyzed, a variety of summaries are created that contain information useful to government agencies and private industry. The original data is too voluminous to be of any real value to anyone. Only after the data has been processed and concentrated does it yield anything of value—the thing that we call information.

People have been using a variety of means for processing data, but increasingly, the computer has become a tool of choice for this task. The computer is able to manipulate the data directly to yield needed information in a timely and cost-effective manner. Following is a list of the types of tasks that are involved in data processing, whether performed by a computer or by some other means:

1. Data collection—the data is recorded by some means, perhaps in a form that is directly readable by an electronic device.
2. Data storage—the data is stored for later use, perhaps on a disk or tape.
3. Data retrieval—the data must be retrieved from storage when needed.
4. Categorization—data is placed into suitable categories to facilitate processing. (For example, in processing census data, people are classified as employed or unemployed, married, single, divorced or widowed, etc.)
5. Computation—direct computations can be made on numeric data. (In the census data, for example, a person's age can be computed from his or her date of birth.)
6. Summarization—various sums, averages, and other statistics can be computed. (This is particularly important when people undertake to winnow information from a large mass of data, such as the census.)
7. Sorting—data can be rearranged from the order in which it was gathered into some more useful sequence. (For example, census data can be sorted by ZIP code to group all people in a given area together, to facilitate the generation of information about that area.)
8. Reporting—information must be reported to potential users in some form, such as a printed report or on a computer display.

As you study programming and problem solving, you will find that much of what you learn is directly related to one or more of these fundamental data processing steps.

In a computing environment, data is organized in a variety of ways to facilitate the processing tasks that must be performed on it. The most basic unit of data is the **character**. A character may be classed as alphabetic (A . . Z, a . . z), numeric (0 . . 9) or other (such as a period, comma, and so forth). Characters are stored in the computer as numeric codes. The most common coding system is called ASCII, which is an abbreviation for American Standard Code for Information Interchange. See Appendix D for a complete listing of the ASCII code. A group of related characters make up a **field** or **data item**. (The two terms are synonyms.) For example, a person's last name, a birth date, a street address, and a ZIP code are examples of fields. A group of related fields is called a **record**. In the census example, all of the data collected for one person would constitute a record made up of numerous fields. A group of related records is called a **file**. The operating system organizes data into files that have names and locations on the storage media. In order to process a file, a program must "know" the name of the file and the layout of its records so that the data items can be properly interpreted and processed. Later in the text, we will see how Turbo Pascal handles tasks related to file processing when the file is contained on a disk. The first programs we will write will process data that the user enters at the keyboard, which is actually considered a special kind of file.

1.5   PROGRAM-DEVELOPMENT SYSTEMS

In order to develop custom programs, it is necessary to have some type of **program-development system** available. Such a system usually includes a text editor of some type to facilitate the task of entering the program, a program translator that translates the program into a form suitable for execution by the machine, and debugging tools to help in the process of finding and removing errors in the program. Turbo Pascal is a program-development system; it has added convenience of incorporating some simple file-manipulation facilities of an operating system as well.

All computers actually execute programs in machine language form. **Machine language** is a numeric language in which each instruction is composed of an operation code (or *op code*) and one or more operands, which are addresses for the data that are to be operated on. For example, let us suppose, for a hypothetical computer, that op code 25 means to load the content of a designated memory location into a temporary storage location called an accumulator. Also, suppose that op code 39 means to add the content of a memory location into the accumulator, and op code 90 means to store the content of the accumulator into a designated memory location. Let us further assume that the memory locations in our computer have three-digit addresses. With these assumptions, a machine language program to compute the sum of the numbers at locations 300 and 505 and store the result in location 400 would be as follows:

    25300   (load content of 300 into accumulator)
    39505   (add content of 505 into accumulator)
    90400   (store content of accumulator into location 400)

Of course, inside the machine, these instructions would be translated into binary—a string of 1's and 0's. This language is classified as a *low-level* programming language because of its direct relationship with the characteristics of the machine that executes the program.

Most of you will probably never write programs in machine language, because it is a cumbersome and difficult way to communicate with a machine. Program-development systems allow you to express your program in symbolic form, using symbols like + for addition and symbolic names for memory locations. Languages that permit the programmer to write using symbols related more closely to the problem being solved than to the machine that will execute the program are called ***high-level* languages**. Thus, in a high-level language, we might express the preceding program as follows:

    Sum := FirstNumber + SecondNumber;

The words FirstNumber, SecondNumber, and Sum are names for memory locations 300, 505, and 400, respectively. The symbol : = means place the value computed by the expression on the right into the location specified on the left. The symbol ; is a delimiter; it separates statements from one another. It is again obvious that this symbolic description of the operation to be performed using ordinary English words and the language of mathematics is much easier to understand and write than the machine language equivalent. It is the responsibility of the program-development system to translate the high-level program statements into the equivalent machine language so that the program can be executed on the computer.

There are two types of program-translation systems: interpreters and compilers. An **interpreter** translates each statement of a program as it is encountered and then executes the resulting language instructions immediately. A **compiler** translates all the program first, generating a completely translated version of the program called an **object program**. (The original version of the program in the high-level language is referred to as a *source program*.) When the object program is completed, it can be loaded into memory and executed completely independently of the program translator. (Note that in an interpretive system, the source program can never be executed without the presence of the interpreter.) Pascal has been implemented using both systems; Turbo Pascal is a compiler rather than an interpreter. This means that the user must first enter a complete program, then issue the command to compile (translate) the program, and, finally, tell the system to execute (run) the program. In practice, only two steps are actually necessary most of the time: First the user enters the program using the Turbo Pascal editor, and then he or she enters the run command. Turbo Pascal automatically compiles the program, and, if there are no syntax errors, the system automatically begins execution of the program. The following diagram illustrates this process:

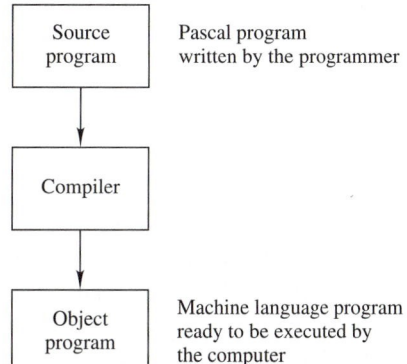

Two of the objections often lodged against compilers as opposed to interpreters are that the user is forced to wait while the compiler translates the program before execution can begin and that the user must manage two versions of the program (the source program and the object program), which take up space on the disk. Both objections are somewhat valid; however, Turbo Pascal has a very fast **in-memory compilation** feature, which helps overcome these problems. Turbo Pascal permits you to generate object programs that are stored as separate files on disk if desired; it also permits you to compile the program and store the object program in the memory of the computer only. The Turbo Pascal compiler is very fast when the latter option is used, thereby permitting the user to begin testing the program very quickly. It also avoids the necessity for storing the object program on disk if this not needed. The system was designed to allow the programmer to use the in-memory compilation feature until the program is completely debugged and tested and then to generate an object program on disk to distribute to program users. In practice, beginning students use the in-memory compilation feature exclusively.[3]

1.6   THE PROGRAM-DEVELOPMENT PROCESS

Although program-development systems are an aid in the task of writing programs, the programmer must perform the essential task of formulating the solution to the problem at hand in terms acceptable to the machine. All programs begin with a problem to be solved, which is equivalent to a task that needs to be accomplished with the aid of the computer. The first thing that a programmer must do is to analyze the problem to make sure that he or she understands all of its parts and all the requirements that will be placed on the program. It is particularly important to understand all the exceptional conditions that may arise and to plan for the program to take care of them with appropriate actions.

Once the problem is thoroughly understood, the programmer plans the solution. This usually involves writing a rough outline of the proposed program to make sure that it will accomplish its intended purpose and to serve as a guideline when the task of writing the actual program code is undertaken. The program at this stage is said to be written in *pseudocode*—a very high level, quite informal description of the program that typically contains the essential elements of the logic of the program, but does not include all the detail that will be required by the actual code. This stage in the problem-solving process is very much like writing an outline before attempting to write a theme or term paper. It serves to focus your ideas and helps you make sure that you have covered all essential points in a logical and orderly manner.

After the pseudocoded version of the program is completed and has been revised in the light of careful analysis of the problem, the programmer writes the program in a high-level programming language, being careful to include all the detail and using the syntax required for that language. Pascal has a definite format that you will have to use in order for your programs to be acceptable to the Pascal compiler. Certain words have to be used in particular places in your program, and certain marks of punctuation must be used very carefully. Once you learn what the compiler expects of you, you will not find these requirements burdensome.

After writing the program in the high-level programming language, the programmer types in the program text using the editor provided by the program-development system. The editor provided by Turbo Pascal makes use of a number of commands that you will need to master to make efficient use of the system. After typing the source program, it is a good idea to save it on a disk, so that if anything goes wrong, you will not have to retype the program.

Once the program has been keyed into the system and stored, you must compile the program. At this point, the compiler may detect incorrect program statements, which it calls *syntax errors*. Turbo Pascal will inform you of the location of syntax errors and will print an error message describing the nature of the error. If syntax errors are encountered, you must return to the editor to make the corrections and compile the program again. Turbo Pascal makes this step easy because the program can be placed on the screen with the cursor positioned at the point at which the error was encountered.

---

[3]Compiling a program to disk is not required until the student begins creating units, a feature described in Chapter 14.

After all syntax errors have been removed, it is necessary to execute the program to determine whether it is indeed a correct solution to the problem for which it is intended. For simple programs such as the ones in this chapter, a glance at the screen will be sufficient to tell you whether the program is correct or not. For more complicated programs, it will be necessary to enter some carefully chosen test data and analyze the results produced by the program to judge whether or not the program is functioning correctly. If the program does not produce the output expected, then it has one or more logical errors, which must be removed. This may necessitate reviewing the problem to be solved, rethinking the overall logical flow of the program, or carefully reviewing the program code to make sure that it is correct. In practice, if the problem has been well understood and the program design has been carefully thought out, the number and severity of logical errors should be minimized. The following diagram summarizes the process of program development:

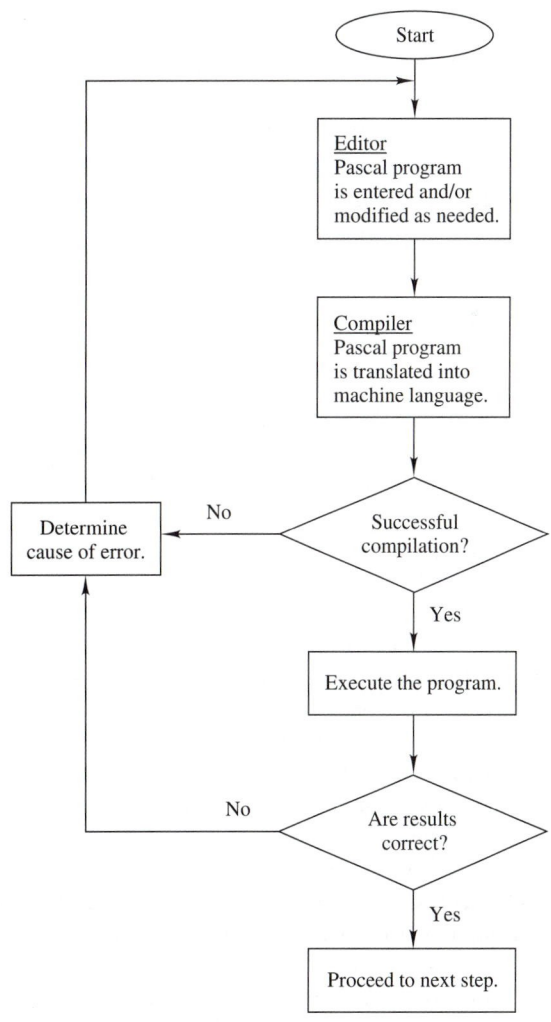

After the programmer has verified that the program performs its intended function correctly, the program can be released to others to use. Usually, it will be necessary to prepare some form of documentation for the intended user describing what the program does and how to use it. After users have the chance to work with the program, minor problems are usually encountered that were overlooked by the programmer. These will necessitate program maintenance. Maintenance involves making changes to the program in the light of errors or changes in program requirements. New versions of the program are prepared and tested before being released to program users. Students often do not have an opportunity to practice this part of the program-development cycle. Once a program has been accepted as being logically correct, they usually leave it and work on another problem. Nevertheless, the task of program maintenance is a very important one in real-world applications of computers; writing programs that ease the maintenance task is an important consideration.

In summary, the **program-development process** can be thought of as containing the following steps:

1. *Problem definition*: The programmer must understand the problem to be solved.
2. *Program design*: An overall plan for the program is developed.
3. *Program coding*: The program is written in a high-level programming language.
4. *Text entry*: Using an editor, the source program is prepared for compilation.
5. *Compilation and removal of syntax errors*: This step is repeated until no more syntax errors are encountered and a complete object program is produced.
6. *Program testing*: Logical errors are removed from the program by using sample data to test the program.
7. *Program documentation and distribution*: Users are informed about the program and provided a copy of it.
8. *Program maintenance:* Minor changes are made to the program as needed.

1.7 PROCEDURES AND ALGORITHMS

By definition, a **procedure** is a set of instructions for accomplishing some task. We deal with procedures on a daily basis for doing everyday things—preparing our favorite cake, driving an automobile or riding a bicycle, putting together a model airplane, curing the hiccups, adding a column of numbers, playing a board game, etc. All these activities can be described by a set of instructions that specify how to accomplish the desired goal. Much of our formal education is spent learning procedures for achieving desirable ends.

Although we deal with procedures on a daily basis, we are not accustomed to writing procedures in a formal way. Often, procedures are expressed verbally in informal and incomplete fashion. We are able to use such procedures because we bring to bear our previous experience and common sense. A computer program is a type of procedure that is formally and precisely stated. Computers are much less able to deal with ambiguous and informal instructions than are human beings. In order to solve a problem with a computer, it is necessary to write the set of instructions in a very precise and logical fashion; the computer does only what it is instructed to do, no more and no less. This means that humans must adjust their thinking somewhat in order to write computer programs. Many things that we take for granted in ordinary problem solving must be spelled out in considerable detail for a computer. It also means that humans must be more logical and precise in their thinking in order to envision the set of steps that the computer will have to carry out to solve a problem.

Some procedures are classified as **algorithms**. An algorithm is a procedure that has the following characteristics:

1. *Precision*: The instructions are unambiguous; any two processors (any machine or person carrying out the procedure) must carry out the instruction in the same way.
2. *Finiteness*: The procedure must ultimately come to a halt; there can be no possibility that the procedure could go on forever.
3. *Effectiveness*: The procedure must be guaranteed to produce a correct solution for the problem it is intended to solve.
4. *Input*: The procedure must call for input; this means that it must solve a general class of problems, not just one specific instance of a problem.
5. *Output*: The procedure must produce output; there must be no possibility of it coming to a halt without producing output that is the solution to the problem.

There are many examples for algorithms in mathematics—how to multiply two numbers, how to convert feet to inches, etc.—but there are very few algorithms in other areas of human endeavor. For example, medical doctors use a great number of well-known procedures for treating various illnesses, but unfortunately, very few of them meet all the criteria for an algorithm. Usually the most difficult criterion to satisfy is effectiveness. In medicine, most procedures are effective only a percentage of the time; in some cases the procedure does not work. This does not mean procedures that are not algorithms are not useful. On the contrary, such procedures may be very useful if people understand their limitations.

The best computer programs are instances of algorithms. The precision with which statements are expressed is guaranteed by the compiler, which rejects ambiguous statements. A good program is guaranteed to halt; one that does not is said to be in an *infinite loop*, i.e., it repeats a set of instructions forever. Programs certainly ought to be effective. One of the basic tasks of programming is to remove logical errors in a program that keep it from doing its job properly. Most programs ask the user to enter data for processing in one form or another. This makes the program more useful than one that otherwise would produce the same output each time it is executed. Finally, a program is relatively useless if it produces no output. How will you know what results have been computed, unless the program produces output of some form?

However, not all computer programs are algorithms. A program might still be useful if it is able to solve some instances of a problem but not others (lack of effectiveness), if it enters an infinite loop from time to time (the user can always turn off the power to the machine or reload the operating system), or if it does not call for input (such as some programs that produce signs or banners). You should treat the preceding criteria as standards for judging the quality of the programs you write, with the understanding that a program may fail to meet one or more of the criteria and still be a useful program.

1.8   WHAT IS TURBO PASCAL?

Pascal is a high-level language originated by Niklaus Wirth in 1971. He developed the language as a means for teaching students how to write good *structured* programs. Structured programs are programs that are easy to develop and maintain. Two of his goals in defining the language were to make it simple to use and to keep it within the capabilities of widely available computers. The language was named in honor of the 17th-century mathematician and inventor, Blaise Pascal, but is otherwise unrelated to him or his work.

At first, interest in the language was strongest among computer science teachers and students, but now Pascal is widely used by programmers for developing commercial software. One version of the language, which is known as *Standard Pascal*, was developed jointly by the American National Standards Institute (ANSI) and the Institute of Electrical and Electronic Engineers (IEEE). The most popular commercial version of the language was a package called **Turbo Pascal**, which was developed by Borland International, a company based in Scotts Valley, California.

Turbo Pascal meets most of the criteria defined by Wirth in his original description of the language in the book, *Pascal User Manual and Report* (by K. Jensen and N. Wirth); the description of Standard Pascal is also followed closely in the Turbo implementation. Turbo Pascal does include a number of extensions to the standard versions of language, primarily in the area of handling alphanumeric data and in a provision for numerous additional standard procedures. Turbo Pascal also includes a text editor and simple operating system interface to make the task of preparing programs easier.

Version 3 of Turbo Pascal has been available for several years, but is no longer in common use. Version 4, in which the editor portion of the package was significantly revised and improved, was released in 1987. Version 5.0, in which an integrated debugging feature was added, was released in 1988. This release was followed by version 5.5, which used the same interface and the data type object was added. Version 6.0, which was released in 1991, made significant improvements to the user interface by adding mouse support and the capability for dealing with multiple windows on the desktop. Version 7.0, released in 1992, added on-screen color highlighting of a program's major syntactic elements. This is the version that we will use in the body of this text, since it is the one most widely used in colleges and universities today. (The details of using versions 5.0 and 5.5 are covered in Appendix E.)

1.9   A SIMPLE PASCAL PROGRAM

In order to begin our study of Pascal, let us examine a very simple Pascal program, shown in Figure 1.4. The purpose of this program is to display a friendly greeting on the screen.

```
program P1a (Output);
begin
     Writeln ('Hello');
     Writeln ('This is my first Turbo Pascal program')
end.
```

Figure 1.4   Program 1a: A first Pascal program.

The text of the greeting is as follows:

```
Hello
This is my first Turbo Pascal program
```

Admittedly, this is not a very useful program; however, by studying it, you will learn a great deal about all Pascal programs, which have the same basic elements and general syntax. The first line in the program is:[4]

```
program P1a (Output);
```

This instruction is used to give the program a name (P1a) and specify that the program will produce output. The word **program** is a Pascal **reserved word** that is always used in the first instruction of every Pascal program. (A reserved word is one that has a special meaning to the Pascal compiler and can be used only in a specific context. A complete list of reserved words in Pascal is shown in Appendix A.) We follow the convention of writing all reserved words using lowercase letters only. The program name is defined by the programmer. It can be any sequence of characters except a reserved word. (We adopt the convention of using the same name in the program statement as the file name assigned to the program on the disk. Thus, the name of this program on the disk that accompanies the text is P1a). We also avoid the names of **standard identifiers** as well. In this text, we follow the practice of capitalizing the names of entities that the programmer defines (such as the program name and the names of variables, constants, and procedures), as well as the names of standard identifiers. In the **program statement**, the program name is followed by the left parenthesis, which in turn is followed by a list of the files that the program will use. (Technically, these are called **program parameters**.) The word Output means that the program will produce output on a standard output device—the CRT screen on most computers. If the program were going to accept input from the standard input device (the keyboard), the list would contain the standard identifier Input and appear as:

```
program Alternate (Input, Output);
```

This statement would specify that the program name is Alternate (an arbitrary choice) and that it would call for input as well as produce output. The next character after the program statement—and, indeed, the character following every complete Pascal statement that will be followed by another Pascal statement—is the **semicolon**. This character

---

[4]We will follow the convention of writing Pascal reserved words in bold in program listings, to help improve readability. This is the same convention used when a program is printed via the Turbo Pascal Print command.

is a delimiter, indicating to the compiler that it has come to the end of one statement and that it can expect another one to follow.

The program statement is followed by the body of the Pascal program, which describes the actions to be performed by the computer when the program is executed. This portion of the program always begins with reserved word **begin** and ends with the reserved word **end**. Additionally, since there are no further statements following the end statement, a **period** must follow the word **end**. Thus, a general layout for simple Pascal programs would be as follows:

```
program program-name (program-parameters);
begin
   statement-sequence
end.
```

We shall use this notation repeatedly in this text to describe the syntax of Pascal programs. The use of italics in the general form means that these portions are to be replaced by the programmer with appropriate entries. Words that are not in italics and marks of punctuation (such as the parenthesis, the semicolon, and the period in the preceding general form) must be used as shown.

In this program, the *statement-sequence* consists of two statements, which tell the computer what to write on the screen. The standard procedure **Writeln** is used to produce output. In this case, the output will be placed on the screen; however, Writeln can be used to produce output on other devices as well. Procedures are invoked by specifying the procedure name followed by a left parenthesis and a list of items (called *parameters*) to be passed to the procedure. The list of parameters is terminated by a right parenthesis. If there are no parameters, then the procedure name is written without the parentheses. In this program, the parameter list in the first statement contains the character string 'Hello'. Note that **character strings** are enclosed in apostrophes (also called *single quotes*; Pascal does not use the usual double quotes). Note that the first Writeln statement is followed by a semicolon, which is required because this statement will be followed by another Writeln statement that writes the character string,

```
This is my first Turbo Pascal program
```

Observe that the second Writeln statement is not followed by a semicolon, because there are no more statements following it; the next entry is end., which signifies the end of the procedure and is not a statement by itself. (It would not have been a serious error to have placed a semicolon following the second Writeln statement. The compiler would have encountered the characters end. and assumed that the statement following the second Writeln statement was a *null*, or *empty*, statement.)

The program in Figure 1.4 produces output on the screen of the computer. If the computer has a printer, and if output is desired, the Writeln statements can be modified as shown in Figure 1.5 to produce output to the printer. This is done by adding the standard identifier **Lst** as the first parameter in the parameter list for the Writeln statement. Thus, the statement

```
Writeln(Lst, 'Hello');
```

```
program P1b (Lst);
uses Printer;
begin
     Writeln (Lst, 'Hello');
     Writeln (Lst, 'This is my first Turbo Pascal program')
end.
```

Figure 1.5 Program 1b: Program with output to the printer.

will produce output on the printer, whereas the statement

```
Writeln('Hello');
```

will produce output on the screen. (The standard identifier Lst is short for List.) Note that when a parameter list contains more than one entry, the items are separated from one another by commas. This is required by Pascal syntax for any list of items.

Beginning with version 4.0, Turbo Pascal incorporated program "**units,**" which contain definitions of standard identifiers and provide useful features that may not be needed in all programs. The standard identifier Lst is defined in the unit Printer. In order to inform the compiler that it must look at the unit Printer, you must include the **uses** statement immediately after the program statement. The general syntax of the uses statement is

```
uses unit-name;
```

where *unit-name* is the name of a Turbo Pascal unit that has been previously written and stored in an appropriate file. To make use of the unit Printer, we must include the statement

```
uses Printer;
```

as shown in the program of Figure 1.5. (*Note:* The uses statement, units, and the identifier Lst are Turbo Pascal extensions to standard Pascal.)

1.10   USING TURBO PASCAL 7.0

Turbo Pascal 7.0 consists of an integrated program-development system and a program-debugging system. The program-development system consists of the following elements:

- an editor used to create files for programs and/or data
- a desktop manager that allows you to manipulate multiple windows (this facility was new in Turbo Pascal 6.0)
- a file manager that allows you to store and retrieve files and execute programs
- a compiler that is used to translate the programs you write into machine language.

This section covers the details of using the program-development system; the details of using the program-debugging system are covered in Appendix G.

1.10.1   Overview

The first step in using Turbo Pascal is to load it into the memory of your computer. The exact details of this operation vary from one computer to another, depending, in part, on which operating system you are using. Detailed instructions are found in the Turbo Pascal reference manuals; your instructor may provide additional instructions.

The screen that you see when you first load Turbo Pascal 7.0 will be similar to that shown in Figure 1.6. Across the top of the screen is the Main Menu bar. Across the bottom of the screen is a series of prompts that help you remember the meaning of the most often used function keys. This line is called the "Status bar." In between the menu bar and the status bar you find an active edit window. The window is partially framed by parallel lines and also contains some additional useful information, including the following:

- the row and column position of the cursor in the lower left-hand corner of the frame; initially, the cursor is in row 1 (the first number) and column 1 (the second number).
- the name of the current file in the top center of the frame; initially, the file name is the default, "NONAME.PAS." When you save the file, you will be prompted to assign a different name to it.
- the window number in the upper right-hand corner of the screen; initially, this will be 1. When you open a second window, the number on that window will be 2, a third window will be numbered 3, and so forth.

Figure 1.6 Initial screen in Turbo Pascal 7.0.

There are two quite different ways to use Turbo Pascal. The first (and usually the most convenient) is to use the mouse. The mouse cursor is positioned by moving the mouse; menu items are selected by positioning the mouse cursor over the desired element and pressing the left mouse button. The second way to use Turbo Pascal is to use the function keys and arrow keys. To select the Main Menu, you press function key 10. (Note the entry "F10 Menu" in the status line.) This activates the Main Menu bar. Items from the Main Menu can be selected by pressing the key corresponding to the highlighted character in a command (for example, pressing F selects the File command), or you can use the arrow key to highlight the desired command and then press the Enter key. In the following discussion, we will assume that you are able to select a command with one of these alternative techniques.

1.10.2   Creating A New Program

In this section, we will describe how to perform the tasks necessary to create, execute, and save a new program. We will use Program 1a, shown in Figure 1.4, as an example.

After starting Turbo Pascal, the first task you perform is changing the default path to the destination to which you will to save the program. In most cases, the default path at the time Turbo Pascal is loaded is the path to the directory in which the software is contained. It is a very good idea to place the programs that you create either in a separate directory on the hard disk or on a floppy disk. For purposes of illustration, we will assume that you will be placing the programs that you write on a disk in drive A. Therefore, the first thing that you need to do is change the default directory to this drive. This task is carried out by selecting the File command, which will display the pulldown menu (sometimes called a submenu), as shown in Figure 1.7. The command that you wish to execute is "Change dir . . . ," so you highlight that item (by clicking on it with the mouse or using the arrow key to move the selection bar). After selecting this option, a screen similar to the one shown in Figure 1.8 will be displayed. This screen shows a "dialog box," which

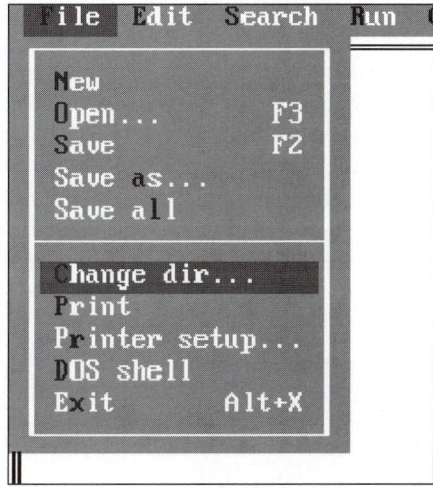

Figure 1.7 The File submenu.

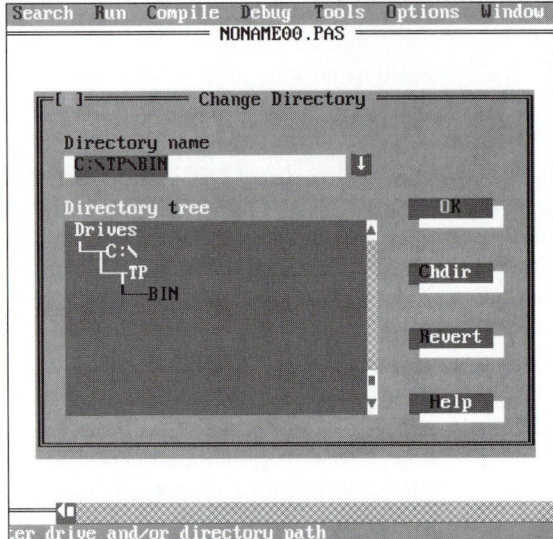

Figure 1.8 The Change Directory dialog box.

you will use to enter the new directory name. The screen shows the current default path to be C:\TP, which means that directory TP on drive C is the current default. (The current default may be different on your system.) To change to a new path, type the new path, which will then replace the old one in the box. The new path will be simply A:, as shown in Figure 1.9. When these characters have been entered, you can select "OK" with the mouse, or simply press Enter. You have now reset the default path so that files can easily be read from or saved to the disk in drive A.

Initially, the cursor is in line 1, position 1. You can now proceed to type the program one line at a time, beginning with the initial position of the cursor. At the end of each line, press Enter to begin the next line of the program on a new line on the screen. After you type the program, the screen will be as shown in Figure 1.10. Pascal reserved words will appear in white; other words will be in yellow. Note that the default file name is still displayed as C:NONAME.PAS. When you save the program, you will be prompted for the name of the file, and this name will become the name displayed in the window frame. At this point, it is a good idea to save the program. This is accomplished by selecting Save from the File menu. A dialog box as shown in Figure 1.11 will be opened to allow you to enter the name of your file. We have chosen to call the file by the same name as is used in the program statement, so we enter "P1A" as the name of the file. (Saving the file before executing the program is a good idea, but is not absolutely necessary. If your program results in some unrecoverable error, making it necessary to reboot the system, then,

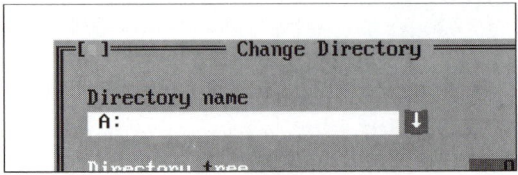

Figure 1.9 Changing the default path in the Directory name box.

File   Edit   Search   Run   Compile   Debug   Tools   Options   Window   Help

```
[■]                          C:NONAME00.PAS                        1=[↕]
program P1a (Output);
begin
    Writeln ('Hello');
    Writeln ('This is my first Turbo Pascal program)
end.




         5:5
```

F1 Help   F2 Save   F3 Open   Alt+F9 Compile   F9 Make   Alt+F10 Local menu

Figure 1.10 Program 1a as entered in the initial edit window.

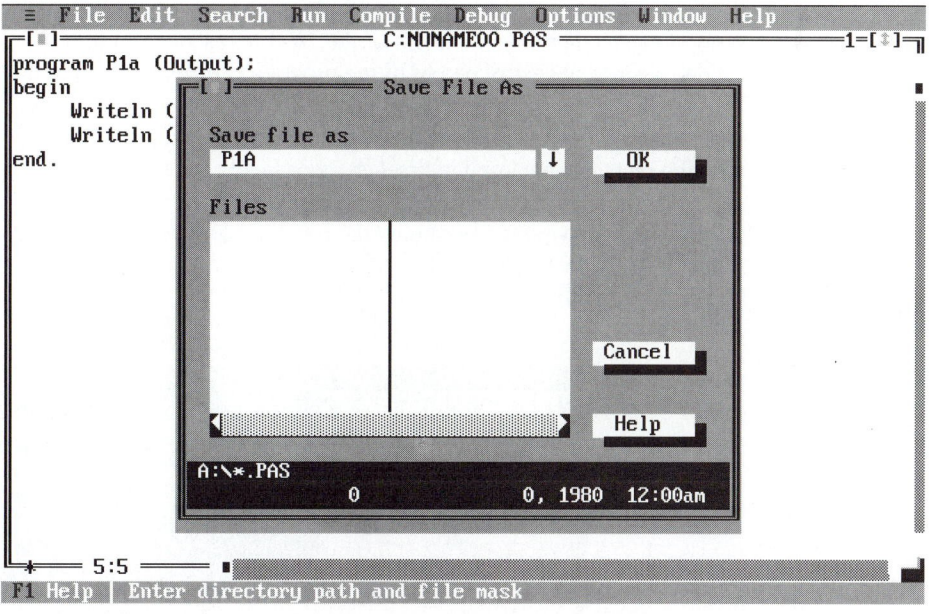

Figure 1.11 The "Save File As" box is used to specify the name of a file to be saved to the current directory.

unless you saved the file, the program will be lost. You will then have to reenter the content of the program. If the file had been saved, then you would be able to reload the file into memory from the disk and continue with the task of determining what went wrong.)

Once you have entered the program, you can execute it by selecting the Run command from the Main Menu. The resulting submenu is shown in Figure 1.12. The first option is Run, which is the one that you select to compile and (if the compilation is successful) execute the program. Note that an alternative way to carry out this task is to use the "hot keys," Ctrl-F9. This means pressing these two keys simultaneously or holding down the Ctrl key and then pressing F9.

Assuming that you made no mistakes in typing the program, the system will automatically proceed from compilation to execution. When the program is executed, the screen will flicker momentarily and then will be restored to the Turbo Pascal display.

What happened to the output produced by the program? It is on a separate screen called the "DOS text screen." You can examine the content of this screen in two ways, both of which involve using the Windows command from the Main menu. Selecting this command results in the submenu shown in Figure 1.13. If you select "User screen" from this menu, you will receive a full view of the DOS user screen, including recently executed DOS commands and possibly output from other programs. A somewhat more desirable alternative is to select "Output" from the Windows submenu. This results in the program's output being displayed in a second window, labeled "Output" as shown in Figure 1.14. The screen now has two windows. The Output window is number 2; the program is in window number 1. The Output window is now the active window. (There can be only one active window at a time. The active window is highlighted by the frame of parallel lines. Note that window 1 is now framed in a single line, indicating that is not the active window. Since the Output window is active, you can use the arrow key to scroll up or down to show other content of the DOS text screen. In this case, it is not necessary to do so, since the entire output of the program is displayed within the window.)

When you are finished with the Output window, it is a good idea to close it. This can be done in one of two ways. The easiest way is to use the mouse to click on the small solid rectangle enclosed in brackets (technically called the "Close box") in the upper left-hand corner of the window. This causes the window to be closed. (If you did the same thing for the window containing the program, you would have an empty desktop with no active window.) The second way to close a window is to select the Close command from the Window submenu.

Figure 1.12 The Run submenu.

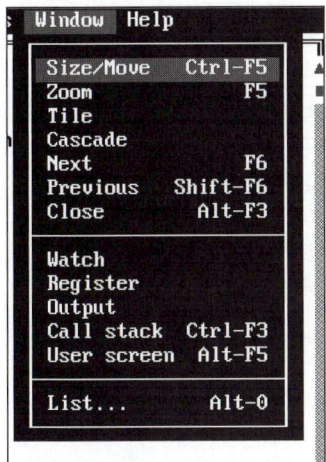

Figure 1.13 The Window submenu.

1.10.3 Time Out

In order to accomplish the following series of exercises, you will need a formatted disk:

1. Start Turbo Pascal. Place your disk in drive A, and change the default drive to A.
2. Type the program shown in Figure 1.4, exactly as shown.

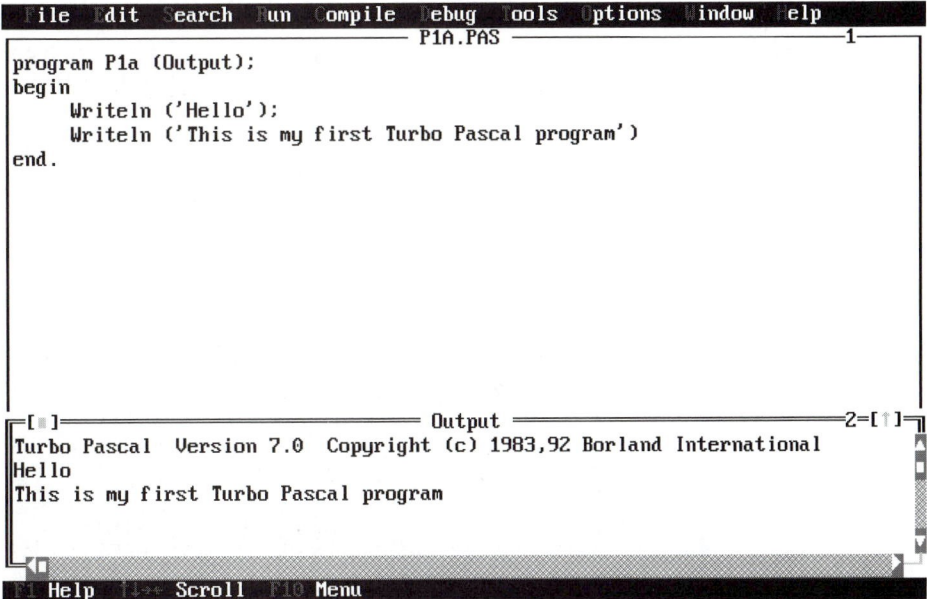

```
  File  Edit  Search  Run  Compile  Debug  Tools  Options  Window  Help
────────────────────────── P1A.PAS ──────────────────────────1─
program P1a (Output);
begin
    Writeln ('Hello');
    Writeln ('This is my first Turbo Pascal program')
end.
```

```
─[■]══════════════════ Output ═══════════════════2=[↑↓]─
Turbo Pascal  Version 7.0  Copyright (c) 1983,92 Borland International
Hello
This is my first Turbo Pascal program
```

```
 F1 Help  ↑↓←→ Scroll  F10 Menu
```

Figure 1.14 The Output window.

3. Save the program to your disk, giving the file a name of your choosing. (Turbo Pascal automatically adds the extension .PAS to the name you choose if your file name has no extension.)

4. Execute the program. If you have made typing errors, a syntax error will result. Examine the program carefully, and correct any statement that causes a problem. (We will discuss syntax errors in greater detail in the next section.)

5. Examine the Output window. Close the window.

6. Examine the full DOS text screen by selecting the User screen from the Windows submenu. You can close this screen by pressing any key. Return to DOS by selecting Exit from the File submenu.

1.10.4 Dealing with Existing Programs

Once you have saved a program, you can return to run or modify it by first using the Change dir command to change the default path to the drive (and directory if appropriate) containing the file and then using the Open command from the File submenu to open the file. Once a file is selected in this manner, it is loaded into an edit window; you can then edit the file or compile and run it, as desired. When you are finished, you can use the Save as command to save the file under a different name or the Save command to replace the previous version of the file with the current version.

Accompanying this text is a disk containing all of the programming examples reproduced in the book. Many of the exercises direct you either to test a particular program or to modify a program in a specified fashion. The disk is organized into 15 directories, corresponding to the 15 chapters in the book. All of the programs for Chapter 1 are located in the directory called C01, the programs for Chapter 2 are located in the directory C02, and so forth.

To illustrate the method required to gain access to these programs, let us describe the process for loading Program 1a, as shown in Figure 1.4. The first step is to use the Change dir command from the File submenu to set the path to directory C01 in drive A. Selecting the Change dir command opens a dialog box, as shown in Figure 1.15. You type A:\C01 in the box. This path is made up of three parts:

The drive designator (A:)

The root directory indicator (\)

The directory name (C01).

After you have set the path to point to the directory containing the file you wish to load, you use the Open command from the File submenu (or press F3). This command will open

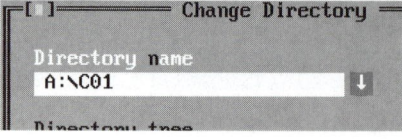

Figure 1.15 Using the Change dir command.

a window that displays a list of files contained in the current directory, as shown in Figure 1.16. You can highlight the file you wish to open with the arrow key or by clicking on the name of the file with the mouse. Then you can open the file by pressing Enter or clicking on the Open box with the mouse as shown in Figure 1.16. At this point, the file will be placed in an Edit window in the same fashion as if you had entered the file yourself. You can then modify the program or run it, as desired.

When you do modify one of the programs supplied with the text, it is a good idea to save the new version under a different name and perhaps on a different disk. Changing the name when the file is saved will retain the original version for future reference. If you try saving files to the disk supplied with the text, you will quickly run out of room. To save the file on a different disk, you can remove the original disk and insert your own formatted disk. Then use the Save as command from the File submenu to save the program under a different name. Using the Save as command automatically resets the current directory to the root directory of the disk in the designated drive and changes the name of the file in the edit window.

1.10.5   *Time Out*

To do the following exercises, you will need the disk that accompanies this text and a formatted disk of your own:

1. Load Turbo Pascal. Insert the disk that accompanies the text in drive A. Use the Change dir command from the File submenu to change the current directory to directory C01 on drive A.

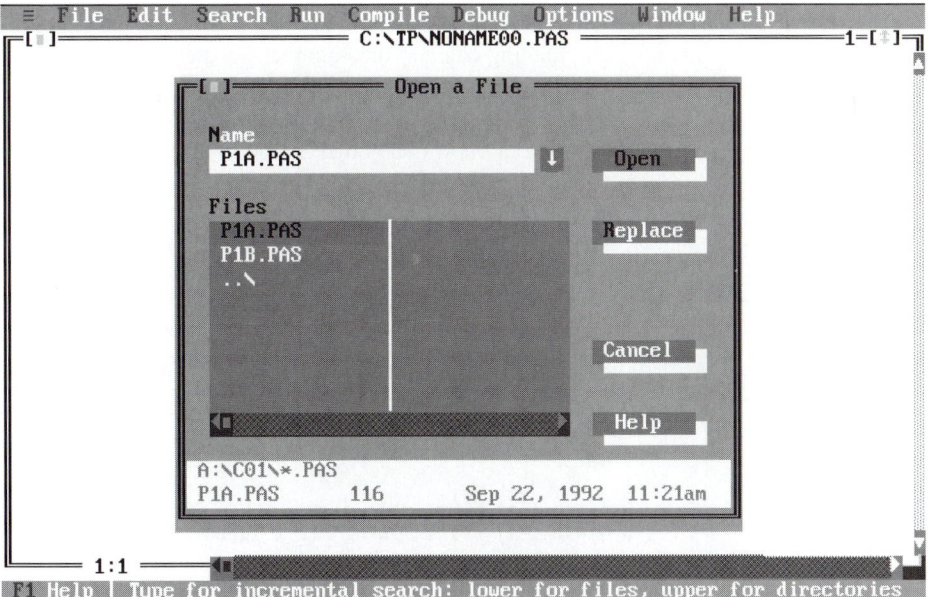

Figure 1.16 Using the Open command.

2. Use the Open command from the File submenu to open the file P1A, which contains Program 1a.

3. Execute this program and examine the Output window. Close the Output window.

4. Replace the disk in drive A with your own formatted disk. Use the Save as command to save Program 1a, under a name of your choosing.

1.10.6   Using Multiple Windows

One of the very nice features of version 7.0 of Turbo Pascal is the ability to have multiple windows on the desktop. These can be Edit windows containing different programs, Output windows showing the output produced by a program, or other types of windows that we will discuss later in the text. Windows can be displayed in several ways, moved, and resized—all under your control.

When you have one program in an Edit window and open another file or start a new file (with the New command from the File submenu), the new window is displayed in front of the old one, as shown in Figure 1.17; this is called *cascade* format. The new window becomes the active window, as indicated by its frame, which is composed of double lines. The previous window is still present and is shown with a frame composed of a single line. Note the window number in the upper right-hand portion of the frame.

An alternative way to display windows is shown in Figure 1.18. This arrangement is the result of using the Tile command from the Windows submenu. Each Window occupies a part of the screen, enabling you to view a portion of each. As before, the frame of the active window is composed of double lines, while other windows are framed in a single line. You can switch back to the cascade display by using the Cascade command from the Windows submenu.

When there are multiple windows on the desktop, you can move back and forth among them, making one and then another the active window. There are two ways to do this. If you click with the mouse on any exposed apart of a window, that window will become the active window. It will be brought to the front of the desktop and may hide other windows from view. (The other windows are still present, even though you cannot see them.) Another way to navigate among windows is to select the Next or Previous command from the Windows submenu. The Next command will make the next sequentially numbered window active. The Previous command will make the window that was previously active the active window.

```
 ≡  File  Edit  Search  Run  Compile  Debug  Options  Window  Help
─────────────────────────── P1A.PAS ──────────────────────1────┐
┌─[■]══════════════════════ P1B.PAS ═══════════════════2=[↑]═┐│
│program P1b (Lst);                                          ▲│
│uses Printer;                                               ■│
│begin                                                        │
│     Writeln (Lst, 'Hello');                                 │
│     Writeln (Lst, 'This is my first Turbo Pascal program')  │
│end.                                                         │
│                                                            ▼│
└────────────────────────────────────────────────────────────┘
```

Figure 1.17   Multiple windows displayed in cascade fashion.

```
≡  File  Edit  Search  Run  Compile  Debug  Options  Window  Help
────────────────────────── P1A.PAS ──────────────────────────1───
program P1a (Output);
begin
    Writeln ('Hello');
    Writeln ('This is my first Turbo Pascal program')
end.




┌[■]═════════════════════════ P1B.PAS ═════════════════════2=[↑]┐
program P1b (Lst);
uses Printer;
begin
    Writeln (Lst, 'Hello');
    Writeln (Lst, 'This is my first Turbo Pascal program')
end.




──── 1:1 ════◄□
 F1 Help  F2 Save  F3 Open  Alt-F9 Compile  F9 Make  F10 Menu
```

Figure 1.18 Multiple windows displayed in tile fashion.

You may have noticed other differences between the frames of an active and an inactive window. In addition to the use of horizontal lines in the frame in place of a single line, the frame of the active window has a "Close button" in the upper left-hand corner, and a single or double arrow in the upper right-hand corner. Clicking on the Close button with the mouse closes the window, so that it is no longer present on the desktop. Clicking on the double-headed arrow (called the zoom box) will change the size of the window from a full-screen display to a smaller display; clicking on the single-headed arrow will display the window in a full-screen format. (This is the equivalent of using the Zoom command from the Windows submenu.)

In addition to the two commands, Cascade and Tile, which change the appearance of windows on the screen, you can resize any active window. There are two ways to accomplish this task. You can use the mouse or the Size/Move command from the Windows submenu. Using the mouse is the most convenient method. The lower right-hand corner of an active window is called the *resize corner*. By pointing to this corner and holding down the left mouse button, you can drag the corner to change the displayed size of the window from very small to a full-screen display. To move the entire window around the desktop, use the top part of the frame. Point to this part of the frame, hold down the left mouse button, and drag the frame in the direction of your choice. When you release the mouse button, the window will stay in position.

One final difference between the frame of an active window and that of an inactive window is the presence of scroll bars on the bottom and right side of the active window. By clicking on the right-hand scroll bar, you can scroll the content of the window up or down to display content that was not previously visible in the window. The bottom scroll bar is used to scroll text from left to right in the window.

Figure 1.19 shows a desktop containing three windows. Window number 1 contains Program 1a. Window number 2 is the Output window, showing the output produced by the execution of this program. Both of these windows have been resized and moved to a convenient location on the desktop. The third window is the active window. It was created by using the New command from the File submenu and is the active window. Note the presence of the double lines, the close box (upper left-hand corner), the zoom box (upper right-hand corner), the resize corner (lower right-hand corner), and the scroll bars (bottom and right-hand borders of the frame).

1.10.7 Time Out

In the following series of exercises, you will gain familiarity with the manipulation of multiple windows in Turbo Pascal. During the exercises, you will create a screen similar to that shown in Figure 1.19.

1. Start Turbo Pascal. Open Program 1a from the disk that accompanies this text. Resize the window using the mouse and the resize corner (or the Size/Move command from the Windows submenu). Make the window roughly the same size as that shown in Figure 1.19.
2. Run the program. Use the Output command from the Windows submenu to open the Output window. Resize and move this window to a position slightly below and to the right of the first window. Note that this window may overlap and thus obscure parts of the window containing the program.

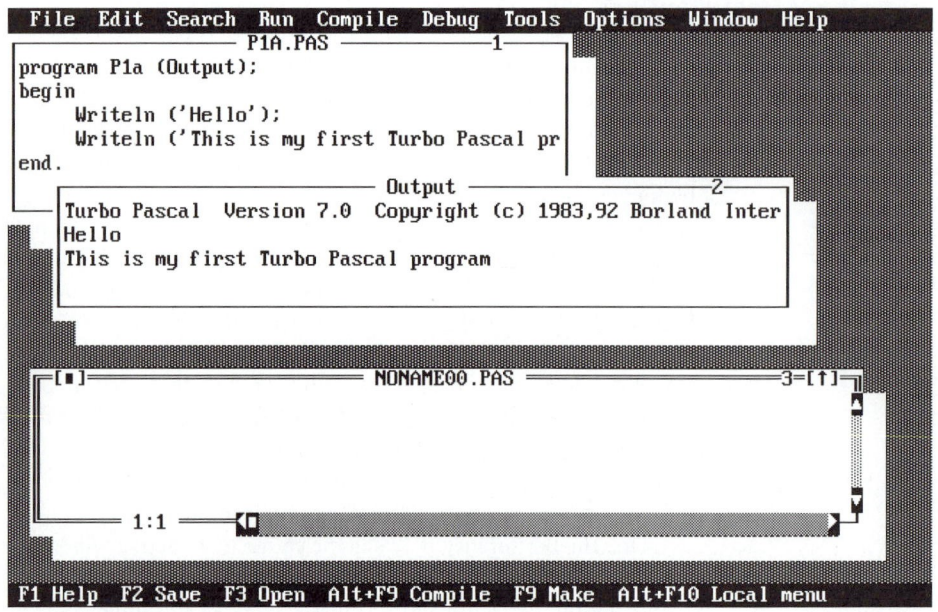

Figure 1.19 Typical desktop containing three windows that have been resized and moved.

3. Use the New command from the File submenu to open a new Edit window. Resize and move this window to a position similar to that shown in Figure 1.19.

4. Practice activating one and then another of these windows. Notice how the frame changes as each window becomes active.

5. Use the zoom box on any one of the windows to change the display to full screen. Note that the single-headed arrow becomes a double-headed arrow when you do this. Then use the zoom box to return to the former display.

6. Use the close box to close each of the windows. When you finish, you will have an empty desktop. Terminate Turbo Pascal and return to the operating system.

1.11   SYNTAX ERRORS

Syntax errors are errors caused by the failure of the programmer to enter program statements that could be translated by the compiler. Pascal has certain rules of syntax that must be followed. Rules such as the following are examples of syntax rules that must be followed for the Pascal compiler to be able to translate your program: The first statement in the program must begin with the reserved word *program*; each statement that will be followed by another Pascal statement must be followed by a semicolon; and the last *end* must be followed by a period. If you make a mistake, the compiler will encounter a statement that it cannot translate and will halt with a syntax error message. You must then determine what caused the problem and make the correction.

Common sources of syntax errors are misspelled words and missing marks of punctuation. For example, suppose the semicolon had been omitted following the program statement in Program 1a, so that the first line of the program read

```
program P1a (Output)
```

rather than the correct form with the semicolon, which is

```
program P1a (Output);
```

If the program is compiled with this error, the screen shown in Figure 1.20 is displayed.

```
 ≡  File  Edit  Search  Run  Compile  Debug  Options  Window
┌─[■]══════════════════════ P1A.PAS ═════════════════════
│ Error 85: ";" expected.
│begin
│     Writeln ('Hello');
│     Writeln ('This is my first Turbo Pascal program')
│end.
```

Figure 1.20 Syntax error resulting from a missing semicolon following a statement.

This screen indicates that the compiler was on line 2 when the error was detected. The message

```
Error 85: ";" expected.
```

means that a semicolon was not found where the compiler expected to find it. (When you press any key, the error message disappears.) In this case, the cursor is placed at the character *b* in *begin* on the second line. It may be confusing at first when the compiler does not place the cursor at the exact location of the error, but you must remember that the compiler can only attempt to translate the text presented to it. It continues forward until it reaches something it cannot translate and then stops. This means that if the error is not at the exact location of the cursor, it is usually close by. In this case, the last character on the preceding line must be a semicolon, to indicate the end of the the program statement.

Another common error is misspelling words. Reserved words and standard identifiers must be spelled exactly as expected by the compiler. For example, suppose we had misspelled the first instance of the standard identifier Writeln by spelling it incorrectly as in

```
Writln ('Hello');
```

If the program is compiled with this error in place, the error message

```
Error 3: Unknown identifier.
```

will be displayed. This error message indicates that an unknown identifier or other syntax error of undetermined origin has been encountered. In this case, when the Escape key is pressed, the cursor returns to the initial *W* of the incorrect word. The actual error, a missing *e*, is to the right of the placement of the cursor, but this placement of the cursor is in keeping with the general rule that the cursor will indicate the first thing in the program that the compiler could not identify.

Programmers sometimes forget that the last *end* in a Pascal program must be followed by a period. If we attempt to compile Program 1a with this error, the following error message will result:

```
Error 10: Unexpected end of file.
```

The compiler expects that the period will be encountered before the end of the source program; hence the message "Unexpected end of file." In this case the cursor is placed directly at the place the error occurs—immediately following the word end.

Recall that character strings must be enclosed in single quotes. For example, if you forget the last quote in the second Writeln statement in program Ch1a, and the statement appears as

```
Writeln ('This is my first Turbo Pascal program)
```

then the error message

```
Error 8: String constant exceeds line.
```

is displayed, and the cursor is placed following the right parenthesis on this line.

As you can see, the Turbo Pascal compiler has quite a number of error messages. Sometimes the content of the message will be immediately helpful to you, and you will be able to make the correction promptly. Sometimes the message will be puzzling to you, and you will have to examine the program very carefully to determine what caused the error. Often a classmate or a laboratory assistant will be able to spot the error after your best efforts have failed, but try not to rely on other people too often. You will learn a great deal by correcting your own errors. Every time you correct an error, you will learn something about Pascal, and you will be less likely to make the same error in the future.

It is important to distinguish between the form of a program (its syntax) and the function of a program (what it does). It is not enough to remove syntax errors from a program so that the compiler can translate it successfully (although this is a necessary step); if the program does not function properly—if it does not solve the intended problem—then it contains other errors, which are called *logical errors*. The compiler cannot find logical errors for you; it is the programmer's job to verify that the program performs the function intended for it. We shall have much more to say about the process of program testing in succeeding chapters.

1.11.1 Time Out

In the following exercises, you will practice correcting syntax errors using Program 1a.

1. Edit Program 1a so that it appears exactly as follows:

```
program P1a (Output)
begin
     Writln('Hello')
     Writeln('This is my first Turbo Pascal program)
end
```

Note that the errors to be introduced include the following:

Missing semicolon at the end of the first line
The word "Writeln" misspelled in the third line
Missing semicolon at the end of the third line
Missing quote at the end of the fourth line
A period missing on the last line.

2. Compile the program and observe each syntax error message. In each case, make the necessary correction and compile the program again. Repeat until the program can be compiled successfully.

3. Introduce still other errors of your own choosing into Program 1a, observe the resulting error messages.

1.12 PRINTING YOUR PROGRAM

From the File submenu, you can select Print to print the current program on the printer. This command activates a program called "PRNFLTR.EXE," which takes your program, adds instructions to print reserved words in bold (and other effects which we will discuss later), and sends the text to the printer. It is your responsibility to make sure that the system can locate this program. It is normally located in the same subdirectory as Turbo Pascal, so if you have not changed the default directory, you should be able to print your program by simply selecting Print from the File submenu. On the other hand, if you have changed the default drive or directory using the Change dir command, you are likely to see a message indicating that the PRNFLTR cannot be found when you try to use the Print command. If this happens to you, select the Printer setup command from the File submenu. This will open a window such as that shown in Figure 1.21. This window shows that the Filter path is the current default path. You can change the Filter path by typing the actual path needed to locate PRNFLTR in the Filter path box. For example, if Turbo Pascal has been installed using default settings, the actual path to PRNFLTR is C:\TP\BIN\PRNFLTR, which indicates that it is in subdirectory BIN, which is a subdirectory of TP on drive C. (The actual path on your system may vary; check with your instructor or lab manager for details.) You should type the correct path in the Filter path box as shown in Figure 1.22. After selecting OK, you will be able to use the Print command, no matter what the default setting for the directory is.

The second line in the Printer setup window is used to configure PRNFLTR to communicate correctly with your printer. This is done by specifying Command line parameters. The parameter $NOSWAP is required. The second parameter that follows the / specifies the type of printer. For example, the Command line shown in Figure 1.21 would be used for an Epson printer, and the command line in Figure 1.22 would be used for a Hewlett Packard (HP) LaserJet printer. The only other type of printer supported is a Postscript type of laser printer (PS). The Epson setting will work with a large percentage of dot matrix printers in use today.

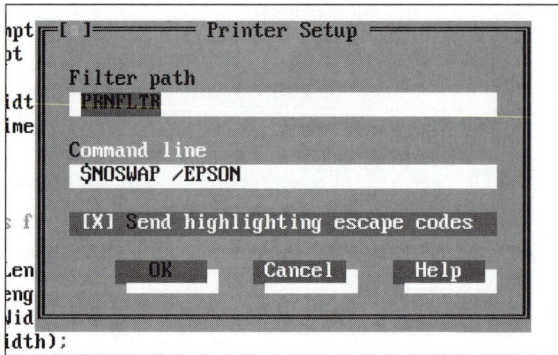

Figure 1.21 Default settings in the Printer Setup window.

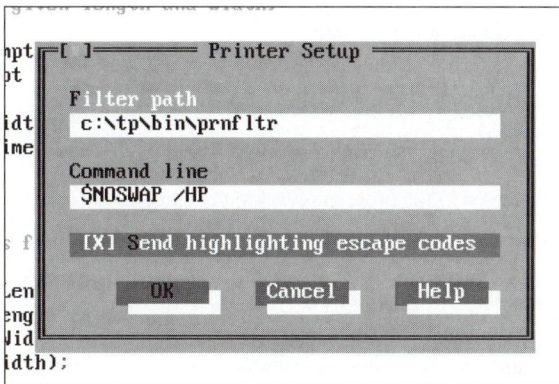

Figure 1.22 Complete path for PRNFLTR and configuration for HP printer. *Note:* The complete path may be different in your system. The Command Line must agree with your printer type (EPSON, HP, PS).

1.12.1 Time Out

If you have a printer connected to your machine, try printing Program 1a. Use the Printer setup command to change the path for PRNFLTR if necessary.

1.13 QUESTIONS AND EXERCISES

1. What is the distinction between computer hardware and software?
2. List the units of a computer and describe the function of each.
3. What is the CPU?
4. Which type of system usually has more processing power—a microcomputer, minicomputer, or mainframe?
5. Distinguish between a microprocessor and microcomputer.
6. Determine the following information about the computer you will be using:
   (a) Brand name and model
   (b) Type of processor (name and model number)
   (c) Amount of memory (How many kilobytes or megabytes?)
   (d) Number and capacity of the disk drives
   (e) Type of floppy disk required
   (f) Capacity of hard disk
7. Distinguish between the function of main memory and secondary memory.
8. Why do we say that main memory is volatile? What limitations on the use of main memory does this entail?
9. What are some guidelines for the care of floppy disks?
10. What is the distinction between system software and application software?
11. What is an application package? Since application packages exist, why is there a need for custom-designed programs?
12. List some of the major functions of an operating system.
13. Which operating system are you using on your computer?

14. Why are program translators necessary?

15. What is machine language? How does it differ from high-level languages?

16. What is the basic difference between an interpreter and a compiler? Which type of system is Turbo Pascal?

17. What is the basic difference between a source program and an object program?

18. List the steps involved in the program-development process.

19. What characteristics of a procedure make it an algorithm? Are all programs algorithms? Why or why not?

20. Who was Pascal? Who designed the programming language Pascal?

21. What is a reserved word? Give some examples.

22. What is a standard identifier? Give an example.

23. What is a program parameter? Where are they used? Give two examples of commonly used program parameters.

24. What is the first statement in every Pascal Program? The last statement?

25. What purpose does the semicolon have in Pascal? The period?

26. What does the procedure Writeln do?

27. How do you direct output to the printer from a Pascal program?

28. Describe the procedure for booting your system. What does *booting a system* mean?

29. What purpose is served by the cursor?

30. Describe the procedure for formatting a disk on your system. How often does this task have to be performed?

31. What is a syntax error? What are some common causes of syntax errors?

32. Explain the meaning of each of the following terms related to the Turbo Pascal desktop manager:

   (a) Cascade format

   (b) Tile format

   (c) Frame

   (d) Active window

   (e) Close button

   (f) Zoom box

   (g) Resize corner

   (h) Scroll bar

33. Define each of the following terms:

   (a) Character

   (b) Field

   (c) Data item

   (d) Record

   (e) File

34. How are data and information related?

35. List the types of tasks required in processing data.

2

Introduction to Pascal: Part 1

Now that you have a reasonable acquaintance with the Turbo Pascal system and its editor, it is time to begin our study of programming and, in particular, programming in Pascal. In this chapter, we explain basic features of Pascal that allow you to write programs involving input, computations, and output. With these facilities, you can write many useful and interesting programs.

2.1   PASCAL IDENTIFIERS: CONSTANTS AND VARIABLES

A program is a description of the steps to be taken as the computer reads data, performs computations, and produces results. An important part of any program is, therefore, the description of the data that the program will process. There are two fundamentally different data constructs in Pascal: constants and variables. A **constant** is a value that will not change during the execution of the program. A **variable** represents a value that may change (perhaps many times) during a program. For example, if you were writing a program to compute the area of a triangle, you would need variables to represent the base and height of the triangle, and you would need the constants 1 and 2 in representing the computation to be performed:

$$\frac{1}{2} \times \text{ base } \times \text{ height.}$$

Variables are assigned symbolic names, which in Pascal are called **identifiers**. An identifier can be any sequence of letters and digits, provided that the first character in the identifier is a letter. (Actually, the underscore character can also be used as a letter, but the use of this character is not recommended because it is easy to overlook and can result in unnecessary errors; we shall ignore the underscore character henceforth.) Identifiers should be chosen to be descriptive of the variable they name. Some reasonably good identifiers for variables would be:

    EmployeeName
    HourlyRate
    BaseOfTriangle
    TestGrade

We use the convention of capitalizing each word in an identifier. Numeric characters can be useful in identifiers when there are several related items. For example, if there were three tests, appropriate names would be:

    TestGrade1
    TestGrade2
    TestGrade3

There are three restrictions on identifiers:

- The first character must be a letter. Thus, the name 1Grade would be invalid, but Grade1 is fine.
- Only the first 63 characters of an identifier are significant. Identifiers may be of any length, but Turbo Pascal will discard excess characters (the 64th and following). Even though extremely long names are permitted, it is better to keep identifiers reasonably short. Long ones are difficult to remember and reproduce correctly and can result in programs that are difficult to read.

- The only valid characters are letters and digits (and the underscore, of course). Perhaps the most common mistakes are to insert spaces and other prohibited characters into identifiers. Thus, the identifier

```
Test Grade
```

is invalid because of the space between Test and Grade, and the identifier

```
Test/Grade
```

is invalid because of the slash between Test and Grade.

Within the limitations just described, the programmer can invent identifiers for variables according to his or her own imagination and common sense. Remember that the goal is to make the program readable not only to the original programmer, but also to anyone else who might need to understand the program. You should be consistent in the way you name variables. (For example, three related test grades shouldn't be called TestGrade1, Test2, and Grade3.) You should make the names descriptive. Identifiers such as Z1F45 and Abc are valid, but in most cases aren't very descriptive and can make the program difficult to comprehend. Finally, you should avoid the standard identifiers and reserved words that have preassigned meanings in Pascal. A complete list of reserved words is provided in Appendix A. Thus, you could not name a variable string or String, because string is a Turbo Pascal reserved word. (Note the upper- and lowercase letters are treated as equivalent by the compiler; we use the distinction between them to enhance readability.) It is permissible, however, to embed a reserved word or standard identifier into your own identifier. For example, the names

```
StringOfCharacters
```

and

```
CharacterString
```

are perfectly valid identifiers, although both contain the reserved word string.

One final word of caution is in order with regard to identifiers. Once you have decided on the name of a variable or other entity in the program, you must use that identifier the next time you wish to reference it. Thus, if you declare that a variable is to be called

```
HoursWorked
```

you cannot later in the program refer to the variable as

```
Hours
```

or as

```
WorkedHours
```

or by any other name except that used in the definition of the identifier. The best way to avoid making this type of mistake is to decide on logical names in the first place; when you need to recall the name, there will be less chance of using a different identifier.

Whereas variables are always assigned an identifier, constants may be assigned an identifier or may be referenced by writing the value of the constant; the choice is up to the programmer. For example, if you wished to compute the number of ounces in a pound, there are two ways to express the number 16, which is a required constant for this computation. You could write the expression as

```
16 * NumberOfPounds
```

in which the constant 16 is referenced explicitly by writing its value into the expression. (The symbol * is used to denote multiplication.) Another approach is to declare a constant with an identifier such as

```
OuncesInAPound
```

with a value 16. Then the expression can be written as

```
OuncesInAPound * NumberOfPounds
```

In this case the first approach probably makes more sense, but as you will see, the second option is useful for long or complicated constants or constants that might change sometime in the future. One constant that has a standard identifier in Turbo Pascal is π, which, as you may recall, has the value 3.14159. . . . The name assigned to this constant is **Pi**, and, since it is a standard identifier, it is provided automatically by the system; you do not have to declare it yourself, as you would with other constants. For example, if you wished to compute the circumference of a circle (recall that the formula is $C = \pi d$), the following expression could be used:

```
Pi * DiameterOfCircle
```

Of course, you could write the equivalent

```
3.14159 * DiameterOfCircle
```

The standard identifier for π is a useful built-in feature of Turbo Pascal, much like the π key on many calculators.

Constants may be numeric, such as the ones just described, or they may be character strings, such as the constants used in Program 1a in Chapter 1, i.e., `'Hello'` and `'This is my first Turbo Pascal program'`. Remember that string constants are enclosed in single quotes; numeric constants are written as numbers, using the usual conventions for writing numerals. Thus, the constants `'123'` and `123` are not the same. The first one is a string constant made up of the characters `'1'`, `'2'`, and `'3'`; the second one is a numeric value. Numeric values are used in expressing arithmetic computations; string constants are used primarily for input and output operations. For example, the expression

```
'2' * RadiusOfCircle
```

is invalid because of the string constant `'2'`; the correct expression to compute the diameter of a circle, given the radius, is

```
2 * RadiusOfCircle
```

2.1.1 *Time Out*

In the following exercises, you will try out what you have learned about identifiers for variables and constants:

1. Using the rules for Pascal identifiers, classify each of the following as valid or invalid. For invalid identifiers, which rule is violated?
   - (a) `FirstNumber`
   - (b) `Student'sName`
   - (c) `TestAverage`
   - (d) `123Go`
   - (e) `C3PO`
   - (f) `R 2 D 2`
   - (g) `ThisIsAVeryLongVariableNameIsItTooLong`
   - (h) `thisidentifierismadeupoflowercasecharacters`
   - (i) `ALLUPPERCASECHARACTERS`

2. Classify each of the following as a numeric constant, a string constant, or invalid. For each invalid example, what rule is violated?
   - (a) `1234`
   - (b) `'How are you?'`
   - (c) `'So long`
   - (d) `1.234`
   - (e) `-8`
   - (f) `+14`
   - (g) `'1234'`
   - (h) `''Hello''`

3. Following are alternative identifiers for variables. Using the criteria outlined above, which choice would be better?
   - (a) `numberofdays`   `NumberOfDays`
   - (b) `C`   `Cost`
   - (c) `RateOfPay`   `RATEOFPAY`
   - (d) `FirstPayRate`   `PayRate1`

2.2   STRUCTURE OF A PASCAL PROGRAM

A Pascal program has three basic parts:

Program heading: Defines program name and program parameters
Declaration part: Defines names for constants and variables (among other things)
Statement part: Describes actions to be performed by the program

Recall that the program heading consists of the reserved word *program*, followed by the program name (which is an identifier that you make up), and then—in parentheses—a list of program parameters, which are identifiers for files that the program will process. Input is assigned to the keyboard; Output is assigned to the screen. Input and Output are two built-in file identifiers that will often be used as program parameters. The program header is terminated by a semicolon. Some typical program headers are:

```
program Sample (Input, Output);
```
The program name is Sample; the program will require input from the keyboard and produce output to the screen.
```
program Sample2 (Output);
```
The program name is Sample2; the program involves output to the screen, but no input is required.

Program parameters are required in standard Pascal, but are optional in Turbo Pascal. We will include them because they serve as a form of documentation regarding the files that the program will process.

In the declaration part, all identifiers for constants and variables and other entities that the programmer wishes to define are given. There are actually five types of declarations possible:

Labels

Constants

Types

Variables

Procedures and functions

At this point, we concentrate on the constants and variables; the other types of declarations are discussed later in the text.

A constant declaration part consists of the reserved word *const* followed by a series of constant assignments in which the identifier for the constant and its value are specified. The general form for a constant assignment is

```
identifier = value;
```

where *identifier* is the name to be assigned to the constant and *value* is the value of the constant. For example, a typical constant declaration part for a program would appear as:

```
const
    OuncesInAPound = 16;
    PoundsInATon = 2000;
    UnitOfMeasure = 'Ounces';
```

In this example, two numeric constants, OuncesInAPound and PoundsInATon, are defined and assigned values 16 and 2,000, respectively. One string constant is defined, called UnitOfMeasure; its value is 'Ounces'. Note that each constant assignment is followed by a semicolon. This is a requirement of Pascal syntax, since other statements will follow the assignment.

The variable declaration part is a little different from the constant declaration part because, for variables, the programmer must declare the data type rather than the value. We referred to data type in the last section in our discussion of string and numeric constants. Variables are formally assigned a data type when the identifier is defined in this part of the program. Four data types with which we will need to work immediately are **Char**, **string**, **Integer**, and **Real**. (In Turbo Pascal, string is a reserved word, but Char, Integer, and Real are standard identifiers; hence, we capitalize the latter identifiers but not the former.) A variable of type Char can store a single character. A variable that is of type string can store a sequence of characters. A variable that is of type Integer can store an integer such as 2, 0, −56, or 123. (No decimal part of a value can be stored in an integer.) A variable that is of type Real can store any number that includes a decimal part, such as 3.4, −1.23, or 23.0. There are other standard data types supported by Pascal, and Pascal gives you the ability to define your own data types. Much more is said about data types later. For now, we concentrate on four of the most useful:

Char: used for storing single characters.

string: used for storing character data such as names or addresses.

Integer: used for storing values that have no decimal part.

Real: used for storing values that have a decimal part.

(*Note:* Data type string is a Turbo Pascal extension of standard Pascal.)

The variable declaration part of a program begins with the reserved word var, which is followed by variable declarations of the form

```
identifier-list : type;
```

The *identifier-list* is a list of identifiers (separated by commas if there is more than one of them) defined to have the data type that follows the colon. The statement is terminated by a semicolon. For example, suppose you wished to declare two variables, Number1 and Number2, to be of type Real, a third variable, Number3, to be of type Integer, and a fourth variable, Code, to be of type Char. Then the variable declaration part could be written as follows:

```
var
      Number1, Number2    : Real;
      Number3             : Integer;
      Code                : Char;
```

The spacing in the above elements is not crucial, but is, instead, a matter of readability. There are lots of other ways that the code could be written; for example, you could write

```
var
      Number1, Number2 : Real;
      Number3 : Integer;
      Code : Char;
```

Or (horrors!) you could write all this information on one line of Pascal code. When you write Pascal code, try to align like elements and use standard conventions for indentation; these practices will help make your programs readable and understandable. String variables can be declared using the type identifier string, as in

```
var
      Name : string;
```

This will reserve space for 255 characters—the maximum length for string variables. You may also specify the maximum number of characters that will be stored in the variable. This is done using the specification

```
string[length]
```

where *length* is an integer in the range 1 to 255 specifying the maximum length for the character string stored in this variable. For example, suppose we wished to define a variable called Name with a maximum length of 20 characters and a variable called Address with a maximum length of 30 characters. The variable declaration part could be coded as follows:

```
var
      Name     : string[20];
      Address  : string[30];
```

Note the required use of the brackets to enclose the length.

If the length of the string is 255, you may omit the length specification entirely. For example, the following specifications are completely equivalent:

```
var
      TextLine : string[255];
```

and

```
var
     TextLine : string;
```

The third major part of a Pascal program is the statement part, which begins with the reserved word **begin** and is terminated by **end**. In between, you write the action part of the program—the instructions that tell the computer how to process the constants and variables you have declared.

Our discussion about the structure of a Pascal program is summarized in Figure 2.1. Every program has three basic parts: the program header, declaration part, and statement part. The program header specifies the program name and provides a list of program parameters. The declaration part includes constants and their values and variables and their types. Four common data types are Integer, which is used for data that contain no decimal part; Real, which is used for data that may contain a decimal part; Char, which is used for data consisting of a single character; and string, which is used for data composed of sequences of characters. The last part of the program is the statement part, which specifies the processing steps to be performed by the program.

2.2.1   Time Out

In the following exercises, you will practice writing constant and variable declarations:

1. Write a constant declaration part for a program that needs the constant 40, which will be called HoursPerWeek, and the constant MinimumRateOfPay, with value 3.35.
2. Write a constant declaration part for a program with the following constants: SchoolName and SchoolLocation. Provide data appropriate for your own school.

```
program program-name (program-parameters);      ⌐ Program heading
uses unit-name...;                               ⌐
const                                            │
     identifier = value;                         │
        .                                        │
        .                                        │
        .                                        │
                                                 │  Declaration part
var                                              │
     identifier-list : type;                     │
        .                                        │
        .                                        │
        .                                        │
begin                                            ⌐
     statement                                   │
        .                                        │
        .                                        │  Statement part
        .                                        │
end.                                             │
```

Figure 2.1 General structure of a Pascal program.

3. Write a variable declaration part for a program defining the following variables: Length and Width are of type Real; NumberOfRectangles is to be of type Integer.

4. Write a variable declaration part for a program defining string variables for CompanyName (maximum length 15 characters), StreetAddress (maximum length 20 characters), City (maximum length 10 characters), and State (2 characters). Also, define a variable Zip of type Integer.

2.3   CONSTANTS: INTEGER, REAL, CHAR, AND STRING

Pascal supports two numeric data types—Integer and Real—and a variety of nonnumeric data types, including Char and string. The fundamental distinction between numeric and nonnumeric data is that arithmetic operations may be performed on numeric data, but not on nonnumeric data. Integer and Real data are said to be operationally compatible, which means that you can write arithmetic expressions involving Integer and Real data without worrying that you are mixing the two data types. Char and string data are incompatible with either Integer or Real.

Integer constants are written as a series of digits optionally preceded by a + or − sign. Integer data must be in the range −32,768 to 32,767. No spaces or other characters may be used in writing an Integer constant. The following are examples of valid Integer constants:

$$-234$$

$$+1098$$

$$6789$$

$$0$$

$$-12345$$

The following are examples of invalid Integer constants (with the reason why each is invalid noted in parentheses):

33000	(too large; maximum value is 32767)
12,345	(imbedded comma)
−33000	(too small; minimum value is −32768)
12.0	(decimal point makes this a Real constant)

Be careful of using the dollar sign. Turbo Pascal accepts a constant such as

```
$1234
```

as a valid Integer constant, but its value will probably not be what you intended. The dollar sign signifies that this is a hexadecimal (base 16) value. (For more information, see the Turbo Pascal reference manual.) Real data are used to represent quantities that have or may have a fractional part. One way to represent a Real constant is as a series of digits (optionally preceded by a sign), a decimal point, and a series of digits. The only mandatory parts of a Real constant are the leading digit (it may be 0), the decimal point, and a decimal digit (it may be 0). The following are examples of valid Real constants:

$$1234.0$$
$$-1234.0$$
$$+1234.0$$
$$12.34$$
$$0.1234$$
$$-0.01234$$

The following are examples of invalid Real constants (with the reason why each is invalid noted in parentheses):

.1234	(no leading digit—correct constant is 0.1234)
12,345.0	(embedded comma—correct constant is 12345.0)
12345	(no decimal point—correct constant is 12345.0)
12345.	(no decimal digits—correct constant is 12345.0)

An alternative way to represent Real data is based on scientific notation, in which numbers are represented using powers of 10 to specify the placement of the decimal point. In Pascal, the character E is used to signify that the number following is an exponent with the base implied to be 10. Consider the number 1,200, which in scientific notation would be expressed as

$$1.2 \times 10^3$$

In Pascal, this number could be written as 1.2E3 or as 0.12E4, 12.0E2, 120.0E1, or 1200.0E0; these are all equivalent to 1,200. This type of notation is called **exponential notation**. The requirements for exponential notation are a Real or Integer constant, followed by the character E, followed by an Integer constant. Turbo Pascal uses this notation as a default when writing out Real data. (You can edit real data for output—more about this later.) For example, consider Program 2a and its output shown in Figure 2.2. The constants A, B, C, D, and E represent five alternative ways to write the value 2,000. Note that the output produced for all five is identical:

```
2.0000000000E+00
```

Figure 2.2 also illustrates that if a constant is coded without a decimal point (the constant F), it is assumed to be an Integer. Note the different form of output used by the system for an Integer: Integer values are represented as a simple sequence of digits. The constants G, H, and I illustrate that in exponential notation, either part of the constant may be negative. The constant G, which is defined as $-0.2E4$, has the value -2000.0; the constant H, which is defined as $0.2E - 4$, has the value 0.00002; the constant I, which is defined as $-0.2E -4$, has the value 0.00002. Note that the sign of the exponent affects the placement of the decimal point.

```
program P2a (Lst);
uses Printer;
const
     A = 2000.0;
     B = 2.0E3;
     C = 0.2E4;
     D = 2E3;
     E = 2.0E3;
     F = 2000;
     G = -0.2E4;
     H = 0.2E-4;
     I = -0.2E-4;
     J = 1.234567896789;          Output produced by Program 2a
begin
     Writeln (Lst, 'A = ', A);       A =    2.0000000000E+03
     Writeln (Lst, 'B = ', B);       B =    2.0000000000E+03
     Writeln (Lst, 'C = ', C);       C =    2.0000000000E+03
     Writeln (Lst, 'D = ', D);       D =    2.0000000000E+03
     Writeln (Lst, 'E = ', E);       E =    2.0000000000E+03
     Writeln (Lst, 'F = ', F);       F = 2000
     Writeln (Lst, 'G = ', G);       G = -2.0000000000E+03
     Writeln (Lst, 'H = ', H);       H =    2.0000000000E-05
     Writeln (Lst, 'I = ', I);       I = -2.0000000000E-05
     Writeln (Lst, 'J = ', J)        J =    1.2345678968E+00
end.
```

Figure 2.2 Program 2a: Example of Real constant declaration and output.

The default format used by Pascal for writing out Real data gives a hint that the number of significant digits used for representing real data by Turbo Pascal is 11. If you attempt to write a longer constant in a program, Turbo Pascal won't object, but the resulting constant will be rounded to 11 digits. This is illustrated by the constant J in the program of Figure 2.2. Note that J is defined as

```
1.234567896789
```

which contains 13 significant digits; Pascal displays the value of the number as

```
1.2345678968E+00
```

which has been rounded to 11 digits. The reason for this is that Pascal reserves a fixed amount of space in memory for each Real data item (constant or variable).

The range of values that can be represented in Real data is $2.9E - 39$ through $1.7E38$. These represent very small and very large values, respectively. You probably will never need numbers this small or large.

Following are examples of invalid Real constants in exponential notation (with the reason that each is invalid in parentheses):

```
1.2E2.        (decimal point in exponent)

1.2 E2        (space before E)

1.2E 2        (space after E)
```

```
1.2E50        (exponent too large)
1.2E-50       (exponent too small)
```

String constants are defined using a single quote, followed by a sequence of characters, followed by a single quote. The maximum length of a string constant (or variable) is 255 characters; the minimum length is zero. A string that contains no characters is called the **null string** and has length zero. If you wish to place a single quote in the midst of the string constant, use two single quotes side by side. For example, in order to create a constant with value

```
John's pay
```

you would write

```
'John''s pay'
```

The system automatically substitutes one single quote for the two that you write. Some examples of valid string constants are as follows (with the length of each in parentheses):

```
'Enter name'     (Length = 10)
'Sally''s'       (Length = 7)
' '              (Length = 0; the null string)
```

Some examples of invalid string constants are as follows (with the reason why each is invalid enclosed in parentheses):

```
'Enter name      (missing quote at end of string)
Enter name'      (missing quote at beginning of string)
'Sally's'        (use two quotes to insert a quote into a string)
```

2.3.1   *Time Out*

1. For each of the following numeric constants, specify whether it is an Integer constant, a Real constant, or invalid.
(**a**) 1234
(**b**) 12.34
(**c**) -.0056
(**d**) +0.000123
(**e**) 98,700
(**f**) 3E4
(**g**) 2.3E3.
(**h**) 3 E4
(**i**) 50000
(**j**) 50000.

(k) 3E40

(l) 40E3

2. For each of the following string constants, specify whether it is valid or invalid. For valid constants, specify the length.

(a) 'John Brown''s Body'

(b) 'Circle'

(c) 'Square

(d) Rectangle'

(e) ''   (Note that there is no space between the single quotes.)

(f) ' ' (Note the space between the single quotes.)

2.4   FUNDAMENTAL LAW OF IDENTIFIERS

In Pascal, extensive use is made of identifiers to name constants, variables, procedures, functions, and other entities. We have discussed constants and variables so far; additional elements are discussed later. Regardless of what is being named, you must obey the **fundamental law of identifiers** when referring to an object:

> An identifier must be defined before it can be referenced.

Identifiers are defined in the Declaration part of the program, which has separate sections for each of the five basic types of objects you can define—labels, constants, types, variables, and procedures and functions. Once an identifier is defined, it can be used in any subsequent statement where it is appropriate.

Consider, for example, Program 2b, shown in Figure 2.3. In this program, the constant A is defined with value 1234, and then the constant A is used in the definition of the constants B, C, and D. Note the values of these constants, as reflected in the output pro-

```
program P2b (Lst);
uses Printer;
const
     A = 1234;
     B = A;
     C = -A;
     D = +A;
     MaxLength = 255;
var
     StudentName : string[MaxLength];
begin
     Writeln (Lst, 'A =', A);
     Writeln (Lst, 'B =', B);
     Writeln (Lst, 'C =', C);
     Writeln (Lst, 'D =', D)
end.
```

```
Output produced by Program 2b

A =1234
B =1234
C =-1234
D =1234
```

Figure 2.3 Program 2b: Example of an application of the fundamental law of identifiers.

duced by the program. Because A was defined first, it can be used as a constant later in the definitions of identifiers for other constants. Because of the fundamental law of identifiers, however, the following constant definition section would be invalid:

```
const
    A = 1234;
    B = C;
    C = A;
```

In the definition of the constant named B, there is a reference to an identifier C, which has not yet been defined. If this program segment were rewritten as

```
const
    A = 1234;
    C = A;
    B = C;
```

it would be perfectly valid because each identifier is defined before it is used.[1]

The program shown in Figure 2.3 also shows how a constant assigned an identifier in the constant declaration part can be used in defining a variable. Recall that a string variable must be declared using the type

string

or

string[*length*]

where *length* is an integer constant that specifies the maximum length of the string to be stored in the variable. In Program 2b, there is a constant defined in the constant declaration part as follows:

```
MaxLength = 255;
```

The constant is then used in the definition of the variable declaration part as follows:

```
StudentName : string[MaxLength];
```

The effect would be the same as using the declaration

```
StudentName : string[255];
```

or

```
StudentName : string;
```

The advantage to the approach used in Program 2b is that if you need to change the

---

[1]Note that arithmetic operations are allowed in constant declarations beginning with Version 6.0. For example, a declaration such as D = C + 2 is valid as long as the constant C has previously been declared.

maximum length of StudentName some time later, all you must do is change the value assigned to the constant called MaxLength and recompile the program. All variable definitions (there might be more than one) that made use of this constant would be automatically adjusted; you would not have to go to each individual declaration and change it.

2.4.1   Time Out

The following program segment contains a syntax error. What is the error and how would you correct it?

```
const
     X = 12;
     Y = X;
     Z = W;
     W = 2;
```

2.4.2   Units and the Uses Statement

Turbo Pascal 4.0 and all subsequent versions make it possible to write program components and store them in a precompiled form called *units*. Each unit has a name and contains constants, variables, procedures, and functions that can be used by any other program that may need access to these items. Several units are supplied with the compiler, and the user can construct others as needed. The supplied units are shown in Figure 2.4.

In order to inform the compiler that a program needs to make use of one or more units, the programmer includes the *uses* statement. The general form of the uses statement is

```
uses unit-name-list;
```

The uses statement is placed immediately after the program statement, as shown in the programs in Figures 2.2 and 2.3. In each of these programs, the Writeln statement directs output to the printer by using the standard file identifier Lst. This identifier is defined in the unit Printer. The first two statements in the programs are required to inform the compiler that the program will reference an identifier that is defined in the unit Printer:

```
program. . . ;
uses Printer;
```

Unit	Contains procedures and functions relating to
Dos	The operating system
Crt	The screen
Printer	The printer (Includes file identifier Lst)
Graph3	Graphics routines from Version 3.
Turbo3	Features not supported in Versions 4.0 and later
Graph	Graphics

Figure 2.4 Standard units in Turbo Pascal.

When a unit is specified in the uses statement, the compiler automatically makes available all the definitions of that unit to the program. You will need to include the uses statement in any program that will send output directly to the printer of your system. Later we investigate other uses of the predefined units.[2]

2.5 THE READLN STATEMENT

The simplest input statement in Pascal is Readln, which is used to read a line of text from an input file. If you make no special provisions in this statement, Readln refers to the keyboard (input is to be entered at the keyboard); however, it can reference other sources of data as well.

The general forms of the Readln statement are:

```
Readln (list-of-variables)
Readln (file-identifier,  list-of-variables)
```

where *list-of-variables* represents a list of the variables into which data read from the file are to be placed and *file-identifier* is an identifier for the file that contains the data. If *file-identifier* is omitted, Turbo Pascal assumes that data is to be read from the file Input, which is a predefined file identifier associated with the keyboard. Thus, instead of writing

```
Readln (Input, list-of-variables)
```

you can write

```
Readln (list-of-variables)
```

which is shorter and more readable.

When a Readln statement that references the keyboard is executed, the program halts until the user enters data. During the data-entry process, the user can use the backspace key to change any part of what has been entered. The data-entry process is terminated by pressing the Enter or Return key.[3] Actually, the data being entered are stored in a special memory area called a *buffer*, which is independent of the computer's main memory. Each keystroke is automatically echoed on the screen; that is, the equivalent character is displayed on the screen. Once the data-entry operation is terminated by the Enter key, the characters you have entered are interpreted by your program, and appropriate values are placed in the variables you specified in the Readln statement's list-of-variables.

---

[2]Many of the facilities provided in the units were standard features of the language in version 3.0. In order to run programs under version 3.0 from the disk that accompanies this text, it will be necessary for you to delete the uses statement when it is present in a program. Thus, the programs in Figures 2.2 and 2.3 will run in version 3.0 if the uses statement is removed. Version 3.0 will treat the uses statement as a syntax error.

[3]On some keyboards the Enter key is labeled "Return." We will refer to this key as the "Enter" key henceforth in this text.

For example, suppose that the following variables have been defined in a program:

```
var
     Number1 : Integer;
     Number2 : Real;
     String1 : string[10];
```

In order to have the user enter a value and store it in the variable Number1, the following Readln statement could be used:

```
Readln (Number1)
```

The device to be used is the keyboard, and one integer value is to be read and stored in the variable Number1. The user types an integer value obeying the same basic rules that were just specified for an integer constant and presses Enter to terminate the procedure. For example, if the user types

```
-12
```

the value stored in Number1 will be -12. Note that there must be no spaces or other characters within the integer value. Thus, if the user typed

```
-1 2
```

the value stored in Number1 would be -1, and the remainder of the characters on the line would be ignored.

In order to enter a real value, the user may type any series of characters that would constitute a real constant of the appropriate value. The only major difference is that the decimal point is not an absolute requirement in data entry, as it is when you are writing a constant in a Pascal program. Thus, if the program contained the statement

```
Readln (Number2)
```

and the user wished to enter the value 2000, any of the following would have the desired effect:

$$2000$$
$$2000.0$$
$$2.0E3$$
$$2E3$$
$$20E2$$
$$0.2E4$$

(This list is not exhaustive; you can probably think of still other ways to enter the value 2000.0.) Note that spaces and other characters such as dollar signs and commas are *not* used in entering numeric values, just as they are not used in writing numeric constants inside a Pascal program.

If the *list-of-variables* in the Readln statement contains more than one variable, the user must enter the required number of values, using at least one space as a delimiter between the individual values in the sequence. For example, suppose the following Readln statement is executed:

```
Readln (Number1, Number2)
```

If the user wished to enter the value 12 for Number1 and -1.23 for Number2, any of the following could be typed:

```
12   -1.23
12      -1.23
12 -0.123E1
```

Note that the number of spaces between the values is not important; the requirement is that there be at least one. Note also that leading spaces are not significant. Any number of spaces may precede the first digit of the first number.

When entering the value of a string variable, the user simply types the desired character sequence and presses Enter when finished. For example, suppose that the following Readln statement is executed with the variables just defined:

```
Readln (String1)
```

If the user types

```
May Jones
```

and presses the Enter key after the *s*, the variable String1 will contain a character string of length 9. If more than the maximum number of characters that can be stored in the string variable are typed (10 in this example), then excess characters on the right are not stored. For example, if the user typed

```
John J. Jones
```

the variable would actually contain the characters

```
John J. Jo
```

a string of length 10—the maximum that can be stored in the variable String1.

If the *list-of-variables* in a Readln statement contains one or more numeric variables followed by a string variable, spaces between the numeric values delimit these fields; the first space following the last numeric value is assumed to be the start of the character string. For example, assume that the following Readln statement is contained in a program:

```
Readln (Number1, Number2, String1)
```

Suppose that the user wishes the value of Number1 to be 12, the value of Number2 to be 1.2, and the value of String1 to be John Doe. The user could type any of the following sequences of characters to enter these desired values:

```
12    1.2 John Doe
12  1.2 John Doe
      12      0.12E1 John Doe
```

Note, however, that the actual content of String1 would be " John Doe", with the leading space as the first character in the string. In other words, the length of the string would be 9 rather than 8.

If the *list-of-variables* in a Readln statement contains a string variable followed by a numeric variable, the user must enter all the characters of the string variable before entering any characters of the numeric value. For example, suppose the following Readln statement occurs in a program:

```
Readln (String1, Number1)
```

In order for the value of String1 to be John Doe and the value of Number1 to be 12, the user would have to type

```
John Doe    12
```

Note the two spaces after the *e*. The actual content of String1 would be "John Doe ", a string of length 10. If the user had typed

```
John Doe 12
```

with one space following the *e*, then the value of String1 would be "John Doe 1" and the value of Number1 would be 2. Because of this problem, it is advisable to construct separate Readln statements for each string variable.

It is likely that you will make mistakes in keying in data from time to time. For example, you might inadvertently type a decimal point when the program expects an integer value, or you might enter an alphabetic character as the value of an Integer or Real variable. When this happens, an execution error occurs. Error 10, which is described as "Error in numeric format," is produced in these cases, and you are returned to the editor, with the cursor placed on the variable for which invalid data was supplied. At this point, you can correct the program if it is in error or exit from the editor and retry the data-entry operation, using greater care in your typing.

2.5.1 *Time Out*

For the following exercises, assume that the variable declaration section of the program reads as follows:

```
var
    Name, Address : string[20];
```

```
        PreviousMeterReading, PresentMeterReading : Integer;
        Rate : Real;
```

1. Would the following Readln statement be advisable? Why or why not?

   ```
   Readln(Name, Address)
   ```

2. Write a Readln statement to permit the user to enter the previous meter reading and present meter reading.
3. Suppose the program contains the Readln statement

   ```
   Readln (Rate)
   ```

   What are some ways that the user could enter the value 0.03 as the value for Rate?
4. Suppose you enter an alphabetic character when you are supposed to be entering numeric characters. If you have not yet pressed Enter, how can you correct the mistake? If you have pressed Enter, how can you correct the mistake?

2.6 THE WRITELN STATEMENT

The **Writeln** statement is a basic output statement used to write a line of text onto a file. Unless you make special provisions for another device, output is sent to the computer screen.

The general forms of the Writeln statement are

```
Writeln (expression-list)
Writeln (file-identifier, expression-list)
```

where *expression-list* is a list of constants, variables, or expressions separated by commas and *file-identifier* is an identifier for the file to which the output is to be directed. The first form of the Writeln statement automatically directs output to the screen. If *file-identifier* is omitted, Turbo Pascal assumes that data is to be written to the file Output, which is a predefined file identifier assigned to the screen. Thus, instead of writing

```
Writeln (Output, expression-list)
```

you can write

```
Writeln (expression-list)
```

which is shorter and more readable. If you wish to write to any other destination (such as the printer), you must use the second form of the statement. For example, in order to direct output to the printer, you could use the file Lst, and your Writeln statement would look like

```
Writeln (Lst, . . .)
```

The identifier Lst is defined in the unit Printer and necessitates the inclusion of a uses statement in the program.

The *expression-list* in a Writeln statement can contain any constant or variable, or any expression involving constants, variables, and mathematical operations. For example, the following Writeln statements will all print the character 4:

```
Writeln (4)          (list contains the Integer constant 4)
Writeln ('4')        (list contains the string constant '4')
Writeln (2+2)        (list contains the expression 2 + 2, which has the value 4)
```

Assuming that the identifier Four has been declared to represent the value 4, and assuming that the variable Count has had the value 4 placed in it, the following Writeln statements will also print the character 4:

```
Writeln (Four)       (list contains the constant Four)
Writeln (Count)      (list contains the variable Count)
```

If more than one item is included in the *expression-list*, then the commas are used between the items to separate them. For example the *expression-list* in the following Writeln statement contains a constant and a variable:

```
Writeln ('Student name is ', Name)
```

When this statement is executed, the characters

```
Student name is
```

are displayed, followed by the content of the variable Name.

One important use of the Writeln statement is to display prompts prior to executing a Readln statement. Recall that the Readln statement causes the system to pause until the user enters required data. But there is no message displayed on the screen informing the user what data is required or, indeed, that the system is halted, waiting for him or her to enter any data at all. The programmer must be careful to write a message to the user telling him or her what data must be entered. Messages of this sort are called *prompts*.

For example, consider Program 2c, shown in Figure 2.5. The purpose of this program is to have the user enter his or her name and age and then respond with the input data in two nicely formatted lines of text. A sample of the screen's appearance during the execution of the program is shown beneath the program. The first Writeln statement in the program prompts the user with the message

```
What is your name?
```

The user types any string of up to 20 characters; in this case, the user has typed

```
John Doe
```

```
program P2c (Input, Output);
var
     Name : string[20];
     Age  : Integer;
begin
     Writeln ('What is your name?');
     Readln (Name);
     Writeln ('How old are you?');
     Readln (Age);
     Writeln;
     Writeln('Your name is ',Name);
     Writeln('You are ',Age,' years old')
end.
```

Sample execution of Program 2c

```
What is your name?
John Doe
How old are you?
17

Your name is John Doe
You are 17 years old
```

Figure 2.5 Program 2c: Example of Writeln and Readln.

The next Writeln statement writes the prompt:

```
How old are you?
```

The Readln statement that follows accepts an Integer value and stores it in the variable Age.

The next Writeln statement does not have an expression list. This causes a blank line to be displayed on the screen. The subsequent two Writeln statements display the content of the variables Name and Age, along with text that is included as string constants in the *expression-list* in each of the statements.

An alternative way of specifying character strings such as prompts is shown in Program 2d, shown in Figure 2.6. This program is functionally equivalent to Program 2c; however, in Program 2d two string constants, NamePrompt and AgePrompt, have been defined with appropriate values. Then, in the statement part of the program, the statement

```
Writeln ('What is your name?');
```

is replaced by

```
Writeln (NamePrompt);
```

The advantage to this approach is that the prompts are readily apparent to anyone reading the program. (They are up front, so to speak, rather than being buried in the depths of the program.) If someone later wished to change the content of the prompt, it would be clear

```
program P2d (Input, Output);
const
     NamePrompt = 'What is your name?';
     AgePrompt = 'How old are you?';
var
     Name : string[20];
     Age  : Integer;
begin
     Writeln (NamePrompt);
     Readln (Name);
     Writeln (AgePrompt);
     Readln (Age);
     Writeln;
     Writeln ('Your name is ',Name);
     Writeln ('You are ',Age,' years old')
end.
```

Figure 2.6 Program 2d: Using named constants as prompts.

to him or her exactly which lines of the program to change. Also, this practice helps keep the statement part of the program from becoming overly long and complex, which in turn helps keep the program readable. Finally, the practice is a good discipline for you, the programmer, since it forces you to play close attention to the content of the prompt to make sure that it says exactly what needs to be said in a clear and concise manner. This is especially valuable if the same string constant is used many times in different parts of the program. However, unless the constant name is very meaningful, reading the code becomes more difficult.

2.6.1   Time Out

1. Compile and execute Program 2c from the program disk accompanying the text.
2. Modify the program so that the last two lines of output are printed on the printer as well as on the screen.
3. Modify the program so that the two lines of output are separated by a blank line.
4. Modify the program so that the output would be similar to the following:

       John Doe is your name and you are 17 years old.

5. Modify the program to include named constants such as the ones used in Program 2d.

2.7   THE ASSIGNMENT STATEMENT

There are two fundamentally different ways that a variable is assigned a value in a program. One way is through input—the user enters a value, and the system stores that value in the variable. The Readln statement is used for this purpose. The other way is through the assignment statement. The **assignment statement** causes the value of the variable to be replaced by a computed value.

An assignment statement has the general form

```
variable := expression
```

The value of the *expression* to the right of := replaces the *variable* to the left. For example, assuming that the variables Alpha and Beta have been declared to be Real, the following statements assign the value 1.2 to the variable Alpha and then place the value of Alpha into Beta:

```
Alpha := 1.2;
Beta := Alpha;
```

(After execution of these statements, the value in both Alpha and Beta will be 1.2.) We have much more to say about expressions in a subsequent section, but for now you need to know that an **arithmetic expression** may be a constant or a variable, as in the preceding examples, or any combination of constants and variables linked by arithmetic operations and grouping symbols (parentheses). The arithmetic operations used for real constants and variables are

+	addition
−	subtraction
*	multiplication
/	division

For example, the following assignment statement will add 2 to the value of Beta and place the result in Alpha:

```
Alpha := Beta + 2
```

Consider another example: Suppose you are writing a program in which you wish to compute the area of a triangle, where the user enters the value of the base and height. You have written the following variable declarations:

```
var
    Base, Height, Area : Real;
```

In the statement part, you begin by prompting the user for the appropriate input and reading the values of the variables. Then you wish to compute the area of the triangle. The appropriate statement would be:

```
Area := 1 / 2 * Base * Height;
```

An alternative way to write this statement would be to use parentheses to indicate which operation is to be performed first, as in the following:

```
Area := (1 / 2) * (Base * Height);
```

In this case there is nothing to be gained by the addition of parentheses, except perhaps making the meaning of the statement clearer to the reader of the program, but in some cases parentheses are necessary. For example, suppose that you need to code the formula for the perimeter of a rectangle. The algebraic formula is usually written as

$$p = 2(l + w)$$

In Pascal, you might write the formula as

```
Perimeter := 2 * (Length + Width);
```

Here the parentheses are necessary because without them the statement would be equivalent to

$$p = 2l + w$$

which is clearly not what is intended. Also, note the necessity for the multiplication operator in the Pascal formula. There is no implied multiplication convention, as there is in algebra.

The assignment statement uses the symbol $:=$ rather than the equals sign (which is used only in the constant declaration section). You should think of the equals sign as meaning "is equivalent to" the symbol $:=$ should be read as "is replaced by." For example, the assignment statement

```
Alpha := Gamma - 16;
```

means that after the value of the expression Gamma $-$ 16 is computed, it replaces the former value of Alpha. Think of variables as memory locations that are capable of storing exactly one value at a time. Thus, if the assignment statement

```
Delta := Delta + 1
```

is executed, and the value contained in Delta was 3 before the statement is executed, then the value will be $3 + 1$, or 4, after the statement is finished executing.

A fundamental limitation on the assignment statement is as follows:

> The data type of the expression must be assignment compatible with the data type of the variable.

Integer is assignment compatible with Real, but Real is not assignment compatible with Integer. Neither is compatible with string or Char data. Thus, assuming that Number2 is a Real variable, it is permissible to write an assignment statement such as

```
Number2 := 3;
```

where the expression is an Integer. The system will make the required modification to the integer value so that it has an appropriate Real form when it is placed in Number2. By contrast, when an attempt is made to place a Real value in an Integer variable, a type mismatch error will result. For example, if Number1 is an Integer variable, the assignment statement

```
Number1 := 3.92;
```

will result in the message "Error 26: Type mismatch." (You must think ahead when declaring variables, to decide which data type is most appropriate for that variable. If there is a possibility that it will contain a decimal part, it should be Real.)

A string variable can be used in an assignment statement to receive a string or Char value. For example, the following statement would assign the value

```
'How old are you'
```

to the string variable String1:

```
String1 := 'How old are you':
```

(There are some string operations that you can use to create string expressions; we cover these in Chapter 8.)

Note, however, that string and numeric data types are not compatible. Thus, an assignment statement that attempts to assign a numeric value to a string variable, such as

```
String1 := 2 + 2;
```

would be invalid, as would a statement assigning a string value to a numeric variable, such as

```
Number1 := 'How old are you';
```

Program 2e, which is shown in Figure 2.7, illustrates the use of assignment statements in the context of a complete program. It is a modification of Program 2c, with the added feature of computing and printing the user's age in months and days as well as in years. The variable AgeInMonths is an Integer variable; its value is computed in the statement

```
AgeInMonths := 12 * Age;
```

The variable AgeInDays is a Real variable; its value is computed in the statement

```
AgeInDays := 365.25 * Age;
```

(Recall that every fourth year is a leap year, so it is appropriate to multiply by 365.25 rather than 365 to compute an estimated number of days in a given number of years.)

Program 2f, which is shown in Figure 2.8, is functionally equivalent to Program 2e, but in this case two constants, MonthsInYear and DaysInYear, have been defined in the

```
program P2e (Input, Output);
const
     NamePrompt = 'What is your name?';
     AgePrompt = 'How old are you?';
var
     Name               : string[20];
     Age, AgeInMonths : Integer;
     AgeInDays          : Real;
begin
     Writeln (NamePrompt);
     Readln (Name);
     Writeln (AgePrompt);
     Readln (Age);
     AgeInMonths := 12 * Age;
     AgeInDays := 365.25 * Age;
     Writeln;
     Writeln ('Your name is ',Name);
     Writeln ('You are ',Age,' years old');
     Writeln ('This is ',AgeInMonths,' months ',
              'or approximately ',AgeInDays,' days')
end.
```

Sample execution of Program 2e

```
What is your name?
John Jones
How old are you?
17

Your name is John Jones
Your are 17 years old
This is 204 months or approximately 6.2092500000E+03 days
```

Figure 2.7 Program 2e: Example of assignment statement.

constant declaration part and then used in the assignment statements:

```
AgeInMonths := MonthsInYear * Age;
AgeInDays := DaysInYear * Age;
```

This program illustrates the use of named constants in assignment statements, but more than that, it illustrates the fact that there is no one correct way to solve a problem. Which of the two programs, 2e or 2f, is the clearer and more logical to you?

Actually, assignment statements can be avoided in some programs by placing the expression that computes the desired value in the list of parameters of the Writeln statement. This is the approach taken in Program 2g, which is shown in Figure 2.9. This program is functionally equivalent to the preceding two programs. There are two drawbacks, however, to the use of expressions in the Writeln statement:

1. The Writeln statement becomes needlessly complex and difficult to understand.
2. The program may be more difficult to modify, since the values being computed are not stored in a variable, where they can be accessed for further computation.

```
program P2f (Input, Output);
const
    NamePrompt = 'What is your name?';
    AgePrompt = 'How old are you?';
    MonthsInYear = 12;
    DaysInYear = 365.25;
var
    Name              : string[20];
    Age, AgeInMonths : Integer;
    AgeInDays         : Real;
begin
    Writeln (NamePrompt);
    Readln (Name);
    Writeln (AgePrompt);
    Readln (Age);
    AgeInMonths := MonthsInYear * Age;
    AgeInDays := DaysInYear * Age;
    Writeln;
    Writeln ('Your name is ',Name);
    Writeln ('You are ',Age,' years old');
    Writeln ('This is ',AgeInMonths,' months ',
              'or approximately ',AgeInDays,' days')
end.
```

Figure 2.8 Program 2f: Example of named constants in assignment statements.

```
program P2g (Input, Output);
const
    NamePrompt = 'What is your name?';
    AgePrompt = 'How old are you?';
    MonthsInYear = 12;
    DaysInYear = 365.25;
var
    Name : string[20];
    Age  : Integer;
begin
    Writeln (NamePrompt);
    Readln (Name);
    Writeln (AgePrompt);
    Readln (Age);
    Writeln;
    Writeln ('Your name is ',Name);
    Writeln ('You are ',Age,' years old');
    Writeln ('This is ',MonthsInYear * Age,' months ',
              'or approximately ',DaysInYear * Age,' days')
end.
```

Figure 2.9 Program 2g: Example of expressions in Writeln statement.

2.7.1 Time Out

For questions 1 and 2, assume the following constant and variable declarations:

```
const
    A = 3.2;
    B = -2;
```

```
var
    C : Integer;
    D : Real;
    E : string[10];
```

1. What will be the value of C, D, and E after execution of each sequence of assignment statements?

   (a)
   ```
   D := A * 2;
   C := B + 4;
   E := 'Alpha';
   ```

   (b)
   ```
   C := A;
   D := (A + 1.5) / 0.2;
   E := '';
   ```

   (c)
   ```
   E := ' ';
   C := -B;
   D := C;
   ```

2. Each of the following assignment statements has an error. Find the error.
   (a) `C = 2;`
   (b) `D := 'Beta';`
   (c) `C := 3(A + B);`
   (d) `E := 4;`
   (e) `2 - 3 := C`

3. Write the Pascal equivalent for each of the following formulas:

   (a) $C = \frac{5}{9}(F - 32)$ (Fahrenheit-to-Celsius conversion)

   (b) $a = \frac{1}{2}h(a + b)$ (area of a trapezoid)

   (c) $c = \pi d$ (circumference of a circle)

4. Modify Program 2c to meet the added requirement that the program must compute and print the age of the user in weeks.

2.8 DESIGNING COMPLETE PROGRAMS

Complete programs usually do not emerge in their final, fully polished states from the mind of a programmer. Just as the writer of an English theme must organize his or her thoughts before writing, the programmer must think about the problem to be solved and the basic steps that will be required before beginning the task of writing the program.

A useful tool for preparing preliminary versions of a program is called *pseudocode* (which means "false code"). **Pseudocode** is an informal language without the rigid rules of syntax of a computer language. Pseudocode serves the same purpose for the programmer that an outline does for the author—it allows him or her to record ideas in an organized fashion. Just as the author of a paper may prepare several versions of the outline before writing, the pseudocoded version of a program will often undergo several transformations until the programmer is satisfied with his or her solution.

There are almost as many versions of pseudocode as there are programmers, because it is an informal language meant only to convey the essence of a program to human readers rather than to a machine. In this text we adopt the convention of numbering each major step in the procedure, as follows:

1.0 Major step 1

2.0 Major step 2

3.0 Major step 3

⋮

As more detail is added to each part of the procedure, we use indentation and the following numbering system:

1.0 Major step 1

    1.1 Detail 1 of step 1

    1.2 Detail 2 of step 1

    ⋮

2.0 Major step 2

    2.1 Detail 1 of step 2

    2.2 Detail 2 of step 2

    ⋮

3.0 Major step 3

⋮

An example will illustrate what we mean. Consider the program in Figure 2.7. The problem being solved may be summarized as follows:

> Write a program to allow the user to enter his or her name and age in years. Compute and print the age first in years, then in months, and then in days. Include the name in appropriately formatted output lines.

Analysis of this problem could lead to the following pseudocode for the required program:

1.0 Read Name and Age

2.0 Convert Age to months and to days

3.0 Write Name, Age, and computed values

This version of the program is quite general and brief. It lacks much of the detail of the completed program, but it illustrates the overall logical form of the program. At this point the programmer might choose to add detail to some of the major steps of the procedure, as follows:

1.0 Read Name and Age

    1.1 Read Name

    1.2 Read Age

2.0 Convert Age to months and to days
   2.1 AgeInMonths = 12 × Age
   2.2 AgeInDays = 365.25 × Age
3.0 Write Name, Age, and computed values

Now the programmer may have a detailed enough plan from which to write the complete program, or he or she might choose to refine the plan further, adding still more detail.

This process of refinement by adding successive layers of detail is called **top-down program design** and is a very important technique that you will want to practice in your programming efforts. The technique is powerful because once you have a general outline of the proposed program, you can concentrate on how to carry out small portions of the procedure without having to worry about the entire program. Top-down program design is an application of the old adage "divide and conquer." A large and complex task is divided into a series of simpler tasks; each of these subtasks is independently divided into still simpler tasks, and so forth, until the entire procedure is expressed in simple enough terms to be able to write the actual program in a computer language. We shall illustrate the process with examples many times, but ultimately, the technique must become your own. No two people use exactly the same pattern of thinking in problem solving, even though the end products may be equivalent if not identical.

2.8.1 Case Study

We illustrate the top-down approach to problem solving for the following programming task:

> Write a program to allow the user to enter the length and width of a rectangle. Compute and print the area and perimeter of the rectangle.

This problem is much like the problem just encountered, because the basic sequence of events will be input, compute, output. More formally, the first pseudocoded version of the program might be as follows:

1.0 Get values for Length and Width
2.0 Compute Perimeter and Area
3.0 Write input values and computed values

A first level of refinement would add detail to each of these major steps in the procedure, as follows:

1.0 Get values for Length and Width
   1.1 Get value for Length
   1.2 Get value for Width
2.0 Compute Perimeter and Area
   2.1 Perimeter = 2 × (Length + Width)
   2.2 Area = Length × Width

3.0 Write input values and computed values
    3.1 Write Length, Width
    3.2 Write Perimeter, Area

A second refinement could be written to provide more detail for the input procedure, which lacks the concept of prompts:

1.0 Get values for Length and Width
    1.1 Get value for Length
        1.1.1 Write prompt for Length
        1.1.2 Read Length
    1.2 Get value for Width
        1.2.1 Write prompt for Width
        1.2.2 Read Width

2.0 Compute Perimeter and Area
    2.1 Perimeter = 2 × (Length + Width)
    2.2 Area = Length × Width

3.0 Write input values and computed values
    3.1 Write Length, Width
    3.2 Write Perimeter, Area

This example shows the top-down design process carried to its ultimate conclusion. For such a simple problem, you might have chosen to stop at the first or second levels of refinement. There is no one way to use the technique; the important thing is that you organize the steps of the procedure before you start to write the actual Pascal program code. As you tackle longer and harder problems, the power of the top-down design process will become apparent.

Let us now turn this procedure into a completed program. We shall call the program "P2h."[4] Since it will involve Input and Output, the program statement will be

```
program P2h (Input, Output);
```

Two prompts are required; we shall declare named constants for them in order to simplify the statement part of the program:

```
const
    LengthPrompt = 'Enter length of rectangle ';
    WidthPrompt = 'Enter width of rectangle ';
```

Analysis of the procedure shows that we need four variables: Length and Width, which are input variables, and Area and Perimeter, which are output variables. We must decide the data type of these variables. Since they represent measurements that can

---

[4]In practice, you may wish to assign more meaningful names to your programs. We use names such as P2h as an aid for the reader to identify the file on the accompanying disk that contains the program.

have a decimal part, we choose to make them Real. Thus, the variable declaration part of the program is as follows:

```
var
        Length, Width, Area, Perimeter : Real;
```

Turning the pseudocoded procedure into Pascal is a very straightforward task, as shown in Figure 2.10.

Note that only the procedural statements at the lowest level are actually translated into Pascal code. Note also that it may be necessary to add still more detail to certain steps when turning them into Pascal code. For example, in steps 3.1 and 3.2, literals are added to identify the output being produced. Do not be confused by the changes in syntax between pseudocode and Pascal. Pseudocode is for your use; you may write whatever symbols and notation that make sense to you, but Pascal demands that you follow its rules of syntax. For example, we translate the pseudocode step

2.1 Perimeter $= 2 \times$ (Length + Width)

into the Pascal equivalent

```
Perimeter := 2 * (Length + Width);
```

The equal sign is translated as $:=$; the multiplication sign, $\times$, used in algebra is translated as *, which is the symbol for multiplication in Pascal, and so forth. The completed program is shown in Figure 2.11, with several sample executions presented in Figure 2.12.

Pseudocode	Pascal
	begin
1.0 Get values for Length and Width	
1.1 Get value for Length	
1.1.1 Write prompt for Length	`Writeln (LengthPrompt);`
1.1.2 Read Length	`Readln (Length);`
1.2 Get value for Width	
1.2.1 Write prompt for Width	`Writeln (WidthPrompt);`
1.2.2 Read Width	`Readln (Width);`
2.0 Compute Perimeter and Area	
2.1 Perimeter $= 2 \times$ (Length + Width)	`Perimeter := 2.0 * (Length + Width);`
2.2 Area $=$ Length $\times$ Width	`Area := Length * Width;`
3.0 Write input values and computed values	
	`Writeln;`
3.1 Write Length, Width	`Writeln ('Length =', Length, 'Width =', Width);`
3.2 Write Perimeter, Area	`Writeln ('Perimeter =', Perimeter, 'Area =', Area)`
	end.

Figure 2.10 Translation of pseudocode into Pascal.

```
program P2h (Input, Output);
const
      LengthPrompt = 'Enter length of rectangle ';
      WidthPrompt = 'Enter width of rectangle ';
var
      Length, Width, Area, Perimeter : Real;
begin
      Writeln (LengthPrompt);
      Readln (Length);
      Writeln (WidthPrompt);
      Readln (Width);
      Perimeter := 2.0 * (Length + Width);
      Area := Length * Width;
      Writeln;
      Writeln ('Length =', Length, ' Width =', Width);
      Writeln ('Perimeter =', Perimeter, ' Area =', Area)
end.
```

Figure 2.11 Program 2h: Area and perimeter of a rectangle.

```
Enter length of rectangle
2
Enter width of rectangle
4

Length = 2.0000000000E+00 Width = 4.0000000000E+00
Perimeter = 1.2000000000E+01 Area = 8.0000000000E+00
Enter length of rectangle
2.37
Enter width of rectangle
A  ◄───────────────────────────────── Error resulted from
Runtime error 106 at 0B31:00E0.                invalid data entered
Enter length of rectangle                       by the user
2.37
Enter width of rectangle
7  ◄───────────────────────────────── Error corrected by
                                                 running the program
Length = 2.3700000000E+00 Width = 7.0000000000E+00    again and entering
Perimeter = 1.8740000000E+01 Area = 1.6590000000E+01  a valid value
```

Figure 2.12 Sample executions of Program 2h.

2.8.2 *Time Out*

1. Compile and execute Program 2h from the program disk accompanying the text.

2. Modify Program 2h to compute the areas and perimeters of two different rectangles. Compute and print the differences between the areas and perimeters of the two rectangles.

3. A program is needed that will compute the cost of carpeting a rectangular room. The cost of the carpet per square yard and the measurements of the room in feet are to be entered by the user. A preliminary pseudocoded version of the program is as follows:

    1.0 Get measurements of room

    2.0 Get price of carpet

3.0 Compute cost of carpet for room

4.0 Write input values and computed cost

Make one level of refinement of this procedure. Recall that there are 9 square feet in a square yard and that the cost of a carpet is the price per square yard times the number of square yards.

4. Using the pseudocode just developed, write a complete Pascal program.

2.9 ARITHMETIC EXPRESSIONS

We have mentioned arithmetic expressions briefly in preceding sections, and you have written a few of them by now. In this section, we discuss arithmetic expressions and the arithmetic operations available in Turbo Pascal in detail. When you have completed the section, you will be able to translate even fairly complex algebraic expressions into Pascal.

An arithmetic expression is a way of expressing a value in a program. An arithmetic expression may be as simple as a single constant or variable, or it may be any number of constants and variables linked by arithmetic operations and grouping symbols. Typical expressions are

```
-23.5
Age
(Grade1 + Grade2) / 2
```

Recall that the grouping symbols used in Pascal are parentheses. They are used to specify that operations within the parentheses are to be performed before operations outside the parentheses.

Pascal provides the usual arithmetic operators of addition ($+$), subtraction ($-$), multiplication ($*$), real division ($/$) and some additional ones, including unary minus (minus with one operand, as in $-A$), integer division (div), and modulus (mod, an operation used to compute an integer remainder). The following sections explain each of these operations in detail.

2.9.1 Unary Minus

The **unary minus** is sometimes read by mathematicians as meaning "the opposite of." The operation is expressed using the minus sign followed by a single operand. It means to compute the opposite, or negative, of the operand. For example, if the value of Number1 is 4, then the value of the expression

```
-Number1
```

is -4. If the value of Number1 is -4, then the value of the expression $-$Number1 is $+4$.

2.9.2 Addition and Subtraction

Addition $(+)$ and subtraction $(-)$ are very straightforward operations. They cause, respectively, the sum and difference of two operands to be computed, exactly as in mathematics. Examples of the translation of algebraic expressions involving addition and subtraction are shown below:

Expression	*Pascal Equivalent*
$a + b$	A + B
$a - b$	A - B
$x + 2$	X + 2

If more than two operations (addition or subtraction) are present, the operations are carried out in order from left to right. Consider, for example, the evaluation of the following expression:

$$2 + 3 - 4 + 5$$
$$\underbrace{}\ \ \ \ \ \ \ \ \ \ \ \ \ $$
$$5 \quad - \quad 4$$
$$1 \quad + \quad 5$$
$$6$$

If you use parentheses, the expression inside the parentheses will be evaluated first. Observe the following two examples:

$$(2 + 3) - (4 + 5) \qquad 2 + (3 - 4) + 5$$
$$5 \quad - \quad 9 \qquad\qquad 2 + \ (-\ 1)$$
$$-4 \qquad\qquad\qquad\qquad 1 \quad + \quad 5$$
$$\qquad\qquad\qquad\qquad\qquad 6$$

When translating algebraic expressions into Pascal, you must be careful to use parentheses if they are needed. If in doubt, use them. Excess sets of parentheses never hurt; missing sets of parentheses will alter the value of the expression dramatically. Study the following examples:

Expression	*Pascal Equivalent*	*Comment*
$a + b + c$	A + B + C	No parentheses required; $(A + B) + C$ and $A + (B + C)$ are equivalent.
$a - (c - b)$	A - (C - B)	Parentheses are required; $A - C + B$ is equivalent to $A - (C - B)$, but $A - C - B$ is not.
$a - (c + b)$	A - (C + B)	Parentheses required; or $A - C - B$, which is equivalent, can be used.

Addition and subtraction are binary operators; that is, they act on two operands. If both operands are Integer, the sum or difference is Integer. If either or both of the operands are Real, then the result is Real. Consider the following examples:

Expression	*Result*	*Type*
2 - 3	-1	Integer
2.0 - 3	-1.0	Real
2 - 3.0	-1.0	Real
2.0 - 3.0	-1.0	Real
2 + 3	5	Integer
2.0 + 3	5.0	Real
2 + 3.0	5.0	Real
2.0 + 3.0	5.0	Real

Most of the time the distinction between Integer and Real results will not be critical to you when performing addition and subtraction, since Integer and Real are operationally compatible data types.

2.9.3 Multiplication

The multiplication symbol in Pascal (and in most programming languages) is the asterisk. No implied multiplication is permitted, as in algebra. For example, the correct translation of the algebraic expression

$$2a$$

is

```
2 * A
```

If there are more than two multiplication operators, the operations are carried out from left to right. For example, to translate the expression

$$abc$$

you could write

```
A * B * C
```

This expression is equivalent to

```
(A * B) * C
```

As with addition and subtraction, multiplication is a binary operator. If the two operands are Integer, the product is Integer. If either or both of the operands are Real, the product will be Real. This property is illustrated in the following examples:

Expression	*Value*	*Type*
3 * 5	15	Integer
3 * 5.0	15.0	Real
3.0 * 5	15.0	Real
3.0 * 5.0	15.0	Real

2.9.4   Division

Pascal provides two division operators. The symbol / is used to obtain the Real quotient of two values; the symbol div is used to obtain the Integer quotient of two Integer operands. The Real quotient contains the fractional result, if any; the Integer quotient contains only the integer (whole-number) portion of the quotient. For example, the value of the expression 5 / 4 (Real quotient) is 1.2; the value of the expression 5 div 4 (Integer quotient) is 1. You will find that the Integer division operation is useful on occasion, but for most ordinary mathematical formulas, you will use the Real division operation.

Real division can be carried out with any mixture of Integer and Real operands. In any case, the result is Real. This principle is illustrated in the following examples:

Expression	*Value*	*Type*
2 / 3	0.66666666666	Real
2.0 / 3	0.66666666666	Real
2 / 3.0	0.66666666666	Real
2.0 / 3.0	0.66666666666	Real

Integer division can be carried out on only two integer operands. For example, the value of 2 div 3 is 0—the integer portion of the quotient. Any attempt to use the div operator with Real operands will be treated as an error.

Successive division operations in an expression are carried out from left to right. Consider, for example, the order of evaluation for the following two expressions:

```
6/4/2            6 div 4 div 2
 \_/              _____/
1.5/2              1    div 2
\____/              _____/
 0.75                  0
```

2.9.5   Modulus

The **modulus** operator, mod, is used to return the integer remainder after dividing the first operand by the second operand. This operation is defined only for two integer operands.

Recall the terminology used in division, as illustrated in the following example:

$$\text{Divisor} \longrightarrow 6\overline{)10} \quad \begin{array}{l} 1 \longleftarrow \text{Quotient} \\ 0 \longleftarrow \text{Dividend} \\ \underline{6} \\ 4 \longleftarrow \text{Remainder} \end{array}$$

As we have seen, the Integer division operator div is used to compute the integer quotient; thus, 10 **div** 6 has the value 1. The modulus operator is used to compute the remainder; for example, 10 **mod** 6 has the value 4.

The sign of the quotient is determined by the ordinary rules of algebra: If the divisor and dividend have the same sign, the quotient is positive; if the divisor and dividend have different signs, the quotient is negative. The sign of the modulus (the result of the mod operation) is always the same as the sign of the dividend. These facts are illustrated in the following examples:

Value Of		*Value Of*	*Value Of*
A	B	A **div** B	A **mod** B
13	4	3	1
-13	4	-3	-1
13	-4	-3	1
-13	-4	3	-1

You will find that the mod operation is very useful for certain programming tasks that are encountered quite frequently. For example, suppose you wish to convert time measured in months to years and months; that is, you want to convert, say, 14 months to 1 year and 2 months. Assuming that the variables TimeIn Years and TimeInMonths are of type Integer, the following two statements will perform the required conversion:

```
TimeInYears  := TimeInMonths div 12;
TimeInMonths := TimeInMonths mod 12;
```

2.9.6   *Time Out*

1. Evaluate each of the following expressions. In each case, specify the data type of the result.

(**a**) 3 - 4.0
(**b**) 3 + 4
(**c**) 3 - 4 + 6.0
(**d**) 3 / 2
(**e**) 3 **div** 2
(**f**) 3.0 / 2
(**g**) 3.0 / 2.0
(**h**) 3 * 2
(**i**) 3 * 2.0
(**j**) 5 **mod** 2
(**k**) -5 **mod** 2

(**l**) −5 **div** 2
(**m**) −4 / 5 / 2
(**n**) −4 **div** 5 **div** 2

2. Translate each of the following algebraic expressions into Pascal:
  (**a**) $x - y - z$
  (**b**) $2(x + y)$
  (**c**) x / y
  (**d**) xy
  (**e**) $x - (y + z + w)$

2.9.7 Precedence

When you write complex expressions, Pascal uses rules of **precedence** to determine, in the absence of parentheses, the order in which the operations are performed. This choice is of critical importance in computing the correct value of an expression. Consider, for example, the expression

$$2 \times 3 + 1$$

If the multiplication is performed first, the value is

$$(2 \times 3) + 1 = 6 + 1 = 7$$

If the addition is performed first, the value is

$$2 \times (3 + 1) = 2 * 4 = 8$$

Actually, multiplication has precedence over addition, so that the expression $2 \times 3 + 1$ should be evaluated as

$$2 \times 3 + 1 = (2 \times 3) + 1 = 6 + 1 = 7$$

There are three levels of precedence in evaluating arithmetic expressions, as shown in Figure 2.13. The highest level is the unary minus. At the next level is a group of operations called **multiplying operators**; these include multiplication (*), Real division (/), Integer division (div), and modulus (mod). At the lowest level are the **adding operators**, including addition (+) and subtraction (−). The basic rules followed by Pascal in evaluating an expression that is without parentheses are as follows:

Operations with higher precedence are carried out before operations with lower precedence. Operations with equal precedence are carried out from left to right.

Precedence Level	Operations
Highest	Unary minus (−)
↕	Multiplying operators (*, /, div, mod)
Lowest	Adding operators (+, −)

Figure 2.13 Precedence of arithmetic operators in an unparenthesized expression.

Consider, for example, the following expression:

```
-A  -  B  *  C  /  D  +  E
```

The operation with highest precedence is the unary minus, so that the first operation to be performed is $-A$:

```
(-A)  -  B  *  C  /  D  +  E
```

Next, the multiplying operators are evaluated. There are two of these—multiplication and division. Since they have equal precedence, they are carried out from left to right; in this case, the multiplication is performed first and then the division:

```
(-A)  -  ((B  *  C)  /  D)  +  E
```

Finally, the adding operators are evaluated. Again, there are two of them, and they are evaluated from left to right—the subtraction first and then the addition:

```
((-A)  -  ((B  *  C)  /  D))  +  E
```

In practice, you may not wish to rely on the rules of precedence when writing arithmetic expressions. You can control the order of evaluation by placing parentheses in the expression as needed. One place that parentheses are needed is to avoid two contiguous (side-by-side) operators. For example, in order to write the Pascal equivalent of the expression

$$a + -3$$

you have to enclose the -3 in parentheses:

```
A  +  (-3)
```

Without the parentheses, there would be two contiguous operators $+$ and $-$, which is prohibited in Pascal. In general, the rule regarding parentheses is

> When in doubt, use parentheses.

There is no penalty for excess parentheses; there will be serious consequences if you need them and they are omitted.

Some algebraic expressions that are written without parentheses must have parentheses inserted in them when translated into Pascal. For example, consider the expression

$$\frac{a + b}{3}$$

The correct way to translate this expression is

```
(A  +  B)  /  3
```

Without the parentheses, the expression would be equivalent to

$$a + \frac{b}{3}$$

which is obviously very different from what was intended.

Some expressions will require several sets of parentheses. Note that the brackets ([ ]) and braces ({ }) that are often found in algebra are not used in the same way in Pascal. Pascal recognizes only parentheses as grouping symbols in arithmetic expressions. You may use as many sets of parentheses as required. In evaluating expressions with multiple sets of parentheses, Pascal evaluates the innermost expression first, then evaluates the next innermost, and so on, until the expression is completely evaluated. For example, consider the algebraic expression

$$3[a - (b + c)]$$

The correct way to translate this into Pascal is

```
3 * (A - (B + C));
```

In evaluating this expression, the value of B + C is computed first, then the quantity A − (B + C); finally, the result is multiplied by 3.

Following are some examples of translated algebraic expressions.

Expression	*Pascal Equivalent*	*Comment*
$\dfrac{a + b}{c - d}$	(A+B)/(C-D)	Parentheses necessary in both numerator and denominator
$\dfrac{2x - y}{-3}$	(2*X-Y)/(-3)	Parentheses required for denominator to avoid contiguous operators
$3x + 4y - z$	3*X+4*Y-Z	No parentheses required
$\dfrac{a}{-(b + c)}$	A/(-(B+C))	Two sets of parentheses required
$3\left[\dfrac{a}{c - d} \cdot \dfrac{b}{c + d}\right]$	3*((A/(C-D))*(B/(C+D)))	This is a complicated expression; note that you must be careful to balance parentheses; for every left parenthesis, you must have a right parenthesis

2.9.8 *Time Out*

1. Evaluate each of the following expressions:

   (**a**) 2 + 3 / 4

   (**b**) 2 - 3 * 4

(c) 3 / 4 * 2

(d) 3 **div** 4 + (-2)

(e) 13 **div** 4 **mod** 2

(f) 2 + 4 **mod** 2

(g) (2 + 4) **mod** 2

(h) 2 - 3 **div** 2 + 13 **mod** 2

2. Translate each of the following expressions into Pascal:

(a) $ab - \dfrac{-3}{d}$

(b) $\dfrac{2(a - b)}{-3}$

(c) $\dfrac{a + b}{2} \cdot \dfrac{c - d}{4}$

(d) $(x - 3)(x + 4)$

(e) $\dfrac{x + y}{x - y}$

2.10   PROGRAM DEBUGGING AND TESTING

The process of ensuring a program's correctness should begin before the first line of program code is written. The programmer should logically execute the procedure while it is still at the pseudocode stage to make sure that the correct output will be produced for a carefully chosen variety of inputs. When choosing sample data to test a procedure, try to choose simple values for which calculations can be made without a great deal of work. For example, in testing one of the programs in Figures 2.7 and 2.9, you might use a value of 10 for age, since it is easy to calculate that the age in months should be $12 \times 10 = 120$ and the age in days should be $365.25 \times 10 = 3652.5$. If you cannot choose input values that yield simple computations, then it is a good practice to verify results with a calculator. Once the program is written, you can use these same values to verify that the program is producing correct results. After the program is written, it is the responsibility of the programmer to verify that it is a correct implementation of the procedure, as expressed in the program plan.

As you have seen, errors in programs may be classified as errors in syntax or logical errors. The compiler catches syntax errors when it cannot correctly translate a statement in your program. The compiler does not, however, detect errors in the logic of the program itself. After you have written a program and successfully removed all syntax errors, you must ensure that the program is logically correct—that is, that it performs its intended function correctly.

The basic approach to **program testing** is to enter data and verify that the output produced by the program is correct. This means that you must know what output to expect when you are testing a program with data. (You can usually use the data that was used to test the pseudocode version of the program as a starting point.) Only when you have verified by independent calculation that the answers produced by a program are correct can you have complete trust in the program. All too often, students neglect this very important part of the programming task. There is an unfortunate tendency to use test data for which expected answers are not known, and if the results that are produced look reasonable (or worse yet, if the output is properly formatted, but no care is paid to the reasonableness of the values), the student accepts the program as correct. In some organizations that develop software, the tasks of devising test data and testing software are carried out by professional software-testing personnel rather than the original programmers. Software testing is not an easy task, but it is absolutely imperative if the resulting product is to have any real value. The old adage "If it can go wrong, it will" is directly applicable to programming. The only way to make sure that your program doesn't have hidden flaws that cause it to produce erroneous output is to test the program with adequate data.

Let us suppose that you have encountered a logical problem in a program on which you are working. What can you do? The first step is to verify all the formulas in the program to see whether you have inadvertently made a mistake in typing a constant or variable in one of them. Often, you will spot the mistake immediately and be able to make the required correction. Sometimes it is helpful to break up long and involved expressions into several parts so that each part is simpler and can be verified independently of the others. For example, if you program contained the assignment statement

```
Alpha := 3 * (Beta - 4) + ( Beta + 2) * (Beta - 1);
```

you might break this up as follows:

```
Result1 := 3 * (Beta - 4);
Result2 := (Beta + 2) * (Beta - 1);
Alpha := Result1 + Result2;
```

Although the alternative requires three lines of code rather than one, each line is simpler, and, of course, simple expressions are less likely to contain errors than complicated ones.

If the formulas appear to be correct, then you may wish to insert some **diagnostic output** into your program to verify that the values of variables are what you expect them to be. This is particularly true if some intermediate results are computed that would not normally be printed out. For example, if you suspected that the problem in a program lay in the preceding assignment statement, you could insert the following diagnostic output:

```
Writeln ('Beta = ',Beta);
Result1 := 3 * (Beta - 4);
Writeln ('Result1 = ', Result1);
Result2 := (Beta + 2) * (Beta - 1);
Writeln ('Result2 = ', Result2);
Alpha := Result1 + Result2;
Writeln ('Alpha = ', Alpha);
```

When using diagnostic output, it is important to label the value being displayed so that you will know what you are looking at; there is nothing more frustrating than trying to make sense out of a screen full of unlabeled numbers. Of course, when you have found the problem, you will want to remove the diagnostic output statements so that the program user is not bothered by extraneous output.

Sometimes your best efforts at locating the source of a logical error in a program will be to no avail. After you have given the problem careful consideration on your own, you may find it helpful to talk to someone else who is knowledgeable about programming. Even if this person does not understand every detail of the problem you are attempting to solve with your program, the act of explaining parts of your program to him or her is often sufficient to enable you to spot the error yourself. But by all means, try to solve the problem on your own. The more you do for yourself, the greater will be your confidence in your own abilities. Debugging programs requires you to use your powers of deduction in somewhat the same way as a detective solves a crime. The more you exercise these powers, the better you will become at it.

Note: Users of Turbo Pascal version 5.0 or later may use the integrated debugging facility's Watch window to perform the diagnostic output described in this section. See Appendix G for details.

2.11 REVIEW QUESTIONS

1. Distinguish between a constant and a variable.
2. List the rules for writing valid identifiers in Pascal.
3. Name the three major parts of a Pascal program.
4. Distinguish between the meanings of = and :=.
5. What is the maximum length of a string constant or variable?
6. What are the rules for writing Integer constants? Real constants? String constants? Char constants?
7. What is exponential notation? Why would you use it?
8. What is the fundamental law of identifiers?
9. What is a file-identifier? In what statements would you use a file-identifier?
10. What is the purpose of an assignment statement?
11. Suppose the value of Real variable A is 3.0 and that of Real variable B is -2.0. What will be the value of Real variable C after execution of each of the following assignment statements?

    (a) `C := 2 * A + 3 - B;`
    (b) `C := A/B;`
    (c) `C := 3 * (A - B) / 2;`
    (d) `C := A * A + B * B;`
    (e) `C := A + 2 / B - 3;`
    (f) `C := A * Pi;`
    (g) `C := 3.2E4;`
    (h) `C := 3.2E-4;`

12. Suppose the value of Integer variable D is 3 and that of Integer variable E is -2. What will be the value of Integer variable F after execution of each of the following assignment statements?

    (a) `F := D **div** E;`
    (b) `F := D **mod** E;`

(**c**) F := D + E;

(**d**) F := -(D + E);

(**e**) F := -D + E;

(**f**) F := 14 **div** 3 **div** 2;

(**g**) F := 14 **mod** 3 **mod** 2;

13. Translate each of the following into Pascal:

   (**a**) Compute the remainder after dividing Hours by 24.

   (**b**) Compute the integer quotient of Hours divided by 24.

   (**c**) Compute the volume of a circular cylinder. If r is the radius of the base and h is the height, then the volume v is given by $v = \pi r^2 h$. *Hint:* Use the fact that $r^2 = r \times r$ when you write the formula in Pascal.

   (**d**) $a = bx^2 + c$

   (**e**) $a = \dfrac{b + c}{d + e}$

   (**f**) $a = 2[3 - (b + c)]$

14. What is pseudocode? What purpose does it serve?

15. What is top-down program design?

16. The following procedure is the first draft of a program to compute the volume of a cylinder for values of the radius and height entered by the user. Refine the procedure to a point at which the program could be written:

   1.0 Get values for Radius and Height

   2.0 Compute Volume

   3.0 Write input values and Volume

17. Is the following statement true or false? Why?

   The programming task is finished when all syntax errors have been removed from the program.

18. What is diagnostic output? Why would you use it?

2.12   PROGRAMMING EXERCISES

1. Write a program to compute the area and circumference of a circle for a value of the radius entered by the user. Recall that $a = \pi r^2$ and $c = 2\pi r$.

2. Look up the currency-conversion factors for your choice of foreign countries. Write a Pascal program to allow the program user to enter an amount of U.S. currency and print out the equivalent amounts in foreign currency. Include appropriate currency designators (for example, pounds for Great Britain, francs for France, etc.).

3. Write a program to convert miles to kilometers, using the fact that 1 mile = 1.61 kilometers.

4. Write a program to compute the batting average and slugging average for a baseball player. Input consists of the number of singles, doubles, triples, home runs, and times at bat. The batting average is the number of hits divided by the number of times at bat. The slugging average is the total bases divided by the number of times at bat. (A single counts as one base, a double as two, a triple as three, and a home run as four.)

5. Let three resistors be connected in parallel, as follows:

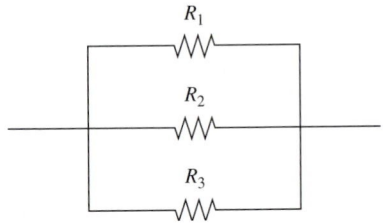

Then the total resistance of the circuit is

$$\frac{1}{\dfrac{1}{R_1} + \dfrac{1}{R_2} + \dfrac{1}{R_3}}$$

Write a program to read values for R_1, R_2, and R_3 and compute the total resistance.

6. Given two integers p and q, where $p > q$, a Pythagorean triplet is formed by

$$p^2 - q^2 \qquad 2pq \qquad p^2 + q^2$$

Write a program to read p and q and compute the corresponding triplet. *Note:* A Pythagorean triplet consists of three integer values that can be the sides of a right triangle. The term is derived from the Pythagorean theorem, which states that for sides a and b and hypotenuse c of a right triangle, $a^2 + b^2 = c^2$. You might wish to verify that the values computed by your program do indeed satisfy this relationship.

7. Write a program to convert a measurement expressed in inches into yards, feet, and inches.

8. Radar can be used to compute the distance of an object in the following manner: The radar signal travels at approximately the speed of light (186,000 miles per second). The difference between the time of transmission and the time the signal returns, divided by 2, is the time it took for the signal to travel to the object. This time multiplied by the speed of light is the distance to the object. Write a program to compute the altitude of a satellite for a ground-based radar site. The trackers use a clock that measures time in seconds. The program user should be able to enter the time at which the signal was sent and the time at which the signal returned. The program must compute the altitude of the satellite.

9. One commonly used angle measure is in radians. There are 2π radians in $360°$. Write a program to convert angle measure in degrees to radians. *Hint:* $1° = \pi/180$ radians.

10. Write a program to compute the number of coins required to make a given amount of change (less than one dollar). For example, 59 cents = 2 quarters, 0 dimes, 1 nickel, and 4 pennies.

11. A retail merchant is planning a sale in which merchandise will be discounted by 6%, 8%, and 10% on successive days. Write a program to allow the merchant to enter the regular price of an item and then compute and print the three sale prices.

12. Write a program to allow a user to enter an amount to be invested and an interest rate. Have the program compute the amount that will be in the account at the end of 1 year, assuming that the amount will be invested for 1 year and that the interest will be compounded quarterly. If $P =$ amount invested and $R =$ interest rate, the required formula is

$$P \times \left(1 + \frac{R}{4}\right)^4$$

13. An employee is paid at the rate of \$6 per hour on a weekly basis. If the employee works more than 40 hours per week, he or she is paid at $1\frac{1}{2}$ times the normal rate of pay. From the employee's paycheck, the following deductions are made:

Federal withholding tax: 13% of gross pay
Social security tax: 6.7% of gross pay
Union dues: \$5.45

Write a program to allow the employee to enter the number of hours he or she worked at the regular rate and the number of hours worked at the overtime rate. Compute and print the gross pay, the amounts of the deductions, and the net pay.

3

Introduction to Pascal: Part 2

In this chapter, you will gain confidence in your ability to solve problems as you expand your knowledge of Pascal. You will be able to add comments to your programs to make them more understandable to yourself and others. You will be able to write more complex arithmetic expressions by adding standard mathematical functions and exponentiation. You will learn about data type Boolean and more about Char. You will be able to exert more control over your input and output operations using the Write procedure, formatting, and screen control procedures. You will learn how to read from and write to text files. You will be able to divide your programs into segments by writing your own procedures.

3.1   COMMENTS

Pascal gives you the option of including comments at virtually any point in your program. Comments are ignored by the compiler; their purpose is strictly to communicate with the person reading the program. Comments are enclosed in braces, which are the symbols { and } appearing on the keyboard of all current microcomputers.[1]

For example, Figure 3.1 shows Program 3a, which is identical to Program 2h with added comments. In order to improve the readability of the program listings in this book we will show comments in italics. In program listings produced by the Turbo Pascal Print command, comments will also appear in italics. On the screen, Turbo Pascal 7.0 displays comments in grey.

The first comment that you should include in every program describes the purpose of the program. This comment should immediately follow the program statement:

```
program P3a (Input, Output);
{Program to compute area and perimeter of a
     rectangle, given length and width}
```

Note that a comment may be on one line or many lines. The comment starts with the left brace, {, and ends with the right brace, }. Using the alternative notation for comments, this portion of the program would appear as follows:

```
program P3a (Input, Output);
(* Program to compute area and perimeter of a
     rectangle, given length and width *)
```

Your instructor may wish you to include more elaborate comments at the beginning of your programs, including your name, the date, the assignment number, and perhaps other information as well.

Comments should be used in the declaration part of a program to explain the purpose of the program elements being defined. In the variable declaration part, for example, it is useful to categorize variables. For instance, a simple program usually has some input variables (variables whose value is supplied by the user) and some output variables (variables whose value is computed and written). In the program shown in Figure 3.1, Length and Width are input variables, whereas Area and Perimeter are output variables. Appropriate comments are included, showing the categorization of these

---

[1]If your keyboard does not have the brace symbols (or even if it does), you can use (* and *) as an alternative. Because the parentheses have other meanings in Pascal, whereas the braces are used exclusively for comments, and because the alternative takes two characters instead of one, we choose to use the braces for comments. You should be aware that others disagree with this choice and recommend using the alternative exclusively. One reason to use the alternative is for compatibility with standard Pascal, which specifies (* and *) for comments. For this reason, many of the Pascal programs you see in magazines and other books use the alternative notation.

```
program P3a (Input, Output);
{Program to compute area and perimeter of a
    rectangle, given length and width}
const
    LengthPrompt = 'Enter length of rectangle ';
    WidthPrompt = 'Enter width of rectangle ';
var
    Length, Width,          {Input variables}
    Area, Perimeter         {Output variables}
        : Real;
begin

{1.0 Get values for Length and Width}

    Writeln (LengthPrompt);
    Readln (Length);
    Writeln (WidthPrompt);
    Readln (Width);

{2.0 Compute Perimeter and Area}

    Perimeter := 2.0 * (Length + Width);
    Area := Length * Width;

{3.0 Write input values and computed values}

    Writeln;
    Writeln ('Length =', Length, ' Width =', Width);
    Writeln ('Perimeter =', Perimeter, ' Area =', Area)
end.
```

Figure 3.1 Program 3a: Example of use of comments.

variables:

```
var
    Length, Width,      {Input variables}
    Area, Perimeter     {Output variables}
        : Real;
```

There are many other ways to write the same comments; for example, the following format would work just as well:

```
var
    {Input variables}
        Length, Width
    {Output variables}
        Area, Perimeter : Real;
```

You can probably think of other ways to accomplish the same purpose. Remember: The goal of comments is to make the program readable to you and anyone else who needs to read and understand it.

Comments can also be used in the statement part of the program to explain the purpose of each statement or sequence of statements. A good approach to take here is to use the pseudocode that you developed for the program as a guide. Each major step from the pseudocode can be translated as a comment, as shown in Figure 3.1. Of course, additional lines of pseudocode or any additional comments that might help the reader understand the program could be included. Note the use of blank lines. These may be used anywhere within the program and often help to make a program more readable. The goal is readability and understandability, not slavish adherence to an inflexible standard.

3.1.1 Time Out

Retrieve Program 2c from the program disk that accompanies the text, and add comments to it in the style illustrated in Figure 3.1.

3.2 MATHEMATICAL FUNCTIONS

A function is an algorithm that performs a computation and returns a single value. Most functions require one or more arguments; these are the values used by the function in performing its work. You have probably studied functions in mathematics and made use of them on your calculator. Pascal provides a variety of the most often used mathematical functions as a standard feature of the language, and it gives you the facility to define your own functions. We will have much more to say on the subject of programmer-defined functions later; in this section, we describe the standard mathematical functions in Pascal.

A summary of the most often used Pascal standard mathematical functions is shown in Figure 3.2. Note that each has a standard identifier and requires one parameter, which is enclosed in parentheses after the function name. This parameter is the argument of the function. In order to make use of a function, all you have to do is write the function with the desired argument in any arithmetic expression. During the execution of the program, the appropriate value will be returned automatically, and that value will (conceptually) take the place of the function reference in the evaluation of the expression. A parameter may be coded as a constant, a variable, or an arbitrarily complex expression. If an expression is used as a parameter, it will be evaluated, and the result will be used as the value of the parameter.

3.2.1 Absolute Value

You may recall that the absolute value of a number is defined mathematically as

$$|x| = \begin{cases} x & \text{if } x > 0 \\ 0 & \text{if } x = 0 \\ -x & \text{if } x < 0 \end{cases}$$

If the argument is positive, the absolute value is the same as the value of the argument; if the argument is negative, the absolute value is the opposite of (or negative of) the argument. The net result is that the absolute value of a number is always positive. For example,

$$|3| = 3 \qquad \text{since } 3 > 0$$

		Data Type		
Function	**Syntax**	**Argument**	**Value**	**Description**
Absolute Value	Abs(*param*)	Integer or Real	Same as argument	Returns the absolute value of argument
Arctangent	Arctan(*param*)	Integer or Real	Real	Returns the arctangent of argument expressed in radians
Cosine	Cos(*param*)	Integer or Real	Real	Returns the cosine of argument which must be expressed in radians
Exponential	Exp(*param*)	Integer or Real	Real	Returns e^{param}, where e is the constant 2.718281 . . .
Fractional part	Frac(*param*)	Integer or Real	Real	Returns the fractional part of the argument
Integer part	Int(*param*)	Integer or Real	Real	If *param* $\geq$ 0, returns greatest integer $\leq$ to *param* If *param* $<$ 0, returns smallest integer $\geq$ to *param*
Logarithm	Ln(*param*)	Integer or Real	Real	Returns the natural logarithm (base e) of argument
Round	Round(*param*)	Real	Integer	Rounds to nearest integer If *param* $\geq$ 0, returns Trunc(*param* + 0.5) If *param* $<$ 0, returns Trunc(*param* − 0.5)
Sine	Sin(*param*)	Integer or Real	Real	Returns sine of argument, which must be expressed in radians
Square	Sqr(*param*)	Integer or Real	Same as argument	Returns $param^2 = param \times param$
Square root	Sqrt(*param*)	Integer or Real	Real	Returns the square root of argument
Truncate	Trunc(*param*)	Real	Integer	If *param* $\geq$ 0, returns greatest integer $\leq$ to *param*. If *param* $<$ 0, returns smallest integer $\geq$ to *param*

Figure 3.2 Summary of Turbo Pascal standard mathematical functions.

and

$$|-3| = -(-3) = 3 \qquad \text{since } -3 < 0$$

In order to compute absolute value in a Pascal program, you write

```
Abs (param)
```

where *param* represents the value of the argument of the function. For example, you could write the following expressions:

Algebraic expression	**Pascal equivalent**
$|-3|$	Abs(-3)
$|x|$	Abs(X)
$|x - 3y|$	Abs(X - 3 * Y)

Note that the argument for a function can be any expression, no matter how complex; it can involve any function references that may be needed. Consider the following example:

Algebraic expression	Pascal equivalent
$\|\|x\| - \|y\|\|$	Abs (Abs (X) - Abs (Y))

There are two data types to be considered in any reference to a function: the data type of the argument and the data type of the value of the function. In the case of the function Abs, the argument may be Integer or Real, and the value of the function will have the same data type as the argument. Consider the following examples:

Expression	Argument type	Value	Type of value
Abs (−3.5)	Real	3.5	Real
Abs (3)	Integer	3	Integer

3.2.2. Trigonometric Functions

Pascal provides three trigonometric functions: sine, cosine, and arctangent. Sine and cosine are quite similar. The general form for references to these two functions is

```
Sin (param)
Cos (param)
```

where *param* represents the argument of the function, expressed in radian measure. Those of you who have studied trigonometry will recall that the formula for converting from degree measure to radian measure is

```
radian = degree / 57.296
```

The constant 57.296 is approximately equal to the number of degrees in 1 radian. Actually, this value is 180/π. Thus, the following Pascal expressions could be used to compute the sine and cosine of an angle measured in degrees:

```
Sin (Degree / (180/Pi))      Cos (Degree / (180/Pi))
```

(Recall that Pi is the standard identifier for the constant π.) The program in Figure 3.3 illustrates a simple application of the trigonometric functions. The user enters the angle measure in degrees, and the program prints out the radian measure and the sine and cosine of the angle.

```
program P3b (Input, Output, Lst);
{Program computes sine and cosine for angles entered by user}
uses Printer;
const
     InputPrompt = 'Enter Angle Measure (in degrees)';
var
     Degree,         {Input variable}
     Radian          {Output variable}
        : Real;
begin
     Writeln (InputPrompt);
     Readln (Degree);
     Radian := Degree/(180/Pi);
     Writeln (Lst,'Degree Measure = ', Degree,
               ' Radian Measure = ',Radian);
     Writeln (Lst, 'Sine = ',Sin(Radian), ' Cosine =  ',Cos(Radian))
end.


                    Sample output from Program 3b

 Degree Measure = 9.0000000000E+01 Radian Measure = 1.5707963268E+00
 Sine = 9.9999999999E-01 Cosine = 0.0000000000E+00
```

Figure 3.3 Program 3b: Example of use of functions Sin and Cos.

The general form for reference to the arctangent function is

```
Arctan (param)
```

where *param* is the value of the tangent of an angle. The function Arctan returns the measure of the angle in radians. The value of the argument may be Integer or Real; the value returned by the function is Real. For example, the following statements could be part of a program to allow a user to compute the arctangent of any desired value:

```
Writeln ('Tangent value = ', TanValue);
Writeln ('Angle = ', Arctan (TanValue),' Radians')
```

3.2.3 Exponential and Logarithmic Functions

Two functions that are closely related are the exponential function Exp, which is used to compute a power of the number e, and the logarithmic function Ln, which is used to compute logarithms to the base e. The constant e, which is approximately equal to 2.7182818285 . . . , is an important number in mathematics. It is an irrational number like π, which means that its decimal representation is nonrepeating and nonterminating. (Because of this, any computations based on these values in a computer must be performed with approximations of the actual value.) A lot of mathematical formulas involve the number e, and it is a convenient base for computing logarithms as well.

In order to compute a power of e, you can use the function Exp, which has the general form

```
Exp (param)
```

The argument of the function is the exponent to be applied to the base e; the value returned will be e^{param}. For example, the value of Exp (1) is $e^1 = 2.7182818285$, which is the value of e correct to 11 significant digits. The argument may be Integer or Real; the value of the function will always be Real. Examples of the use of this function in translating algebraic expressions are as follows:

Algebraic expression	Pascal equivalent
e^{x+y}	Exp (X + Y)
$\dfrac{1}{e^{x+y} - e^{x-y}}$	1 / (Exp (X + Y) - Exp (X - Y))

The natural logarithm (base e) of a number can be computed using the function Ln, which has general form

```
Ln (param)
```

where *param* is an Integer or Real value. The value returned will be Real. Recall that a logarithm is actually an exponent required to produce the value of its argument. For example, we know that

$$e^1 = 2.7182818285\ldots$$

This implies that the logarithm to the base e of 2.7182818285 . . . is 1; that is, Ln (2.7182818285) is approximately 1. Because logarithms actually represent exponents, and because any power of a positive base is greater than zero, the argument of the function Ln must be greater than zero. If you attempt to evaluate the function Ln with an argument that is negative or zero, an appropriate error message will result. (In Turbo Pascal, this message is "Runtime error 207 at . . . .") Following are some examples of the use of the Ln function:

Algebraic expression	Pascal equivalent
$\ln(a)$	Ln (A)
$\ln(e^a)$	Ln (Exp (A))

You should note that the functions Ln and Exp are closely related; in fact, mathematicians call them inverse functions, which means that each "undoes" the action of the other. That is, $\ln(e^a) = a$ and $e^{\ln(a)} = a$. You can verify this by writing values of the expressions

```
Ln (Exp (A)) and Exp (Ln(A))
```

for appropriate values of A.

3.2.4 Square and Square Root

Two very useful functions are square, which returns the value of the argument squared (multiplied by itself), and square root, which returns the square root of the argument. The general form of the square function is

```
Sqr (param)
```

where the argument is an Integer or Real value; the value returned will have the same data type as the argument and will be equal to $param^2 = param \times param$. Following are examples:

Expression	Type of argument	Value	Type of value
Sqr (3)	Integer	9	Integer
Sqr (-4.2)	Real	17.64	Real
Sqr (10.0)	Real	100.0	Real

The Sqr function is useful in translating mathematical expressions that make use of powers of 2. For example, consider the following:

Algebraic expression	Pascal equivalent
$x^2 + 3x - 4$	Sqr (X) + 3 * X - 4
$(2x)^2 - (x + y^2)^2$	Sqr (2 * X) - Sqr (X + Sqr (Y))

Note that it is always possible to write an expression correctly without the Sqr function; for example, x^2 can be translated as X * X instead of Sqr (X). The power of the Sqr function comes in its similarity to the mathematical notation, so the Pascal expression is very close to the original algebra. The Sqr function can be used to compute other powers, as in the following examples:

Algebraic expression	Pascal equivalents
x^3	X * Sqr (X), or X*X*X
x^4	Sqr (Sqr (X)), or X*X*X*X
x^6	Sqr(X) * Sqr (Sqr(X)), or X*X*X*X*X*X

The next major section in this chapter covers an alternative method for computing powers.

Square root is the inverse function of square. The general form of the function reference is

```
Sqrt (param)
```

where *param* is of type Integer or Real and has a value that is not less than zero. The value of the function is Real and is equal to $\sqrt{param}$. (The restriction on the value of the argument is necessary because the square root of a negative number is not a real number. Pascal does not handle complex or imaginary numbers as a standard data type. Turbo Pascal will write the following error message if, during the execution of a program, an attempt is made to evaluate the square root of a negative number: "Error 207: Invalid floating point operation.") Following are some examples of the evaluation of the Sqrt function:

Expression	Value
Sqrt (4)	2.0
Sqrt (2.0)	1.4142135
Sqrt (Sqrt(16))	2.0

The Sqrt function is useful in expressing algebraic formulas involving radicals and powers of $\frac{1}{2}$, as shown in the following examples:

Algebraic expression	Pascal equivalent
$\sqrt{x+y}$	Sqrt (X + Y)
$x - (y + z)^{1/2}$	X - Sqrt (Y + Z)

As with Exp and Ln, Sqr and Sqrt are inverse functions. Thus, $\sqrt{x^2} = x$ and $(\sqrt{x})^2 = x$. You can verify these identities by writing the values of the expressions

```
Sqrt (Sq (X)) and Sqr (Sqrt (X))
```

for appropriate values of X.

3.2.5 Integer and Fractional Parts

Occasionally, it is useful to be able to separate a number into its two parts—the integer part that lies to the left of the decimal point and the fractional or decimal part that lies to the right of the decimal point. For example, consider the number 3.45. The integer part is 3 and the fractional part is 0.45. Pascal provides functions to perform these tasks—Int computes the integer portion of a value and Frac computes the fractional part of a value.

The general form of the Integer function is

```
Int (param)
```

where the argument may be Integer or Real. The value is Real and is computed as follows:

> If the value of the argument is greater than or equal to 0, the function returns the greatest integer less than or equal to the argument. If the value of the argument is negative, the function returns the smallest integer greater than or equal to the argument.

This description may seem complicated, but a few examples will help you see the logic behind the rule:

Expression	Value	Comment
Int(3.2)	3.0	3.0 is the largest integer value ≤ 3.2
Int (3)	3.0	3.0 is the largest integer value ≤ 3; note that the value of the function is always Real
Int (-3.2)	−3.0	−3.0 is the smallest integer value ≥ -3.2
Int (-3)	−3.0	−3.0 is the smallest integer value ≥ -3

The general form of the Fractional function is

```
Frac (param)
```

where the argument may be Integer or Real. The value of the function is the fractional part of the argument:

```
param - Int (param)
```

The value of the function is Real. Following are some examples of the evaluation of this function:

Expression	Value	Comment
Frac (3.2)	0.2	$3.2 - \text{Int }(3.2) = 3.2 - 3.0 = 0.2$
Frac (3)	0.0	$3 - \text{Int }(3) = 3 - 3.0 = 0.0$
Frac (-3.2)	−0.2	$-3.2 - \text{Int }(-3.2) = -3.2 - (-3.0) = -0.2$
Frac (-3)	0.0	$-3 - \text{Int }(-3) = -3 - (-3.0) = 0.0$

Often Int and Frac are used together, as in the following example: Suppose you wish to separate a currency amount into dollars and cents, where the currency amount was contained in a Real variable. (This operation is necessary, for example, in writing checks, wherein the written description of the check amount has separate parts for the dollar amount and the cents.) Assuming that the variables DollarAmount, CentsAmount and CurrencyAmount are all Real, the following statements could be used to perform the task:

```
DollarAmount := Int (CurrencyAmount);
CentsAmount := Frac (CurrencyAmount);
```

3.2.6   Truncate and Round

The Truncate and Round functions are unlike any of the other functions covered in this section because, whereas the argument of the function is of type Real (as was the case with the other functions), the value of the function is of type Integer. These two functions allow you to convert a Real value to Integer form.

The general form of the truncate function is

```
Trunc (param)
```

where the argument must be of type Real. The value of the function is of type Integer and is computed in exactly the same way as the Int function:

If the value of the argument is greater than or equal to 0, the function returns the greatest integer less than or equal to the argument. If the value of the argument is negative, the function returns the smallest integer greater than or equal to the argument.

The only difference between the Trunc function and the Int function is that although the value of the Int function is Real, the value of the Trunc function is Integer, as shown in the following examples:

Expression	Value	Expression	Value
Trunc (2.56)	2	Int (2.56)	2.0
Trunc (-2.56)	-2	Int (-2.56)	-2.0

The Round function rounds a Real argument to the nearest Integer. The general form of the round function is

```
Round (param)
```

where the argument must be Real. The value of the function is computed as follows:

If the argument is greater than or equal to zero, the function returns the value Trunc (*param* + 0.5). If the argument is negative, the function returns the value Trunc (*param* − 0.5).

The following are examples of how Round works:

Expression	Value	Comment
Round (3.2)	3	Trunc $(3.2 + 0.5) =$ Trunc $(3.7) = 3$
Round (3.6)	4	Trunc $(3.6 + 0.5) =$ Trunc $(4.1) = 4$
Round (-3.2)	-3	Trunc $(-3.2 - 0.5) =$ Trunc $(-3.7) = -3$
Round (-3.5)	-4	Trunc $(-3.5 - 0.5) =$ Trunc $(-4.0) = -4$

The Round function can be used to round a Real value to any desired number of decimal places. For example, suppose we wish to round the value of CurrencyAmount to two decimal places. Then the following expression could be used:

```
Round (CurrencyAmount * 100) / 100
```

As an example, if CurrencyAmount has the value 3.607, the evaluation of this expression would proceed as follows:

```
Round (3.607 * 100) / 100
Round (   360.7   )
        361            / 100
              3.61
```

The Truncate function can be used in a similar manner to truncate a Real value to any desired number of decimal digits:

```
Trunc (3.607 * 100) / 100
Trunc (   360.7   )
        360            / 100
              3.60
```

3.2.7 *Time Out*

1. Evaluate each of the following expressions, assuming that the variable A is Real and has the value 3.6.
   (a) `Abs (A)`
   (b) `Sqr (A)`
   (c) `Sqrt (25)`
   (d) `Sqr (Sqrt (A))`
   (e) `Int (A)`
   (f) `Int (-A)`
   (g) `Frac (A)`

(**h**) `Trunc (A)`

(**i**) `Round (A)`

(**j**) `Exp (Ln (A))`

(**k**) `Ln (Esp (A)`

2. Translate each of the following expressions into Pascal.

   (**a**) $|x - y|$

   (**b**) $3x^2 + 4y^2$

   (**c**) $\sqrt{x^4 - y^3}$

   (**d**) $\sin(x) - \cos(x)$

   (**e**) $\arctan(x)$

   (**f**) $e^x - e^{-x}$

   (**g**) $\ln(x^2)$

   (**h**) $\sin^2(x)$

   (**i**) Round the value of x to the nearest thousandth.

   (**j**) Round the value of x to the nearest hundred.

3. Write a short Pascal program to verify that Sqr and Sqrt and Exp and Ln are inverse functions.

3.3   EXPONENTIATION: PROBLEM AND SOLUTION

Pascal is probably the only high-level programming language that does not have an arithmetic operator for **exponentiation**. Yet exponentiation is a very common mathematical process; you will need to accomplish it to implement mathematical formulas related to business, finance, and statistics, as well as most branches of science and mathematics.

We have discussed one approach to the problem: You can use the definition of exponentiation as repeated multiplication in some cases. For example, the algebraic expression x^3 can be implemented either as X * X * X or as X * Sqr (X). For large values of the exponent, this method is quite tedious. Also, the method does not work for fractional exponents such as $x^{1/3}$. Some fractional exponents can be handled using the Sqrt function. For example, the expression $x^{1/2}$ can be implemented as Sqrt (X), and the expression $x^{1/4}$, which is equivalent to $(x^{1/2})^{1/2}$, can be translated as Sqrt (Sqrt(X)). This approach is also applicable only for certain special expressions and does not offer a solution to the general problem.

A much more general problem is the use of a variable as an exponent. How can we implement expressions such as x^n? The answer lies in the use of logarithms, which—before the advent of calculators and computers—were commonly used as an aid to performing exponentiation. Performing exponentiation in expressions such as

$$(4^2)^3$$

can be accomplished by multiplying the exponents:

$$(4^2)^3 = 4^{2 \times 3} = 4^6$$

Logarithms are actually exponents. Combining these two ideas leads to the following rule:

> The logarithm of a power can be computed by multiplying the logarithm of the base by the exponent.

Thus, $\ln(3^2) = 2 \times \ln(3)$. This property holds for real exponents as well as integer exponents, e.g.,

$$\ln(3^{1/2}) = \tfrac{1}{2} \times \ln(3)$$

and, in general,

$$\ln(x^n) = n \times \ln(x)$$

Of course, this expression is the logarithm of the power; in order to compute the actual value of the power, it is necessary to find the inverse logarithm of the result. This is done by raising the logarithm base (e in the case of natural logarithms) to the power of the logarithm. The method is summarized in the following equations:

$$x^n = e^{\ln(x^n)} = e^{n \ln(x)}$$

Thus, an appropriate way to implement exponentiation in a Pascal program is as follows:

```
Exp (exponent * Ln (base))
```

where *base* must be positive. The following examples illustrate the use of this method:

Expression	Pascal equivalent
x^n	Exp (N * Ln (X))
$y^{1/4}$	Exp (0.25 * Ln (Y))
$z^{1/n}$	Exp ((1 / N) * Ln (Z))

The major drawback to this method is the restriction that the argument of the function Ln be greater than zero. In some situations it is more appropriate to use repeated multiplication, which is valid for positive and negative values of the variable. But when repeated multiplication is not appropriate, the use of logarithms is a readily available alternative.

3.3.1 Time Out

Translate each of the following expressions into Pascal:
1. $a^n - b^n$
2. $\sqrt[3]{x}$
3. x^{a+b}
4. $\dfrac{x^a}{y^b}$

5. ax^b

6. $(x + y)^{2n}$

3.4 WRITE AND WRITELN

There are two procedures that can be used to direct output to a file: Write and Writeln. Up until now, you have used Writeln for output. This procedure executes a sequence of control characters that cause carriage return (Cr) and line feed (Lf) to be inserted at the end of every line of text. (Control characters are used to send commands to a device, rather than to send characters to be displayed by the device.) Carriage return causes the next output to a device to appear at the beginning of a line. Line feed causes the next output to begin on the next line. When output is directed to the screen, the Cr code causes the cursor to return to the beginning of a line; the Lf code causes the cursor to go to the next line.[2] Taken together, the **Cr/Lf** combination causes the cursor to be placed at the beginning of the next line on the screen so that the next screen operation (either input or output) will take place beginning at that point. A similar operation takes place when the Cr/Lf combination is directed to the printer. The print head returns to the beginning of a line, and the paper is advanced one line so that it is ready for new output at the beginning of a new line. (When the Writeln procedure addresses a disk file, the actual codes for Cr and Lf are inserted into the text; more will be said on this in Section 3.11.)

The **Write** procedure does essentially the same thing as the Writeln procedure, except that the Cr/Lf codes are not inserted at the end of each line of text. The general forms of the Write statement are essentially the same as those of the Writeln statement:

```
Write (expression-list)
Write (file-identifier, expression-list)
```

where *expression-list* is a list of constants, variables, or expressions separated by commas and *file-identifier* is an identifier for the file to which the output is directed.

For example, suppose you wished to write the characters

```
ABC
```

in a line of text on the screen and position the cursor so that the next output would begin at the beginning of the next line. One way to do this, of course, is to use the statement

```
Writeln ('ABC');
```

The actual sequence of characters transmitted by this statement to the screen are

```
ABC (Cr)(Lf)
```

---

[2]The Cr/Lf combination of codes is sometimes referred to as the End Of Line or EOL marker.

The system intercepts the codes for Cr and Lf and performs the desired action rather than displaying output on the screen. Another way that this task could be done would be as follows:

```
Write ('A');
Write ('B');
Writeln ('C');
```

The first Write statement causes the character A to be displayed on the screen. The cursor advances automatically to the next position and waits for more output. The next Write statement causes the character B to be displayed on the screen; as before, the cursor advances one position and waits. The Writeln statement causes the character C to be displayed on the screen, followed by Cr and Lf; the cursor is positioned at the beginning of the next line and waits for the next operation. This is obviously a trivial example; no one would use three statements to do the job of one. However, the Write statement is useful in a variety of instances because it gives you more flexibility in writing your program and greater control over the placement of output on the screen.

For example, the Write statement allows you to divide up a long and complicated Writeln statement into several parts. You can use a sequence of Write statements for the basic output and then follow the sequence with a single Writeln statement to cause a carriage return and line feed. For example, the following statement sequences are equivalent:

```
Writeln (A, B, C, D);   Write (A);
                        Write (B, C);
                        Write (D);
                        Writeln;
```

(You can make this example realistic by replacing A, B, C, and D by complicated strings or expressions.)

As another example, consider Program 3c, shown in Figure 3.4, which is a revision of Program 3a. In the previous version of the program, the Writeln statement was used to display prompts for data entry; in this version, the Write statement is used to display these prompts:

```
Write (LengthPrompt);
Readln (Length);
Write (WidthPrompt);
Readln (Width);
```

The first statement causes the sequence of characters contained in LengthPrompt to be displayed, and the cursor waits in the next available position for the user to type data; a similar sequence of events occurs in the second data-entry operation. The appearance of the screen after execution of the program is shown in the lower portion of Figure 3.4. Typing data immediately following a prompt is a much more natural way for most users to enter data than typing the data on the line below the prompt.

```
program P3c (Input, Output);
{Program to compute area and perimeter of a
     rectangle, given length and width}
const
     LengthPrompt = 'Enter length of rectangle ';
     WidthPrompt = 'Enter width of rectangle ';
var
     Length, Width,          {Input variables}
     Area, Perimeter         {Output variables}
        : Real;
begin

{1.0 Get values for Length and Width}

{Note use of Write statements in this segment of the program}
     Write (LengthPrompt);
     Readln (Length);
     Write (WidthPrompt);
     Readln (Width);

{2.0 Compute Perimeter and Area}

     Perimeter := 2.0 * (Length + Width);
     Area := Length * Width;

{3.0 Write input values and computed values}

     Writeln;
     Writeln ('Length =', Length, ' Width =', Width);
     Writeln ('Perimeter =', Perimeter, ' Area =', Area)
end.
```

Sample execution of Program 3c

```
Enter length of rectangle 3
Enter width of rectangle 4.5

Length = 3.0000000000E+00 Width = 4.5000000000E+00
Perimeter = 1.5000000000E+01 Area = 1.3500000000E+01
```

Figure 3.4 Program 3c: Example of use of the Write statement for input prompts.

3.4.1. Time Out

Modify Program 2h to make use of the Write statement for the input prompts, as shown in Figure 3.4. Also, break up the last two Writeln statements into a series of Write statements using only Writeln statements to produce Cr/Lf.

3.5 FORMATTED OUTPUT

You may have noticed that you seem to be somewhat at the mercy of the system when it comes to the appearance of the output produced by your programs. Pascal gives you the option of specifying **formatting** information in the list of arguments in your Write and Writeln statements. This option allows you to exert a measure of control over the appearance of the values written by your program in terms of the number of characters on the line allocated to the value and, for Real values, the choice of ordinary or exponential format. A value of any type can be formatted; however, the details differ from type to type.

3.5.1 Formatting String Values

A string value is formatted by writing a colon followed by an integer expression after a string-valued parameter in a Write or Writeln parameter list. The value of the integer expression, called *field-width* in the following general form, specifies the number of characters to be used in the line for the value of the string:

```
string-parameter: field-width
```

For example, suppose you had a string variable called StudentName and wished to have the system write the value of the variable using 20 positions on the output line. Then the following Writeln statement could be used:

```
Writeln (StudentName: 20);
```

If the content of StudentName is less than 20 characters in length, the output will be right justified in the field and padded on the left with spaces. For example, if the content of StudentName is 'Mary Smith', which is 10 characters in length, the output would have 10 spaces followed by the characters 'Mary Smith'. The output would appear as follows:

$$\text{|\_|\_|\_|\_|\_|\_|\_|\_|\_|\_|M|a|r|y|\_|S|m|i|t|h|}$$

If the content of the string is longer than the value of *field-width*, the output will consist of actual characters. For example, the output produced by the statement

```
Writeln (StudentName:5);
```

would be

$$\text{|M|a|r|y|\_|S|m|i|t|h|}$$

since the length of StudentName is greater than 5. Program 3d, shown in Figure 3.5, illustrates both of these rules in the output produced by its first two Writeln statements.

Note that any string-valued parameter can be formatted; that is, a string constant, variable, or expression can make use of a format descriptor. For example, the following Writeln statement could be used:

```
Writeln ('Heading':30);
```

This would cause the characters 'Heading' to be right justified in a field of length 30,

```
program P3d (Lst);
{This program demonstrates formatted output}
uses Printer;
const
      StringValue = 'This is a string';
      PositiveInteger = 1235;
      NegativeInteger = -1235;
      PositiveReal = 12.86;
      NegativeReal = -12.86;
begin
      Writeln (Lst, '*', StringValue:20, '*');
      Writeln (Lst, '*', StringValue:1, '*');
      Writeln (Lst);
      Writeln (Lst, '*', PositiveInteger:8, '*');
      Writeln (Lst, '*', NegativeInteger:8, '*');
      Writeln (Lst, '*', PositiveInteger:3, '*');
      Writeln (Lst, '*', NegativeInteger:3, '*');
      Writeln (Lst);
      Writeln (Lst, '*', PositiveReal:8, '*');
      Writeln (Lst, '*', NegativeReal:8, '*');
      Writeln (Lst, '*', PositiveReal:14, '*');
      Writeln (Lst, '*', NegativeReal:14, '*');
      Writeln (Lst);
      Writeln (Lst, '*', PositiveReal:10:4, '*');
      Writeln (Lst, '*', NegativeReal:10:4, '*');
      Writeln (Lst, '*', PositiveReal:8:1, '*');
      Writeln (Lst, '*', NegativeReal:8:1, '*');
      Writeln (Lst, '*', PositiveReal:6:0, '*');
      Writeln (Lst, '*', NegativeReal:6:0, '*')
end.
```

```
Output from Program 3d

*    This is a string*
*This is a string*

*    1235*
*   -1235*
*1235*
*-1235*

* 1.3E+01*
*-1.3E+01*
* 1.2860000E+01*
*-1.2860000E+01*

*   12.8600*
*  -12.8600*
*    12.9*
*   -12.9*
*     13*
*    -13*
```

Figure 3.5 Program 3d: Examples of formatted output.

which would be toward the middle of the line. This is a much more convenient way to accomplish this objective than the alternative. Without formatting, you would write a string constant of length 30 consisting of 23 spaces followed by the characters 'Heading'.

Note also that, although the use of integer constants is common in specifying formatting information, you can actually write any integer-valued expression for this purpose. Thus, assuming that FieldLength is an Integer constant or variable, the following statements would be syntactically correct:

```
Writeln (StudentName:FieldLength);
Writeln (StudentName:FieldLength+2);
```

In each case, the value of the expression would be calculated at the time of execution of the statement, and this value would be used to determine the appearance of the output.

3.5.2 Formatting Integer Values

Integer-valued expressions can be formatted in a manner similar to the one used for string values. The general form is

integer-parameter:field-width

where *field-width* is an Integer expression that is used to determine the number of characters to be used for the value of *integer-parameter*. If the value of *integer-parameter* takes fewer characters than the value of *field-width*, they will be right justified in the field and padded on the left with spaces. For example, suppose that the value of the Integer variable TestGrade is 78. Then the output produced by the statement

```
Writeln (TestGrade:5);
```

would be

```
      7 8
```

If the value of *integer-parameter* takes more characters than specified in the value of *field-width*, then the actual value is written without regard to the value of *field-width*. For example, the output produced by the statement

```
Writeln (TestGrade:1);
```

would be

```
7 8
```

Both of these cases are illustrated in the output of the sample program shown in Figure 3.5.

3.5.3 Formatting Real Values

Real values can be formatted for either exponential output, which resembles unformatted output, or in a fixed-decimal-point format. If you wish to produce exponential output, the general form is

```
real-parameter: field-width
```

where the value of *field-width* determines the number of characters to be used for the value of *real-parameter*. The minimum value for *field-width* is 8. The real value will be rounded to fit into the field. Following are some examples of this format option, assuming that the value of the Real variable TestAverage is 76.83 and the value of the Real variable ClassAverage is 78.00:

Statement	Output
Writeln(TestAverage:8)	7 . 7 E + 0 1
Writeln(TestAverage:10)	7 . 6 8 3 E + 0 1
Writeln(TestAverage:13)	7 . 6 8 3 0 0 0 E + 0 1
Writeln(TestAverage-ClassAverage:8)	- 1 . 2 E + 0 0
Writeln(TestAverage-ClassAverage:12)	- 1 . 1 7 0 0 0 E + 0 0

Further examples of this type of formatting are shown in the sample program of Figure 3.5.

Fixed-decimal-point output of Real values is also possible. You specify the field width, as before, and also the number of digits to the right of the decimal point, using the general form

```
real-parameter: field-width: decimal-places
```

where *field-width* and *decimal-places* are Integer expressions that determine the total width of the field and the number of digits to be printed to the right of the decimal point. The value of *real-parameter* will be rounded to the prescribed number of decimal places. Assuming that the values for the Real variables TestAverage and ClassAverage are as described before, the following are some examples of fixed-decimal-point formatting:

Statement	Output
Writeln(TestAverage:7:2);	76.83
Writeln(TestAverage:7:4);	76.8300
Writeln(TestAverage-ClassAverage:5:2);	-1.17
Writeln(TestAverage-ClassAverage:6:1);	-1.2

If the value of *decimal-places* is zero, then the value will be rounded to the nearest integer, and no decimal point will be printed, as shown in the following examples.

Statement	Output
Writeln(TestAverage:7:0);	77
Writeln(TestAverage-ClassAverage:7:0);	-1

Further examples of this type of formatting are shown in the sample program of Figure 3.5.

The use of fixed-point format for Real values can considerably enhance the readability of the output produced by your programs. For example, suppose we replace the last two output statements of the program in Figure 3.4 with the following:

```
Writeln('Length =', Length:6:2,' Width =', Width :6:2);
Writeln('Perimeter =', Perimeter:8:2,' Area =', Area:8:2)
```

A sample of the output produced by the revised program is shown in Figure 3.6. Compare this output with that shown in Figure 3.4, and you will see immediately that the revision has contributed greatly to making the output understandable to the average person. But note also that the output produced by the program no longer reflects the actual values entered by the user. Instead, all the values are rounded to two decimal places. If it is important that the program be able to cope with varying numbers of significant digits, then the best choice is still the exponential output form.

```
Enter length of rectangle 5.789
Enter width of rectangle 8.784

Length =  5.79 Width =  8.78
Perimeter =  29.15 Area =  50.85
```

Note that values have been rounded to two decimal places

Figure 3.6 Sample output using fixed-point format for Real values.

3.5.4   *Time Out*

1. Show the output produced by each of the following statements, assuming that A is a string variable with value 'ABC', B is an Integer variable with value -123, and C is a Real variable with value 23.4896.
   (a) `Writeln (A:5);`
   (b) `Writeln (A:1);`
   (c) `Writeln (B:6);`
   (d) `Writeln (B:2);`
   (e) `Writeln (C:8);`
   (f) `Writeln (C:8:3);`
   (g) `Writeln (C:8:2);`
   (h) `Writeln (B+C:4:0);`
2. Modify Program 2h, using formatted output where appropriate.

3.6   MORE ON DATA TYPES CHAR AND STRING

Up until now, we have usually used the data type string for a variable that will store character data. This method will work in all cases, but remember that standard Pascal does not support the data type string for storing characters. The only data type supported in standard Pascal for character data is Char. A variable of type Char is capable of storing exactly one character. This data type is essentially equivalent to data type

string[1]

For example, in order to declare a variable X to be of type Char, you would write

var
        X : Char;

In this case the variable X can store exactly one character, which may be placed there by an assignment statement such as

        X := 'A';

or an input statement such as

```
Readln (X);
```

Just as Integer and Real data are said to be compatible, data types Char and string are compatible. For example, you can use a character constant or variable to specify the value of a variable of type string, as in the following example (assume that Y is of type string[3]):

```
X := 'A';
Y := X;
```

It is not permissible to use a string constant or variable to specify the value of a variable of type Char. For example, the statement

```
X := 'ABC';
```

will be rejected as a "type mismatch" error by the compiler.

Two questions are probably on your mind right now:

1. What good is data type Char if you can always use string[1] as a substitute?
2. If standard Pascal supports only data type Char, how can you deal with character strings of greater length in standard Pascal programs?

There is good reason for using data type Char instead of string[1] when you need to declare a variable that will store only a single character: Data type Char is simpler and more straightforward. Also, if you ever want to convert your Turbo Pascal program into standard Pascal, you will have no problem with any variable of data type Char; however, you will have to make appropriate substitutions for data type string.

And speaking of substitutions, in a standard Pascal program you might see the following declaration for a variable that will store a sequence of characters:

```
StudentName : packed array [1..20] of Char;
```

This is the equivalent of the Turbo Pascal statement

```
StudentName : string[20];
```

The term *array* means a sequence of related items; the term *packed* means that the data are represented in the most efficient manner possible; the sequence 1..20 means that there will be 20 characters numbered from 1 to 20. We cover arrays in detail in Chapter 9. Our purpose in bringing up the subject at this point is so you can read Pascal programs from other sources with some understanding. The string data type is a significant enhancement to the Pascal standard; it makes many operations on character strings much easier than if you use packed arrays. However, it is possible to do everything that needs to be done using the packed array method for declaring character variables.

3.7   DATA TYPE BOOLEAN

A data type that you will find useful from time to time is type Boolean, which is named for the 19th-century mathematician George Boole. A Boolean variable has only two possible values: True and False. The words *True* and *False* are standard identifiers for the two **Boolean constants**. A Boolean variable is declared using the data type Boolean. For example, the following code declares the variables X and Y to be of type Boolean:

```
var
     X, Y : Boolean;
```

The variables X and Y can be assigned a value using the assignment statement in much the same way that other variables are assigned values. For example, the following two statements set X to True and Y to False:

```
X := True;
Y := False;
```

(Assignment statements are the only way that Boolean variables can be assigned a value; you cannot enter values into Boolean variables using Readln.)

It is also possible to declare Boolean constants by setting the constant equal to True or False. For example, the following code declares a Boolean constant called Answer with the value True:

```
const
     Answer = True;
```

Boolean values can be printed out using the ordinary Write or Writeln statement. The characters TRUE and FALSE are printed, as appropriate, when a Boolean expression is included as a parameter of Write or Writeln. Assuming that the values of the variables X and Y and the constant Answer are as specified before, consider the following examples:

Statements	Output
Writeln (X);	TRUE
Writeln (Y, Answer);	FALSETRUE

You will not often have the need to write out the values of Boolean expressions, but this facility is useful occasionally for debugging purposes.

3.7.1   Logical Operations

Pascal supports **logical operations** that can act on Boolean values. The logical operators are

not
and
or
xor

(All but xor are part of standard Pascal; xor is a Turbo Pascal extension.)

The operation **not** is a unary[3] operation that acts on a single Boolean value and serves to negate it: that is, to return the opposite of the value acted on. Thus, the value of "not True" is "False", and the value of "not False" is "True". The general form for using the not operator is

not *expression*

The value of the not operation is defined in the following table:

expression	**not** *expression*
True	False
False	True

For example, suppose Answer is a Boolean constant with value True and X is a Boolean variable. Then the following statement would place the negation of Answer in X:

X := **not** Answer;

The value of X would be False after execution of the statement.

The operation **and** is a binary operation operating on two Boolean expressions. The resulting expression has the general form

expression-1 **and** *expression-2*

The resulting expression is True if both *expression-1* and *expression-2* are True; if either or both of these two expressions is False, then the resulting expression is False. This rule is summarized in the following table:

expression-1	*expression-2*	*expression-1* **and** *expression-2*
True	True	True
True	False	False
False	True	False
False	False	False

---

[3]The term *unary* means that the operation requires only one operand. An operation that acts on two operands is called a *binary* operation.

For example, suppose the value of Answer is True and the value of Y is False. Then after execution of the statement

```
X := Answer and Y;
```

the value contained in X will be False because the value of True and False is False.

The operation **or** is also a binary operation operating on two Boolean expressions. The resulting expression has the general form

```
expression-1 or expression-2
```

The resulting expression is True if either or both of *expression-1* and *expression-2* are True; if both are False, the value of the expression is False. This rule is summarized in the following table:

expression-1	*expression-2*	*expression-1* **or** *expression-2*
True	True	True
True	False	True
False	True	True
False	False	False

For example, suppose the value of Answer is True and the value of Y is False. Then after execution of the statement

```
X := Answer or Y;
```

the value of X will be True because the value of True or False is True.

The operation **xor** (for exclusive or) is another binary operation operating on two Boolean expressions. The resulting expression has the general form

```
expression-1 xor expression-2
```

The resulting expression is True if either of *expression-1* and *expression-2* is True; if both are True or both are False, the value of the expression is False. This rule is summarized in the following table:

expression-1	*expression-2*	*expression-1* **xor** *expression-2*
True	True	False
True	False	True
False	True	True
False	False	False

For example, suppose the values of both Answer and Y are true. Then after execution of the statement

```
X := Answer xor Y;
```

the value of X will be False because the value of True xor True is False. (Note how this differs from the inclusive or, where the values of True or True is True.).

You should be aware of the fact that all of the preceding operations are defined on Integer data as well as logical data. Beginning programmers probably will not have an occasion to use the Integer versions of these operations, which act on the binary (base 2) representations of Integer values, but if you write an expression such as

```
3 or 4
```

it will not be treated as a syntax error. For more information, see the Turbo Pascal reference manual.

As with arithmetic operations, there are rules of precedence for determining which logical operation is to be performed when more than one operation is present in an expression. The **precedence of logical operations** is as follows:

Precedence	Operation
High	not
↕	and
Low	or, xor

The basic rules are the same for these operations as for arithmetic operations:

> Expressions within the innermost sets of parentheses are evaluated first. In an expression with no parentheses, operations with higher precedence are evaluated before operations with lower precedence. If two operations have equal precedence, they are evaluated from left to right.

These rules are illustrated in the evaluation of the following expressions (assume that X and Answer have the value True and Y has the value False):

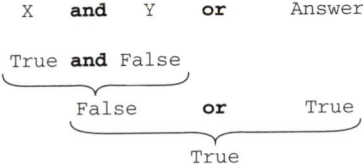

Comment: X **and** Y is evaluated first because and has higher precedence than or.

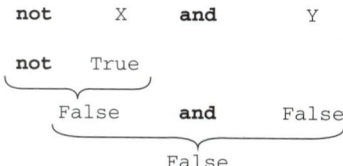

Comment: Not has higher precedence than and.

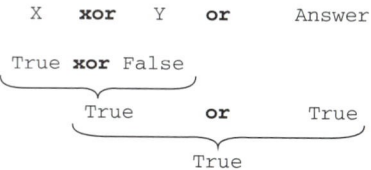

Comment: Xor and or have the same precedence; therefore the operations are evaluated from left to right.

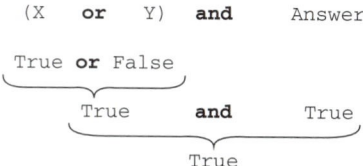

Comment: The expression inside the parentheses is evaluated first.

At this point you are probably saying to yourself, "So what? What good are Boolean variables and logical operations?" This is a good question, but one that we are not yet in a position to answer convincingly. The real utility of Boolean variables and logical operations will come in specifying the flow of control within a program. Thus far, all your programs have been straightforward sequential sets of instructions that are executed one after another. There has been no branching; that is, there has been no selection of alternative paths through the instructions. This topic receives attention in the next chapter. When you get there, you will be equipped with a basic knowledge of Boolean variables and logical operations and will be able to put them into practical use within your programs. So for now, postpone judgment on the utility of these programming tools; we will be using them very shortly.

3.7.2 Formatting Char and Boolean Output

Char and Boolean values can be formatted by specifying a field width in the parameter list in the Write or Writeln statement. The general form for doing this is

```
character-expression: field-width
logical-expression: field-width
```

where *field-width* is an integer expression.

Recall that a variable or constant of type Char is of length 1; if the value of *field-width* is greater than 1, the character will be right justified in the field and padded on the left with spaces. The output of data of type Char is illustrated in the sample program shown in Figure 3.7.

If a logical expression is present in the list of parameters of a Write or Writeln statement, its value is represented on the output line as TRUE or FALSE. If the *field-width* specified for a logical expression is longer than that needed for the output (4 or 5 characters), the output will be right justified in the field and padded on the left with spaces. If the value is less than that needed for the output, the characters TRUE and FALSE are written without regard to the value of *field-width*. These rules are illustrated in the output produced by Program 3e, shown in Figure 3.7.

Note: The ability to write the value of a Boolean variable or logical expression is a Turbo Pascal extension of standard Pascal.

```
program P3e (Output);
{The purpose of this program is to illustrate
    Char and Boolean constants and data}
const
    BooleanConstant = True;
    CharacterConstant = 'A';
var
    BooleanVariable : Boolean;
    CharacterVariable : Char;
begin
    Writeln ('BooleanConstant    *', BooleanConstant, '*');
    Writeln ('BooleanConstant:8 *', BooleanConstant:8, '*');
    BooleanVariable := not BooleanConstant;
    Writeln ('BooleanVariable    *', BooleanVariable, '*');
    Writeln ('BooleanVariable:2 *', BooleanVariable:2,'*');
    Writeln;
    Writeln ('CharacterConstant    *', CharacterConstant, '*');
    Writeln ('CharacterConstant:3 *', CharacterConstant:3,   '*');
    Writeln;
    Write ('Enter a character ');
    Readln (CharacterVariable);
    Writeln ('CharacterVariable    *', CharacterVariable, '*')
end.
```

Sample execution of Program 3e

```
BooleanConstant    *TRUE*
BooleanConstant:8 *    TRUE*
BooleanVariable    *FALSE*
BooleanVariable:2 *FALSE*

CharacterConstant    *A*
CharacterConstant:3 *  A*

Enter a character a
CharacterVariable    *a*
```

Figure 3.7 Program 3e: Output of Boolean and Char data.

3.7.3 Time Out

1. Assume that A, B, and C are Boolean variables and that the values of A and B are True, whereas the value of C is False. Evaluate each of the following expressions.

   (a) A **and** C

   (b) A **or** C

   (c) **not** A

   (d) A **xor** C

   (e) A **or** B **and** C

   (f) A **and** B **or** C

   (g) A **xor** B **and** C

   (h) A **or** (**not** B)

   (i) **not** (A **or** B **xor** C)

2. Assume that A and B are Boolean variables with the value True and X is a variable of type Char with the value A. Show the output produced by each of the following statements.

   (a) Writeln (A);

   (b) Writeln (B:1);

   (c) Writeln (B:6);

   (d) Writeln (X:4);

   (e) Writeln (**not** A **or** B);

   (f) Writeln (**not** (A **and** B):8);

3.8 PROCEDURES

Recall that in the pseudocoded version of a program, you break down the problem to be solved into a set of smaller tasks, each of which is well defined and somewhat independent of the other tasks. Pascal gives you the ability to implement your program as a series of well-defined and separately defined tasks called **procedures**. A procedure is a separately written program segment that is invoked when it is needed to do the task it was designed to do.

Actually, you have been using Pascal **standard procedures** all along. Procedures such as Readln, Writeln, Write, and so forth are built-in procedures that perform very useful functions for you. You invoke them using the procedure call statement, which has the general form.

```
procedure-name (parameter-list)
```

where the parentheses and the *parameter-list* are omitted if they are not needed. We have seen, for example, that in order to write two variables A and B, we use the procedure call statement

```
Writeln (A, B);
```

which has two parameters. On the other hand, if we want to write a blank line, we use the statement

```
Writeln;
```

which invokes the procedure called Writeln with no parameters.

Turbo Pascal has quite a number of other standard procedures that perform the following:

- Input and output operations
- Operations on strings
- File manipulation
- Screen management
- Graphics-related tasks
- A variety of miscellaneous tasks

All these are described in detail in the Turbo Pascal reference manual. For example, some of the more useful screen-management procedures, all of which require the unit Crt, are listed next.

Procedure	*Function*
ClrScr	Clear screen: Erases the screen and returns the cursor to the upper left-hand corner. The ClrScr procedure is often used to begin data entry. It makes sure that the user is not bothered by output left over from previous programs.
DelLine	Delete line: Deletes the content of the line containing the cursor and moves other lines up one line.
InsLine	Insert line: Inserts a blank line at the cursor position and moves all lines below down one line.

None of these procedures require parameters.

Another interesting and useful screen-management procedure is the GotoXY procedure, which allows you to place the cursor at any desired position on the screen. The general form for invoking this procedure is

```
GotoXY (column-position, row-position)
```

where *column-position* and *row-position* are Integer expressions specifying the X (column) and Y (row) positions of the cursor. Screens differ in size. Most have 80 columns and 25 rows. The address of the position in the upper left-hand corner is 1,1; the address of the position in the upper right-hand corner (column 80, row 1) is 80,1; the address of the lower left-hand corner (column 1, row 25) is 1,25; and so forth. For example, to position the cursor at column 1 of line 19, you could use the statement

```
GotoXY (1, 19);
```

Note that the GotoXY procedure does not perform input or output operations; all it does is position the cursor on the screen. The next input or output operation takes place at this location on the screen. The GotoXY procedure can be used to cause output to appear at different parts of the screen instead of sequentially—one line at a time from top to bottom.

Another standard procedure that can be of value is **Delay**. This procedure causes the program to pause an amount of time that you specify as an argument to the procedure. The general form for invoking this procedure is

```
Delay (time-value)
```

where *time-value* is an integer expression. The amount of time is approximately the number of milliseconds (thousandths of a second) specified by *time-value*; however, since machines vary, you will have to experiment to find out how this procedure will work on your machine. For example, in order to delay execution of a program for about 2 seconds, you would write

```
Delay (2000);
```

The Delay function is often used to slow down the execution of a program to give users a chance to react to what is on the screen. Sometimes computers do tasks so quickly that users can be a bit bewildered.

For example, many programs feature a welcome screen. The welcome screen tells you the name of the program, the company name, the copyright information, and so forth. This screen is displayed for a period of time; then it is replaced with another screen, which is used to enter data and get results from the program. The Delay procedure could be used to keep the screen in place long enough for the user to read it.

The procedure for displaying a welcome screen could be summarized as follows:

1.0 Clear the screen

2.0 Display welcome message

3.0 Delay

4.0 Clear the screen

This procedure is implemented in Program 3f, shown in Figure 3.8. Note the use of the GotoXY procedure in the implementation of Step 2.0. This enables the program to display the output in the center of the screen.

3.8.1 Time Out

1. Execute Program 3f, which is contained on the disk that accompanies the text. If the delay is too short to be able to read the screen on your machine, increase the value in the Delay statement; if the screen lasts too long, decrease the value in the Delay statement.

2. Add your name and address at an appropriate location on the screen.

3. Add Delay statements in Step 2.0 so that the user can read the various words as they are being displayed on the screen.

4. Position the cursor in the middle of the screen just below the title of the book. Use repeated InsLine statements to cause the lines in the lower half of the screen to scroll off the bottom of the screen.

5. Move the cursor to the top row of the screen and use the DelLine procedure repeatedly to cause the book title to scroll up and off of the screen.

```pascal
program P3f (Output);
{Program to display a welcome screen}
uses Crt;
begin

{1.0 Clear the screen}

     ClrScr;

{2.0 Display welcome message}

     GotoXY (28,10);
     Write ('Welcome to');
     GoToXY(6,12);
     Write('STRUCTURED PROGRAMMING IN TURBO PASCAL, Second Edition');
     GotoXY (6,15);
     Write ('By Lister W. Horn');
     GotoXY (42,15);
     Write ('Prentice Hall, Inc.');
     GotoXY (42,16);
     Write ('Publisher');
     GotoXY (28,18);
     Write ('Copyright 1995');

{3.0 Delay}

     Delay (10000);

{4.0 Clear the screen}

     ClrScr

end.
```

```
                    Output from Program 3f
    +----------------------------------------------------------+
    |                       Welcome to                         |
    |                                                          |
    |     STRUCTURED PROGRAMMING IN TURBO PASCAL, Second Edition|
    |                                                          |
    |                                                          |
    |     By Lister W. Horn                Prentice Hall, Inc. |
    |                                      Publisher           |
    |                                                          |
    |                    Copyright 1995                        |
    |                                                          |
    +----------------------------------------------------------+
```

Figure 3.8 Program 3f: Welcome screen program.

3.9 OVERVIEW OF FILES

A **file** is designed to facilitate the storage and retrieval of data on devices that are external to the processor. All the data types with which we have dealt up to now have been concerned strictly with data as it is represented in the main memory of the computer. But we know that data must come from some source that is external to the computer's processing unit and must be stored in some form that is also external to the processor in order to be of any value to the computer user. We have routinely used the keyboard of the computer as the source of data and the screen as the destination. We must now turn to a detailed examination of this process so that your programs can utilize disk files for data storage and processing.

One basic principle of all computers is that the operating system handles all input and output operations for a program. When an input operation is performed from your program, what actually happens is that the program formulates a request for data and sends the request to the operating system. The operating system actually executes the input task and transmits the data back to the program, which then proceeds with its next operation. A similar technique is used when an output operation is performed by a program. When the operating system receives an input or output request from a program, it must know the source of or destination for the data. Input may be requested from the keyboard or from a file that is stored on disk. Output may be sent to the screen, the printer, or a disk file. The operating system can handle any of these transfers, but it must be told which file is being addressed. To facilitate this process, the operating system has a list of predefined **file names** that are standard and used by all software to send data to the keyboard, the screen, the printer, and other physical devices that may be part of the system. Files that are located on a disk must also have a name, but that name is assigned by the user. A directory of all the files contained on a disk is maintained, so that the operating system can locate the file on the disk when a user requests access to such a file.

It is useful to distinguish between the name of a file known to the operating system (let's call this the *external file name*) and the name of the file used by a program (let's call this the *internal file name*). These are both ways of identifying a file, but they are used in different contexts. All entities in Pascal (including files) are assigned identifiers. Turbo Pascal includes a number of predefined file identifiers that are used by default in input and output statements. You can write programs that process files without being conscious of the names of the files that you are addressing (although we have made it a habit to list all the files that a program is to process in the program statement). The following are some of the standard file identifiers built into Turbo Pascal:

File identifier (internal name)	Assignment (external name)
Input	Con (Console: ordinarily the keyboard)
Output	Con (Console: the screen)
Lst	Prn (System list device, usually the printer)

Notice that we have also listed the device to which the file is assigned. The assignment refers to the operating system's standard file names—the names that we have previously called external file names.

When you define a file in a program, it is necessary not only to give it a name (an identifier that constitutes its internal name), but also to communicate the location of the file to the operating system (that is, we must associate the internal name with some external name). In Pascal, this process is called *assignment*. As we have seen, the operating system has a list of standard identifiers that are permanently associated with the screen, the keyboard, the printer, and other physical devices associated with the system. The standard Turbo Pascal files are all assigned to one of the operating system's standard identifiers. When you write a program that accesses data from some source that has no standard file name, then your program will be responsible for assigning the (internal) file identifier to the (external) file name so that the operating system can locate the file for you.

Any processing of a file actually involves three distinct steps:

1. Open the file. (Inform the operating system of the external name of the file, and ready the file for processing.)

2. Process the file. (Execute input and/or output operations on the file.)

3. Close the file. (Inform the operating system that the program is finished processing the file.)

When you are using Turbo Pascal standard files, you do not have to be concerned with opening or closing a file; these operations will be carried out automatically for you. However, when you are working with a nonstandard file, you will have to accomplish the open procedure before you can process the file, and your program will need to close the file when the processing is completed.

Many programming languages include a single statement or procedure to open a file. In Turbo Pascal, the open operation is accomplished in two steps. The first step is to use the **Assign procedure** to establish the linkage between the (internal) file variable and the (external) file name. The second step is to ready the file for processing. This is done with the **Rewrite procedure** if the file is to be processed as an output file (the file will be created by the program) or the **Reset procedure** if the file is to be processed as an input file (the file exists and will be read by the program). We cover the details of these procedures in the next sections.

Processing a file is accomplished by the procedures **Read** and **Readln** (to perform input) and Write and Writeln (to perform output). We are already accustomed to using Write, Writeln, and Readln to process standard files. (The relationship between the procedures Read and Readln is similar to the relationship between the procedures Write and Writeln; the details are covered in Section 3.12. With all input and output procedures, the first parameter in the list of parameters is the file identifier; if the file identifier is omitted, a standard file is assumed. The standard file identifier that is assumed for Read and Readln is Input; the standard file identifier that is assumed for Write and Writeln is Output. One example of the use of file identifiers has been covered previously: Recall that to address output to the printer, the standard file identifier Lst was used in the Writeln statement, as in Writeln (Lst, . . .). In general, it will be necessary to include the file identifier in any input or output procedure parameter list if the procedure is to process any file other than the associated standard file.

After a file has been processed, the program should close the file. This is a simple task that the procedure **Close** performs. Closing a file informs the operating system that the program no longer needs to have access to the file; the operating system then makes an appropriate modification in the directory entry for the file.

A Pascal file must be assigned a base type. The base type of a file specifies what kind of data is contained in the file. A file may consist of a sequence of items of any type (except file). There is one file type identifier that is standard (**Text**); you can create other file types to meet the unique needs of your programs. A Text file consists of a sequence of characters; one byte for each character. (In some contexts, such files are called *ASCII files* because the ASCII code is used for each character in the file.) Files of other types are usually referred to as *binary* files, because the coding used for the content of the file is the same as the binary code used in the memory of the computer to represent data items of a variety of types.

In the following sections, we will consider Text files. Procedures for creating and processing binary files are deferred until Chapter 10.

3.10   FILE NAMES

The rules for writing external file names are governed by the operating system. In MS/PC DOS a complete external file name is made up of four parts, three of which are optional:

- Drive designator (optional)
- Path (optional)
- Basic file name
- Extension (optional)

The basic name of the file is a sequence of from one to eight characters that can be either alphabetic ('a' through 'z', 'A' through 'Z') or numeric ('0' through '9'). Other characters can (but should not) be used in file names. Upper- and lowercase letters are treated as equivalent by the operating system.

Following the basic file name is an optional extension of up to three characters (alphabetic or numeric only). If present, the extension is separated from the basic file name by a period. File extensions are often used to help identify the contents of a file. Some software packages add an extension to the basic name automatically when they create a file. The Turbo Pascal editor, for example, adds the extension .PAS to every file name if you give the file a name that does not have an extension already. Following are some examples of valid file names:

```
SAMPLE
SAMPLE.PAS
INVENTOR.DAT
MONTH2.DTA
```

Following are some examples of invalid file names:

`INVENTORY.DAT`	(basic name is too long)
`MONTH 2`	(embedded space in file name)
`PAYROLL.DATA`	(extension has too many characters)

The first component of a file name is the optional drive specification. The floppy disk drives are labeled A and B. The hard disk is labeled C. (Your system may also make use of RAM disks—simulated disks that are in the memory of the computer. In this case, you may also use drive designators such as D and E). If a file name is entered without a drive designator, the operating system uses the default drive (also called the system drive) for the file. If you wish the file to be located on a different disk, you can write the drive designator, followed by a colon in front of the basic file name. For example, the file name B:PAYROLL.DAT indicates that the file is to be located on drive B, regardless of what drive is currently designated as the system drive. In order to make sure that your program will locate the desired file in all circumstances, it is a good idea to form the habit of prefacing any file name with the drive designator.

The second part of an external file name is the optional path. When there are a great many files present on a disk, it is useful to divide the disk content into various subdirectories, each of which is assigned a name. Only one directory will be active at any one time; files will automatically be located in that directory by default. If you wish to address a file in a subdirectory other than the current one, you place that directory name, surrounded by the character \ (called a *backslash*), in front of the basic file name. For example, a complete address for a file PAYROLL.DAT located in the subdirectory PERSONEL on drive B would be

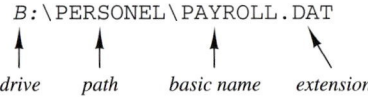

3.11 TEXT FILES

Text files are very useful because they can be created and processed by a variety of methods. The format of a Pascal Text file is the same as the ASCII format of the files created by the Turbo Pascal program editor and virtually every other word processor and editor in common use. This means that you can create a file using any available software and process the file with a Pascal program. It also means that you can use another Pascal program, the Pascal program editor, or any other piece of software that operates on ASCII files to access a Text file that has been created by a Pascal program. (The same statement cannot be made for binary files created by Pascal programs; generally, the only way to process such files is through another Pascal program.)

A Text file can be visualized as sequences of characters (called lines) separated by special control codes—the carriage return (Cr) and line feed (Lf)—which we refer to collectively as *end-of-line* (abbreviated as EOL) codes. The EOL codes are always present in the file, but are not printed when a Text file is printed on the printer or displayed on the screen; the codes are interpreted by the devices and cause the content of the file to be listed as separate lines. The last line in the file is terminated by two control codes—the usual EOL and an end-of-file marker, which is abbreviated EOF. When you are typing a text file at the keyboard of the computer, the EOL codes are automatically generated when you press the Enter key to terminate a line. The EOF marker can be generated by pressing Ctrl-Z (press both keys simultaneously). Because of this, the EOF marker is sometimes referred to as Ctrl-Z or ^Z, where the symbol ^ indicates a control character. A simple Text file containing three lines is illustrated in Figure 3.9.

Note that in a Text file the lines are variable in length; only the number of characters actually used is included in the file. Note also that a space is a character and does take up one byte in the file.

To facilitate the processing of a file, Pascal maintains an internal pointer (called a **File-position pointer**) to indicate the next available component in a file.[4] When a Text file is opened, the pointer points to the first character in the first line of the file. As data is read from the file, the pointer is updated by the system until at last it points to the byte containing the EOF code. When a file is created as the output of a program, the pointer is used to keep track of the next available space into which data can be placed. Ordinarily, the existence of this pointer is transparent to the programmer, since it is maintained by the system and cannot be manipulated directly by the program. There are, however, ways that the program can exert influence over the position of the pointer, as we shall see. The existence of the pointer and how program statements affect its position should be understood from the outset. This will help you avoid many common misunderstandings and programming problems.

The first step in writing a program that will process a file is to declare a variable of type file. For Text files, this can be accomplished quite simply by using the standard identifier Text as the type of the file variable. For example, the following declaration would declare the identifier DataFile to be a Text file:

```
var
    DataFile : Text;
```

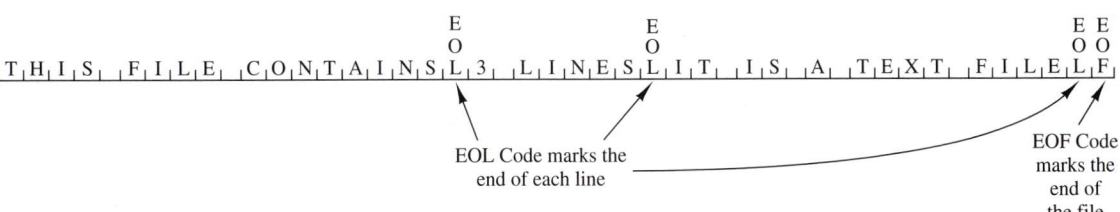

Figure 3.9 Example of a Text file.

---

[4]Technically, the File-position pointer points to a position in the buffer assigned to the file. When a file is read, many characters from the file are actually read and stored in the buffer, but only a few of them may be transferred into variables for processing. Similarly, when a file is being written, the program fills the buffer before data is actually written onto the file itself.

This declaration makes DataFile a variable that, like other variables, has a type; in this case the type is Text, which is a standard identifier for a file type that is made up of a sequence of characters and control codes. In some other respects, the variable DataFile is unlike other variables. There are no statements that can be used to process variables of a file type. (Even the assignment statement is forbidden.) A file-type variable is used as the internal file name of the file that exists or will exist in some external form.

The next step in writing a program to process a Text file is to assign the file variable to the (external) file name—the one by which the file is known to the operating system. This is accomplished using the Assign procedure, which has the general form

```
Assign (file-variable, file-name)
```

where *file-variable* is any variable declared with a file type and *file-name* is a string variable or expression that contains the external name of the file. For example, suppose the external name of our file is `'PAYROLL.DAT'`. Then the file DataFile could be assigned to this file by the statement

```
Assign (DataFile, 'PAYROLL.DAT');
```

The trouble with this form of assignment is that each time the program is executed, exactly the same file would be processed. Often the user will want to enter the external name of the file during the execution of a program. Assume that FileName is a string variable containing the external name of the file; then the following Assign statement would assign that name to DataFile:

```
Assign (DataFile, FileName);
```

Note that the maximum length for a file name without a path designator is 14 characters (including the drive designator, basic file name, extension, colon, and period). In a program that uses a variable to store a file name, an appropriate declaration would be

```
var
    FileName : string[14];
```

(Of course, this assumes that path names will not be used. If they are used, the file name will have to be longer.)

The next task that must be accomplished by a program in processing a Text file is to make the file ready for processing. The operating system must locate the file or begin a directory entry for the file. The program must initialize the File-position pointer. These tasks are accomplished in one of two ways, depending on the intended usage of the file. A Text file can be opened only for input or output. That is, you must decide whether the program will read the data from a file that already exists or create a new file.

If the file is assumed to exist and the program needs to read its content, the Reset procedure is invoked. The general form of this procedure reference is

```
Reset (file-variable)
```

where *file-variable* has been previously assigned to a file name. The Reset procedure performs the following functions:

1. The specified directory is searched for the file.

2. If the file exists, the File-position pointer is set to point to the first character in the file, and processing continues.

3. If the file does not exist, the program is terminated with an execution-time input/output error.

If the file is to be created as output from the program, then the Rewrite procedure is invoked. The general form of the Rewrite procedure reference is

```
Rewrite (file-variable)
```

where *file-variable* has been previously assigned to a file name. The Rewrite procedure causes the operating system to begin a new directory entry for the file and positions the File-position pointer to the first available space for data in the file. Any previous file (in the current directory) with the same name will be erased.

Thus far, we have covered the means by which a file variable is declared and how a file is opened. Remember that opening a file is accomplished in two steps: the Assign procedure is used to assign an external name to the file, and then either the Reset (for an input file) or Rewrite (for an output file) procedure is invoked. Once the file is opened, the procedures Read and Readln are used to read data from an input file, and the procedures Write and Writeln are used to write data to an output file. In each case, the file variable must be the first parameter in the parameter list. Note that if the Reset procedure is invoked, the Write and Writeln procedures are invalid for that file. In like manner, if the Rewrite procedure is invoked, the Read and Readln procedures are invalid. A Text file *must* be used exclusively as an input file or an output file.

Once processing is terminated, the program must close the file using the Close procedure. The general form for invocation of this procedure is as follows:

```
Close (file-variable)
```

The Close procedure informs the operating system that the program is finished processing the file. If the file was an output file, the EOF code is written following the last line of the file, and the directory entry for the file, which was begun when the Rewrite procedure was invoked, is completed. For an input or output file, closing the file frees up the operating system's *handle* that was attached to the file when the file was opened. (The operating system allocates to each open file an area of memory called an I/O buffer and a pointer to the area on the disk that actually contains the file's content; these elements collectively constitute a handle. When the file is closed, the handle is deactivated and can therefore be reallocated to another file. The operating system is configured for only a limited number of open files at any time and hence has only a few handles available.) Closing an output file is more critical than closing an input file. If an output file is not closed, then the EOF code will not be written to the file, but, worse yet, the directory entry will not be completed for the file, so that you may not be able to access the contents of the file later.

3.11.1   Program Example: Text Files for Input

Let us revise Program 3a to seek its input from a file, rather than having the user enter the data at the keyboard. Recall that this program computes the area and perimeter of a rectangle from values of the length and width entered by the user. We will create a Text file called MEASURE.DAT that will contain two lines; the first line will have the value of the length and the second will have the value of the width. (The Turbo Pascal editor handles this task readily; when the file is saved, it is given the appropriate name, including the extension. Remember that the Turbo Pascal editor automatically adds the extension .PAS to the file name if you do not specify an extension.) A sample of the content of the file MEASURE.DAT is

```
12
10
```

Now consider the program that will process this file. It will need a variable of type Text for the file. We will call this variable DataFile. Its declaration will appear as

```
DataFile : Text;
```

The program's first task is to open the file. Then it can read the content of the file, process the data, and produce the required results. Opening the file is accomplished in two steps:

```
Assign (DataFile, 'MEASURE.DAT');
Reset (DataFile);
```

Remember that the Reset procedure is used whenever a file is to be opened for input. Now the program will be able to read the data from the file, using the statements

```
Readln (DataFile, Length);
Readln (DataFile, Width);
```

When the first statement is executed, the first line in the file is read and the value is stored in the variable Length. After execution of the first Readln statement, the File-position pointer points to the second line in the file, which is read by the second Readln statement. The last task that the program performs is to close the file using the Close statement:

```
Close (DataFile)
```

Remember that closing an input file is a good practice, but not absolutely necessary for the program to function correctly.

The completed program is shown in Figure 3.10 as Program 3g. The output produced by the program for the sample data presented before is shown in Figure 3.11.

```
program P3g (DataFile, Output);
{Program to compute area and perimeter of a
    rectangle with input from a text file}
var
    Length, Width,        {Input variables}
    Area, Perimeter       {Output variables}
       : Real;
    DataFile : Text;      {File variable}
begin

{1.0 Open input file}

    Assign (DataFile, 'MEASURE.DAT');
    Reset (DataFile);

{2.0 Get values for Length and Width}

    Readln (DataFile, Length);
    Readln (DataFile, Width);

{3.0 Compute Perimeter and Area}

    Perimeter := 2.0 * (Length + Width);
    Area := Length * Width;

{4.0 Write input values and computed values}

    Writeln;
    Writeln ('Length =', Length:6:2, ' Width =', Width:6:2);
    Writeln ('Perimeter =', Perimeter:8:2, ' Area =',  Area:8:2);

{5.0 Close input file}

    Close (DataFile)

end.
```

Figure 3.10 Program 3g: Reading data from a Text file.

```
Length = 12.00 Width = 10.00
Perimeter = 44.00 Area =120.00
```

Figure 3.11 Sample output from Programs 3g, 3h, and 3i.

3.11.2 *Time Out*

1. Using the Turbo Pascal editor, create the file MEASURE.DAT and verify its content. Then run Program 3g and observe its output.
2. Using the editor, modify the content of the file MEASURE.DAT and save the file. Now run Program 3g, and verify that the data it is processing is coming from the new version of the data file.
3. Create a file MYDATA.DAT with two values of Length and Width of your choosing. Modify Program 3g to process this file. (Change the file name in the Assign statement).

3.11.3   Program Example: Text Files for Output

Let us modify Program 3g so that instead of addressing its output to the screen, the output is placed in a text file, which we will call RECTANGL.RPT. (We will use the extension RPT as an abbreviation for *report* to designate files that contain information produced as output from a program.) The program will need a second file variable for this file. We will use the identifier OutputFile for this variable and add it to the list of identifiers declared to be of type Text:

```
DataFile, OutputFile : Text;
```

The program must open the file for output before writing to it. Opening the file for output is a two-step process:

```
Assign (OutputFile, 'RECTANGL.RPT');
Rewrite (OutputFile);
```

Remember that Rewrite is used for an output file, whereas Reset is used for an input file. Information can be written to the file by adding the file identifier to the list of arguments in the Writeln statements:

```
Writeln (OutputFile);
Writeln (OutputFile, 'Length =' . . .);
Writeln (OutputFile, 'Perimeter =' . . .);
```

Finally, the Close statement is used to close the file:

```
Close (OutputFile)
```

Remember that closing an output file is absolutely necessary for the file to be added to the directory and thereby to be available after termination of the program.

The completed program is shown as Program 3h in Figure 3.12. The content of the file RECTANGL.RPT is as shown in Figure 3.11 for the sample content of MEA-SURE.DAT described previously. Notice that when the content of RECTANGL.RPT is displayed on the screen, it appears the same as if the program had produced the output directly on the screen. The advantage to creating a file to contain the program's output is that the information is now permanent and can be viewed, printed, or incorporated into some other file, such as a report created by a word-processing program.

3.11.4   Time Out

1. Run Program 3h. Using the Turbo Pascal editor, view the file RECTANGL.RPT.
2. Modify Program 3h to process the file MYDATA.DAT and produce a report MYREPT.RPT. If you haven't done so already, create the file MYDATA.DAT with data

```
program P3h (DataFile, OutputFile);
{Program to compute area and perimeter of a
    rectangle with input from a text file and output to a text file}
var
    Length, Width,        {Input variables}
    Area, Perimeter       {Output variables}
      : Real;
    DataFile, OutputFile : Text;      {File variables}
begin

{1.0 Open input file}

    Assign (DataFile, 'MEASURE.DAT');
    Reset (DataFile);

{2.0 Open output file}

    Assign (OutputFile, 'RECTANGL.RPT');
    Rewrite (OutputFile);

{3.0 Get values for Length and Width}

    Readln (DataFile, Length);
    Readln (DataFile, Width);

{4.0 Compute Perimeter and Area}

    Perimeter := 2.0 * (Length + Width);
    Area := Length * Width;

{5.0 Write input values and computed values}

    Writeln (OutputFile);
    Writeln (OutputFile,'Length =', Length:6:2, ' Width =',  Width:6:2);
    Writeln (OutputFile,'Perimeter =', Perimeter:8:2, ' Area  =', Area:8:2);

{6.0 Close files}

    Close (DataFile);
    Close (OutputFile)

end.
```

Figure 3.12 Program 3h: Writing information to a text file.

of your choosing. Then execute the revised program and verify the content of MYREPT.RPT.

3.11.5 Program Example: File Names Entered by the User

One of the not so nice features of each of Programs 3g and 3h is that the external names of the files are built into the program as literals in the Assign statements. This makes it necessary to revise the program itself if you want to process any file other than the ones described in the program. To avoid this problem, it is possible to have the user enter the names of the files that the program will use for its input and output. This is done by declaring a string type variable for the external names—we will call these variables InputFileName and OutputFileName. In response to an appropriate prompt, the user can enter the name of each of the files. The Assign statement then uses the variable instead of a literal as its second argument. For example, to open DataFile for input, the following sequence of statements could be used:

```
Write ('Enter name of input file');
Readln (InputFileName);
Assign (DataFile, InputFileName);
Reset (DataFile);
```

A similar sequence of statements would be used for the output file.

Program 3i, shown in Figure 3.13, is a revision of Program 3h that allows the user to enter the names of the input and output files in response to prompts from the program.

```
program P3i (Input, Output, DataFile, OutputFile);
{Program to compute area and perimeter of a
    rectangle with input from a text file and output to a text file.
    In this version of the program, the user enters the names of the
    files to be used for input and output}
const
    InputPrompt = 'Enter name of input file ';
    OutputPrompt = 'Enter name of output file ';
var
    Length, Width,       {Input variables}
    Area, Perimeter      {Output variables}
      : Real;
    DataFile, OutputFile : Text;              {File variables}
    InputFileName, OutputFileName : string;   {Variables for file names}
begin

{1.0 Open input file}

    Write (InputPrompt);
    Readln (InputFileName);
    Assign (DataFile, InputFileName);
    Reset (DataFile);

{2.0 Open output file}

    Write (OutputPrompt);
    Readln (OutputFileName);
    Assign (OutputFile, OutputFileName);
    Rewrite (OutputFile);
    .
    .
    .
end.
```

Figure 3.13 Program 3i: File names entered by the user.

3.11.6 Time Out

1. Run Program 3i. Supply file names of your choice in response to the prompts from the program.

2. Try running Program 3i with the name of an input file that does not exist. Note the error message that is produced.

3.12   READ AND READLN

As you have seen, there are two output procedures that can be used for Text files: Write and Writeln. These two procedures differ in the way that they handle the end-of-line (EOL) character sequence. Recall that Writeln causes EOL to be written as the last character transmitted to the file, whereas Write does not transmit this character sequence. Corresponding to these two output procedures are two input procedures: Read and Readln.

Like Write and Writeln, Read and Readln differ in how they handle the EOL character sequence. This difference can be summarized in the following general statements:

> When a Readln operation is terminated, the File-position pointer is advanced past the next EOL character sequence to point to the next line of the file.

> When a Read operation is completed, the file position pointer points to the first character not required to supply values for the argument list.

These principles apply whether the file being read is Input (the keyboard) or a Text file on disk. A simple example will help you understand the differences between the two procedures. Consider the following Text file, which we will call SampleFile:

When the file is opened for input, the File-position pointer points to the first character in the first line in the file. Now, suppose the following statement is executed, assuming that A is declared as a Real variable:

```
Readln (SampleFile, A);
```

The first line of the file has two values in it. The first of these values will be placed in the variable A. The next value will be skipped because of the way that Readln handles the File-position pointer, which is advanced to the first character following EOL, thus:

The next Read or Readln statement will begin processing the data with the first value on the second line of the file.

Occasionally, it is useful to advance the File-position pointer to the beginning of the next line. This can be done by using the statement

```
Readln (SampleFile);
```

which has no variables in its argument list.

Now suppose that the following statement is executed instead of the Readln (we assume that the file has just been opened and the File-position pointer is pointing to the first character in the file):

```
Read (SampleFile, A);
```

The first value (12) will be stored in A, but the File-position pointer will point to the space following 12:

$$1\,2\quad-3\,0\,E\,O\,L\,6\quad3\,1\quad E\,O\,L\,E\,O\,F$$

↑ File-position pointer

This means that the next Read or Readln statement will begin translating the content of the file with the second value on the first line.

Despite the differences in Read and Readln, they do share a very important characteristic. All input in Pascal is list directed; that is, the system seeks to locate data to place in each of the variables in the list of arguments specified by the program. The basic principle is as follows:

> Read and Readln will read as many lines of text as are required to supply values for the variables in the argument list.

For example, consider the Text file SampleFile used in the previous examples. We assume that the file has just been opened, so that the File-position pointer is pointing to the first item in the first line. Suppose the following statement is executed (assuming that A, B, and C are declared as Real variables):

```
Readln (SampleFile, A, B, C);
```

The values of the three variables will be 12, -30, and 6, respectively. After execution of the statement, the File-position pointer will point to EOF, since Readln will advance past the next EOL.

No matter how many lines of the file are required, Readln will attempt to locate a value for each variable in its list of parameters. You may have noticed this characteristic of Readln in your own use of Pascal programs. For example, if the parameter list in a Readln statement contains two variables, the user can enter the value for the first variable, followed by the value for the second, or the user can enter the value, press Enter (which transmits EOL), and then enter the second value and press Enter. The user has responded to one Readln statement with two lines of text. If, instead, the Read statement had been used in the program, the user would have the same two options, since, in this respect, Read and Readln behave in exactly the same way. However, after execution of the Read statement, the File-position pointer would be pointing to the second item on the second line, rather than to EOF.

3.12.1 Time Out

For the following exercises, assume in each case that the File-position pointer is pointing to the beginning of the first line in the file, which is called Sample2 and contains the following data:

$$3 \, 4 \quad A \, B \, C \, E \, O \, L - 3 \quad 2 \, E \, O \, L \, E \, O \, F$$

File-position pointer

Also, assume that the variable X is of type Integer, Y is of type string, and Z is of type Real. Show the values of each variable and the position of the File-position pointer after execution of each statement or sequence of statements.

1. `Readln (Sample2, X, Y);`

2. `Read (Sample2, X);`
   `Readln (Sample2, Y, Z);`

3. `Read (Sample2, X);`
   `Readln (Sample2);`

4. `Readln (Sample2, X);`
   `Read (Sample2, Z);`

5. `Readln (Sample2);`
   `Read (Sample2, X, Z);`
   `Readln;`

Using the general principles outlined in this section, explain why the following two program segments are equivalent:

6. `Readln (Sample2, X, Y);` and

```
Read(Sample2, X);
Read(Sample2, Y);
Readln;
```

7. `Readln (Sample2, X, Y, Z);` and

```
Read (Sample2, X, Y);
Readln (Sample2);
Read (Sample2, Z);
Readln (Sample2);
```

3.13 PROGRAMMER-WRITTEN PROCEDURES

Not only does Pascal provide a variety of standard procedures; it also gives you the ability to define procedures in your own programs. This facility makes it possible to segment the program into relatively independent modules, write a procedure for each module, and then invoke the procedure by specifying its name in the same way as standard procedures are referenced. The procedures you write may or may not require parameters. In this section, we will describe procedures without parameters; procedures with parameters are covered later (see Chapter 5).

Procedures are included in the declaration part of a program. A general form for a program that includes a procedure is as follows:

```
program-header;
uses unit-name . . . ;
constant-declaration-part;
variable-declaration-part;
procedure-declaration-part;
begin
    statement;
       .
       .
       .

end.
```

A general form of a **procedure declaration part** for a procedure that does not involve parameters is as follows:

```
procedure procedure-name;
const
    constant-declaration;
       .
       .
       .

var
    variable-declaration;
       .
       .
       .

begin
    statement;
       .
       .
       .

end;
```

Note that the form for declaring a procedure follows very closely the form used to declare a complete program, with two exceptions: (1) A procedure declaration begins with the procedure statement, and (2) the end statement that concludes the statement part is followed by a semicolon rather than a period. (This is in keeping with the general rule that a program statement is terminated by a semicolon if other statements will follow.)

For example, consider Program 3c, shown in Figure 3.4. This program computes the area and perimeter of a rectangle. Each of the three main program modules could be implemented as a separate procedure. Let us construct a procedure for Module 1.0, which performs the input function for the program. You should name procedures with reasonably short but descriptive names. We choose to call this module GetValues. Thus, the first statement in the declaration is

```
procedure GetValues;
```

Procedure GetValues will make use of two constants. We could make the constants global by including them in the constant declaration part of the main program, but since they are needed only by this procedure, it makes sense to declare them as part of the procedure. (**Global** means "known throughout the program.") This makes the identifiers known only within Procedure GetValues (or any procedure that might be subordinate to it; more on this later); such identifiers are called **local identifiers**. With this in mind, the procedure declaration now looks like the following:

```
procedure GetValues;
(Procedure to get values for Length and Width)
const
    LengthPrompt = 'Enter length of rectangle ';
    WidthPrompt = 'Enter width of rectangle ';
```

Note that you should include comments in procedures, just as you would include comments in any program unit. Next, you might be tempted to include variable declarations for Length and Width. This would be an error, however, because that would make these variables local to the procedure GetValues. The variables must be global because they will be referenced not only in the procedure GetValues, but also in other parts of the main program. Therefore, the variables Length and Width are declared in the ordinary variable declaration part of the main program. (If you want to see the finished product to see where Length and Width are defined, look at the complete program in Figure 3.14.) If there were local variables to be declared, these would come next. In this case there are none, so we continue with the statement part of the procedure. The completed procedure now looks like the following:

```
procedure GetValues;
{Procedure to get values for Length and Width}
const
    LengthPrompt = 'Enter length of rectangle ';
    WidthPrompt = 'Enter width of rectangle ';
begin    {GetValues}
    Write (LengthPrompt);
    Readln (Length);
    Write (WidthPrompt);
    Readln (Width)
end;      {GetValues}
```

```pascal
program P3j (Input, Output);
{Program to compute area and perimeter of a
    rectangle given length and width. This version of the program
    illustrates the use of a procedure.}

var

    Length, Width,      {Input variables}
    Area, Perimeter     {Output variables}
       : Real;

{*********************************************************************}

    procedure GetValues;
    {Procedure to get values for Length and Width}

    const

         LengthPrompt = 'Enter length of rectangle ';
         WidthPrompt = 'Enter width of rectangle ';

    begin {GetValues}

         Write (LengthPrompt);
         Readln (Length);
         Write (WidthPrompt);
         Readln (Width)

    end; {GetValues}

{*********************************************************************}

begin   {Main Program}

{1.0 Get values for Length and Width}

    GetValues;

{2.0 Compute Perimeter and Area}

    Perimeter := 2.0 * (Length + Width);
    Area := Length * Width;

{3.0 Write input values and computed values}

    Writeln;
    Writeln ('Length =', Length:6:2, ' Width =', Width:6:2);
    Writeln ('Perimeter =', Perimeter:8:2, ' Area =', Area:8:2)

end. {Main Program}
```

Figure 3.14 Example of programmer-defined procedures.

Note two things in this code. First, we have included the name of the procedure as a comment with the begin and end statements. Since there will now be several begin and end statements in the program, it is important to denote what is being begun and ended with this particular begin or end statement. For the main program, we will use the formats

begin {*Main Program*}
.
.
.
end {*Main Program*}

The second thing to remember is that the end statement that terminates the statement part of a procedure declaration is terminated by a semicolon, not a period.

The completed program is shown in Figure 3.14. We have added some blank lines to enhance readability and comments consisting of rows of asterisks to delineate the procedure-declaration part of the program visually. We recommend that you use a similar practice in your programs. Note the way in which Module 1.0 is implemented in the main program:

```
{1.0 Get values for Length and Width}
    GetValues;
```

The name of the procedure is used to cause the execution of the procedure in exactly the same way that you invoke the standard procedures described in the preceding section.

Of course, we could choose to implement Modules 2.0 and 3.0 as separate procedures as well. Such a version of the program is shown in Figure 3.15. We use the convention of inserting comments consisting of rows of dashes between the declarations of different procedures in the procedure declaration part of the program. We suggest that you follow this pattern in your programs. Note that the use of a comment on each begin and end statement becomes more important because there are now quite a few in the program. Since each module of the program has been implemented as a separate procedure, the statement part of the main program is exceedingly simple, as shown in Figure 3.15. The only executable statements now are procedure calls to the three procedures defined in the program: GetValues, ComputePerimArea, and WriteValues.

How do you know when to put detail statements into the statement part of the main program and when to write separate procedures for a module? To a certain extent, this is a judgment call on the part of the programmer. Certainly, when the statement part of the program gets too long to fit one screen or one printed page, it needs to be broken down into procedures. In a short program a procedure is called for if a module is complicated, such as one that involves numerous computations or extensive detailed input/output statements. The goal is to keep the program readable and understandable. If placing a particular body of code into a procedure contributes to this goal, then you should write a separate procedure; if a separate procedure makes the program more difficult to read or comprehend, put the detailed statements in the statement part of the main program.

3.13.1   *Time Out*

1. Revise Program 3f to include a procedure for Step 2.0 of the program.

```
program P3k (Input, Output);
{Program to compute area and perimeter of a
     rectangle, given length and width. This version of the program
     illustrates the use of multiple procedures.}

var

     Length, Width,        {Input variables}
     Area, Perimeter       {Output variables}
        : Real;

{*******************************************************************}

     procedure GetValues;
     {Procedure to get values for Length and Width}

     const

          LengthPrompt = 'Enter length of rectangle ';
          WidthPrompt = 'Enter width of rectangle ';

     begin    {GetValues}

          Write (LengthPrompt);
          Readln (Length);
          Write (WidthPrompt);
          Readln (Width)

     end;    {GetValues}
{-----------------------------------------------------------------}
     procedure ComputePerimArea;
     {Procedure to compute Perimeter and Area}

     begin    {ComputePerimArea}

          Perimeter := 2.0 * (Length + Width);
          Area := Length * Width;

     end;    {ComputePerimArea}
{-----------------------------------------------------------------}
     procedure WriteValues;
     {Procedure to write input and computed values}

     begin    {WriteValues}

          Writeln;
          Writeln ('Length =', Length:6:2, ' Width =',  Width:6:2);
          Writeln ('Perimeter =', Perimeter:8:2, ' Area =',  Area:8:2)

     end;    {WriteValues}

{*******************************************************************}
```

Figure 3.15(a) Program 3k: Example of a program with multiple procedures (part 1 of 2 parts).

2. Retrieve Program 2e, and revise it to include three procedures—one for the input function, one for computations, and one for output.

```
begin   {Main Program}

{1.0 Get values for Length and Width}

    GetValues;

{2.0 Compute Perimeter and Area}

    ComputePerimArea;

{3.0 Write input values and computed values}

    WriteValues

end.   {Main Program}
```

Figure 3.15(b) (Part 2 of 2 parts).

3.14   STRUCTURE DIAGRAMS

When a program is made up of multiple procedures, a diagram can be useful in helping you visualize the relationships among the procedures. Such diagrams are called **structure diagrams** because they show you the structure of your program. Structure diagrams are composed of rectangles in which the name of each procedure of the program is written. The block representing the main program is placed at the top of the diagram, and blocks representing other procedures are placed below. A line is drawn to connect the rectangles when one procedure invokes another.

For example, consider the program shown in Figure 3.14. This program contains a main program and one subordinate procedure, GetValues. The structure diagram for the program is shown in Figure 3.16. For identification purposes, we will use the convention of writing the program name in the block representing the main program module.

When there are multiple procedures subordinate to the main program, as in the program of Figure 3.15, the structure diagram shows the relationships among the procedures (see Figure 3.17). It is customary to list the procedures in the structure diagram in their order of invocation from left to right.

At this point the structure of the programs we have studied is relatively simple, so that structure diagrams add very little to our understanding of the whole program.

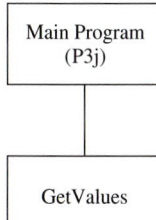

Figure 3.16 Structure diagram for the Program 3j.

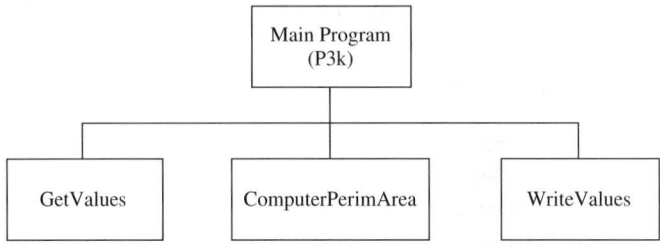

Figure 3.17 Structure diagram for Program 3k.

However, as programs become longer and more complex, with numerous procedures and additional levels of subordination, the structure diagram can be an important asset in gaining an insight into the overall structure of the program.

3.14.1   Time Out

Draw structure diagrams for the two programs you modified in the exercises in Section 3.13.1.

3.15   Case Study: Monthly Payment for a Mortgage

■ **Problem Statement.**   Write a program to compute the amount of the monthly payment required to pay off a loan, where the user enters the loan amount (the principal), the interest rate, and the length of the loan in years. The formula for computing the monthly payment is as follows:

$$M = \left[\frac{R(1 + R)^N}{(1 + R)^N - 1} \right] \times P$$

where P = principal, R = monthly rate, N = number of payments, and M = monthly payment. The monthly rate is the yearly rate divided by 12. The number of payments is the length of the loan times 12. The user should enter his or her name, and the output should include the user's name, the input data, and the monthly payment. After the computer completes its display, the system should wait with the information on the screen.

■ **Problem Analysis.**   This problem requires the user to enter data (name and mortgage information). The program then performs the required computations and produces the specified output. An initial version of the procedure is as follows:

1.0 Get user name

2.0 Get mortgage data

3.0 Compute payment amount

4.0 Write input data and payment

5.0 Wait

At this point, it is necessary to decide on variable names. Let us use the following dictionary:

Variable Name	Type	Comment
Principal	Real	Amount of loan
Rate	Real	
Time	Real	Time in years
First	string	User's first name
Last	string	User's last name
MiddleInitial	Char	User's middle initial (1 character)
Payment	Real	Monthly payment amount

With these definitions in mind, we can now add some detail to the procedure as follows:

1.0 Get user name
    1.1 Read First
    1.2 Read MiddleInitial
    1.3 Read Last
2.0 Get mortgage data
    2.1 Read Principal
    2.2 Read Rate
    2.3 Read Time
3.0 Compute payment amount
4.0 Write input data and payment
    4.1 Write name
    4.2 Write mortgage data
    4.3 Write Payment
5.0 Wait

Now let us turn our attention to the module that computes the payment amount. We know the formula, but in order to use it, several operations will need to be performed on the input data. In particular, the monthly rate must be computed from the yearly rate, and the number of payments must be derived from the number of years. After these computations are performed, the formula can be used to compute the value for Payment. Our procedure can now be rewritten as follows:

1.0 Get user name
    1.1 Read First
    1.2 Read MiddleInitial
    1.3 Read Last
2.0 Get mortgage data
    2.1 Read Principal
    2.2 Read Rate
    2.3 Read Time

3.0 Compute payment amount
  3.1 Compute monthly rate
  3.2 Compute number of payments
  3.3 Compute Payment
4.0 Write input data and payment
  4.1 Write name
  4.2 Write mortgage data
  4.3 Write Payment
5.0 Wait

We note that the formula for computing the monthly payment is fairly complicated. It would be advisable to break it into parts by computing the numerator, $R(1 + R)^N$, and denominator, $(1 + R)^N - 1$, and then combining these in a much simpler formula to compute the monthly payment. We therefore revise the procedure one more time to add this detail to Module 3.3, Compute Payment:

1.0 Get User Name
  1.1 Read First
  1.2 Read MiddleInitial
  1.3 Read Last
2.0 Get mortgage data
  2.1 Read Principal
  2.2 Read Rate
  2.3 Read Time
3.0 Compute payment amount
  3.1 Compute monthly rate
  3.2 Compute number of payments
  3.3 Compute Payment
    3.3.1 Compute Numerator
    3.3.2 Compute Denominator
    3.3.3 Payment = Numerator/Denominator * Principal
4.0 Write input data and payment
  4.1 Write name
  4.2 Write mortgage data
  4.3 Write Payment
5.0 Wait

This version of the procedure now has sufficient detail to enable us to begin writing the actual program.

■ **Problem Solution.**   In designing the program for this problem, we will choose to implement Module 3.0 using a separate procedure because it involves numerous calculations and because it requires several variables that are not needed in the remainder of the program. We will also choose to write an initial version of the program that does not contain this procedure, in order to test the relatively simpler input and output code. A preliminary version of the program is shown as Program 3l in Figure 3.18. It contains all of the pseudocode of the completed program, but no implementation of Module 3. It also does not include the output statement in Module 4 for the payment amount, since this will be computed in Module 3. Writing one or more preliminary versions of a program is a very useful technique because it allows you to find and correct errors in incremental steps. In

```pascal
program P3l (Input, Output);
{Program to compute the amount of a mortgage payment,
    given Principal, Rate, and Time}
uses Crt;
var
    Principal, Rate : Real;            {Input variables}
    Time          : Integer;
    First, Last   : string[10];
    MiddleInitial : Char;
    Payment       : Real;              {Output variable}

begin

{1.0  Get user name}

    ClrScr;
    Write ('Enter First Name ');
    Readln (First);
    Write ('Enter Middle Initial ');
    Readln (MiddleInitial);
    Write ('Enter Last Name ');
    Readln (Last);

{2.0  Get mortgage data}

    Write ('Enter Loan Amount ');
    Readln (Principal);
    Write ('Enter Yearly Interest Rate in form 0.dddd ');
    Readln (Rate);
    Write ('Enter Term of Loan in Years ');
    Readln (Time);

{3.0  Compute payment amount}

{4.0  Write input data and payment}

    Writeln;
    Writeln ('Mortgage computation for ', First, ' ',
            MiddleInitial, '. ', Last);
    Writeln ('Principal = ', Principal:10:2);
    Writeln ('     Rate = ', Rate*100:10:2, '%');
    Writeln ('    Years = ', Time:10);

{5.0  Wait}

    Write ('Press <Enter> to continue');
    Readln

end.
```

Figure 3.18 Program 3l: A preliminary version of the mortgage payment program.

this case, once Program 3l is debugged and we add the procedure for computing the mortgage payment, we know that any errors that are encountered will be in the new part of the program.

In Program 3l, note how we implemented the requirement that the system wait until the user views the information the program has produced. We write a message and then execute a Readln statement with no arguments. This causes the system to wait until the user has transmitted EOL by pressing the Enter key before proceeding. Such a technique is very useful because of the way Turbo Pascal causes the user screen to disappear immediately after completion of the program. Of course, the user can recall the user screen by issuing appropriate commands to the Turbo Pascal system, but this is something of a nuisance and can be avoided by the simple wait procedure used in the program.

The completed program is shown as Program 3m in Figure 3.19. Note in the procedure ComputePayment that we have defined a local constant called PaymentsPerYear and used that constant in the computation of MonthlyRate (Rate / PaymentsPerYear) and NumberPayments (Time * PaymentsPerYear). The rationale behind writing the program in this way is as follows: If someone later wishes to modify the program to work with quarterly payments (four payments per year), all he or she will have to do is change the one line of code defining the constant PaymentsPerYear. The alternative would be to

```pascal
program P3m (Input, Output);
{Program to compute the amount of a mortgage payment,
    given Principal, Rate, and Time}
uses Crt;
var
    Principal, Rate : Real;            {Input variables}
    Time            : Integer;
    First, Last     : string[10];
    MiddleInitial;  : Char;
    Payment         : Real;            {Output variable}

{*************************************************************************}

    procedure ComputePayment;
    {Procedure to compute payment, given Principal, Rate, and Time}
    const
        PaymentsPerYear = 12;
    var
        {Local variables used in computing monthly payment}
        Numerator, Denominator, MonthlyRate, NumberPayments : Real;
    begin   {ComputePayment}
        MonthlyRate := Rate / PaymentsPerYear;
        NumberPayments := Time * PaymentsPerYear;
        Numerator := MonthlyRate *
                        Exp (NumberPayments * Ln(1 +  MonthlyRate));
        Denominator := Exp (NumberPayments * Ln  (1+MonthlyRate)) - 1;
        Payment := Numerator / Denominator * Principal
    end;    {ComputePayment}

{*************************************************************************}
```

Figure 3.19(a) Program 3m: Completed mortgage payment program. (Part 1 of 2 parts)

```
begin {Main Program}

{1.0  Get user name}

      ClrScr;
      Write ('Enter First Name ');
      Readln (First);
      Write ('Enter Middle Initial ');
      Readln (MiddleInitial);
      Write ('Enter Last Name ');
      Readln (Last);

{2.0  Get mortgage data}

      Write ('Enter Loan Amount ');
      Readln (Principal);
      Write ('Enter Yearly Interest Rate in form 0.dddd ');
      Readln (Rate);
      Write ('Enter Term of Loan in Years ');
      Readln (Time);

{3.0  Compute payment amount}

      ComputePayment;

{4.0  Write input data and payment}

      Writeln;
      Writeln ('Mortgage computation for ', First, ' ',
               MiddleInitial, '. ', Last);
      Writeln ('Principal = ', Principal:10:2);
      Writeln ('     Rate = ', Rate*100:10:2, '%');
      Writeln ('    Years = ', Time:10);
      Writeln ('  Payment = ', Payment:10:2);

{5.0  Wait}

      Write ('Press <Enter> to continue');
      Readln

end.   {Main Program}
```

Figure 3.19(b) (Part 2 of 2 parts)

change each line of code that depended on this constant, which opens up the possibility that one line might be changed but the other one missed. Also, since the constant is named and appears prominently in the program listing, it is more obvious that this change can be made than if the constant 12 were used in the two related computational statements.

A sample execution of Program 3m is shown in Figure 3.20.

3.15.1   *Time Out*

1. Test Program 3m with input of your choosing.
2. Modify Program 3m so that the program's output produced in Module 4.0 is placed in the center of the screen (use GotoXY).

```
Enter First Name Joe
Enter Middle Initial A
Enter Last Name Jones
Enter Loan Amount 45000
Enter Yearly Interest Rate in form 0.dddd 0.1250
Enter Term of Loan in Years 30

Mortgage computation for Joe A. Jones
Principal = 45000.00
     Rate =    12.50%
    Years =       30
  Payment =   480.27
Press <Enter> to continue
```

Figure 3.20 Sample execution of Program 3m.

3. Modify the program to allow for quarterly payments rather than monthly payments.

4. Modify the program so that the number of payments per year is an input variable. Should you rename any of the variables in the program?

5. Would it be appropriate to clear the screen as the initial step in Module 4.0? Try this and test the program. Does this affect the usability of the program? Why?

3.16   PROGRAM DEBUGGING AND TESTING

In the programs you have written thus far, you probably have been able to proceed immediately from the pseudocoded version of a program to a completely coded functioning program. For the small programs we have written, this has indeed presented no problems. But for larger problems, you may wish to proceed from the pseudocode to the complete program by coding and testing your program a little at a time. That is, it is often valuable to code and test some program modules before all modules have been coded. This practice makes it possible to concentrate on smaller segments of a program in your search for errors. Once you have debugged a portion of the program, you can add another module and test the program. It is most likely that any errors you encounter in the new version of the program will be isolated in the module that you just added. By repeating this process—add a module to the program and then test the program—until the program is fully implemented, you will eventually arrive at a complete and fully debugged program. The work of debugging and testing the program will have been accomplished in parallel with the task of implementing the program.

Let us use the program for computing a mortgage payment (Program 3m) as an example. We assume that the program has been completely thought out and pseudocoded. It is now time to begin implementing the program. A strategy that is often effective is to code and test the input modules first. This ensures that data will be read correctly. In order to verify the correctness of the input, it is necessary to include some output as well. At this stage in the development process, the program could appear as was shown in Figure 3.18.

Now we can begin to add modules one or two at a time. In this case, we probably would want to add the module that computes the monthly payment. Since this module has intermediate variables—variables that are computed, but that are not specified as part of the output of the completed program—you might want to insert some diagnostic output inside the module so that you can verify that the formulas are correct. This diagnostic output will, of course, be removed in the completed program. The initial portion of this version of the program would appear as shown in Figure 3.21.

Once you have verified that the data are being read properly and the calculations are being performed correctly, you can complete the program by writing the output module with detailed formatting and labels. After final testing, all diagnostic output can be removed, and the program will be ready for use. While this may seem like a roundabout method for developing a program, you will find in practice that it makes the ultimate task of debugging and testing the program much easier. One additional advantage is that the method enables you to spot errors early in the development process and correct them right away. If the error is sufficiently serious, you may have to return to the pseudocode and

```pascal
program P3n (Input, Output);
{Program to compute the amount of a mortgage payment,
     given Principal, Rate, and Time}
{This version of the program illustrates the use of diagnostic
     output that is often useful in debugging a program}
uses Crt;
var
     Principal, Rate : Real;              {Input variables}
     Time            : Integer;
     First, Last     : string[10];
     MiddleInitial   : Char;
     Payment         : Real;              {Output variable}
{*********************************************************************}
     procedure ComputePayment;
     {Procedure to compute payment, given
          Principal, Rate, and Time}
     {Procedure includes diagnostic output of the values
          of intermediate variables}
     const
          PaymentsPerYear = 12;
     var
          {Local variables used in formula for computing monthly payment}
          Numerator, Denominator, MonthlyRate,  NumberPayments : Real;
     begin   {ComputePayment}
          MonthlyRate := Rate / PaymentsPerYear;
          Writeln ('MonthlyRate = ',MonthlyRate:6:4);
          NumberPayments := Time * PaymentsPerYear;
          Writeln ('NumberPayments = ', NumberPayments:6:0);
          Numerator := MonthlyRate *
                         Exp (NumberPayments * Ln(1 + MonthlyRate));
          Writeln ('Numerator = ', Numerator);
          Denominator := Exp (NumberPayments * Ln  (1+MonthlyRate)) - 1;
          Writeln ('Denominator = ', Denominator);
          Payment := Numerator / Denominator * Principal;
          Writeln ('Payment = ',Payment:8:2);
     end;   {ComputePayment}
{*********************************************************************}
```

Figure 3.21 Program 3n: Use of diagnostic output in developing the mortgage payment program. Screened statements will be removed in completed program.

revise one or more parts of the program plan. If you are using the **stepwise program-development** technique outlined in this section, you have not wasted time coding a complete program that is fundamentally flawed.

Note: Users of Turbo Pascal 5.0 and later may use the watch window to output values of variables during the development process. See Appendix G for details.

3.17 REVIEW QUESTIONS

1. What purpose do comments serve in a program? What are the two methods for coding comments in Turbo Pascal? Which method is found in standard Pascal?

2. For this exercise, assume that the following constant declarations have been made:

```
const
        A = 16;
        B = -4;
        C = 1.7;
        D = -2.3;
```

Evaluate each of the following expressions.

(a) `Abs (B)`

(b) `Abs  (C  -  D)`

(c) `Sqr  (B)`

(d) `Sqrt  (A)`

(e) `Int  (C)`

(f) `Fract  (D)`

(g) `Trunc  (C)`

(h) `Round  (C)`

3. Write Pascal code for each of the following expressions.

(a) $\sqrt{x - y^2}$

(b) $\sin^2(x)$

(c) e^{-x}

(d) a^{x+y}

(e) $ax^n - by^n$

4. Explain the difference between Write and Writeln. Why would you want to use Write in a program?

5. For this exercise, assume that the following constant declaration is in place:

```
const
        A = -123;
        B = 1.46;
        C = True;
        D = 'XYZ';
```

Show the output produced by each of the following statements.

(**a**) `Write (A:5);`

(**b**) `Write (B:8);`

(**c**) `Write (B:8:1);`

(**d**) `Write (C:6);`

(**e**) `Write (D:6);`

6. How does a variable of type Char differ from one of type string[1]?

7. For this exercise, assume that the following constant declaration is in place:

```
const
    A = True:
    B = False;
```

Evaluate each of the following expressions.

(**a**) A **or** B

(**b**) **not** A

(**c**) **not** (A **and** B)

(**d**) A **xor** B

(**e**) **not** A **xor** B

(**f**) A **or** (**not** B) **and** B

8. What function is served by each of the following standard procedures?

(**a**) `ClrScr`

(**b**) `InsLine`

(**c**) `DelLine`

(**d**) `GotoXY`

(**e**) `Delay`

(**f**) `Assign`

(**g**) `Reset`

(**h**) `Rewrite`

(**i**) `Close`

9. In a Pascal program, where is the procedure declaration part placed?

10. In what way is a procedure declaration different from a Pascal program specification? In what ways are they the same?

11. What is the difference between a global identifier and a local identifier? Why do you specify some constants and variables to be local?

12. What purpose is served by a structure diagram?

13. Describe stepwise program implementation. Of what value is this technique?

14. Explain the difference between Read and Readln.

15. What purpose is served by EOL in a Text file?

16. What purpose is served by EOF in a Text file?

17. When creating a Text file from the keyboard, how does the user transmit the EOL codes?

18. How is the external file name associated with the file variable in a Pascal program?

19. What two statements are required to open a file for input? for output?

20. Why is it important to close an output file?

3.18 PROGRAMMING EXERCISES

1. Write procedures to print each letter of your initials in a large format. For example, the letter A should be composed of all A's as shown:

```
        A
      A   A
     A     A
     AAAAAAA
    A         A
   A           A
```

Write a main program to print your initials, using each of the procedures as needed.

2. Write a program to compute the distance between two ships, where the program user enters the x- and y-coordinates of each ship. If X_1 and Y_1 are the coordinates of ship 1, and X_2 and Y_2 are the coordinates of ship 2, the distance is

$$\sqrt{(X_1 - X_2)^2 + (Y_1 - Y_2)^2}$$

3. Write a program to compute the integer quotient and remainder for two integer values entered by the user.

4. An accountant needs a program to compute the annual depreciation rate for office equipment. She wishes to enter the original price, the resale price, and the age in years of the equipment. The formula for computing the depreciation rate is

$$R = 1 - \left(\frac{P_2}{P_1}\right)^{1/N}$$

where R = the depreciation rate, P_1 is the original price, P_2 is the resale price, and N is the age.

5. Write a program to compute the principal of a loan, given the payment, interest rate, and length of the loan. The required formula is

$$P = \frac{M \times 12}{I} \times \left[1 - \frac{1}{(1 + I/12)^N}\right]$$

where P is the principal, M is the monthly payment, I is the interest rate, and N is the total number of payments (length of the loan times 12).

6. An individual retirement account (IRA) allows a person to deposit an amount each year into an account that will accumulate tax free to provide a retirement income. Let us assume that the person will contribute the same amount each year. Write a program to compute the future value of the account, given the amount of the annual deposit, the interest rate, and the number of years until retirement. The required formula is

$$T = R \left[\frac{(1 + I)^Y - 1}{I}\right]$$

where T is the total value, R is the amount of the annual deposit, Y is the number of years, and I is the interest rate.

7. Write a program to compute the area of a regular hexagon, given the perimeter. *Note:* A regular hexagon is composed of six equilateral triangles, as shown in the following figure:

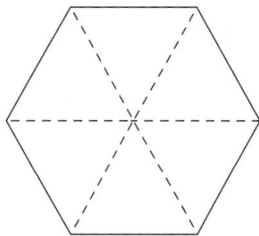

In order to compute the area of the hexagon, first compute the area of each triangle and then multiply by 6.

8. Write a program to compute the annualized rate of return on a short-term investment. Input consists of the amount invested, the amount returned, and the number of days of the investment. Print the annualized rate as a percentage. The required formula is

$$R = 365 \left(\frac{A_2 - A_1}{T A_1} \right)$$

where R is the rate, A_1 is the amount invested, A_2 is the amount returned, and T is the length of the investment in days.

9. Write a program to compute the payoff amount for a loan using the following technique which is sometimes referred to as the "Rule of 78." Input consists of the number of payments in the original loan, the monthly payment amount, the amount borrowed, and the number of payments yet to be made. The required formula is

$$P = M \times (N - K) - \frac{(N \times M - A) \times (N - K + 1) \times (N - K)}{N \times (N + 1)}$$

where N is the number of payments in the payments in original loan, M is the monthly payment amount, A is the amount of the original loan, K is the number of payments made to date, and P is the payoff amount.

10. Write a program to verify that not (X or Y) is equivalent to (not X) and (not Y). *Hint:* Declare X and Y as Boolean variables. Create a procedure that will print out the values of the two expressions. In your main program, execute the output procedure after setting X and Y to each of the following combinations of values:

X	Y
True	True
True	False
False	True
False	False

11. Write a program to compute the volume in cubic yards and cubic feet and the capacity in gallons of cylindrical tank. Input consists of the diameter and height of the tank in feet. (*Note:* There are 231 cubic inches in a gallon.)

12. The amount that must be invested for a specified number of years in order to have a desired amount of money can be determined by the formula

$$\frac{F}{(1 + R)^N}$$

where F = future value of the investment, R = interest rate, and N = number of years. Write a program to allow the user to enter values for F, R, and N and compute the required payment.

13. Use the Turbo Pascal editor to create a file containing your initial in the style illustrated in Programming Exercise 1. Write a program to read this file and display its contents on the screen.

14. A file contains two lines. The first line consists of a student name and the second of five test grades. Write a program to process the data in this file and create a report showing the student's name and grades and the average grade. The output should be placed in a Text file.

15. Modify Program 3m to process a Text file containing the data that the present version of the program gets interactively from the user. Your program should allow the user to enter the name of the file that contains the data to be processed.

4

Control Structures: Selection

Thus far we have said little about the word *structured*, which is the first word in the title of this text. Actually, the programs you have already written have been structured; you accomplished this naturally by following the examples we presented in the text. In this chapter, you will learn about structured programming in a more formal sense. You will also learn about the if and case statements, which will add to your ability to solve a wider range of problems—problems that require selection among two or more alternative courses of action.

4.1   STRUCTURED PROGRAMMING

The term **structured programming** refers to a collection of programming practices that have been shown to yield programs that are easy to understand and maintain and that are less likely to contain logical errors than programs developed using other techniques. There are four basic ideas at the heart of structured programming:

1. Program modularity
2. Top-down program design
3. Use of a restricted set of program structures
4. Standards for readability

Let us examine each of these concepts in turn.

A **program module** is a portion of a program that carries out a single well-defined task. In a structured program, a module has a single entry point and a single exit point; that is, control passes to the first statement in the module, the module accomplishes its task, and control passes from the last statement in the module to the next element of the program. The important thing is for the module to exhibit a high degree of cohesiveness—the content of the module must be strongly related to the task at hand. There are many ways to implement a program module in Pascal. A module may be a sequence of statements in the statement part of a procedure. Or you may wish to write a separate procedure or function (more on functions later) to implement a module. For example, consider the program shown in Figure 3.15. It is clear that this program is made up of three modules that have been implemented as three separate procedures: GetValues, which carries out input operations; ComputePerimArea, which performs the program's computations; and WriteValues, which performs output operations.

A second major concept in structured programming is **top-down program design**. This is the technique by which a program is initially specified as a sequence of high-level tasks; then each task is broken into smaller tasks and so forth, until the complete program is designed. Top-down program design has been illustrated in previous chapters using pseudocoded versions of programs that are repeatedly refined until a complete program plan is evolved. You will find that this is a very powerful technique because it enables you to postpone decisions about some of the details of a program until later on in the design process; you have to focus on only one level of detail at a time. You will particularly appreciate this advantage as programs become longer and more involved. Another advantage to top-down program design is that, when properly applied, it leads naturally to program modules with a high degree of cohesiveness.

A very important component in the theory and practice of structured programming is the restriction placed on the use of **program structures**. A program structure is a pattern for the flow of control within a program. The programs you have written up to now have made use of the sequence structure: The program statements have been executed one after the other in a sequential fashion. Other structures are possible; indeed, much of the power of a computer lies in its ability to select among alternative courses of actions and to repeat sets of instructions. Both of these capabilities require that the next instruction to be executed will not be the next instruction in the program. One of the fundamental theoretical conclusions of structured programming is that there are only three **control structures** needed to solve any problem:

1. *Sequence:* A sequence of instructions is executed, one after the other.
2. *Selection:* One of a number of alternative paths is selected.
3. *Iteration:* A sequence of statements is repeated in a controlled fashion.

In most modern programming languages (including Pascal), the goto statement is not required to implement any of these structures. Pascal does include the goto statement for those times you must use it, but most programmers never need it. In fact, Pascal was designed with this aspect of structured programming in mind. The language includes very powerful facilities to enable programmers to implement selection and iteration structures in a wide variety of circumstances; there is little or no need to try out structures of your own design. The goal of this restriction is to keep the control structures simple and predictable, thereby making programs easier to understand, debug, and maintain. Pascal makes it natural for you to stick to the three permitted program structures and thereby write good structured programs.

A final concept in structured programming is adherence to standards for program readability. We have already discussed some of the practices that we feel contribute to program readability. For example, you have been encouraged to write variable names that are short and descriptive. You make sure that each statement in a program starts on a new line, and you use levels of indentation to show the relation of statements to each other. You incorporate white space in the form of blank lines and comments at appropriate points in the program. All these practices enhance program readability; the fact that you follow the same set of standards all the time gives the programs a predictable format, which in itself contributes to the readability of your programs.

4.1.1 Program Flowcharts

Very early in the history of computers, it became apparent that some means of planning programs was needed; it was then (and still is) very difficult to write a program without some sort of preliminary plan. We have described pseudocode as an appropriate vehicle for this task. Another method that predates the use of pseudocode is the program flowchart. A **program flowchart** is a diagram showing the steps in a procedure, with lines showing the flow of control. Because a flowchart renders a program's structure in a visual format, it was (and to some extent continues to be) a useful tool.

The symbols shown in Figure 4.1 have been adopted as the standard symbols for program flowcharts. Differently-shaped blocks are used for different types of program statements. Computational statements are placed in rectangular blocks. For example, the

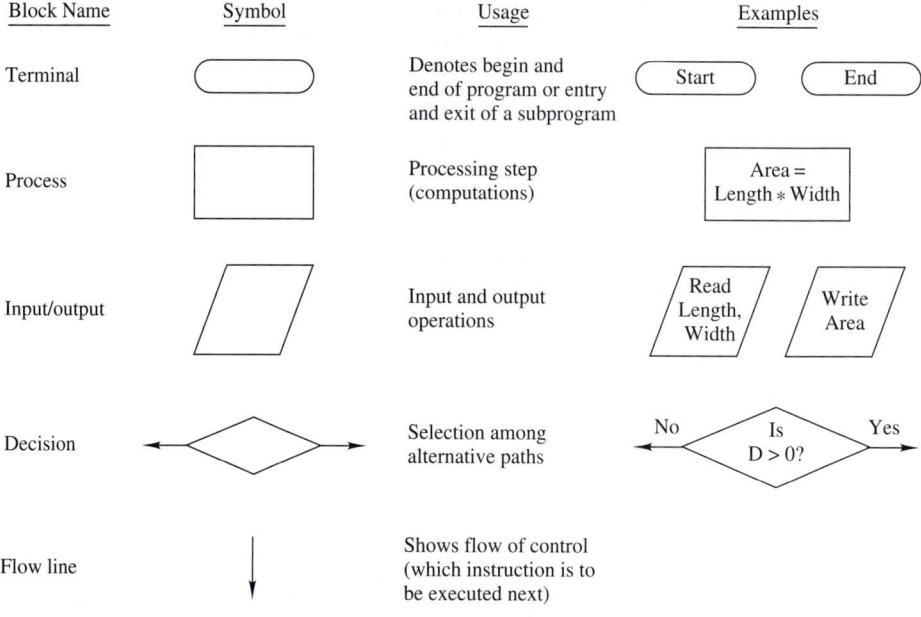

Figure 4.1 Summary of program flowchart symbols.

following are typical:

(As with pseudocode, the level of detail in a flowchart may vary.) Input and output statements are placed in parallelograms. Some examples are:

The beginning and end of the procedure are denoted using oval-shaped blocks:

The flow of control within the procedure is denoted by the line segments that connect the blocks. For example, the following procedure, which is presented in both pseudocode and flowchart forms, could be used to compute and print an employee's gross pay based on hours worked and rate of pay:

1.0 Get Hours and Rate

2.0 Compute GrossPay

3.0 Write Hours, Rate, and GrossPay

Start

Get
Hours, Rate

Compute
GrossPay

Write Hours,
Rate, GrossPay

Stop

Decision points that denote places at which alternative paths through a procedure are to be selected are marked using the diamond-shaped symbol:

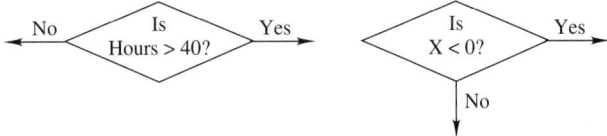

A decision symbol will show the two alternative paths that can be selected, based on the specified condition. In the example on the left, if the value of the variable Hours is greater than 40, the next program action will be selected by following the flow line labeled "Yes"; otherwise, the next action is selected by following the line labeled "No." In the example on the right, one of the two alternative paths is to be selected based on the value of the variable X. If X is negative, the "Yes" path will be taken; otherwise, the "No" path is selected.

As an example, consider the problem of computing an employee's pay with the additional consideration that all hours worked over 40 are to be paid at $1\frac{1}{2}$ times the usual hourly rate. This means that there must be two different procedures for computing gross pay—one if the hours worked are greater than 40 and one if the hours worked are less than or equal to 40. The plan for this program is similar to that for the program described before, but Module 2.0 must be refined as shown in the following pseudocode:

1.0 Get Hours and Rate

2.0 Compute GrossPay

    2.1 If Hours > 40 then

        2.2   GrossPay $=$ 40*Rate $+$ 1.5*Rate*(Hours $-$ 40)

2.3 Else
2.4   GrossPay = Rate*Hours
2.5 End if
3.0 Write Hours, Rate, and GrossPay

In flowchart form, this procedure would appear as shown in Figure 4.2.

Program flowcharts make it possible to describe any control structure that you can devise, because flow lines can be drawn at will. For long and complicated programs, the flowchart becomes a maze of intersecting flow lines, leading to the derisive term "spaghetti code" to describe nonstructured programs that make use of programmer-defined control structures. The use of structured programming techniques has made program flowcharting less useful as a program-planning tool. The permitted control structures can be described quite nicely in pseudocode. Pseudocode can be manipulated using computer-based word processors or editors; flowcharts usually have to be drawn manually using a flowchart template. For these reasons, flowcharting has been largely replaced by pseudocode as a program-planning tool. Flowcharting remains as a way to describe a procedure or part of a procedure in a visual fashion. Often, the old saying that a picture is worth a thousand words is as true when describing the flow of control in a program as it

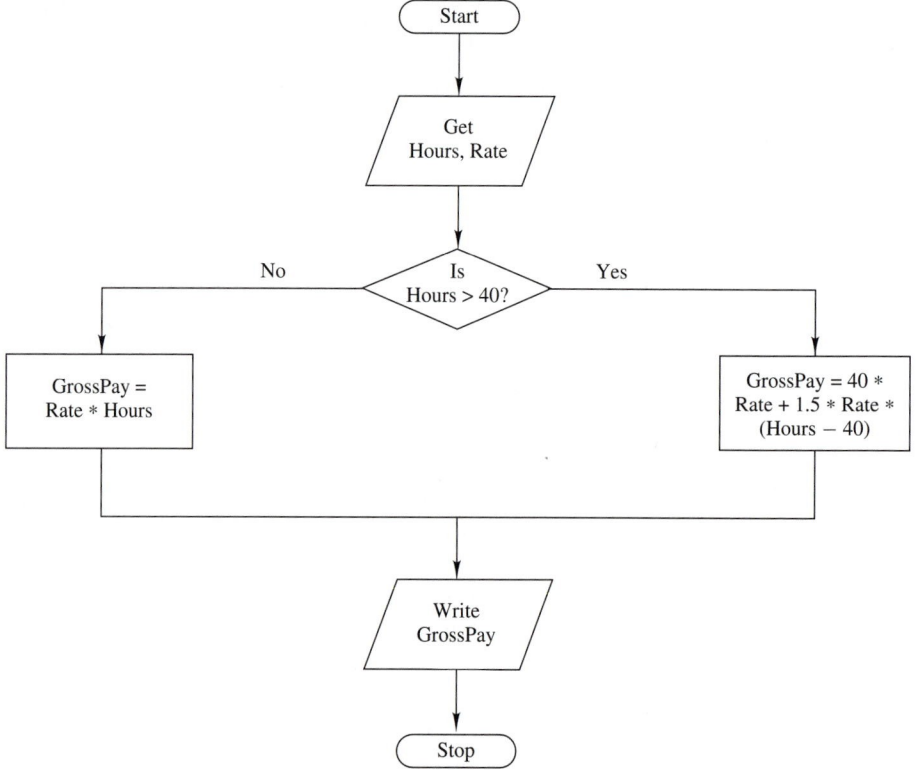

Figure 4.2 Flowchart of payroll procedure.

is in other areas of human endeavor. We will use program flowcharts occasionally in this text when they seem appropriate to illustrate a point. We do not use flowcharts as a primary programming tool in our own work, and we certainly do not advise you to do so.

4.2 THE SELECTION STRUCTURE

One of the fundamental principles of structured programming is that three program structures are sufficient to write any program. The three fundamental structures—sequence, selection, and iteration—are summarized in Figure 4.3. You have used the sequence structure in the programs you have written so far in your study of programming. The **selection structure** allows you to introduce decision-making capabilities into a program; that is, the program can behave differently, depending on circumstances. The iteration structure allows a program to repeat a block of code, which makes possible the use of several very powerful problem-solving techniques. In this section, we shall concentrate on the selection structure; iteration structures are covered in detail in Chapter 6.

Selection is always based on a condition that will be either True or False. The **condition** is expressed in terms of one or more **relations** between two expressions. In Pascal, a variation on the usual mathematical notation for relations is used, as shown in the following table:

Symbol	Meaning
$=$	Equal to
$<$	Less than
$>$	Greater than
$<=$	Less than or equal to
$>=$	Greater than or equal to
$<>$	Not equal to

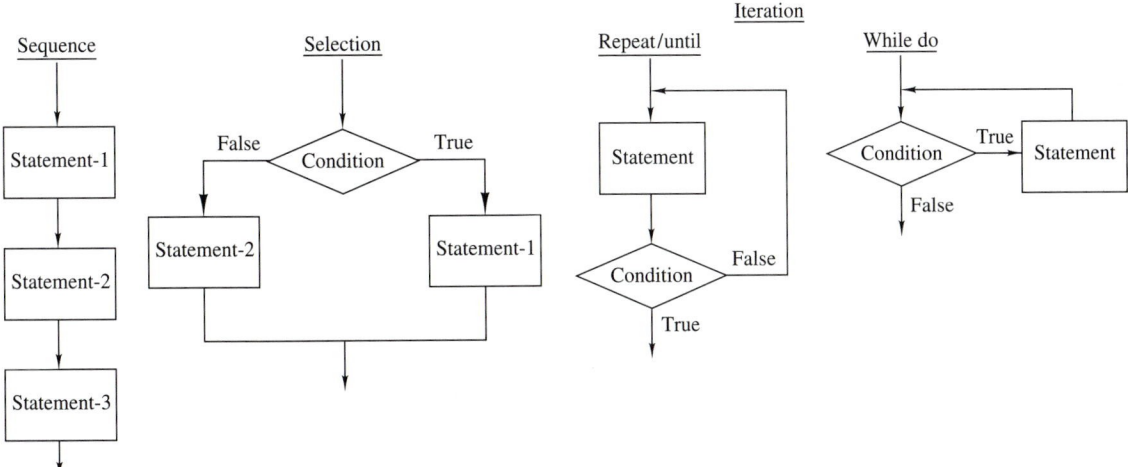

Figure 4.3 Summary of fundamental control structures.

A condition is classed as simple if it involves one relation, as in the following examples:

A < 0	Condition will be True when A is negative.
(A - B) >= C	Condition will be True when the value of A − B is greater than or equal to the value of C.

A condition is said to be **compound** if it involves more than one relation and at least one logical operation (and, or, xor, not), as in the following examples:

(A < 0) and (B < 0)	Condition will be True when both A and B are negative.
(A = 3) or (B = 5)	Condition will True when either A has the value 3 or B has the value 5 or both.

In pseudocode, the selection structure is written using the If statement. The If statement has two general forms, as shown in Figure 4.4.

Form 1 of the If statement is useful when there is some set of actions that must be carried out if the condition is true and not if the condition is false. For example, let us design a program that will compute the commission for a salesperson who is paid on the following basis: A basic commission of 10% on gross sales is earned. If the amount of gross sales is over $1,000, a bonus of $50 is paid. Input to the program is the name and gross sales amount for a salesperson; the output should be the input values and the amount of the commission.

A first plan for this program could be as follows:

1.0 Get Name and Sales

2.0 Compute Commission

3.0 Write Name, Sales, and Commission

Module 2.0 needs refinement because the rule specified for computing the commission is somewhat complicated. Upon reflection about the problem, we revise the pseudocode as follows:

COMMISSION PROGRAM, VERSION 1

1.0 Get Name and Sales

2.0 Compute Commission

    2.1 Commission $= 0.10 *$ Sales

    2.2 If Sales > 1000 then

    2.3   Add 50 to Commission

    2.4 End If

3.0 Write Name, Sales, and Commission

Note that if Sales are *not* greater than or equal to 1,000 (that is, if Sales are less than

Form 1

If   *condition* then
       statement-1
         .
         .
         .

End If

Form 2

If   *condition* then
       statement-1
         .
         .
         .

Else

       statement-n
         .
         .
         .

End If

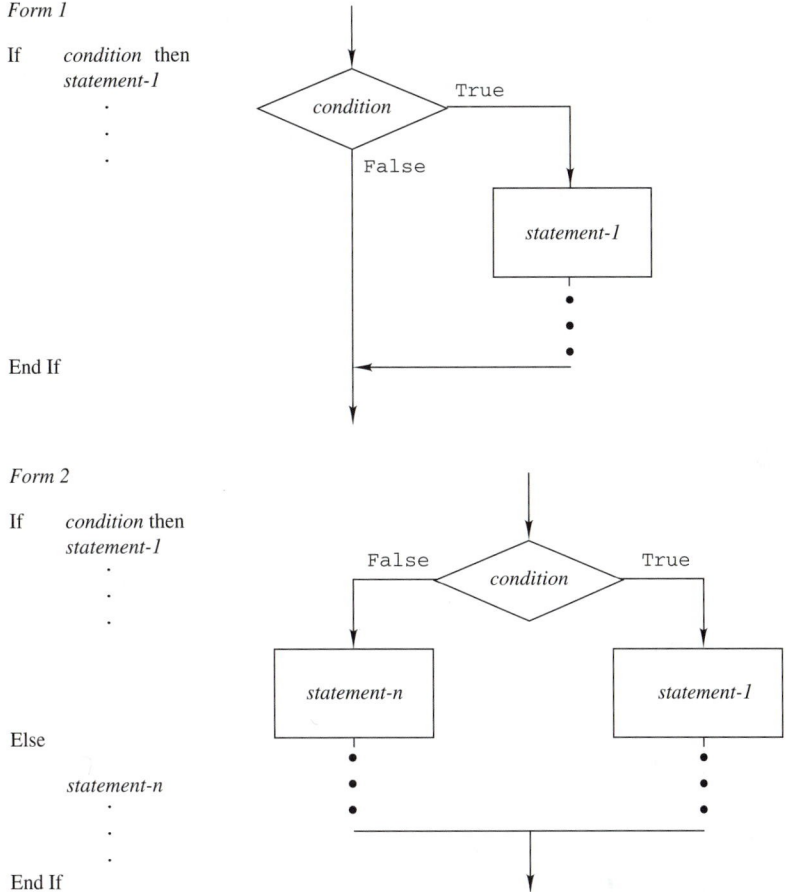

Figure 4.4 General forms of pseudocode If statement.

1,000), statement 2.3 is bypassed. An important point about the If statement is that no matter whether the condition is true or false, after all statements in the range of the statement have been executed, control passes to the statement following the End If statement. End If is called a *scope delimiter* for the If statement. It specifies the end of the selection structure.

Often, several If statements will be needed to select among more than two alternative courses of action. For example, let us return to the problem of paying the salesperson, with the following rule for computing the commission:

If gross sales are under $500, the commission is $50.

If gross sales are between $500 and $1,000 inclusive, the commission is 10% of gross sales.

If gross sales are greater than $1,000, the commission is 11% of gross sales.

We must revise the program as follows:

COMMISSION PROGRAM, VERSION 2

1.0 Get Name and Sales

2.0 Compute Commission
    2.1 If Sales < 500 then
    2.2   Commission = 50
    2.3 End If
    2.4 If (Sales >= 500) and (Sales <= 1000) then
    2.5   Commission = 0.10 * Sales
    2.6 End If
    2.7 If Sales > 1000 then
    2.8   Commission = 0.11 * Sales
    2.9 End If

3.0 Write Name, Sales, and Commission

In this example, note the use of the compound condition

$$(Sales >= 500) \text{ and } (Sales <= 1000)$$

This condition will be true when both relations are true; if either relation is false, the condition is false. Note further that exactly one of the conditions

$$Sales < 500$$
$$(Sales >= 500) \text{ and } (Sales <= 1000)$$
$$Sales > 1000$$

will be true for any given value of Sales. Accordingly, this set of conditions is said to be *mutually exclusive*.

    Form 2 of the If statement is useful if you need to select from among two alternative courses of action based on some condition. If the condition is true, you wish the program to choose one set of statements; if the condition is false, an alternative set of statements is to be executed. In either case, control passes to the statement following the End If statement. For example, let us return to the problem of paying a salesperson, but with a different rule for computing the commission:

    If gross sales are over $1,000, the commission is paid at the rate of 11%; otherwise the commission is 10%.

    The same basic program outline as before is appropriate, but now Module 2.0, which computes the commission, should be revised as shown in the following pseudocode:

COMMISSION PROGRAM, VERSION 3

1.0 Get Name and Sales

2.0 Compute Commission
    2.1 If Sales > 1000 then

2.2   Commission = 0.11 * Sales
2.3 Else
2.4   Commission = 0.10 * Sales
2.5 End If
3.0 Write Name, Sales, and Commission

In this case, one of the statements 2.2 or 2.4 will be executed, depending on the value of Sales. Note again that after execution of either part of the If statement, control passes to the statement following the End If. That is, if, during a sample execution of the program, the value of Sales is greater than 1,000, statement 2.2 will be selected for execution because the condition Sales > 1000 is true. After statement 2.2 is executed, control passes to statement 3.0. Alternatively, if the value of Sales is less than or equal to 1,000, the condition Sales > 1000 will be false, and statement 2.4 will be executed, followed by Statement 3.0 Thus, there are two paths through this procedure:

$$1.0, 2.1, 2.2, 3.0 \qquad \text{(if Sales } > 1000)$$
$$1.0, 2.1, 2.4, 3.0 \qquad \text{(if Sales } \leq 1000)$$

Now consider again Version 2 of the commission program. Remember that the rule for paying the commission was based on sales under $500, between $500 and $1,000, and over $1,000. In Version 2 of the program, we used a sequence of three Form 1 If statements. An alternative way to write the procedure involves using nested Form 2 If statements—Form 2 If statements, some of which are wholly contained within the range of others. For example, an alternative way of coding Module 2.0 in this example is shown in the following version of the program:

COMMISSION PROGRAM, VERSION 4

1.0 Get Name and Sales
2.0 Compute Commission
    2.1 If Sales < 500 then
    2.2   Commission = 50
    2.3 Else
    2.4   If Sales <= 1000 then
    2.5   Commission = 0.10 * Sales
    2.6   Else
    2.7   Commission = 0.11 * Sales
    2.8   End If
    2.9 End If
3.0 Write Name, Sales, and Commission

This technique avoids the use of compound conditions (conditions using and, or, and not) but adds an extra measure of complexity to the code.

4.2.1   Time Out

1. Draw program flowchart equivalents for Module 2 of Versions 1, 2, 3, and 4 of the commission program.
2. Consider Version 2 of the commission program. If the value of Sales is less than 500, the execution path for the procedure is 1.0, 2.1, 2.4, 2.7, 3.0. Write two other execution paths. Under what circumstances will each be selected?
3. A student's letter grade is assigned on the basis of a test score as follows:

Test Score	Letter Grade
90–100	A
80–89	B
70–79	C
60–69	D
0–59	F

Design a program that will allow a user to enter a test score and that will output the corresponding letter grade.

4.3   CONDITIONS

As we have seen, conditions play a fundamental role in the selection structure. In this section, we describe the Pascal conventions for writing conditions. In the next section, we use this information to write Pascal if statements.

A condition must have a Boolean value (True or False). A condition may indeed be specified as a Boolean constant or variable or logical expression. Another way to form a condition is to use a relation. A **relation** has the general form

```
expression-1 relational-operator expression-2
```

where the expressions must be of compatible data types and the **relational-operator** is one of the following symbols:

Symbol	Meaning
=	Equal to
<	Less than
>	Greater than
<=	Less than or equal to
>=	Greater than or equal to
<>	Not equal to

For example, assume that the following constant declarations are in place:

```
const
     X = -2;
     Y = 4.2;
```

Then the following relations are valid and represent a variety of the possibilities in writing relations:

```
     X <= Y
    -2 <= 4.2
```
True

Comment: This relation involves Integer and Real constants, which are compatible.

```
Sqr(X)        >       Y + 3
Sqr(-2)             4.2 + 3
```
```
   4          >       7.2
```
False

Comment: Arithmetic operations are carried out and functions are evaluated before the evaluation of the relational operator.

The last example raises the issue of the precedence of relational operators, compared with arithmetic operators. Certainly, we would like to be able to write relations such as

```
Sqr (A) + Sqr (B) = Sqr (C)
```

with the understanding that the expressions on the left and right are to be evaluated and then compared. This is indeed the way in which this relation will treated, because Pascal assigns a precedence relationship among all of the operators (arithmetic, logical, and relational), as shown in Figure 4.5.

Using the precedence table, you can determine the order of evaluation for relations that are quite complex, as shown in the following example:

```
     -X div 2 <= Y / 2
    -(-2)
```
```
       2 div 2     4.2/ 2
```
```
          1      <=   2.1
```
True

We noted earlier that compound conditions are made up of simple conditions connected by logical operators. Pascal offers you the logical operators not, and, or, and xor. You have

Precedence	Operator
High	Unary minus (−)
↑	not
	Multiplying operators (*, /, div, mod, and)
↓	Adding operators (+, −, or, xor)
Low	Relational operators (<, >, =, < >, <ψ=, > =)

Figure 4.5 Precedence for arithmetic, logical, and relational operators.

already seen how these can be used with Boolean constants and variables. They can also be used with relations to form compound conditions. The value of the resulting expression is determined using the same rules presented previously (see Chapter 3, Section 6), which are summarized for you in Figure 4.6

For example, suppose you wished to write a condition that would be True when the value of X was negative and the value of Y was positive. The required condition would be

```
(X < 0) and (Y > 0)
```

It is very important to note the use of parentheses in this condition. Recall that any expression within parentheses is evaluated first. In this case, assuming the values of X and Y defined before, the expression-evaluation process will proceed as follows:

```
(X < 0) and    (Y > 0)
 −2 < 0         4.2 > 0
 ⌣              ⌣
True    and    True
        ⌣
       True
```

The parentheses are required because of the relative precedences of the relational and the logical operators. All the logical operators have higher precedence than the relational operators. If we attempted to write the condition as

```
X < 0 and Y > 0
```

e	**not** e
True	False
False	True

$e-1$	$e-2$	$e-1$ **and** $e-2$	$e-1$ **or** $e-2$	$e-1$ **xor** $e-2$
True	True	True	True	False
True	False	False	True	True
False	True	False	True	True
False	False	False	False	False

Figure 4.6 Summary of evaluation of logical operators.

The first operation to be carried out would be and, which would be followed by $<$ and $>$; this is clearly an error.

Following are some examples of the evaluation of compound conditions, assuming the values of X and Y declared previously:

```
(X <> 0) or     (Y <> 0)
-2 <> 0         4.2 <> 0

   True     or     True

          True
```

Comment: This condition will be True when either X or Y or both are not equal to zero.

```
not (X = 0)
    -2 = 0

not False

   True
```

Comment: Note that **not** (X = 0) and X <> 0 are equivalent.

```
(X > 0) xor     (Y > 0)
-2 > 0          4.2 > 0

False    xor    True

         True
```

Comment: This condition will be True when X and Y have different signs; it will be false when both X and Y are positive or both X and Y are negative.

4.3.1   Time Out

Assume that A is an Integer variable with value 0 and that B is a Real variable with value −4.5. Evaluate each of the following:

1. A < 0
2. B <= A
3. B + A > 0
4. A = 0
5. (A = 0) **and** (B > 0)
6. Abs (B) > A
7. (A < B) **or** (B < 0)
8. (A < 0) **xor** (B < 0)

9. not (A = 0)

10. not (A < 0) **or** (B > 0)

4.3.2   Comparing Character Data

All the examples presented so far in this section have dealt with comparing numeric expressions (Integer and Real, which are compatible data types). Character data (string and Char, which are also compatible data types) can also be compared.

Character-type data are represented in memory using the American Standard Code for Information Interchange (ASCII) code. The details of this code are described in Appendix D. Basically, each character is coded as a string of binary digits. When two characters are compared, the system actually compares the binary codes representing the characters. The characters are therefore assigned a ranking based on the value of the code used to represent them. For example, if you check the table in Appendix D, you will find that the decimal value for the binary code that represents the character A is 65, and the corresponding value for the character B is 66. Therefore, we say that A is less than B; in other words, the value of the condition

```
'A' < 'B'
```

is True. The ranking of characters in a system is called its collating sequence. The ASCII **collating sequence** for numeric and alphabetic characters is as follows:

```
' ' < '0' < '1' . . . < '9' < 'A' < 'B' < . . . <'Z' < 'a' < 'b' < . . .
< 'z'
```

All representable characters are actually present in the collating sequence, as shown in Appendix D. In particular, the space character, represented by a code with decimal value 32, is less than all the numeric and alphabetic characters.

When comparing two character strings, the system compares characters from left to right. The first character found that differs between the strings determines the relationship between the strings. Two strings must contain identical characters and have the same length to be classed as equal. A shorter string that has the same characters as the initial characters of a longer string is considered to be less than the longer string. These rules are illustrated in the following examples:

'ABC' = 'ABC'	The strings are identical in content and length.
' AB' < 'ABC'	The first comparison is between ' ' in the first string and 'A' in the second; since ' ' < 'A,' this establishes the relationship between the two strings.
'abc' > 'ABC'	Since 'a' > 'A', the first string is greater than the second.
'ABc' > 'ABC'	The strings are equal up to the last character; since 'c' > 'C', the first string is greater than the second.
'AB' < 'AB '	The first string is of length 2 and the second string is of length 3; the first two characters of the strings are equal;

	therefore, the shorter string is less than the longer.
`'D' > 'ABCD'`	The first comparison ('D' > 'A') determines the relationship between the two strings.
`'2' > '1'`	This is as expected
`'2' > '12'`	This is unexpected; the system is comparing the character codes used in the strings, not the values of the numbers being represented.

Note: String comparison is a feature of Turbo Pascal not found in Standard Pascal.

For purposes of comparison, variables of type Char are treated as the equivalent of string[1]. You may mix variables of type string and Char in writing a relation, since they are compatible data types. For example, let assume that the variable LastName has been declared to be of type string[10] and contains the character string 'Jones', and the variable MiddleInitial of type Char has been declared and has value 'J'. Following are some examples of conditions involving these variables:

```
LastName > 'JONES'
'Jones'  > 'JONES'
         True
```

Comment: This relationship is established at the second comparison, where 'o' > 'O'.

```
MiddleInitial < LastName
      'J'      < 'Jones'
           True
```

Comment: The first string is equal to the first character of the second one, but the first string is shorter.

```
MiddleInitial <> ''
      'J'      <> ''
           True
```

Comment: This condition could be used to test for the presence of a middle initial.

4.3.3 *Time Out*

For the following, assume that X has the value `'Washer'` and Y has the value `'W'`. Evaluate each condition.

1. Y <= X

2. X > 'WASHER'

3. X >= 'Washer'

4. `Y > '1'`
5. `Y = 'W'`

4.4 THE IF STATEMENT

In Pascal, the selection structure is implemented by the **if statement**, which is the equivalent of the If statement in pseudocode. The general forms of the Pascal if statement are:

Form 1

```
if condition then
    statement
```

Form 2

```
if condition then
    statement-1
else
    statement-2
```

The words *if*, *then*, and *else* are Pascal reserved words and hence are written with lowercase letters, following our convention for reserved words. Note that there is no End If statement in Pascal. The if statement is terminated in the same way as any other statement—usually by a semicolon, but sometimes by a reserved word such as *else* or *end*. Note also that the then clause and the else clause of the statement contain a single Pascal statement. This is a restriction that is not faced in pseudocode, where the two parts of the statement are free to contain as many statements as desired. (In the next section, we will see how to effectively avoid this restriction on the Pascal if statement by using a compound statement.)

For example, consider Module 2.0 of Version 1 of the commission program described in Section 2. The relevant pseudocode was as follows:

2.0 Compute Commission
    2.1 Commission = 0.10 * Sales
    2.2 If Sales > 1000 then
    2.3   Add 50 to Commission
    2.4 End If

The Pascal equivalent for this module is the following:

```
{2.0 Compute Commission}
    Commission := 0.1 * Sales;
    if Sales > 1000 then
        Commission := Commission + 50;
```

The complete program, is shown in Figure 4.7. Sample executions are shown in Figure 4.8.

In the program, Form 1 of the if statement is required. The semicolon after the statement Commission := Commission + 50 serves the same purpose as the End If statement does in pseudocode—it acts as a scope delimiter for the if statement. When the compiler encounters the semicolon, it knows that this is the end of the if statement.

A sequence of Form 1 if statements is required in the implementation of Module 2.0 of Version 2 of the commission program. The required code is shown in Figure 4.9; the remainder of the program is identical to Program 4a, shown in Figure 4.7. Note the use of

```
program P4a (Input, Output);
{Commission program version 1;
    example of Form 1 if statement}
const
    NamePrompt = 'Enter Salesperson Name ';
    SalesPrompt = 'Enter Sales Amount ';
var
    Name : string[20];      {Input Variables}
    Sales,
    Commission              {Output Variable}
        : Real;
{*********************************************************************}
    procedure Wait;
    begin    {Wait}
        Write ('Press <Enter> to continue');
        Readln
    end;     {Wait}
{*********************************************************************}
begin    {Main Program}

{1.0 Get Name and Sales}

    Write (NamePrompt);
    Readln (Name);
    Write (SalesPrompt);
    Readln (Sales);

{2.0 Compute Commission}

    Commission := 0.1 * Sales;
    if Sales > 1000 then
       Commission := Commission + 50;

{3.0 Write Name, Sales, and Commission}

    Writeln;
    Writeln ('Salesperson : ',Name);
    Writeln ('      Sales $ ',Sales:8:2);
    Writeln (' Commission $ ',Commission:8:2);

{4.0 Wait}

    Wait

end.    {Main Program}
```

Figure 4.7   Program 4a: Example of Form 1 if statement.

```
Enter Salesperson Name Joe Jones
Enter Sales Amount 450

Salesperson : Joe Jones
      Sales $   450.00
 Commission $    45.00
Press <Enter> to continue
Enter Salesperson Name Mary Smith
Enter Sales Amount 1200

Salesperson : Mary Smith
      Sales $  1200.00
 Commission $   170.00
Press <Enter> to continue
```

Figure 4.8 Sample executions of Program 4a.

```
program P4b (Input, Output);
{Commission program, Version 2;
    example of sequence of Form 1 if statements}
    .
    .
    .
{2.0 Compute Commission}

    if Sales < 500 then
       Commission := 50;
    if (Sales >= 500) and (Sales <= 1000) then
       Commission := 0.1 * Sales;
    if Sales > 1000 then
       Commission := 0.11 * Sales;

    .
    .
    .
end.   {MainProgram}
```

Figure 4.9 Program 4b: Example of a sequence of Form 1 if statements.

parentheses to code the compound condition

```
(Sales >= 500) and (Sales <= 1000)
```

in the second if statement. In pseudocode it is possible to omit these parentheses, but in Pascal they are required because the relational operators have lower precedence than the logical operator *and*. Note that in this code there is a sequence of three semicolons that delimit the three separate if statements.

An example of Form 2 of the Pascal if statement is found in the implementation of Module 2.0 in Version 3 of the commission program. The relevant pseudocode is as follows:

2.0 Compute Commission
  2.1 If Sales > 1000 then

2.2 Commission = 0.11 * Sales
2.3 Else
2.4 Commission = 0.1 * Sales
2.5 End If

Note that we could code the constant one-tenth as 0.1 or 0.10. In Pascal, the two constants are equivalent. The Pascal equivalent of this module is

```
{2.0 Compute Commission}
    if Sales > 1000 then
       Commission := 0.11 * Sales
    else
       Commission := 0.1 * Sales;
```

The relevant parts of the program are shown in Figure 4.10.

The importance of the semicolon in terminating the if statement cannot be emphasized too strongly. Most of the statements you have written so far have been contained on one line, so you may have developed a habit of placing a semicolon at the end of every line of code. Although the if statement usually is placed on several lines of code for clarity, it is still only one statement and therefore is separated from the next statement in the program by one semicolon. For example, suppose you coded the preceding module incorrectly as

```
if Sales > 1000 then
   Commission : = 0.11 * Sales; ←  Note added semicolon
else
   Commission : = 0.1 * Sales;
```

The difference may appear small (what can one small semicolon more or less matter?),

```
program P4c (Input, Output);
{Commission program, Version 3;
    example of Form 2 if statement}
    .
    .
    .
{2.0 Compute Commission}

    if Sales > 1000 then
       Commission := 0.11 * Sales
    else
       Commission := 0.1 * Sales;
    .
    .
    .
end.    {Main Program}
```

Figure 4.10 Program 4c: Example of Form 2 if statement.

but to the compiler, there is a large problem. The first semicolon effectively serves to terminate the if statement. The compiler assumes at this point that another statement will follow and thus that you have written a Form 1 if statement without the else clause. What, then, can be made of the reserved word *else* that the compiler interprets next? It is normally associated with a Form 2 if statement, but the compiler has just concluded a Form 1 if statement! In fact, the compiler cannot interpret the *else*, and therefore, a syntax error will result. When coding if statements in Pascal, you must be very careful to use the semicolon properly: The statement in the then clause is never followed by a semicolon if an else clause is present.

There are no restrictions on what Pascal statements can be part of the then or else clauses of an if statement. It is often useful to embed an if statement in one or the other parts of an if statement. An example is found in Module 2.0 of Version 4 of the commission program. The relevant pseudocode is as follows:

2.0 Compute Commission
    2.1 If Sales < 500 then
    2.2 Commission = 50
    2.3 Else
    2.4 If Sales <= 1000 then
    2.5   Commission = 0.10 * Sales
    2.6 Else
    2.7   Commission = 0.11 * Sales
    2.8 End If
    2.9 End If

The Pascal implementation of this code is shown in Figure 4.11. A sample execution of the program (4d) is shown in Figure 4.12. In this case, the inner if statement is embedded

```
program P4d (Input, Output);
{Commission program, Version 4;
    example of nested if statements}
        .
        .
        .
{2.0 Compute Commission}

        if Sales < 500 then
            Commission := 50
        else
            if Sales <= 1000 then
                Commission := 0.1 * Sales
            else
                Commission := 0.11 * Sales;
        .
        .
        .
    end.    {Main Program}
```

Figure 4.11 Program 4d: Example of nested if statement.

```
Enter Salesperson Name Joe Jones
Enter Sales Amount 450

Salesperson : Joe Jones
      Sales $  450.00
 Commission $   50.00
Press <Enter> to continue
Enter Salesperson Name Mary Smith
Enter Sales Amount 1200

Salesperson : Mary Smith
      Sales $  1200.00
 Commission $   132.00
Press <Enter> to continue
```

Figure 4.12 Sample executions of Program 4d.

in the else clause of the outermost if statement. The semicolon that terminates the inner if statement also terminates the outer if statement.

An if statement can also be contained in the then clause of an if statement. You can see this if you write the Pascal equivalent of the following pseudocode module:

1.0 If A = B then

2.0   If C < D then

3.0   Write C

4.0   Else

5.0   Write D

6.0   End If

7.0 Else

8.0   Write 'A not equal to B'

9.0 End If

The Pascal equivalent is

```
if A = B then
   if C < D then
      Writeln (C)
   else
      Writeln (D) ←    Note: No semicolon is used here.
else
   Writeln ('A not equal to B');
```

In this case, the inner if statement is not followed by a semicolon because it is followed by the else clause of the outer if statement. A semicolon following the statement Writeln (D) would have signified not only the end of the inner if statement, but also the end of the outer if statement. The compiler would then register a syntax error when it encountered the reserved word *else* on the next line of code.

4.4.1 Time Out

1. Translate each of the following pseudocode modules into Pascal.

(a) 1.0 If SexCode = 'M' then
   2.0   Write 'Male'
   3.0 Else
   4.0   Write 'Female'
   5.0 End If

(b) 1.0 If PayRate < 7.50 then
   2.0   Add 50 to bonus
   3.0 End If

(c) 1.0 If (SexCode = 'M') or (SexCode = 'm') then
   2.0   Write 'Male'
   3.0 Else
   4.0   If (SexCode = 'F') or (SexCode = 'f') then
   5.0   Write 'Female'
   6.0   Else
   7.0   Write 'Invalid Sex Code'
   8.0   End If
   9.0 End If

(d) 1.0 If $A^2 + B^2 = C^2$ then
   2.0   Write 'Right Triangle'
   3.0 Else
   4.0   Write 'Not a Right Triangle'
   5.0 End If

2. Modify Program 4a to compute the commission on the following basis:

> The commission is $50 if sales are in the range from $500 to $1,000 (inclusive). If sales are less than $500, the commission is $20. If sales are more than $1,000, the commission is 5% of sales.

3. The management of the company that uses Program 4a has decided to make the following modification to the way in which it pays its sales force: Each salesperson is assigned a bonus code (A, B, or C), which, together with the amount of sales, will determine the commission. The rule is:

> If bonus code = A, the rate is 5% of sales; if bonus code = B, the rate is 5% of sales if sales are less than $1,000 and 6% otherwise; if bonus code = C, the rate is 6% of sales.

Modify Program 4a to accommodate this change.

| **4.** Write a Pascal program for the grade problem described in Exercise 3 of Section 4.2.1.

4.5   COMPOUND STATEMENTS

Recall that one of the major restrictions on the if statement is that each clause in it must contain one statement. As promised, there is a way to avoid this restriction: You simply write a **compound statement**. The compiler treats a compound statement as a single statement and thereby enables you to meet the restriction on the syntax of the if statement, but you can place as many statements as you wish inside the compound statement. The general form of a compound statement is

```
begin
    statement-1;
        .
        .
        .
end
```

The compound statement is terminated by the reserved word *end*, which is followed by a semicolon (if another Pascal statement will follow) or a Pascal reserved word such as *else* or *end*. Any number of statements of any type may be in a compound statement. Compound statements may be used in any context in which a simple statement is used.

For example, consider the following pseudocode module:

1.0 If HourlyRate < 7.50 then
2.0   Add 50 to Bonus
3.0   Write 'Bonus of $50 included'
4.0 End If

There are two things to be accomplished if the condition is true. In order to code this in Pascal, we will write a compound statement containing two statements:

```
begin
    Bonus := Bonus + 50;
    Writeln ('Bonus of $50 included')
end
```

Then we can use the compound statement in an if statement, as follows:

```
if HourlyRate < 7.50 then
    begin
```

```
        Bonus := Bonus + 50;
        Writeln ('Bonus of $50 included')
  end; {if}
```

The semicolon after *end* signifies the end of the if statement. It is customary to include a comment following the *end* statement signifying what is being ended—in this case, the if statement—so the line is coded as

```
end; {if}
```

The practice enhances the readability of your program by making it read more like pseudocode.

Often, compound statements are used in both clauses of an if statement. For example, consider the following pseudocode:

1.0 If HourlyRate < 7.50 then
2.0   Add 50 to Bonus
3.0   Write 'Bonus of $50 included'
4.0 Else
5.0   Multiply bonus by 1.10
6.0   Write 'Bonus of 10% included'
7.0 End If

This module requires two compound statements when the Pascal if statement is written:

```
if HourlyRate < 7.50 then
  begin
      Bonus := Bonus + 50;
      Writeln ('Bonus of $50 included')
  end
else
  begin
      Bonus := 1.1 * Bonus;
      Writeln ('Bonus of 10% included')
  end; {if}
```

In this code, only three semicolons are required. You would not normally include a semicolon at the end of the two Writeln statements, because they are each followed by *end*. (If you did, Pascal would insert a null statement, which would have no effect on the execution of the program.) The last *end* is followed by a semicolon because it will be followed by a Pascal statement. The first *end* is not followed by a semicolon because the next program element is the else clause of the if statement. (If you inserted a semicolon here, the if statement would be terminated and a syntax error would result.)

Let us write a program that will ensure that two values A and B are always such that A $\le$ B; that is, we desire a program such that if the input is 2 and 3 or 3 and 2, the output will be 2 and 3.

The first version of the program would be:

1.0 Enter A and B

2.0 Resequence A and B if needed

3.0 Write A and B

The task of resequencing (also called interchanging) needs to be accomplished only if A is greater than B. We therefore rewrite the program as

1.0 Enter A and B

2.0 Resequence A and B if needed

    2.1 If A $>$ B then

    2.2   Interchange A and B

    2.3 End If

3.0 Write A and B

The task of interchanging two values requires that a third temporary, or holding, location be established to "hold on" to one of the values when its variable is replaced by the second value. The required procedure is as follows:

Hold $=$ A

A $=$ B

B $=$ Hold

The first statement transfers the value of A to Hold; the second statement replaces the value of A by the value of B; the third statement replaces the value of B by the previous value of A, which is now in Hold. Thus, the complete plan for this program, with this routine in place, is as follows:

1.0 Enter A and B

2.0 Resequence A and B if needed

    2.1 If A $>$ B then

    2.2   Interchange A and B

        2.2.1 Hold $=$ A

        2.2.2 A $=$ B

        2.2.3 B $=$ Hold

    2.3 End If

3.0 Write A and B

An implementation for Module 2.0 in Pascal would require a compound statement for the interchange procedure, as in the following:

```
{2.0 Resequence A and B if needed}
    if A > B then
        begin
            Hold := A;
            A := B;
            B := Hold
        end;  {if}
```

4.5.1   Time Out

1. Translate each of the following into Pascal.

  (a) **1.0** If A = B then
      2.0   Add 1 to C
      3.0   Write C
      4.0 End If

  (b) **1.0** If A < B then
      2.0   Add 1 to C
      3.0   Write A
      4.0 Else
      5.0   Add 2 to C
      6.0   Write B
      7.0 End If

  (c) **1.0** If TestGrade > 90 then
      2.0   Lettergrade = 'A'
      3.0   QualityPoints = 4
      4.0 End If

2. In the following Pascal coding segment, numbers enclosed in circles are located in places where you might be tempted to use a semicolon. Which of the numbers should be replaced by semicolons? Give a reason for each response.

```
begin
    Writeln (InputPrompt) (1)
    Readln (A, B) (2)
    if A > B then
        begin
            Hold := A (3)
            A := B (4)
            B := Hold (5)
        end (6) {if}
    Writeln ('Values in sequence are ',A,B) (7)
end.
```

3. Write a program to place two values entered by the program user into ascending sequence.

4.5.2   Program Example

■ **Problem Statement.**   Professor X has created Text files containing the following information (on separate lines) about his students:

Name
Social security number
Registration type (U = undergraduate, G = graduate)
Three test scores

For example, the following is a sample file containing information about a graduate student Mary Jones, whose social security number is 111111111 and whose test scores are 80, 90, and 95:

Mary Jones
111111111
G
80 90 95

A program is needed to compute the final grade. Undergraduate students must have an average greater than 70 to pass, while graduate students must have a grade greater than 75 to pass. The program should create appropriately formatted output on the screen and wait after the output is produced. The program should also allow the professor to enter the name of the file to be processed.

■ **Problem Analysis.**   A plan for the program is as follows:

GRADING PROGRAM (PROGRAM 4E)

1.0 Open data file
2.0 Read data
3.0 Process data
4.0 Close data file
5.0 Wait

Let us consider the tasks involved in step 3. It would be a useful feature if the program printed an error message if a type other than G or U is encountered. If a valid value for the registration type is found, we first compute the test average. If the registration type is U, the computation is made using one rule; otherwise the computation is made using an alternative rule. This is summarized in the following refinement of step 3:

3.0 Process data
    3.1 If registration type is valid then
    3.2   Compute the average
    3.3   If registration type = 'U' then
    3.4   Passing grade = 70
    3.5   Else
    3.6   Passing grade = 75
    3.7   End If
    3.8   If average > passing grade then
    3.9   Grade = 'Pass'
    3.10   Else
    3.11   Grade = 'Fail'
    3.12   End If
    3.13   Write input data and grade
    3.14 Else
    3.15   Write error message
    3.16 End If

■ **Problem Solution.**   A solution to this problem is shown as Program 4e in Figure 4.13. The output produced by the program for the sample data described before is

```pascal
program P4e (Input, Output, DataFile);
{Program processes student information to compute pass/fail grade;
    program illustrates use of compound statement}
const
    FileNamePrompt = 'Enter name of file ';
    ErrorMessage = 'Invalid registration type ';
    UndergraduatePass = 70;
    GraduatePass = 75;
var
    Name, SSN              : string;     {Input variables}
    RegistrationType       : Char;
    Test1, Test2, Test3    : Real;
    Grade                  : string;     {Output variable}
    PassingGrade, Average  : Real;       {Control variables}
    DataFile               : Text;
    FileName               : string;
{***********************************************************************}
    procedure Wait;
    begin   {Wait}
        Write ('Press <Enter> to continue ');
        Readln
    end;    {Wait}
{***********************************************************************}
```

Figure 4.13(a) Program 4e: Illustrates use of compound statement (Part 1 of 2 parts).

```
begin      {Main Program}

{1.0 Open data file}

     Write (FileNamePrompt);
     Readln (FileName);
     Assign (DataFile, FileName);
     Reset (DataFile);

{2.0 Read data}

     Readln (DataFile, Name);
     Readln (DataFile, SSN);
     Readln (DataFile, RegistrationType);
     Readln (DataFile, Test1, Test2, Test3);

{3.0 Process the data}

     if (RegistrationType = 'U') or (RegistrationType = 'G') then
          begin
               Average := (Test1 + Test2 + Test3) / 3;
               if RegistrationType = 'U' then
                    PassingGrade := UndergraduatePass
               else
                    PassingGrade := GraduatePass;
               if Average > PassingGrade then
                    Grade := 'Pass'
               else
                    Grade := 'Fail';
               Writeln;
               Writeln ('Name :':20, Name:15);
               Writeln ('SSN :':20, SSN:15);
               Writeln ('Registration type :':20, RegistrationType:15);
               Writeln ('Test grades :':20,
                         Test1:5:0, Test2:5:0, Test3:5:0);
               Writeln ('Average :':20, Average:15:0);
               Writeln ('Final grade :':20, Grade:15)
          end
     else
          Writeln (Errormessage, RegistrationType:3);

{4.0 Close file}

     Close (DataFile);

{5.0 Wait}

     Wait

end.     {Main Program}
```

Figure 4.13(b) (Part 2 of 2 parts).

shown in Figure 4.14. Note the use of a compound statement in the implementation of step 3. This compound statement is composed of a replacement statement, two if statements, and several Writeln statements.

```
Enter name of file grades.dat

             Name :      Mary Jones
              SSN :       111111111
 Registration type :              G
      Test grades :    80   90   95
          Average :             88
      Final grade :           Pass
Press <Enter> to continue
```

Figure 4.14 Sample execution of Program 4e.

Although this program performs its stated function, it would not be used in practice. To use the program, it is necessary to create a separate file for each student—a very tedious task indeed. A much better approach would be to place the data for all students in one file and have the program process each set of items in succession. This would require the use of an iteration structure to cause the processing steps to be repeated for each set of data items. We will return to this problem in Chapter 6, which is devoted to the iteration structure, and discuss a number of different ways in which the program can accomplish the task.

4.5.3   Time Out

Create five data files containing data as required for Program 4e. In two of the files, have a registration type 'U' (one with grades that average greater than 70 and the other with grades that average less than 70). In two other files, have a registration type 'G' (one with grades that average greater than 75 and the other with grades that average less than 75). In the fifth file, have an invalid registration type. Test Program 4e with each of your files. Note that five files are required to test each of the five distinct execution paths in this program. (This exercise should convince you of the impracticality of using the program to process the data represented by one class of students, much less by an instructor's full complement of classes.)

4.6   MULTIPLE SELECTION STRUCTURE

As we have seen, an if statement may be part of the then clause or the else clause (or both) of another if statement; this situation is called a *nested if statement*. Unfortunately, if the practice is carried to an extreme, the resulting program structure becomes difficult to read and understand. Also, the standards for indentation specify that each if and its associated else should be placed on one margin and the statements in the then and else clauses be placed on a margin to the right. If there are multiple levels of nesting, you can quickly run out of room on the line. There is another format that you will find useful when you need to select among several alternatives. This format is called a **multiple selection structure** and has the following general form:

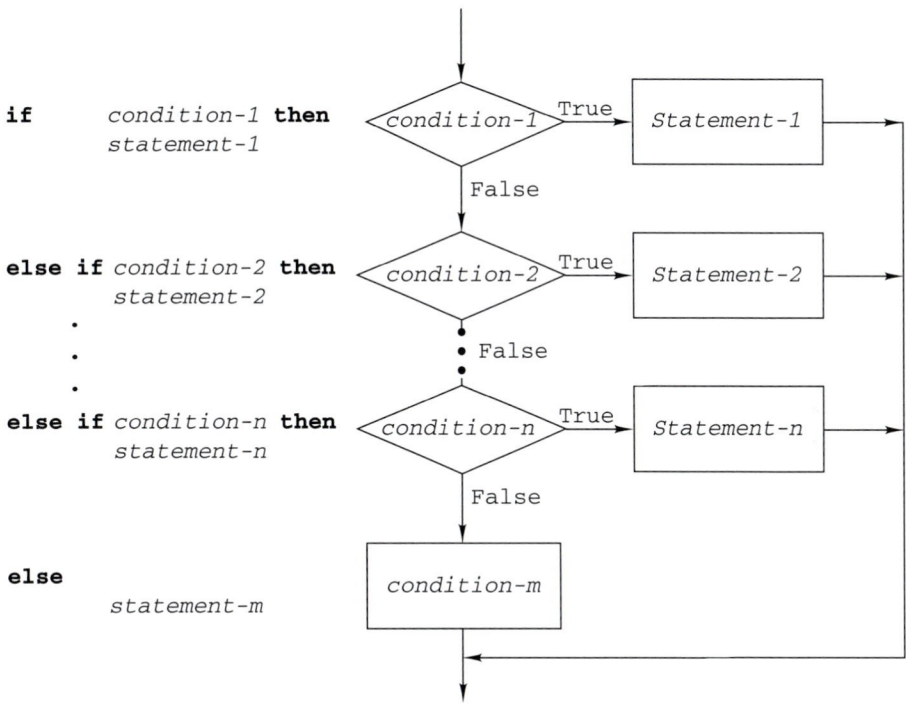

This program structure specifies that *statement-1* is to be executed if *condition-1* is true, *statement-2* is to be executed if *condition-2* is true, and so forth. If none of the conditions included in the list is true, then *statement-m* is executed. Note that the last else clause is optional if you want no action at all when all of the conditions in the list are false. Note also that the evaluation for the conditions takes place in the order you specify. The first one that is true determines the action to be taken. In any case, execution resumes with the statement following the if statement, as shown in the flowchart of the structure.

As an example of this structure, consider the following problem: write a program to classify a year as a leap year or not a leap year. Input to the program consists of the year (e.g., 1992); output should be the year and the appropriate designation. The rule for determining a leap year is as follows: A year is a leap year if it is divisible by 4 and not by 100; and every fourth century year is a leap year (these are years that are divisible by 400). "Divisible by" means that the remainder after division is 0. The following examples illustrate the application of this rule:

Year

1992	Leap year	(divisible by 4 and not by 100)
1900	Not leap year	(divisible by 4 and 100, not by 400)
1993	Not leap year	(not divisible by 4)
2000	Leap year	(divisible by 400)

A first version of the program could be as follows:

1.0 Read Year

2.0 Determine whether Year is a leap year or not

3.0 Write Year and Label

The rule for determining whether a year is a leap year can be summarized in the following decision table:

Year divisible by 4?	Year divisible by 100?	Year divisible by 400?	Leap year?
Yes	No		Yes
Yes	Yes	No	No
Yes	Yes	Yes	Yes
No			No

Step 2 can be refined as shown in the following complete program plan:

1.0 Read Year

2.0 Determine whether Year is a leap year or not
    2.1 If Year is divisible by 4 and not by 100 then
    2.2   Label = 'Leap Year'
    2.3 Else If Year is divisible by 100 and not by 400 then
    2.4   Label = 'Not a Leap Year'
    2.5 Else If Year is divisible by 400 then
    2.6   Label = 'Leap Year'
    2.7 Else If Year is not divisible by 4 then
    2.8   Label = 'Not a Leap Year'
    2.9 End If

3.0 Write Year and Label

Recall that the mod operator computes the remainder after dividing one Integer by another. Therefore, a way to implement the condition

Year divisible by 4

would be

```
Year mod 4 = 0
```

assuming, of course, that Year is an Integer variable. An implementation of Module 2.0 makes use of the multiple selection structure as follows:

```
{2.0 Determine if Year is a leap year or not}
        if      (Year mod 4 = 0) and (Year mod 100 <> 0) then
```

```
            Label := 'Leap Year'
    else if (Year mod 100 = 0) and (Year mod 400 <> 0) then
            Label := 'Not a Leap Year'
    else if   Year mod 400 = 0 then
            Label := 'Leap Year'
    else if   Year mod 4 <> 0 then
            Label := 'Not a Leap Year';
```

Note that this is not the only solution to the problem, but it does have the advantage of bearing a direct relationship to the decision table. (Each condition corresponds to one line in the decision table.) The solution is also easy to read because of the regularity of its structure.

The entries in the decision table actually represent mutually exclusive conditions; that is, only one of them can be true for a given year. We have seen before that when we have a set of mutually exclusive conditions, we can write a simple series of separate if statements. Why, then, should we go to the extra bother of the multiple selection structure? It is worth doing because it is clear to the reader in the multiple selection that it is the intention of the programmer that only one of the outcomes will occur. This may indeed be the result of a series of simple if statements as well, but the alternative approach does not communicate this to the reader as well as the multiple selection structure does. What happens if some programmer later begins to modify the conditions? With the multiple selection structure, there will be at most one action selected no matter what; with the sequence of if statements, there is the possibility of selecting any number of actions.

4.6.1 *Time Out*

1. Using a multiple selection structure, translate the following module into Pascal:

1.0 If (Character $>=$ '0') and (Character $<=$ 9) then
2.0   Write 'Numeric character'
3.0 Else If (Character $>=$ 'A') and (Character $<=$ 'Z') then
4.0   Write 'Uppercase alphabetic character'
5.0 Else If (Character $>=$ 'a') and (Character $<=$ 'z') then
6.0   Write 'Lowercase alphabetic character'
7.0 Else
8.0   Write 'Character not alphabetic or numeric'
9.0 End If

Would it be possible to implement this module using a series of simple if statements? Why or why not?

2. Using the multiple selection structure, translate the following module into Pascal:

1.0 If (A $>=$ B) and (B $>=$ C) then
2.0   Write A, B, C

3.0 Else If (A >= C) and (C >= B) then
4.0   Write A, C, B
5.0 Else If (B >= A) and (A >= C) then
6.0   Write B, A, C
7.0 Else If (B >= C) and (C >= A) then
8.0   Write B, C, A
9.0 Else If (C >= A) and (A >= B) then
10.0   Write C, A, B
11.0 Else If (C >= B) and (B >= A) then
12.0   Write C, B, A
13.0 End If

Describe the problem being solved in this module. Are the conditions mutually exclusive?

3. Write a program to determine whether a given year is leap year, using the method outlined previously. Can you improve on the method?

4.6.2   Program Example

Let us consider again the grading problem described in Section 4.5.2. Recall that the processing step produced one of five different outcomes, shown in the following table:

Registration Type	Average	Grade
U	> 70	Pass
U	<= 70	Fail
G	> 75	Pass
G	<= 75	Fail
other than G, U		Error

An alternative way to implement the processing module in the solution to this problem is to build a multiple selection structure based on the preceding table. This is the approach taken in Program 4f, which is shown in Figure 4.15. A multiple selection structure is used to assign a value 'Pass', 'Fail', or 'Error' to the variable Grade. Then the value of Grade is tested. If it is not 'Error', the ordinary output of valid data is produced. However, if the value of Grade is 'Error', then the appropriate error message is produced. In this program, the variable Grade serves a double purpose: It is used as an output variable for valid data and as an error flag to enable appropriate action to be taken for invalid data.

4.6.3   Time Out

1. Try out Program 4f with the data files you used to test Program 4e. The output should be the same in all cases.
2. Modify Program 4f to include output of all of the input data for both valid and invalid data. For invalid data, write 'Error' in place of the grade 'Pass' or 'Fail'.

```
program P4f (Input, Output, DataFile);
{Program processes student information to compute pass/fail grade;
     program illustrates multiple selection structure}
     .
     .
     .
{3.0 Process the data}

     Average := (Test1 + Test2 + Test3) / 3;
     if       (RegistrationType = 'U') and
              (Average > UndergraduatePass) then
                 Grade := 'Pass'
     else if (RegistrationType = 'U') and
              (Average <= UndergraduatePass) then
                 Grade := 'Fail'
     else if (RegistrationType = 'G') and
              (Average > GraduatePass) then
                 Grade := 'Pass'
     else if (RegistrationType = 'G') and
              (Average <= GraduatePass) then
                 Grade := 'Fail'
     else
                 Grade := 'Error';
     if Grade <> 'Error' then
        begin
            Writeln;
            Writeln ('Name :':20, Name:15);
            Writeln ('SSN :':20, SSN:15);
            Writeln ('Registration type :':20, RegistrationType:15);
            Writeln ('Test grades :':20,
                    Test1:5:0, Test2:5:0, Test3:5:0);
            Writeln ('Average :':20, Average:15:0);
            Writeln ('Final grade :':20, Grade:15)
        end
     else
        Writeln (Errormessage, RegistrationType:3);
     .
     .
     .
end.    {Main Program}
```

Figure 4.15 Program 4f: Illustrates multiple selection structure. Note the vertical alignment of multiple conditions.

4.7 THE CASE STATEMENT

The **case statement** is a specialized statement in Pascal for implementating the multiple selection structure. It is appropriate when exactly one action or set of actions is to be selected, depending on a set of conditions relating to a single expression. The if statement, of course, can be used to implement this structure, as we saw in the preceding section: however, the case statement has many advantages and additional features that make it a valuable tool.

The following general form of the case statement may appear a bit intimidating at first, but we will explain and illustrate each part in due course:

```
case expression of
    case-list-1 : statement-1;
        .
        .
        .
    case-list-n : statement-n
    else
        statement-list
end
```

The *expression* is called the *selector*; its value is used to select among the alternative actions represented by statements 1 through *n*. A **case-list** is a list of potential values of the expression. The *expression* and the constants used in the case lists must be of the same data type. Any data type except Real may be used. If the value of the *expression* is equal to one of the values in a *case-list*, then the corresponding statement is selected for execution, and control passes to the statement following the case statement. If none of the values in any of the case lists matches the value of *expression*, then the statement(s) in the else clause is executed. The else clause is optional in Turbo Pascal and is not a part of standard Pascal.

In its simplest form, a *case-list* consists of a single constant, which must be of the same data type as the *expression*. For example, suppose we wish to compute quality points associated with a letter grade, using the following association:

Letter grade	Quality points
A	4
B	3
C	2
D	1
F	0

(Quality points are often used in computing grade-point averages.) Assuming that LetterGrade is of type Char, the following case statement could be used:

```
case LetterGrade of
    'A' : QualityPoints := 4;
    'B' : QualityPoints := 3;
    'C' : QualityPoints := 2;
    'D' : QualityPoints := 1;
    'F' : QualityPoints := 0
end; {case}
```

Note carefully the placement of semicolons in this statement. A semicolon is placed after each statement in the list of alternatives, except the one that precedes *end*. (This is in keeping with the general rule that a statement should end with a semicolon if another statement will follow.) The semicolon placed after end assumes that another statement will follow this one in the program. The comment following end is in keeping with the general practice of signifying what is being ended; here, it is the case statement that is terminated.

In this example, if the value of LetterGrade is none of 'A' through 'F', then none of the statements will be selected. The else clause can be used to take appropriate action when none of the conditions is satisfied. For example, if you wished to write an error message and assign a value of 0 to QualityPoints, you could revise the preceding code as follows:

```
case LetterGrade of
      'A' : QualityPoints := 4;
      'B' : QualityPoints := 3;
      'C' : QualityPoints := 2;
      'D' : QualityPoints := 1;
      'F' : QualityPoints := 0
    else
          Writeln ('Error in value of LetterGrade :',
                     LetterGrade);
          Quality Points := 0
  end; {case}
```

Note that the else clause can contain one or more statements (separated by semicolons, as usual, if there is more than one). Note also that the statements following the case lists must be single statements (which can, of course, be compound statements if needed; more on this later).

At this point, it is useful to compare a module written with the case statement with one coded using nested if statements. For example, compare the preceding code with the following equivalent code:

```
if       LetterGrade = 'A' then
         QualityPoints := 4
else if LetterGrade = 'B' then
         QualityPoints := 3
else if LetterGrade = 'C' then
         QualityPoints := 2
else if LetterGrade = 'D' then
         QualityPoints := 1
else if LetterGrade = 'F' then
         QualityPoints := 0
else
         begin
             Writeln ('Error in Letter Grade : ',LetterGrade);
             QualityPoints := 0
         end; {if}
```

Plainly, the case statement is much easier to read and understand than the alternative. Moreover, the case statement is less work for the programmer because there is less typing and fewer lines of code; consequently, there are fewer chances for making typing mistakes that result in annoying syntax errors. Where it is appropriate, the case statement is of considerable value as an aid in writing readable code in a painless fashion.

But the case statement is even more powerful, because you can construct case lists that represent multiple possible values for the selector. As usual, a list consists of elements separated by commas. In this instance, the list must be of constants of the same type as the selector expression. For example, suppose you wish to compute the number of days in a month, given the month number, as shown in the following table:

Month name	Month number	Number of days
January	1	31
February	2	28
March	3	31
April	4	30
May	5	31
June	6	30
July	7	31
August	8	31
September	9	30
October	10	31
November	11	30
December	12	31

There is no obvious functional relationship between the month number and the number of days in the month; however, we note that month 2 has 28 days, months 4, 6, 9, and 11 have 30 days, and the rest have 31 days. Accordingly, we could perform the computation with a case statement as follows:

```
case MonthNumber of
    2              : NumberDays := 28;
    4, 6, 9, 11  : NumberDays := 30
    else
                    NumberDays := 31
end; {case}
```

An alternative to this code, which makes provision for the existence of invalid month numbers, is the following:

```
case MonthNumber of
    2                      : NumberDays := 28;
    4, 6, 9, 11          : NumberDays := 30;
    1, 3, 5, 7, 8, 10, 12    : NumberDays := 30
    else
```

```
            Writeln ('Error in month number : ',MonthNumber);
            NumberDays := 0
end;    {case}
```

Another element that may be used in case lists is the **subrange**, which has the general form

```
constant-1..constant-2
```

A subrange includes all values between *constant-1* and *constant-2*, including the endpoints. For example, the subrange `'A'..'Z'` includes all the uppercase letters, and the subrange `1..5` includes the Integer values 1, 2, 3, 4, and 5. A subrange may be included in a range list either by itself or in any desired mixture with other constants.

For example, suppose we wish to classify a character as either a numeric character, an uppercase alphabetic character, or a lowercase alphabetic character. Assuming that Character is of type Char, the following case statement could be used:

```
case Character of
    '0'..'9' : Writeln ('Numeric character');
    'A'..'Z' : Writeln ('Uppercase alphabetic character');
    'a'..'z' : Writeln ('Lowercase alphabetic character')
    else
                Writeln ('Other character')
end; {case}
```

As noted before, a subrange may be included in a range list along with other elements. This can help shorten lists when a sequential pattern exists among the elements in the list. For example, suppose a company pays its salespeople a different percentage based on a product code associated with each item in inventory as follows:

Product code	Commission rate
A–J, R, S	5%
K, M–P, X, Y, Z	6%
All others	7%

Then the following statement could be used to compute CommissionRate based on ProductCode:

```
case ProductCode of
    'A'..'J', 'R', 'S'              : CommissionRate := 0.05;
    'K', 'M'..'P', 'X'..'Z'        : CommissionRate := 0.06
        else
                CommissionRate := 0.07
end; {case}
```

We pointed out earlier that the else clause of the case statement could contain a list of statements, but the statements selected by the case lists must be single statements. A compound statement may be used to get around this limitation in the same way that we used the compound statement to avoid a similar problem with the if statement. Consider the following example, which also illustrates the case statement in pseudocode.

■ **Problem Statement.** Write a program that will compute the letter grade and associated points for a test score entered by the program user. The following table shows the required association:

Test score	Letter grade	Quality points
0–59	F	0
60–69	D	1
70–79	C	2
80–89	B	3
90–100	A	4

■ **Problem Analysis.** An initial version of the program is similar to others we have written:

1.0 Read TestScore

2.0 Compute LetterGrade and QualityPoints

3.0 Write TestScore, LetterGrade, and QualityPoints

Module 2.0 requires selection among five alternatives based on the value of TestScore. The Case statement is a natural way to make the selection:

1.0 Read TestScore

2.0 Compute LetterGrade and QualityPoints
    2.1 Case TestScore of
    2.2   0–59: LetterGrade = F; QualityPoints = 0
    2.3   60–69: LetterGrade = D; QualityPoints = 1
    2.4   70–79: LetterGrade = C; QualityPoints = 2
    2.5   80–89: LetterGrade = B; QualityPoints = 3
    2.6 90–100: LetterGrade = A; QualityPoints = 4
    2.7 End Case

3.0 Write TestScore, LetterGrade, and QualityPoints

■ **Problem Solution.** In coding Module 2.0, we must use a compound statement for each statement associated with a case list because there are two actions to be carried out for each range of test scores. The complete program module will appear as follows:

```
{2.0    Compute LetterGrade and QualityPoints}
     case TestScore of
         0..59   :  begin
                         LetterGrade  :=  'F';
                         QualityPoints  :=  0
                    end;
         60..69  :  begin
                         LetterGrade  :=  'D';
                         QualityPoints  :=  1
                    end;
         70..79  :  begin
                         Lettergrade  :=  'C';
                         QualityPoints  :=  2
                    end;
         80..89  :  begin
                         LetterGrade  :=  'B';
                         QualityPoints  :=  3
                    end;
         90..100 :  begin
                         LetterGrade  :=  'A';
                         QualityPoints  :=  4
                    end
     end;    {case}
```

This is Program 4g, which is shown in Figure 4.16.

It should be noted that when the range lists are mutually exclusive, they can appear in any order in the case statement. The order in which the lists are given becomes important when the lists do not represent mutually exclusive conditions. Pascal actually evaluates the conditions in the order presented; the first one that is found to be true (i.e., the first time the selector expression matches a value in a *case-list*) causes the associated statement to be executed. If more than one condition could be true, the first one encountered is the one selected. For example, consider the following contrived example:

```
case Value of
    1..3 : X := 1;
    3..5 : X := 2
end; {case}
```

If Value = 3, this statement will result in X being assigned the value 1. On the other hand, if the statement had been written as

```
case Value of
    3..5 : X := 2;
    1..3 : X := 1
end; {case}
```

```
program P4g (Input, Output);
{Program to compute letter grade and quality points from
    a test score; illustrates case statement}
uses Crt;
const
    InputPrompt = 'Enter test score ';
var
        TestScore  : Integer;      {Input Variable}
        LetterGrade : Char;        {Output Variables}
        QualityPoints : Real;
{*********************************************************************}
    procedure Wait;
    begin    {Wait}
        Write ('Press <Enter> to continue');
        Readln
    end;     {Wait}
{*********************************************************************}
begin    {Main Program}

{1.0 Read TestScore}

    ClrScr;
    Write (InputPrompt);
    Readln (TestScore);

{2.0 Compute LetterGrade and QualityPoints}

    case TestScore of
        0..59   : begin
                        LetterGrade := 'F';
                        QualityPoints := 0
                  end;
        60..69  : begin
                        LetterGrade := 'D';
                        QualityPoints := 1
                  end;
        70..79  : begin
                        LetterGrade := 'C';
                        QualityPoints := 2
                  end;
        80..89  : begin
                        LetterGrade := 'B';
                        QualityPoints := 3
                  end;
        90..100 : begin
                        LetterGrade := 'A';
                        QualityPoints := 4
                  end
    end;    {case}

{3.0 Write TestScore, LetterGrade, QualityPoints}

    Writeln;
    Writeln ('   Test score : ',TestScore:2);
    Writeln (' Letter grade : ',LetterGrade:2);
    Writeln ('Quality points: ',QualityPoints:2:0);

{4.0 Wait}

    Wait

end.
```

Figure 4.16 Program 4g: Illustration of the case statement.

then if Value = 3, the statement will cause X to be assigned the value 2. It is usually a logical error to have overlap in the values contained in range lists in a case statement.

4.7.1 Restriction on Case Statement and Subranges

The expression used as the selector in a case statement must have an ordinal type, and the values listed in the case-lists must be of a compatible ordinal type. An ordinal type is a type that has a predecessor/successor relationship among its elements. Integer is an ordinal type: The successor of 1 is 2, and the predecessor of 1 is 0. Char is also an ordinal type: The successor of 'B' is 'C', and the predecessor of 'B' is 'A', as defined by the ASCII code used to represent characters. On the other hand, Real is *not* an ordinal type: The successor of 1.0 is ambiguous. (Is it 1.1, 1.01, 1.001, or . . . ?) Thus, the expression used as a selector in the case statement must not be Real. For the same reason, subranges composed of Real values, such as 1.0 . . 2.0, are invalid.

4.7.2 *Time Out*

1. Consider the following arbitrary case statement. Numbers enclosed in circles are placed in locations where you might be tempted to write a semicolon. Which numbers must be replaced by semicolons?

```
case V of
    1..4, 7    : X := 1 (1)
    5, 6       : begin
                     X := 3 (2)
                     Writeln   (X) (3)
                 end (4)
    10..20     : X := 9 (5)
    else
                 X := 10 (6)
                 Writeln (X) (7)
end
```

2. For each of the following, what value will assigned to X as a result of the execution of the preceding case statement?
   (a) V = 3
   (b) V = 19
   (c) V = −1
   (d) V = 6

3. Modify Program 4g to carry out the following actions if the value of TestScore is outside the range 0 to 100:

```
Write an error message
LetterGrade = space
QualityPoints = 0
```

4. Modify Program 4g to accommodate the following grading system:

Test score	Letter grade	Quality points
0–59	F	0
60–67	D	1
68–69	D+	1.5
70–77	C	2
78–79	C+	2.5
80–87	B	3
88–89	B+	3.5
90–100	A	4

5. Write a program to allow a user to enter a month number and have the program respond with the number of days in the month.

6. Modify the program written for Exercise 5 to allow the user to enter the month number and the year. Have the program respond with the number of days in the month, taking into account leap years.

4.8   Case Study: Geometric Computations

So far, all the programs we have written have performed a single function. Very often, however, programs are needed to perform multiple related functions that the user can select as needed. Such programs need a means by which the user can communicate his or her wishes to the program so that it can carry out the proper function(s). One way that this can be done is through a set of command codes entered by the user. Each code corresponds to one of the functions that can be performed by the program. Typically, the program presents the user with a list of possible functions and associated codes and then prompts the user to enter one of the codes. (This list of functions and codes is called a **menu**.) Based on the value of the code, the program selects one of its possible functional modules for execution. Because the user may key in a code that cannot be recognized by the program, it is important to validate the user's response. This requires the program to check the user's response against the list of valid codes. If the response is one of the codes, the program can proceed with its work; if the response is invalid, an error message should be written, and the program can terminate. A general plan for a multifunction program is as follows:

MULTIFUNCTION PROGRAM PLAN

1.0 Get program option from user

2.0 Validate option

3.0 Select program function based on option

    3.1 If option is valid, then

    3.2   Carry out appropriate program function

    3.3 End If

We will use this basic plan in the solution of the following problem:

■ **Problem Statement.** Write a program to perform a variety of computations relating to geometric figures. The program should allow the user to compute either the area or the perimeter of a square, rectangle, or triangle.

■ **Problem Analysis.** The basic plan for this program has just been outlined. Because the problem is reasonably involved, we should plan to divide the program into procedures very early in the design process. Based on the general plan outlined before, we can identify the following procedures that will be required:

Procedure name	Purpose
GetOptions	Display the menu and get user's choices
ValidateOption	Test validity of options entered by user
SquareComputations	Perform computations for a square
RectangleComputations	Perform computations for a rectangle
TriangleComputations	Perform computations for a triangle

All these procedures will be subordinate to the main program, which will execute them as needed to solve the problem. The structure diagram for the program is shown in Figure 4.17.

The user must enter two codes: one to select a figure and one for the calculation to be performed. Insofar as possible, the codes used should relate to the option being selected. One method that works well when each option begins with a different letter is to use the first character of the word as the code. (This is the way Turbo Pascal's menus are designed.) In this case, the figure options are Square, Rectangle, and Triangle, so we can use the codes S, R, and T to represent the corresponding figures. Similarly, we can use the code values A and P to represent Area and Perimeter. Of course, we will need two variables (of type Char) for these two user options; let us call these variables FigureOption and CalculationOption. To make the program more user friendly, we should allow either an uppercase or lowercase character as a code. For example, we want the program to treat s and S as equivalent. Thus, the procedure for entering

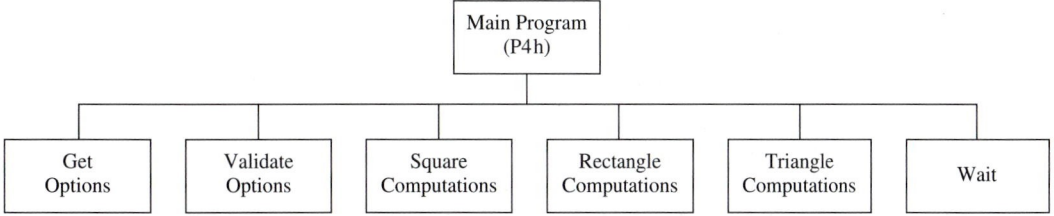

Figure 4.17 Structure diagram for geometric computations program (Program 4h).

program options is as follows:

PROCEDURE GETOPTIONS

1.0 Display figure option menu
2.0 Get figure option
3.0 Display calculation option menu
4.0 Get calculation option

After the options are entered, the program's next task is to validate the values of FigureOption and CalculationOption. One approach to this task is to use a program flag. A flag is a variable that is used to control the operation of a program. Typically, the program sets the value of the flag at one point and then tests the flag at another point. Flags are often implemented as Boolean variables and assigned a value True or False, as appropriate. In the case of this program, we will need two flags of type Boolean; let's call them ValidFigureOption and ValidCalculationOption. The value of Valid-FigureOption should be set to True if FigureOption contains one of the recognizable figure codes ('S', 's', 'R', 'r', 'T', or 't') and False otherwise; a similar operation is required to set the value of ValidCalculationOption. At the time that an invalid option is detected, it is appropriate to write an error message. The procedure for validating options is as follows:

PROCEDURE VALIDATEOPTIONS

1.0 Test FigureOption
    1.1 If FigureOption has a valid value then
    1.2   ValidFigureOption = True
    1.3 Else
    1.4   ValidFigureOption = False
    1.5   Write error message
    1.6 End If
2.0 Test CalculationOption
    2.1 If CalculationOption has a valid value then
    2.2   ValidCalculationOption = True
    2.3 Else
    2.4   ValidCalculationOption = False
    2.5   Write error message
    2.6 End If

The procedures for performing the operations of the program are quite similar. In each case, the user must be prompted for the values of the variables required to perform the computation. The program should echo the input, carry out the required operations, and then present the results. (To *echo* the input means to display the data entered by the user. This is important so that the user understands exactly what data has been received by the program to use as a basis of its computations.) A general plan for a procedure to carry out computations is shown next:

PROCEDURE TO CARRY OUT COMPUTATIONS

1.0 Get input data required for computation

2.0 Echo input

3.0 Perform calculations and print results

■ **Problem Solution.** This program is shown as Program 4h in Figures 4.18(a)–(e). A sample execution is shown in Figure 4.19.

The initial portion of the program is shown in Figure 4.18(a). This portion contains the definition of the global variables.

The procedure GetOptions is also shown in Figure 4.18(a). The menu lines and prompts are declared as named constants for readability.

The procedure ValidateOptions is shown in Figure 4.18(b). We have used the case statement as a convenient way to test whether the variables contain valid values. Module 1.0 could have been implemented using an if statement as follows:

```
if (FigureOption = 'T') or
    (FigureOption = 't') or
    (FigureOption = 'R') or
    (FigureOption = 'r') or
    (FigureOption = 'S') or
    (FigureOption = 's')       then
          ValidFigureOption := True
else
     begin
          ValidFigureOption := False;
          Writeln ('Invalid figure option : ',FigureOption)
     end; {if}
```

Clearly, the case statement is a more concise and readable way to perform this task. Another way such an operation could have been carried out is as follows: Since a condition has a Boolean value, we could write an assignment statement assigning the value of the condition to a Boolean variable. In that case, we could have written

```
ValidFigureOption := (FigureOption = 'T') or
                     (FigureOption = 't') or
                     (FigureOption = 'R') or
                     (FigureOption = 'r') or
                     (FigureOption = 'S') or
                     (FigureOption = 's');
if not ValidFigureOption then
     Writeln ('Invalid figure option : ',FigureOption);
```

From a logical standpoint, there is certainly nothing wrong with this approach. (In Chapter 7, we shall see that sets can be used to good advantage for problems of this type.)

```pascal
program P4h (Input, Output);
{Program to perform a variety of computations for
    geometric figures}
uses Crt;
var
    FigureOption,                        {Input variables}
    CalculationOption : Char;
    ValidFigureOption,                   {Control variables}
    ValidCalculationOption  :  Boolean;
{*********************************************************************}
    procedure GetOptions;
    {Procedure to display the menu and get user's choices}
    const
        MenuLine1 = 'Main Menu';
        MenuLine2 = 'Geometric Figure    Code';
        MenuLine3 = 'Square              S';
        MenuLine4 = 'Rectangle           R';
        MenuLine5 = 'Triangle            T';
        FigureOptionPrompt = 'Enter Code for desired figure : ';
        MenuLine6 = 'Calculation Options    Code';
        MenuLine7 = 'Area                   A';
        MenuLine8 = 'Perimeter              P';
        CalculationOptionPrompt = 'Enter Code for desired calculation : ';
    begin     {GetOptions}

    {1.0 Display figure option menu}

        ClrScr;
        Writeln (MenuLine1);
        Writeln;
        Writeln (MenuLine2);
        Writeln (MenuLine3);
        Writeln (MenuLine4);
        Writeln (MenuLine5);
        Writeln;

    {2.0 Get figure option}

        Write (FigureOptionPrompt);
        Readln (FigureOption);

    {3.0 Display calculation option menu}

        Writeln;
        Writeln (MenuLine6);
        Writeln (MenuLine7);
        Writeln (MenuLine8);
        Writeln;

    {4.0 Get calculation option}

        Write (CalculationOptionPrompt);
        Readln (CalculationOption)

    end;    {GetOptions}
{-----------------------------------------------------------------------}
```

Figure 4.18(a) Program 4h: Global variables and GetOptions procedure (Part 1 of 5 parts).

```
procedure ValidateOptions;
{Procedure to test validity of options entered by user}
begin    {ValidateOptions}

{1.0 Test FigureOption}

    case FigureOption of
         'T', 't', 'R', 'r', 'S', 's' : ValidFigureOption := True
            else
                ValidFigureOption := False;
                Writeln ('Invalid figure option : ',FigureOption)
    end;   {case}

{2.0 Test CalculationOption}

    case CalculationOption of
         'A', 'a', 'P', 'p' : ValidCalculationOption := True
            else
                ValidCalculationOption := False;
                Writeln ('Invalid calculation option : ',
                              CalculationOption)
    end    {case}

 end;   {ValidateOptions}
{-------------------------------------------------------------------}
```

Figure 4.18(b) Program 4h: ValidateOptions procedure (Part 2 of 5 parts).

Figures 4.18(c) and (d) contain the procedures for calculations for squares and rectangles, respectively. Although the details are somewhat different, the overall structures of these two procedures are quite similar. Note the use of the case statement to select the proper formula for evaluation. The if statement could have been used instead. Note also that it is not logically necessary to provide an else clause in the case statement, since the value of CalculationOption has been previously validated. The main program does not execute these procedures unless both of the options entered by the user are valid.

Figure 4.18(e) contains a program stub for the procedure TriangleComputations. A **stub** is a dummy procedure lacking the complete logic needed to perform its function. Stubs are often used in program development to test the overall logical flow of the program prior to adding details. The procedure has a name and can therefore be referenced in the main program, but the only statement in the procedure is a warning to the program user that this program module has not yet been completed. We shall leave the completion of this procedure to you (see Section 4.8.1, "Time Out").

Figure 4.18(e) also contains the statement part of the main program. Note the use of the compound condition in the if statement in Module 3.0. The condition

```
ValidCalculationOption and ValidFigureOption
```

will be true when both of the Boolean variables are True. Note also that Module 3.0 contains a case statement nested in the if statement. This structure has not been used before in the text, but it is a perfectly satisfactory way to do the task that needs to be done.

```
procedure SquareComputations;
{Procedure to perform computations for a square}
const
    DataPrompt = 'Enter length of side of square : ';
var
    Side,                {Input variable}
    Area, Perimeter      {Output variables}
        : Real;
begin    {SquareComputations}

{1.0 Get value for side}

    Writeln;
    Write (DataPrompt);
    Readln (Side);
    Writeln;

{2.0 Echo input}

    Writeln ('Figure : ':30,'    Square');
    Writeln ('Length of side : ':30, Side:10:2);

{3.0 Perform calculations and print results}

    case CalculationOption of
        'A', 'a' :  begin
                        Area := Sqr (Side);
                        Writeln ('Area : ':30, Area:10:2)
                    end;
        'P', 'p' :  begin
                        Perimeter := 4 * Side;
                        Writeln ('Perimeter : ':30,
                                    Perimeter:10:2)
                    end
    end    {case}

end;    {SquareComputations}
{----------------------------------------------------------------------}
```

Figure 4.18(c) Program 4h: SquareComputations procedure (Part 3 of 5 parts).

4.8.1   *Time Out*

1. Test Program 4h with sample data. Try to test all the possible functions, including the entry of invalid options.

2. Finish the coding of the procedure TriangleComputations. Note that this procedure differs somewhat from the other two because the data that the user is required to enter is dependent on the computational option that was chosen.

3. People who use a program often object to having a menu displayed each time commands are to be given. This objection is based on the fact that menu displays are time consuming and unnecessary when the user already knows the codes. Some programs make use of alternative means of communicating the functions and the associated codes to the user.

   (a) One option is to incorporate the command list and options in the prompt line. For

```
procedure RectangleComputations;
{Procedure to perform computations for rectangle}
const
     LengthPrompt = 'Enter length of rectangle : ';
     WidthPrompt = 'Enter width of rectangle : ';
var
     Length, Width,       {Input variables}
     Area, Perimeter      {Output variables}
        : Real;
begin     {RectangleComputations}

{1.0 Get length and width}

     Write (LengthPrompt);
     Readln (Length);
     Write (WidthPrompt);
     Readln (Width);
     Writeln;

{2.0 Echo input}

     Writeln ('Figure : ':30,' Rectangle');
     Writeln ('Length : ':30, Length:10:2);
     Writeln ('Width : ':30, Width:10:2);

{3.0 Perform calculations and print results}

     case CalculationOption of
         'A', 'a' :  begin
                          Area := Length * Width;
                          Writeln ('Area : ':30, Area:10:2)
                      end;
         'P', 'p' :  begin
                          Perimeter := 2 * (Length + Width);
                          Writeln ('Perimeter : ':30,
                                      Perimeter:10:2)
                      end
     end   {case}

end;    {RectangleComputations}
{-----------------------------------------------------------------}
```

Figure 4.18(d) Program 4h: RectangleComputations procedure (Part 4 of 5 parts).

example, in the current program, the prompt for the calculation option could be

```
Enter (A)rea or (P)erimeter:
```

This approach is appropriate when the number of options is short enough to appear on one line. Revise procedure GetOptions in Program 4h using this type of prompt line for both options. Which version of the program seems more appropriate, the original or the revised?

```
        procedure TriangleComputations;
        begin    {TriangleComputations}

               {This procedure is incomplete. Student may complete
                this portion of the program as an  assignment.}
               Writeln ('Calculations for triangle not yet implemented.')

        end;     {TriangleComputations}
{---------------------------------------------------------------------}
        procedure Wait;
        begin    {Wait}
               Write ('Press <Enter> to continue');
               Readln
        end;     {Wait}
{*********************************************************************}
begin    {Main Program}

{1.0 Get program options from user}

        GetOptions;

{2.0 Validate options}

        ValidateOptions;

{3.0 Select program function based on option}

        if ValidCalculationOption and ValidFigureOption then
           case FigureOption of
              'S', 's' : SquareComputations;
              'R', 'r' : RectangleComputations;
              'T', 't' : TriangleComputations
           end;    {case}

{4.0 Wait}

        Wait

end.     {Main Program}
```

Figure 4.18(e) Program 4h: Miscellaneous procedures and statement part (Part 5 of 5 parts).

(b) Another option for commands is to present the prompt without any on-screen help and allow the user to enter a supplementary command to get help in the form of a menu (and perhaps other information as well). For example, the program prompt for the calculation option could be

```
Enter calculation code (? for help) :
```

If the user enters a ?, the program displays the menu and then prompts the user for an option code (perhaps without the help feature being available this time). This requires a logical revision of the program module responsible for the task, as

```
Main Menu

Geometric Figure     Code
Square                S
Rectangle             R
Triangle              T

Enter Code for desired figure : r

Calculation Options     Code
Area                     A
Perimeter                P

Enter Code for desired calculation : A
Enter length of rectangle : 4.5
Enter width of rectangle : 3.42

                    Figure : Rectangle
                    Length :     4.50
                    Width  :     3.42
                    Area   :    15.39
Press <Enter> to continue
```

Figure 4.19 Sample execution of Program 4h.

outlined in the following pseudocode segment:

Write 'Enter calculation code (? for help) : '
Read Calculation Code
If CalculationCode = '?' then
      Write menu
      Write 'Enter calculation code : '
      Read CalculationCode
End If

Revise the procedure GetOptions in Program 4h using this technique. Which of the three versions of the program now seems to be the most appropriate? How would you decide which of these techniques is best in any given situation?

4.9 PROGRAM DEBUGGING AND TESTING

The process of testing a program requires that you devise a set of sample data that test all possible execution paths through the program. The more distinct paths there are, the more difficult this task becomes. For example, in the case of Program 4a, there are two paths—one for values of Sales $\leq$ 1000 and one for values of Sales $>$ 1000. Both of these paths are tested in the sample data shown in Figure 4.8. Similarly, Program 4g has five paths corresponding to five possible outcomes; an adequate test of this program should actually test the endpoints of each group of TestScore values and perhaps one intermediate value (although theoretically, if the program functions properly for the endpoints of each interval, it will give correct results for intermediate values).

Devising sample data to test Program 4h is somewhat more complex because of the numerous combinations of options that can be selected by the user. To perform an exhaustive test of this program, you would need to test all combinations of valid values for FigureOption, plus one invalid one (for a total of seven values), with all possible valid values of CalculationOption, plus an invalid one (for a total of five possible values); this would mean a total of $5 \times 7 = 35$ tests. Actually, some of these trials are redundant because in this program the data-validation module is independent of the calculation module, so that testing all combinations of a valid value of FigureOption with an invalid value of CalculationOption is unnecessary; a similar comment is true with regard to testing all possible combinations of valid values of CalculationOption with an invalid value of FigureOption.

Part of the job of a programmer is to analyze a program and devise a adequate testing scheme to verify that the program will perform its intended function. Unfortunately, the number of possible combinations of input values tends to increase to unmanageable size very quickly, making it necessary at times to rely on sampling techniques and testing with actual users who report errors that are encountered. (When programmers or other data processing professionals test a program, the process is called **alpha testing**. When users test a program under operational conditions, the process is called **beta testing**.) Unfortunately, despite the best efforts of everyone involved in the development of a program, there are often errors remaining that are not encountered until after the program is distributed to intended users. This makes it necessary to revise the program and issue new versions on a continuing basis.

We have seen that one technique that can be valuable in correcting errors is the use of diagnostic output. These are output statements placed at strategic points in a program so that you can observe the values of relevant variables. The trouble with this technique is that the statements must be removed from the program once the program is corrected—a task requiring a great deal of work on the part of the programmer. Also, it is very annoying to have just removed numerous diagnostic output statements from a program and then discover an error that had been overlooked previously and have to add the diagnostic statements laboriously again. Some of the work and frustration of working with diagnostic output can be avoided by making each statement conditional, that is, by placing each diagnostic output statement in an if statement with an appropriate condition. For example, a common technique is to define a Boolean constant with a name such as Debug and give it a value True. Then each diagnostic output statement looks like

```
if Debug then
    Writeln( . . .);
```

When you have debugged the program successfully, you then change the value of the Boolean constant to False (which is a simple operation) and leave all the diagnostic output statements in place. Since the value of the condition in each is now False, none of the diagnostic output will be produced. If you need the diagnostic output later, it is a simple matter to change the value of the Boolean constant back to True to secure the diagnostic output once again.

An alternative to writing your own diagnostic output statements is to use the Turbo Pascal debugging features described in Appendix G. One advantage to using the Turbo Pascal debugger is that you avoid the increased program size that results when adding your own debugging statements.

4.9.1 Time Out

1. Part of the complexity in testing Program 4g comes from the fact that we admit upper-case and lowercase values for each of the control variables. This means that we have to test combinations of upper- and lowercase values that all lead to the same basic program function. Some of this complexity can be avoided by revising the option input procedure to eliminate the lowercase values of the variables. The UpCase function is very useful for this task. This function accepts an argument of type Char and returns the uppercase equivalent of the argument if it exists; otherwise the value of the argument is returned. Sample evaluations of this function are as follows:

Expression	*Value*	*Comment*
UpCase('a')	'A'	Lowercase converts to uppercase
UpCase('A')	'A'	Uppercase argument not changed
UpCase('1')	'1'	Function acts only on characters 'a'. .'z'; all others are not changed

For example, we could modify Module 2.0 of the procedure GetOptions of Program 4g as follows:

```
{2.0 Get figure option}
    Write (FigureOptionPrompt);
    Readln (FigureOption);
    FigureOption := UpCase (FigureOption);
```

Now, in the remainder of the program, we can ignore the possibility of lowercase values for the variable FigureOption.

Revise Program 4g by making both FigureOption and CalculationOption uppercase immediately after the option is entered. Observe that the program becomes noticeably less complex. What effect does this change have on your plan for testing the program?

2. Add conditional diagnostic output to Program 4a, using a Boolean constant Debug, as described before. Test the program twice, once with Debug = True and again with Debug = False.

4.9.2 A Final Word

By now, you have discovered that programming requires you to describe every detail of the problem being solved. You might be thinking, "If I have to go to all this trouble to solve a problem, I would just as soon solve the problem and not bother with the program."

For certain problems that need to be solved only once, you may be right: A program may not be worth the effort. But remember that when the program is completed, the user can solve the problem again and again by simply executing the program and supplying relevant data. If the problem arises on a continuing basis, the work of developing a program becomes worth the effort. Once the task is programmed, the speed with which the computer can execute the program is the machine's primary value. The computer allows all who have access to the program to benefit from the work that went into the development process.

4.10 REVIEW QUESTIONS

1. Define the term *structured programming*.
2. What is a program module?
3. Why is top-down program design a valuable tool?
4. What is a control structure?
5. What three control structures are sufficient for implementing any program?
6. What are some programming practices that contribute to the readability of a program?
7. What is a program flowchart? Of what value is it?
8. Draw the flowchart equivalent of the following program:

   1.0 Read A, B
   2.0 Write the smaller of A and B
       2.1 If A < B then
       2.2   Write A
       2.3 Else
       2.4   Write B
       2.5 End If

9. What symbols are used as relational operators?
10. Assume that X = 3 and Y = −2. Evaluate each of the following conditions:
    (a) `(X > 0)` **or** `(Y < 0)`
    (b) **not** `(X > Y)`
    (c) `(X <> 0)` **xor** `(Y <> 0)`
    (d) `(X <= Y)` **and** `(Y < 0)`
11. Evaluate each of the following conditions:
    (a) `'a' > 'A'`
    (b) `'abc' < 'bcd'`
    (c) `'abc' > 'ab'`
    (d) `'Abc' = 'abc'`
    (e) `' ab' = 'ab'`
    (f) `'2' > '10'`
    (g) `'A' = UpCase ('a')`

12. The following Pascal coding segment should implement Module 2.0 in Problem 8; however, it contains a syntax error. Find the error.

```
{2.0 Write the smaller of A and B}
    if A < B then
        Writeln (A);
    else
        Writeln (B);
```

13. What is a compound statement? Why does Pascal need to provide for compound statements?

14. Design a program to find the smallest of three values entered by the user. The following represents a preliminary plan:

    1.0 Get values for A, B, and C

    2.0 Let Small = smallest of A, B, C

    3.0 Write Small

    Complete the program plan.

15. What is a multiple selection structure? What are two ways such a structure can be implemented in Pascal?

16. What is a case-list? How are case-lists used in the case statement?

17. What part of the Turbo Pascal case statement is not found in standard Pascal?

18. What are subranges? Of what value are they?

19. What is a program menu? List several alternative ways to communicate a menu to the user.

20. What is data validation? Why is it necessary?

21. What are program stubs? Why are they useful?

22. What is an execution path? When testing a program, why is it important to know what the possible execution paths in the program are?

23. Why is it a good idea to place diagnostic output in a conditional statement?

24. What purpose is served by the UpCase function?

4.11   PROGRAMMING EXERCISES

1. Write a program to sort (from smallest to largest) three values entered by the user.

2. Write a program to solve quadratic equations of the form

$$ax^2 + bx + c = 0$$

for user-entered values of a, b, and c. Recall that the solutions are dependent on the value of the discriminant $d = b^2 - 4ac$:

If $d < 0$, there are no solutions.

If $d = 0$, then there is one solution: $x = \dfrac{-b}{2a}$.

If $d > 0$, there are two solutions:

$$x_1 = \frac{-b + \sqrt{d}}{2a} \qquad x_2 = \frac{-b - \sqrt{d}}{2a} = cr$$

Note: if $a = 0$, then the equation is not quadratic.

3. Look up the currency conversion factors for foreign countries of your choice. Write a program to allow the user to enter a U.S. currency amount and select from a menu the foreign currency to which he or she wishes to convert.

4. A "magic" number is an integer in which the number is equal to the sum of the cubes of its digits. Write a program to determine whether a number entered by the user is a magic number.

5. Linear equations of the form

$$a_1 x + b_1 y = c_1$$
$$a_2 x + b_2 y = c_2$$

can be solved using the formulas

$$x = \frac{c_1 b_2 - c_2 b_1}{a_1 b_2 - a_2 b_1} \qquad y = \frac{a_1 c_2 - a_2 c_1}{a_1 b_2 - a_2 b_1}$$

provided that $a_1 b_2$ is not equal to $a_2 b_1$. Write a program to allow the user to enter values for a_1, b_1, c_1, a_2, b_2, and c_2 and compute the solutions if they exist.

6. Write a program to compute the positive difference of two values A and B entered by the user. *Note:* If $A < B$, the positive difference $= B - A$, if $A > B$, the positive difference $= A - B$, if $A = B$, the positive difference $= 0$.

7. First-class postage costs $.29 for the first ounce and $.23 for each additional ounce or part thereof. Write a program to read a letter weight by the user and compute the postage. Some examples are shown in the following table:

Weight	Cost
0.5	.29
1.0	.29
1.1	.52
2.0	.52
2.9	.75

8. A method for computing the area of a triangle is as follows: If a, b, and c represent the sides of a triangle, then the area is given by

$$A = \sqrt{s(s-a)(s-b)(s-c)}$$

where s is the semiperimeter, defined by

$$s = \frac{a+b+c}{2}$$

Write a program to allow the user to enter values of a, b, and c and compute the area of the triangle. Note that if $s(s-a)(s-b)(s-c) < 0$, the values a, b, and c cannot represent the sides of a triangle.

9. Data-processing systems often incorporate a check digit into each account number assigned to customers in the system. The purpose of the check digit is to be able to determine whether the account number is valid or not without having to search through external records. There are many ways to compute a check digit, but typically, the digit is formed as a mathematical function of the other digits in the account number. One method is as follows: Let us assume that we wish to have three-digit account numbers, with a fourth digit computed as a check digit. Then the account number may be expressed as

$$d_1\, d_2\, d_3\, d_{ck}$$

where d_{ck} is the ones digit of the value

$$1 \times d_1 + 2 \times d_2 + 3 \times d_3$$

By analyzing any four digit number, a program can determine whether or not the number represents a valid account number in the system.

For example, the number 2345 is invalid because the check digit should be 0 (the one's digit of $1 \times 2 + 2 \times 3 + 3 \times 4 = 2 + 6 + 12 = 20$), the number 2340, on the other hand, is a valid account number.

Write a program to allow the program user to enter a four-digit account number and determine whether or not the account number is valid.

10. Write a program to determine whether or not three values entered by a user could represent the sides of a triangle and, if so, whether they could represent the sides of a right triangle. The program should write out one of three messages following the three values entered by the user:

    Can represent the sides of a triangle
    Can represent the sides of a right triangle
    Cannot represent the sides of a triangle

    Note: you cannot assume that the values are in any sequence, e.g., from smallest to largest.

11. Write a program to process a Text file containing a student's name and three test scores. Calculate the student's average test score, and then print out the average and one of the following messages: Unsatisfactory if the average is not more than 50 or Satisfactory for any other average.

12. In a certain checking account, there is no service charge if the balance is at least $300. However, if the balance is less than $300, but greater than or equal to $200, the service charge is $3; if the balance is less than $200, the service charge is $4. Write a program to read a Text file containing a customer's name and balance and print out these items, together with the amount of the service charge.

13. A gas company charges customers based on the following rate table:

	Charge
Usage $\leq$ 10 ft^3	$8.00
10 ft^3 < Usage $\leq$ 30 ft^3	$8.00 + $.90 for each cubic foot over 10
Usage > 30 ft^3	$26.00 + $1.00 for each cubic foot over 30

Write a program to compute the charge for the usage entered by the program user.

14. Write a program to compute gross pay, where values for employee name, hours worked during one week, and hourly rate of pay are read from a Text file. If hours worked are not greater than 40, then gross pay is hours worked times the hourly rate. If hours worked are greater than 40, then the employee is paid at the hourly rate for the first 40 hours and 1 1/2 times the hourly rate for the hours worked over 40.

Programmer-Defined Procedures

5

At this point, you have written several programs that made use of programmer-written procedures. You have seen how they help to segment a program into modules of manageable size and complexity. But there is an additional feature of Pascal that will enable your procedures to be even more useful. This feature is the *parameter list*, which is an optional part of the definition of a procedure. In this chapter, we will see how procedures with parameter lists can make a program simpler and perform more work with less effort on the part of the programmer. Additionally, we will describe *data-flow diagrams*, an enhancement to structure diagrams that will make them more useful as a program design tool.

5.1   TOP-DOWN PROGRAM DESIGN AND DEVELOPMENT: A REVIEW

One of the basic ideas of structured programming is that top-down program design and development are very effective ways to design and implement a program. Top-down program design involves the refinement of one module of a program at a time by adding successive levels of detail until the design is complete. At each stage in the design process, you have a complete version of the program; however, some portions of the program may be expressed at a very high level (with little detail), whereas others may be expressed with greater detail. You have seen how pseudocode is an effective tool for expressing a program's design through the various iterations of the design process.

Top-down program development is a process that parallels the top-down design process. In order to use top-down program development, the programmer writes the main portion of the program as a series of modules and codes each of the modules as a program stub. A stub, as you will recall, is a module that is incomplete; typically, it has enough detail to be syntactically correct (so that you can compile the program without syntax errors), but it lacks some or all the detailed statements required to do its work. After testing the initial version of the program, the programmer adds detail to the various procedures (usually one at a time) and tests the new version of the program. The major advantage to top-down program implementation is that each time a new version of the program is tested, errors tend to be isolated in untested portions of the program and hence are easy to locate. This makes the tasks of correcting logical errors and verifying the correctness of the final version of the program much more manageable than would otherwise be possible.

Implicit in both top-down program design and top-down program implementation are the identification and isolation of program modules. A **program module** is a program segment that has a clearly defined task. In structured programming, we insist that a module have a single entry point (the beginning of the module) and a single exit point (the end of the module). In Pascal a program module may be implemented as a single statement, as a sequence of statements, or as a procedure. One advantage of using procedures is that they are clearly identified in the program. Often, a logical error in a program can be traced to the responsible procedure by examining the nature of the error. A procedure can be executed by invoking its name; this tends to make other portions of the program much shorter and more understandable. A procedure tends to hide the detail of a particular task from other parts of a program. Variables and constants that are needed only in a particular procedure are declared in that procedure. There are two advantages to this practice: It makes the lists of constants and variables for the larger program unit shorter and easier to understand, and it protects the procedure's variables from inadvertent modification by other portions of the program.

It is sometimes possible to identify program modules that perform essentially the same operation on different data. For example, suppose a company pays its employees biweekly, but computes pay, including overtime for all hours over 40, on a weekly basis. A program to perform the latter task could be as follows:

COMPUTE PAY

1.0 Compute pay for first week

2.0 Compute pay for second week

3.0 Compute total pay

A refinement of this program illustrates the parallelism between Modules 1.0 and 2.0:

COMPUTE PAY

1.0 Compute pay for first week
    1.1 If Hours for week 1 $\leq$ 40 then
    1.2   Pay for week 1 = Hours for week 1 * Rate
    1.3 Else
    1.4   Overtime hours for week 1 = Hours for week 1 $-$ 40
    1.5   Pay for week 1 = 40 * Rate + 1.5 * Rate * Overtime hours for week 1
    1.6 End If
2.0 Compute pay for second week
    2.1 If Hours for week 2 $\leq$ 40 then
    2.2   Pay for week 2 = Hours for week 2 * Rate
    2.3 Else
    2.4   Overtime hours for week 2 = Hours for week 2 $-$ 40
    2.5   Pay for week 2 = 40 * Rate + 1.5 * Rate* Overtime hours for week 2
    2.6 End If
3.0 Compute total pay

It is clear that Modules 1.0 and 2.0 are essentially similar. For an implementation of this program in Pascal, it would be very useful to be able to write a single procedure that could perform the calculation of pay for one week only, but with data supplied at the time the procedure is invoked. In this way, the weekly pay procedure could be coded once but used twice, thereby saving time for the programmer and making the whole program smaller and more manageable. This is exactly the facility offered by writing a parameter list for a procedure. The parameter list contains the values that we wish to pass to the procedure and/or the variables that we wish the procedure to return. In the case of the preceding example, we want to pass the hours worked to the weekly pay procedure, and the amount of pay for the week's work should be returned. By invoking the procedure twice with different parameters, the program can compute both weeks' pay so that the total pay can be computed in Module 3.0. The next section contains specific detail on how to write procedures with parameter lists.

5.2 PARAMETER LISTS FOR PROCEDURES

If you wish to write a procedure that will be invoked with a parameter list, you place a list of **formal parameter** declarations in parentheses after the procedure name in the procedure declaration statement, and you write a corresponding list of **actual parameters** in parentheses after the procedure name when the procedure is to be executed.

A general form for the **procedure declaration** statement is

```
procedure procedure-name (formal-parameter-section);
```

where the *formal-parameter-section* is made up of a series of parameter declarations (separated by semicolons if two or more are present). A parameter declaration can have either of the following general forms:

```
    identifier-list : type
var identifier-list : type
```

A parameter declaration of the first form defines **value parameters**; a parameter declaration of the second form (one that is preceded by "var") defines **variable parameters**. A value parameter is a parameter that the procedure uses as input; that is, value parameters are used to pass values to the procedure. We say that these values are **imported** into the procedure for processing. A variable parameter is used by the procedure to communicate with the calling program; that is, variable parameters are used to pass values from the procedure to the calling program. These are the **exports** of the procedure. Often, a variable parameter serves as both an import and an export. That is, a procedure may take the content of a variable parameter, process it, and return the modified value to the calling program.

For example, consider the following (arbitrary) example of a procedure declaration:

```
procedure Sample1 (A, B : Real;
                   C     : Integer;
            var    D     : Char;
            var    E, F : Integer);
```

In this example, A, B, and C are value parameters, and D, E, and F are variable parameters. Variables A and B are Real, variables C, E, and F are Integer, and the variable D is of type Char. (Variables of any type may be declared in a formal parameter section.) Note that the value parameters and variable parameters are listed in separate declarations, even when they have the same type. Note also that each declaration of variable parameters is preceded by var. Declarations of value parameters and variable parameters may be mixed in any desired order. For example, the following procedure declaration is syntactically valid:

```
procedure Sample2 (G : Real; var H : Integer; I : Char);
```

In this case, the variables G and I are value parameters and the variable H is a variable parameter.

Although value and variable parameters may be listed in any sequence in a *formal-parameter-section,* the list of parameters supplied in a procedure invocation statement (which are called the actual parameters, or arguments) must match the order of the associated variables in the procedure declaration. For example, in order to execute procedure Sample2 successfully, there would have to be three actual parameters. The first parameter is a value parameter, so the actual parameter could be a Real constant, variable, or expression.

(At the time of invocation, the value of the first expression in the list of arguments becomes the value of the first formal parameter.) The second parameter is a variable parameter, so the associated actual parameter would have to be an Integer variable. (It would be an error to use a constant or expression to specify a variable parameter, since the procedure will use the actual variable specified for the variable parameter to receive a value that will then become known to the calling program.) The third parameter is a value parameter, so its value could be specified by a variable of type Char or by an appropriate constant or expression. Four important rules are brought out in the preceding example:

1. Actual parameters and formal parameters are associated in order from left to right.
2. The number of actual parameters must equal the number of formal parameters.
3. The data type of an actual parameter must match that of the corresponding formal parameter. (The only exception to this rule is that an Integer-type actual parameter may correspond to a value parameter of type Real.)
4. Actual parameters corresponding to value parameters may be specified by any expression of the appropriate data type; actual parameters corresponding to variable parameters must be variables of the appropriate data type.

For example, given the procedure declaration for procedure Sample2, the following procedure invocation statements would be valid (we assume that the variable R is of type Real, I is of type Integer, and C is of type Char):

```
Sample2 (R, I, C);
```
Each actual parameter is specified by a variable of appropriate type.
```
Sample2 (3.4, I, 'A');
```
The two value parameters are specified by constants of the appropriate type (Real and Char); the variable parameter is specified by an Integer variable.
```
Sample2 (Sqr(R) + 2.0, I, C);
```
The first argument is specified by an expression with a real value.
```
Sample2 (3, I, C);
```
The first argument is specified by an Integer type constant, which is permissible.

With the assumptions just outlined, the following procedure invocation statements would not be valid, for the reasons noted:

```
Sample2 (I, R, C);
```
The second argument does not match the data type of the second formal parameter.
```
Sample2 (R, 3, 'A');
```
The second argument must be an Integer variable, not an Integer constant, since it corresponds to a variable parameter.
```
Sample2 (R, I);
```
There are three formal arguments, so there must be three actual arguments.

The variable listed in a *formal-parameter-section* are not defined further in the procedure; that is, they are not listed in the variable declaration part of the procedure—to do so would be to attempt to define the identifier a second time, which is prohibited by Pascal. The identifiers used in a *formal-parameter-section* may be the same as those defined in the calling program, or they may be different. If they are the same, the formal parameter declaration takes the place of the similarly named identifier and blocks access in the procedure to the externally defined identifier. Usually, you will attempt to give formal parameters names that are descriptive, but not specific. Using the biweekly payroll procedure of the last section as an example, we might choose the identifiers HoursWeek1 and HoursWeek2 for the variables that will store the input data for the two weeks, but in the procedure to compute pay, we might choose to call the variable representing the hours worked in a week by the name Hours.

When writing a procedure involving a parameter list, the formal parameters are treated much as ordinary variables. The major difference is that a change made in the value of a variable parameter is communicated to the corresponding actual parameter. Normally, a procedure would not change the content of a value parameter, but if it did, the change would have no effect on the value of the corresponding actual parameter. Let us illustrate the process of writing a procedure with parameters by returning to the commission program used in Chapter 4.

■ **Problem Statement.**   A company pays its salespeople every 2 weeks, based on the total commission earned for each week. Each week's commission, which is based on sales, is computed as follows:

	Commission
Sales < 500	$50
500 ≤ Sales ≤ 1,000	10% of Sales
1,000 < Sales	11% of Sales

Input to the program should be the salesperson's name and the amount of sales for two weeks. The program should compute the total commission.

■ **Problem Analysis.**   An initial plan for the program is as follows:

COMMISSION PROGRAM, VERSION 5

1.0 Get Name and Sales

2.0 Compute Commission

3.0 Write Name, Sales, and Commission

The process of computing the commission involves three steps, as shown in the following revision of the program plan:

COMMISSION PROGRAM, VERSION 5

1.0 Get Name and Sales

2.0 Compute Commission

    2.1 Compute commission for first week

2.2 Compute commission for second week

2.3 Compute total commission

3.0 Write Name, Sales, and Commission

We note that the procedure for computing commission for the two weeks is the same, except for the basis on which the computation is made: In the first case, the commission is based on sales for week 1, and in the second case the sales are based on sales for week 2. This leads us to conclude that it would be advantageous to design a separate procedure for this task—a procedure that could be executed with different arguments. The procedure should accept as its input the value of sales for one week and produce as output the amount of the commission for one week. The pseudocode version of this procedure is as follows:

PROCEDURE COMPUTE COMMISSION (IMPORT : SALES;
EXPORT : COMMISSION)

1.0 If Sales < 500 then

2.0   Commission = 50

3.0 Else

4.0   If Sales <= 1000 then

5.0   Commission = 0.10 * Sales

6.0   Else

7.0   Commission = 0.11 * Sales

8.0   End If

9.0 End If

Note the use of the header in the pseudocoded procedure. The list of items following "Import" correspond to the variables that will be value parameters in the Pascal implementation of this procedure. The list of items following "Export" correspond to the variable parameters in the Pascal implementation. The Pascal equivalent is as follows:

```
procedure ComputeCommission (Sales   : Real;
                        var Commission : Real);
{Procedure to compute commission for one week's sales}
begin {ComputeCommission}
     if Sales < 500 then
        Commission := 50
     else if Sales <= 1000 then
             Commission := 0.1 * Sales
     else
             Commission := 0.11 * Sales
end;   (ComputeCommission)
```

■ **Problem Solution.**   The complete program is shown in Figure 5.1. Sample executions of the program are shown in Figure 5.2. Note the use of the procedure Compute-

Commission in implementing Module 2.0 in the Main Program:

```
{2.0  Compute Commission}
     ComputeCommission (SalesWeek1, CommissionWeek1);
     ComputeCommission (SalesWeek2, CommissionWeek2);
     TotalCommission := CommissionWeek1 + CommissionWeek2;
```

The first execution of the procedure ComputeCommission provides the value of SalesWeek1 for the formal parameter Sales. The procedure ComputeSales places an appropriate value in the formal parameter Commission, which corresponds to CommissionWeek1. Since Commission is a variable parameter, its value becomes that of the associated actual parameter—CommissionWeek1. When the TotalCommission is computed, the value of the variable CommissionWeek1 is in place from the first execution of ComputeCommission, and the value of the variable CommissionWeek2 is in place from the second execution of ComputeCommission.

5.2.1   *Time Out*

1. Assume that a procedure has been defined by the following procedure declaration:

```
procedure Sample3    (X : Real;
               var   Y : Integer;
                     Z : Boolean);
```

Classify each of the following procedure invocation statements as valid or invalid, assuming that R is a real variable, I is an Integer variable, and B is a Boolean variable.
(a) `Sample3 (R, I, B);`
(b) `Sample3 (3.4, I, True);`
(c) `Sample3 (I, R, B);`
(d) `Sample3 (R, -2, B);`
(e) `Sample3 (R, I);`
(f) `Sample3 (R, I, R <> 4.0);`
(g) `Sample3 (3, I, B)`

2. Write a program to implement a solution to the payroll problem outlined in Section 5.1. An initial pseudocode version of the program is as follows:

BIWEEKLY PAYROLL PROGRAM

1.0 Get Employee name, Hours for week 1, Hours for week 2, and Hourly Rate
2.0 Compute Pay
    2.1 Compute pay for first week
    2.2 Compute pay for second week
    2.3 Compute total pay
3.0 Write input data and total pay

Use a procedure with a parameter list to compute pay for one week.

```pascal
program P5a (Input, Output);
{Commission program,Version 5;
    program illustrates procedures with argument list}
uses Crt;
const
     NamePrompt = 'Enter Salesperson Name ';
     SalesPrompt1 = 'Enter Sales Amount for First Week ';
     SalesPrompt2 = 'Enter Sales Amount for Second Week ';
var
     Name : string[20];       {Input Variables}
     SalesWeek1,
     SalesWeek2,
     CommissionWeek1,         {Computational Variables}
     CommissionWeek2,
     TotalCommission          {Output Variable}
          : Real;
{*****************************************************************}
     procedure ComputeCommission (Sales : Real; var Commission :  Real);
     {Procedure to compute commission for one week's sales}
     begin    {ComputeCommission}
         if Sales < 500 then
             Commission := 50
         else if Sales <= 1000 then
                 Commission := 0.1 * Sales
             else
                 Commission := 0.11 * Sales
     end;    {ComputeCommission}
{-----------------------------------------------------------------}
     procedure Wait;
     begin    {Wait}
         Write ('Press <Enter> to continue');
         Readln
     end;     {Wait}
{*****************************************************************}
begin    {Main Program}

{1.0 Get Name and Sales}

     ClrScr;
     Write (NamePrompt);
     Readln (Name);
     Write (SalesPrompt1);
     Readln (SalesWeek1);
     Write (SalesPrompt2);
     Readln (SalesWeek2);

{2.0 Compute Commission}

     ComputeCommission (SalesWeek1, CommissionWeek1);
     ComputeCommission (SalesWeek2, CommissionWeek2);
     TotalCommission := CommissionWeek1 + CommissionWeek2;

{3.0 Write Name, Sales and Commission}

     Writeln;
     Writeln ('      Salesperson : ',Name);
     Writeln (' First Week Sales $ ',SalesWeek1:8:2);
     Writeln ('Second Week Sales $ ',SalesWeek2:8:2);
     Writeln ('       Commission $ ',TotalCommission:8:2);

{4.0 Wait}

     Wait

end.    {Main Program}
```

Figure 5.1 Program 5a: Example of procedure with a parameter list.   **225**

```
Enter Salesperson Name Jones Jones
Enter Sales Amount for First Week 500
Enter Sales Amount for Second Week 1200

      Salesperson : John Jones
 First Week Sales $    500.00
Second Week Sales $   1200.00
       Commission $    182.00
Press <Enter> to continue




Enter Salesperson Name Mary Smith
Enter Sales Amount for First Week 400
Enter Sales Amount for Second Week 600

      Salesperson : Mary Smith
 First Week Sales $    400.00
Second Week Sales $    600.00
       Commission $    110.00
Press <Enter> to continue
```

Figure 5.2 Sample executions of Program 5a.

5.3   VALUE AND VARIABLE PARAMETERS

Understanding the difference between value and variable parameters is important to an overall understanding of how to use procedures in Pascal programs. Recall that we use value parameters to import values into a procedure and variable parameters to export values to the calling program. The actual parameter corresponding to a variable parameter must be a variable of the appropriate type, whereas actual parameters corresponding to value parameters may be any expression of the appropriate type. A close look at the mechanics of the implementation of value and variable parameters in Pascal will help you understand why these restrictions are imposed.

5.3.1   Value Parameters

When a procedure is called with a value parameter, the system evaluates the corresponding actual parameter and passes the value that has been computed to the procedure. The procedure stores that value in a local variable named by the corresponding formal parameter. For example, consider the following Pascal program:

```
program Ch5Example1 (Output);
var
    I : Integer;
    R : Real;
{ ****************************************************************}
```

```
procedure Sample4 (J : Integer;
                   K : Real);
              .
              .
              .
{*******************************************************************}
begin{Main Program}
       .
       .
       .
end. {Main Program}
```

In this example, the procedure Sample4 has two value parameters: J and K. An invocation of this procedure in the Main Program, such as

```
Sample4 (I, R);
```

would cause the value of the variable I to be copied into the variable J and the value of the variable R to be copied into the variable K. Any manipulation of the variables J and K in procedure Sample4 would have no effect on the values of the variables I and R. (However, the variables I and R are global variables; the procedure could change the value of either simply by using one of them in an input operation or assignment statement.) Because actual parameters corresponding to value parameters are evaluated at the time the procedure is executed, these parameters can be any desired expression (of the appropriate type, of course). For example, it would be permissible to invoke procedure Sample4 with a statement such as

```
Sample4 (3 + 2, Sqrt (25.0));
```

In this case, the value 5 is computed for the first parameter, and this becomes the value of J inside Sample4; the value of K would become 5.0.

5.3.2 Time Out

1. What output would be produced by the following program? Explain why the value of the variable A does not change.

```
program Ex1 (Output);
var
    A : Integer;
{*******************************************************************}
    procedure Alpha ( Z : Integer);
    begin
        Z := Z = 1;
        Writeln (Z)
    end;
{*******************************************************************}
```

```
begin
    A := 3;
    Alpha (A);
    Writeln (A)
end.
```

2. What output would be produced by the following program, assuming that the user has entered 3 and 4 as the values of C and D, respectively? Explain why the output might not be as the programmer might expect.

```
program Ex2 (Input, Output)
var
    C, D :  Integer;
{*****************************************************************}
    procedure Swap (First, Second : Integer);
    var
        Temp : Integer;
    begin
        Temp := First;
        First := Second;
        Second := Temp
    end;
{*****************************************************************}
begin
    Readln (C, D);
    Swap (C, D);
    Writeln (C, D)
end.
```

3. What output will be produced by the following program?

```
program Ex3 (Output);
const
    E = 5;
{*****************************************************************}
    procedure Beta (P : Integer);
    begin
        if P > 5 then
            P := 1
        else
            P := 0;
        Writeln (P)
    end;
{*****************************************************************}
begin
    Writeln (E);
    Beta (E);
    Writeln (E)
end.
```

5.3.3 Variable Parameters

The situation is quite different with variable parameters. When a procedure with a variable parameter is called, the address of the actual parameter takes the place of the corresponding formal parameter. Variable formal parameters are, in a sense, placeholders for the address of the variable, which is the actual parameter. This means that any manipulation of the formal parameter actually manipulates the corresponding actual parameter directly. The programmer can thus think of formal variable parameters as new names of the corresponding actual parameters throughout the execution of the procedure. For example, consider the following Pascal program outline:

```
program Ch5Example2 (Output);
var
     I : Integer;
     R : Real;
{****************************************************************}
     procedure Sample5    (var J : Integer;
                           var K : Real);
                .
                .
                .

{****************************************************************}
begin {Main Program}
                .
                .
                .

end. {Main Program}
```

In this case, variables J and K in procedure Sample5 are variable parameters, so that if the procedure is invoked by a statement such as

```
Sample5 (I, R);
```

any change made to the variable J within Sample5 will actually manipulate I, which is the corresponding actual parameter; similarly, any change made to variable K is actually going to change R. The variables J and K do not actually exist as separate memory locations in the same way that other variables do. Formal parameters such as J and K, which represent variable parameters, are sometimes called *pseudovariables* or *dummy variables*, because they stand for the address of an actual variable. Because of this difference between value and variable parameters, it becomes clear why Pascal does not permit you to use anything but a variable in the actual parameter list to specify a variable parameter. It is anticipated that the procedure will change the value of a variable parameter; hence, a valid address must be available in the corresponding formal parameter so that the change can be stored in memory.

5.3.4 *Time Out*

1. What output would be produced by the following program? Explain why the value of the variable A changes. Compare this result with the answer given for Exercise 1 in Section 5.3.2.

```pascal
program Ex1a (Output);
var
    A : Integer;
{*****************************************************************}
    procedure Alpha (var Z : Integer);
    begin
        Z := Z + 1;
        Writeln (Z)
    end;
{*****************************************************************}
begin
    A := 3;
    Alpha (A);
    Writeln (A)
end.
```

2. What output would be produced by the following program, assuming that the user has entered 3 and 4 as the values of C and D, respectively. Compare this answer with that given for Exercise 2 in Section 5.3.2.

```pascal
program Ex2a (Input, Output)
var
    C, D   : Integer;
{*****************************************************************}
    procedure Swap (var First, Second : Integer);
    var
        Temp : Integer;
    begin
        Temp := First;
        First := Second;
        Second := Temp
    end;
{*****************************************************************}
begin
    Readln (C, D);
    Swap (C, D);
    Writeln (C, D)
end.
```

3. What is wrong in the following program? Why does this program have a serious error, whereas the similar program listed in Exercise 3 in Section 5.3.2. has no errors?

```pascal
program Ex3a (Output);
const
    E = 5;
{*****************************************************************}
    procedure Beta (var P : Integer);
    begin
        if P > 5 then
```

```
                        P := 1
                else
                        P := 0;
                Writeln (P)
        end;
{***********************************************************************}
begin
        Writeln (E);
        Beta (E);
        Writeln (E)
end.
```

4. Consider the following Pascal program:

```
program Ch5Example3 (Output);
var
        I : Integer;
        C : Char;
{***********************************************************************}
        procedure Sample6 (N : Integer;
                                P : Char);
        begin
                Writeln ('Line 1 ', N, P);
                N := 1;
                P := 'Z';
                Writeln ('Line 2 ', N, P)
        end;
{***********************************************************************}
begin {Main Program}
        I := 0;
        C := 'A';
        Sample6 (I, C);
        Writeln ('Line 3 ', I, C)
end. {Main Program}
```

What output will be produced by the program? (If you have trouble with this exercise, type in the program and observe the results.)

5. Suppose the procedure declaration for procedure Sample6 in the previous exercise is modified as follows:

```
procedure Sample6 (var N : Integer;
                        var P : Char);
```

What effect will this have on the output produced by the program? Explain what happens to change the output.

5.4 DATA-FLOW DIAGRAMS

Recall that structure diagrams help you visualize the structure of a program when procedures are included in its implementation. The main program and each procedure are represented in the diagram by rectangles; line segments connecting the blocks represent the flow of control. For example, the structure diagram for version 5 of the commission program version presented in Figure 5.1 is shown in Figure 5.3. Note that the block labeled ComputeCommission is present twice in the structure diagram, even though there is only one procedure in the actual program. This is because the structure diagram represents not only the parts of the program and their hierarchical relationship, but also the flow of control. Control is passed to the procedure ComputeCommission twice; therefore, it is present in the structure diagram twice.

A procedure typically imports some values from the calling program and exports others back to the program. This represents a flow not only of control, but also of data from the calling program to the procedure and from the procedure to the calling program. This flow of data can be represented in a modified structure diagram by listing those items being passed to the procedure with an arrow pointing from the block representing the calling program to the block representing the procedure. The values being returned to the calling program can be represented similarly, but the arrow would point from the procedure to the calling program. The resulting diagram is called a **data-flow diagram**; it resembles a structure diagram in many ways, but with added detail.

For example, suppose a procedure Sample7 imports variables A and B from the main program. The data-flow diagram for this situation could be drawn as

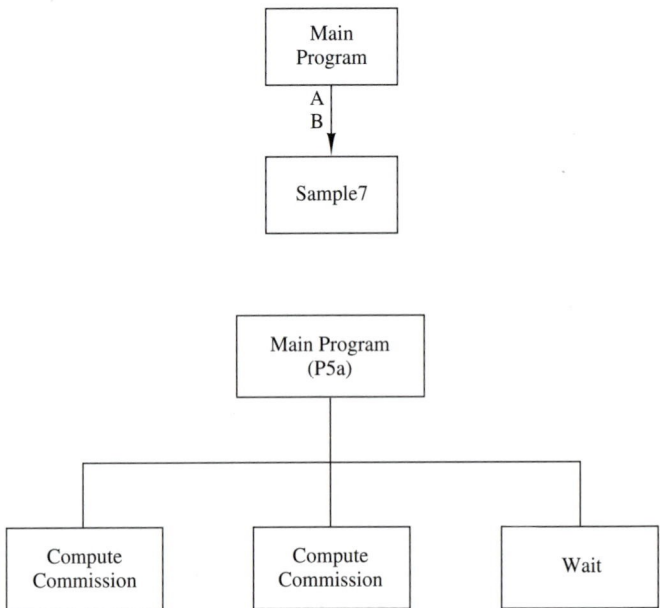

Figure 5.3 Structure diagram for Program 5a.

As another example, suppose a procedure Sample8 exports variábles C, D, and E to the main program. The data-flow diagram for this situation could be drawn as

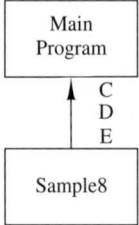

If a procedure both imports and exports items, then there will be two arrows with appropriate variable lists. For example, suppose a procedure Sample9 imports a variable F and exports variables G and H. Then the data-flow diagram would appear as

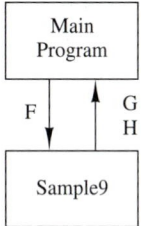

If a variable is used as both an import and an export, it is listed twice. For example, suppose the procedure Sample9a imports and exports the variable J from the Main Program. Then the data-flow diagram would appear as

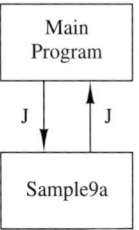

The data-flow diagram for the program of Figure 5.1 is shown in Figure 5.4. Note that the variable names listed in a data-flow diagram are those defined in the calling program, not the ones in the subordinate program unit. That is, we always use the names of the actual parameters in data-flow diagrams, not the names of formal parameters.

Data-flow diagrams can be a useful design tool to help you visualize not only the hierarchy of a program's procedures, but also the data that passes among them. It is often helpful to draw a data-flow diagram after the program is completely designed, but before work on actual coding begins. The diagram will help you code suitable program stubs.

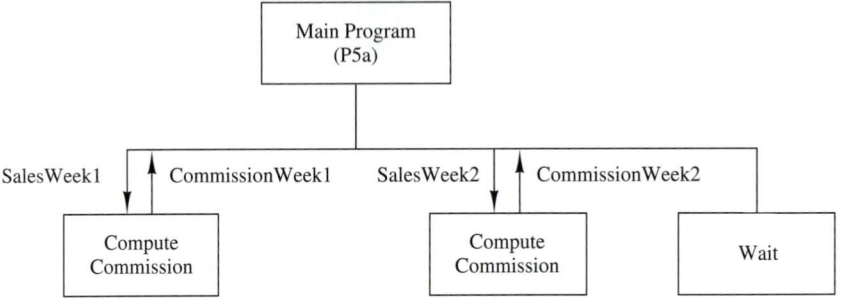

Figure 5.4 Data-flow diagram for Program 5a.

Thus, when a procedure imports or exports a value to or from a calling program, you must provide suitable sample values in the program stub. For example, if you were designing a program stub for the procedure ComputeCommission of the program shown in Figure 5.1, you would have to provide a value for its export—Commission. A suitable stub could be:

```
procedure ComputeCommission (Sales : Real;
                        var Commission : Real);
begin
    Commission := 0
end;
```

This will cause the value zero to be returned to the calling program every time; the programmer can verify that the overall logical structure of his or her program is correct before attending to the details of ComputeCommission. Used in this way, data-flow diagrams can be a helpful guide in implementing the top-down program development technique.

5.4.1   Time Out

1. Draw a data-flow diagram for the following sample program:

```
program Ch5Example4 (Input, Output);
var
    A, B, C : Real;
{***************************************************************}
    procedure Sample10 (J, K : Real);
        .
        .
        .
{-------------------------------------------------------------}
    procedure Sample11 (L : Real; var M : Real);
        .
        .
        .
{-------------------------------------------------------------}
```

```
     procedure Sample12 (var N, P : Real);
        .
        .
        .

{*****************************************************************}
begin {Main Program}
     Sample12 (A, B);
     Sample10 (A, B);
     Sample11 (A, C)
end.    {Main Program}
```

2. Draw a data-flow diagram for the payroll program described in Exercise 2 of Section 5.2.1.

5.5   Case Study: Difference Between Two Dates

■ **Problem Statement.**   Write a program to compute the difference in days between two dates in the same year. This is information that is needed in a number of financial calculations, such as the computation of short-term interest. For example, the difference between January 1 (the first day in the year) and January 30 (the 30th day in the year) is $30 - 1 = 29$ days. The difference between January 30 and December 31 (the 365th day) is $365 - 30 = 335$ days. Input to the program should be two dates in numeric form. For example, January 30 would be entered as 1 30, December 31 would be entered as 12 31, and so forth.

■ **Problem Analysis.**   A technique that yields a reasonably simple solution to this problem is to use the Julian date instead of the calendar date to perform computations. The Julian date is defined to be the day of the year. For example, the Julian date for January 1 is 1, the Julian date for January 31 is 31, the Julian date for February 1 is 32, the Julian date for December 31 is 365, and so forth. (We will ignore the existence of leap years in this discussion. You can add this consideration later if desired.) Thus, if we convert calendar dates to Julian dates, we can subtract to find the difference. (Attempting to solve this problem without reference to Julian dates makes the problem much more difficult than it need otherwise be.)

With these considerations in mind, we can construct a rough outline of the required program:

DATE DIFFERENCE PROGRAM (P5b)

1.0 Get dates

2.0 Compute and write Julian date for each date

3.0 Compute and write difference

4.0 Wait

One problem that needs to be addressed early in the design of this program is the possibility of invalid dates—dates in which the month number is not in the range 1 to 12 or the day number is not valid for a given month (e.g., 1 32). This determination should be made prior to computing the Julian date, and if either of the dates is invalid, the computation of the difference should not be attempted. The best way to handle the communication of the existence of invalid data is to use a flag with the value True if the data is valid and False if the data is invalid. Since there are two dates, we will need two flags, one for each date.

A basic dictionary of the variables required for this program will help in writing the next version of the program:

Variable	*Comment*
Day1, Month1	Calendar date for first date
Day2, Month2	Calendar date for second date
ValidDate1, ValidDate2	Validity flags for the two dates
JulianDate1, JulianDate2	Julian dates for the two dates
Difference	Difference in days between dates

Since the computation of the Julian date is a task that must be used twice in the program, it is sensible to design a procedure to accomplish this task. (Even if the task were needed only once, it might make sense to write it as a procedure because it would make the procedure more readable.) Let us call the procedure ComputeJulianDate and give it two tasks:

1. Determine whether a date is valid.
2. If the date is valid, compute the Julian equivalent.

The main program can call for the execution of this procedure twice, once for the first date and a second time for the second date. With this decision in mind, we can redesign the main program as follows:

DATE DIFFERENCE PROGRAM (P5b)

1.0 Get dates
2.0 Compute and write Julian date for each date
    2.1 Compute Julian date for first date
    2.2 If first date is valid then
    2.3   Write JulianDate1
    2.4 End If
    2.5 Compute Julian date for second date
    2.6 If second date is valid then
    2.7   Write JulianDate2
    2.8 End If
3.0 Compute and write difference
    3.1 If both dates are valid then
    3.2   Difference = JulianDate2 − JulianDate1

3.3   Write Difference
3.4 Else
3.5   Write error message
3.6 End If
4.0 Wait

Let us now turn our attention to the procedure to compute the Julian date. This procedure will need to import the day and month numbers for the date and export the Julian date and the validity flag. A design for the procedure is as follows:

PROCEDURE COMPUTEJULIANDATE (IMPORT : CALENDARMONTH, CALENDARDAY; EXPORT : VALIDDATE, JULIANDATE)

1.0 Validate CalendarMonth

2.0 If CalendarMonth is valid then

3.0   Validate CalendarDay

4.0 End If

5.0 If ValidDate then

6.0   Compute JulianDate

7.0 End If

Note that the variable names in this procedure are descriptive, but none is identical to any variable used in the main part of the program that was previously designed. This is done primarily for clarity; it is clear to the reader that this is not the same variable as was described previously. (It is our practice to use the same variable names in the actual program as are used in the pseudocode; we suggest that you adopt the same practice to the extent possible.)

The processes of validating the month and day are sufficiently complex to warrant the construction of separate procedures for each. The procedure ComputeJulianDate can use the flag ValidDate to communicate with the respective validation procedures. Thus, the design of the procedure ValidateMonth, which will import the month number and export the validity flag, can appear as follows:

PROCEDURE VALIDATEMONTH (IMPORT : MONTH; EXPORT : VALIDMONTH)

1.0 ValidMonth $=$ True if Month ≥ 1 and Month ≤ 12 and False otherwise

2.0 If not ValidMonth then

3.0   Write error message

4.0 End If

The procedure for validating the day requires that we compute the largest valid day for the month. For example, we know that the largest day for January is 31, so that a date such as 1 32 is invalid. Thus, the procedure for validating the value of Day must import the values of Month and Day and export a Boolean-valued validity flag. The design of this procedure can now be written:

PROCEDURE VALIDATEDAY (IMPORT : MONTH, DAY;
EXPORT : VALIDDAY)

1.0 Compute number of days in Month

2.0 ValidDay = True if Day $\geq$ 1 and Day $\leq$ number of days in Month
      and False otherwise

3.0 If not ValidDay then

4.0   Write error message

5.0 End If

It is instructive at this point to analyze the data-flow diagram for this program, as shown in Figure 5.5. The main program executes the procedure ComputeJulianDate twice. The first time, Day1 and Month1 are imported, and ValidDate1 and JulianDate1 are returned by the procedure. The second time, similar variables related to the second date are sent and received.

■ **Problem Solution.**   The completed program is shown in Figure 5.6. Sample output from the program is shown in Figure 5.7.

Figure 5.6(a) shows the initial portion of the program, which defines the variables, along with input prompts. These variables are global variables—variables defined throughout

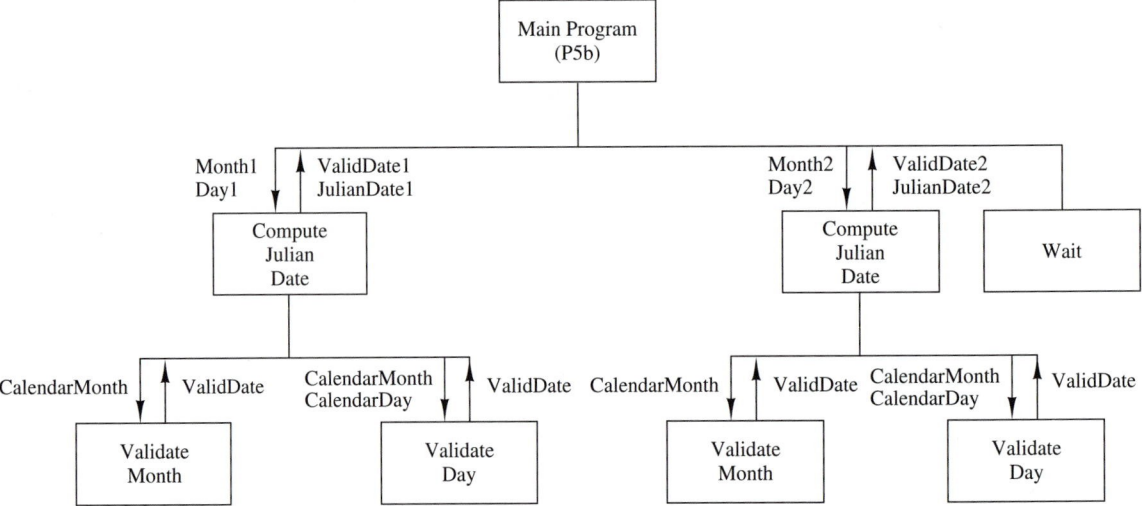

Figure 5.5 Data-flow diagram for calculation of difference between two dates (Program 5b).

```
program P5b (Input, Output);
{Program to compute the difference between two dates in the
     same year}
uses Crt;
const
     DatePrompt1 = ' Enter First Date in form mm dd : ';
     DatePrompt2 = 'Enter Second Date in form mm dd : ';
var
     Month1, Day1, Month2, Day2,     {Input Variables}
     JulianDate1, JulianDate2,       {Computational Variables}
     Difference                      {Output Variable}
          : Integer;
     ValidDate1, ValidDate2          {Control Variables}
          : Boolean;
{*********************************************************************}
```

Figure 5.6(a) Program 5b: Constant and variable declarations (Part 1 of 3 parts).

the rest of the program. Note, however, that the procedures use parameter lists as a vehicle for communication; they do not refer to the global variables at all.

Figure 5.6(b) shows the procedure ComputeJulianDate, which includes the declaration of the two procedures ValidateMonth and ValidateDay. Note that these procedures are defined as part of the procedure ComputeJulianDate, since they are needed only within the context of that procedure and are not needed by the main program. In the procedure ValidateMonth, note the use of the assignment statement

```
ValidMonth := (Month >= 1) and (Month <= 12);
```

to implement the much more cumbersome pseudocode equivalent:

1.0 ValidMonth = True if Month $>=$ 1 and Month $<=$ 12 and
　　　　　　　　　　False otherwise

A similar technique is used in the procedure ValidateDay to assign a value to ValidDay. Note also the use of the case statement in the procedure ValidateDay to compute the number of days in a month by grouping all months with the same number of days into one case list. February is the only month with 28 days, so the case list corresponding to NumberDays := 28 contains only the number 2. April, June, September, and November all have 30 days, so the case list corresponding to Number-Days := 30 contains the numbers 4, 6, 9, and 11. The case list corresponding to NumberDays := 31 contains the other month numbers.

In the statement part of the procedure ComputeJulianDate, note the use of the case statement to compute the initial value of JulianDate. This value corresponds to the number of days that have elapsed prior to the first day of the month. Prior to January 1, there have been zero days, so the value of JulianDate is 0 when Month is 1. Prior to February 1, there have been 31 days, so the value of JulianDate is set to 31 when Month is 2, and so forth for the rest of the months. The correct Julian date is then computed by adding the value of CalendarDay to JulianDate.

```
procedure ComputeJulianDate (CalendarMonth,
                             CalendarDay : Integer;
                        var ValidDate   : Boolean;
                        var JulianDate  : Integer);
{Procedure to compute the Julian date}
{-----------------------------------------------------------------}
    procedure ValidateMonth (Month : Integer;
                        var ValidMonth : Boolean);
    {Procedure to determine if a month is valid}
    begin   {ValidateMonth}
        ValidMonth := (Month >= 1) and (Month <= 12);
        if not ValidMonth then
            Writeln ('Invalid Month Number : ', Month)
    end;    {ValidateMonth}
{-----------------------------------------------------------------}
    procedure ValidateDay (Month, Day : Integer;
                      var ValidDay : Boolean);
    {Procedure to validate day of a month}
    var
        NumberDays : Integer;
    begin   {ValidateDay}
        case Month of
            2                  : NumberDays := 28;
            4,6,9,11           : NumberDays := 30;
            1,3,5,7,8,10,12    : NumberDays := 31
        end;    {case}
        ValidDay := (Day >= 1) and (Day <= NumberDays);
        if not ValidDay then
            Writeln ('Invalid Day Number : ', Day)
    end;    {ValidateDay}
{-----------------------------------------------------------------}
begin   {ComputeJulianDate}
    ValidateMonth (CalendarMonth, ValidDate);
    if ValidDate then
        ValidateDay (CalendarMonth, CalendarDay, ValidDate);
    if ValidDate then
        begin
            case CalendarMonth of
                1  : JulianDate := 0;
                2  : JulianDate := 31;
                3  : JulianDate := 59;
                4  : JulianDate := 90;
                5  : JulianDate := 120;
                6  : JulianDate := 151;
                7  : JulianDate := 181;
                8  : JulianDate := 212;
                9  : JulianDate := 243;
                10 : JulianDate := 273;
                11 : JulianDate := 304;
                12 : JulianDate := 334
            end;    {case}
            JulianDate := JulianDate + CalendarDay ;
        end     {if}
end;    {ComputeJulianDate}
{-----------------------------------------------------------------}
```

Figure 5.6(b) Program 5b: The procedure ComputeJulianDate (Part 2 of 3 parts).

```
      procedure Wait;
      begin   {Wait}
          Write ('Press <Enter> to continue');
          Readln
      end;   {Wait}
{**********************************************************************}
begin {Main Program}

{1.0 Get Dates}

    ClrScr;
    Write (DatePrompt1);
    Readln (Month1, Day1);
    Write (DatePrompt2);
    Readln (Month2, Day2);

{2.0 Compute and write Julian date for each date}

    Writeln;
    ComputeJulianDate (Month1, Day1, ValidDate1 ,JulianDate1);
    Write ('Date 1 : Month = ',Month1,' Day = ',Day1);
    if ValidDate1 then
       Writeln(' Julian Date = ', JulianDate1)
    else
       Writeln;
    ComputeJulianDate (Month2, Day2, ValidDate2, JulianDate2);
    Write ('Date 2 : Month = ',Month2,' Day = ',Day2);
    if ValidDate2 then
       Writeln(' Julian Date = ', JulianDate2)
    else
       Writeln;

{3.0 Compute and write difference}

    if ValidDate1 and ValidDate2 then
       begin
           Difference := JulianDate2 - JulianDate1;
           Writeln ('      Difference in days : ', Difference)
       end
    else
       Writeln ('Difference not computed due to invalid date(s)');

{4.0 Wait}

    Wait

end.   {Main Program}
```

Figure 5.6(c) Program 5b: Statement part (Part 3 of 3 parts).

Figure 5.6(c) shows the statement part of the main program. Note that we are careful to take appropriate action if the date happens to be invalid. Module 2.0 echos the input data and, if it is valid, writes the appropriate Julian dates. Recall that the specific error messages for invalid data are the responsibility of the appropriate data-validation procedure. Although this is a relatively complex program, you will observe that much of the complexity is buried in the subordinate procedures. The main program remains a straightforward reflection of our original program design.

```
 Enter First Date in form mm dd : 04 30
Enter Second Date in form mm dd : 12 01

Date 1 : Month = 4 Day = 30 Julian Date = 120
Date 2 : Month = 12 Day = 1 Julian Date = 335
    Difference in days : 215
Press <Enter> to continue




 Enter First Date in form mm dd : 01 32
Enter Second Date in form mm dd : 13 02

Invalid Day Number : 32
Date 1 : Month = 1 Day = 32
Invalid Month Number : 13
Date 2 : Month = 13 Day = 2
Difference not computed due to invalid date(s)
Press <Enter> to continue
```

Figure 5.7 Sample executions of date-difference program (Program 5b).

5.5.1 Time Out

1. Execute Program 5b. Verify that the output for the dates you enter is correct. Attempt to enter invalid dates, and observe the results.

2. Add a consideration of leap years to Program 5b. This will involve adding additional input items (Year1 and Year2) and procedures to determine whether the year is a leap year, to validate the day number (for month = 2), and to compute the Julian date (when month is greater than 2). Think carefully about the design and placement of the procedure for determining whether a year is a leap year or not. Should it be defined along with ValidateMonth and ValidateDay as part of the procedure-declaration portion of ComputeJulianDate, or should it be defined as part of the procedure declaration part of the main program? What should the imports and exports of the procedure be? Draw a data-flow diagram of the revised program.

5.6 SCOPE OF IDENTIFIERS

We have already discussed the fundamental law of identifiers in Pascal:

> An identifier must be declared before it can be referenced.

This rule is true for all identifiers, whether they be identifiers for constants, variables, or procedures. However, not all identifiers defined in a program are available to every procedure, even if the definition of the procedure follows the definition of the identifier. Associated with every identifier is a *scope*—that is, a segment of the program in which that identifier can be referenced. In any program, the constants, variables, and procedures defined in the declaration part of the main program are defined throughout the program. We say that the scope of these identifiers is *global*. We have seen that identifiers for constants and variables defined within a procedure are defined only within that procedure; we say that the scope of these identifiers is *local* to the procedure.

Because procedures can contain procedure declarations of their own, there is a need to make a finer description of the scope of an identifier than just global or local. It is useful to conceive of a program as being composed of a series of nested blocks. The main program unit makes up the outer block, and each procedure makes up an inner block. Each inner block is wholly contained in a larger block. For example, the block structure of Program 5b is shown in Figure 5.8. Recall that the procedure ComputeJulianDate makes use of two procedures—ValidateMonth and ValidateDay—that are defined in its procedure declaration part. Thus, the outer block, which corresponds to the main program, encompasses one inner block corresponding to ComputeJulianDate. The block corresponding to ComputeJulianDate contains two blocks, corresponding to ValidateMonth and ValidateYear. Another way to visualize the block structure of the program is to use the familiar outline notation that we have used in writing pseudocode:

MAIN PROGRAM (P5a)

1.0 ComputeJulianDate
    1.1 ValidateMonth
    1.2 ValidateDay
2.0 Wait

The following general principle regarding the **scope of an identifier** makes use of the concept of program blocks:

> An identifier is defined only within the block of its declaration.

A corollary to this principle is the following:

> An identifier is also defined in any block that is contained in the block where it is declared (an inner block), but is undefined in an outer block.

For example, with respect to Program 5b, the identifiers DatePrompt1, DatePrompt2, Month1, etc., which are in the initial declaration part of the program, are defined not only in the outer block, but also in all inner blocks: ComputeJulianDate and its subordinates, ValidateMonth and ValidateDay. By "defined within," we mean that the program can reference the identifier, and if the identifier is a variable, an assignment or input statement could change the value of the variable; if the identifier is for a procedure, the program could invoke that procedure.

The identifiers CalendarMonth, CalendarDay, ValidDate, JulianDate (which are the formal parameters for the procedure ComputeJulianDate), and ValidateMonth and

```
program P5b (Input, Output);                                        ┐  Scope of
uses Crt;                                                              DatePrompt1
const                                                                  DatePrompt2
    DatePrompt1 = ' Enter First Date in form mm dd : ';                Month1
    DatePrompt2 = 'Enter Second Date in form mm dd :';                 Day1
var                                                                    Month2
    Month1, Day1, Month2, Day2    {Input Variables}                    Day2
    JulianDate1, JulianDate2,     {Computational Variables}            JulianDate1
    Difference                    {Output Variable}                    JulianDate2
        : Integer;                                                     Difference
    ValidDate1, ValidDate2        {Control Variables}                  ValidDate1
        : Boolean;                                                     ValidDate2
                                                                       ComputeJulianDate
                                                                       Wait
    procedure ComputeJulianDate (CalendarMonth,                     ┐  Scope of
                                 CalendarDay : Integer;                CalendarMonth
                            var  ValidDate   : Boolean;                CalendarDay
                            var  JulianDate : Integer;                 ValidDate
                                                                       JulianDate
        procedure ValidateMonth (Month   : Integer;                    ValidateMonth
                            var  ValidMonth : Boolean);                ValidateDay
            . . .                                                   ┐  Scope of
        end; {ValidateMonth}                                           Month
                                                                       ValidMonth
        procedure ValidateDay (Month, Day : Integer;               ┐  Scope of
                            var  ValidDay : Boolean);                  Month
            . . .                                                      Day
        end; {ValidateDay}                                             ValidDay
                                                                       NumberDays
    begin {ComputeJulianDate}
        . . .
    end; {ComputeJulianDate}

    procedure Wait;
        . . .
    end; {Wait}

begin {Main Program}
    . . .
end.   {Main Program}
```

Figure 5.8 Block structure of Program 5b.

ValidateDay (procedures that are defined within ComputeJulianDate) are defined within the block constituted by ComputeJulianDate and, consequently, are undefined outside this block. Thus, the main program could neither reference any of the identifiers used as formal parameters nor invoke either of the procedures ValidateMonth or ValidateDay. On the other hand, any block that is subordinate to this one can reference any of the identifiers in this list (provided, of course, that the identifier has been previously defined). For example, the procedure ValidateDay could reference the procedure ValidateMonth (if it needed to) because ValidateDay constitutes an inner block; an identifier is defined not only in the block of its declaration, but also in any block subordinate to that block. However, the procedure ValidateMonth could *not* invoke ValidateDay, because the definition of this procedure follows the definition of ValidateMonth and would therefore be a violation of the first principle of identifiers: An identifier must be defined before it can be used.

5.6.1 *Time Out*

1. Draw a data-flow diagram for Program 5c, shown in Figure 5.9.
2. What output will be produced by Program 5c? After going through the program by hand, execute it to verify your answer.
3. The block structure of Program 5c is shown in Figure 5.10. Summarize the structure of this program, using the outline form decribed in this section.

```pascal
program P5c (Output);
const
     A = 3;
     B = 4;
var
     C : Integer;
{*********************************************************************}
     procedure W (D, E : Integer);
     const
          F = 5;
     var
          G : Integer;
     {---------------------------------------------------------------}
          procedure X (var H : Integer);
          begin   {X}
               Writeln ('Procedure X : H = ',H)
          end;    {X}
     {---------------------------------------------------------------}
          procedure Y (I : Integer);
          const
               J = 6;
          begin   {Y}
               Writeln ('Procedure Y : I = ', I, ' J = ',J)
          end;    {Y}
     {---------------------------------------------------------------}
     begin    {W}
          Writeln ('Procedure W : D = ', D,
                                  ' E = ', E,
                                  ' F = ', F);
          X (D);
          Y (F)
     end;     {W}
     {---------------------------------------------------------------}
     procedure Z (K : Integer);
     begin    {Z}
          Writeln ('Procedure Z : K = ',K)
     end;     {Z}
{*********************************************************************}
begin  {Main Program}

     W (A, B);
     Z (A)

end.    {Main Program}
```

Figure 5.9 Program 5c: Sample program showing nested procedures.

```
program P5c (Output);
const
        A = 3;                                    ─── Main Program
        B = 4;
var
        C : Integer;


        procedure W (D, E : Integer);             ─── 1.0
        const
                F = 5;
        var
                G : Integer;


                procedure X (var H : Integer);    ─── 1.1
                begin   {X}
                        . . .
                end;


                procedure Y (I : Integer);        ─── 1.2
                const
                        J = 6;
                begin   {Y}
                        . . .
                end;     {Y}


        begin   {W}
                . . .
        end;     {W}


        procedure Z (K : Integer);                ─── 2.0
        begin   {Z}
                . . .
        end;     {Z}

begin   {Main Program}
        . . .
end.    {Main Program}
```

Figure 5.10 Block structure of Program 5c.

5.6.2   Technical Note

One way to help you understand how Pascal handles identifiers is to look at how the system maintains its symbol table during the compilation process. A **symbol table** is used by the compiler to keep track of which identifiers have been declared and what they represent. (Compilers refer to identifiers as *symbols* because the actual identifier is usually replaced by a coded symbol, which the compiler finds easier to manage than the sequence of characters used in the program.) For purposes of this discussion, let us ignore many of the details of symbol tables and concentrate on how the compiler "knows" which identifiers can be referenced at any given point.

A symbol table is a list of the identifiers that have been declared within a program. Because program blocks can be nested, the symbol table must reflect the structure of the program's blocks in order to show which symbols can be referenced at any point in the compilation. The Pascal symbol table is a tree structure that has the program identifier as its root. The identifiers for the main program block constitute a branch of the tree at the highest level in the structure. When a procedure is declared, the identifiers within that procedure are shown as a branch in the tree, which is one level lower than that of the identifier for the procedure. As an example, the symbol table for Program 5c is shown in Figure 5.11.

In the notation used for this illustration, the identifiers are listed from left to right in the order that they are encountered by the compiler. The identifier W is the name of a procedure that contains various identifiers; these are shown as a branch emanating from W at level 2 in the chart. X and Y are also identifiers for procedures that are defined within procedure W; they result in branches that form a third level in the tree.

When an identifier is declared, the compiler adds it to the symbol table. When an identifier is encountered (for example, in an assignement statement), the compiler examines the symbol table to determine whether the identifier is defined. The compiler searches the table in the following manner: First, identifiers that have been defined in the present procedure are examined. (These correspond to identifiers found on the branch of the tree corresponding to the procedure.) If the identifier in question is not found on the present branch, the identifiers that have been defined in the branch of the tree at the next previous level are examined. The process of examining symbols in successively higher branches is continued, until the compiler locates the identifier or determines that the identifier has not been previously declared and hence is invalid. (You have probably encountered invalid symbols by now—they happen because we misspell a word, make a typing error, or neglect to declare an identifier.)

The compiler builds the symbol table as it scans the program. The table shown in Figure 5.11 is the result of the entire compilation. The symbols that are valid at any given point are those to the left of the symbol in question on the present branch (they have been previously declared) and those lying to the left on branches that bear a direct relationship to the present one at higher levels in the tree. For example, let us use the table to determine which symbols would be valid during the translation of procedure X. The identifiers for X are at level 3 in the symbol table. Therefore, the identifiers that are valid are the identifiers declared in X (the identifier H), the identifiers that have been previously declared in the level 2 branch above (these are D, E, F, G, and X), and the identifiers that

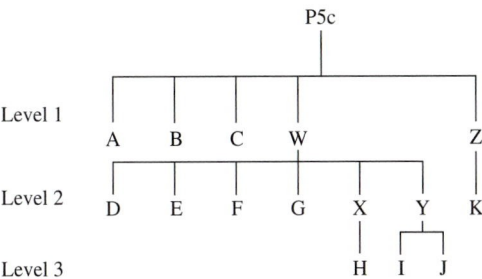

Figure 5.11 Symbol table for Program 5c.

have been previously declared in the level 1 branch still higher in the tree (these are A, B, C, and W). The portion of the tree that is circled in Figure 5.12 shows branches of the tree that contain identifiers defined for procedure X.

As another example, consider the valid identifiers for procedure Z. The identifiers declared in this procedure are at level 2 (the identifier K). Additionally, identifiers at the next higher branch (level 1) that have been previously declared would also be valid (these include A, B, C, and W). Note that the identifiers that are subordinate to W are inaccessible from the procedure Z. The symbol table is searched only for identifiers previously declared as part of the procedure presently being compiled and for identifiers previously declared on branches directly related to the present one at successively higher levels in the tree. The portion of the tree circled in Figure 5.13 shows the branches of the tree that have identifiers that are valid for procedure Z.

5.6.3 Time Out

Refer to Figure 5.11 to answer the following questions.

1. List the identifiers that may be referenced within each of the program blocks.
2. Could procedure W invoke procedure Z? Explain.
3. Could procedure Z invoke procedure W? Explain.
4. Could procedure Y invoke procedure Z? Explain.
5. Could procedure Z invoke procedure Y? Explain.
6. Could procedure X reference constant F? Explain.
7. Could procedure X reference constant J? Explain.
8. Could procedure Z reference constant J? Explain.

5.6.4 Implications for Program Design

When you are designing a program, you have a choice of many ways in which the blocks of the program can be structured. In general, the best rule to follow is to make the block structure of the program reflect the control structure. That is, if procedure X will be exe-

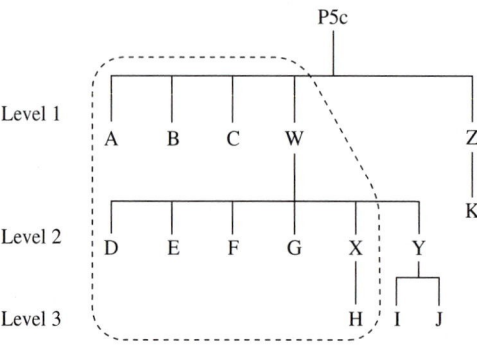

Figure 5.12 Identifiers defined in procedure X.

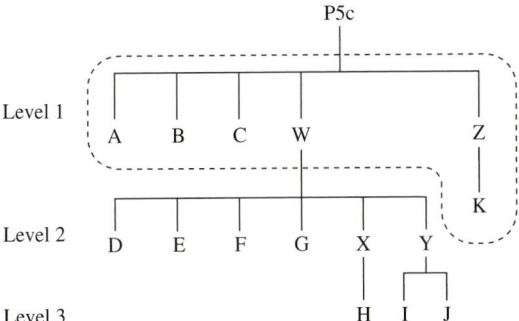

Figure 5.13 Identifiers defined in procedure Z.

cuted only by procedure Y, then procedure X should be declared as part of procedure Y. On the other hand, if procedure X will be executed by procedures Y and Z, then procedure X should be declared at the lowest level in the hierarchy such that both procedures Y and Z can have the required access.

For example, Figure 5.14 shows an alternative arrangement of the procedure declaration section of Program 5b. In this alternative, the three procedures ValidateMonth, ValidateDay, and ComputeJulianDate are defined as three separate procedures in the procedure declaration part of the main program. The program is syntactically correct and performs the same function as it did previously; however, this design is less desirable than the one used in the original version of the program. The reason for this is that the alternative program violates the design rule just specified. The procedures ValidateMonth and ValidateDay are executed only from ComputeJulianDate; therefore, the best place for these procedures is as subordinate procedures within ComputeJulianDate.

The block structure of the alternative program is shown in Figure 5.15. Compare this structure with that of the original program, shown in Figure 5.8. You will note that the alternative version has four distinct blocks nested within the outer block, whereas the original version has two blocks nested within the outer block and two blocks nested within the first intermediate block. These relationships can also be seen by examining the block structure in outline form, as follows:

MAIN PROGRAM (P5b)

1.0 ComputeJulianDate
    1.1 ValidateMonth
    1.2 ValidateDay
2.0 Wait

MAIN PROGRAM (P5d)

1.0 ValidateMonth
2.0 ValidateDay
3.0 ComputeJulianDate
4.0 Wait

As was noted earlier, in the alternative version of the program, the procedures ValidateMonth and ValidateDay are within the scope of the main program (because they are declared as part of the procedure declaration part of the main program), as well as the procedure ComputeJulian Date (because they are previously defined at the same level as ComputeJulianDate), even though they are needed only by the procedure Compute-JulianDate. The problem that is created by this situation is as follows: The procedure ComputeJulianDate is incomplete without ValidateMonth and ValidateDay. If you wished

```
program P5d (Input, Output);
{Program to compute the difference between two dates in the same year;
    program illustrates alternative design without nested procedure
    declarations}
    .
    .
    .
(*************************************************************************)
    procedure ValidateMonth (Month : Integer;
                            var ValidMonth : Boolean);
    {Procedure to determine whether a Month is valid}
    begin    {ValidateMonth}
    .
    .
    .
    end;     {ValidateMonth}
{---------------------------------------------------------------------}
    procedure ValidateDay (Month, Day : Integer;
                            var ValidDay : Boolean);
    {Procedure to validate day of a month}
    .
    .
    .
    end;   {ValidateDay}
{---------------------------------------------------------------------}
    procedure ComputeJulianDate (CalendarMonth,
                                 CalendarDay : Integer;
                            var ValidDate    : Boolean;
                            var JulianDate   : Integer);
    {Procedure to compute Julian date}
    .
    .
    .
    end;   {ComputeJulianDate}
{---------------------------------------------------------------------}
    .
    .
    .
end.   {Main Program}
```

Figure 5.14 Program 5d: Alternative design for date-difference program.

to use this procedure in another program, you would have to copy all three procedures. As programs become larger and more complex, you will appreciate the fact that a procedure should be self-contained so that it can be used whenever it is needed. Often, it is possible to copy a previously coded and tested procedure from one program to another, thereby saving a great deal of time and effort; a self-contained procedure will be much easier to copy and integrate into another program than one that is dependent on a number of other independent procedures.

Sometimes, a program will require the same procedure to be accessible from two or more other procedures. When this happens, the procedure in question should be placed at the lowest level in the block structure that is consistent with providing the required access. For example, consider the procedure to determine whether a year is a leap year, which was added to Program 5b as part of Exercise 2 of Section 5.5.1. The procedure

```
program P5d (Input, Output);
uses Crt;
     DatePrompt1 = ' Enter First Date in form mm dd : ';
     DatePrompt2 = 'Enter Second Date in form mm dd : ';
var
     Month1, Day1, Month2, Day2,      {Input Variables}
     JulianDate1, JulianDate2,        {Computational Variables}
     Difference                       {Output Variable}
         :  Integer;
     ValidDate1, ValidDate2           {Control Variables}
         :  Boolean;


     procedure ValidateMonth (Month     : Integer;
                          var ValidMonth : Boolean);
         . . .
     end;   {ValidateMonth}


     procedure ValidateDay (Month, Day : Integer;
                          ValidDay : Boolean);
     var
         NumberDays : Integer;
         . . .
     end;   {ValidateDay}


     procedure ComputeJulianDate (CalendarMonth,
                             CalendarDay : Integer;
                         var ValidDate   : Boolean;
                         var JulianDate : Integer);
         . . .
     end;   {ComputeJulianDate}


     procedure Wait;
         . . .
     end;   {Wait}


     . . .

end.   {Main Program}
```

Scope of
DatePrompt1
DatePrompt2
Month1
Day1
Month2
Day2
JulianDate1
JulianDate2
Difference
ValidDate1
ValidDate2
ComputeJulianDate
Wait

Scope of
Month
ValidMonth

Scope of
Month
Day
ValidDay
NumbersDays

Scope of
CalendarMonth
CalendarDay
ValidDate
JulianDate

Figure 5.15 Block structure of Program 5d.

LeapYear was needed by ValidateDay and by ComputeJulianDate. Thus, an appropriate way to design the block structure of the program is as follows:

MAIN PROGRAM (MODIFICATION OF P5b)

1.0 ComputeJulianDate
  1.1 LeapYear
  1.2 ValidateMonth
  1.3 ValidateDay
2.0 Wait

It would not be appropriate to declare LeapYear as part of ValidateDay, since it would be accessible only within that procedure and would be inaccessible to the procedure ComputeJulianDate. Note that the procedure for LeapYear must precede ValidateDay in order to provide access to LeapYear from ValidateDay.

5.7 FILE VARIABLES AS PARAMETERS

As we have seen, the general rule when choosing to declare a formal parameter as value or variable in a procedure declaration is to consider whether or not any change in the value of the variable is to be returned to the calling program. If it is, then the parameter must be a variable parameter. Remember that the system makes a local copy of a value parameter, so that a change to it is not communicated back to the calling program.

A special situation arises with respect to file variables. The rule to remember is

> In a formal parameter declaration, a variable with a file type must be declared as a variable parameter.

The basic reason for this restriction is that a file variable represents a file that exists externally to the program. Because of this, it is not possible for the system to make a local copy of the variable (and the underlying file), which would be required of a value parameter. To avoid the problem, Turbo Pascal makes the restriction that all file type parameters must be variable parameters, whether the variable will be changed by the procedure or not.

5.7.1 Program Example

Let us consider again Programs 4e and 4f, which process a file containing data regarding a student's registration status and grades. The variable DataFile is of type Text and thus is a file-type variable. In both programs, Module 1.0 opens the file for input. Suppose we wish to implement this module as a procedure. The actual parameter would be the file variable DataFile. The corresponding formal parameter would have to be a variable parameter, such as that in:

```
procedure OpenInputFile (var InputFile : Text);
```

The completed procedure is shown as Program 5e in Figure 5.16. Notice that within this procedure, all references to the file are made by means of the local variable InputFile.

The procedure OpenInputFile would need to make InputFile a variable parameter, regardless of the restriction imposed by the language, since the procedure makes changes to the variable that must be communicated to the calling program. Consider now the procedure ReadInput from Program 5e. The purpose of this procedure is to read data from a file and return the data to the calling program. Obviously, the variables that will be read from the file must be variable parameters, since their primary function is to return a series of values to the calling program. But notice that the file variable GradeFile is also declared

```pascal
program P5e (Input, Output, DataFile);
{Program processes student information to compute pass/fail grade;
    program illustrates use of a file variable as a parameter}
const
    ErrorMessage = 'Invalid registration type ';
    UndergraduatePass = 70;
    GraduatePass = 75;
var
    Name, SSN               : string;     {Input variables}
    RegistrationType        : Char;
    Test1, Test2, Test3     : Real;
    Grade                   : string;     {Output variable}
    PassingGrade, Average   : Real;       {Control  variables}
    DataFile                : Text;
{******************************************************************}
    procedure OpenInputFile (var InputFile : Text);
    {Procedure opens a Text file for input}
    const
        FileNamePrompt = 'Enter name of file ';
    var
        FileName : string;
    begin    {OpenInputFile}
        Write (FileNamePrompt);
        Readln (FileName);
        Assign (InputFile, FileName);
        Reset (InputFile)
    end;      {OpenInputFile}
{-----------------------------------------------------------------}
    procedure ReadData (var GradeFile : Text;
                        var N, S : string;
                        var RT : Char;
                        var T1, T2, T3 : Real);
    {Procedure reads data from student grade file}
    begin    {ReadData}
        Readln (GradeFile, N);
        Readln (GradeFile, S);
        Readln (GradeFile, RT);
        Readln (GradeFile, T1, T2, T3)
    end;      {ReadData}
{-----------------------------------------------------------------}
    procedure Wait;
    begin    {Wait}
        Write ('Press <Enter> to continue ');
        Readln
    end;      {Wait}
{******************************************************************}
begin    {Main Program}

{1.0 Open data file}

    OpenInputFile (DataFile);

{2.0 Read data}

    ReadData (DataFile, Name, SSN, RegistrationType,
              Test1, Test2, Test3);
    .
    .
    .
end.      {Main Program}
```

Figure 5.16 Program 5e: Using a file variable as a parameter.

to be a variable parameter in the procedure header:

```
procedure ReadData (var GradeFile : Text;
                    var N, S : string;
                    var RT : Char;
                    var T1, T2, T3 : Real);
```

In this header, GradeFile must be declared as a variable parameter, even though the procedure makes no change to it. This declaration is a direct requirement for file-type variables: They must be declared as variable parameters.

5.7.2 Time Out

1. Test Program 5e. (Remember that you must have a file available for the program to process.)
2. Try making GradeFile a value parameter in the declaration of ReadData. What happens when you try to compile the program?
3. Draw a data-flow diagram for Program 5e.
4. Modify Program 5e to create an output file for the information produced by the program. Add a procedure to open an output file and a procedure to produce the actual output.

5.8 GLOBAL IDENTIFIERS

The basic purpose of parameters is to communicate between a procedure and a calling program. This makes it unnecessary for the program to refer to variables defined in the calling program for just that purpose. Programs without parameters that we wrote in previous chapters made liberal use of references to global variables for the same purpose—a necessity at the time because we had not yet introduced the concept of parameters.

Henceforth, we will adhere to the following programming practice:

> A procedure must not reference identifiers for constants or variables defined outside itself.

It is strongly suggested (and your instructor will surely insist) that you follow the same rule in your programs.

You may be wondering why global identifiers for constants and variables should be avoided so scrupulously. After all, the rules of scope of definition of identifiers make it clear that references to identifiers defined at a higher level in the symbol table are available for any descendant procedure to use—Nicklaus Wirth designed the language this way.

The problem with having a procedure make a reference to a global identifier is that you reduce the likelihood that the procedure can be reused in a different program. One of the advantages of creating a procedure to perform a particular task is economy of effort. Not only can the procedure be used several times in the current program, but also when the same task must be carried out at another time, you (or someone else) may be able to use the procedure at that time in a different and unrelated program. For example, consider the procedure OpenInputFile in Program 5e. These steps are fairly standard for opening any Text file for which the user will enter the name of the file to be opened. You can therefore extract this procedure and use it in other programs. Moreover, since it makes no reference to any identifier outside itself, the procedure is all that you have to copy. Note that we moved the definition of the constant FileNamePrompt and the variable FileName into this procedure when we rewrote Program 4f. If we had left either of these identifiers declared in the Main Program's constant or variable declarations, the procedure would still have worked. But if you wished to move the procedure to another program, it would be necessary also to move the declarations on which it depends—a small problem in this case, but a very large problem when many global references are made. The use of references to globally defined identifiers severely limits the portability of your code and thus should be avoided. You can avoid the problem by following two practices:

> Declare constants and variables that are needed only in a procedure in the declaration part of the procedure.

> Handle communication of data between a procedure and a calling program by parameter lists.

Global variables also contribute to other problems in developing a program. In many instances, large programs are written by programming teams. If global variables are used, the team must work together much more closely than is otherwise necessary. (When communication among parts of a program is handled by parameter lists, a programmer needs to know only the list of parameters and the purpose to be served by the procedure being written; actual names used for variables in other parts of the program are of no concern.) If global variables are used, a change in the name of a variable must be propagated throughout the whole program, rather than just in the block in which the variable is defined. There is always the chance that one instance of the variable will be missed, which will result in a syntax error or debugging problem. If global variables are used, there is also the chance that a procedure will inadvertently change the value of a variable such that a logical error results that may be difficult to diagnose and correct. (When this happens, we say that the procedure has produced *side effects*—unintended consequences of the execution of the procedure that affect other parts of the program.)

Be aware that Turbo Pascal does not warn you when you make reference to a global variable in a program. It is up to the programmer to avoid this practice by making sure that all identifiers used in a procedure are defined within the procedure, either in the formal parameter section or in the procedure's other declarations.

5.8.1 *Time Out*

1. Consider the procedure GetValues in Program 3j. This procedure refers to Length and Width—identifiers for variables defined in the calling program. Revise the procedure

GetValues to eliminate these global references by including a parameter list for the procedure GetValues.

2. Using parameter lists, eliminate global references in the procedures GetValues, ComputePerimArea, and WriteValues in Program 3k.

3. Revise the declaration of the procedure ComputePayment in Program 3m to eliminate global references.

4. In Program 4h, the variables FigureOption, CalculationOption, ValidFigureOption and ValidCalculationOption are treated as global identifiers by the procedures in the program. Add parameter lists as needed to these procedures to eliminate global references.

5.8.2   Using Named Constants as Global Identifiers

While the prohibition against using global identifiers that has just been discussed can contribute to highly portable code, it is common practice to permit references to globally defined constants. This practice is useful because it contributes to a program's readability (the same identifier is used for the same value everywhere in the program) and maintainability (if the constant ever changes, it can be changed once, and the change is then propagated throughout the program). For example, suppose you are writing a program dealing with the computation of pay and taking into account FICA withholding. Although the FICA withholding rate changes from time to time, it will probably be treated as a constant in the program. Furthermore, it may be needed in many parts of the program. It then makes sense to define this value as a named constant once and use it wherever it is needed in either the main program or any procedure. When following this practice, however, you should be aware that any procedure which refers to this identifier is not readily portable, because any program making use of the procedure must have a like-named identifier in place. It is a good idea to note such dependencies in the comments of a procedure, so that anyone wishing to use that code will be aware of what is required.

5.9   PRECONDITIONS AND POSTCONDITIONS

One of the reasons we use procedures is that they allow us to focus on what task is to be accomplished, rather than how it is to be done. The details of the how are hidden in the code of the procedure; the calling program has to know only what needs to be done and that the procedure accomplishes the desired end. Computer scientists call this concept **procedural abstraction**; when used carefully, it contributes greatly to our ability to solve complex problems.

However, most procedures cannot be used without setting up certain conditions prior to invoking them; these are called **preconditions**. Often, this entails nothing more than supplying appropriate data via the parameters passed to the procedure, but if the job is not performed correctly, the procedure will not carry out its task properly. After the procedure has been executed, certain things will have been accomplished; these things are called **postconditions**. We say that if the preconditions are true, then, after execution of the procedure, the postconditions will also be true.

For example, consider the procedure ValidateDay in Program 5b, as shown in Figure 5.6(b). This procedure imports Month and Day and exports a Boolean variable ValidDay. The value of ValidDay will be True if Day is an appropriate day number for the value of Month. Additionally, the procedure prints a warning message if the value of ValidDay is False. The precondition for using the procedure is that the value of the first parameter (Month) be in the range 1 to 12. The postcondition is that the value of the third parameter (ValidDay) will be True if the value of Day is found to be appropriate, and if the value of Day is inappropriate, the value of ValidDay will be False, and an error message will be printed. If the precondition is met, then the postcondition will necessarily follow. It is sometimes recommended that preconditions and postconditions be incorporated into Pascal code in the form of comments. In this case, we might rewrite the procedure as follows:

```
procedure ValidateDay (Month, Day : Integer;
                 var ValidDay : Boolean);
{Procedure to validate day of a month.
    Precondition:  Value of Month is in range 1 to 12.
    Postcondition: ValidDay will be True if Day is appropriate
                   to value of Month; otherwise ValidDay will be
                   False, and an error message will be printed.}
        .
        .
        .
end; {ValidateDay}
```

Whether or not you actually write preconditions and postconditions into your code, you should think about them as you design and code your programs. You must make sure that preconditions are met prior to executing a procedure, in order to expect that the postconditions will be true. In this example, if the precondition is not satisfied (if Month is not in the range 1 to 12), the value of ValidDay is unpredictable, since the value of NumberDays will not be computed.

The concept of a precondition and postcondition is often very useful when debugging a program that involves procedures. When it appears that a procedure is not doing what you intended it to do, you should consider one of two possible types of error: (1) The preconditions for that particular procedure are not satisfied. (2) There is an error in the procedure itself. If you have been programming for any length of time, you will find yourself staring at code that is not working properly, but that appears to you to be perfectly correct. The problem is quite often found in unmet preconditions—sometimes because these conditions can be subtle, but more often because you simply failed to think about preconditions at all.

5.9.1   *Time Out*

1. Write appropriate preconditions and postconditions for the following procedures in Program 5b: ComputeJulianDate, ValidateMonth, Wait.
2. Write appropriate preconditions and postconditions for the procedure ComputeCommission in Program 5a.

3. Write appropriate preconditions and postconditions for procedures OpenInputFile and ReadData found in Program 5e.

5.10 PROGRAM DEBUGGING AND TESTING

One particular problem of which you should be aware when debugging a program that makes use of procedures is the phenomenon known as **blocked access**. As you know, the best practice to use in designing a program is to write unique identifiers through-out the program. However, this is not a practice that will be enforced by the compiler. The compiler insists that the identifiers declared in the constant and variable declara-tion parts of a particular procedure be unique, and all procedures in a given declara-tion part must have unique identifiers. (In terms of the symbol table, these identifiers appear on the same branch of the tree.) Identical identifiers can be used in different procedures with no problems (because they appear on different branches of the sym-bol table tree). For example, Program 5b uses the identifier Month as a formal para-meter in both the procedures ValidateDay and ValidateMonth; there is no ambiguity, since each identifier is a local variable within each procedure (that is, they are on dif-ferent branches of the symbol table tree). Blocked access occurs when a procedure declares an identifier that is the same as one that has been previously declared in a higher level block containing the procedure. This is not treated as an error by the com-piler; any reference to the symbol in the procedure in question is treated as a reference to the entity defined within that procedure and not as a reference to the previously defined item. We say that the local identifier blocks the program's access to what would otherwise be available to it.

For example, consider the following program segment:

```
procedure X (var A, B : Real);
const
    C = 3;
    {-------------------------------------------------------}
    procedure Y (D : Real);
    const
        C = 4;
    begin     {Y}
        .
        .
        .
    end;      {Y}
    {-------------------------------------------------------}
begin {X}
    .
    .
    .
end;       {X}
```

In this case, the definition of the constant with identifier C within the procedure Y takes precedence over the constant with the same name defined in procedure X. Without the local definition of C in Procedure Y, the identifier C would be global; that is, a reference to C within procedure Y would be a reference to the constant C defined in the constant declaration part of procedure X. Access to this constant is blocked by the definition of the local constant with the same identifier.

An analysis of the symbol table for this segment will help you understand why blocked access happens. The symbol table for the preceding program segment is as follows:

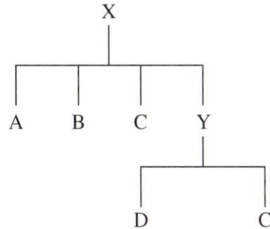

Consider how the compiler seeks to resolve a reference to the symbol C within the statement part of procedure Y. It first searches the branch of the tree representing identifiers defined within Y. There is a match; therefore, the search is terminated. If the identifier C had not been present on this branch of the tree, then the compiler would search the branch from which the branch for Y descends and find the identifier C on that branch.

The phenomenon of blocked access actually causes problems only in programs in which global references are used. If you avoid global references, then it will not matter whether a procedure uses an identifier that is the same as one used in a surrounding program block. Turbo Pascal allows the use of qualified identifiers to eliminate blocked access. To qualify an identifier, write the name of the procedure in which the identifier is defined, followed by a period, followed by the identifier. For example, in the foregoing example, procedure Y could reference identifier C by using the qualified reference X.C.

Another potentially bothersome problem in debugging a program that makes use of procedures is the potential for unwanted recursion. A procedure uses **recursion** when it invokes itself. (You may have noticed that the identifier for a procedure is defined within the procedure itself.) Used properly, recursion is a very powerful tool that can simplify the solution to many interesting problems; we will discuss recursion in depth in Chapter 8. On the other hand, if you inadvertently use recursion, it can result in a program that enters an infinite loop—one that never terminates. The usual symptom of this problem is a program that "locks up"; that is, it continues forever, and there appears to be no way for you to regain control to go back to the Turbo program-development system.

5.11   REVIEW QUESTIONS

1. In what way does top-down program development reflect top-down program design?
2. What are some advantages in coding a program module as a procedure?

3. Distinguish between a value parameter and a variable parameter. When should a parameter be a variable parameter, and when should it be a value parameter?

4. When should a value that is imported into a procedure be declared as a variable parameter?

5. Under what circumstances can the number of actual parameters differ from the number of formal parameters?

6. Under what circumstances can the data type of an actual parameter differ from the data type of a formal parameter?

7. How can actual parameters that correspond to value parameters differ from actual parameters that correspond to variable parameters?

8. A procedure is free to change the value of both value and variable parameters, but there is a fundamental difference in the result of the two types of changes. What is this difference?

9. How do data-flow diagrams differ from structure diagrams? How can data-flow diagrams help you in program development?

10. What is a Julian date?

11. What is meant by the scope of an identifier?

12. What are three general principles that will help you determine whether an identifier is defined within a given program block?

13. What is a symbol table?

14. What order is used by the Pascal compiler in searching its symbol table when it needs to determine the meaning of an identifier?

15. What design principle should be used to determine the best block structure for a program?

16. What is blocked access? How can it be avoided?

17. What is recursion? How can it lead to problems in debugging a program?

18. What restriction is placed on file variables in the declaration of formal parameters?

19. Why should global references to variables be avoided in procedures? How can references to globally defined constants contribute to program readability and maintainability?

20. Define the term *procedural abstraction*.

21. How can a careful consideration of preconditions and postconditions aid in writing bug-free programs?

5.12   PROGRAMMING EXERCISES

1. Write a procedure to swap two variable parameters. Use this procedure to sort three values (from smallest to largest) entered by the user.

2. Write a program to allow the user to select output from among the following geometric symbols:

   Line (15 units long)

   Square (7 units by 7 units)

   Rectangle (15 units by 5 units)

   Triangle (9 units at the base by 5 units high)

   Use asterisks to construct the geometric shapes.

3. The time value of money is the change in the value of money over a period of time due to interest earned or paid. The equation for the future value of money for a single-payment loan or

investment is

$$\text{Future Value} = \text{Present Value} \times \left(1 + \frac{i}{n}\right)^{nt}$$

where i = interest rate, n = number of compounding periods, and t = number of years. A program is needed that will enable a user to compare two alternative savings programs. For each investment, the user will enter the initial deposit, the length of the investment, the number of compounding periods, and the interest rate. The program should calculate and print the future value of both investments and should inform the user which option is best.

4. A pair of socks costs $1.05 each, $10.25 per dozen, or $110 per gross (144). Write a program to allow the user to enter the number of pairs of socks to be purchased and calculate the optimum number of socks to purchase and the price. Note that it costs more to purchase 11 pairs of socks than it does a dozen; therefore the optimum purchase if the user needed 11 pairs would be a dozen.

5. Modify Program 3m to allow users to compare the monthly payments of two different loans.

6. Modify Program 5e to write the letter-grade equivalent for each test and the average grade computed by finding the sum of the quality points for each test and dividing by 3.

6

Control Structures: Iteration

Thus far, we have explored two of the basic control structures required in structured programming: sequence and selection. In this chapter, we add the third basic structure: iteration. This structure opens up a rich variety of possibilities in problems that you will be able to solve.

In the simplest possible terms, **iteration** involves a structure in which the execution of a sequence of statements is repeated in some controlled fashion. The number of ways in which this control can be implemented is virtually infinite; in structured programming we use only certain standardized methods in order to make programs simpler and more understandable. Pascal offers three statements that you can use to implement an iteration structure:

1. while
2. repeat
3. for

Each of these enables your program to enter a controlled loop. In a *loop*, a sequence of statements is executed a number of times. (The statements being repeated are called the **body of the loop**.) A loop is *controlled* if the program exits when some condition is satisfied. The opposite of a controlled loop is an *infinite loop*, in which there is no means for the program to exit from the loop; the body of the loop is repeated forever (or until the user interrupts the program by some means such as typing ⟨Ctrl⟩⟨C⟩. Normally, we avoid infinite loops in favor of controlled loops. The three statements just listed, if used correctly, can implement controlled loops in a program.

In this chapter, we examine each of these statements in detail. When you finish the chapter, you will be able to choose which one of them is appropriate for a given programming task, and you will be able to use them to solve problems requiring iteration.

6.1 PRETEST VERSUS POSTTEST

All three loop control statements make use of some condition (which is stated either explicitly or implicitly) to enable the program to exit from the loop. There are two points at which the condition can be tested: at the beginning of the loop (before any of the statements in the body of the loop have been executed, called a **pretest**) or at the end of the loop (after the statements in the body of the loop have been executed, called a **posttest**). The difference between these two methods of loop control can be effectively illustrated with flowcharts showing the following two structures:

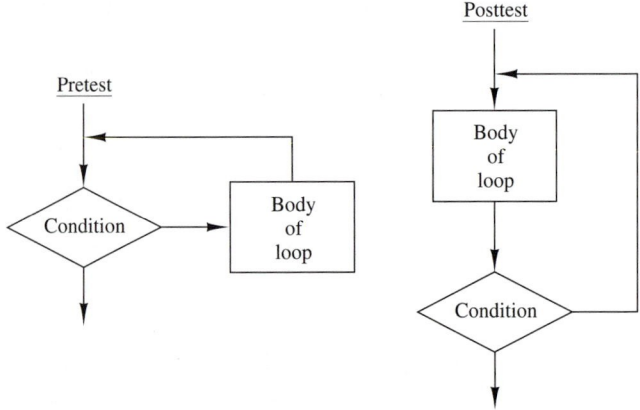

When a pretest structure is used, the body of the loop may not be executed at all, depending on the circumstances of a particular program. The loop will not be executed at all if the condition controlling the loop is satisfied initially. This may be useful if there is no need to execute the statements in the loop under some circumstances but the statements are needed under others. When a posttest structure is used, the body of the loop will be executed at least once because the condition used to control the loop is not tested until after the statements have been executed the first time. When the condition is tested, the loop may be continued or terminated, but it will always be carried out at least one time. It turns out that while and for make use of the pretest structure, whereas repeat makes use of the posttest structure. From a practical point of view, this means that loops controlled by while and for will be executed zero or more times, whereas a loop controlled by repeat will be executed one or more times. There are other consequences of the use of pretest versus posttest for loop control, which we will discuss when each statement is covered in detail.

6.2 THE WHILE STATEMENT

The **while** statement enables a program to repeat the execution of a statement while some condition is true; when the condition becomes false, the program proceeds with the next statement. The while statement makes use of the pretest structure; this means that the condition is tested before the execution of the statement that constitutes the body of the loop. The general form of the while statement and the flowchart equivalent are:

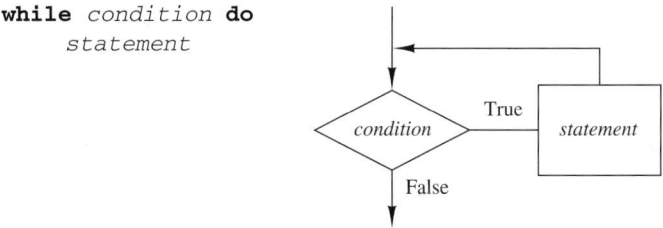

```
while condition do
        statement
```

Note that the while statement controls only a single statement; when more than one action is to be included in the body of the loop, a compound statement must be used, yielding the following general form:

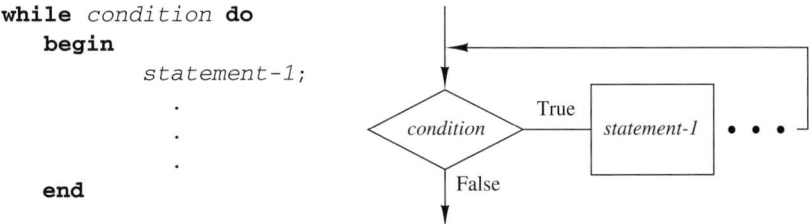

```
while condition do
    begin
            statement-1;
                .
                .
                .
    end
```

For example, let us write a program segment that would **count** from 1 to 10. This involves using a variable (called a *counter*) that starts at the value 1 and is incremented by

1 until it reaches the value 10. Assuming that the variable Count has been declared as an Integer variable, the following program segment could be used:

```
Count := 1;
while Count <= 10 do
    Count := Count + 1;
```

The sequence of values assumed by the variable Count will be 1, 2, 3, 4, 5, 6, 7, 8, 9, 10, 11. Each time the condition Count ≤ 10 is tested, it will be True, until the value of Count finally becomes larger than 10. At this point, the condition Count ≤ 10 is False, and the loop is terminated.

Several things should be noted with regard to this simple example:

1. The initial value of the condition controlling a while loop must be established before execution of the while statement. In the preceding example, this task was accomplished by setting Count to 1, so that initially Count ≤ 10 will be True.
2. The body of the loop being controlled by a while statement must take some action that affects the condition used to control the loop. In the preceding example, this was done by modifying the value of Count, so that eventually the condition Count ≤ 10 becomes False and the loop terminates.
3. The body of the loop controlled by a while statement is a single statement; if other statements follow, the while statement is followed by a semicolon, as shown in the example.

Let us modify the preceding program segment to generate a listing of the numbers from 1 to 10. The same basic idea can be used, except that in this case the body of the loop must contain two statements—one to increment the counter and the other to write the desired output. This requires the use of a compound statement:

```
Count := 1;
while Count <= 10 do
    begin
        Writeln (Count);
        Count := Count + 1
    end;            {while}
```

Note the use of the comment in this example; it will be our practice to denote the end of the while statement in this way, to clarify the body of the loop controlled by the statement for the reader of the program. In this example, note also the importance of using a compound statement. Remember that the while statement controls only a single statement—which may be simple or compound, but is still a single statement. The following coding segment may appear to be equivalent to the preceding one, but in fact, it will result in an infinite loop:

```
Count := 1;
while Count <= 10 do
      Writeln (Count);
      Count := Count + 1;
```

In this example, the while statement actually controls only one statement (Writeln (Count)), not the two-statement sequence, which was probably the intention of the programmer. This means that the value of Count never changes, so the output from the program will be an endless series of 1's. This program segment violates one of the basic principles of using the while statement: The loop body must take some action that affects the controlling condition. If it does not, an infinite loop will result. (The foregoing example represents a common mistake in using the while statement, one that you can avoid by remembering that while controls only one statement. If you want while to control multiple statements, you must start the body of the loop with begin and terminate it with end—that is, you must make the body of the loop a compound statement.)

6.2.1 Program Example

Following is an example of the use of the while statement in the context of a complete program:

■ **Problem Statement.** Write a program to compute the sum of a series of values entered by the program user. The user will enter the value zero to terminate the input, at which point the program should print the computed sum.

■ **Problem Analysis.** The technique required to solve this problem is called **accumulation**. We will declare a variable Sum (called an *accumulator*) and place an initial value of zero in it. As each number is read, we will add it to the accumulator, thereby keeping a running total of the numbers. When all numbers have been entered, the value in the accumulator will be the required sum. With this strategy in mind, we can write a preliminary plan for the program, assuming that the accumulator will be called Sum and the input value will be called Number:

ACCUMULATION PROGRAM

1.0 Initialize Sum
2.0 Accumulate sum of numbers entered by user
3.0 Write Sum
4.0 Wait

Step 2.0 is the point in the program that requires an iteration structure. This step requires that the first number be read and then that the repetition of a series of actions (adding Number to Sum and reading the next Number) commence, and continue as long as the value of Number is not equal to zero. This can be incorporated into the program plan as follows:

ACCUMULATION PROGRAM

1.0 Initialize Sum

2.0 Get first number

3.0 Accumulate sum of numbers entered by user

    3.1 While Number $<> 0$ Do

    3.2   Add Number to Sum

    3.3   Read Number

    3.4 End While

4.0 Write Sum

5.0 Wait

(This syntax is customary in describing While loops in pseudocode; the body of the loop is indented, and the scope of the structure is denoted by *End While*.)

■ **Problem Solution.** Program 6a, shown in Figure 6.1, is a solution to this problem. A sample execution of the program is shown in Figure 6.2. Note particularly the while statement used to implement Module 3.0. The statement controlled by the while must be a compound statement, since three actions are required. Note also that we are careful to make sure that all the considerations in using while that were described before are satisfied. The initial value of Number is established when the user enters it; this ensures that the initial value of the condition Number $<> 0$ that governs the while loop is established. (If the user entered 0 as the first value, then the body of the loop would never be executed, because, presumably, the user had no values to add up.) The body of the loop contains a statement that affects the condition governing the loop. The last action taken in the loop is to have the user enter another value for Number. When at last the value 0 is entered, the loop is terminated.

    Note also the statement used to implement Module 3.2 (Add Number to Sum):

```
Sum := Sum + Number;
```

This statement means the following: Take the current content of Sum, add the content of Number, and place the result back into Sum. This causes the value of Sum to change continuously during the execution of the program, as shown in the following table:

Number	Sum	Comment
	0	Initial value
8	8	$8 = 0 + 8$
−2	6	$6 = 8 + (−2)$
9	15	$15 = 6 + 9$
45	60	$60 = 15 + 45$
0		Program terminates

```pascal
program P6a (Input, Output);
{Program to compute the sum of a sequence of numbers entered
    by the user}
uses Crt;
const
    InputPrompt = 'Enter Number (0 to stop) ';
var
    Number,       {Input Variable}
    Sum           {Output Variable}
        : Integer;
{*********************************************************************}
    procedure Wait;
    begin   {Wait}
        Write ('Press <Enter> to continue ');
        Readln
    end;    {Wait}
{*********************************************************************}
begin     {Main Program}

{1.0 Initialize Sum}

    Sum := 0;

{2.0 Get first Number}

    ClrScr;
    Write (InputPrompt);
    Readln (Number);

{3.0 Accumulate sum of numbers entered by user}

    while Number <> 0 do
            begin
                Sum := Sum + Number;
                Write (InputPrompt);
                Readln (Number)
            end;   {while}

{4.0 Write Sum}

    Writeln ('Sum of numbers is ', Sum);

{5.0 Wait}

    Wait

end.     {Main Program}
```

Figure 6.1 Program 6a: A program using accumulation.

Accumulation is a fundamental problem-solving tool that you will find useful in a wide variety of problems.

6.2.2   *Time Out*

1. Examine each of the following program segments. Assuming that the variables X and Y have been declared as Integer, what output will be produced? (*Hint:* Construct a table

```
Enter Number (0 to stop) 8
Enter Number (0 to stop) -2
Enter Number (0 to stop) 9
Enter Number (0 to stop) 45
Enter Number (0 to stop) 0
Sum of numbers is 60
Press <Enter> to continue
```

Figure 6.2 Sample execution of Program 6a.

such as that shown previously as you trace the execution of each segment.)

(a) X := 3;
```
   while X < 10 do
        X := X + 2;
   Writeln (X);
```

(b) Y := 10;
```
   while Y >= 0 do
        begin
             Writeln (Y);
             Y := Y - 1
        end;    {while}
```

(c) Y := 0;
```
   X := 1;
   while X <= 5 do
        Y := Y + X;
   Writeln (X, Y)
```

(d) Y := 0;
```
   X := 5;
   while X > 0 do
        begin
           Y := Y + X;
           Writeln (X, Y);
           X := X - 2
        end; {while}
```

(e) X := 5;
```
   while X <> 0 do
        begin
           Writeln (X);
           X := X - 2
        end;    {while}
```

(f) Y := 10;
```
   while Y <> 0 do
```

```
begin
   Writeln (Y);
   Y := Y - 1
end;     {while}
```

2. Execute Program 6a from the disk that accompanies this text with sample data of your choosing.
3. Draw the program flowchart equivalent of the while statement in Program 6a.
4. Modify Program 6a to compute the sum of exactly five values entered by the program user.
5. Modify Program 6a to compute the average of the values entered by the user.

6.2.3 Another Example

For another example of the use of the while statement, let us return to Program 4h, which, as you may remember, performs computations for a variety of geometric figures. The program is menu driven, but does not incorporate the concept of a loop. This means that in order for the user to perform another computation after one is completed, it is necessary to execute the program again. Also, if the user enters one incorrect code, the program terminates. An improvement to this program would be to add a fourth option to the Main Menu option list; the new option would be Quit. The program would then return to the Main Menu after performing a computation; the user could select Quit when there were no more computations to be performed. This approach to the problem will require that the program accept and validate the figure option separately from the calculation option, since the figure option now will do double duty: It will be used to select a figure, and it will be used to terminate execution of the program. In the revised program, we should also like the user to be able to correct errors in typing in codes without having the program terminate.

With these goals in mind, we can revise the plan for the program as follows:

**GEOMETRIC COMPUTATIONS (ALTERNATIVE 1),
PRELIMINARY PLAN**

1.0 Get initial FigureOption

2.0 While FigureOption <> Quit, Process user requests
    2.1 While FigureOption <> Quit Do
    2.2   Get ComputationOption
    2.3   Case FigureOption Of
    2.4   Square: Square Computations
    2.5   Rectangle: Rectangle Computations
    2.6   Triangle: Triangle Computations
    2.7   End Case
    2.8   Wait
    2.9   Get FigureOption
  2.10 End While

You may have noticed that there is no provision for validating the various options in this plan, as there was in our original version of the program. It is possible to place the burden for validation on the procedure responsible for getting the option, so that only a valid option is returned to the main program. One advantage to this is that the main program can be simpler. Another advantage is that the user will be able to repeat the entry of an option if he or she inadvertently types an incorrect value. Thus, the process of prompting the user, reading an option, and validating the option should be repeated as long as the option is invalid. When a valid option is entered, the procedure can terminate and pass the option back to the main program. With these considerations in mind, we can design the procedure for getting a value for FigureOption as follows:

PROCEDURE GET FIGURE OPTION, PRELIMINARY PLAN (EXPORT: FIGUREOPTION)

1.0 Display Menu
2.0 While option is invalid, get an option
    2.1 While not ValidOption Do
    2.2   Write prompt
    2.3   Read FigureOption
    2.4   Validate FigureOption
    2.5 End While

This procedure would make use of two procedures—one to display the menu (Display-Menu) and another to validate the figure option (ValidateFigureOption). The latter procedure should import the value of FigureOption and export a Boolean variable ValidOption, which would be True if the value of FigureOption was one of the permitted values and False otherwise. This Boolean variable provides the clue to controlling the while loop in Module 2.0. We can initialize the value of ValidOption to False outside the loop and then have the procedure ValidateFigureOption reset the variable to True when the user has succeeded in entering a recognizable code. These ideas lead us to revise the plan for procedure GetValidFigureOption as follows:

PROCEDURE GETVALIDFIGUREOPTION (EXPORT: FIGUREOPTION)

1.0 Display Menu
2.0 Initialize ValidOption to False
3.0 While option is invalid, get an option
    3.1 While not ValidOption Do
    3.2   Write prompt
    3.3   Read FigureOption
    3.4   ValidateFigureOption (FigureOption, ValidOption)
    3.5 End While

A similarly constructed procedure, which we might call GetValidComputationOption, would be required for the CalculationOption.

Let us now revise the plan for the main program as follows:

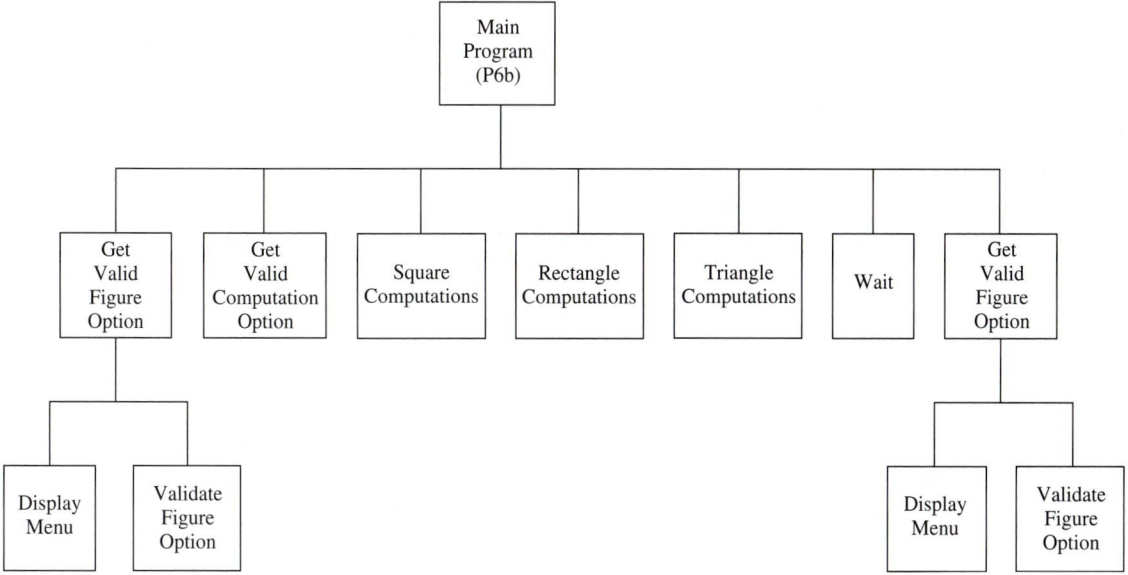

Figure 6.3 Structure diagram for alternative computations program (Program 6b).

GEOMETRIC COMPUTATIONS (ALTERNATIVE 1), FINAL PLAN

1.0 GetValidFigureOption (FigureOption)

2.0 While FigureOption <> Quit process user requests

  2.1   While FigureOption <> Quit Do

  2.2   GetValidComputationOption (CalculationOption)

  2.3   Case FigureOption of

  2.4   Square: SquareComputations (CalculationOption)

  2.5   Rectangle: RectangleComputations (CalculationOption)

  2.6   Triangle: TriangleComputations (CalculationOption)

  2.7   End Case

  2.8   Wait

  2.9   GetValidFigureOption (FigureOption)

  2.10 End While

The structure diagram for the revised program is shown in Figure 6.3.

A preliminary version of the required program is shown in Figure 6.4. Figure 6.4(a) shows the initial portion of the program, including the definition of the variables FigureOption and CalculationOption, and the procedure GetValidFigureOption, including the two procedures declared as part of this procedure: DisplayMenu and ValidateFigure-Option. The statement part of GetValidFigureOption contains the program segment of greatest interest:

```
DisplayMenu;
ValidOption := False;
```

```
program P6b (Input, Output);
{Program to perform a variety of computations for
    geometric figures; this version illustrates an
    alternative method for performing the validation of
    user-entered options and for overall program control
    using a while loop.}
uses Crt;
var
    FigureOption,
    CalculationOption : Char;              {Input Variables}
{*********************************************************************}
    procedure GetValidFigureOption (var FigureOption : Char);
    {Procedure to display the menu and get user's choice}
    const
        FigureOptionPrompt = 'Enter desired option ';
        VerificationPrompt = 'Are you sure you wish to quit ? (Y/N)';
    var
        ValidOption : Boolean;              {Control Variable}
        Verify : Char;
    {------------------------------------------------------------------}
        procedure DisplayMenu;
            .
            .
            .
        end;         {DisplayMenu}
    {------------------------------------------------------------------}
        procedure ValidateFigureOption (Option : Char;
                                    var ValidOption : Boolean);
        {Procedure to test validity of figure option entered
            by user}
        begin   {ValidateFigureOption}
            if (Option = 'R') or (Option = 'S') or
               (Option = 'T') or (Option = 'Q') then
                    ValidOption := True
            else
                begin
                    ValidOption := False;
                    Writeln ('Invalid figure option : ',Option)
                end    {if}
        end;     {ValidateFigureOption}
    {------------------------------------------------------------------}
    begin      {GetValidFigureOption}
        DisplayMenu;
        ValidOption := False;
        while not ValidOption do
            begin
                Write (FigureOptionPrompt);
                Readln (FigureOption);
                FigureOption := UpCase (FigureOption);
                ValidateFigureOption(FigureOption,ValidOption);
                if FigureOption = 'Q' then
                    begin
                        Write (VerificationPrompt);
                        Readln (Verify);
                        if UpCase (Verify) <> 'Y' then
                            ValidOption := False
                    end    {if}
            end      {while}
    end;     {GetValidFigureOption}
{------------------------------------------------------------------}
```

Figure 6.4(a) Program 6b: Declarations of variables and procedures (Part 1 of 2 parts).

```
        .
        .
        .
{***********************************************************************}
begin    {Main Program}

{1.0 Get initial FigureOption}

     GetValidFigureOption (FigureOption);

{2.0 While FigureOption <> 'Q', process user requests}

     while FigureOption <> 'Q'  do
          begin
               GetValidComputationOption (CalculationOption);
               case FigureOption of
                    'S' : SquareComputations (CalculationOption);
                    'R' : RectangleComputations (CalculationOption);
                    'T' : TriangleComputations (CalculationOption)
               end;   {case}
               Wait;
               GetValidFigureOption (FigureOption)
          end    {while}

end.     {Main Program}
```

Figure 6.4(b)   Program 6b: Statement part (part 2 of 2 parts).

```
    while not ValidOption do
         begin
              Write (FigureOptionPrompt);
              Readln (FigureOption);
              FigureOption := UpCase (FigureOption);
              ValidateFigureOption(FigureOption, ValidOption);
              .
              .
              .
         end {while}
```

In this segment, note how we have been careful to follow the principles established earlier regarding the use of the while statement. We have been careful to establish an initial value for the condition; this is done here by assigning the value False to ValidOption. When the while statement is executed initially, the value of not ValidOption is True (not False is True), so that the body of the loop is executed at least once, giving the user a chance to enter a value for FigureOption. We have also been careful to ensure that the body of the loop can change the value of the condition. In this case, the procedure ValidateFigureOption returns a value of True or False in the variable ValidOption. If ValidOption is False, the body of the loop will be executed again; when ValidOption becomes True, the value of the condition not ValidOption will be False, and the loop will terminate.

One additional feature that is implemented in this procedure is the verification of the Quit command. If the user enters 'Q', the program requests a verification that that is the action intended. This task is carried out in the following program segment:

```
if FigureOption = 'Q' then
    begin
        Write (VerificationPrompt);
        Readln (Verify);
        if UpCase (Verify) <> 'Y' then
            ValidOption := False
    end {if}
```

The reason for adding this extra step is for the convenience of the program user. If the user inadvertently enters the Quit command, the program allows him or her to have a change of mind and continue with another option.

Note how handy the UpCase function is in this procedure. It enables us to deal with only the uppercase character in the program, while allowing the user to enter either the uppercase or the lowercase character from the keyboard.

The statement part of the main program is shown in Figure 6.4(b). We use the value of FigureOption to continue processing (if the value of FigureOption is not equal to 'Q') or, alternatively, allow the user to continue selecting a CalculationOption and carrying out desired computations.

Program 6b is based on Program 4h, but adds two major improvements. We have already discussed the first of these: the use of iteration structures. The second major improvement is the elimination of references to global variables in the procedures. This change was made by adding parameter lists to each procedure declaration. In Program 6b, all communication between a procedure and its calling program is made by means of the parameter lists. This change is in keeping with our principle of avoiding references to global variables, so as to enhance the portability and reusability of our code.

6.2.4   Time Out

1. Test Program 6b with both valid and invalid responses. Note that many portions of the program are stubs.
2. Implement the program stubs in Program 6b. Use relevant portions of Program 4h as a guide.
3. Draw a data-flow diagram for GetValidFigureOption from Program 6b.

6.3   THE EOF FUNCTION

When a program accesses data from a file, it is almost always necessary to use an iteration structure to continue processing the file while it contains more data. The program usually terminates only when all of the data from the file has been read and processed. Turbo Pascal provides a function called Eof (which stands for *End Of File*) that enables the program to determine whether there is more data in the file. The following program example will describe how this function is used in a typical file-processing task.

■ **Problem Statement.**   Write a program to read a Text file and list its content to the screen of the computer.

■ **Problem Analysis.**   In order to make the program general, we want to have the user enter the name of the file to be processed. The program will then open that file as an input file, read each line, and write the line on the screen. Let us use the file variable DataFile as the internal name of the file. The pseudocode for this program is as follows:

TEXT FILE LISTING PROGRAM

1.0 Open DataFile for input
2.0 Process DataFile
3.0 Wait
4.0 Close DataFile

The program will need a string variable to store the name of the file (DataFileName) and a string variable to store each line of text as it is read from DataFile (Data).

■ **Problem Solution.**   Following is a partial listing of the required program:

```
program TextFileList (DataFile, Output);
{Program reads a Text file and prints its content on the screen}
const
    FileNamePrompt = 'Enter name of file';
var
    DataFile : Text;
    DataFileName, Data : string;
    .
    .
    .
begin    {Main Program}
{1.0 Open DataFile for input}
    .
    .
    .
{2.0 Process DataFile}
    while not Eof (DataFile) do
        begin
            Readln (DataFile, Data);
            Writeln (Data)
        end; {while}
{3.0 Wait}
    Wait;
{4.0 Close DataFile}
    Close (DataFile)
end.      {Main Program}
```

Module 2.0 of the pseudocode specifies simply that the file is to be processed. This requires reading each line from the file and writing the line to the screen. The process should continue until the end-of-file code is reached, at which point the loop should terminate. To determine when end of file has been reached, Turbo Pascal provides a Boolean-valued function Eof, which will return True if the next available character in the file is the EOF code and False otherwise. The general form of the **Eof function** reference is

```
Eof (file-variable)
```

Recall that the system maintains the File-position pointer, which points to the next available component of a file. The Eof function simply evaluates the character pointed to by this pointer. If that character is the EOF code, the function returns True; otherwise the function returns False.

Using the Eof function, we can control the loop using a while statement as follows:

```
while not Eof (TextFile) do
    begin
        Readln (TextFile, Data);
        Writeln (Data)
    end; {while}
```

The Eof function enables the program to "look ahead" at the next available character in the file. If it is not EOF, then it is appropriate to read the next line from the file; if it is the EOF code, then the program should not attempt to read the next line, because there is no more data to be read.

It is instructive to trace the execution of this program with a sample data file. After execution of the Reset procedure, the File-position pointer points to the first character of the first line of the file, as shown in Figure 6.5. At this point, the value of Eof (TextFile) is False (since the pointer does not point to the EOF code), so the Readln procedure is executed for the first time. Readln causes an entire line of the file to be read, including the EOL code. This leaves the File-position pointer pointing to the first character of the next line. The content of the first line is transferred to the variable Data, and the value of this variable is written onto the screen. Now the Eof function is evaluated again; again it returns the value False, so that the next line of the file is read and written to the screen. At this point, the File-position pointer points to the first character of the third line of the file. Again the Eof function evaluates as False, and the third line is read and written. Now the File-position pointer points to the character beyond the third line, which is the EOF code. When the Eof function is evaluated now, it returns the value True, and the loop is terminated. Finally, the Close procedure closes the file and the program terminates.

6.3.1 *Time Out*

1. Implement fully the Text file-listing program described in this section. Test it with a Text file of your choice. (The program can work with any ASCII file, including all .PAS files created by the Turbo Pascal editor. The program can list its own source code if you wish.)

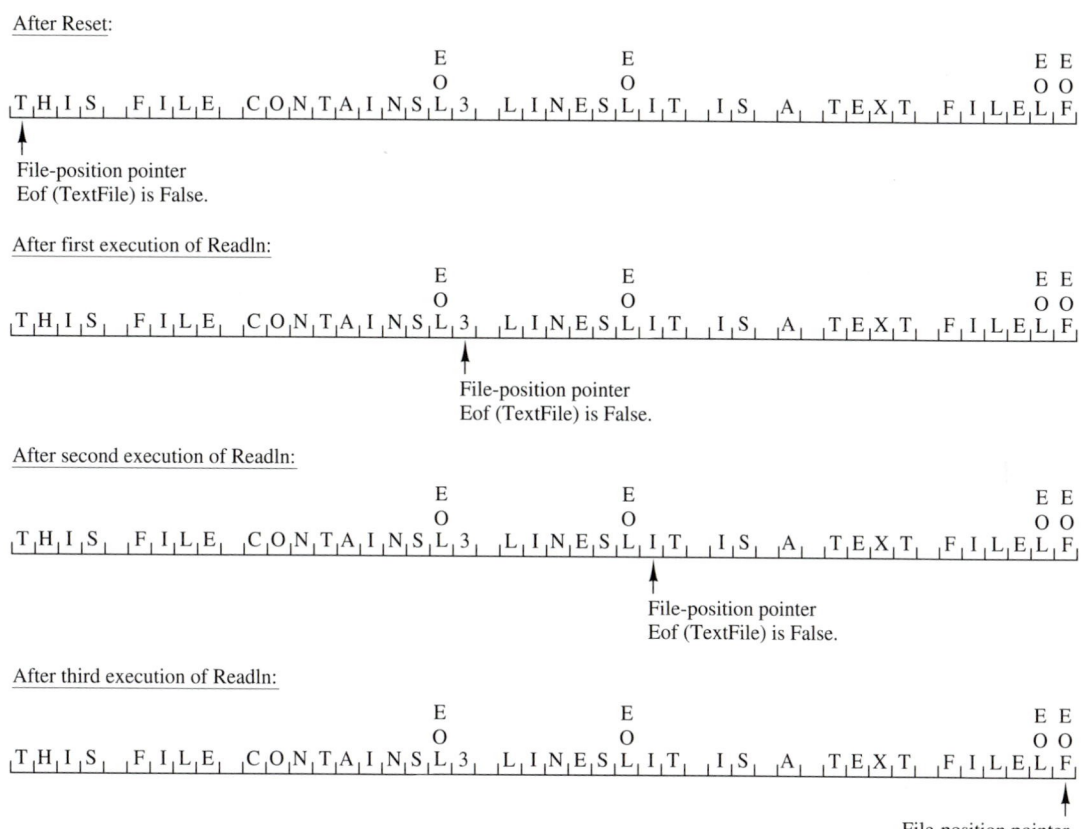

Figure 6.5 Execution of Text file listing program with a sample file.

2. If you have access to a printer, modify the program to list the file to the printer instead of (or in addition to) the screen. You may wish to give the user a choice.

6.3.2   Processing Data from a Text File

A primary reason for having files located on secondary storage devices such as disks is that they are permanent. That is, unlike data stored in primary memory, which will disappear when the next program is loaded, data stored in a disk file will be there the next time it is required. Thus, a primary usage of files is for long-term storage of data. The data must, of course, be entered at the keyboard or some other source the first time, but thereafter, any program that needs access to the data can obtain that access by declaring a file and reading the data.

Reading a Text file is conceptually the same as reading data entered at the keyboard of the computer. In fact, the default file Input, which is the means by which keyboard input is obtained. is classed as a Text file. The Readln statement reads lines of characters, beginning at the current position of the file-position pointer and concluding with the EOL codes that terminate the last line read. (Remember that the EOL codes in a Text file are equivalent to pressing the Enter key at the keyboard.) Then the content of the input line(s) is translated as needed into internal representations of data and stored in the variables that were specified in the execution of the Readln procedure. This process is illustrated in the program example that follows.

In Section 4.5.2, we described a grading problem in which the data was to be processed from a Text file. At the time, we had not introduced the iteration structure, so the program could process only one set of data items. We pointed out that this is not a practical approach to the problem. Now let us revise the program that we wrote for this problem so that it processes multiple sets of data items from the same file. We will use the Eof function to control the processing loop. As long as the function returns the value False, the program will read the next set of data items and process the data. Program 6c, shown in Figure 6.6, reflects this modification.

Figure 6.6(a) shows the declaration of variables and the procedures OpenInputFile, ReadData, and Wait. Note that we use parameter lists to communicate data between the main program and the procedures. Also, remember that a file variable must be declared as a variable parameter in a procedure declaration; this requirement is reflected in each procedure header, which requires the file variable. Figure 6.6(b) shows the procedures ComputeGrade and WriteData. In this version of the program, we have implemented these two modules as separate procedures, rather than placing them in the body of the main program. This practice helps keep the main program from being overly long. Figure 6.6(c) shows the statement part of the main program. The primary feature of this part is the while loop that controls the processing of the file in the implementation of Module 2.0. A second feature of interest is control over the screen output. The problem one encounters when generating output to a screen is that there may be too much output to fit on one screen. This will cause the output to flow off the screen—usually so fast that the information cannot be read by the user. To counter the problem, we observe that in this case there is room for output of only three sets of data items on the screen. So each time the screen fills up, we wait until the user is ready to proceed. This is done by using a counter, which is initialized to zero prior to entering the loop. Each time a set of items is processed, the program adds 1 to the counter. When the counter is divisible by 3, a screen full of information has been produced, so the program waits. The following program segment accomplishes this task:

```
Count := Count + 1;
if Count mod 3 = 0 then
    begin
        Wait;
        ClrScr
    end  {if}
```

Figure 6.7 shows the result of executing the program with a file containing information about four students. The output for the first three students appears on the first screen. When the user presses Enter, the screen is cleared, and the information from the fourth student is displayed.

```
program P6c (Input, Output, DataFile);
{Program processes student information to compute pass/fail grade;
    program illustrates use of the Eof function to control
    processing of a file}
uses Crt;
var
    Name, SSN                : string;      {Input variables}
    RegistrationType         : Char;
    Test1, Test2, Test3      : Real;
    Grade                    : string;      {Output variable}
    PassingGrade, Average    : Real;        {Control variables}
    DataFile                 : Text;
    Count                    : Integer;
{*************************************************************************}
    procedure OpenInputFile (var InputFile : Text);
    {Procedure opens a Text file for input}
    const
        FileNamePrompt = 'Enter name of file ';
    var
        FileName : string;
    begin   {OpenInputFile}
        Write (FileNamePrompt);
        Readln (FileName);
        Assign (InputFile, FileName);
        Reset (InputFile)
    end;    {OpenInputFile}
{-----------------------------------------------------------------------}
    procedure ReadData (var GradeFile : Text;
                        var N, S : string;
                        var RT : Char;
                        var T1, T2, T3 : Real);
    {Procedure reads data from student grade file}
    begin   {ReadData}
        Readln (GradeFile, N);
        Readln (GradeFile, S);
        Readln (GradeFile, RT);
        Readln (GradeFile, T1, T2, T3)
    end;    {ReadData}
{-----------------------------------------------------------------------}
    procedure Wait;
    begin   {Wait}
        Write ('Press <Enter> to continue ');
        Readln
    end;    {Wait}
{-----------------------------------------------------------------------}
```

Figure 6.6(a) Program 6c: Variable and procedure declarations (part 1 of 3 parts).

6.3.3   *Time Out*

1. Create a sample file for several students in the format required by Program 6c. Recall that four lines are required for each student:

Student Name
Social Security Number

```
    procedure ComputeGrade (T1, T2, T3 : Real;
                               RT : Char;
                          var Av : Real;
                          var G : string);
  {Procedure computes average and grade}
  const
        UndergraduatePass = 70;
        GraduatePass = 75;
  begin    {ComputeGrade}
        Av := (T1 + T2 + T3) / 3;
        if      (RT = 'U')  and (Av > UndergraduatePass) then
                G := 'Pass'
        else if (RT = 'U') and (Av <= UndergraduatePass) then
                G := 'Fail'
        else if (RT = 'G') and (Av > GraduatePass) then
                G := 'Pass'
        else if (RT = 'G') and (Av <= GraduatePass) then
                G := 'Fail'
        else
                G := 'Error'
  end;      {ComputeGrade}
{------------------------------------------------------------------------}
  procedure WriteData (N, S : string;
                          RT : Char;
                          T1, T2, T3, Av : Real;
                          G : string);
  {Procedure produces output for one set of data items}
  const
        ErrorMessage = 'Invalid registration type ';
  begin    {WriteData}
        Writeln;
        Writeln ('Name :':20, N:15);
        Writeln ('SSN :':20, S:15);
        Writeln ('Registration type :':20, RT:15);
        Writeln ('Test grades :':20,
                    T1:5:0, T2:5:0, T3:5:0);
        Writeln ('Average :':20, Av:15:0);
        if G <> 'Error' then
                Writeln ('Final grade :':20, G:15)
        else
                Writeln (Errormessage, RegistrationType:3)
  end;      {WriteData}
{**********************************************************************}
```

Figure 6.6(b) Program 6c: Procedures ComputeGrade and WriteData (part 2 of 3 parts).

Registration Status

Three Test Grades

Test Program 6c with your sample data.

2. Add the following features to Program 6c:
   (a) Write out the number of students processed by the program
   (b) Compute and print the overall average for all students
   (c) Compute and print the number of students that pass and the number that fail.

```
begin      {Main Program}

{1.0 Open data file}

    OpenInputFile (DataFile);

{2.0 Read and process the data}

    ClrScr;
    Count := 0;
    while not Eof (DataFile) do
        begin
            ReadData (DataFile, Name, SSN, RegistrationType,
                    Test1, Test2, Test3);
            ComputeGrade (Test1, Test2, Test3, RegistrationType,
                    Average, Grade);
            WriteData (Name, SSN, RegistrationType,
                    Test1, Test2, Test3, Average, Grade);
            Count := Count + 1;
            if Count mod 3 = 0 then
                begin
                    Wait;
                    ClrScr
                end    {if}
        end;    {while}

{3.0 Close file}

    Close (DataFile);

{4.0 Wait}

    Wait

end.    {Main Program}
```

Figure 6.6(c) Program 6c: Statement part (part 3 of 3 parts).

6.4   THE EOLN FUNCTION

Earlier we noted that there is an input procedure, Read, which is related to Readln in much the same way that Write and Writeln are related. (Remember that the Writeln procedure writes a line of text and ends the line with the EOL combination (Cr/Lf), whereas the Write procedure writes text, but does not write the EOL combination.) Like Writeln, the Readln procedure takes special action with regard to EOL; it reads one or more lines of text, up to and including the Cr/Lf, which terminates the last line that is read. The File-position pointer is left pointing to the first character at the beginning of a new line. Like Write, the Read procedure takes no special action with regard to EOL. Rather, it causes a sufficient number of lines of text to be read to place values in each of the actual variables specified by the program, but, when this process is finished, the Read procedure leaves the file-position pointer pointing to the next character in the file. This character might be the EOL sequence, or it might be the beginning of the value of the next data item in a line.

```
              Name :        Joe Jones
               SSN :        111111111
 Registration type :                U
       Test grades :    23   67    89
           Average :               60
       Final grade :             Fail

              Name :       Mary Smith
               SSN :        222222222
 Registration type :                G
       Test grades :    90   78    34
           Average :               67
       Final grade :             Fail

              Name :      Sue Strange
               SSN :        333333333
 Registration type :                U
       Test grades :    90   90    90
           Average :               90
       Final Grade :             Pass
 Press <Enter> to continue



              Name :       Sam Black
               SSN :        333333333
 Registration type :                Y
       Test grades :    67   45    90
           Average :               67
 Invalid registration type    Y
 Press <Enter> to continue
```

Figure 6.7 Sample output from Program 6c.

An illustration will help you remember the difference between Read and Readln. Suppose the following lines of text are in a file (DataFile) with the File-position pointer pointing to the beginning of a line, as shown:

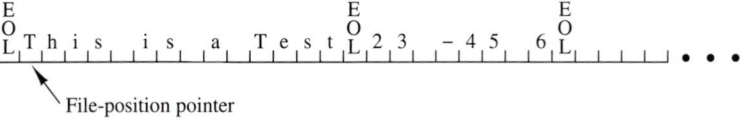

Suppose also that ST is a string variable and that I and J are integer variables. Suppose further that the following statement is executed:

```
Readln (DataFile, ST, I, J);
```

The Readln statement will read a value for ST from the first line of text; it will then skip over the EOL that terminates this line and read a value for I and J from the next line (the values will be 23 and −45, respectively). Then the File-position pointer will be positioned to point to the beginning of the next line of text. It does not matter that there may be other data on the line last read; all these characters will be ignored and the file-position pointer will be moved past them and past the EOL sequence and placed at the beginning of the next line of text. The status of the variables and the File-position pointer at the conclusion of this action will be as follows:

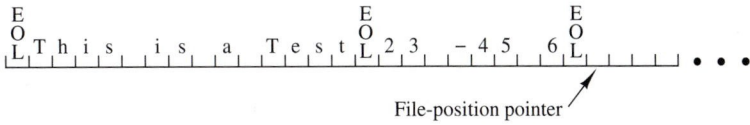

File-position pointer

ST = 'This is a Test'

I = 23

J = −45

Now suppose the file is in the same initial status, with the file-position pointer pointing to the first character of the first line. Suppose also that the following statement is executed:

```
Read (DataFile, ST, I, J);
```

Again, a sufficient number of lines of text will be read to provide values for each variable in the list, but this time the File-position pointer will be left pointing to the next character following the last value read:

File-position pointer

ST = 'This is a Test'

I = 23

J = −45

The next Read or Readln procedure call could now store the last value on the line into some variable. For example, if the statement

```
Read (DataFile, K);
```

is executed next, then the value 6 would be stored in K (assume that K is of type Integer), and the file-position pointer would be left pointing to the EOL sequence:

File-position pointer

ST = 'This is a Test'

I = 23

J = −45

K = 6

In any program that uses the Read procedure, it is usually necessary to determine when the File-position pointer is pointing to the EOL. This can be done by using the Boolean function **Eoln**. The general form for the invocation of this function is as follows:

```
Eoln (file-variable)
```

The function returns the value True if the File-position pointer is currently pointing to the EOL sequence in the file assigned to *file-variable* and returns False otherwise. For example, after the execution of the statement

```
Read (DataFile, ST, I, J);
```

in the preceding example, the value of Eoln (DataFile) would be False, since the file-position pointer is pointing to a character in the line other than EOL. After execution of the additional statement

```
Read (DataFile, K);
```

the value of Eoln (DataFile) will be True, since the file-position pointer will be pointing to EOL.

For example, suppose we wish to perform an analysis on the characters in a Text file. To keep things simple, let us write a program to count the number of E's in the file. (We will treat uppercase and lowercase E's as the same for this purpose.) The problem requires that we be able to process each character individually from each line in the file. When we reach the end of a line, we need to skip over the EOL characters and proceed with the characters on the next line. The Eoln function allows us to determine when the File-position pointer is pointing to the EOL character sequence. Thus, when the Eoln function returns True, we need to advance past the EOL characters and begin with the next line—a task that we can do with the Readln statement.

Following is the partial text of a program to solve this problem:

```
program CharacterCount (TextFile, Output);
{Program counts E's in a Text file}
const
     FileNamePrompt = 'Enter name of file';
var
     DataFile : Text;
     Character : Char;
     Count : Integer;
     .
     .
     .

begin {Main Program}
{1.0 Open DataFile for input}
     .
     .
     .
```

```
{2.0 Count E's in DataFile}
    Count := 0;
    while not Eof (DataFile) do
        begin
            while not Eoln (DataFile) do
                begin
                    Read (DataFile, Character);
                    if UpCase (Character) = 'E' then
                        Count := Count + 1
                end; {while}
            Readln (DataFile)
        end; {while}
{3.0 Print number of E's}
    Writeln ('Number of E''s = ', Count);
{4.0 Wait}
    Wait;
{5.0 Close DataFile}
    Close (DataFile)
end. {Main Program}
```

Remember that the statement

```
Readln (DataFile);
```

will cause the file-position pointer to advance past the EOL sequence to the beginning of the next line. If this statement were not present, then the value of Eoln (DataFile) would be True for the next pass through the loop.

6.4.1   Time Out

1. Complete the program outlined in the preceding section. Test it with a data file of your choosing.
2. Modify the new program to count the number of vowels in the Text file.
3. Modify the program again to allow the user to choose which letter he or she wishes to count.
4. The program just described outlines a general strategy that you can use in processing the lines of a text file. Actually, when you only want to process individual characters, you could dispense with the inner loop controlled by the detection of EOL. The Read statement will return the Cr/Lf characters at the end of each line. They will not be the character being counted, so they will essentially be ignored by the program. Try out the following implementation of Module 2.0:

```
Count := 0;
while not Eof (DataFile) do
    begin
        Read (Datafile, Character);
        if UpCase (Character) = 'E' then
            Count := Count + 1
    end {while}
```

6.4.2 Program Example

- **Problem Statement.** A Text file contains two lines for each student in a class. The first line contains the student's name, and the second line contains a sequence of grades. Write a program to process this file and create a report showing each student's name and grades and the average of the test grades. A sample of the desired report is shown in Figure 6.8. Note that it is possible that a student has no grades at all, in which case his or her average should be 0.

- **Problem Analysis.** Let us use the variable GradeFile to refer to the file to be processed. The file must be opened as an input file. After all of the data has been processed, the program should Wait and then close GradeFile. This plan is summarized in the following pseudocode:

GRADE AVERAGE PROGRAM (P6d)

1.0 Open GradeFile
2.0 Process GradeFile
3.0 Wait
4.0 Close GradeFile

What makes this problem different from any we have encountered previously is that the number of elements to be read from one line is variable. We will need a variable Grade to store each value as it is read and a counter N to keep track of how many values have been read. We will use the Eoln function to control the loop that reads the values from the line containing grades. As each grade is read, it must be added to an accumulator (Average), and we will add 1 to the counter N. After an entire line is read, we will divide Average by N to determine the average of the grades read.

```
Enter name of file containing grades P6D.DAT
      Joe Jones  23   45   56
        Average  41

     Mary Smith  78   90   99   78
        Average  86

      Sue Brown  67   89
        Average  78

      Sam Spade
        Average   0

   Thomas White  56   78   90   100   100 34 90
        Average  78

Press <Enter> to continue
```

Figure 6.8 Sample grade summary report.

■ **Problem Solution.** A solution to this problem is shown as Program 6d in Figure 6.9. Of particular interest is the portion of the implementation of Module 2.0 that processes one set of grades:

```
N := 0;
Average := 0;
while not Eoln (GradeFile) do
    begin
        Read (GradeFile, Grade);
        Write (Grade:4:0);
        N := N + 1;
        Average := Average + Grade
    end;   {while}
```

Here, the variable N is used as a counter, and the variable Average is used as an accumulator. Note that it is imperative that these variables be initialized to zero before processing each set of grades. Note also that if the line is empty, the Eoln function will return True, and no data will be read. To avoid a division by zero, we test the value of N before dividing to compute the average:

```
if N <> 0 then
    Average := Average / N
else
    Average := 0;
```

Observe that for this program to function correctly, the line in the file containing the name must be followed by a line containing grades. If a student had no grades, the second line would contain only EOL (which is generated by [Enter] when the file is created with an editor).

6.4.3   Time Out

1. Assume that the following program segment is in place:

```
var
    A, B, C : Integer;
    FileVar : Text;
```

Assume also that FileVar is opened as an input file and the following lines of text are in the file:

File-position pointer

Show the content of the relevant variables, the status of the file-position pointer, and the value of Eoln (FileVar) after execution of each of the following sequences of statements:

(a) Read (FileVar, A);
      Readln (FileVar, B);

```pascal
program P6d (Input, Output, GradeFile);
{Program to compute average grades for a variable number
    of grades per student}
uses Crt;
var
    GradeFile : Text;           {Input Variables}
    StudentName : string;
    Grade,
    Average                     {Output Variable}
        : Real;
    N : Integer;                {Number of grades for a student}
    .
    .
    .
begin     {Main Program}

{1.0 Open GradeFile}

    OpenInputFile (GradeFile);

{2.0 Process GradeFile}

    while not Eof (GradeFile) do
        begin
            Readln (GradeFile, StudentName);
            Write (StudentName:15);
            N := 0;
            Average := 0;
            while not Eoln (GradeFile) do
                begin
                    Read (GradeFile, Grade);
                    Write (Grade:4:0);
                    N := N + 1;
                    Average := Average + Grade
                end;   {while}
            Readln (GradeFile);
            if N <> 0 then
                Average := Average / N;
            else
                Average := 0;
            Writeln;
            Writeln ('Average':15,Average:4:0);
            Writeln;
        end;   {while}

{3.0 Wait}

    Wait;

{4.0 Close GradeFile}

    Close (GradeFile)

end.     {Main Program}
```

Figure 6.9 Program 6d: Example of using Eof and Eoln functions.

(b) `Readln (FileVar, A);`
    `Read (FileVar, B, C);`
(c) `Read (FileVar, A, B);`
    `Readln (FileVar);`
(d) `Readln (FileVar, A, B, C);`
(e) `Read (FileVar, A);`
    `Readln (FileVar);`
    `Read (FileVar, B, C);`

2. Create a sample file with data in the format required by Program 6d. Test Program 6d with your data.

3. Sometimes it is possible to test programs that were intended to process Text files by entering data at the keyboard. This is done by entering the file name "CON" as the name of the file to be processed. Then all Read and Readln statements that request data from the file will address the keyboard. When a Read or Readln statement is executed, the data is taken from the keyboard buffer instead of the file. You end each line of text by pressing Enter. This transmits the EOL codes. (The process can get confusing because, normally, there are no prompts that one expects from an interactive program, but you can usually tell when a program is expecting input.) To transmit the end-of-file code, you use ⟨Ctrl⟩⟨Z⟩ (press the Ctrl key, and, while holding it down, press Z) and then press Enter. On the screen, you will see ^Z. In memory, you will have entered the EOF code. Try out this process with Program 6d. The output will not be very attractive, but you can determine that the program is working.

6.5   THE REPEAT STATEMENT

The **repeat** statement makes it possible for a program to repeat one or more statements until some condition is met. As long as the condition is False, the loop is repeated; when the condition becomes True, the loop is terminated. The repeat statement makes use of the posttest structure; this means that the condition is tested after the body of the loop has been executed. The general form of the repeat statement, with its flowchart equivalent, is as follows:

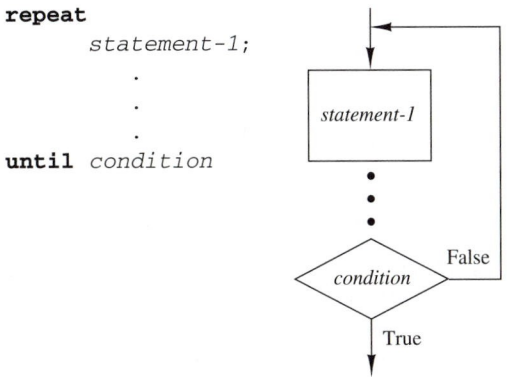

```
repeat
        statement-1;
            .
            .
            .
until condition
```

Unlike the while statement, the body of the loop for the repeat statement can be any number of statements. Because the test is made after the statements have been executed at least once, the repeat statement is not well suited to a situation where, under certain circumstances, the loop should not be executed at all. On the other hand, repeat can be used without setting up the value for the condition prior to executing the statement. The value of the condition must, however, be established by the time the condition is tested at the bottom of the loop.

For example, let us write a program segment that would count from 1 to 10. As before, we will use a counter that must be initialized outside the loop. The following program segment could be used:

```
Count := 1;
repeat
    Count := Count + 1
until Count = 10;
```

The sequence of values assumed by Count would be 1, 2, 3, 4, . . . 9, 10. When Count has the value 10, the condition Count = 10 is True, and the loop is terminated. In this case, the body of the loop contains one statement, so there is no need to place a semicolon after that statement. Note that a semicolon is usually needed after the condition, since other statements usually follow.

One very nice feature of the repeat statement is that it is not necessary to write a compound statement to contain the statements forming the body of the loop. For example, if we wished to add a Writeln statement to the preceding program segment, we would have:

```
Count := 1;
repeat
    Writeln (Count);
    Count := Count + 1
until Count = 10;
```

The values written for Count would be 1, 2, 3, 4, 5, 6, 7, 8, 9. When Count becomes 10, the loop terminates. Note that there is a semicolon after the Writeln statement, since another statement will follow.

In order to generate a list of the values 1 to 10, the following program segment would be required:

```
Count := 1;
repeat
    Writeln (Count);
    Count := Count + 1
until Count > 10;
```

When Count becomes 10, the Writeln statement will not have been executed yet, so it is necessary to repeat the loop one more time. This time, the value 10 is written, Count becomes 11, and the loop is terminated, since Count > 10 is now True.

There are three major considerations in using the repeat statement:

1. The body of the loop will always be executed at least once. (If this is not desired, you should use a while statement to implement the loop.)
2. The body of the loop must take some action that affects the condition controlling the loop. If this is not done, the loop will be executed either one time (in case the condition turns out to be True) or forever (in case the condition is False).
3. The body of the loop may be multiple statements terminated by the reserved word until.

6.5.1 Program Example

Following is an example of the repeat statement in the context of a complete program:

■ **Problem Statement.**   The factorial of a number N is defined as

$$N! = 1 \times 2 \times 3 \times \ldots \times (N - 1) \times N$$

For example, $6! = 1 \times 2 \times 3 \times 4 \times 5 \times 6 = 720$. The factorial of 0 is defined to be 1, i.e., $0! = 1$. Write a program to allow the user to enter a value for N and compute $N!$.

■ **Problem Analysis.**   A plan for this program is as follows:

FACTORIAL PROGRAM, PRELIMINARY PLAN

1.0 Get value for Number
2.0 Compute Factorial of Number
3.0 Write Factorial
4.0 Wait

The solution to this problem will require a counter to generate the numbers 1, 2, 3, . . . , N and an accumulator, which we call Factorial, to accumulate the product. We will initialize Factorial to have the value 1 and generate the numbers 1, 2, 3, 4, . . . using a counter called I. For each value of I, we will take the present value of Factorial, multiply by I, and make this the new value of Factorial. The process continues until all the required values of I (from 1 to N) have been processed. Module 2.0 requires an iteration structure to generate the values of the variable I from 1 to Number:

FACTORIAL PROGRAM, FINAL PLAN (P6e)

1.0 Get value for Number
2.0 Compute Factorial of Number
    2.1 Initialize Factorial to 1
    2.2 Initialize I to 1
    2.3 Do
    2.4   Factorial = Factorial * I

2.5   I = I + 1
2.6 Until I > Number
3.0 Write Factorial
4.0 Wait

For example, when Number has the value 6, the successive values of the variables I and Factorial are as shown in the following table:

Number	Factorial	I	Comment
6	$\cancel{1}$		Initial values
	$\cancel{1}$	$\cancel{1}$	$1 = 1 \times 1$
	$\cancel{2}$	$\cancel{2}$	$2 = 1 \times 2$
	$\cancel{6}$	$\cancel{3}$	$6 = 2 \times 3$
	$\cancel{24}$	$\cancel{4}$	$24 = 6 \times 4$
	$\cancel{120}$	$\cancel{5}$	$120 = 24 \times 5$
	720	$\cancel{6}$	$720 = 120 \times 6$
		7	I > Number is True, so loop halts

■ **Problem Solution.** The program for this problem (Program 6e) is shown in Figure 6.10. Sample executions are shown in Figure 6.11. Since *N*! becomes large very quickly, it is necessary to make the variable Factorial a Real variable, even though it will have no decimal part. Note the similarity between the pseudocode version of the loop in Module 2.0 and the Pascal equivalent. In pseudocode, it is customary to write Do/Until instead of the Pascal repeat, but the two constructs are otherwise equivalent. Note that this program produces the correct value for 0! and 1!, namely, 1.

6.5.2   *Time Out*

1. Show the output produced by each of the following program segments. Assume that X and Y are Integer variables.

(a)
```
X := 1;
repeat
      X := X + 2;
      Writeln (X)
until X = 10;
```

```
program P6e (Input, Output);
{Program to compute the factorial of a number}
const
     InputPrompt = 'Program computes N factorial: Enter N ';

var
     Number,         {Input Variable}
     I               {Control Variable}
         : Integer;
     Factorial : Real;    {Output Variable}
{*********************************************************************}
     procedure Wait;
     begin     {Wait}
         Write ('Press <Enter> to continue ');
         Readln
     end;      {Wait}
{*********************************************************************}
begin    {Main Program}

{1.0 Get value for Number}

     Write (InputPrompt);
     Readln (Number);

{2.0 Compute Factorial of Number}

     Factorial := 1;
     I := 1;
     repeat
         Factorial := Factorial * I;
         I := I + 1
     until I > Number;

{3.0 Write Factorial}

     Write ('Factorial of ', Number);
     Writeln (' is ', Factorial:10:0);

{4.0 Wait}

     Wait

end.     {Main Program}
```

Figure 6.10 Program 6e: Factorial program illustrating the repeat statement.

```
Program computes N factorial: Enter N 3
Factorial of 3 is          6
Press <Enter> to continue
Program computes N factorial: Enter N 6
Factorial of 6 is        720
Press <Enter> to continue
Program computes N factorial: Enter N 10
Factorial of 10 is    3628800
Press <Enter> to continue
```

Figure 6.11 Sample executions of Program 6e.

(b)
```
Y := 20;
repeat
      Y := Y - 5;
      Writeln (Y)
until Y = 0;
```

(c)
```
X := 5;
Y := 0;
repeat
      Y := Y + X;
      X := X - 1
until X < 1;
Writeln (Y);
```

(d)
```
X := 5;
Y := 0;
repeat
      Y := Y + 1
until X = 0;
Writeln (Y);
```

2. Execute Program 6e, and test it with values of your choice. In particular, verify that it makes the correct computation for 0! and 1!.

3. Insert a Writeln statement into Module 2.0 to make the program produce a table of factorials for I from 1 to Number.

4. Change the data type of Factorial to Integer, and test the program as before. What is the upper limit of the value of N for which the factorial can be computed?

5. Change Module 2.0 so that the program will count backward from Number to 1. Test the program as before. Make sure the program works for 0! and 1!. Which method is better for this problem?

6.5.3   Another Example

Let us return to the geometric computations program (Program 4h) for an example of repeat statements in the context of a larger program. In Section 6.2.3, we redesigned this program to incorporate loops in two of its parts: The main program uses a loop to enable the user to repeat computations, and the procedure for entering options incorporates a loop to ensure that a valid option is entered by the user. These portions of the program can be redesigned using repeat loops, which may result in more natural and logical code.

The main program can be summarized in one sentence.

**GEOMETRIC COMPUTATIONS (ALTERNATIVE 2),
PRELIMINARY PLAN**

1.0 Process user requests until FigureOption = Quit

This can be refined as follows:

GEOMETRIC COMPUTATIONS (ALTERNATIVE 2), FINAL PLAN

1.0 Process user requests until FigureOption = Quit
   1.1 Do
   1.2   GetValidFigureOption (FigureOption)
   1.3   If FigureOption not = Quit then
   1.4   GetValidComputationOption (CalculationOption)
   1.5   Case FigureOption of
   1.6   Square: SquareComputations (CalculationOption)
   1.7   Rectangle: RectangleComputations (CalculationOption)
   1.8   Triangle: TriangleComputations (CalculationOption)
   1.9   End Case
   1.10   Wait
   1.11   End If
   1.12 Until FigureOption = Quit

Recall that when we used the while loop to implement the procedure GetValid-ComputationOption in the previous version of this program, it was necessary to initialize the value of ValidOption prior to entering the loop. The reason for this is that the while statement performs a pretest. Because the repeat statement performs a posttest, this initialization is not necessary, making the design of the new procedure much cleaner:

PROCEDURE GET VALID FIGURE OPTION (EXPORT: FIGUREOPTION)

1.0 Display menu
2.0 Do
3.0   Get FigureOption
4.0   Validate FigureOption
5.0 Until ValidOption

An implementation of this program using repeat statements is shown as Program 6f in Figure 6.12. The procedure GetValidFigureOption is similar to the previous version, except for the use of the repeat statement for loop control. The relevant part of this procedure is:

```
DisplayMenu;
repeat
     Write (FigureOptionPrompt);
     Readln (FigureOption);
     FigureOption := UpCase (FigureOption);
     ValidateFigureOption (FigureOption, ValidOption);
     .
     .
     .
until ValidOption
```

```
program P6f (Input, Output);
{Program to perform a variety of computations for
    geometric figures; this version illustrates overall
    program control using repeat.}
    .
    .
    .
    begin      {GetValidFigureOption}
        DisplayMenu;
        repeat
            Write (FigureOptionPrompt);
            Readln (FigureOption);
            FigureOption := UpCase (FigureOption);
            ValidateFigureOption(FigureOption,ValidOption);
            if FigureOption = 'Q' then
                begin
                    Write (VerificationPrompt);
                    Readln (Verify);
                    if UpCase (Verify) <> 'Y' then
                        ValidOption := False
                end   {if}
        until ValidOption
    end;    {GetValidFigureOption}
    .
    .
    .
{*********************************************************************}
begin    {Main Program}

{1.0 Process user requests until FigureOption = 'Q'}

    repeat
        GetValidFigureOption (FigureOption);
        if FigureOption <> 'Q' then
            begin
                GetValidComputationOption (CalculationOption);
                case FigureOption of
                    'S' : SquareComputations (CalculationOption);
                    'R' : RectangleComputations (CalculationOption);
                    'T' : TriangleComputations (CalculationOption)
                end;   {case}
                Wait;
            end    {if}
    until FigureOption = 'Q'

end.    {Main Program}
```

Figure 6.12 Program 6f: Illustrates repeat statement in the geometric figures program.

If you compare this portion of the program to the equivalent statements in Figure 6.4(a), you will note the simplicity of this approach. The repeat structure fits the logic required in this program segment very nicely. The body of the loop must be executed at least once. The value of ValidOption is essentially undefined until a value of FigureOption is available. Thus, it makes sense to test the condition at the bottom of the loop rather than at the top of the loop, as was necessary when a while statement was used.

The relevant portion of the main program is as follows:

```
repeat
      GetValidFigureOption;
      if FigureOption <> 'Q' then
         begin
            .
            .
            .
         end {if}
until FigureOption = 'Q'
```

During the execution of the program, the user enters an option. If the option is not Q or q, then the request for computation is serviced; the controlling condition will be False, and the loop will continue. If the option is Q or q, then the servicing of the request is bypassed; the controlling condition will be True, and the program will terminate. A comparison of the statement portion of this program with the equivalent version shown in Figure 6.4(b) does not lead to the conclusion that the repeat structure is any better suited to the program than the while. With while, it is necessary to get an initial value for FigureOption prior to entering the loop. This is not necessary with the repeat version. On the other hand, in the repeat version, it is necessary to use a selection structure inside the loop to avoid having the user enter a ComputationOption when he or she has selected Quit, a complication that was not needed in the while version of the program. In general, it is better to write programs with as few structures as possible, because the resulting program is more likely to be simple and easier to understand. With this criterion in mind, the while version of the geometric figures program is probably to be preferred over the repeat version.

6.5.4 *Time Out*

1. Implement the program stubs of Program 6e. (If you wrote the program suggested in Exercise 2 of Time Out Section 6.2.4, you can edit that program to carry out this assignment.)
2. Reconsider again the Text File List program described in Section 6.3. An alternative technique for controlling the loop required in Module 2.0 is the repeat statement:

```
repeat
      Readln (DataFile, Data);
      Writeln (Data)
until Eof (DataFile);
```

This technique is somewhat easier because it does not require a begin/end program block and you don't have to write a negated condition (while not Eof (DataFile) do . . .). The only trouble with the repeat approach is that it assumes that there is at least one line in the file. Rewrite this program using the repeat statement for loop control, and compare the two versions of the program.

6.5.5   A Final Word

Thus far, we have examined two different iteration statements: while and repeat. Following is a summary of the primary differences between these two statements:

1. While creates a pretest loop; repeat creates a posttest loop.

2. A while loop will be executed as long as the condition is true; when the condition becomes false, the loop is terminated. A repeat loop will be executed as long as the condition is false; when the condition becomes true, the loop is terminated.

3. A while statement is considered to be more general than a repeat statement, since it handles the possibility that the loop may not be executed at all. The body of a repeat loop is always executed at least once.

6.6   THE FOR STATEMENT

Several of the examples presented in preceding sections have used counting as a means of loop control. Using either the while or repeat statement, it is possible to generate any desired sequence of values, such as 1, 2, 3, 4, 5, . . . , 10 or 10, 9, 8, . . . , 2, 1, by initializing a variable outside the loop and then either incrementing by 1 (to get the ascending sequence) or decrementing by 1 (to get the descending sequence). Because this is such a common occurrence in programming, most programming languages provide a statement that performs the tasks of initializing, incrementing or decrementing, and testing the variable automatically for the program. In Pascal, this statement is the **for** statement, which has two variations, as shown in the following general forms:

Form 1
```
for control-variable := initial-value to final-value do
    statement
```

Form 2
```
for control-variable = initial-value downto final-value do
    statement
```

The *control-variable, initial-value*, and *final-value* must all have the same data type. Any ordinal data type can be used. (This, of course excludes Real, which is not an ordinal type, as explained in Section 4.7.1.) Most commonly, Integer or Char data is used with the for statement. A Form 1 statement is used for generating an ascending sequence; a Form 2 statement is used for generating a descending sequence. The for statement controls a single statement, which is repeated once for each value of the *control-variable*. If multiple actions are to be repeated, a compound statement must be used. The value of the *control-variable, initial-value*, and *final-value* must not be modified by statements within the body of the loop.

For example, assume that Count is an Integer variable. Then the following program segment could be used to write a list of the numbers 1, 2, 3, . . . , 9, 10:

```
for Count := 1 to 10 do
    Writeln (Count);
```

The actions taken by the system in implementing this program segment are shown in Figure 6.13. Note that the for loop is implemented using a pretest. This means that when using a Form 1 statement, if the *initial-value* is greater than the *final-value*, the body of the loop will not be executed at all. For example, the following program segment will produce no output, because *initial-value* (11) is greater than *final-value* (10):

```
for Count := 11 to 10 do
    Writeln (Count);
```

As noted before, a Form 2 for statement can be used to generate a descending sequence. For example, the sequence 10, 9, 8, . . . , 2, 1 would be produced by the following program segment:

```
for Count := 10 downto 1 do
    Writeln (Count);
```

In flowchart form, the actions taken to implement this program segment are shown in Figure 6.14.

When downto is specified in a for statement, the body of the loop will not be executed if the *initial-value* is less than the *final-value*. For example, the following program segment will produce no output, because *initial-value* (1) is less than *final-value* (10):

```
for Count := 1 downto 10 do
    Writeln (Count);
```

The body of a loop controlled by a for statement can be a simple statement, as shown in the preceding examples, or it can be a compound statement. For example, the

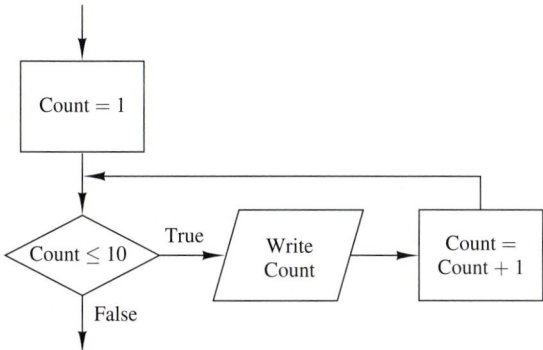

Figure 6.13 Flowchart of for/to example.

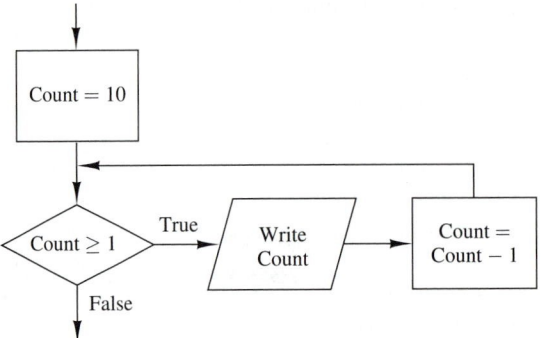

Figure 6.14 Flowchart of for/downto example.

following program segment could be used to allow a user to compute the sum of five numbers entered one at a time (assuming that all variables are of type Integer):

```
Sum := 0;
for I := 1 to 5 do
    begin
        Write ('Enter Number : ');
        Readln (Number);
        Sum := Sum + Number
    end; {for}
Writeln ('Sum is : ', Sum);
```

(Note the use of the comment at the end of the body of the loop; this is consistent with our previously established convention denoting what is being ended by the end statement.) In this case, the body of the loop controlled by the for statement is the compound statement containing three simple statements. This compound statement is repeated five times. Since the value of the *control-variable* is not used in the loop, this segment could just as easily have been written using for/downto, as follows:

```
Sum := 0;
for I := 5 downto 1 do
    begin
        .
        .
        .
    end; {for}
Writeln ('Sum is : ',Sum);
```

In order to make the program a bit more flexible, we could prompt the user to enter the number of values for which the sum is desired, as shown in the following program segment:

```
Write ('Enter number of values : ');
Readln (Limit);
```

```
Sum := 0;
for I := 1 to Limit do
    begin
        Write ('Enter Number : ');
        Readln (Number);
        Sum := Sum + Number
    end; {for}
Writeln ('Sum is : ', Sum);
```

The *initial-value* and *final-value* may be written using any expression having the appropriate data type. In the preceding example, *initial-value* was written as a constant and *final-value* was written as a variable. This is a fairly common pattern, but more complicated expressions can be used if needed.

One of the valuable characteristics of the for statement is that it does perform a pretest to avoid execution of the body of the loop when it is not needed. In the case of the preceding program segment, if the user entered 0 as the value of Limit, the body of the loop would not be executed, and the output would be

```
Sum is : 0
```

which is appropriate in this event.

We noted earlier that a variable with an ordinal type could be used for the control variable in a for statement. Real data do not qualify, since, as we discussed previously, the successor of a Real number such as 1.0 is unclear; that is, what is the next Real number following 1.0—is it 1.1 or 1.01 or 1.001? In fact, there are (theoretically) infinitely many Real numbers between any two Real numbers. The for/to statement actually generates the successor of the current value of the control variable, while the for/downto generates the predecessor of the current value of the control variable, for each repetition of the loop. Another ordinal data type that you have used is type Char. This is a set of discrete elements ordered according to the collating sequence defined by the ASCII code (see Appendix D). Because of this ordering, it is possible and sometimes useful to use a control variable of type Char with a for statement to generate a sequence of characters. For example, the following program segment would produce a line containing the lowercase characters (assuming that the variable Character is of type Char):

```
for Character := 'a' to 'z' do
    Write (Character);
Writeln;
```

6.6.1   Program Example

Let us examine the use of the for statement in the context of a complete program.

■ **Problem Statement.**   Write a program to produce a table of areas and circumferences of a circle for radial values varying from 1 to 20 in increments of 1.

■ **Problem Analysis.**   An initial plan for this program is as follows:

TABLE PROGRAM, INITIAL PLAN

1.0 Write heading for table
2.0 Write table
3.0 Delay

Module 2.0 requires an iteration structure to generate the values for the radius. Since the required values are a simple arithmetic sequence (1, 2, 3, . . . , 20), the For statement is a natural method to use to control the loop. A final plan for the program is as follows:

TABLE PROGRAM, FINAL PLAN (P6g)

1.0 Write heading for table
2.0 Write table
    2.1 For Radius = 1 To 20
    2.2   Compute Area
    2.3   Compute Circumference
    2.4   Write Radius, Area, Circumference
    2.5 End For
3.0 Delay

Note the similarity between the For statement used in pseudocode and the for statement in Pascal. The major difference is that in pseudocode we use the End For statement to denote the end of the body of the loop.

■ **Problem Solution.**   The required program is shown in Figure 6.15 as Program 6g. The output produced by this program is shown in Figure 6.16. Note that the limit for the table is established as a named constant (TableLimit) to facilitate later changes that may be necessary in the program. For example, by changing TableLimit to a variable and reading a value for it, you can make the program generate tables of different length.

    An alternative version of this program is shown in Figure 6.17, with output shown in Figure 6.18. In this program, the for/downto statement is used to produce a table in which the radial values are generated in descending sequence.

6.6.2   *Time Out*

1. Consider each of the following program segments. What output is produced by each? Assume that X and Y are Integer variables and C is type Char.

(a)
```
X := 0;
for Y := 1 to 5 do
   begin
       X := X + Y;
       Writeln (X, Y)
   end;   {for}
```

```
program P6g (Output);
{Program to produce a table of areas and circumferences of a
    circle for radial values varying from 1 to TableLimit}
uses Crt;
const
    TableHead = 'Radius    Area    Circumference';
    TableLimit = 20;
var
    Area, Circumference : Real;       {Output Variables}
    Radius              : Integer;
begin

{1.0 Write heading for table}

    ClrScr;
    Writeln (TableHead);

{2.0 Write table}

    for Radius := 1 to TableLimit do
        begin
            Area := Pi * Sqr(Radius);
            Circumference := Pi * 2 * Radius;
            Writeln (Radius:4, Area:10:2, Circumference:15:2)
        end; {for}

{3.0 Delay}

    Delay (5000)

end.
```

Figure 6.15 Program 6g: Table program illustrating for/to.

Radius	Area	Circumference
1	3.14	6.28
2	12.57	12.57
3	28.27	18.85
4	50.27	25.13
5	78.54	31.42
6	113.10	37.70
7	153.94	43.98
8	201.06	50.27
9	254.47	56.55
10	314.16	62.83
11	380.13	69.12
12	452.39	75.40
13	530.93	81.68
14	615.75	87.96
15	706.86	94.25
16	804.25	100.53
17	907.92	106.81
18	1017.88	113.10
19	1134.11	119.38
20	1256.64	125.66

Figure 6.16 Output produced by Program 6g.

```
program P6h (Output);
{Program to produce a table of areas and circumferences of a
     circle for radial values varying from TableLimit to 1}
        .
        .
        .
{2.0 Write table}

     for Radius := TableLimit downto 1 do
         begin
              Area := Pi * Sqr(Radius);
              Circumference := Pi * 2 * Radius;
              Writeln (Radius:4, Area:10:2, Circumference:15:2)
          end; {for}

        .
        .
        .
 end.
```

Figure 6.17 Program 6h: Table program illustrating for/downto.

```
Radius    Area    Circumference
  20    1256.64       125.66
  19    1134.11       119.38
  18    1017.88       113.10
  17     907.92       106.81
  16     804.25       100.53
  15     706.86        94.25
  14     615.75        87.96
  13     530.93        81.68
  12     452.39        75.40
  11     380.13        69.12
  10     314.16        62.83
   9     254.47        56.55
   8     201.06        50.27
   7     153.94        43.98
   6     113.10        37.70
   5      78.54        31.42
   4      50.27        25.13
   3      28.27        18.85
   2      12.57        12.57
   1       3.14         6.28
```

Figure 6.18 Output produced by Program 6h.

(b) for X := 3 **downto** -3 **do**
       Writeln (X);

(c) Y := 1;
   for X := 1 **to** 5 **do**
     begin
         Y := Y * X;
         Writeln (X, Y)
     end; {for}

(d) for X := 5 **to** 1 **do**
         Writeln (X);

(e) for Y := 1 **downto** 5 **do**
         Writeln (Y);

(f) Y := 3;
    for X := Y **to** Y + 3 **do**
         Writeln (X);

(g) for C := 'A' **to** 'E' **do**
         Writeln (C);

(h) for C := 'Z' **downto** 'A' **do**
         Write (C);
      Writeln;

2. Modify Program 6g to allow the user to enter the value for TableLimit.
3. Revise Program 6a to allow the user to enter the number of values to be added. Compute and write the average of the values.
4. Revise Program 6e to incorporate a for statement to generate the values of I used in computing the value of Factorial. Could either form of the for statement be used in this program? Try both methods.
5. Revise Program 6h to produce the table of values of radii varying from 10 to 1 in decrements of 0.5. Is a for statement appropriate in this case?

6.6.3   System Note

The flowcharts shown in Figures 6.13 and 6.14 represent a somewhat simplified picture of the internal implementation of the for statement. In actuality, the system computes the number of iterations required to complete the loop prior to beginning execution of the loop and then repeats the loop that number of times, regardless of the values taken on by the *control-variable*.

The number of **repetitions of a for loop** is computed as

$$|\textit{final-value - initial-value}| + 1$$

For example, the for statement

    for I := 1 **to** 10 **do**

will cause the loop to be repeated $|10 - 1| + 1 = 9 + 1 = 10$ times. The for statement

    for I := 10 **downto** 0 **do**

will cause the loop to be repeated $|0 - 10| + 1 = |-10| + = 10 + 1 = 11$ times.

When the data type Char is used for the *control-variable* and the expressions in the for statement, the ASCII value is used in computing the iteration count. For example, the for statement

```
for C := 'a' to 'e' do
```

will cause the loop to be repeated five times because the ASCII value of 'a' is 97, the ASCII value of 'e' is 101, and $|101 - 97| + 1 = 4 + 1 = 5$. (See Appendix D for a complete list of these values.)

The internal implementation of the for loop in Turbo Pascal is as follows:

TURBO IMPLEMENTATION OF FOR STATEMENT

1.0 Iteration-Count $= |final\text{-}value - initial\text{-}value| + 1$

2.0 While loop has not been executed Iteration-Count times Do

3.0   If first pass through loop then

4.0   *control-variable* $= initial\text{-}value$

5.0   Else

6.0   Compute next value of *control-variable*

7.0   End If

8.0   Execute statements(s) in body of loop

9.0 End Do

In standard Pascal, the value of *control-variable* becomes undefined after the loop has been terminated. This is not true in Turbo Pascal. As implied in the general procedure, the value of *control-variable* is normally the same as that of *final-value* when the loop is terminated. It would not, however, be good practice to write a program that depends on this identity, since that program would not run properly if compiled in another Pascal system.

One of the restrictions imposed on the for loop is that the programmer must not modify the value of the *control-variable* inside the loop. In Turbo Pascal, if you do this, it does not affect the number of executions of the loop, since that number is computed prior to executing the loop the first time. Similarly, you should not modify the values of variables that control *initial-value* and *final-value*, but again, such a modification will have no effect on the number of repetitions of the loop because those values are computed outside the loop and are based on the initial values of these expressions.

6.7 Case Study: Approximation of Square Root

■ **Problem Statement.** The square root of a number cannot be computed exactly in many cases. This is because square roots are often irrational numbers—numbers whose decimal representations are nonrepeating and nonterminating. (Some numbers, such as 4,

16, and 25, do have rational square roots, but many others, such as 2, 3, and 5, do not.) In a computer, it is necessary to approximate the square root of a number, since the value cannot, in general, be computed exactly. One method that is sometimes used is to compute a number of terms of the following sequence, which converges to the square root of A:

$$x_0 = \frac{A}{2}$$

$$x_1 = \frac{1}{2}\left(x_0 + \frac{A}{x_0}\right)$$

$$x_2 = \frac{1}{2}\left(x_1 + \frac{A}{x_1}\right)$$

$$\vdots$$

$$x_{i+1} = \frac{1}{2}\left(x_i + \frac{A}{x_i}\right) \qquad \text{for } i = 0, 1, 2, \ldots$$

In mathematical terms, the values of x_i become closer and closer to the square root of A as i becomes larger. Each term of this sequence can be considered an approximation to the square root of A. The more terms of the sequence that are computed, the better the approximation becomes.

Write a program to compute approximations for numbers entered by the program user by computing five terms of this sequence. The program should continue until the user enters a value 0. (As a by-product of the program, also produce a table showing the successive approximations.)

■ **Problem Analysis.** The overall solution to this problem can be summarized as follows:

SQUARE ROOT APPROXIMATION (P6i)

1.0 Get initial Number
2.0 While Number not = zero perform computation and get next number
    2.1 While Number not = zero Do
    2.2   Perform computation and write table
    2.3   Write Approximation
    2.4   Get next Number
    2.5 End While

Let us design a separate procedure to perform the task specified in Module 2.2. The main program will export the value of Number to the procedure and import the value of Approximation from the procedure. A preliminary plan for this procedure is as follows (we will use the notation of the mathematical statement described earlier):

PROCEDURE APPROXIMATESQUAREROOT (IMPORT : A; EXPORT : X)

1.0 Compute initial value of X
2.0 Write heading for table
3.0 Compute five terms of sequence

Module 3.0 of this plan must reflect the computational method described in the problem statement: The new value for X is computed from the old value of X using the following formula:

$$X = \frac{1}{2}\left(X + \frac{A}{X}\right)$$

Note that we have dropped the subscripts because we are interested in knowing only the value of the last value of X, not the intermediate values. (Pascal does have the capability for implementing subscripted variables using an array; see Chapter 9.) Module 3.0 requires an iteration structure to repeat the loop five times; it seems natural to use a For loop to do this task. Thus, a completed plan for the procedure ApproximateSquareRoot can now be written:

PROCEDURE APPROXIMATESQUAREROOT (IMPORT : A; EXPORT : X)

1.0 Compute initial value of X
   1.1 X = A / 2
2.0 Write heading for table
3.0 Compute five terms of sequence
   3.1 For I = 1 to 5
   3.2 $\qquad X = \frac{1}{2}\left(X + \frac{A}{X}\right)$
   3.3 $\qquad$ Write X
   3.4 End For

The data-flow diagram for this program is shown in Figure 6.19.

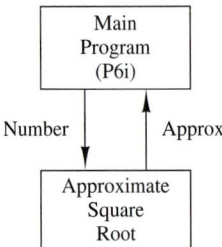

Figure 6.19 Data-flow diagram for Program 6i.

■ **Problem Solution.** The completed Program, 6i, is shown in Figure 6.20, with a sample execution shown in Figure 6.21. In the procedure ApproximateSquareRoot, note that the constant N has been declared with value 5. This was done to facilitate later changes to the number of terms that may be desired.

A basic problem with this approach to computing the square root of a number is that when the computation is finished, the user has no way of knowing or even guessing how many significant digits there are in the estimation. Based on the output shown in Figure 6.21, we see that the third term of the sequence gives us the square root of 16 correct to the nearest hundredth (two decimal places), whereas the fourth term gives us the value correct to six decimal places. Notice the fourth and fifth terms in the sequence in the computation of the square root of 27. The difference between these terms is less than 0.0001. This would lead us to conclude that the fifth term is correct to four decimal places, since succeeding terms of the sequence seem unlikely to have any effect on these four digits of the value. These observations, in turn, lead us to the following rule of thumb with regard to the accuracy of an estimation produced by using a converging sequence: If the difference between two successive approximations is less than 10^{-n}, then the approximation is probably correct to n decimal places. Keep in mind that this is a rule of thumb. It is true most of the time, but not always. Each sequence has its own characteristics of convergence that must be investigated mathematically. However, the rule is true often enough to be of value. (The area of mathematics that is primarily concerned with problems of this type is called numerical analysis.)

Let us incorporate this observation into a revision of the procedure ApproximateSquareRoot. We will repeat the loop an undetermined number of times (instead of a fixed number of times, as in Program 6i), using the criterion described before to terminate the loop: The loop should stop when the difference between the previous term in the sequence (the old approximation) and the present term (the new approximation) differs by less than a prescribed value, such as 0.0001 or 0.00001. (This value is usually represented by the Greek letter ϵ, so we call it epsilon.) This revision of the procedure would compute the initial approximation as before. Since the loop must be repeated at least once, a Repeat structure would seem logical: The loop will continue until the difference between approximations is less than the specified amount. The first action within the loop would be to "hold on" to the current value by placing it into another location, so that when the new approximation is computed, the difference between the previous approximation and the new approximation can be computed. These ideas are summarized in the following revision of ApproximateSquareRoot:

**PROCEDURE APPROXIMATESQUAREROOT
(IMPORT : A; EXPORT : X)**

1.0 Compute initial value of X
2.0 Write heading for table
3.0 Produce approximation
    3.1 Do
    3.2   OldX = X
    3.3 $X = \dfrac{1}{2}\left(X + \dfrac{A}{X}\right)$

```
program P6i (Input, Output);
{Program to approximate the square root of a number entered
    by the user}
uses Crt;
const
     InputPrompt = 'Enter number (0 to stop) : ';
var
     Number,                  {Input Variable}
     Approx  : Real;          {Approximation for Square Root of Number}
{*****************************************************************}
     procedure ApproximateSquareRoot(A : Real; var X : Real);
     {Procedure to approximate square root of A}
     const
          N = 5;    {Iteration count}
     var
          I : Integer;   {Loop control variable}
     begin     {ApproximateSquareRoot}

     {1.0 Compute initial value of X}

          X := A / 2;

     {2.0 Write heading for table}

          Writeln ('Initial Approximation for square root of ',A:10:6,
                  ' is ', X:10:6);
          Writeln ('Iteration   Approximation');

     {3.0 Compute N terms of sequence}

          for I := 1 to N do
               begin
                    X := 1 / 2 * (X + A / X);
                    Writeln (I:4,' ':10, X:10:6)
               end    {for}

     end;        {ApproximateSquareRoot}
{*****************************************************************}
begin    {Main Program}

{1.0 Get initial Number}

     ClrScr;
     Write (InputPrompt);
     Readln (Number);

{2.0 While Number not = zero perform computation and get next Number}

     while Number <> 0 do
            begin
                 ApproximateSquareRoot (Number, Approx);
                 Writeln ('Approximation for square root is ', Approx:10:6);
                 Writeln;
                 Write (InputPrompt);
                 Readln (Number)
            end     {while}

end.    {Main Program}
```

Figure 6.20 Program 6i: Square root approximation program.

```
Enter number (0 to stop) : 16
Initial Approximation for square root of 16.000000 is  8.000000
Iteration    Approximation
   1             5.000000
   2             4.100000
   3             4.001220
   4             4.000000
   5             4.000000
Approximation for square root is  4.000000

Enter number (0 to stop)  : 27
Initial Approximation for square root of  27.000000 is  13.500000
Iteration    Approximation
   1             7.750000
   2             5.616935
   3             5.211914
   4             5.196176
   5             5.196152
Approximation for square root is  5.196152

Enter number (0 to stop) : 0
```

Figure 6.21 Sample execution of Program 6i.

3.4   Write OldX, X, OldX − X
3.5 Until |OldX − X| < Epsilon

Note the use of the absolute value in the condition that controls this loop. We really don't care if the difference is a small negative value or a small positive value, as long as the difference is close to zero.

Program 6j, shown in Figure 6.22, is a modification of Program 6i that makes use of the revised version of the procedure ApproximateSquareRoot. Note that Epsilon is declared as a constant in the procedure to facilitate later modifications of the program that may be needed. It would be possible to make Epsilon a variable and allow the user to enter different values to observe the values being computed. A sample execution of Program 6j is shown in Figure 6.23. Note that the differences between terms of the sequence are themselves a sequence that converges fairly rapidly to zero. Note also the use of the function Abs. This is a built-in function that returns the absolute value of a real argument.

6.7.1   *Time Out*

1. Execute Program 6i, using sample data of your choosing. Increase the number of iterations, and observe the effect on the values computed. Add a line to the table of approximations to show the difference between successive approximations, and observe the differences thus computed.

2. A method for approximating the cube root of a number can be found in the following sequence, which converges to the cube root of A:

$$x_0 = \frac{A}{2}$$

$$x_{i+1} = \frac{1}{3}\left(2x_i + \frac{A}{x_i^2}\right), \qquad i = 0, 1, 2, 3, \ldots$$

```
program P6j (Input, Output);
{Program to approximate the square root of a number entered
    by the user to prescribed degree of accuracy}
    .
    .
    .
    procedure ApproximateSquareRoot(A : Real; var X : Real);
    {Procedure to approximate square root of A to prescribed
        degree of accuracy}
    const
        Epsilon = 0.00001;   {Governs accuracy of approximation}
    var
        OldX : Real;   {Previous term of sequence}
    begin    {ApproximateSquareRoot}

    {1.0 Compute initial value of X}

        X := A / 2;

    {2.0 Write heading for table}

        Writeln ('Initial Approximation for square root of ',A:10:6,
                ' is ', X:10:6);
        Writeln ('Old Term':16, 'New Term':16, 'Difference':16);

    {3.0 Produce approximation}

        repeat
            OldX := X;
            X := 1 / 2 * (X + A / X);
            Writeln (OldX:16:9, X:16:9, OldX-X:16:9)
        until Abs (OldX - X) < Epsilon

    end;    {ApproximateSquareRoot}
    .
    .
    .
end.   {Main Program}
```

Figure 6.22 Program 6j: Alternative version of the square root approximation program.

Write a program similar to Program 6i to approximate the cube root of a value entered by the user.

3. Modify the program you wrote to approximate cube roots to make use of the alternative method for terminating the loop, as shown in Program 6j. Experiment with various values of Epsilon to determine the effect this value has on the output produced by your program.

6.8 Case Study: Multiplication Table

■ **Problem Statement.** Write a program to produce multiplication tables for the integers from 1 to 10.

```
Enter number (0 to stop) :  16
Initial Approximation for square root of 16.000000 is  8.000000
        Old Term        New Term        Difference
      8.000000000     5.000000000     3.000000000
      5.000000000     4.100000000     0.900000000
      4.100000000     4.001219512     0.098780488
      4.001219512     4.000000186     0.001219326
      4.000000186     4.000000000     0.000000186
Approximation for square root is   4.000000


Enter number (0 to stop)  :  27
Initial Approximation for square root of  27.000000 is   13.500000
        Old Term        New Term        Difference
     13.500000000     7.750000000      5.750000000
      7.750000000     5.616935484      2.133064516
      5.616935484     5.211913542      0.405021942
      5.211913542     5.196176254      0.015737288
      5.196176254     5.196152423      0.000023831
      5.196152423     5.196152423      0.000000000
Approximation for square root is   5.196152

Enter number (0 to stop) :  0
```

Figure 6.23 Sample execution of Program 6j.

■ **Problem Analysis.**   One approach to this problem is to produce multiplication tables in the form of multiplication facts, such as

$$2 \times 3 = 6$$

for all 100 multiplication facts, which range from 1×1 to 10×10. If printed one per line, these would more than fill up the computer's screen, so let us generate each set of 10 facts on a single screen. Each screen can then be displayed in turn, with a suitable pause between screens so that the user can read what has been displayed. The various multiplication facts can be computed by multiplying two variables, which we can call I and J. If I is equal to 1, then by varying J from 1 to 10, we can produce the following multiplication facts:

I	J	I*J
$1 \times 1 = 1$		
$1 \times 2 = 2$		
$\vdots$		
$1 \times 10 = 10$		

These considerations lead us to the following preliminary program plan:

MULTIPLICATION FACTS PROGRAM (PRELIMINARY PLAN)

1.0 Write multiplication facts
    1.1 For I = 1 to 10
       1.2   Clear the Screen

    1.3   Write multiplication facts for I
    1.4   Wait
    1.5 End For

Module 1.3 in this plan will require an iteration structure in order to generate the values for J; a For loop similar to the one used to generate the values of I can be used:

MULTIPLICATION FACTS PROGRAM (P6k)

  1.0 Write multiplication facts
    1.1 For I = 1 to 10
    1.2   Clear the Screen
    1.3   Write multiplication facts for I
        1.3.1 For J = 1 to 10
        1.3.2   Product = I * J
        1.3.3   Write I, J, Product
        1.3.4 End For
    1.4   Wait
    1.5 End For

■ **Problem Solution.**   Program (6k) for this problem is shown in Figure 6.24. A sample of the program's output is shown in Figure 6.25. Note the use of named constants in the program. The table limit (10) is declared to facilitate changing this value if desired. The constant Time is used to specify the delay. Increasing or decreasing this value will increase or decrease the time interval between screens. Note the way in which each line of output is positioned on the screen. The statement

```
GoToXY(30, J + 7);
```

is executed prior to each Write. This causes the cursor to be positioned in column 30 and row J + 7. When J is 1, the output begins in column 30, row 8; when J is 2, the output begins in column 30, row 9, and so forth. The net effect is to cause the set of 10 output lines to be centered on the screen. (Don't be afraid to use GoToXY to produce interesting output effects.)

6.8.1   Time Out

1. Execute Program 6k.
2. Change one or both of the for/to statements to for/downto statements, and observe the effect this has on the output produced by the program.
3. Modify the for statement that controls the value of J as follows:

```
for J = I to Limit do
```

What effect does this have on the output produced by the program? How many lines of output are produced by this version of the program?

```
program P6k (Output);
{Program to produce multiplication facts;
    illustrates nested for loops}
uses Crt;
const
    Limit = 10;       {Limit for table}
var
    I, J, Product : Integer;
{*********************************************************************}
    procedure Wait;
    begin   {Wait}
        Write ('Press <Enter> to continue ');
        Readln
    end;    {Wait}
{*********************************************************************}
begin    {Main Program}

    for I := 1 to Limit do
        begin
            ClrScr;
            for J := 1 to Limit do
                begin
                    Product := I * J;
                    GoToXY(30,J+7);
                    Writeln (I:3,' X',J:3,' =',Product:3)
                end;    {for}
            Wait
        end;    {for}
    Writeln ('Program finished');
    Wait

end.     {Main Program}
```

Figure 6.24 Program 6k: Multiplication facts program illustrating nested for loops.

```
                                        10 X  1 = 10
                                        10 X  2 = 20
                                        10 X  3 = 30
                                        10 X  4 = 40
                                        10 X  5 = 50
                                        10 X  6 = 60
                                        10 X  7 = 70
                                        10 X  8 = 80
                                        10 X  9 = 90
                                        10 X 10 =100
Press <Enter> to continue
Program finished
Press <Enter> to continue
```

Figure 6.25 A sample of the output produced by Program 6k.

6.8.2   An Alternative Solution

■ **Problem Statement.**   Write a program to produce multiplication tables for the integers from 1 to 10.

■ **Problem Analysis.**   An alternative approach to this problem is to produce a multiplication table with 10 rows and 10 columns, showing all of the 100 multiplication facts. At first glance, this would seem to imply that the program would need 100 variables in which to store the products. Although this is indeed one type of solution, it is not really necessary because we can write output to any part of the screen, thereby making it possible to perform the computation, compute the placement of the data on the screen, and write the data at the location computed. If we do not write other values at that screen location, that content remains while other screen locations are written. With this in mind, we can write an alternative plan for the program:

MULTIPLICATION TABLE PROGRAM (P6l)

1.0 Clear the Screen

2.0 For I = 1 to 10

3.0   For J = 1 to 10

4.0   Compute Product I and J

5.0   Locate position for Product of I and J

6.0   Write Product at position

7.0   End For

8.0 End For

9.0 Wait

■ **Problem Solution.**   Program 6l, which is shown in Figure 6.26, makes use of this plan. The output produced by the program is shown in Figure 6.27. The implementation of Module 5.0 from the plan is the most interesting part of the program. The screen is divided into 80 columns and 25 lines. We can use I to determine the line number for each of the products for I. (That is, the products for 1 will appear on line 1, the products for 2 will appear on line 2, and so forth.) If each number that is printed takes five positions, then there is room for a maximum of 16 numbers on one line. In particular, we can use 5*J to determine the position of the Jth product on the line. (The products for J = 1 will begin in position 5, the products for J = 2 will begin in position 10, and so forth.) Using these ideas, we can position the cursor for the product for any combination of I and J by the following GoToXY statement:

```
GoToXY (5*J, I);
```

For example, when I is 10 and J is 10, the product 10 × 10 = 100 will be written in column 50, line 10. When I is 1 and J is 1, the product 1 × 1 = 1 will be written in column 5 of line 1. In general, each product is assigned a unique position on the screen. In Program 6l, the actual GoToXY statement uses the named constant Tab, which is also used

```
program P61 (Output);
{Program to produce full multiplication table}
uses Crt;
const
     Limit = 10;      {Limit for table}
     Tab = 5;         {Spacing for table entries}
     Time =100;       {Delay for each table element}
var
     I, J, Product : Integer;
{**********************************************************************}
     procedure Wait;
     begin    {Wait}
          Write ('Press <Enter> to continue ');
          Readln
     end;        {Wait}
{**********************************************************************}
begin      {Main Program}

     ClrScr;
     for I := 1 to Limit do
         for J := 1 to Limit do
             begin
                  Product := I * J;
                  GoToXY (J*Tab+10, I+8);
                  Write (Product:Tab);
                  Delay (Time)
             end;    {for}
     GoToXY (1, 24);
     Wait

end.    {Main Program}
```

Figure 6.26 Program 6l: Alternative multiplication table program.

	1	2	3	4	5	6	7	8	9	10
1	1	2	3	4	5	6	7	8	9	10
2	2	4	6	8	10	12	14	16	18	20
3	3	6	9	12	15	18	21	24	27	30
4	4	8	12	16	20	24	28	32	36	40
5	5	10	15	20	25	30	35	40	45	50
6	6	12	18	24	30	36	42	48	54	60
7	7	14	21	28	35	42	49	56	63	70
8	8	16	24	32	40	48	56	64	72	80
9	9	18	27	36	45	54	63	72	81	90
10	10	20	30	40	50	60	70	80	90	100

Press <Enter> to continue

Figure 6.27 Output produced by Program 6l.

in the format for the Write statement to facilitate writing tables of different size and form. By changing the value of Tab, the user can increase or decrease the size of the field allocated to each value and, at the same time, change the location of each value on the screen by an appropriate and compensating amount.

6.8.3   *Time Out*

1. Execute program 6l. The delay that follows the write statement provides you an opportunity to observe the order in which the table is filled. If the table fills up too slowly, decrease the value of Time; if it fills up too fast, increase the value of Time.

2. Change the value of Limit. What is the maximum table size that can be accommodated? Is it also necessary to change the value of Tab?

3. Experiment with the program by changing first one, then the other, and then both of the for/to statements to for/downto statements. How do you account for the fact that the table ends up looking the same no matter what combination of for/to and for/downto statements that you use? How would you make a fundamental change in the organization and appearance of the table?

4. What happens to the table if you make the following substitution for the second for statement?

```
for J := I to Limit do
```

With this substitution in place, also change the GoToXY statement as follows:

```
GoToXY (I*Tab, J);
```

What change is made in the resulting table? Why does this happen?

6.9   CHOOSING AMONG ITERATION STATEMENTS

When you are solving a problem that requires an iteration structure, you must choose among the three iteration statements available in Pascal. We have seen that some programming tasks can be accomplished equally well with all three statements, whereas other tasks seem to lend themselves more naturally to one statement or the other. How do you choose which statement is "best" for a given task?

In order to answer this question, we must take into account the characteristics and limitations of the statements themselves. We know, for example, that the for statement requires that the number of loop repetitions be known prior to entering the loop. The for statement is especially useful for generating ascending or descending sequences of values of type Integer or Char. The while and repeat statements are useful when the number of loop repetitions cannot be established prior to catering the loop. The while statement is useful when there is a possibility that the body of the loop will not be executed at all; the repeat is useful when the body of the loop must be executed at least once. The while statement requires that the program establish the value of the condition used to control the loop prior to entering the loop; the repeat statement does not make this stipulation.

Often you can "make do" with any one of the three statements to perform a particular programming task, but your program will tend to be cleaner and more elegant if you try to choose the statement that most clearly fits the requirements of the task at hand. In sum, you should use a for statement to generate a sequence or repeat a loop a fixed number of times. Use a while when there is the possibility that the body of the loop may not need to be executed at all; use repeat when the body of the loop must be executed at least once.

6.10 PRECONDITIONS AND POSTCONDITIONS

Just as a consideration of preconditions and postconditions is important in thinking about procedures, the same concepts can help us understand iteration structures. Preconditions are conditions that must be true prior to execution of the program module containing the iteration structure in order for the postconditions to be true after execution of the module.

For example, consider the following program segment:

```
Sum := 0;
for I := 1 to 5 do
     begin
          Writeln (InputPrompt);
          Readln (Number);
          Sum := Sum + Number
     end {for}
```

This program segment computes the sum of five values entered by the user. The precondition for the loop is that the value of Sum is set to zero; the postcondition is that the value of Sum will be the required sum of values entered by the user. If the precondition is not met prior to beginning the loop (say, for some reason, the program did not set the value of Sum to 0), then the postcondition will not be true.

Similar preconditions and postconditions can be specified for any program loop. When you are designing and coding a program, it is a good idea to think about these conditions to verify that the required preconditions will be satisfied before the program enters a loop. When debugging a program involving a while, repeat, or for statement, you should always consider not only the content of the statements in the body of the loop, but also the preconditions that may be required for the loop to accomplish its intended purpose. Often, program problems can be traced to unsatisfied preconditions, particularly when no fault can be found with the body of a loop.

6.10.1 Time Out

1. Write preconditions and postconditions for the while loop used in Module 3.0 of Program 6a, as shown in Figure 6.1.
2. Write preconditions and postconditions for the repeat loop used in Module 2.0 of Program 6e, as shown in Figure 6.10.

3. Write preconditions and postconditions for the for loop used in Module 2.0 of Program 6g, as shown in Figure 6.15.

6.11   PROGRAM DEBUGGING AND TESTING

Debugging a program that involves one or more loops can be frustrating and difficult if you do not make use of the techniques we have presented to help in the debugging process. Diagnostic output is especially useful in debugging a program in which a loop appears to be functioning improperly. Usually, you should place diagnostic output before the beginning of the loop, inside the body of the loop, and after the loop-control statement. The variables directly involved in the loop-control condition are the ones of most interest. You need to observe what is happening to these variables as the loop progresses. Occasionally, you may wish to write out the value of the condition being used to control the loop. Remember that you can write the value of an expression with a Boolean value; the system responds with TRUE if the expression is True and FALSE otherwise.

What can go wrong in a program involving a loop? Usually, the problems that you will encounter are directly traceable to ignoring one or more of the limitations and characteristics of the various statements. Following is a list of some of the more common problems that you may encounter and some suggestions as to what may have gone wrong.

■ **Program Enters an Infinite Loop.**   This problem is usually evident in one of two ways: If there is output inside the loop, the output continues indefinitely on the screen or printer; if there is no output in the loop, the system appears to "lock up." In Turbo Pascal version 4.0 and later, you can terminate the program by entering ⟨Ctrl⟩ ⟨Break⟩.[1]

The cause of the infinite loop is almost always traceable to the fact that the program is not changing the condition that controls the loop in the body of the loop. Either you forgot to put the appropriate statement(s) in the body of the loop, or you made a mistake in writing the condition that controls the loop. Check the condition that controls the loop first; it is usually the easiest thing to change. If it is correct, then look carefully at what is happening inside the loop.

■ **Program Does Not Enter the Loop At All.**   This problem occurs with the for statement and the while statement because both of these perform pretests to determine whether the condition is satisfied before ever executing any of the body of the loop. In the case of the for statement, look for inappropriate use of the to and downto options. For example, if you meant to write

```
for I := 1 to 5 do
```

---

[1] In version 3.0, the computer will be unresponsive to the keyboard unless you have used the compiler option {$U+}, in which case you will be able to interrupt the program with ⟨Ctrl⟩⟨C⟩. (For this reason, we recommend that you always use {$U+} when testing a program that involves a loop in Turbo Pascal 3.0.)

but instead wrote

```
for I := 1 downto 5 do
```

you would find that the program will not execute the loop at all. In the case of the while statement, you need to examine carefully the program segment that is supposed to establish the initial value of the condition. You will find that either this segment was inadvertently omitted or its execution was bypassed for some reason. Another possible cause of this problem is that you have not written the condition in the while statement correctly.

■ **Loop is Not Executed the Correct Number of Times.** This is a potential problem with all three loop-control statements. In the for statement, look at the initial value and final value very carefully, since these determine the number of repetitions of the loop. In the while and repeat statements, diagnostic output is usually most helpful in understanding the logic of the program segment that constitutes the body of the loop. It is this segment that governs the ultimate value of the condition controlling the loop; if the logic is faulty, the condition may be set inappropriately, and the loop will not terminate when it should.

6.12   REVIEW QUESTIONS

1. Define the terms *loop* and *body of a loop*.
2. Distinguish between a controlled loop and an infinite loop.
3. Which Pascal loop-control statements utilize a pretest? Which utilize a posttest?
4. Draw the flowchart equivalent of the following program segment (assume A is type Integer):

```
A := 0;
while A = 0 do
      Readln (A);
```

5. What will cause the termination of the loop in the program segment in Question 4?
6. How many statements are in the body of the loop controlled by a while statement?
7. Draw the flowchart equivalent of the following program segment (assume X and Sum are type Integer):

```
Sum := 0;
repeat
      Readln (X);
      Sum := Sum + X
until Sum > 25;
```

8. How many values of X must the user enter before the loop in the program segment in Question 7 is terminated?
9. Show the output that will be produced by each of the following program segments (assume X is of type Integer):

    (a) ```for X := -5 to 0 do
         Writeln (X);```

(b) for X := 0 **downto** -5 **do**
   Writeln (X);

(c) for X := 4 **downto** 7 **do**
   Writeln (X);

(d) for X := 7 **to** 4 **do**
   Writeln (X);

10. Show the output that will be produced by each of the following program segments (assume that C is of type Char):

   (a) for C := 'a' **to** 'e' **do**
      Writeln (C);

   (b) for C := 'E' **downto** 'A' **do**
      Writeln (C);

11. Which iteration statement would be most appropriate in each of the following programming situations?

   (a) A loop must be executed N times, where N is an Integer variable.

   (b) A loop must be executed at least once, with the value of the loop-control condition established within the body of the loop.

   (c) A loop may or may not be executed, depending on the value of a condition that has an initial value established outside the body of the loop.

12. What is the probable cause of each of the following program errors?

   (a) No output is produced in a program segment that makes use of a for loop.

   (b) A program that uses a while loop locks up during execution.

   (c) A program that uses a repeat loop begins to generate the same output over and over.

   (d) A program segment that is controlled by a for loop is not repeated the correct number of times.

13. Determine the number of repetitions of the loop for each of the following (assume I is type Integer and C is type Char):

   (a) for I := 2 **to** 5 **do**

   (b) for I := 5 **to** -5 **do**

   (c) for C := 'C' **to** 'D' **do**

   (d) for C := 'w' **downto** 'e' **do**

14. Each of the following program segments is intended to implement a loop that will be repeated five times. In each case, there is a flaw in the code. Find and correct the errors. (Assume that I is type Integer and C is type Char.)

   (a) for I := 0 **to** 5 **do**

   (b) I := 5;
      while I >= 0 **do**
         Writeln (I);

   (c) I := 0;
      repeat
            Writeln (I);
            I := I + 1
      until I > 5;

   (d) for C := 'e' **to** 'j' **do**

   (e) for I := 5 **downto** 0 **do**

15. What codes terminate each line in a Text file? What code terminates the file?

16. What is the File-position pointer? How is it used?

17. Distinguish between Read and Readln. How are they similar? How are they different?

18. What is the Eoln function? How can a program advance to the beginning of a new line if Eoln is True?

19. What is the Eof function? How can it be used to control the processing of a file?

20. What is the keyboard equivalent of EOL? of EOF?

21. How can a consideration of preconditions and postconditions help you in writing while, repeat, and for statements that perform their intended functions correctly?

22. Determine the output of the following program segment:

```
for I := 1 to 4 do
    for J := 6 to 8 do
        for K := 100 downto 98 do
            Writeln (I*J*K);
```

6.13   PROGRAMMING EXERCISES

1. Mary Smith plans to begin an individual retirement account (IRA) in which she will deposit $2,000 per year to the account for 20 years. If interest is credited yearly at the rate of 10%, how much will she have at the end of 20 years? Print a schedule showing the status of the account at the end of each year.

2. A perfect number is one that is equal to the sum of its divisors, other than itself. Six is a perfect number, since $6 = 1 + 2 + 3$. The ancient Greeks attached mystical significance to such numbers. In the first century A.D., the numbers were separated into abundant numbers, in which the sum of the divisors is greater than the number itself (e.g., 12 is abundant, since $1 + 2 + 3 + 4 + 6 > 12$), and deficient numbers, in which the sum of the divisors is less than the number (e.g., 9 is deficient, since $1 + 3 < 9$). Write a program to list all integers in the range 1 to 100 and classify them as abundant, deficient, or perfect.

3. Write a program to list all distinct factors of a number N entered by the user. For example if N $= 6$, then the output should be 1, 2, 3, 6. Use the value N $= 0$ to terminate execution of the program.

4. It is interesting to note that perfect squares can be generated by adding odd numbers to the preceding perfect square. For example, examine the pattern in the following:

$$1^2 = 0 + 1 = 1$$
$$2^2 = 1 + 3 = 4$$
$$3^2 = 4 + 5 = 9$$
$$\vdots$$

Use this technique to write a list of the first 10 perfect squares.

5. The Pythagorean theorem states that for a right triangle with sides a and b and hypotenuse c,

$$a^2 + b^2 = c^2$$

A Pythagorean triplet is three integer numbers a, b, c that satisfy this condition. Two well-known Pythagorean triplets are 3, 4, 5 (since $3^2 + 4^2 = 5^2$) and 5, 12, 13 (since $5^2 + 12^2 = 13^2$). Write a program to determine all Pythagorean triplets with $1 \le a < b \le 30$. One approach to this problem is as follows: For each pair of values in the given range, compute c. If c is an integer, then a, b, c is a Pythagorean triplet.

6. Write a program to produce a table of the areas and circumferences of a circle for varying values of the radius. The user should enter the initial, terminating, and increment values for the radius. Validate the user's choice of these values. If the increment is positive, then the initial value should be less than the terminating value; if the increment is negative, then the initial value should be greater than the terminating value. You may wish to use two different procedures to produce the table—one if the increment is positive and another if the increment is negative.

7. Look up the currency-conversion factors for your choice of foreign countries. Write a program to allow the user repeatedly to select a country from a menu and then convert any desired number of U.S. currency amounts into the currency of that country. Include an option "Quit" on the main menu. Have the user enter zero to terminate the series of conversions for a given main menu choice.

8. Write a program to draw a rectangle on the screen, allowing the user to choose the coordinates of the upper left-hand corner of the rectangle and the vertical and horizontal sizes of the rectangle. Include error messages if the coordinates are too close to the edge of the screen to draw a rectangle of the size selected by the user. Use any character of your choice (such as *) to construct the figure.

9. Consider the sum

$$1 + \frac{1}{2} + \frac{1}{3} + \frac{1}{4} + \dots$$

It takes 4 terms of the sequence for the sum to exceed $2 (1 + \frac{1}{2} + \frac{1}{3} + \frac{1}{4} > 2)$, and 11 terms of the sequence for the sum to exceed $3 (1 + \frac{1}{2} + \frac{1}{3} + \dots + \frac{1}{10} + \frac{1}{11} > 3)$. Create a table showing the number of terms of the sequence required for the sum to exceed the values 2, 3, . . . , 10. The table should appear as follows:

Sum	Number
2	4
3	11
⋮	⋮
10	

Caution: the number of terms increase dramatically as the value of Sum increases.

10. It can be shown that

$$\frac{\pi}{2} = \frac{2}{1} \times \frac{2}{3} \times \frac{4}{3} \times \frac{4}{5} \times \frac{6}{5} \times \frac{6}{7} \times \frac{8}{7} \times \dots$$

Use this relationship to produce an approximation for π correct to three decimal places. *Hint:* Terminate the accumulation process when the difference between successive approximations is less than some small value (e.g., 0.01, or 0.001). Experiment with various values to determine which one will give you accuracy to three decimal places.

11. Write a program to compute

$$1^2 + 2^2 + 3^2 + \ldots + N^2$$

for a value of N entered by the user. Terminate execution of the program when the value of 0 is entered.

12. In some business applications, a quantity known as the capital recovery factor is defined by

$$\frac{i(1+i)^n}{(1+i)^n - 1}$$

where i is the interest rate and n represents the length of the investment. Write a program to print a tabulated set of values of the capital recovery factor for values of n ranging from 1 through a maximum value. The maximum value for n and the value for i are entered by the program user.

13. Write a program to produce a conversion table between miles and kilometers, using the fact that 1 mile = 1.61 kilometers. Include appropriate headings. The program user should enter the beginning and ending values and the increment desired for the miles column.

14. The first few terms of the Fibonacci sequences are as follows:

$$1, 1, 2, 3, 5, 8, 13, 21, 34, \ldots$$

Each term is formed by adding the two preceding terms. Stated formally

$$f_1 = 1$$
$$f_2 = 1$$
$$f_i = f_{i-1} + f_{i-2} \qquad \text{for } i = 3, 4 \ldots$$

Write a program to list the first N terms of the Fibonacci sequence, where the value of N is entered by the program user. *Note:* The terms of the sequence become large fairly rapidly. Consider carefully whether to use Integer or Real variables.

15. Write a program to produce a depreciation schedule. The user should enter the value of the item (V) and (N), which represents useful life of the item being depreciated. Use the double-declining-balance method. In this method, the depreciation for a year is $2/N$ times the value at the beginning of the year. For example, if $V = 1,000$ and $N = 5$, your output should be similar to the following:

Year	Value at beginning of year	Depreciation amount	Value at end of year
1	1000	400	600
2	600	240	360
3	360	144	216
⋮	⋮	⋮	⋮

16. Write a program to find the largest and smallest values in a sequence entered by the user.

17. It is known that the natural logarithm (logarithm to the base e) of x can be approximated by the series

$$\ln x = \frac{(x-1)^1}{1} - \frac{(x-1)^2}{2} + \frac{(x-1)^3}{3} - \frac{(x-1)^4}{4} + \cdots$$

Write a program to use this method to produce an approximation for ln 2 that is correct to two decimal digits. (*Caution:* This series converges very slowly.)

18. The golden mean was used by ancient Greek architects in the design of structures. A building in which the ratio of the length to the width equaled the golden mean was believed to be aesthetically pleasing. It can be shown that the limit of the ratio of successive terms of the Fibonacci series is equal to the golden mean. Write a program to compute terms of the Fibonacci sequence and the ratio of each number to its predecessor. How many terms of the sequence are required before the difference between successive ratios is less than 0.01? 0.001? 0.0001? 0.00001?

19. Determine the number of years required for an investment to double in value. Input to the program should be the amount invested (P) and the interest rate (R). Assuming that interest is compounded once a year, the formula for determining the amount of an investment A after N years is

$$A = P(1 + R)^N$$

20. Modify the program written for Exercise 19 to create a table showing the time required to double an investment for interest rate varying from 5% to 12% in increments of 1%.

21. A Text file containing data regarding each item produced and sold by a business has been created. There are two lines for each item. The first contains the item description, and the second contains the production amount followed by the sales amount. Sample listing of the content of the file is the following:

```
Widgets
34 56
Gidgets
47 68
Zidgets
10 4
Digits
9 3
```

Write a program to produce a report, with appropriate headings, showing the content of this file.

22. Write a menu-driven utility program to allow the user to create or list a Text file. A plan for the required program is as follows:

TEXT FILE UTILITY PROGRAM

1.0 Repeat
2.0   Get Choice
3.0   Case Choice of
4.0   List : List a file
5.0   Create : Create a file
6.0   End Case
7.0 Until Choice is Quit

(If you have access to a printer, you may wish to add a third option to allow the user to print the file.)

23. Write a program to analyze a Text file to determine the number of words it contains. Words are separated from one another by one or more spaces or by EOL.

24. Create a Text file in which each line contains the make of a car, the distance traveled in a month, and the number of gallons of gas consumed. Write a program that will create a report showing the data contained in the file and the miles per gallon obtained by each car. Compute the average gas mileage for each car. In a separate report, list those cars with gas mileage in excess of 5 miles per gallon above the average and those cars with less than 5 miles per gallon below the average.

25. Create a Text file containing basic data for each employee in a business that pays its employees on an hourly basis. The first line for each employee contains the employee name. The next line contains the following data: hours worked, hourly rate, income tax withholding rate. Write a program to create a report showing each employee's gross earnings and net pay, with the following assumption: If the employee works more than 40 hours, he or she earns time and a half for hours over 40. Use a FICA withholding rate of 6.87%.

26. Create a Text file containing the transactions for a checking account for a month. The first line in the file contains the owner's name. The second line contains the beginning balance. Successive lines contain transactions coded as follows: transaction code, transaction date, transaction amount. Use transaction code 'D' to indicate a deposit and 'C' to indicate a check. Write a program to create a register showing the status of the account after each transaction.

7

Data Types

One of the strengths of Pascal is the richness of the data types that it makes available to the programmer. Where other programming languages may support three or four distinct data types, Pascal supports all the basic data types found in other languages, plus many others that are well suited for specific tasks. In this chapter, we review the data types with which you are already familiar and set the stage for the discussion of additional types. Also, the chapter will cover a new data type (Byte), user-defined data types, and sets.

7.1 OVERVIEW OF DATA TYPES

Thus far in the text, you have used data types Integer, Real, Char, Boolean, and string. In Turbo Pascal, integer-type data are useful for representing values in the range $-32,768$ to $+32,767$. Integer data have no capability for representing a number with a decimal part. In Turbo Pascal, real-type data are capable of representing values in the range 10^{-39} to 10^{+38}, correct to 11 significant digits. Real data are often an approximation of the actual values being represented. Char-type data are used to represent single characters. String-type data are used to represent series of characters of maximum length 255. Boolean-type data are used for data that can have one of two possible values: True or False. Recall that Integer, Real, Char, and Boolean data types are standard in all versions of Pascal, whereas string is a Turbo Pascal feature that is not found in all versions of Pascal.

In order to put the concept of data type into perspective, it is useful to classify further the data types supported by Turbo Pascal. The language supports four basic kinds of data types, as shown in Figure 7.1:

Simple

String

Structured

Pointer

Simple data types are the building blocks for other data types. Of the data types with which you are familiar, Integer, Char, Boolean, and Real are all simple types.

The simple data types are all scalar. The word *scalar* is borrowed from mathematics and is based on the word *scale*. A scale is a way of ordering values. Perhaps the most common scale is the number line. Each real number can be represented on the number line by a point. The placement of points reflects the order of the numbers being represented. That is, if real number a is less than real number b, then the point representing a lies to

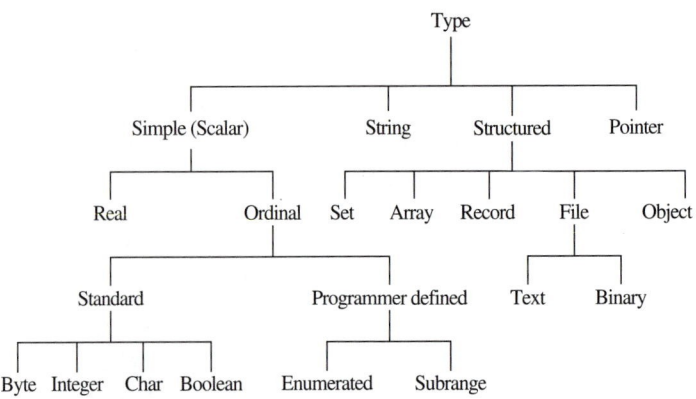

Figure 7.1 Categorization of Turbo Pascal data types.

the left of the point representing *b*. When a Pascal data type is called scalar, we mean that there is a well-defined ordering of the individual data items that make up that type. Thus, Integer is a scalar type because the integers are ordered: $-32{,}768 < -32{,}767 < \cdots < 0 < 1 < 2 \cdots < 32{,}767$. Char is a scalar type because all the characters are ordered, based on the ASCII value of the code used to represent the character. Boolean is ordered, with False $<$ True. Although it is not possible to write an explicit list of all the Real values, real values are ordered in such a way that for Real values *a* and *b*, exactly one of the relations $a < b$, $a = b$, and $a > b$ will be true.

Although all the simple data types are scalar, not all are ordinal. The word *ordinal* is also borrowed from mathematics and means that objects are ordered in such a way that it is possible to determine which one is the first, which is the second, which is the third, and so forth. (The ordinal numbers are first, second, third, fourth, etc.) In the context of Pascal, the term *ordinal* implies that it is possible to determine the successor and predecessor of any value (except those at the beginning and end of the sequence of data items). All the standard scalar types except Real are classed as ordinal. Thus, the successor of the Integer 1 is 2; the predecessor of 1 is 0. The successor of the character 'b' is 'c'; its predecessor is 'a'. The successor of the Boolean value False is True; the predecessor of True is False. Data type Real is not classed as ordinal, because this successor-predecessor relationship does not exist for real values. (What real number immediately follows 1.0? Is it 1.1 or 1.01 or 1.001 or . . .? Mathematically speaking, there are infinitely many real numbers between any two real numbers; because of this, it is not possible to talk about the successor or predecessor of a real number.)

A way to classify simple data types is as either standard or programmer defined. All the simple types with which you are familiar are standard data types; this means that they are built-in parts of Turbo Pascal with predefined identifiers. Pascal also gives you the ability to define simple data types to your own specifications and assign identifiers to those data types. You have already encountered one of these programmer-defined data types in a different context: the subrange. Recall that a subrange is based on one of the ordinal data types and is expressed by writing the beginning value, two periods, and the ending value. (For example, 1..10 is a subrange based on type Integer and 'a'..'z' is a subrange based on type Char.) Another user-defined data type is the enumerated type. In this type, you list explicitly (that is, you enumerate) all instances of the data. For example, the standard data type Boolean is actually an enumerated type consisting of (False, True). Programmer-defined enumerated types are described in detail in this chapter.

Let us leave the simple types for a moment and turn our attention to other basic categories of types. One with which you are already familiar is the string type. This type is a nonstandard feature of Turbo Pascal that enables a program to store up to 255 characters in a variable. Chapter 8 covers strings in greater detail than has been previously presented.

Another large category of types is the structured types. The term *structured* means that each of these types is based on an organized collection of data items of other types. For example, a *set* is a group of data items of a specified ordinal type such as Integer or Char. Thus, you can create a set of Integers or a set of characters. Sets are discussed later in this chapter. An *array* is a sequence of data items of a particular type that can be accessed by specifying one or more subscripts. Arrays are discussed in Chapter 9. A *record* is a grouping of data of various types that can be processed as a single unit. A *file* is a grouping of data stored externally to the program (usually on disk, but, as we have seen, files can also be assigned to the keyboard, the screen, and the printer). We have already discussed Text files, which are files based on character sequences that are separated from one another by the EOL sequence. Records and files based on other types of data are discussed in Chapter 11. *Objects* are the newest data type in Turbo Pascal; they were first supported in Turbo Pascal 5.5. An object is based on a collection of data items of various types, together with procedures and functions that process the data. Objects are discussed in Chapter 15.

The last major classification of data types is the pointer. A pointer is a data item that points to (that is, contains the address of) a location in memory. Pointers are often used to define specialized data structures that are useful for carrying out a variety of operations of data. Pointers are discussed in Chapter 12.

As you can see, much of the remainder of this book is concerned with the characteristics and uses of various data types. At this point, you should have a general knowledge of the available data types and the vocabulary used to describe them. We will use this vocabulary quite frequently in the remainder of the text.

7.2 DATA TYPE BYTE: A NONSTANDARD FEATURE OF TURBO PASCAL

In computer terminology, the word **byte** refers to the basic unit of storage in a computer. A byte is made up of 8 bits (binary 1's and 0's). We have already seen the relationship between character data and the byte. Each character occupies 1 byte and is represented by an ASCII code. In Turbo Pascal, it is possible to use a byte to store numbers as well as characters. This data type is called *Byte*; the range of values that can be represented in Byte data is from 0 to 255. This represents the decimal value of all the bit combinations from 00000000_2 to 11111111_2. (Data type Byte is not implemented in standard Pascal.)

For example, the following program segment would declare the variables X to Y to be of type Byte:

```
var
     X, Y : Byte;
```

These variables could take on any value in the range 0 to 255. Data-type Byte is compatible with Integer in all cases, *except* when data are being passed as parameters. Thus, the variables X and Y could be used in assignment statements or arithmetic expressions in exactly the same way as Integer variables would be used. For example, if Z is an Integer variable, the following statements would be valid:

```
Z := X + Y;
X := Z;
Y := 2 * Z + Y div 2;
```

In all these statements, X and Y are used exactly as they would have been had they been declared as type Integer.

Data types Byte and Integer are not compatible when data are passed as parameters. For example, the following program segment would be invalid:

```
program Example (Input, Output);
var
        X : Byte;
        .
        .
        .
{*****************************************************************}
        procedure P(Z: Integer);
        .
        .
        .
{*****************************************************************}
begin                                    Data-type mismatch; procedure expects
        .                                the parameter to be of type Integer.
        .
        .
        P(X);
        .
        .
        .

end.
```

The data type Byte is useful when you want to increase the efficiency of memory utilization. If the range of values that a variable will take on is from 0 to 255, why declare the variable to be of type Integer, which will occupy 2 bytes of memory? Such a variable can be declared to be of type Byte and thereby occupy only 1 byte of memory. You probably would never notice the saving of a single byte of memory, but if a large number of variables are involved (such as when a large array is being created), the differences in memory requirements may be substantial and significant. In such a case, the use of Byte data type could make the difference between a program that is feasible on a given computer and one that is not feasible because it requires more memory than is available on the system. In Turbo Pascal, no more than 64k bytes can be reserved for variables, so such issues are important for some applications. (Additional nonstandard data types available in Turbo Pascal, are described in Appendix F.)

7.3   ENUMERATED DATA TYPES

In the same way that you can declare identifiers for constants and variables, Pascal allows you to declare an identifier for a data type. The identifiers thus declared can then be used in the same way that standard data types are used. That is, when a variable is declared, the type specification can be either a standard data type or a data type that the programmer has declared. The general form of the **type declaration** is as follows:

```
type
     identifier = type;
     .
     .
     .
```

When present in a program segment, type declarations usually precede constant and variable declarations. In a type declaration, the specification of *type* can be one of the standard data types, but more often it will be a programmer-defined data type. In this section, we will describe one of the options you have in defining a data type—the enumerated data type.

Often, it is useful to restrict the values that a variable can assume to some well-defined set. For example, if a variable is to represent the day of a week, there are seven possible values for the variable—one for each day of the week. Sometimes such variables are assigned a numeric code, such as 1 for Sunday, 2 for Monday, and so forth. This approach works fine as long as the value of the variable stays in the range 1 to 7 and the programmer remembers the rule used to make the association between the day of the week and the value of the variable. On the other hand, if it were possible to define a variable that could take on only the values Sunday, Monday, Tuesday, etc., both potential problems with the numeric coding scheme would be solved: There would only be seven possible values for the variable, and the meaning of each value would be explicitly stated.

Pascal makes it possible to create a variable that meets the requirements just outlined. To do this, you first declare a data type and list all the possible values that will be associated with a variable of that type. This is called an **enumerated data type**. The word *enumerated* is derived from *numbered*, which implies that there are a finite number of values and that they can be explicitly ordered from smallest to largest. To declare an enumerated data type, you decide on an appropriate identifier for the type and, in the type declaration, specify *type* as a list of the possible values enclosed in parentheses and separated by commas. The values thus defined are actually identifiers and hence are *not* enclosed in quotes. For example, to declare a data type called DayOfWeek, the following type declaration could be written:

```
type
     DayOfWeek = (Sunday, Monday, Tuesday, Wednesday,
                  Thursday, Friday, Saturday);
```

With this declaration in place, it is now possible to declare variables with this data type. For example, the following program segment would declare variables WeekDay and WeekEndDay to be of type DayOfWeek:

```
var
     WeekDay, WeekEndDay : DayOfWeek;
```

The program can now process the variables WeekDay and WeekEndDay in many of the ways that other variables are processed. For example, the variables can be used in assignment statements. The following statements would assign the value Monday to WeekDay and Saturday to WeekEndDay:

```
WeekDay := Monday;
WeekEndDay := Saturday;
```

In this context, Monday and Saturday are constants of data type DayOfWeek. Notice that these constants are not character strings, so that the following statements are invalid:

```
WeekDay := 'Monday';
WeekEndDay := 'Saturday';
```

The only possible values that these two variables can take on are contained in the list of identifiers given when the data type DayOfWeek was defined.

An enumerated data type is a scalar type, which means that the values are ordered. The ordering of the values is actually given when the data type is defined. In the case of data type DayOfWeek, the ordering is

```
Sunday < Monday < Tuesday < Wednesday < Thursday < Friday < Saturday
```

Thus, assuming that the value of WeekDay is Monday and the value of WeekEndDay is Saturday, the relation

```
WeekDay > WeekEndDay
```

is False. On the other hand, the compound condition

```
(WeekEndDay = Saturday) or (WeekEndDay = Sunday)
```

is True.

An enumerated data type is also an ordinal data type. This means that there is a successor-predecessor relationship defined for the values of this type. Such a relationship is defined explicitly when the data type is defined. For example, in the case of the data type DayOfWeek, the first element is Sunday, its successor is Monday, and so forth. Because of this relationship, an enumerated data type may be used where any other ordinal data type is valid. One of these places is in a for statement. For example, the following statement would generate the values Monday, Tuesday, . . . , Friday:

```
for Weekday := Monday to Friday do
    . . . ;
```

Similarly, the following statement would generate the sequence of values Friday, Thursday, . . . , Tuesday:

```
for Weekday := Friday downto Tuesday do
    . . . ;
```

Although a program can use a variable with an enumerated data type in many ways, it cannot use such a variable in an arithmetic expression or directly in an input or output operation. Thus, the following statements would be invalid:

```
Readln (WeekDay);
Weekday := Weekday + 1;
Writeln (WeekDay);
```

Input and output of data stored in the program as variables with an enumerated data type must be accomplished indirectly. For example, suppose the program user is directed to enter the day of the week as a numeric code with value 1 through 7. The program can then assign an appropriate value to the variable WeekDay using the following program segment (assume that the variable DayNumber is of type Byte or Integer):

```
Readln (DayNumber);
case DayNumber or
        1 :  WeekDay := Sunday;
        2 :  WeekDay := Monday;
        3 :  WeekDay := Tuesday;
        4 :  WeekDay := Wednesday;
        5 :  WeekDay := Thursday;
        6 :  WeekDay := Friday;
        7 :  WeekDay := Saturday
    else
        Writeln ('Invalid day number')
end    {case}
```

In order to accomplish output for a variable with an enumerated data type, a similar procedure is required:

```
case WeekDay of
    Sunday      : Writeln('Sunday');
    Monday      : Writeln('Monday');
    Tuesday     : Writeln('Tuesday');
    Wednesday   : Writeln('Wednesday');
    Thursday    : Writeln('Thursday');
    Friday      : Writeln('Friday');
    Saturday    : Writeln('Saturday')
end; {case}
```

Note in the preceding program segment that it is not necessary to include an else clause, because all the possible values of the variable WeekDay have been listed.

At this point, you are probably wondering about the ultimate value of an enumerated data type, given the problems associated with input and output. Enumerated data types are valuable for two reasons:

1. *Program readability.* Because the value of an enumerated data type does not depend on remembering some coding scheme, the meaning of the value of a variable is

more explicit. This can make a great contribution to the readability of a program. It is much clearer to write

```
if WeekDay; = Monday then
    . . . ;
```

than to write the logically equivalent

```
if DayNumber = 2 then
    . . . ;
```

2. *Program maintainability.* Of course, the underlying code must be present in the program at some point—usually as part of the input routine when a coded value is used to assign the value to the variable with the enumerated data type, but the coding scheme does not need to be repeated each time the data is referenced. This can make a great contribution to the maintainability of a program because, if the coding scheme changes, it is necessary to change only the input (and perhaps the output) procedure. The rest of the program can continue to function as before because it has been insulated from the actual codes used in the data being processed.

As an example of this latter point, consider a program that must process a code representing a person's sex. Let us assume that we instruct the user to enter the character M to represent male and F to represent female. The following program makes use of an enumerated data type Sexes with two possible values: Male and Female. A variable SexOfClient is defined to be of data type Sexes. A Char variable SexCode is used as an input variable. Based on the value of SexCode, an appropriate value is assigned to the variable SexOfClient. In subsequent processing of the data, all references to SexCode is made through the variable SexOfClient:

```
program Sample (Input, Output);
type
    Sexes = (Male, Female);
var
    SexCode : Char;
    SexOfClient : Sexes;
    .
    .
    .
begin
    .
    .
    .
    repeat
        Write ('Enter sex code (M)ale or (F)emale ');
        Readln (SexCode);
        if SexCode = 'M' then
            SexOfClient := Male
```

```
            else if SexCode = 'F' then
                  SexOfClient := Female
            else
                  Writeln ('Invalid Sex Code')
      until (SexCode = 'M') or (SexCode = 'F');
         .
         .
         .
      if SexOfClient = Male then
            . . . ;
         .
         .
         .
   end.
```

Now let us assume that at some later time the program user wishes to change the code used for entering sex to upper- or lowercase letters, or perhaps change to a numeric code, such as 1 for female and 2 for male. In either case, the program must be modified, but the modification is restricted to the input procedure. The remainder of the program (which processes the meaning of the data rather than the actual code used to represent the data) can remain unchanged. This means that it is likely that the program modification will be accomplished more quickly and with less of a likelihood for error than would otherwise be the case. (As programs become longer, the task of ferreting out all instances of the usage of the coded meaning of a variable becomes more of a problem, and the likelihood of overlooking one or more instances increases.)

7.3.1   *Time Out*

1. Modify the input procedure of program Sample shown earlier to allow the user to enter upper- or lowercase letters for the sex code.

Consider the following program segment in answering Questions 2–5:

```
type
      Suit = (Club, Diamond, Heart, Spade);
var
      Card : Suit;
```

2. List the constants defined for data type Suit.
3. Which of the following assignment statements are valid?
   (a) `Card := Suit;`
   (b) `Suit := Card;`
   (c) `Card := Diamond;`
   (d) `Card := 'Club';`
   (e) `Card := Card - 1;`

4. Assume that the value of Card is Heart. Evaluate each of the following expressions:
   (a) `Card > Diamond`
   (b) `Card <= Spade`
   (c) `(Card = Club)` **or** `(Card = Heart)`
5. What values of Card will be generated by each of the following?
   (a) for `Card := Club` **to** `Heart` **do**

        `. . . ;`

   (b) for `Card :=` `Spade` **downto** `Club` **do**

        `. . . ;`
6. Define a data type called Seasons that will allow you to declare a variable with one of four values representing the seasons of the year.

Consider the following program segment in answering questions 7 and 8:

```
type
      MakerOfCar = (GeneralMotors, Ford, Chrysler, Toyota,
                       Nissan, BMW, Volkswagen);
var
      Car : MakerOfCar;
      CarCode : Char;
```

7. Write a program segment allowing the user to enter a value for CarCode and assigning an appropriate value to the variable Car. Detect invalid values for CarCode.
8. Write a program segment to output an appropriate character string based on the value of the variable Car.

7.3.2.   A Complete Example

Let us turn to Program 5b, which is used to compute the difference between two dates, for an example of the use of an enumerated data type. Recall that this program allows the user to enter two dates, and it computes the difference between them in days. The program is constructed around a procedure called ComputeJulianDate, which is used to compute the Julian date for each of the two dates so that the difference can be computed. This procedure imports Integer values called CalendarMonth and CalendarDay and exports the Boolean variable ValidDate and the Integer variable JulianDate. CalendarMonth is an example of a coded value: 1 represents January, 2 represents February, and so forth. It would be sensible to declare an enumerated data type that could take on values representing the months of the year and convert the value in CalendarMonth to a variable of the enumerated data type. Subsequent processing of the data could then be based on the value of the new variable.

     An alternative version of the procedure ComputeJulianDate from Program 5b is contained in Program 7a, shown in Figure 7.2, with the corresponding data-flow diagram shown in Figure 7.3. The declaration part of ComputeJulianDate creates the data type MonthNameType, which takes on values from the list of three-character abbreviations of the month names. A variable called Month is declared to have type MonthNameType. This

```
program P7a (Input, Output);
uses Crt;
{Program to compute the difference between two dates in the
      same year. This version of the program illustrates the use
      of an enumerated data type in the procedure ComputeJulianDate.}
      .
      .
      .
      procedure ComputeJulianDate (CalendarMonth,
                                   CalendarDay : Integer;
                           var ValidDate    : Boolean;
                           var JulianDate   : Integer);
      {Procedure to compute the Julian Date}
      type
          MonthNameType = (Jan, Feb, Mar, Apr, May, Jun, Jul,
                           Aug, Sep, Oct, Nov, Dec);
      var
          Month : MonthNameType;
      {----------------------------------------------------------------}
          procedure ValidateMonth (MonthNumber : Integer;
                              var ValidMonth : Boolean;
                              var NameOfMonth : MonthNameType);
          {Procedure to determine whether a month is valid and convert
               the month number to month name}
          begin    {ValidateMonth}
              ValidMonth := (MonthNumber >= 1) and (MonthNumber <= 12);
              case MonthNumber of
                      1  : NameOfMonth := Jan;
                      2  : NameOfMonth := Feb;
                      3  : NameOfMonth := Mar;
                      4  : NameOfMonth := Apr;
                      5  : NameOfMonth := May;
                      6  : NameOfMonth := Jun;
                      7  : NameOfMonth := Jul;
                      8  : NameOfMonth := Aug;
                      9  : NameOfMonth := Sep;
                      10 : NameOfMonth := Oct;
                      11 : NameOfMonth := Nov;
                      12 : NameOfMonth := Dec
                    else
                          Writeln('Invalid Month Number : ',MonthNumber)
              end    {case}
          end;     {ValidateMonth}
      {----------------------------------------------------------------}
          procedure ValidateDay (Month : MonthNameType;
                                 Day : Integer;
                            var ValidDay : Boolean);
          {Procedure to validate day of a month}
          var
              NumberDays : Integer;
          begin  {ValidateDay}
              case Month of
                  Feb                  : NumberDays := 28;
                  Sep, Apr, Jun, Nov : NumberDays := 30;
                  else
                                        NumberDays := 31
              end;    {case}
              ValidDay := (Day >= 1) and (Day <= NumberDays);
              if not ValidDay then
                  Writeln ('Invalid Day Number : ', Day)
          end;   {ValidateDay}
      {----------------------------------------------------------------}
```

Figure 7.2(a) Program 7a: Declaration part showing use of an enumerated data type (part 1 of 2 parts).

```
    begin    {ComputeJulianDate}
        ValidateMonth (CalendarMonth, ValidDate, Month);
        if ValidDate then
            ValidateDay (Month, CalendarDay, ValidDate);
        if ValidDate then
            begin
                case Month of
                    Jan  : JulianDate := 0;
                    Feb  : JulianDate := 31;
                    Mar  : JulianDate := 59;
                    Apr  : JulianDate := 90;
                    May  : JulianDate := 120;
                    Jun  : JulianDate := 151;
                    Jul  : JulianDate := 181;
                    Aug  : JulianDate := 212;
                    Sep  : JulianDate := 243;
                    Oct  : JulianDate := 273;
                    Nov  : JulianDate := 304;
                    Dec  : JulianDate := 334
                end;  {case}
                JulianDate := JulianDate + CalendarDay;
            end  {if}
    end;  {ComputeJulianDate}
    .
    .
    .
end.  {Main Program}
```

Figure 7.2(b) Program 7a: Statement part (part 2 of 2 parts).

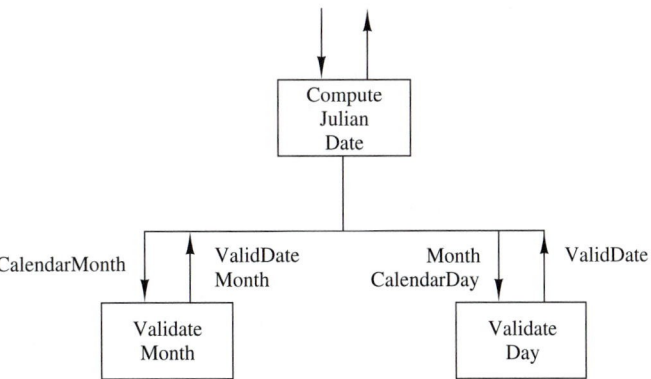

Figure 7.3 Data-flow diagram for procedure compute JulianDate in Program 7a.

variable will be used to import the name of the month from the procedure ValidateMonth and export it to the procedure ValidateDay; it will also be used in the final computation of the Julian date.

The procedure ValidateMonth imports an Integer value MonthNumber and exports a Boolean variable ValidMonth and a variable of type MonthNameType called Name-OfMonth. If the month is valid—i.e., if the value of MonthNumber is in the range of 1 to

12—then the procedure returns a value True in ValidMonth and places the appropriate value in NameOfMonth, using the case statement to select which of the values to place there.

The procedure ValidateDay imports a value called Month of type MonthNameType and the integer value Day. It exports the Boolean variable ValidDay. By means of a case statement, this procedure uses the value contained in Month to compute the maximum number of days that are valid for a given month:

```
case Month of
      Feb                     : NumberDays := 28;
      Sep, Apr, Jun, Nov : NumberDays := 30;
      else
            NumberDays :=  31
end; {case}
```

This program segment is much more readable and understandable than the equivalent code that was used in the original version of the program.

The content of the variable Month is also used in the computation of the Julian date in the statement part of the procedure. The value of Month is used instead of the month number to select the appropriate value for the variable JulianDate. This makes the case statement used for this purpose more understandable and contributes to making the procedure seem less technical and easier to read.

Note that MonthNameType is local to the procedure ComputeJulianDate; it would not be defined in the main program. MonthNameType is, however, defined within the two subordinate procedures ValidateMonth and ValidateDay. This data type is used freely within these procedures in much the same way as any standard data type would be used. For example, the variable parameter NameOfMonth in the procedure ValidateMonth is of type MonthNameType, and the value parameter Month in the procedure ValidateDay is of type MonthNameType.

7.3.3   Unnamed Enumerated Data Types

In all the examples of enumerated data types that we have presented thus far, we have first declared the type in the type declaration and thereafter referred to the type using an identifier. Although this is a common practice, it is not absolutely necessary; an enumerated data type can be defined directly in the variable declaration, as is illustrated in Program 7b, shown in Figure 7.4. In this program, variable X can take on values A and B and therefore is of an (unnamed) enumerated data type.

A fundamental restriction on a variable with an **unnamed enumerated data type** is that it cannot be passed to a procedure as a parameter. In a procedure parameter list, the data type of each parameter *must* be specified as an identifier; thus, a specification such as

```
procedure P ( Y : (A, B) ) ;
```

is invalid. This means that if a variable with an enumerated data type is to be passed to a procedure, it must have a named data type, as in Program 7c, which is shown in Figure 7.5.

```
program P7b;
{Program illustrates the declaration of an unnamed enumerated
        data type}
var
     X : (A, B);
begin
     X := A
end.
```

Figure 7.4 Program 7b: Declaration of an unnamed (anonymous) enumerated data type.

```
program P7c;
{Program illustrates a named enumerated type}
type
     T = (A, B);
var
     X : T;
{********************************************************}
     procedure P (Y : T);
     begin
     end;
{********************************************************}
begin    {Main Program}
     X := A;
     P (X)
end.     {Main Program}
```

Figure 7.5 Program 7c: Example of a named enumerated data type.

Because of this restriction on the use of an unnamed enumerated data type, it is advisable to use the type declaration to declare a name for the data type any time enumerated data types are used in a program. Unnamed types are sometimes referred to as *anonymous* types.

7.3.4   *Time Out*

1. Modify Program 4h to make use of variables with enumerated data types to represent the options for figure and calculation.

7.4   SUBRANGE DATA TYPES

Another type of programmer-defined data type is the **subrange**. A subrange can be formed from any ordinal data type and is expressed by writing the first value in the range, two periods, and the last value in the range. (A basic restriction is that the first value must be less than or equal to the last value.) The ordinal data types are Byte, Boolean, Char, Integer, and enumerated data types. For example, a subrange of the Integers from 1 to 10 is written as 1..10; a subrange of all capital letters is written as 'A'..'Z'. Enumerated data types are also ordinal and therefore can be used in a subrange. For example, suppose the following type declaration is part of a program:

```
type
     CardName = (Two, Three, Four, Five, Six, Seven,
                 Eight, Nine, Ten, Jack, Queen, King, Ace);
```

Subranges of base type CardName include Five .. Nine, Queen .. Ace, and so forth.

We have seen that subranges can be useful in simplifying the case statement. Another potential use for a subrange is in the specification of a data type. That is, it is possible to specify either a named or unnamed data type as a subrange of another data type. For example, suppose there is a variable in a program that can take on only the values 'A', 'B', 'C', 'D', 'E', and 'F'. Then you could declare that variable in the variable declaration section as

```
var
     X : 'A'..'F';
```

The base type of the variable X would be Char; X would be constrained, however, to have values only in the range 'A' through 'F'. The variable X would be compatible with other Char variables and operations on Char data. For example, you could use X as the parameter for a procedure that has data type Char specified as the data type of the associated formal parameter.

Another option is to declare a named data type using the subrange. For example, suppose there are variables Y and Z that can take on values 1 through 5. A way to specify these variables would be

```
type
     T = 1..5;
var
     Y, Z : T;
```

The base type for a variable of type T is Integer, which means that these variables are compatible with operations on Integers, including usage as a parameter in a procedure that has the associated formal parameter declared as type Integer.

As noted earlier, a subrange of an enumerated data type can also be written. Consider the following example:

```
type
     MonthNameType = (Jan, Feb, Mar, Apr, May, Jun,
                      Jul, Aug, Sep, Oct, Nov, Dec);
     SummerMonthName = Jun..Aug;
var
     X : MonthNameType;
     Y : SummerMonthName;
```

In this program, the variable X is of type MonthNameType, and the variable Y is of type SummerMonthName. This means that X and Y are compatible, since they have the same base type, but Y can take on only the values Jun, Jul, and Aug.

We have said that a variable with a subrange data type is constrained to have its value lie within the specified range. In Turbo Pascal, this is actually an option that the programmer can control. The concept is called **range checking**. When range checking is active, any attempt to assign a value to a variable that is outside the range specified in its data type results in an execution-time error. The program is terminated, and an appropriated error message is displayed. When range checking is inactive, a variable with a subrange data type is treated just like any other variable of the base type: No check is made on values assigned to the variable, and the program will continue as usual if a value outside the prescribed range is assigned to the variable.

The compiler option that governs range checking is the R option. In order to activate range checking, place the statement {R+} or (*R+*) in your program. In order to deactivate range checking, place the statement {$R−} or (*$R−*) in the program. For example, Program 7d, shown in Figure 7.6, produces the error message depicted in Figure 7.7 because of the attempt to assign an inappropriate value to the variable Y. Range checking can be turned on and off as many times as desired in a program, as is illustrated by Program 7e, shown in Figure 7.8. In this case, range checking is active for the first two statements, which assign appropriate values to the variables. Range checking is then turned off prior to the last statement, which assigns an inappropriate value to the variable Y; because range checking is inactive at this point, the program runs with no error message.

Note, however, that range checking, as specified by the R compiler option, affects the code that the compiler generates; the option cannot be turned on or off during the actual execution of the program.

Beginning programmers are often confused about when to use subrange data types. In Turbo Pascal, such data types are essentially ignored by the compiler unless the programmer invokes range checking, so it might be suggested that subranges can be safely ignored in writing programs. Indeed, it is possible to write any desired program without a subrange data type; however, the data type does have a contribution to make to the process of writing and debugging programs. The basic value of subrange data types is to make the system detect errors that would otherwise show up as logical errors in a program. For

```
program P7d;
{Program illustrates active range checking}
type
        MonthNameType = (Jan, Feb, Mar, Apr, May, Jun,
                         Jul, Aug, Sep, Oct, Nov, Dec);
        SummerMonthNameType = Jun..Aug;
var
        X : MonthNameType;
        Y : SummerMonthNameType;
begin
        {$R+}         {Activate range checking}
        X := Jan;
        Y := X
end.
```

Figure 7.6 Program 7d: Example of active range checking.

Figure 7.7 Execution of Program 7d showing range check error.

```
program P7e;
{Program illustrates activating and deactivating range checking}
type
        MonthNameType = (Jan, Feb, Mar, Apr, May, Jun,
                           Jul, Aug, Sep, Oct, Nov, Dec);
        SummerMonthNameType = Jun..Aug;
var
        X : MonthNameType;
        Y : SummerMonthNameType;
begin
        {$R+}      {Activate range checking}
        X := Jan;
        Y := Jun;
        {$R-}      {Deactivate range checking}
        Y := X
end.
```

Figure 7.8 Program 7e: Example of activating and deactivating range checking.

example, if a variable MonthNumber is used in the program, and by some means it takes on the value 13, this is an error that will be reflected in some way in the output produced by the program. If MonthNumber is defined as a subrange data type, such as

```
var
        MonthNumber : 1..12;
```

and if range checking is active, then program execution will be terminated at the point at which the value of MonthNumber falls outside the allowable range. The cursor will then be positioned at the point in the program where the error occurred. This makes it easier to spot the cause of the error than if we wait for the error to show up in some other way (which may necessitate extensive analysis of the program to determine the cause of the error).

Thus, the basic value of subrange data types is in making the debugging process easier. One often-repeated bit of advice to programmers is to activate range checking during the debugging process and then deactivate it for the production version of the program. One reason for this advice is that range checking consumes time and space. It takes time for the system to check each value assigned to a subrange type variable; a program that involves range checking will run more slowly than a program that does not. The program that is generated is larger if range checking is invoked because of the extra instructions that must be generated to take care of the required testing.

Beginning programmers are sometimes tempted to substitute subrange type variables and range checking for data validation. For example, if a particular input value must be in the range 'a' through 'e', it is possible (but not desirable) to proceed as shown in the following program segment:

```
var
     Data : 'a'..'e';
begin
     {R+}
     .
     .
     .
     Write ('Enter Data (a..e) ');
     Readln (Data);
     .
     .
     .
end.
```

The trouble with this approach is that if the user enters any value other than 'a' through 'e', the program will terminate, and the user will have no opportunity to enter the data again. Such a program is extremely user unfriendly. (One might even call it user hostile.) A much better approach is shown in the following program segment:

```
type
     FirstLetters = 'a'..'e';
var
     Data : FirstLetters;
{$R+}
{ ******************************************************************}
     procedure GetData (var ValidData : FirstLetters);
     var
          InputCharacter : Char;
     begin     {GetData}
          repeat
               Write ('Enter Data (a..e) ');
               Readln (InputCharacter);
               case InputCharacter of
                    'a'..'e' : ValidData := InputCharacter;
                         else
                              Writeln ('Invalid Data')
               end {case}
          until (Data = 'a') or (Data = 'b') or (Data = 'c') or
               (Data = 'd') or (Data = 'e')
     end;     {GetData}
{ ******************************************************************}
```

```
begin {Main Program}
    .
    .
    .
    GetData (Data);
    .
    .
    .
end.    {Main Program}
```

After data entry is completed, the program can process the content of Data. The primary advantage to this scheme is that it provides an extra check on the internal logic of the program. Any attempt to assign a value to Data that is outside the allowable range will result in an execution-time error, and the source of the error will be immediately apparent.

Aside from the value of subrange data type for program debugging, there is an additional advantage in improving the readability and the maintainability of a program. When a reader encounters a variable declared with a subrange data type, the intended range of values for that variable is immediately apparent. This improves the maintainability of the program because the programmer who is charged with making changes to the program has a clearer idea of the intended function of such variables.

7.4.1 Time Out

Use the following program segment in answering questions 1–3:

```
type
    ProgrammingLanguage = (Assembler, Fortran, COBOL,
                            Basic, Pascal, C);
    IntegerRange = 5..9;
    FirstHalf = 'A'..'M';
var
    Language : Fortran..Pascal;
    X : IntegerRange;
    Y : FirstHalf;
```

1. What is the base type for IntegerRange? for FirstHalf?
2. List the values that are valid for the variables Language, X, and Y.
3. What will happen when the following statement is executed? What determines the outcome of the statement?

```
X := 10;
```

4. Modify Program 4g to use a subrange data type for the variable TestScore. (Restrict the values to 0 through 100.) Write a procedure to validate the data entered by the user. The value of TestScore should be exported from the procedure to the main program. Use the procedure GetData as a model.

7.5   ORDINAL FUNCTIONS: ORD, PRED, AND SUCC

Recall that we defined the term ordinal as denoting a type of data in which there was a natural predecessor-successor relationship among the data elements. The ordinal data types are Byte, Integer, Char, Boolean, and enumerated data types. In each case, there is a next element and a previous element for all data items except the smallest (the first one) and the largest (the last one). Pascal provides three functions that allow the program to make use of the ordered nature of ordinal data: **Ord**, which returns an Integer value representing the position of an ordinal value relative to other data items of the same type; **Pred**, which returns the predecessor of its argument; and **Succ**, which returns the successor of its argument.

The function Ord requires one argument, which can be of any ordinal data type (any scalar type except Real). The value returned by the function is of type Integer and represents the position of the argument in the range of values possible for that data type. For example, consider the data type MonthNameType, defined as

```
type
    MonthNameType =  (Jan, Feb, Mar, Apr, May, Jun,
                      Jul, Aug, Sep, Oct, Nov, Dec);
```

The value of Ord (Jan) is 0, the value of Ord (Feb) is 1, the value of Ord (Mar) is 2, and so on. (The ordinal value of the first element of an enumerated data type is always 0. This may seem odd at first, but you will find in working with computers that we often begin counting with 0.) One very practical way to use the Ord function with an enumerated data type is in writing out the value of a variable for diagnostic output. We know that a variable of type MonthNameType cannot be written directly and that it takes a fairly elaborate procedure to translate the identifier into a character string for output purposes. Suppose that you have a variable Month of type MonthNameType. Then the following statement would be sufficient for diagnostic purposes to allow you to examine the value of Month:

```
Writeln ('Month = ',Ord(Month));
```

For example, if the value of Month is Jan, the output will be Month = 0, which is sufficient for the purpose at hand.

The ordinal value of a character is equivalent to the value of the ASCII code used to represent the character, as shown in Appendix D. For example, the value of Ord ('A') is 65, and the value of Ord (' ') is 32. Consider the following coding segment, assuming that C is a variable of type Char:

```
for C := 'A' to 'Z' do
    Writeln (Ord(C));
```

The output would be a list of numbers from 65 through 90.

The Boolean values are False and True, with False < True. Thus, the value of Ord (False) is 0 and the value of Ord(True) is 1.

The Ord function is most often used with character, Boolean, and enumerated data types, but it can be used with Byte and Integer data as well, since they are ordinal data types. Thus, if Z is a variable of type Byte with value 12, the value of Ord (Z) is 12, but it is of type Integer. (Since Byte and Integer are compatible, the distinction is rarely of importance.) If the argument of the Ord function is of type Integer, the value returned is the same as the value of the argument.

Sometimes it is useful to access the successor or predecessor of a particular ordinal value. The function Succ returns the successor of its argument, whereas the function Pred returns the predecessor of its argument. The value returned always has the same type as the argument. For example, assuming data type MonthNameType defined earlier, the value of Pred (Feb) is Jan and the value of Succ (Jan) is Feb. The function Pred returns an invalid value if the argument is the lowest valued (the first) of its type. Similarly, the function Succ returns an invalid value if its argument is the highest valued (the last) of its type. For example, if range checking is active, then the following statement will result in an execution-time error:

```
Month := Succ (Dec);
```

If range checking is not active, then this statement will place the value 12 into Month, a value that does not correspond to any of the enumerated values specified for a variable of type MonthNameType!

For data types Integer and Byte, the functions Succ and Pred are equivalent to adding 1 and subtracting 1, respectively. For example, the value of Succ (2) is $2 + 1$, and the value of Pred (2) is $2 - 1$.

For data type Char, the successor and predecessor of a value are defined by the ASCII code. For example, the value of Succ ('B') is 'C', and the value of Pred ('B') is 'A'. The successor is found by adding 1 to the value of ASCII code for a character, and the predecessor is found by subtracting 1.

In general, if X is any ordinal value, Ord (Succ (X)) = Ord (X) + 1, whereas Ord(Pred (X)) = Ord (X) − 1. For example, recall that Ord ('A') = 65. By this property, the ordinal value of the successor of 'A' should be $65 + 1 = 66$. As a check, the value of Succ ('A') is 'B', and the value of Ord ('B') is indeed 66.

7.5.1 Time Out

What is the value of each of the following expressions, assuming the following declarations?

```
type
    ProgrammingLanguage = (Assembler, Fortran,
                           COBOL, Basic, Pascal, C);
```

1. Ord (COBOL)

2. Pred (Pascal)

3. `Succ (Basic)`

4. `Ord ('Z')`

5. `Succ ('E')`

6. `Ord (True)`

7. `Ord (Succ (Assembler))`

8. `Ord (Pred (C))`

7.6   TYPE CONVERSION

Pascal is often described as a strongly typed language. This means that the language generally requires that constants and variables have the same (or compatible) data types in order to be able to perform arithmetic operations, assignment, and parameter passing. Sometimes these requirements can present obstacles to writing logical and efficient programs. For this reason, you may need to convert data from one type to another.

We have already discussed one form of type conversion: The **Ord function** computes an Integer value for an ordinal data item. Three other functions that perform related operations are Round, which rounds a Real value to the nearest Integer, Trunc, which truncates the decimal part of a Real value, and Chr, which converts an Integer value to the associated character. Additionally, there is a nonstandard general type-conversion facility in Turbo Pascal that allows you to convert from any scalar type (except Real) to another scalar type, based on the ordinal values of the data items.

The **Round function** accepts a Real parameter and returns an Integer value that has been rounded to the nearest whole number. For example, the value of Round (1.6) is 2, the value of Round (−1.2) is −1, and the value of Round (2.5) is 3. The technique used in rounding a positive number is to add 0.5 to it and then truncate (or cut off) the decimal part of the sum. To round a negative number, the system adds −0.5 to it and then truncates the decimal portion of the sum.

The **Trunc function** accepts a Real parameter and returns an Integer value that is obtained by truncating the decimal part of the number. For example, the value of Trunc (1.6) is 1, the value of Trunc (−1.2) is −1, and the value of Trunc (2.5) is 2.

The **Chr function** returns a Char value based on the value of its Integer parameter; the value of the function is derived from the ASCII value of the code used to represent the character. For example, Chr (65) has value 'A' because the value of the ASCII code used to represent 'A' is 65 (see Appendix D). Note that Chr and Ord perform inverse functions on Char data. Thus, the value of Ord ('Z') is 90, and Chr (90) has the value 'Z'. Using these two functions, you can convert freely between character data and related Integer values of the ASCII code. For example, Ord (Chr (65)) is 65, and Chr (Ord ('A')) is 'A'.

These functions represent the limit of type conversion supported by standard Pascal. In order to facilitate writing efficient programs, Turbo Pascal supports a nonstandard retyping facility called **value typecasting** that can be used to convert from any ordinal type to any other. The standard types that can be used for this purpose are Integer, Byte, Char, and Boolean. Enumerated data types with a declared identifier can also be used. The syntax for value typecasting is similar to a function reference:

```
type (scalar-value)
```

The value returned is of type *type* and has the same ordinal value as *scalar-value*. For example, when *type* is Char and *scalar-value* is of type Integer, this facility performs exactly the same function as the Chr function described before. Thus, Char (65) has the value 'A' because the ordinal value of the argument is 65 and the ordinal value of 'A' is 65. The typecasting feature is, of course, much more powerful than any single function because it allows you to transfer from any type to any other type.

Suppose that the following declaration is part of a program segment:

```
type
    MonthNameType = (Jan, Feb, Mar, Apr, May, Jun,
                     Jul, Aug, Sep, Oct, Nov, Dec);
    CapitalLetter = 'A'..'Z';
```

Then the following examples make use of value typecasting as shown:

Expression	Value	Comment
MonthNameType(1)	Feb	The ordinal value of Feb is 1.
Integer('A')	65	The ordinal value of 'A' is 65.
CapitalLetter(65)	'A'	When a type is declared using a subrange, the ordinal values of the elements are derived from the ordinal values of the base type—Char in this case.
Boolean(1)	True	Ord(True) is 1.
Byte(False)	0	Ord(False) is 0.

The typecasting feature is often useful in reducing the length of a program. For example, consider the procedure ValidateMonth in the revised version of the program to compute the Julian date, as shown in Figure 7.2(a). In this procedure, the value of the variable MonthNumber is used to assign a value to the variable NameOfMonth, which is of type MonthNameType. The computation requires a relatively complicated case statement:

```
case MonthNumber of
    1  : NameOfMonth := Jan;
    2  : NameOfMonth := Feb;
    .
    .
    .
    12 : NameOfMonth := Dec
    . . . ;
```

```
program P7f (Input, Output);
{Program to compute the difference between two dates in the
      same year.  This version of the program illustrates the use
      of typecasting in procedure ValidateDate.}
          .
          .
          .
          procedure ValidateMonth (MonthNumber : Integer;
                                var ValidMonth : Boolean;
                                var NameOfMonth : MonthNameType);
          {Procedure to determine whether a Month is valid and convert
           the month number to month name}
          begin    {ValidateMonth}
              ValidMonth := (MonthNumber >= 1) and (MonthNumber <= 12);
              if ValidMonth then
                  NameOfMonth := MonthNameType (MonthNumber - 1)
              else
                  Writeln ('Invalid Month Number : ',MonthNumber)
          end;     {ValidateMonth}
          .
          .
          .
end.      {Main Program}
```

Figure 7.9 Program 7f: Example of use of Turbo Pascal typecasting.

with typecasting, this can be written as one statement:

```
NameOfMonth := MonthNameType (MonthNumber - 1);
```

For example, when MonthNumber has the value 1, the value of MonthNumber − 1 is 0, and MonthNameType (0) has the value Jan because the ordinal value of Jan is 0. A complete version of the procedure ValidateMonth is contained in Program 7f, which is shown in Figure 7.9. This program is functionally equivalent to the procedure of the same name in Program 7a, shown in Figure 7.2.

7.6.1 Time Out

For the following exercises, assume the following declarations:

```
type
      CardName = (Two, Three, Four, Five, Six, Seven, Eight,
                    Nine, Ten, Jack, Queen, King, Ace);
      CharSeq = 'a'..'z';
```

What are the value and data type of each of the following expressions?

1. Round (1.3 + 4.5)
2. Trunc (4.5)
3. Chr (48)

4. `Ord (Chr (48))`

5. `CardName (1)`

6. `CharSeq (97)`

7. `Char (49)`

8. `Integer ('a')`

9. `Integer (True)`

10. `Integer (Ace)`

11. `Boolean (0)`

7.7   SETS AND SET OPERATIONS

Pascal is rather unique among major programming languages in offering data type set. A set is defined as a group of items of a particular type. For example, we can speak of a set of automobiles, a set of integers, or a set of characters. In Pascal, a set is denoted by enclosing a list of the elements of the set in brackets. For example, the set of the first 10 integers can be denoted as

```
[1, 2, 3, 4, 5, 6, 7, 8, 9, 10]
```

or, by using the subrange notation, as

```
[1..10].
```

Subrange notation may be mixed freely with other list elements in specifying a set. For example, the following are equivalent ways of specifying a set containing the integers 1 through 10:

```
[1..5, 6..10]
[1, 2, 3..8, 9, 10]
[1..9, 10]
```

The set of lowercase characters that are vowels could be denoted as

```
['a', 'e', 'i', 'o', 'u'].
```

A set is a structured data type; this means that it is made up of elements of a simple type. Thus, we might construct a set of base type Integer or Char, as shown here, or the base type could be any ordinal type, including enumerated types. For example, suppose type DayName is defined as

```
type
    DayName = (Sun, Mon, Tue, Wed, Thr, Fri, Sat);
```

Then a set of elements of base type DayName that represents weekdays would be `[Mon..Fri]` or `[Mon, Tue, Wed, Thr, Fri]`. A set of elements that represents weekend days would be `[Sun, Sat]` or `[Sat, Sun]`. The order in which elements are listed in a set is unimportant. The two sets representing weekend days are equal—that is, they represent the same set. In the same way, the following sets of integers would be equal:

```
[1..5]
[5, 4, 3, 2, 1]
[5, 3, 2, 1, 4]
```

A basic restriction on sets in Turbo Pascal is that their maximum size is 256, and the ordinal value of each element must be in the range 0 to 255. Because of this restriction, the maximum value of an integer in a set of integers would be 255, and you could not construct a set containing negative integers. A set with no elements, which is called the **empty set**, is denoted by [ ]. (*Caution:* A subrange specification in which the first value is greater than the second, such as 5..1, can result in the specification of an empty set; that is, the set [5..1] is equal to [ ].)

Another basic restriction on sets is that an element cannot be present in the set more than once. Thus, the set ['a', 'a'] is the same as the set ['a']; both sets contain exactly one element. A set must be based on only one type; it is not possible to mix elements of different types in the same set. A set such as [1, 'a'] is invalid because of this restriction.

A fundamental property of set theory is that for a given element *x* and set *A*, either *x* is an element of *A* or *x* is not an element of *A*. For example, 1 is an element of the set [1..10], whereas the character 'a' is not an element of the set ['A'.. 'Z']. Pascal provides a relational operator, **in**, which you can use to test set membership. For example, the relation

```
'a' in ['a', 'e', 'i', 'o', 'u']
```

is True. The relational operator **in** is most often used to test the content of a variable. For example, if Character is of type Char, then you can write the following statement to determine whether Character is a vowel or consonant;

```
if Character in ['a', 'e', 'i', 'o', 'u'] then
   Writeln ('Vowel')
else
   Writein ('Consonant');
```

This use of set membership avoids the following equivalent, but messy, compound condition;

```
if   (Character = 'a') or (Character = 'e') or
     (Character - 'i') or (Character = 'o') or
     (Character = 'u') then
     ...;
```

Consider the following relation, where X is of type Integer:

```
(X >= 1) and (X <= 10)
```

This relation is True when X is in the range 1 to 10. An alternative (and simpler) way to write the relation is

```
X in [1..10]
```

This condition is True when the value of X is one of the values in the set consisting of the integers 1, 2, ... , 10.

7.7.1   Time Out

1. Write a set containing the first 10 even integers.
2. Write a set containing the upper- and lowercase letters of the alphabet.
3. Suppose the following declaration is part of a program:

```
type
     MonthNameType = (Jan, Feb, Mar, Apr, May, Jun,
                      Jul, Aug, Sep, Oct, Nov, Dec);
```

Write the set of winter months.

4. Suppose Y is of type Integer and has the value 10. Is each of the following conditions True or False?
   (a) Y in [1..10]
   (b) Y in [0..5, 8..12]
   (c) not (Y in [1..5])
   (d) (Y in [1..5]) and (Y in [8..12])

5. Write a simpler version of each of the following conditions. (Assume that Y is of type Integer, Month is of type MonthName, and Character is of type Char.)
   (a) (Y = 2) or (Y = 4) or (Y = 6)
   (b) (Y >= 5) and (Y <= 10)
   (c) (Month = Mar) or (Month = Apr) or (Month = May)
   (d) ((Character >= 'A') and (Character <= 'Z')) or ((Character >= 'a') and (Character <= 'z'))

7.7.2   Set Type, Variables, and Assignment

It is possible to declare variables with a set data type. This can be done directly in the variable declaration part of a program or by declaring a named set data type and using that name in the variable declaration. The general form for declaring a set data type is

```
set of type
```

where *type* can be any ordinal data type. For example, the variable CharacterSet could be declared to be a set of base type Char by the following program segment:

```
var
      CharacterSet : set of Char;
```

There are many ways to specify *type* in this context. One possibility is with a subrange. For example, the variable SmallIntegers is declared to be a set of Integers in the range 1 to 10 by the declaration

```
var
      SmallIntegers : set of 1..10;
```

A set can be based on a named or unnamed enumerated data type, as shown in the following segment:

```
type
      MonthNameType = (Jan, Feb, Mar, Apr, May, Jun,
                       Jul, Aug, Sep, Oct, Nov, Dec);
var
      Months : set of MonthNameType;
      Days   : set of (Sun, Mon, Tue, Wed,
                       Thr, Fri, Sat);
```

In this segment, Months is a set-type variable of base type MonthNameType, and Days is a set-type variable of an unnamed enumerated base type consisting of the seven identifiers for the days of the week.

Another way to specify a set-type variable is to declare a name for the set type and then use this name in the variable declaration. For example, the following coding segment is an equivalent way of declaring Months and Days to be set-type variables:

```
type
      MonthNameType = (Jan, Feb, Mar, Apr, May, June,
                       Jul, Aug, Sep, Oct, Nov, Dec);
      SetofMonths = set of MonthNameType;
      SetOfDays = set of (Sun, Mon, Tue, Wed, Thr,
                          Fri, Sat);
var
      Months : SetOfMonths;
      Days   : SetOfDays;
```

An advantage to this latter method of declaring variables is that these variables can be passed as parameters to procedures, provided that the procedure uses the same type specification for its argument. (The type specification for a formal argument in a procedure must be a single identifier; a specification such as "set of MonthNameType" is not permitted.)

Note that declaring a variable such as Months to be a set-type variable does not place any value into the variable. As with other variables in Pascal, this variable's value is undefined until the program causes some value to be placed in it. Set-type variables cannot be assigned a value by an input or output statement (Readln or Writeln), but they can have a value placed in them by an assignment statement. The value on the right side of the assignment statement must be a set-valued expression—that is, a set constant, a set variable, or a set computed as the result of set operations (more on these later).

For example, the following statement places the summer month names into the variable Months;

```
Months := [Jun, Jul, Aug];
```

The value of the variable Months is the set containing the three specified identifiers. Thus, the relation

```
Jun in Months
```

would be True, whereas the relation

```
Jan in Months
```

would be False. Occasionally, you will want to initialize a set variable to be the empty set, this is accomplished by the following statement, which sets the variable Days to be empty:

```
Days := [ ];
```

Now suppose that a second variable, WeekEndDays, has been declared to be of type SetOfDays. Then the following statement would place the content of Days into WeekEndDays:

```
WeekEndDays := Days
```

Note that the statement

```
Days := Tue;
```

would be invalid. Only another set can be placed into the variable Days; Tue is a constant of type DayName, so it would have to be placed into a variable with type DayName. The following statement would, of course, be valid:

```
Days := [Tue];
```

This statement assigns a set containing one element as the value of the variable Days.

An example of the use of sets in the context of a complete program is contained in Program 7g, shown in Figure 7.10. This is a revision of the procedure ValidateDay from the program that computes the difference between two dates. This version of the procedure is functionally identical to the procedure of the same name shown in Figure 7.2. The purpose of the procedure is to determine whether the value of Day is valid for a Month of MonthNameType. The approach taken in the revised version is to declare a type GroupOfMonths as a set of MonthNameType and then declare two variables, Month28

```
program P7g (Input, Output);
{Program to compute the difference between two dates in the
      same year.  This version of the program illustrates the use
      of sets in procedure ValidateDay.}
            .
            .
            .
          procedure ValidateDay (Month : MonthNameType;
                             Day : Integer;
                         var ValidDay : Boolean);
          {Procedure to validate day of a month}
          type
              GroupOfMonths = set of MonthNameType;
          var
              NumberDays : Integer;
              Month28, Month30 : GroupOfMonths;
          begin   {ValidateDay}
              Month28 := [Feb];
              Month30 := [Sep, Apr, Jun, Nov];
              if       Month in Month28 then
                          NumberDays := 28
              else if Month in Month30 then
                          NumberDays := 30
              else
                          NumberDays := 31;
              ValidDay := (Day >= 1) and (Day <= NumberDays);
              if not ValidDay then
                 Writeln ('Invalid Day Number : ', Day)
          end;   {ValidateDay}
            .
            .
            .
end.      {Main Program}
```

Figure 7.10 Program 7g: Example of use of sets.

and Month30, to be of type GroupOfMonths. Then, in the statement part of the procedure, values are assigned to these two variables as follows:

```
Month28 := [Feb];
Month30 := [Sep, Apr, Jun, Nov];
```

Month28 represents the set of months having 28 days; Month30 represents the set of months having 30 days. The decision structure that follows these assignments computes the value of NumberDays based on the value of Month, using relations based on set membership:

```
if Month in Month28 then
    NumberDays := 28
else if Month in Month30 then
    NumberDays : = 30
else
    NumberDays := 31;
```

In this program, the use of a named type, GroupOfMonths, is not really necessary, since the variables of this type are not used as arguments for a procedure call. The following declarations would have been sufficient:

```
var
     NumberDays : Integer;
     Month28, Month30 : set of MonthNameType;
```

In fact, this procedure could dispense with the named variables for sets entirely, since we could write the basic decision structure as follows:

```
if Month in [Feb] then
    NumberDays := 28
else if Month in [Sep, Apr, Jun, Nov] then
    NumberDays := 30
else
    NumberDays := 31;
```

7.7.3   *Time Out*

For these exercises, assume the following declarations:

```
type
     SmallIntegers = set of 1..10;
     CharacterSet = set of Char;
var
     X, Y : SmallIntegers;
     Z    : CharacterSet;
```

Show the content of variable X, Y, or Z after execution of each of the following statements:

1. X := [ ];
2. Y := [1, 3..5];
3. Z := ['a'..'e'];

Assuming the preceding values of variables X, Y, and Z, specify whether each of the following conditions is True or False:

4. 1 **in** X
5. 4 **in** Y
6. 'A' **in** Z

Each of the following statements is invalid. Why?

7. X := 2;
8. if X **in** Y **then**
        . . . ;

7.7.4 Set Operators

Pascal offers a number of operations that can be performed on sets. These operations are **set intersection** (*), **set union** (+), and **set difference** (−). Additionally, you can test for set equality (=) and various forms of inequality, including not equal to (<>) and subset (<= and >=). In all cases, these operations require two sets of the same type as operands.

Set intersection is defined to be the set of elements in common to two sets. In Pascal, the symbol for intersection is *. For example, [1, 2, 3, 4] * [2, 4, 6] is equal to [2, 4] because the two elements that are contained in both sets are 2 and 4. If there are no elements in common between two sets, then the intersection is the empty set. For example, ['a'..'z'] * ['A'..'Z'] is equal to [ ] because there are no characters in common to both sets. The relationship between two sets is often presented in visual form using Venn diagrams. In these diagrams, sets are represented as overlapping circles surrounding elements. The intersection of two sets is represented as that portion of two circles that overlap, as shown in Figure 7.11.

Set union is defined as the set of elements contained in either of two sets. In Pascal, the symbol for union is +. For example, [1, 2, 3, 4] + [2, 4, 6] = [1, 2, 3, 4, 6], which represents the set of elements that are contained in one or the other or both of the sets. (Remember that sets are made up of discrete elements; the elements 2 and 4 are in both sets, but are in the union exactly once. The union of two sets is shown in Venn diagram form by shading all the circles representing the two sets.

Set difference is defined to be elements in the first set that are not contained in the second set. For example, [1, 2, 3, 4] − [2, 4, 6] = [1, 3] because after removing the elements that are common to the two sets, the elements 1 and 3 are the only ones left. In Venn diagram form, the difference is shown by shading that portion of the first set that does not overlap the second set.

For example, suppose the following declarations are in a program:

```
type
     DayNames = (Sun, Mon, Tue, Wed, Thr, Fri, Sat);
     SetOfDays = set of DayNames;
var
     Week, WorkDays, WeekEndDays : SetOfDays;
```

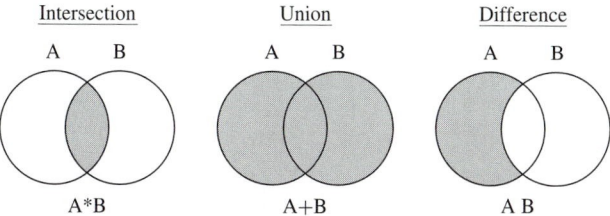

Figure 7.11 Venn diagrams for set operations.

Consider the following program segment;

```
WorkDays := [Mon, Tue, Wed, Thr, Fri];
WeekEndDays := [Sun, Sat];
Week := WorkDays + WeekEndDays;
```

At the end of execution of this segment, the content of Week is [Sun, Mon, Tue, Wed, Thr, Fri, Sat], the union of WorkDays and WeekEndDays.

Suppose the following statement is executed:

```
Week := WorkDays * WeekEndDays;
```

Now the content of Week would be the empty set, because there are no elements in common between WorkDays and WeekEndDays.

Next, suppose the following statement is executed:

```
Week := WorkDays - [Fri, Sat, Sun];
```

Then the value of Week would be [Mon, Tue, Wed, Thr], which represents all the elements of WorkDays except the ones in common with the set that was subtracted.

The following table summarizes set operations (assume that all variables are of type set of 1..10):

A	B	A * B	A + B	A - B
[1..4]	[5..7]	[]	[1..7]	[1..4]
[1..10]	[2,4]	[2,4]	[1..10]	[1,3,5..10]
[1..10]	[]	[]	[1..10]	[1..10]
[3,7,9]	[3,6,10]	[3]	[3,6,7,9,10]	[7,9]
[1..3]	[1..3]	[1..3]	[1..3]	[]

In addition to set operations that act on the elements of sets, you can test for various relations using the relational operators =, <>, <=, and >=. Two sets are equal if they have exactly the same elements. For example, the condition

```
[1, 2, 3] = [2, 1, 3]
```

is True. (Remember that the order of listing elements in a set is not important.) The condition

```
[1, 2, 3] = [1, 2]
```

is False because the two sets do not contain exactly the same elements. In fact, the condition

```
[1, 2, 3] <> [1, 2]
```

is True.

Set A is said to be a subset of set B if all the elements of A are also elements of B. For example, [1, 2] is a subset of the set [1, 2, 3]. You can test for subset relations using the relational operator $<=$ or $>=$. The relation A $<=$ B will be True if A is a subset of B. For example, the condition

```
[1, 2] <= [1, 2, 3]
```

is True, but the condition

```
[1, 2, 4] <= [1, 2, 3]
```

is False because the first set contains an element that is not in the second set.

The relation A $>=$ B will be True if B is a subset of A. For example, the condition

```
['A'..'Z'] >= ['A', 'E', 'I', 'O', 'U']
```

is True. (This is another way of saying that the set of vowels is a subset of the set of letters.)

The following table summarizes set relational operators (assume that all variables are of type set of 1..10):

A	B	A = B	A <> B	A <= B	B <= A
[1..4]	[5..7]	False	True	False	False
[1..10]	[2,4]	False	True	False	True
[1..10]	[]	False	True	False	True
[3,7,9]	[3,6,10]	False	True	False	False
[1..3]	[1..3]	True	False	True	True

7.7.5 *Time Out*

For the following exercises, assume the given declarations:

```
type
      A = set of Char;
      B = set of 1..20;
var
      X, Y, Z, W, V : A;
      Q, R, S, T, U : B;
```

Also, assume that the value of X is ['a'..'e'] and the value of R is [1..5]. Show the value of the relevant variable after execution of each of the following:

1. `Y := X + ['A'..'E'];`

2. `Z := X - ['a', 'f'];`

3. `W := X + X;`

4. `V := X * ['a', 'f'];`

5. `Q := R * [1..10];`

6. `S := R + [1..10];`

7. `T := R - [1..10];`

8. `U := R - R;`

Is each of the following conditions True or False?

9. `['a'..'c'] <= X`

10. `['a'..'c'] >= X`

11. `X + X = X`

12. `[1..20] >= R`

13. `R <= [1..9]`

14. `R - R = [ ]`

What is wrong with each of the following statements?

15. `if 'a' <= X then`

    `. . . ;`

16. `X := X + 'f'`

17. `R := R + ['a']`

7.7.6 Programming with Sets

Sets can be useful in solving certain problems wherein there is a need to store a limited number of elements for later reference. Sets are particularly appropriate when the logic of the problem dictates that duplicates in the data being stored should be ignored and when the order of the elements is not important. (Recall that an element cannot be present in a set more than once.) This use of sets is illustrated in the solution to the following problem.

■ **Problem Statement.** Write a program to allow the user to enter any desired sequence of capital letters. The program should return a list of the capital letters that the user has *not* entered.

■ **Program Analysis.** A reasonable approach to this problem is to use a set to store the characters that have been entered by the user. A set is appropriate in this case because (1) the data items being stored fit the restrictions placed on sets by Turbo Pascal (i.e., the ordinal values must be in the range 0 to 255) and (2) duplicate entries are to be ignored (i.e., the output of the program is not affected if the user enters a particular letter one time or many times). Once the data-entry process has been completed, the program can scan the set to determine which letters are not elements of it; these letters form the output from the program.

In order to use a set to store input, we must make use of a set-builder routine, which operates in much the same way as the logic required in the accumulation of a sum of numbers. We will need to initialize the accumulator set to the empty set prior to the entry of any data. Then, for each data item, we will "add" it to the set using set union. For example, if DataSet is a set of an appropriate type and Data is a data item, then the statement

```
DataSet := DataSet + [Data];
```

would form the union of DataSet and the set containing Data and place the result in DataSet. If the element Data is already in DataSet, then the operation replaces DataSet with itself; if the element Data is not in DataSet, then it is incorporated into DataSet, and this new set becomes the value of DataSet.

With these considerations in mind, we can construct a program plan as follows:

SET EXAMPLES PROGRAM (P7h)

1.0 Initialize set of input characters

2.0 Clear the screen

3.0 Read and store the characters entered by the user

4.0 Output all capital letters not entered by user

5.0 Wait

■ **Problem Solution.**   Program 7h, shown in Figure 7.12, is a solution to this problem. An example of its use is shown in Figure 7.13. In this program, the set of input characters is implemented using the variable InputCharacters, which is declared to be of type set of Capital-Letters. This variable is initialized, as required in step 1.0 of the procedure, in the statement

```
InputCharacters := [ ];
```

In implementing Module 3.0, we must decide on some means to control the loop. The method chosen makes use of the Eoln function to determine when the end of the sequence of characters entered by the user has been reached:

```
while not Eoln do
    begin
        Read (Character);
        . . .
    end;    {while}
Readln;
```

```
program P7h (Input, Output);
uses Crt;
{Program to determine which letters are missing from
    a set of letters entered by the user}
type
    CapitalLetters = 'A'..'Z';
const
    InputPrompt = 'Enter character string ';
var
    Character : Char;
    InputCharacters : set of CapitalLetters;
    .
    .
    .
begin     {Main Program}

{1.0 Initialize set of input characters}

    InputCharacters := [ ];

{2.0 Clear the screen}

    ClrScr;

{3.0 Read and store characters entered by user}

    Writeln (InputPrompt);
    while not Eoln do
          begin
                Read (Character);
                if Character in ['A'..'Z'] then
                     InputCharacters := InputCharacters + [Character]
          end;     {while}
    Readln;

{4.0 Output all capital letters not entered by user}

    Writeln('Capital letters that you have not entered are :');
    for Character := 'A' to 'Z' do
        if not (Character in InputCharacters) then
           Write (Character:2);
    Writeln;
    .
    .
    .
end.      {Main Program}
```

Figure 7.12 Program 7h: Example of use of sets.

```
Enter character string
Now Is The Time For All Good Men (And Women Too). . .
Capital letters that you have not entered are :
 B C D E H J K L O P Q R S U V X Y Z
Press <Enter> to continue
```

Figure 7.13 Sample execution of Program 7h.

When the Eoln function is used without a parameter, it refers to file Input assigned to the keyboard. The first execution of the Read statement allows the user to enter as many characters as desired. These characters are stored in an input buffer for processing. Subsequent executions of Read take data from the buffer and cause the File-position pointer to be moved to the next character in the buffer. When the pointer points to the EOL character sequence, the Eoln statement returns True. The Readln statement advances the pointer past the EOL characters and effectively clears the buffer to accept more input.

For valid characters, the set accumulation is accomplished in the body of the loop as follows:

```
if Character in [ 'A'..'Z'] then
    InputCharacters := InputCharacters + [Character]
```

Recall that a set cannot be used directly in an input or output operation. Thus, in order to perform the requirement of step 4.0, it is necessary to generate all possible elements of the set and test to determine whether each element is in the set. If it is not, then this element is printed. An appropriate way to generate all possible elements in the set is to use the for statement:

```
for Character := 'A' to 'Z' do
    . . .;
```

In the body of the for loop, the test for membership for each value of Character is accomplished as follows:

```
if not (Character in InputCharacters) then
    . .
```

7.7.7 *Time Out*

1. Compile and execute Program 7h.
2. Modify Program 7h to operate with both upper- and lowercase characters.
3. Modify Program 7h to allow the user to choose to output either a list of the characters that have been entered or a list of the characters that have *not* been entered.
4. An alternative approach to this problem is to initialize a set to contain a list of all possible characters and then use set difference to remove each character entered by the user. When finished, the elements remaining in the set would represent the characters that the user has not entered. Write a program to solve this problem, using the alternative approach.

7.8 *Case Study: Relative Primes*

■ **Problem Statement.** Two integers are said to be *relatively prime* if their only common factor[1] is 1. For example, consider the numbers 7 and 9. The factors of 7 are 1 and 7. The factors of 9 are 1, 3, and 9. The only factor they have in common is 1; therefore,

---

[1]The integer a is a factor of b if a is a divisor of b—that is, if b mod a is equal to 0.

they are relatively prime. On the other hand, the integers 8 and 18 are not relatively prime. The factors of 8 are 1, 2, 4, and 8. The factors of 18 are 1, 2, 3, 9, and 18. Since the common factors are 1 and 2, the numbers 8 and 18 are not relatively prime.

Write a program to determine whether number pairs entered by the user are relatively prime.

■ **Problem Analysis.**   We would like to have a program that will process more than one pair of numbers; this leads us to a preliminary program plan:

PRELIMINARY PLAN FOR RELATIVE PRIMES PROGRAM

1.0 Get Numbers

2.0 Process numbers and read next numbers

One way to state the condition required for two numbers to be relatively prime is in terms of sets. If X is the set of factors of the number a and Y is the set of factors of the number b, then a and b are relatively prime if the intersection of X and Y is the set [1]. Stated another way, if $X * Y = [1]$, then a and b are relatively prime.

This analysis leads naturally to the use of Pascal sets in the required program. We can compute the set of factors for each number and then form the intersection of the two sets. If this intersection is the set [1], then the numbers are relatively prime. With this analysis in place, we can now formulate a more complete plan for the program:

RELATIVE PRIMES PROGRAM (P7i)

1.0 Get Numbers

2.0 Process numbers and read next numbers

    2.1   While Numbers not = 0 Do

    2.2   Compute Factors of Number 1

    2.3   Compute Factors of Number 2

    2.4   If Intersection of two sets of factors = [1] Then

    2.5   Write 'Numbers are relatively prime'

    2.6   Else

    2.7   Write 'Numbers are not relatively prime'

    2.8   End If

    2.9   Read Numbers

    2.10 End While

Note that the program will require the computation of factors for two different numbers. A procedure would be appropriate for this task. The procedure will import the Number and export the SetOfFactors of it. One technique for computing the elements of SetOfFactors is to examine all the numbers from 1 to Number and add each factor of Number to the set as we encounter it. A plan for the procedure that we will call Factor is as follows:

PROCEDURE FACTOR (IMPORT : NUMBER,
EXPORT : SETOFFACTORS)

1.0 Initialize SetOfFactors to empty set

2.0 For N = 1 to Number Do

3.0   If N is a factor of Number Then

4.0   Add [N] to SetOfFactors

5.0   End If

6.0 End For

■ **Problem Solution.** The required program is shown as Program 7i in Figure 7.14, with a sample execution shown in Figure 7.15. One of the basic restrictions on this solution to the problem is the restriction on the values of numbers with which it can operate. The ordinal values of elements of a set must be in the range 0 to 255. This means that the program cannot work with a number outside this range. (Remember that every number has at least two factors: 1 and itself.)

This program illustrates the passing of a variable of set type as an argument in a procedure. Pascal requires that the actual parameter and formal parameter have the same type. This is accomplished by declaring the following types:

```
type
    NumberRange = 1..255;
    Factors = set of NumberRange;
```

The two variables used as actual parameters and the formal parameter of the procedure Factor are all declared to be of type Factors.

7.8.1 Time Out

1. Execute Program 7i, and test it with data of your choosing.
2. Modify Program 7i to produce a list of the factors of each number. (Write a procedure that imports the set of factors for a number and produces this list.)
3. Modify Program 7i to produce a list of the factors in common to the two numbers. Can the procedure written for Exercise 2 be used for this task without modification?

7.9 TYPED CONSTANTS: A NONSTANDARD FEATURE OF TURBO PASCAL

There are times when it would be convenient to create a variable that will have an initial value when the execution of a program begins. Turbo Pascal provides you with a way to accomplish this task by means of typed constants. A typed constant is declared in the

```
program P7i (Input, Output);
{Program to determine whether two numbers are relatively prime,
     using sets of factors for each number}
uses Crt;
type
    NumberRange = 1..255;
    Factors = set of NumberRange;
const
    InputPrompt = 'Enter two numbers (0 0 to stop) ';
var
    Number1, Number2 : NumberRange;    {Input Variables}
    FactorsOfNumber1, FactorsOfNumber2 : Factors;
{*****************************************************************************}
    procedure Factor (Number : NumberRange;
                      var FactorsOfNumber : Factors);
    {Procedure to compute factors of number}
    var
        N : NumberRange;
    begin    {Factor}
        FactorsOfNumber := [ ];
        for N := 1 to Number  do
            if Number mod N = 0 then
                FactorsOfNumber := FactorsOfNumber + [N];
    end;      {Factor}
{*****************************************************************************}
begin    {Main Program}

{1.0 Get Numbers}

    ClrScr;
    Write (InputPrompt);
    Readln (Number1, Number2);

{2.0 Process numbers and read next numbers}

    while (Number1 <> 0) and (Number2 <> 0 ) do
        begin
            Factor (Number1, FactorsOfNumber1);
            Factor (Number2, FactorsOfNumber2);
            Write (Number1, ' and ', Number2);
            if FactorsOfNumber1 * FactorsOfNumber2 = [1] then
                Writeln (' are relatively prime.')
            else
                Writeln (' are not relatively prime.');
            Writeln;
            Write (InputPrompt);
            Readln (Number1, Number2)
        end;    {while}

end.     {Main Program}
```

Figure 7.14 Program 7i: Relative primes program.

constant declaration along with ordinary (untyped) constants by using the following form:

$$identifier\ :\ type\ =\ value;$$

By adding the specification of *type*, the *identifier* actually names a variable that will have *value* as its content when the program is loaded.

```
Enter two numbers (0 0 to stop)  8 18
8 and 18 are not relatively prime.

Enter two numbers (0 0 to stop)  2 3
2 and 3 are relatively prime.

Enter two numbers (0 0 to stop)  7 9
7 and 9 are relatively prime.

Enter two numbers (0 0 to stop)  0 0
```

Figure 7.15 Sample execution of Program 7i.

For example, consider the following declarations:

```
type
    DayOfWeek = (Sun, Mon, Tue, Wed, Thr, Fri, Sat);
const
    Sum : Real = 0.0;
    Count : Integer = 0;
    Character : Char = 'A';
    Continue : Boolean = True;
    Day : DayOfWeek = Sun;
```

This segment declares five typed constants of types Real, Integer, Char, Boolean, and DayOfWeek, respectively. Even though typed constants are declared in the constant declaration part of a program, they are actually variables. This means that, unlike constants, their values can change as a result of an input operation or assignment statement. Thus, a statement such as

```
Sum := Sum + Data;
```

Would cause the value of the typed constant Sum to change; a statement such as

```
Readln (Character);
```

would cause the value of Character to change. The only thing that is provided by creating a typed constant is the initial value of the variable; the program is free to change the value of the typed constant in the same way as the value of any other variable is changed. (The term *typed constant* is misleading, although it is the term used in the Turbo Pascal reference manual. A much more descriptive term would be *initialized variable*).

When a typed constant is used in a procedure, the initial value is place in the variable when the program is compiled and placed in memory; it is *not* placed in the variable each time the procedure is executed. This means that if the procedure needs to have a variable initialized each time it is executed, it must have this action performed by an appropriate assignment statement.

One way in which typed constants can be useful is to provide default values for variables in an easily located portion of a program (the declaration part). Using a typed constant rather than an ordinary constant makes it possible for the program to change the value of the typed constant if needed and makes it possible to use the typed constant as a variable parameter in a procedure invocation; neither of these actions are possible with ordinary untyped constants.

In all the examples of typed constants presented so far, *type* has been a scalar type (either standard or programmer defined). These are classed as unstructured typed constants. It is also possible to create a structured typed constant using type string, set, record, or array. For example, the following declaration declares CompanyName as a string typed constant with initial value 'ABC, Inc.':

```
const
     CompanyName : string[10] = 'ABC, Inc.';
```

Typed constants of sets are often useful for providing an initial set of values for reference in a program. (Note that it is not possible to declare an ordinary untyped constant of a set type.) For example, the following declaration would declare the typed constant Vowel to contain a set of characters representing lowercase vowels:

```
const
     Vowel : set of 'a'..'z' = ['a','e','i','o','u'];
```

This would allow the program to use the statement

```
if Character in Vowel then
   . . . ;
```

rather than either of the two alternatives shown next, each of which is more cumbersome (assume that Vowel has been declared to be a variable of the appropriate type):

```
Vowel := ['a', 'e', 'i', 'o', 'u'];
if Character in Vowel then
     . . . ;

if Character in ['a', 'e', 'i', 'o', 'u'] then
     . . . ;
```

One benefit of the use of typed constants is to make a program more efficient. Consider, for example, the version of the procedure ValidateDay contained in Program 7j; shown in Figure 7.16. In order to make use of set membership in the if statement, the variables Month28 and Month30 are initialized using assignment statements:

```
Month28 := [Feb];
Month30 := [Sep, Apr, Jun, Nov];
if Month in Month28 then
     . . . ;
```

```
program P7j (Input, Output);
{Program to compute the difference between two dates in the
        same year.  This version of the program illustrates the use
        of structured typed constants in procedure ValidateDay.}
        .
        .
        .
        procedure ValidateDay (Month : MonthNameType;
                                    Day : Integer;
                              var ValidDay : Boolean);
        {Procedure to validate day of a month}
        type
            GroupOfMonths = set of MonthNameType;
        const
            Month28 : GroupOfMonths = [Feb];
            Month30 : GroupOfMonths = [Sep, Apr, Jun, Nov];
        var
            NumberDays : Integer;
        begin   {ValidateDay}
            if      Month in Month28 then
                        NumberDays := 28
            else if Month in Month30 then
                        NumberDays := 30
            else
                        NumberDays := 31;
            ValidDay := (Day >= 1) and (Day <= NumberDays);
            if not ValidDay then
                Writeln ('Invalid Day Number : ', Day)
        end;   {ValidateDay}
        .
        .
        .
end.   {Main Program}
```

Figure 7.16   Program 7j: Example of use of typed constants.

The problem with this code is that these two assignment statements must be executed each time the procedure is executed, even though the values of Month28 and Month30 never change. A more efficient technique is to use a typed constant for Month28 and Month30, as in the version of ValidateDay shown in Figure 7.16. In this procedure, structured type constants Month28 and Month30 are declared as follows:

```
const
        Month28 : GroupOfMonths = [Feb];
        Month30 : GroupOfMonths = [Sep, Apr, Jun, Nov];
```

These declarations provide the appropriate values for Month28 and Month30, which will be in place when the program is loaded. The compiler translates the declarations one time; it is not necessary for the program to make the assignments each time the procedure is executed.

Two words of caution are in order with regard to typed constants;

1. Typed constants are not a part of standard Pascal. Thus, a program using them must be revised to run in standard Pascal.

2. Use typed constants only when they are the most logical and effective tool for accomplishing a task. A typed constant is really a variable that can be changed (either on purpose or inadvertently) during the execution of the program, whereas an untyped constant cannot be modified by any action taken during the execution of a program. Untyped constants are safer to use because they are protected. The use of typed constants can make a program very difficult to debug.

7.9.1 Time Out

1. Compile and test Program 7k, which is shown in Figure 7.17. This expected output is the value 1.

```
program P7k (Output);
{Program illustrates that the value of a typed constant
    can be changed by a program}
const
    X : Integer = 0;
begin
    X := X + 1;
    Writeln (X)
end.
```

Figure 7.17 Program 7k: Changing the value of a typed constant.

7.10   REVIEW QUESTIONS

1. List two data types provided by Turbo Pascal that are not provided by standard Pascal.

2. Define the terms *scalar* and *ordinal*. What data types are scalar? What data types are ordinal?

3. What range of values can be represented in Byte-type data?

4. In what ways are Byte data compatible with Integer data? In what way are the two types incompatible?

5. What are the basic advantages to declaring a data type using a type declaration?

6. Define the term *enumerated*. What is an enumerated data type? What are the restrictions placed on data with an enumerated data type?

7. What Pascal statements cannot process data with an enumerated data type?

8. What is an unnamed enumerated data type? What restrictions are placed on a variable with an unnamed enumerated data type?

9. What restrictions are placed on the base type of a subrange data type? What restrictions are placed on the values in a subrange?

10. What is range checking? How is it turned on and off in Turbo Pascal? What guideline should be followed in using range checking?

11. What purpose is served by the function Ord? Pred? Succ? Round? Trunc?

12. Explain how generalized type conversion is performed in Turbo Pascal.

13. What is a set? What restrictions are there on set data type in Pascal?

14. What relational operators are available for set data type?

15. Explain the meaning of each of the following set operations: intersection, union, difference. How is each of these carried out in Pascal?

16. What is the empty set? How is the empty set useful in building a set from elements entered by a program user?

17. What is a typed constant?

18. List features of Turbo Pascal relating to data types that are not features of standard Pascal.

7.11   PROGRAMMING EXERCISES

1. A series of integer numbers in the range 1 to 250 is to be entered by the program user. (Use value 0 to terminate the data-entry process.) The program should print a list of all prime numbers that the user has entered. (A prime number is a number that is divisible only by 1 and itself.) *Hint:* Use a set to store each prime number as it is encountered.

2. Two words are to be entered by the program user. A space is used to mark the end of the first word. Write a program to:

    (a) Write an alphabetical list of the letters in each word.

    (b) Write a list of the letters that appear in both words.

    (c) Write a list of the letters that occur in either word.

    (d) Determine whether all the letters in one of the words are contained in the other.

3. Write a program to compute a student's grade-point average (GPA). Input data contains the credit hours and letter grade for each course a student has taken. Assume that letter grades are converted to quality points, using the following table:

Grade	Quality points
A	4
B	3
C	2
D	1
F	0

The number of quality points earned for a course is equal to the credit hours times the quality points for the grade. The GPA is the total quality points earned divided by the total number of credit hours. For example, suppose a student has taken a three-credit-hour course and earned an A and a four-credit-hour course and earned a C. The required computations are as follows:

Credit hours	Grade	Quality points for grade	Quality points for course
3	A	4	3 ← 4 = 12
4	C	2	4 ← 2 = 8
Totals: 7			20

$$\text{GPA} = \frac{20}{7} = 2.857$$

4. Write a program to classify characters entered by the user as a consonant or a vowel. Write an appropriate message if the character is not a letter. Terminate execution when a character that is not a letter has been entered.

5. Write a program that will compute and print the name of a card based on a number in the range 1 to 52 entered by the user. Numbers in the range 1 to 13 represent clubs, 14 to 26 represent hearts, 27 to 39 represent diamonds, and 40 to 52 represent spades. The first number in each range represents the ace, the second number represents the two, and so forth.

6. Write a program to allow the user to enter numbers representing five cards. Have the program list the cards in sequence by name. For example, if the input values are 51, 12, 27, 2, and 3, the output should be

```
Club: Two Three Queen
Heart:
Diamond: Ace
Spade: Queen
```

7. Write a program to allow the user to enter two numbers and an operation symbol (+, −, *, or /). Perform the indicated operation on the numbers, and write the result.

8. Write a program to allow the user to enter any desired sequence of letters. The program should print all distinct combinations of two letters from the set entered by the user. (*Note: AB* and *BA* are *not* distinct.) For example, if the input contains the letters *A*, *E*, and *B*, the output should be *AB*, *AE*, and *BE*.

9. Write a program to verify the following relations for sets A and B:
   (a) A − B is a subset of A.
   (b) A − B = A − (A*B)
   (c) A * B is a subset of both A and B.
   (d) (A − B)*(B − A) = [ ]

10. Write a program to read a sentence from a Text file. After the sentence is entered, have the program print a report similar to the following:

```
INPUT:  The red car drove 20 miles to town!
OUTPUT: Uppercase letters: 1
        Lowercase letters: 24
        Digits: 2
        Other characters:  1
```

11. Write a program to encode a message read from a Text file. The encoding method (which is called the Caesar substitution method) requires that each letter in the message be replaced by a letter that is two letters higher in the alphabet. For example, replace *A* by *C*, *B* by *D*, and so forth. Treat the alphabet as circular; that is, replace *X* by *A* and *Z* by *B*. Lowercase letters should be replaced by their uppercase equivalents before encoding. Ignore all nonalphabetic characters in the message.

12. Repeat Exercise 11, except replace each letter by the ASCII value of the letter that is two letters higher in the alphabet.

13. Write a program to allow the user to enter a month number (1 through 12); the program should respond with the month name (January for 1, February for 2, and so forth) and the season. For purposes of this problem, treat December, January, and February as winter months. March, April, and May as spring months, June, July, and August as summer months, and September, October, and November as fall months.

8

String Data and Functions

In this chapter, we focus on processing string data and on the general topic of functions. You have already used a few functions; in the last chapter we discussed Ord, Succ, Pred, Int, Round, and Trunc, and you have also used mathematical functions such as Sqrt and Sqr. There are a number of very useful functions (and procedures as well) for processing string data. Understanding these will enable you to solve some very interesting problems. Turbo Pascal includes a function to generate random numbers. This function can be used to solve problems in which the computer is used to simulate a process that is understood only in terms of probabilities. Pascal makes it possible for you to define your own functions in much the same way that you have been defining procedures. Finally, Pascal supports a feature called recursion, by which a function or procedure can invoke itself. Recursion makes it possible for you to solve certain problems in fresh and interesting ways.

8.1 PROCESSING STRING DATA

Recall that string data type is a structured data type supported by Turbo Pascal (but is not part of standard Pascal). A string can contain from 1 to 255 characters. The maximum length of a string must be declared using one of the general forms

string[*length*] or **string**

where *length* is an integer constant in the range 1 to 255. For example, the following declarations specify variables X and Y to be string type with maximum length 80 and 255, respectively:

```
var
    X : string[80];
    Y : string[255];
```

Omitting *length* will create a variable capable of storing the maximum number of characters—255. Thus, the declaration

```
Y : string;
```

is equivalent to

```
Y : string [255];
```

The base type for string data is Char, and string variables and constants are compatible with Char variables and constants.

The value of *length* specified when a variable is declared is the maximum number of characters that can be contained in the variable. The actual length of the string can vary from 0 to *length*. A string of length 0, which is denoted by ' ', is called the null string. String variables may be used in input, output, and assignment statements.

When specified as a parameter in Read or Readln, the characters contained in the variable are governed by the value of *length* or by the end of the line. For example, suppose a program contains the statement

```
Readln (X);
```

where X is defined as before. The content of X could be any string entered by the user, up to 80 characters in length. When the user presses the Enter key, the sequence of characters is terminated (because end of line is transmitted). When specified as a parameter in a Write or Writeln statement, a string variable takes up a number of characters in the output line equal to the length of the string.

As an example of string input and output, let us design a program that will enable you to create a Text file. You will be able to use the computer as a simple editor to enter lines of text, editing the characters with the backspace key and retyping as necessary. When you press Enter, the line will be written to the specified file, and you will be able to enter another line of text.

We wish the program to print some initial instructions to the program user. As part of these instructions, the user will enter the name of the file to be created, which the program will open for output. Terminating the program presents something of a problem; we will permit the user to enter the null string to end the program. (This corresponds to pressing the Enter key at the beginning of a line.) The plan for the program is as follows:

TEXT FILE CREATION (P8a)

1.0 Write instructions and open file

2.0 Wait until the user is ready to begin

3.0 Read and write lines of text

4.0 Close file

A solution to this problem is Program 8a, shown in Figure 8.1. Note that we use a null string to terminate data entry:

```
repeat
   .
   .
   .
until TextLine = '';
```

When the user presses the Enter key in response to the Readln statement, the effect is to transmit the null string as the value of TextLine.

We have chosen an alternative method to implement the wait procedure required in Module 2.0. Earlier in the text, we used a Readln statement, which required the user to press the Enter key to proceed. In this program, we use a method that allows the user to press any key (well, *almost* any key) to proceed. This is accomplished with the function ReadKey, which is contained in the Crt unit. This function returns the character in the keyboard buffer pointed to by the File-position pointer for the file Input. If the buffer is empty (as it will be after the execution of a Readln statement, which advances the file-position pointer past the EOL sequence), the function causes the system to halt until a character key is pressed by the user. This character is not echoed to the screen in the usual fashion, but rather becomes the value of the function ReadKey. ReadKey also advances the file-position pointer past the character just read, in the same way as does an ordinary Read procedure. One minor drawback to the ReadKey function is that it reacts only to keys that actually transmit data to the buffer. Keys that act as modifiers, such as Shift, Ctrl, Alt, and the like, do not actually transmit data, but rather change what is transmitted when used in conjunction with another key. Thus, pressing one of these keys will not be sensed by ReadKey; this is why we said that the user can press "almost any key" to continue. Since ReadKey is a function rather than a procedure, we can use it in a replacement statement

```
program P8a (Input, Output, OutputFile);
{Text file creation program; illustrates processing of string data and
    the function ReadKey}
uses Crt;
var
    TextLine : string;
    OutputFile : Text;
{*******************************************************************}
    procedure OpenOutputFile (var MyFile : Text);
    var
        FileName : string;
    begin    {OpenOutputFile}
        Writeln ('Enter name of file to be created ');
        Readln (FileName);
        Assign (MyFile, FileName);
        Rewrite (MyFile)
    end;     {OpenOutputFile}
{-----------------------------------------------------------------}
    procedure AlternateWait;
    var
        Ch : Char;
    begin    {AlternateWait}
        Write ('Press any key to continue ');
        Ch := ReadKey
    end;     {AlternateWait}
{*******************************************************************}
begin    {Main Program}

{1.0 Write instructions and open file}

    Writeln ('Text file creation program');
    OpenOutputFile (OutputFile);
    Writeln;
    Write ('Exit program by pressing <Enter> ');
    Writeln ('at the beginning of a line');
    Writeln ('If you are directing output to the printer ');
    Writeln ('make sure printer is ready before proceeding');

{2.0 Wait until user is ready to begin}

    AlternateWait;
    ClrScr;

{3.0 Read and write lines of text}

    repeat
        Readln(TextLine);
        if TextLine <> '' then
            Writeln (OutputFile, TextLine)
    until TextLine = '';

{4.0 Close file}

    Close (OutputFile);

end.    {Main Program}
```

Figure 8.1 Program 8a: Text file creation program.

or in any other context permitting a character type expression. Thus, in the procedure AlternateWait in Program 8a, we declare a Char type variable named Ch. The procedure contains the following two statements:

```
Write ('Press any key to continue ');
Ch := ReadKey
```

The second statement actually causes the system to wait until the key is pressed. After the key is pressed, the character is returned as the value of ReadKey and placed in the variable Ch. In another context, you might then test the value of this variable and use it for some purpose. For example, you might use the technique when prompting a user to select an item from a menu. The character that is entered is transmitted directly, without the necessity for the user to press the Enter key. But use this method with caution. Using a traditional Readln statement to request data gives the user a chance to change his or her mind about the character that has been entered. In contrast, the ReadKey function takes the character immediately after the key is pressed; there is no chance to change one's mind.

A function that is related to ReadKey is KeyPressed, which is also in the Crt unit. This function returns True when a key is pressed and False otherwise. The usual way to use the function is in a loop such as

```
repeat
until KeyPressed
```

As long as KeyPressed is False, the loop continues; when KeyPressed becomes True, the loop is terminated. The result is somewhat similar to that of ReadKey, except that the character entered by the user is still present in the keyboard buffer and may be read by subsequent statements, such as Read or Readln. Because of this characteristic, the KeyPressed function should be used with care and only in situations (such as at the end of a program) when the program will not read any further data from the keyboard.

8.1.1   *Time Out*

1. Test Program 8a to create a disk file with a name of your choosing. Use the Turbo Pascal editor to examine the file after you have created it.
2. By entering PRN as the file name, you can use Program 8a as a typewriter. It will print on the printer each line of text that you enter. If you have access to a printer, try out this way of using the program.
3. By entering CON as the file name, you can cause the text that you enter to be displayed on the screen immediately below the line on which it was entered. Although this is not particularly useful, the technique can help in debugging programs that create output to a Text file. Try this with Program 8a.
4. Because of the way Program 8a is written, it is not possible to transmit an empty line of text to the file. One way that you could use to get around this problem is to have the user enter a specific character, such as "$", as the content of the line to terminate the program. Make this modification to Program 8a.

5. Modify Program 8a to allow the user to enter the character that he or she wishes to use to terminate the data-entry process. This would be done as part of the preliminary instructions before or after the output file is opened.

8.1.2   String Concatenation

Pascal allows you to perform the concatenation of two strings, using the operator $+$. The word *concatenation* means "a bringing together." When you concatenate two strings, you bring them together to make one string. For example, the value of 'A' + 'BC' is 'ABC'. Concatenation is the only operation that you can perform on string data.

Concatenation can be performed with string constants or variables. For example, suppose the following declarations are in effect:

```
var
     X, Y, Z : string[10];
```

Then the following statements would cause the value 'XYZ, Inc.' to be stored in Z:

```
X := 'XYZ,';
Y := 'Inc.';
Z := X + ' ' + Y;
```

Strings can be used as "accumulators" in a way somewhat analogous to the accumulation concept we used with numeric and set variables. You would initialize the string variable to contain the null string and then concatenate strings to it. For example, the following program segment could be used to construct a sentence from a sequence of words entered by the user:

```
var
     Sentence, Word : string;
          .
          .
          .
begin
     Sentence := '';
     repeat
          Writeln ('Enter word ');
          Readln (Word);
          if Word <> '' then
               Sentence := Sentence + Word + ' ';
     until Word = '';
```

The only restriction on this program is that the maximum length of the sentence be 255 characters. If the length of the string expression exceeds the size of the string variable into which it is placed, the string will be truncated on the right. For example, assume that S is defined as follows:

```
var
    S : string[5];
```

Then after execution of the statement

```
S := 'ABCDEF';
```

the value contained in S will be 'ABCDE'.

The function Concat is also available to perform concatenation. The general form for invoking this function is

```
Concat (string-1, string-2, ..., string-n)
```

where each of the parameters is a string variable, constant, or expression. At least two parameters must be included, but you can include as many as are needed. The value returned by the function is a string constructed by concatenating the content of the parameters from left to right. For example, the following two statements are equivalent (assuming X, Y, and Z are defined as shown before):

```
Z := X + ' ' + Y;
Z := Concat (X, ' ', Y);
```

Most programmers find the use of the concatenation operator more convenient than the concatenation function; the Turbo Pascal reference manual states that the function Concat is included primarily for compatibility with other versions of Pascal.

8.1.3   *Time Out*

1. Show the content of the variable A or C after each of the following assignment statements has been executed. Assume the following declarations:

```
const
    B = 'Turbo';
var
    A : string[15];
    C : string[3];
```

(a) A := B + ' is great';
(b) A := B + ' ' + B;
(c) A := Concat (B, ' ', 'Pascal');
(d) C := B;

2. Implement the sentence-building procedure just outlined in a simple program. Add to the program the ability to count the number of words in the sentence. Write out the sentence and number of words contained in the sentence.

3. Write a program to construct a string consisting of all consonants entered by the user. Ignore any vowels or other characters that are entered. Write out the string when all characters have been entered.

8.1.4   String Indexing

Pascal allows you to process individual characters in a string through the mechanism of string indexing. In this section, we examine this facility and describe the Length function, which is used in most processing of strings; it enables you to determine the number of characters in the string.

The Length function is invoked using the general form

```
Length (string)
```

where *string* is a string variable. The value of the function is an integer in the range 0 to 255 representing the number of characters in the string. The length of the null string is 0. For example, suppose X and Y are declared as

```
var
     X, Y : string[10];
```

and suppose the following statements are executed:

```
X := 'XYZ, Inc.';
Y := '';
```

Then the value of Length (X) would be 9, and the value of Length (Y) would be 0.

Pascal allows you to access the content of individual characters in a string using indexing, which has general form

```
string [index]
```

where *string* is a string variable and *index* is an integer expression. For example, if the string variable X has the value 'XYZ, Inc.', as just shown, the value of X[1] would be 'X', the value of X[2] would be 'Y', and so forth. The value of X[Length(X)] would be '.'; the value of X[Length(X) − 1] would be 'c'.

The indexing of string elements allows you to manipulate, test, and replace any desired character within a string. For example, the following procedure would count all of the vowels in a string of characters (assume Sentence is a string variable, Index and Count are Integer variables, and Vowels is a set of base type Char):

```
Vowels := ['A', 'E', 'I', 'O', 'U', 'a', 'e', 'i', 'o', 'u']
Count := 0;
```

```
for Index := 1 to Length (Sentence) do
    if Sentence[Index] in Vowels then
        Count := Count + 1;
```

An indexed string element can be used in an assignment statement to receive a value; the value must be a single character and will replace the character previously at that position. For example, if X has value 'XYZ, Inc.', then the following statements would change the content of X to 'ABC, Inc.':

```
X[1] := 'A';
X[2] := 'B';
X[3] := 'C';
```

In the following program segment, all vowels in the string Sentence will be replaced by a space (assume that Sentence, Vowels, and Index are as specified before):

```
for Index := 1 to Length (Sentence) do
    if Sentence[Index] in Vowels then
        Sentence[Index] := ' ';
```

Note that indexing cannot be used to change the length of a string; it allows you only to replace one character by another within a string.

The following program illustrates the use of string indexing to solve a problem.

■ **Problem Statement.**   Write a program to allow the user to enter a message consisting of any sequence of words. The maximum length of the message is 255 characters. The program must encode the message using a simple substitution scheme, as shown.

Character	Substitute
A	Z
B	Y
C	X
.	.
.	.
.	.
Z	A

Use a similar substitution rule for lowercase letters. Leave all other characters in the message unchanged.

■ **Problem Analysis.**   This program requires that the user enter the message to be encoded; it also requires that the new message be printed after the encoding process has been carried out. A preliminary plan for the program is as follows:

PRELIMINARY PLAN FOR MESSAGE-ENCODING PROGRAM

1.0 Read Message

2.0 Encode Message

3.0 Write Message

Step 2.0 in this procedure will entail examining each character in the message to make the appropriate substitution. If the character is an uppercase letter, there will be one substitution rule; if the character is lowercase, there will be another substitution rule. We can therefore revise the plan as shown next:

PLAN FOR MESSAGE-ENCODING PROGRAM (P8b)

1.0 Read Message

2.0 Encode Message

    2.1 For each Character in Message Do

    2.2   If Character is uppercase then

    2.3   Make uppercase substitution

    2.4   Else

    2.5   If Character is lowercase then

    2.6   Make lowercase substitution

    2.7   End If

    2.8   End If

    2.9 End For

3.0 Write Message

4.0 Wait

■ **Problem Solution.** Program 8b, which is shown in Figure 8.2, is a solution to this problem. Note particularly the statements that implement the actual character substitutions. These statements make use of the ordinal value of the character. The formula is derived from an observation of the relationships implied in the following table:

Character	Ord(Character)	Substitute	Ord(Substitute)
A	65	Z	90
B	66	Y	89
C	64	X	88
.	.	.	.
.	.	.	.
.	.	.	.
Z	90	A	65

Observe that Ord(Substitute) $= 90 + 65 -$ Ord(Character), or Ord('Z') $+$ Ord('A') $-$ Ord(Character). A similar relationship exists for the lowercase letters.

```pascal
program P8b (Input,Output);
{Message-encoding program; illustrates operations on string data}
uses Crt;
var
   Message : string;
   Index : Integer;
{*************************************************************************}
   .
   .
   .
   procedure Encode (var CharString : string);
   var
        Index : Integer;
   begin    {Encode}
        for Index := 1 to Length(CharString) do
        if CharString[Index] in ['A'..'Z'] then
            CharString[Index] :=
             Chr (Ord('Z') + Ord('A') - Ord(CharString[Index]))
        else if CharString[Index] in ['a'..'z'] then
            CharString[Index] :=
             Chr (Ord('z') + Ord('a') - Ord(CharString[Index]))
   end;     {Encode}
{*************************************************************************}
begin    {Main Program}

{1.0 Read Message}

    Writeln ('Enter message for encoding');
    Readln (Message);

{2.0 Encode Message}

    Encode (Message);

{3.0 Write Message}

    Writeln (Message);

{4.0 Wait}

    AlternateWait

end.     {Main Program}
```

Figure 8.2 Program 8b: Message-encoding program.

8.1.5 *Time Out*

1. Test Program 8b with data of your choosing.
2. Modify Program 8b to substitute the character '/' for each space in the message.
3. Modify Program 8b to replace all lowercase letters with uppercase before encoding the message. Replace all nonalphabetic characters by spaces.

8.1.6 **Internal Representation of Strings**

Turbo Pascal allocates a sequence of bytes in memory for a string; the number of bytes (that is, memory locations) to be allocated is determined by the variable declaration. As you have seen, not all of the possible positions in a string are necessarily used for storing data. The actual length of a string can vary from 0 to the length specified in the declaration.

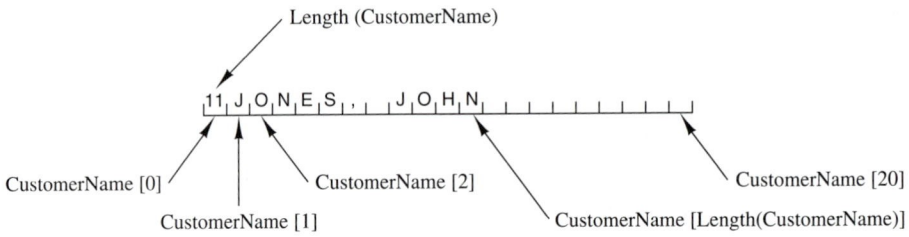

Figure 8.3 Internal representation of a string.

Internally, Turbo keeps track of the number of characters in a string using the first byte of the sequence of locations allocated for the string variable. The content of this byte is a number representing the length of the string. For example, suppose a program contains the following declaration:

```
var
    CustomerName : string[20];
```

Suppose also that the content of this variable is 'Jones, John'. Then the length of Customer Name is 11, and the internal representation of the string can be visualized as shown in Figure 8.3.

As shown in Figure 8.3, CustomerName[1] references the first character in the string, CustomerName[2] references the second character in the string, and so forth. The content of CustomerName[0] is the length of the string. In fact, Length(CustomerName) is equal to Ord(CustomerName[0]). If you change the value of the zeroth character in a string (which is *not* a recommended programming practice), you will have the effect of changing the length of a string. It is definitely the best policy to allow Pascal to compute the length of a string and maintain the content of the zeroth byte of the string for you; if you do modify this byte inadvertently, you run the risk of losing characters in a string.

8.1.7 String Functions

In addition to the functions Length (which returns the value of the length of a string) and Concat (which forms the concatenation of two or more strings), Turbo Pascal provides two other functions that can be useful in processing strings. These functions are **Copy**, which allows you to extract substrings from a string, and **Pos**, which allows you to locate substrings.

A **substring** is defined to be a sequence of characters within a string. For example, consider the string 'ABCD'. The following list contains all possible substrings of this string:

```
A
B
C
D
AB
BC
```

```
CD
ABC
BCD
ABCD
```

The Copy function allows you to extract any desired substring from a string. The general form for invocation of this function is

```
Copy (string, position, number)
```

where *string* is a string variable, *position* is an integer expression that represents the location within *string* of the beginning of the substring, and *number* is an integer expression that is the length of the substring. For example, suppose X is a string variable with content 'ABCD'. Following are some examples of the use of the Copy function to reference substrings of X:

Expression	Value
Copy (X, 1, 1)	'A'
Copy (X, 2, 3)	'BCD'
Copy (X, 2, 2)	'BC'

If the value of *position* + (*number* − 1) exceeds the length of the string, then the function returns a substring beginning at *position* and ending at the end of the string. For example, if X is defined as before, the value of Copy (X, 3, 3) would be 'CD' because 3 + (3 −1) is greater than 4, the length of the string. (This makes sense because the function would otherwise have to return a character beyond the end of the string.)

As an example of the use of the Copy function, let us write a program segment that would write out all substrings of a given string X. It is clear that the following statements would generate all substrings of length 1 from X (assume Position is an Integer variable):

```
for Position := 1 to Length (X) do
    Writeln (Copy(X, Position, 1));
```

In order to generate substrings of varying lengths, it will be necessary to vary the third parameter of the Copy function. The lengths of substrings of X vary from 1 to Length(X). Substrings of length 1 can begin at any position within X. Substrings of length 2 can begin at any position from 1 to Length(X) − 1. In general, a substring of length N can begin at any position in X from 1 to Length(X) − (N − 1). Using this analysis, we can write the following segment to perform the required task:

```
for N := 1 to Length(X) do
    for Position := 1 to Length(X) - (N - 1) do
        Writeln (Copy (X, Position, N) );
```

In this program segment, N represents the lengths of the substrings and Position represents the position within X for a particular substring. When N is equal to 1, the value of Position ranges from 1 to Length(X), thereby generating all substrings of length 1. When N is equal to 2, the value of Position ranges from 1 to Length(X) − 1, which generates all substrings of length 2. When N is equal to Length(X), Position assumes only the value 1, which causes the output of the only substring of length Length(X), which, of course, begins in position 1 of the string.

The function Pos (an abbreviation for Position) allows you to locate instances of a given substring within a string. A general form for invocation of this function is

```
Pos (object, string)
```

where *object* is a string-valued expression that represents the substring to be found and *string* is a string variable in which the search is to be made. The function returns an integer value representing the position of *object* within *string* if it exists; if the substring is not found, then the value of the function is 0. For example, suppose X is a string variable with value 'ABCD' and Y is a string variable with value 'CD'. Following are some examples of the use of the Pos function:

Expression	Value	Comment
Pos ('C',X)	3	'C' is in position 3
Pos ('AB',X)	1	'AB' begins in position 1
Pos (Y,X)	3	'CD' begins in position 3
Pos (X,Y)	0	Y does not contain 'ABCD'

As an example of the use of the Pos function, consider the problem of replacing all instances of one character by another within a string. For example, let us replace all instances of the space character within a string variable TextLine by the character '/'. One method that could be used is to search TextLine repeatedly for spaces and, when one is found, perform the required replacement. The following program segment could be used (assume Position is an Integer variable):

```
Position := Pos (' ', TextLine);
while Position <> 0 do
      begin
          TextLine[Position] := '/';
          Position := Pos (' ', TextLine)
      end; {while}
```

Although this technique is not as efficient as a simple sequential search of the characters in TextLine, it has the advantage of being quite flexible. It enables you to search for substrings of any length and (when combined with the procedures Delete and Insert, described in the following section) allows you to perform any desired operation on the substrings that are located.

8.1.8 Time Out

Assume that R is a string variable with value `'JOHN'` and S is a string variable with value `'MARY AND JOHN'`. What is the value of each of the following expressions?

1. Copy (S, 6, 3)
2. Copy (R, 3, 3)
3. Pos ('AND', S)
4. Pos (R, S)
5. Pos ('M', R)
6. Copy (S, 1, Pos (' ', S))

8.1.9 String Procedures: Delete and Insert

Turbo Pascal supports two procedures that provide additional very powerful string-processing capabilities. The procedure Delete allows you to delete any substring from a string; the procedure Insert allows you to insert a substring into the midst of a string.

The procedure Delete is useful for eliminating any substring from a string. The general form for executing this procedure is

```
Delete (string, position, number)
```

where *string* is a string variable, *position* is an integer-valued expression designating the position of the substring to be deleted, and *number* is the length of the substring. The content of *string* is returned by the procedure with the indicated substring removed; the length of the new value of *string* will be the old length minus *number*. For example, suppose X is a string variable with value 'ABCD'. Following are some examples of the use of Delete for various substrings of X:

Statement	New value of X
Delete (X, 2, 1)	'ACD'
Delete (X, 2, 2)	'AD'
Delete (X, 1, 3)	'D'
Delete (X, 1, 4)	' '(null string)

If the substring to be deleted extends beyond the actual end of the string, the characters from *position* to the end of the string will be deleted. For example, the result of the statement Delete (X, 3, 3) is 'AB'.

As an example of the use of the Delete procedure, let us delete all instances of the space character in a string variable TextString. The first task is to locate each space (the Pos function will enable us to do this) and then use the Delete procedure to delete a string of length 1 in each location. The following program segment could be used:

```
Position := Pos(' ', TextString);
while Position <> 0 do
    begin
        Delete (X, Position, 1);
        Position := Pos (' ', TextString)
    end; {while}
```

A simple variation of this technique allows you to delete all occurrences of a substring of any length. Let us write a program segment to remove all instances of multiple spaces between words in a string variable TextString. That is, we wish to replace all sequences of two or more spaces by a single space. For example, if the content of TextString was

'This is a test'

the new content should be

'This is a test'

We can accomplish this task by repeatedly locating all instances of two spaces and deleting one of the spaces. The following program segment could be used:

```
Position := Pos (' ', TextString);
while Position <> 0 do
    begin
        Delete (TextString, Position, 1);
        Position := Pos (' ', TextString)
    end; {while}
```

The procedure Insert allows you to insert any substring into a string. The general form for executing this procedure is

Insert (*object*, *string*, *position*)

where *object* is a string-valued expression that constitutes the substring to be inserted, *string* is the string in which the substring is to be inserted, and *position* is the location within the string for the insertion of the substring. For example, if X is a string variable with content 'ABCD', following are some examples of the use of the Insert procedure and its effect on the content of X:

Statement	New content of X
Insert ('E', X, 2)	'AEBCD'
Insert ('EE', X, 1)	'EEABCD'
Insert ('Z Z', X, 4)	'ABCZ ZD'

If *position* is greater than the length of *string*, then the effect is to concatenate *object* to *string*. For example, after execution of the statement

```
Insert ('E' X, 5)
```

the content of X would be 'ABCDE'. In general, the length of *string* after execution will be the length of *string* before execution plus the length of *object*.

As an example of the use of the Insert procedure, let us write a program segment that will insert a space following each character in a string. That is, suppose the string variable TextString contains 'Test'. Then the new content should be 'T e s t'. Note that the new character is to be inserted at positions 2, 4, 6, and so forth. With this in mind, we can write the following program segment:

```
Position := 2;
while Position < Length (TextString) do
        begin
                Insert (' ', TextString, Position);
                Position := Position + 2
        end; {while}
```

A combination of Delete and Insert can be used to replace all occurrences of one substring by another. For example, suppose we wish to replace all instances of two spaces in TextString by a single dash ('−'). We can locate each substring, delete it, and then insert the new substring. The following program segment could be used:

```
Position := Pos ('  ', Textstring)
while Position <> 0 do
        begin
                Delete (TextString, Position, 2);
                Insert ('-', TextString, Position);
                Position := Pos ('  '; TextString)
        end;          {while}
```

8.1.10   *Time Out*

1. Assume that the string variable R has the value 'JOHN' and the string variable S has the value 'MARY AND JOHN'. Show the value of the appropriate variable after execution of each of the following:
   (a) Delete (R, 2, 2)
   (b) Delete (S, Length(S) - 1,2)
   (c) Insert (' ', R, 1)
   (d) Insert (R + ' AND', S, 1)
   (e) Insert (' ', R, 6)
   (f) Delete (R, 3, 3)
2. Modify Program 8b to remove all spaces between words as part of the process of encoding the message.

3. Modify Program 8b to insert a space in the encoded message between every three characters, that is, the output should be of the form

        xxx xxx xxx . . .

4. Modify Program 8b to remove all instances of more than two spaces between words before writing the line of text that the user has entered.

8.1.11 String Procedures Str and Val

Turbo Pascal provides two procedures that you can use to convert between the character representation of a numeric value and the internal representation, as contained in a variable of type Real or Integer. The Str procedure converts from internal form to character form; the Val procedure converts from character form to internal form. These procedures can be useful in editing numeric output, and they provide additional latitude for the entry of numeric data by program users.

The Str procedure imports a numeric value and exports a string that contains the character representation of that value. Additionally, you can provide formatting information in the parameter list of the Str procedure similar to that provided in the parameter list of a Write or Writeln procedure. The general format for invocation of the Str procedure is

```
Str (write-parameter, string)
```

where *write-parameter* is a numeric expression of type Integer or Real, optionally followed by the format specifications, and *string* is a string variable. The Str procedure returns the character representation of *write-parameter* in *string*.

Following are some examples of the use of the Str procedure showing the content of the string variable after execution of the procedure. (Assume that X is an Integer variable with value -134, Y is a Real variable with value 12.3456, and Z is a string variable.)

Statement	Value of Z
`Str (X, Z)`	`'-134'`
`Str (X:6, Z)`	`'  -134'`
`Str (Y:7:4, Z)`	`'12.3456'`
`Str (Y:8:2, Z)`	`'   12.35'`

One way in which the Str procedure can be of value is in providing special formatting of numeric output. For example, suppose an account number is five digits in length, and we wish to print it out in the form

```
xx xx x
```

Then, using the Str procedure, we could convert the account number to character form, followed by inserting spaces at the desired locations with the Insert procedure. The following program segment could be used (assume AccountNumber is of type Integer and AccountNumberString is of type string):

```
Str (AccountNumber:5, AccountNumberString):
Insert(' ', AccountNumberString, 3);
Insert(' ', AccountNumberString, 6);
Writeln (...,AccountNumberString,...);
```

The Val procedure allows you to convert a string representing an Integer or Real numeric value into internal form and store the result in a numeric variable of the appropriate type. A general form for invocation of the Val procedure is

```
Val (string, variable, error-code)
```

where *string* is a string expression, *variable* is an Integer or Real variable, and *error-code* is an Integer variable. The Val procedure converts the content of *string* into numeric form and places the result in *variable*. The value of *error-code* will be 0 if no error occurs in the translation process. If the content of *string* is not a valid number of the same type as *variable*, then the content of *error-code* will be the position within *string* where the error was encountered, and the content of *variable* will be undefined.

Following are some examples of the use of the Val procedure and the results produced. (Assume that X and Code are Integer variables, Y is a Real variable, and S is a string variable with content '−123'.)

| Statement | Value of | | | Comment |
	X	Y	Code	
`Val ('12',X,Code)`	12		0	Valid Integer
`Val ('-1.23',Y,Code)`		−1.23	0	Valid Real
`Val (S,X,Code)`	−123		0	Valid Integer
`Val ('1.2',X,Code)`			2	Decimal point is invalid in an Integer value
`Val ('0.1.2',Y,Code)`			4	Second decimal point is invalid in a Real value
`Val ('1A',X,Code)`			2	Alphabetic character is invalid in a numeric value

One way to use the Val procedure is to make a program very specific in the error message presented to the user when invalid data have been entered. The program can read all input in string form and then use Val to extract the value of the variables from the data entered by the user. The value of *error-code* can then be used to determine if the data is valid or, if not, the position of the error. The following program segment could be used to enter and validate the value of an integer variable DataItem (assume ErrorCode is of type Integer and DataString is of type string):

```
ErrorCode := 1;
while ErrorCode <> 0 do
      begin
           Write ('Enter data value ');
           Readln (DataString);
           Val (DataString, DataItem, ErrorCode);
           if ErrorCode <> 0 then
                Writeln ('Error encountered in position ',
                     ErrorCode, ' of the value just entered')
      end; {while}
```

Another advantage of the Val procedure is that it allows the user great flexibility in the choice of characters for entering numeric data. For example, novice users sometimes enter commas in large numbers (e.g., '12,345' instead of the required '12345') or dollar signs (e.g., '$12.34' instead of the required '12.34'). A program could edit out offending characters before using the Val procedure to translate the data into internal form. The following program segment removes all commas and dollar signs from DataString before using the Val procedure to translate the input into internal form:

```
Write ('Enter data value ');
Readln (DataString);
Position := Pos ('$', DataString);
while Position <> 0 do
      begin
           Delete (DataString, Position, 1);
           Position := Pos ('$'; DataString)
      end; {while}
Position := Pos (',', DataString);
while Position <> 0 do
      begin
           Delete (Datastring, Position, 1);
           Position := Pos (',',DataString)
      end; {while}
Val (DataString, DataItem, ErrorCode);
if ErrorCode <> 0 then
      ...;
```

8.1.12 *Time Out*

Assume that A is an Integer variable with value 456, B is a Real variable with value −45.6789, and S is a string variable. Show the value of S after execution of each of the following:

1. `Str(A:6, S)`

2. `Str(B:8:2, S)`

3. `Str(123.7:6:0, S)`

4. `Str((-A+B):8:1, S)`

Assume that T is a string variable with value '−2.789', D and C are Integer variables, and R is a Real variable. Show the values of relevant variables after execution of each of the following:

5. `Val (T, R, C)`

6. `Val ('-12345', D, C)`

7. `Val ('123-', D, C)`

8. `Val ('$2.34', R, C)`

9. Modify the program segment in Section 8.1.11 to remove all alphabetic characters from DataString before performing the conversion of the content of DataString to numeric form.

10. Write a program segment that will edit the real numeric variable RealData as follows:

   `$xx,xxx.xx`

   If the two leading digits are zeros, a space should be printed instead of a comma.

8.2 STRING-TYPE PARAMETERS

As you know, Pascal normally requires the types of formal and actual parameters to match. If they do not, a compilation-time error results. In the case of string parameters, the normal requirement is that the same type identifier must be used in the declaration of both the formal parameter and the actual parameter. The following program outline illustrates this practice:

```
type
     TextString : string(80);
var
     ActualParameter1, ActualParameter2 : TextString;
```

Note: **same type**

```
{*************************************************************************}
     procedure StringProcessor(...FormalParameter : TextString;...);
```

```
{*************************************************************************}
begin
```

```
     StringProcessor (...ActualParameter1...);
```

```
     StringProcessor (...ActualParameter2...);
```

```
end.
```

Turbo Pascal relaxes the preceding requirement for string type parameters in two ways: For value parameters, the only requirement is that the actual and formal parameters be string type; for variable parameters, the more rigid standard is normally enforced by the compiler. However, by using the V compiler directive, you can direct the compiler to use the more relaxed standard for variable parameters. The default setting for the V directive is {$V+}, meaning that rigorous type checking is to be required. If you reset the option to negative, using the directive {$V−}, then the only requirement for string variable parameters is that the formal and actual parameters be of type string. The use of this directive is illustrated in the following program outline:

```
{$V-}
type
     TextString : string[80];
var
     ActualParameter1 : string[12];
     ActualParameter2 : string[30];
```

Note: **different types**

```
{******************************************************************}
      procedure StringProcessor(...var FormalParameter : TextString;...);
             .
             .
             .
{******************************************************************}
begin
             .
             .
             .
          StringProcessor (...ActualParameter1...);
             .
             .
             .
          StringProcessor (...ActualParameter2...);
             .
             .
             .
end.
```

The use of the V compiler directive is illustrated in the context of a complete program in the solution to the following problem.

■ **Problem Statement.**   Write a program to convert decimal numbers to binary (base 2).

■ **Problem Analysis.**   A procedure that can be used to convert from base 10 (decimal) to base 2 (binary) is illustrated in Figure 8.4. You divide the decimal number by 2, retaining the remainder as a binary digit. The process is repeated, using the integer quotient of the preceding division until the quotient is zero. The remainders form the digits of the binary numeral. Given the limits of the number of digits in an Integer data item (32,767 is the greatest Integer), it is necessary to represent the binary numeral as a string. Thus, a procedure for converting from decimal to binary can retain the binary digits by concatenating each new digit, as it is computed, to a string variable that has been initialized to the null string. When the quotient is zero, the string variable will contain the accumulated bits (*bi*nary digi*t*s) that make up the binary numeral. A plan for a procedure, which we will call

Figure 8.4 Conversion of a base-10 number to binary using repeated division.

Convert, is as follows:

PROCEDURE CONVERT (IMPORT : DECIMAL, EXPORT : BINARY)

1.0 Binary = null string

2.0 While Decimal <> 0 Do

3.0   Digit = Remainder after dividing Decimal by 2

4.0   Decimal = Decimal divided by 2

5.0   Concatenate character representation of Digit to Binary

6.0 End While

The main program that is needed for this procedure is quite simple: We will terminate data entry when the user enters the value 0. The plan for the main program is as follows:

PLAN FOR DECIMAL-TO-BINARY CONVERSION PROGRAM (P8c)

1.0 Clear the screen

2.0 Read Decimal number

3.0 While not last number, convert to binary and read next number

     3.1 While Decimal number <> 0 Do

     3.2   Convert Decimal number to binary

     3.3   Write Decimal number and Binary equivalent

     3.4   Read Decimal number

     3.5 End While

■ **Problem Solution.**   The solution to this problem is shown in Figure 8.5 (Program 8c). Note in this program that the formal parameter for the procedure Convert is declared to be of type TextString, and the actual parameter BinaryString is declared as type string[16]. Ordinarily, this would result in a compilation error; however, the inclusion of the compiler directive {$V−} avoids the problem and allows the program to compile and execute without any errors. Note also in the procedure Convert that the Str procedure is used to compute the character representation (which is stored in the string variable Bit) of the Integer variable Digit. The statement that follows concatenates each Bit onto the left of the existing content of Binary.

8.2.1   Time Out

1. Compile and execute Program 8c. Test the program with data of your choice.

2. Change the V compiler directive to positive (substitute {$V+} for {$V−}). Attempt to compile the program again, and note the error message that results.

3. Add a procedure to Program 8c that will convert from binary to decimal. An appropriate procedure can be derived from observing the following relationship:

$$11010_2 = 1 \times 2^4 + 1 \times 2^3 + 0 \times 2^2 + 1 \times 2^1 + 0 \times 2^0$$
$$= ((((1 \times 2) + 1) \times 2 + 0) \times 2 + 1) \times 2 + 0 = 26_{10}$$

Allow the user of the new program to choose which function he or she wishes to perform.

```
program P8c (Input, Output);
{Program converts decimal values entered by the user to binary}
{$V-}  {Relax parameter type matching for variable string parameters}
uses Crt;
const
    InputPrompt = 'Enter decimal number (0 to quit) ';
type
    TextString = string[80];
var
    BinaryString : string[16];
    DecimalValue : Integer;
{*********************************************************************}
    procedure Convert (Decimal : Integer;
                  var Binary : TextString);
    {Procedure to convert decimal to binary}
    var
        Digit : Integer;
        Bit : string[1];
    begin      {Convert}
        Binary := '';
        while Decimal <> 0 do
            begin
                Digit := Decimal mod 2;
                Decimal := Decimal div 2;
                Str (Digit, Bit);
                Binary := Bit + Binary
            end;    {while}
    end;   {Convert}
{*********************************************************************}
begin {Main Program}

{1.0 Clear the screen}

    ClrScr;

{2.0 Read Decimal number}

    Write (InputPrompt);
    Readln (DecimalValue);

{3.0 While not last number, convert to binary and read next number}

    while DecimalValue <> 0 do
        begin
            Convert (DecimalValue, BinaryString);
            Writeln ('The value of ', DecimalValue, ' base 10 is ',
                    BinaryString, ' base 2');
            Writeln;
            Write (InputPrompt);
            Readln (DecimalValue)
        end;    {while}

end.   {Main Program}
```

Figure 8.5 Program 8c: Decimal-to-binary conversion program.

8.3   RANDOM NUMBERS

Often, there is a need to solve problems in which there is an element of uncertainty. We deal with such problems on a daily basis; for example, when we invest money or play games, there is no way to predict the outcome with certainty. In such situations, we measure the uncertainty in terms of probability. Thus, when a coin is flipped, we assume that there is a 50% probability that the result will be a head and a like probability that the result will be a tail. When a card is dealt from a deck of 52 cards, we assume that the probability of getting any particular card is 1/52. When we invest money in a stock, we may not have a formal estimate of the probability of the stock reaching a desired level, but we attempt to assess the probability informally by taking into account the past history of the stock, the state of the economy, and so forth.

We can simulate such events on the computer by using random numbers. A **random number** is a number that has characteristics of unpredictability. Turbo Pascal provides two ways to generate random numbers. The function **Random**, when invoked without specifying an argument, returns a real random number in the range 0 to 1. For example, the following program segment prints a list of 10 such random numbers (assume X is a Real variable);

```
for I := 1 to 10 do
    begin
        X := Random;
        Writeln (X)
    end;  {for}
```

The values of X will be greater than or equal to 0 and less than 1.

The second alternative is to use the function Random with an Integer argument, according to the general form

```
Random (number)
```

In this case, the function returns an integer value greater than or equal to 0 and less than the value of *number*. For example, the following program segment will print a list of 10 random numbers in the range 0 through 9 (assume Y is an Integer variable):

```
for I := 1 to 10 do
    begin
        Y := Random (10);
        Writeln (Y)
    end;  {for}
```

The values of Y will all be from the set [0, 1, 2, 3, 4, 5, 6, 7, 8, 9], but there will be no apparent pattern to the sequence; that is, they will appear to be drawn at random.

In both cases, what the system is actually doing is generating terms of a sequence based on an initial value called a *seed*. This seed value is normally the same each time the program is loaded. Thus, each time the program is recompiled and executed, the same sequence will be generated. If it is executed without recompilation, the sequence will be different because the seed is not reset. (Technically, the sequence is one of *pseudorandom numbers*, because the numbers are repeatable; true random number sequences cannot be repeated. Pseudorandom numbers are useful because they have other characteristics of randomness attributed to true random numbers.) The procedure Randomize can be invoked prior to execution of either of the preceding program segments to have the system generate a seed value at random. For example, the following program segment will simulate the tossing of a coin 20 times; each time the program is recompiled and executed, a different sequence of outcomes is expected:

```
Randomize;
for I := 1 to 20 do
    if Random(2) = 0 then
        Write ('H')
    else
        Write ('T');
Writeln;
```

In some situations, it may be necessary to transform the output of the random number generator slightly to yield a value more appropriate to the problem being solved. For example, in a program that simulates the throwing of a die, which has six possible outcomes (1 through 6), the following program statement would be appropriate:

```
Die := Random (6) + 1;
```

The value Random (6) will be in the range 0 through 5. Adding 1 will transform the value so that the range will be 1 through 6. In order to generate a Real random number in the range 0 to 2, the following statement could be used:

```
X := 2 * Random;
```

In this case, the value of Random will be in the range 0 to 1. Multiplying by 2 will transform the value so that the range is 0 to 2, as desired.

The following example illustrates the use of random numbers to give an estimate of a player's chances of winning a game played with dice.

■ **Problem Statement.** Two players begin playing a game with $20 each and a pair of dice. Each player rolls one of the dice. If the numbers on the two dice match, Player 2 pays Player 1 twice the face value of one of the dice. (For example, if they both roll threes, the second player pays the first player 2 × 3 = $6.) If the numbers on the dice do not match, then Player 1 pays Player 2 an amount equal to the difference between the two dice. (For example, if one player rolls 5 and the other player rolls 2, Player 1 owes 5 − 2 = $3 to Player 2. Note that it does not matter which player rolled the larger value. The amount owed to Player 2 is the absolute value of the difference between the two values.) The game stops when one of the players is bankrupt. The player who wins all the money is the winner of the game. What are the chances of each player winning this game?

■ **Problem Analysis.**   Intuitively, we might suspect that Player 2 has an advantage in this game because the probability that two dice will not match is much greater than the probability that they will, and hence, Player 2 will receive money more frequently than Player 1. Attaching a particular number to this probability is quite difficult because of the ways in which the players are paid and the limit on the bankroll for each player. In order to gain an estimate of the probability, we can simulate the playing of the game repeatedly and keep track of the number of times each player wins. For example, if we play the game 100 times and find that Player 1 has won 12 games, then we can estimate Player 1's chances of winning at $(12/100) \times 100 = 12\%$. (This is, by the way, approximately Player 1's chances of winning the game.) With this analysis in mind, we can design the program as follows:

DICE GAME SIMULATION PROGRAM (P8d)

1.0 Initialize counters for each player's wins

2.0 Play game a number of times

3.0 Write estimate of each player's chances of winning

4.0 Wait

Let us turn our attention to the task of playing one game. Each player starts with the same amount of the money, and play continues until one of the players has won all the other player's money. Following the rules of play just outlined, we can design a procedure to determine a winner of a game as follows:

PROCEDURE PLAYGAME (EXPORT: WHOWON)

1.0 Initialize each player's money supply

2.0 While neither player is bankrupt Do

3.0   Roll dice

4.0   If dice are equal Then

5.0   Add appropriate amount to Player1's money and subtract from Player2

6.0   Else

7.0   Add appropriate amount to Player2's money and subtract from Player1

8.0   End If

9.0 End While

10.0 If Player1 is bankrupt Then

11.0   WhoWon = 2

12.0 Else

13.0   WhoWon = 1

14.0 End If

■ **Problem Solution.**   A solution to this problem is shown in Figure 8.6 (Program 8d). In this case, the number of games played is set to 100, which is the value contained in the constant NumberGames. This is an arbitrarily chosen number. Clearly, we must play the game many times in order to get an accurate estimate of the probability. The choice of the number of repetitions needed for the program to give a "good" estimate of the actual probability is difficult. A theoretical basis exists for making this decision, but

```pascal
program P8d (Output);
{Program to simulate playing of a dice game}
uses Crt;
type
    WinnerType = 1..2;
const
    NumberGames = 100;
var
    Game       : Integer;      {Game Number}
    Winner     : WinnerType;
    Win1, Win2 : Real;           {Number wins for each player}
{*********************************************************************}
    procedure PlayGame (var WhoWon : WinnerType);
    {Procedure to play game one time}
    const
        BankRoll = 20;
    var
        Play1, Play2,          {Current winnings for each player}
        Die1, Die2 : Integer; {Random variables}
    begin   {PlayGame}
        Play1 := BankRoll;
        Play2 := BankRoll;
        while (Play1 > 0) and (Play2 > 0) do
              begin
                    Die1 := Random (6) + 1;
                    Die2 := Random (6) + 1;
                    if Die1 = Die2 then
                        begin
                              Play1 := Play1 + 2 * Die1;
                              Play2 := Play2 - 2 * Die1;
                        end
                    else
                        begin
                              Play1 := Play1 - Abs(Die1-Die2);
                              Play2 := Play2 + Abs(Die1-Die2)
                        end    {if}
              end;   {while}
            if Play1 > 0 then
                WhoWon := 1
            else
                WhoWon := 2;
    end;   {PlayGame}
    .
    .
    .
{*********************************************************************}
```

Figure 8.6(a) Program 8d: Dice game simulation. Declaration part (part 1 of 2 parts).

```
begin    {Main Program}

{1.0 Initialize counters for each player's wins}

     Win1 := 0;
     Win2 := 0;

{2.0 Play game a number of times}

     Randomize;
     Write ('Game # ');
     for Game := 1 to NumberGames do
         begin
             PlayGame (Winner);
             if Winner = 1 then
                Win1 := Win1 + 1
             else
                Win2 := Win2 + 1;
             Write (Game:4)
         end;   {for}

{3.0 Write estimate for each player's chances of winning}

     Writeln;
     Writeln('Player 1 won ',Win1:4:0, ' of ',NumberGames,' games');
     Writeln('Player 2 won ',Win2:4:0, ' of ',NumberGames,' games');
     Writeln;
     Writeln('Estimated probability for Player 1 winning is ',
             Win1 * 100 / NumberGames:4:2, '%');
     Writeln('Estimated probability for Player 2 winning is ',
             Win2 * 100 / NumberGames:4:2, '%');

{4.0 Wait}

     AlternateWait;

end.   {Main Program}
```

Figure 8.6(b) Program 8d: Dice game simulation. Statement part (part 2 of 2 parts).

the details are beyond the scope of the text. (Any book on the subject of simulation can provide details on the topic.)

8.3.1   *Time Out*

1. Write a simple program to list 20 Real random numbers in the range 0 to 1. Modify the program to list numbers in the range 0 to 3. Modify the program to list numbers in the range 1 to 3.

2. Write a program to list 20 Integer random numbers in the range 0 to 1. Modify the program to list numbers in the range 0 to 5. Modify the program to list numbers in the range 1 to 6.

3. Compile and execute Program 8d. Execute the program a second time without recompiling. Is the second result identical to the first? Is this to be expected?

4. Change the number of games played in Program 8d in increments of 100 from 100 to 500. What effect does this have on the value of the probability estimate?

5. A way to make the dice game fairer is to change the multiplier used to determine the amount of money awarded to Player 1 when the dice are equal. Revise Program 8d to vary this number from 2 to 4 in increments of 0.5. Observe the effect this change has on the estimate of the probability that Player 1 will win. At what point would you estimate that the game is "fair," i.e., that each player has an approximately equal chance of winning?

8.4 PROGRAMMER-DEFINED FUNCTIONS

We have often had occasion to write a procedure that imports several values and uses one variable to export the result of a computation to the calling program. In such cases, we could have written a function rather than a procedure. A function is a specialized type of subprogram that accepts values of arguments and returns a single value. The advantage of using a function as opposed to a procedure to accomplish the same purpose is that a function can be incorporated into an expression and hence offers a large measure of flexibility in its usage (compared with a procedure, which is always invoked by a separate statement). You have used a number of functions provided as a standard part of Turbo Pascal; after studying this section, you will be able to write your own.

A function declaration closely resembles a procedure declaration, except that the heading is a function heading rather than a procedure heading. The general form of a function declaration is as follows:

```
function-heading;
declaration-part;
begin
    statement;
    .
    .
    .
end;
```

A **function-heading** has one of two general forms:

Form 1

```
function function-name: type;
```

Form 2

```
function function-name (formal-parameter-section) : type;
```

A Form 1-type function heading is used when there are no parameters for the function. (We have seen a few standard functions that do not require parameters—e.g., Random and KeyPressed). Form 2 function headings are probably more common. The syntax of *formal-parameter-section* is exactly the same for a function as it is for a procedure. A function usually makes use of value parameters only, but Pascal syntax permits variable parameters as well. The major difference between a procedure heading and a function heading is in the concluding specification of *type,* which must be a type identifier. This specifies the data type of the function; it governs the type of the data that will be returned to the calling program when the function is executed.

For example, let us write a heading for a function F, which will accept one Integer parameter X and a Real parameter Y, and which will return a Real value. The following heading could be used:

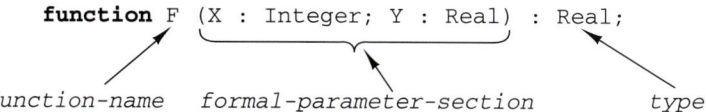

```
function F (X : Integer; Y : Real) : Real;
```

$\qquad$ function-name   formal-parameter-section   type

In this case, both parameters are value parameters. If the function needed to change the value of one or more of these parameters, then the appropriate parameter would be declared as a variable parameter, using one of the following statements:

```
function F (var X : Integer; Y : Real) : Real;
function F (X : Integer; var : Real) : Real;
function F (var X : Integer; var Y : Real) : Real;
```

Normally, functions do not change the values of their parameters.

Any scalar, string, or pointer data type can be used as the type of a function. (In standard Pascal only simple types can be returned by a function.) The specification of the type of the function must be made by an identifier. For other types, such as string with a specified length or a programmer-defined data type, it is necessary to declare an identifier for the data type prior to declaring the function. For example, suppose we desire to create a function S that will return a string value of maximum length 80. Then the following declaration would be invalid:

```
function S (...) : string [80];
```

Instead, in order to create the desired function, you would have to declare an identifier for the data type and use the identifier in the function heading, as follows:

```
type
    StringType = string[80];
    .
    .
    .
    function S (...) : StringType;
    .
    .
    .
```

Within the statement part of a function, the **value of the function** is computed, and that value is assigned to *function-name* in an assignment statement. The general form of this statement is

```
function-name := expression
```

It is important that *function-name* be used on the left side of the statement only. In some respects, *function-name* acts as a variable. It receives and stores a value, just as a variable does. But if *function-name* is used as part of an expression, the system assumes that you mean to invoke the function rather than use its current value as you would a variable. Invocation of a function by itself is called recursion and, although possible in Pascal, this technique must be used with deliberation and care. (We discuss recursion in Section 8.6.) For the present, you should avoid having a function reference itself.

For example, consider the very simple function that would compute the sum of two Integer numbers. The value to be returned is to be an Integer. The following function declaration would define this function:

```
function Add (X, Y : Integer) : Integer;
begin {Add}
    Add := X + Y
end; {Add}
```

In this case, X and Y are value parameters. The only statement in the statement part of the declaration assigns the value $X + Y$ to the function, using the function name on the left side of the assignment statement. This function could be invoked in a large number of ways by a program that included the function itself among its declarations. For example, all the following would be legitimate uses of the function Add (assume all variables are of type Integer):

```
A := Add (B, C); {Equivalent to A := B + C}
B := Add (A+B, C+2*D); {Equivalent to B := A + B + C + 2*D}
C := Add (Add (A, 4), Add(B, -2)); {Equivalent to C := A + 4 + B + (-2)}
```

It may be necessary to define a variable within the function declaration to be used in doing the computation of the value of the function and then assign that value to the function as a last step before returning to the calling program. This is especially true if the computation uses any form of accumulation. For example, let us write a Real-valued function to compute the factorial of an Integer argument. Recall that the factorial of a number N is defined as

$$N! = 1 \times 2 \times 3 \times \ldots \times (N-1) \times N$$

For example, $3! = 1 \times 2 \times 3 = 6$ and $5! = 1 \times 2 \times 3 \times 4 \times 5 = 120$. An appropriate procedure for computing a factorial is to use accumulation. The accumulator is initialized to 1 and then replaced by its current value times each of the integers from 1 to N. The following plan can be used:

1.0 Fact = 1
2.0 For I = 1 to N Do
3.0   Fact = Fact * I
4.0 End For

This plan can be implemented as a Pascal function as follows:

```
function Factorial (N : Integer) : Real;
var
     Fact   : Real;
     I      : Integer;
begin    {Factorial}
     Fact := 1.0;
     for I := 1 to N do
             Fact := Fact * I;
     Factorial := Fact
end;        {Factorial}
```

In this case, the use of the intermediate variable Fact is imperative to the design of the function. A statement such as Factorial := Factorial * I would result in an error because the compiler would understand this to be an invocation of the function Factorial itself.

You may use as many statements of the form

```
function-name := expression
```

as needed in defining the value of a function. Consider the following example. The procedure PlayGame in Program 8d could have been implemented as a function, since it returns a single value to the calling program. Let us revise this procedure and make it a function. Note that the procedure imports no values from the calling program; hence, the function needs no parameter list. The following program segment could replace the definition of the procedure PlayGame in Program 8d:

```
function WhoWon : WinnerType;
{Function to determine winner of a game}
const
     BankRoll = 20;
var
     Play1, Play2, Die1, Die2 : Integer;
begin     {WhoWon}
     .
     .
     .
     if Play1 > 0 then
             WhoWon := 1
```

```
                else
                    WhoWon := 2
        end;    {WhoWon}
```

Note the use of two statements to specify the value to be returned by the function. If this function is included in Program 8d, then Module 2.0 of the main program would be revised as follows:

```
{2.0 Play game a number of times}
    Write ('Game # ');
    for Game := 1 to NumberGames do
        begin
            if WhoWon = 1 then
                Win1 := Win1 + 1;
            else
                Win2 := Win2 + 1;
            Write (Game:4)
        end; {for}
```

As this example shows, it is often possible to carry out a programming task using either a procedure or a function. How do you determine which is best in a given set of circumstances? Unfortunately, there is no easy answer to this question, because it is often a matter of style and taste. The following guideline, however, is sensible and is a rule often used:

Use a function if there is a single variable parameter; if there is more than one variable parameter, use a procedure.

As a corollary to this rule, you should avoid using variable parameters in a function. A function should not change the value of its parameters. If you are forced by the logic of a problem into writing a function with a variable parameter, consider writing a procedure with two variable parameters instead.

8.4.1   Time Out

1. A programmer has written the following function to compute the largest of two real arguments. The code contains one syntax error and one logical error. Find each error.

```
function Big (A, B : Real);
var
    Large : Real;
begin
    if A > B then
        Large := A
    else
        Large := B
end;
```

2. Write a Real-valued function SumOdd that will compute the sum of the odd integers less than or equal to the value of an Integer parameter.

3. Write a string-valued function Reverse that would reverse the characters in its string-valued parameter.

4. Modify Program 8d to make use of the function WhoWon described earlier. The output produced by the program should not change by making this substitution.

8.5 Case Study: Twin Primes

■ **Problem Statement.** A prime number is an integer that is divisible only by 1 and itself. The first few primes are 2, 3, 5, 7, 11, and 13. The number 1 is not considered to be a prime number. Primes that are consecutive odd integers are called *twin primes*. For example, 3 and 5 are twin primes, as are 11 and 13. Write a program to list the first 15 twin primes.

■ **Problem Analysis.** A technique that can be used to solve this problem is to examine successive pairs of odd integers. When a pair of integers that are both prime are located, these should be written. The loop can be controlled by counting, since we must locate 15 of the pairs. The program will also need to make use of counting to generate odd integers for testing. The following program plan can be used:

PRELIMINARY PLAN FOR TWIN PRIME PROGRAM

1.0 Initialize variables

2.0 Write report heading

3.0 Repeat search for twin primes until desired numbers have been found

Let us use the variable Count to count the number of twin primes located so far and the variable Number to generate odd integers for examination. Count will be incremented by 1 each time a twin prime is located; Number will be incremented by 2 to generate the next odd integer for examination. We can refine the preliminary plan as follows:

PLAN FOR TWIN PRIME PROGRAM (P8e)

1.0 Clear the screen

2.0 Initialize variables

    2.1 Count = 0

    2.2 Number = 3

3.0 Write report heading

4.0 Repeat search for twin primes until desired numbers have been found

    4.1 Do

    4.2   While Number and Number + 2 are not prime Do

    4.3   Number = Number + 2

    4.4   End While

4.5   Write Number and Number + 2
4.6   Number = Number + 2
4.7   Count = Count + 1
4.8 Until Count = 15
5.0 Wait

In this program, it will be necessary to determine whether a number is prime or not in a convenient fashion. We can design a function Prime that will accept an Integer-valued argument and return True if the argument is prime and False if it is not. A technique that can be used to determine whether a number is prime is to divide by successive integers, beginning with 2 and ending with half the number. If a divisor is found, then the number is not prime; if no divisor is found in this range, then the number is prime. We can summarize such an analysis in the following plan for the function Prime, which will return a Boolean value:

BOOLEAN FUNCTION PRIME (IMPORT : NUMBER)

1.0 Prime = True
2.0 For Divisor = 2 to Number / 2 Do
3.0   If Divisor is a divisor of Number Then
4.0   Prime = False
5.0   End If
6.0 End For

■ **Problem Solution.**   A complete program for solving this problem is shown in Figure 8.7 as Program 8e. Note the convenience of using a function in this case. Module 3.0 in the Main Program invokes the function in a very descriptive fashion:

```
while not (Prime (Number) and Prime (Number + 2)) do
       . . . ;
```

In other words, when both numbers aren't prime, continue the search for two numbers that are prime.

In this program, the number of pairs to be found is contained in the constant NumberOfTwinPrimes. You will find that when this value is reasonably small, the program produces its output in short order, but as this value increases, the program takes longer and longer to produce its output for larger primes. Although nothing can be done to change this characteristic completely (it will always take longer to determine whether a large number is prime than to determine whether a small number is prime), there are two things that can be done to the program to produce noticeably improved performance.

In the function Prime, the for loop actually generates many more tests than are necessary much of the time: All that is required to terminate the loop is to find one divisor; if one is found, we do not care how many more might exist. Thus, we can revise the plan by omitting the for loop and using counting to generate the possible divisors of Number. The

```
program P8e (Input, Output);
{Program to find twin primes}
uses Crt;
const
     NumberOfTwinPrimes = 15;
var
     Number, Count : Integer;
{*********************************************************************}
     function Prime (Number : Integer) : Boolean;
     {Function returns True if Number is Prime and False otherwise}
     var
         Divisor : Integer;
     begin    {Prime}
         Prime := True;
         for Divisor := 2 to Number div 2 do
             if Number mod Divisor = 0 then
                 Prime := False;
     end;    {Prime}
     .
     .
     .
{*********************************************************************}
begin   {Main Program}

{1.0 Clear the screen}

     ClrScr;

{2.0 Initialize variables}

     Count := 0;
     Number := 3;

{3.0 Write report heading}

     Writeln ('Following numbers are twin primes');

{4.0 Repeat search for twin primes until desired numbers have been found}

     repeat
         while not (Prime (Number) and Prime (Number + 2)) do
             Number := Number + 2;
         Writeln (Number:5, Number + 2:5);
         Number := Number + 2;
         Count := Count + 1
     until Count = NumberOfTwinPrimes;

{5.0 Wait}

     AlternateWait

end.   {Main Program}
```

Figure 8.7 Program 8e: Twin Primes Program.

loop will continue while the value of the function continues to be True and the value of Divisor is less than Number divided by 2. The revised plan for the function is as follows.

ALTERNATIVE PLAN FOR BOOLEAN FUNCTION PRIME (IMPORT : NUMBER)

1.0 Prime = True

2.0 Divisor = 2

3.0 While Prime and Divisor < Number / 2 Do

4.0   If Divisor is a divisor of Number Then

5.0   Prime = False

6.0   End If

7.0   Divisor = Divisor + 1

8.0 End While

When this plan is implemented in Pascal, it will be necessary to use an intermediate variable to contain the value of the function and then assign this value to Prime prior to returning control to the calling program. The reason that this will be necessary is that a statement such as

```
while Prime and (Divisor < Number div 2) do
       . . .
```

will be treated by the compiler as an invocation of the function Prime.

Another way to make Program 8e more efficient is to avoid testing Number + 2 to see whether it is Prime if it has already been determined that Number is not prime. (If Number is not prime, then it does not matter whether Number + 2 is prime, since the pair cannot be a twin prime pair.) Unfortunately, in evaluating the logical expression

```
not (Prime (Number) and Prime (Number + 2))
```

the system determines a value for Prime (Number) and Prime (Number + 2) before determining the value for the whole expression.[1] We can modify the design of Module 4.0 of the program plan to avoid this problem as follows:

4.0 Repeat Search for twin primes until desired number have been found

    4.1 Do

    4.2   If Number is prime Then

    4.3   If Number + 2 is prime Then

    4.4   Write Number and Number + 2

    4.5   Count = Count + 1

---

[1]The use of short-circuit evaluation of Boolean expressions, which is available in Versions 4 and later of Turbo Pascal, can be of value solving this problem. See Appendix F, Section F.2, for details.

4.6   End If
4.7   End If
4.8   Number = Number + 2
4.9 Until Count = 15

In this way, the only time that Number + 2 is tested is when we have a potential twin prime—that is, when Number has been found to be prime.

8.5.1   *Time Out*

1. Execute Program 8e. Change the value of NumberOfTwinPrimes, and observe the behavior of the program. *Caution*: If you set this value to a very large number, the program will appear to enter an infinite loop.
2. Revise function Prime in Program 8e, using the alternative plan just described. Test the program again. What effect does the change have on execution speed?
3. Revise Module 4.0 in Program 8e, using the suggestion just outlined. Test the program. Compare execution speed with tests of previous versions of the program.
4. Write a function to do the message-encoding task of Program 8b.
5. Change procedure Convert in Program 8c to a function.

8.6   RECURSION

Recursion is a problem-solving tool in which a function (or procedure) invokes itself. Unlike some other programming languages, Pascal allows you to write programs using recursion in a very natural and direct way. Theoretically, any problem that can be solved with recursion can be solved without recursion. Despite this fact, recursion is useful because some problems have a very simple and understandable solution when solved using recursion and a very complex and difficult solution without recursion.

Recursive definitions are frequently used in mathematics. For example, consider the factorial function. One way to define the function is the familiar nonrecursive definition:

$$n! = 1 \times 2 \times 3 \times \cdots \times (n - 1) \times n$$

Another way to define the function is as follows:

$$n! = \begin{cases} 1 & \text{if } n = 1 \\ n \times (n - 1)! & \text{if } n > 1 \end{cases}$$

In this definition, the value of 3! is expressed as $3 \times 2!$; in other words, to compute the factorial of 3, we must compute the factorial of another number, 2. Again, by this definition, $2! = 2 \times 1!$. Since 1! is defined to have the value 1, we see that $3! = 3 \times 2 \times 1$, which is exactly the same value derived from the nonrecursive definition of the function. This recursive definition of the factorial shares one thing in common with all recursive definitions: A recursive definition must be conditional; that is, there must be a point at which you can stop. In this case, you stop when the value of the argument is 1.

Let us implement the recursive definition of the factorial function as a Pascal function. The function will accept one Integer argument N and return a Real value. (The reason that the function should have a Real value is that the values of factorials increase dramatically for very small values of N). The following function could be used:

```
function Factorial (N : Integer) : Real;
begin {Factorial}
      if N = 1 then
         Factorial := 1
      else
         Factorial := N * Factorial (N - 1);
end;        {Factorial}
```

Notice that the value of the function is assigned as we have previously done—by using the name of the function on the left side of an assignment statement. But in this case, one of the assignment statements invokes the function, which calls for the evaluation of the factorial of another, smaller number (N − 1). This function is shown in the context of a complete program in Figure 8.8 (Program 8f).

During the execution of this program (and any program involving recursion), the system builds a list of values, called a *stack*, so that when the recursion terminates, the program can return to the appropriate location to complete the calculations that have been temporarily pushed aside. For example, consider the calculation of 3!. Since N is greater than 1, the calculation Factorial := 3 * Factorial (2) must be completed. But this calculation requires the evaluation of Factorial (2). So that information on the last calculation is not lost when the Factorial function is executed with the new argument, the stack now contains the equivalent of

```
3 * Factorial (2)
```

which is the calculation required to complete the function. The function is now invoked with the argument 2. Since N > 1, the value of Factorial is 2 * Factorial (1). As before, this calculation is placed on the stack, which now contains two entries:

```
2 * Factorial (1)
3 * Factorial (2)
```

The function is now invoked with argument value 1. This value can be computed and has the value 1. When the function is completed, the calculation at the top of the stack (the last one placed on the stack) is removed, and that calculation is completed. The value of 2 * Factorial (1) is 2 * 1 = 2, and the function is completed again. This time the stack contains one entry—the calculation 3 * Factorial (2)—which is completed as 3 * 2 = 6. Now the stack is empty, and control returns to the point in the program at which the function was originally invoked.

All this may seem like a great deal of trouble to perform such a simple task, and in this case it is. The nonrecursive technique for computing the factorial is preferable to the recursive. But the example is useful because it points out the process used by the system

```
program P8f (Input, Output);
{Program to compute factorial using recursion}
uses Crt;
const
    InputPrompt = 'Enter positive integer (0 to stop) ';
var
    Number : Integer;
{***********************************************************************}
    function Factorial (N : Integer) : Real;
    {Function computes N! using recursive calls to itself}
    begin   {Factorial}
          if N = 1 then
             Factorial := 1
          else
             Factorial := N * Factorial (N - 1);
    end;    {Factorial}
{***********************************************************************}
begin   {Main Program}

{1.0 Clear the screen}

    ClrScr;

{2.0 Read Number}

    Write (InputPrompt);
    Readln (Number);

{3.0 While Number > 0 compute N! and read Number}

    while Number > 0 do
          begin
                Writeln ('The factorial of ', Number, ' is ',
                          Factorial (Number):6:0);
                Writeln;
                Write (InputPrompt);
                Readln (Number)
          end;    {while}

end.    {Main Program}
```

Figure 8.8 Program 8f: Factorial computation using recursion.

when recursion is involved. The system must build a stack, so that when the process comes to completion, the value that has been computed can be returned to the appropriate calculation. Although this process is automatic, it is not without a price. The stack requires memory. In a long program, there may not be sufficient memory available. The process requires time. A number of data items are moved to and from the stack each time a calculation is placed on the stack or removed from the stack. Generally, a program that performs a computation without using recursion is more efficient in both time and memory utilization than one that uses recursion. Despite these drawbacks, recursion remains a useful tool because it enables the program to be concise and directly related to the original definition of the process. (Compare the mathematical definition of the factorial function with the statement part of the function Factorial.)

Following is another example of a problem that has a natural solution using recursion.

■ **Problem Statement.**   Write a program to compute any desired term of the Fibonacci sequence. The first two terms of this sequence have the value 1. Each term thereafter is formed as the sum of the two preceding terms. The first few terms of the sequence are:

$$1, 1, 2, 3, 5, 8, 13, 21, 34 \ldots$$

A mathematical definition of this sequence is as follows:

$$f_1 = 1$$
$$f_2 = 1$$
$$f_n = f_{n-1} + f_{n-2} \qquad \text{for } n = 3, 4, 5, \ldots$$

By this definition, the value of the third term is computed as

$$f_3 = f_2 + f_1 = 1 + 1 = 2$$

The value of the fourth term is

$$f_4 = f_3 + f_2 = 2 + 1 = 3$$

■ **Problem Analysis.**   The main program is relatively straightforward; we will use a value of 0 entered by the user to terminate. The plan for the main program is as follows.

FIBONACCI SEQUENCE PROGRAM (P8g)

1.0 Clear the screen
2.0 Read Number of term desired
3.0 While Number $\neq$ 0 compute term and read Number

If we use recursion, the function subprogram is a simple restatement of the mathematical definition of the sequence:

REAL FUNCTION FIB (IMPORT : N)

1.0 If N $<=$ 2 Then
2.0   Fib = 1
3.0 Else
4.0   Fib = Fib (N − 1) + Fib (N − 2)
5.0 End If

■ **Problem Solution.**   Program 8g, which is shown in Figure 8.9, solves this problem. In order to determine the efficiency of the program, we have inserted a write statement at the beginning of the function to write out the value of the parameter each time the function is invoked. For example, consider the calculation of the fifth term of the sequence. This

```
program P8g (Input, Output);
{Program computes terms of the Fibonacci sequence
     using recursion}
uses Crt;
const
     InputPrompt = 'Enter Term of Sequence desired (0 to stop) ';
var
     Number : Integer;
     FibNumber : Real;
{************************************************************************}
     function Fib (N : Integer) : Real ;
     {Function computes Nth term of Fibonacci sequence
          using recursion}
     begin    {Fib}
          Write (N : 2);
          if N <= 2 then
             Fib := 1
          else
             Fib := Fib (N - 1) + Fib (N - 2);
     end;    {Fib}
{************************************************************************}
begin    {Main Program}

{1.0 Clear the screen}

     ClrScr;

{2.0 Read Number of term desired}

     Write (InputPrompt);
     Readln (Number);

{3.0 While Number <> 0 compute term and read Number}

     while Number > 0 do
          begin
               FibNumber := Fib (Number);
               Writeln;
               Writeln ('Term number ',Number,' of the sequence is ',
                        FibNumber:2:0);
               Writeln;
               Write (InputPrompt);
               Readln (Number)
          end;    {while}

end.    {Main Program}
```

Figure 8.9 Program 8g: Fibonacci sequence computation with recursion.

requires the calculation of the fourth and third terms, but each of these requires the calculation of other terms. In all, the calculation of the fifth term requires the calculation of other terms. In all, the calculation of the fifth term requires that the function be invoked nine times, as shown in the sample output in Figure 8.10. This example illustrates the inefficiency of the use of the recursion in this case. The advantage, of course, is that the function subprogram is logical and easy to understand.

```
Enter Term of Sequence desired (0 to stop) 5
 5 3 1 2 4 2 3 1 2
Term number 5 of the sequence is 5

Enter Term of Sequence desired (0 to stop) 0
```

Figure 8.10 Sample execution of Program 8g.

8.6.1 Time Out

1. Add output to the function Factorial in Program 8f. Execute the program for sample values of Number. Explain the output values produced from the function.

2. An alternative technique for computing terms of the Fibonacci sequence is to keep track of three terms at a time: the current term and two preceding terms. This technique is used in the following procedure.

REAL FUNCTION ALTERNATIVEFIBONACCI (IMPORT : N)

1.0	If N $<=$ 2 Then
2.0	AlternativeFibonacci = 1
3.0	Else
4.0	A = 1
5.0	B = 1
6.0	F = A + B
7.0	Count = 3
8.0	While Count $<=$ N Do
9.0	A = B
10.0	B = F
11.0	F = A + B
12.0	Count = Count + 1
13.0	End While
14.0	AlternativeFibonacci = F
15.0	End If

Write a Pascal program using this procedure to compute terms of the sequence. Compare the efficiency of this technique with the recursive technique. Compare the simplicity of the two techniques.

3. Consider the following sequence :

$$1, 1, 1, 3, 5, 9, 17, 31 \ldots$$

The fourth term is formed by adding the first, second, and third terms; the fifth term is the sum of the second, third and fourth ; and so forth. Modify Program 8g to compute this sequence, which is sometimes called the "Tribonacci" sequence. Modify the program plan given in problem 2 to compute this sequence. Comment on the relative simplicity of the two approaches.

8.6.2 Case Study: String Reversal

■ **Problem Statement.** Write a program that will print the reversal of any string of characters entered by the program user. For example, if the user enters 'ABCD', the output should be 'DCBA'.

■ **Problem Analysis.** We will choose to write a function Reverse that will accept a string parameter and return the desired value to the calling program. We can use recursion as a problem-solving tool in this case by noting the following facts:

- The reverse of a single character is that character; the reverse of the null string is the null string.

- The reverse of a string of more than one character can be formed by concatenating the first character to the right of the other characters and then reversing the other characters. Thus, Reverse ('ABC') is equal to Reverse ('BC') + 'A'. Following this example one step further, Reverse ('BC') is equal to Reverse ('C') + 'B', which is 'CB'. Thus, Reverse ('ABC') = Reverse ('BC') + 'A' = Reverse ('C') + 'B' + 'A' = 'C' + 'B' + 'A' = 'CBA', which is the desired result.

This analysis leads us to the following program plan for the function Reverse with parameter Str:

FUNCTION REVERSE (IMPORT : STR)

1.0 If the length of Str $<= 1$ Then
2.0   Reverse = Str
3.0 Else
4.0   Let Ch = first character of Str
5.0   Delete the first character in Str
6.0   Reverse = Reserve (Str) + Ch
7.0 End If

Note that, as with all recursive algorithms, this one has a terminating condition: When the length of the parameter becomes less than or equal to 1, the recursion stops.

■ **Problem Solution.** The solution to the problem is shown in Figure 8.11 as Program 8h.

```
program P8h (Input, Output);
{Program reverses string of characters entered by the user;
    illustrates use of recursion in function Reverse}
var
    Data: string;
{********************************************************************}
    function Reverse (Str : string) : string;
    var
        Ch : string[1];
    begin    {Reverse}
        if Length (Str) <= 1 then
            Reverse := Str
        else
            begin
                Ch := Str[1];
                Delete (Str, 1, 1);
                Reverse := Reverse (Str) + Ch
            end   {if}
    end;    {Reverse}
{********************************************************************}
begin    {Main Program}
    Writeln ('Enter character string');
    Readln (Data);
    Writeln (Data, ' ', Reverse(Data));
    Readln
end.      {Main Program}
```

Figure 8.11 Program 8h: String reversal using recursion.

8.6.3 Time Out

1. Try out Program 8h with sample data of your choosing.
2. Insert output statements in the function Reverse to examine the values taken on by Str. Test the program again, and justify the output produced by the new version of Reverse.
3. An alternative way to terminate the recursion in the function Reverse is to test for the null string. If the value of Str is equal to the null string, then this is the value returned by the function; otherwise, we continue as before. Revise the function Reverse to use this scheme. Are there any advantages to this approach over the one originally used? Are there any disadvantages?
4. Think about alternative ways of computing the reversal of a string. Are there advantages to the recursive approach? Are there any disadvantages?
5. Apply the approach described in this section for reversing a string to the task of reversing an integer. Write a function to do this task, and test it with a suitable main program.

8.7 REVIEW QUESTIONS

1. How is the maximum length of a string-type variable specified?
2. Is the following statement true or false? The actual length of a string is always the same as the length declared for the variable. Explain.
3. What is the null string?

4. What is the upper limit on the length of a string?

5. What purpose is served by the function KeyPressed? Why would you use it in a program?

6. In what two ways is string concatenation performed in Turbo Pascal? Which method is usually preferred?

7. Name the function that allows a program to determine the length of a string.

8. What is a string index? Under what circumstances is this facility useful?

9. If X is a string-type variable, what is contained in X[0]?

10. What is a substring?

11. What is the purpose of the Copy function?

12. What is the function that allows you to search a string for occurrences of a substring?

13. Suppose X is a string-type variable, and suppose that Pos (' ',X) has the value 0. What can you conclude?

14. What is the procedure that allows you to remove any substring from a string?

15. What is the procedure that allows you to insert any substring into a string?

16. What procedure converts a value from internal form to character form? What procedure converts from character form to internal form?

17. In what ways does Turbo Pascal relax the usual rules for passing parameters of type string?

18. What purpose is served by the compiler directive V?

19. Comment on the following statement: In Pascal, the function Random returns pseudorandom numbers.

20. What purpose is served by the procedure Randomize?

21. How is a function heading different from a procedure heading?

22. Why is the use of variable parameters for a function discouraged?

23. How is a function assigned a value in the statement part of the function declaration?

24. What restriction is placed on the use of the function name in the statement part of the function declaration?

25. Define recursion.

26. Is recursion a necessary technique for solving problems? Of what value is recursion?

27. What are some drawbacks in the use of recursion in solving a problem?

8.8 PROGRAMMING EXERCISES

1. The Euclidean algorithm for calculating the largest common factor of two positive integers A and B is as follows:

EUCLIDEAN ALGORITHM

1.0 Do
2.0   D = remainder after dividing A by B
3.0   A = B
4.0   B = D
5.0 Until B = 0

When this procedure terminates, the value of A is the largest common factor.

Implement this algorithm as a function with parameters A and B. (Make sure that the function does not change the value of its actual arguments.) Test your program with a main program that allows the user to enter values of A and B and that outputs the largest common factor of the two.

2. Cardano's method for finding a solution S to a cubic equation of the form

$$x^3 + Px + Q = 0$$

is as follows:

CARDANO'S METHOD

1.0 $D = \dfrac{4P^3 + 27Q^2}{27}$

2.0 $U = \sqrt[3]{\dfrac{-Q + \sqrt{D}}{2}}$

3.0 $V = \dfrac{-P}{3U}$

4.0 $S = U + V$

Note that if $D < 0$, the solution is complex. Write a program to solve cubic equations for values of P and Q entered by the user.

3. The least common multiple (LCM) of two numbers A and B is the smallest number divisible by both A and B. For example, the LCM of 4 and 6 is 12. Write a function to compute the LCM. Test it first with a main program that allows the user to enter values of A and B and writes out the LCM. Then write a main program that will allow users to perform addition of fractions. That is, the user enters values of A, B, C, and D to compute the sum

$$\frac{A}{B} + \frac{C}{D}$$

The program should use the LCM of B and D as the least common denominator, convert both fractions to this denominator, and add the numerators.

4. Write a program to simulate the throwing of a die 100 times. The output should be 1, 2, ..., 6 chosen randomly. Verify that all possible values occur with approximately equal frequency.

5. An approximation to the factorial function is given by the Stirling's formula: $n! \approx n^n e^{-n} \sqrt{2\pi n}$. Write a program to generate values for n in the range 1 to 20 and compare the actual value computed for $n!$ with the approximated value.

6. Write a program to approximate the value of π using the following method, which is known as the Monte Carlo method. The equation $x^2 + y^2 = 1$ represents a circle with center at the origin and radius equal to 1. The area of this circle is π, and therefore, the area of that part of the circle contained in the first quadrant is $\pi/4$.

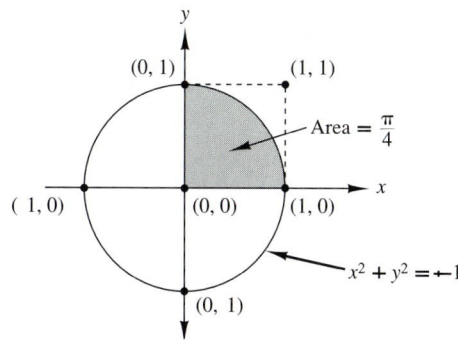

One way to approximate the area of that portion of the circle in the first quadrant is to choose values of x and y in the range 0 to 1 at random. If $x^2 + y^2 \leq 1$, then the point with coordinates (x, y) lies on or below the curve. If $x^2 + y^2 > 1$, then the point lies outside the circle. By repeatedly choosing such points and keeping track of how many lie on or below the circle, we can compute the proportion p of points lying on or below the circle as

$$p = \frac{\text{number of points on or below circle}}{\text{total number of points sampled}}$$

Since the area of the square from which the points were sampled is 1, it follows that $p \cdot 1 = p$ is an estimate of the area of the circle in the first quadrant; hence, p is approximately equal to $\pi/4$ or $4p$ is approximately equal to π. The accuracy of the estimate should improve as the sample size increases. Use sample sizes of 100, 1,000, and 5,000 in your program.

7. Adapt the Monte Carlo method described in Exercise 6 to write a program to approximate the area under the curve $y = x^2$ in the interval 0 to 2, as shown:

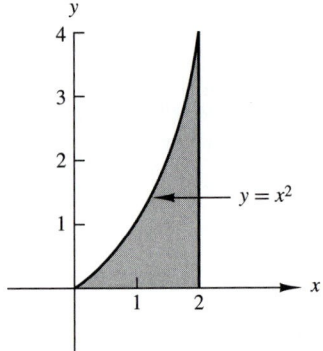

Note: The total area of the rectangle containing the desired area $2 \times 4 = 8$.
The expected value is

$$\int_0^2 x^2 dx = \frac{x^3}{3} \Big|_0^2 = \frac{8}{3} = 2.66\ldots$$

8. Write a program to display the largest common prefix for two strings. The following table shows some examples:

Input		Output
ABC	ABD	AB
1A*	1B*	1
123	12	12
01	34	(No common prefix)

9. Write a program to compute the values of Roman numerals. The values of the symbols used in Roman numerals are as shown in the following table:

Roman numeral	Value
I	1
V	5
X	10
L	50
C	100
D	500
M	1000

10. A drunken student leaves a party (at point A in the map below) and attempts to walk to his dorm (at point B). Unfortunately, the campus is surrounded by busy streets. If the student wanders into the street, he will be run over by a car. Assume that the student goes from one point to another adjacent point in the map with each step he takes, but the direction (N, S, E, W) of each step is chosen at random. What are the student's chances of making it to the dorm without an accident?

11. Write a program to act as a simple calculator. The user should be able to enter expressions in the form

```
integer operator integer
```

where the *operator* can be +, −, *, or / and *integer* is any sequence of numeric digits. The program should respond with the value of the expression or an error message if the string that has been entered is not in the required form. The following table gives some examples.

Input	Output
12 + 3	15
14 *	Error
100 / 11	9
−34	Error
17	Error

12. An alternative method for expressing the Euclidean algorithm for finding the greatest common factor makes use of recursion, as follows:

$$GCF\ (M, N) = \begin{cases} GCF\ (N, M) & \text{if } N > M \\ M & \text{if } N = 0 \\ GCF\ (N, M \bmod N) & \text{otherwise} \end{cases}$$

Write a program to compute the GCF of two integers entered by the program user. Compare this program with the program written for Exercise 1.

13. Write a program to allow the user to enter his or her full name in the form

    `first-name middle-name last-name`

The program should locate the *first-name*, *middle-name*, and *last-name* and assign each value to a separate variable. Write out the name in the following forms:

    `last-name first-name middle-initial`
    `first-initial middle-initial last-initial`

14. Write a program to allow the user to enter any string of text and then find the number of occurrences of any desired character sequence. For example, if the text is

    Now is the time for all good men

and the user requests the system to find *the*, the response should be

    `the occurs 1 time(s)`

If the user requests the system to find *z*, the response should be

    `z occurs 0 time(s)`

15. Write a program to convert input of the forms

    `hours : minutes AM`
    `hours : minutes PM`

into 24-hour time. For example, '2:15PM' should be converted to 1415; and '2:00AM' should be converted to 0200.

16. A palindrome is a sequence of characters that is the same from left to right as from right to left. Examples of such strings include

    toot

    madam

    pop

Write a program to read a string and determine whether it is a palindrome.

17. It can be shown that

$$\sin^{-1} x = x + \frac{1x^3}{2 \cdot 3} + \frac{1 \cdot 3x^5}{2 \cdot 4 \cdot 5} + \frac{1 \cdot 3 \cdot 5x^7}{2 \cdot 4 \cdot 6 \cdot 7} + \frac{1 \cdot 3 \cdot 5 \cdot 7x^9}{2 \cdot 4 \cdot 6 \cdot 8 \cdot 9} + \cdots$$

Write a program to approximate $\sin^{-1}x$ correct to three decimal places for a value of x in the range -1 to 1 entered by the program user.

18. Write a program to compute

$$1 - \frac{1}{3} + \frac{1}{5} - \frac{1}{7} + \frac{1}{9} + \cdots + \frac{1}{N}$$

where N is an odd number. Use a function. Terminate the program if a value of N entered by the user is not an odd number.

19. Write a program to compute

$$2 + 4 + 6 + \cdots + N$$

for values of N entered by the program user. Reject any value of N that is not an even number.

20. Write a program to calculate the number of combinations C that can be found in N things taken R at a time (where $N > R$). The formula is:

$$C = \frac{N!}{R!(N - R)!}$$

21. Legendre polynomials are defined as follows:

$$P_0 = 1$$
$$P_1 = x$$
$$\vdots$$
$$P_i = \left(\frac{2i - 1}{i}\right) P_{i-1}x - \left(\frac{i - 1}{i}\right) P_{i-2} \qquad \text{for } i > 1$$

Write a program to produce a table of $P_0, P_1, \ldots, P_{10}$ for values of x entered by the user.

22. A function known as Ackerman's function is of theoretical importance in computer science. The definition of this function is as follows:

$$\text{ACK}(M, N) = \begin{cases} N + 1 & \text{if } M = 0 \\ \text{ACK}(M - 1, 1) & \text{if } N = 0 \\ \text{ACK}(M - 1, \ \text{ACK}(M, N - 1)) & \text{otherwise} \end{cases}$$

Write a program to evaluate Ackerman's function. Test your program for $M = 2, N = 2$. The expected output is 7. Include output in the function to examine the intermediate values assumed by M and N. *Caution:* The number of recursive calls increases dramatically as M and N increase.

23. Consider the following function declaration:

FUNCTION F (IMPORT : N)

1.0 If N = 1 Then
2.0   F = 1
3.0 Else
4.0   If N is odd Then
5.0   F = F (3*N +1)
6.0   Else
7.0   F = F (N/2)
8.0   End If
9.0 End If

It is an unproven conjecture (called the Collatz conjecture) that this function always returns the value 1, regardless of the value of N (assume that N is a positive integer). Write a Pascal implementation of the Collatz function, and call it for values of N in a suitable range. Verify that the value of the function is 1 in each case. By placing an output statement in the function, you can investigate the range of values assumed by the function argument before it finally returns the value 1.

9
Arrays

One of the most useful structured data types is the array. Arrays allow you to create multiple elements of another type (called the *base type* of the array) and access these elements by the use of a subscript in much the same way that you can access each character of a string by specifying the location of the character within the string. In fact, a string in Turbo Pascal is in reality an array of characters. (In other versions of Pascal that lack the string data type, you must use an array to represent a sequence of characters.) In this chapter, we explore ways in which arrays of various base types can be of value in solving problems.

9.1   ARRAY DECLARATION

When you need to store multiple data items of a particular type in the memory of the computer and give the program access to those items, you may create an **array**. For example, suppose you need to store 10 product names. Then you can create an array of 10 elements that you could visualize as follows:

ProductName[1]	Widgits
ProductName[2]	Gidgits
ProductName[3]	Digits
.	.
.	.
.	.
ProductName[10]	Zidgits

Access to the data in this array is provided by a common identifier (ProductName) and a **subscript**. The subscript is always enclosed in square brackets. The base type of the array is string because each element of the array is of type string. In another program, you might need to store a number of responses to a survey you have conducted. Assuming that the responses are Integer numbers, you would need an array of base type Integer. The size of the array must be declared in the program, so you must specify a number of elements that is at least as big as the number of responses you will be storing. Let us assume that there will be no more than 100 responses. With this assumption, the resulting array could be visualized as

Response[1]	
Response[2]	
Response[3]	
.	.
.	.
.	.
Response[99]	
Response[100]	

Not all the elements of the array need be used during each execution of the program, but no more than 100 elements can be stored unless the program is revised.

An array is created using a type declaration of the following general form:

array[*index-type*] **of** *component-type*

where *index-type* can be any ordinal type (except Longint) and *component-type* can be any type (except file). The specification of *component-type* governs the type of each element of the array. The specification of *index-type* governs two aspects of the structure:

1. The data type of the subscript that will be used to reference elements of the array.
2. The number of elements in the array—there will be one element in the array for each possible value of the subscript.

Pascal permits a very wide range of actual array definition techniques within the general syntax just described. One very common technique is to use a subrange to specify *index-type*. It is also common for the *component-type* to be a simple type such as Integer or Real or a structured type such as string. In the examples that follow, we shall use this technique; in later sections, we shall illustrate some other more "exotic" **array declaration** techniques.

For example, let us declare the array of product names illustrated earlier. There are 10 elements in the array, and we wish to use integer subscripts in the range 1 to 10 to reference these elements; therefore, the specification or *index-type* would be the subrange 1..10. Each element of the array is a string with a maximum length of 20 characters, so the **base type** of the array as specified in *component-type* would be **string**[20]. Thus, a complete declaration of the variable ProductName could be

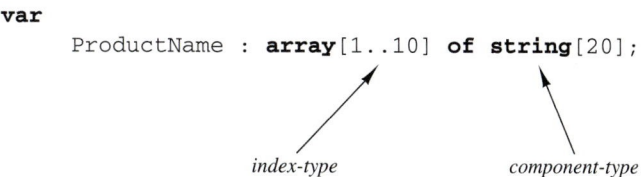

```
var
      ProductName : array[1..10] of string[20];
```

There are a number of alternatives to this coding segment that have equivalent results. We could, for example, create named types for the subrange 1..10 and the string type **string**[20] and use the identifiers for these named types in the declaration of the type of ProductName. This technique is shown next:

```
type
      IndexType = 1..10;
      ProductType = string[20];
var
      ProductName : array[IndexType] of ProductType;
```

Another alternative is to declare the array type as a named type and use the type identifier thus defined in declaring the type of ProductName. This alternative could be implemented as follows:

```
type
      IndexType = 1..10;
      ProductType = string[20];
      ProductArrayType = array[IndexType] of ProductType;
```

```
var
      ProductName : ProductArrayType;
```

Although this technique is a bit longer than the others, it is quite general and can keep you from having data-type mismatch problems later in the program.

Consider the array for storing survey responses described earlier. This array could be created by any number of different Pascal program segments. A very simple technique would be

```
var
      Response : array[1..100] of Integer;
```

A somewhat more elaborate technique would be

```
type
      ArrayOfInteger = array[1..100] of Integer;
var
      Response : ArrayOfInteger;
```

There are several advantages to using the more elaborate alternative to accomplish the task. One advantage is that the type ArrayOfInteger can be used later in the program, as needed, without writing the more complicated description array[1..100] of Integer. Another advantage is that if the variable Response is to be passed to a procedure or function as a parameter, the type specification in the list of formal parameters must be the type identifier ArrayOfInteger; if the formal parameter is not assigned this data type, then a data-type mismatch error will occur.

In all the examples thus far, the subscript has been an Integer. Although this is quite common, Pascal allows you to use other ordinal data types as a subscript, including Byte, Char, Integer, Boolean, enumerated data types, and, of course, subranges based on any of these types. For example, suppose we wish to create an array to store the words used in place of letters in some communications systems (A—Alpha, B—Bravo, and so forth). In this case, it would be convenient to use subscripts of type Char. The structure could be created by the following coding segment:

```
type
      Letters = 'A'..'Z';
      Codes = string[10];
      CodeArray = array[Letters] of Codes;
var
      LetterCode : CodeArray;
```

Remember that the entry made in *index-type* specifies not only the type of the subscript, but also the number of elements in the array. In the preceding case, the subscript type would be Char, and the array would contain 26 elements—one for each letter in the range

'A'..'Z'. You could visualize this array as follows:

```
LetterCode['A']        ┌──────────┐
                       └──────────┘
LetterCode['B']        ┌──────────┐
                       └──────────┘
            .              .
            .              .
            .              .
LetterCode['Z']        ┌──────────┐
                       └──────────┘
```

Note that the mere declaration of an array does not provide any particular content for the array elements. This is the responsibility of the program, as we shall see in subsequent sections.

9.1.1   Time Out

1. Describe the structure that is created by each of the following coding segments.

   (a) **type**

   ```
   SubscriptRange = -3..3;
   ArrayTypeA = array[SubscriptRange] of Real;
   ```
   var
   ```
   ArrayA : ArrayTypeA;
   ```

   (b) **type**

   ```
   ArrayTypeB = array['a'..'e'] of Integer;
   ```
   var
   ```
   ArrayB : ArrayTypeB;
   ```

   (c) **var**

   ```
   ArrayC : array[10..20] of Integer;
   ```

   (d) **type**

   ```
   Day = (Sun, Mon, Tue, Wed, Thr, Fri, Sat);
   ```
   var
   ```
   ArrayD : array[Day] of string[10];
   ```

2. Write Pascal coding segments to create an appropriate array for each of the following:
   (a) A program will process temperature readings taken at hourly intervals over a period of one day.
   (b) A simple substitution encoding scheme is to be used in a program. There will be a substitute assigned for each upper- and lowercase character. An array will be used to associate each character with its substitute.
   (c) Two tables of state names are required in a program. One table contains the two-character state name abbreviation, and the other contains the full name of the state.
   (d) A program needs to represent two vectors of up to 10 components.

9.2 ARRAYS FOR TABLE LOOKUP

The declaration of an array does not assign values to the elements of the array. This task must be undertaken by the program. Array elements can be assigned values in three essentially different ways:

1. The values assigned to the elements can be constants.
2. The array elements can be used to store the results of computations.
3. The array elements can be used to store the values of data items entered by the user or read from some other source.

In this section, we will explore some of the potential for using an array that is assigned constant values. In succeeding sections, we will address other ways for using an array.

In order to access the content of an array element, the program uses a subscript of the appropriate type and in the range allowed by the specification of *index-type* in the array declaration. Great latitude is allowed in the way a subscript can be written. It can be a constant, a variable, or any expression involving constants and/or variables. For example, suppose the following declarations have been made in a program:

```
type
     ArrayType = array[1..10] of Integer;
var
     X, Y : ArrayType;
     I, J : Integer;
```

Then the elements of arrays X and Y can be referenced by subscripts that are Integer constants. The following statements would assign the value 3 to the first element of X and the value -2 to the third element of Y:

```
X[1] := 3;
Y[3] := X[1] - 5;
```

The elements of arrays X and Y can also be referenced by subscripts that are Integer variables. Just as before, the following statements would assign the value 3 to the first element of X and the value -2 to the third element of Y:

```
I := 1;
X[1] := 3;
J := 3;
Y[J] := X[I] - 5;
```

Indeed, any expression with an Integer value can be used as a subscript, as shown in the following segment, which will have exactly the same effect as the preceding two segments:

```
I := 2;
X[I - 1] := 3;
Y[I + 1] := X[I - 1] - 5;
```

In this segment, the value of I − 1 is 1; therefore, X[I − 1] = X[1], and the value 3 is assigned to the first element of X. In a similar way, the value of I + 1 is 3, so Y[I + 1] = Y[3], and the value −2 is placed in Y[3].

One way that arrays can be useful is to store data in a table format for ready access by the program when needed. For example, consider the example of the array of product names that was described in the preceding section. One way to declare this array is as follows:

```
type
     ProductArrayType = array[1..10] of string[20];
var
     ProductName : ProductArrayType;
```

The purpose of this array is to store product names so that when the program needs the name of, say, the third product, the array reference ProductName[3] will return the name of that product. Before the array can be used in this manner, however, it is necessary for the program to store the proper names into the array. This task is called initializing the array or loading the array. It is a task that needs to be done only once, and it must be carried out before any access to the content of the array will be valid. A procedure to load the appropriate values into the array ProductName would be similar to the following:

```
procedure LoadProductNames: (var ProductName : ProductArrayType);
begin
     ProductName[1] := 'Widgits';
     ProductName[2] := 'Gidgits';
     ProductName[3] := 'Digits';
                       .
                       .
                       .
     ProductName[10] := 'Zidgits';
end;
```

Once this procedure has been executed, the values of the various components of ProductName will be in place and can then be referenced as needed by the program. For example, suppose ProductCode is an Integer value entered by the user. Then the following program segment would write out the associated product name:

```
if ProductCode in [1..10] then
   Writeln (ProductName[ProductCode])
else
   Writeln ('Invalid Product Code');
```

If the value of ProductCode is 1, then the output will be the content of ProductName[1], if the value of ProductCode is 2, then the output will be the content of ProductName[2], and so forth. If ProductCode is outside the allowable range for subscripts of this array (outside the range 1 to 10), then the output will be an error message.

It is important that the program validate the value of the subscript before making the array reference, in order to avoid referencing a part of memory that is outside the boundaries set up for the array or to avoid program termination. The **R compiler directive** is used to activate subscript range checking so that an out-of-range subscript value will result in termination of the program with an appropriate error message. To activate range checking use the compiler directive {$R+}. This means that a check will be made to see that the value of a subscript is within the prescribed range. In order to deactivate range checking, you use the directive {$R−}. When range checking is active, the system will check each subscript value against the range specified in the array declaration; if it is outside the range, the program will terminate and an error message will be produced.

The use of an array to store a table of constants is illustrated in the context of a complete program by the solution to the following problem.

■ **Problem Statement.** Write a program to allow the user to enter a series of dates in the form *mm dd yy*, where these numbers represent the month, day, and year, respectively. The program should convert this data into a descriptive format in which the name of the month is substituted for the month number and the year is written as 19*yy*. Examples of the desired output for sample inputs are shown:

Input	Output
01 23 89	January 23, 1989
03 01 90	March 1, 1990
12 20 08	December 20, 1908

■ **Problem Analysis.** The solution to this problem can be greatly simplified by using a table of constants for the month names. There is a natural relationship between the month number and the associated name; we can use this relationship to facilitate looking up the name associated with the month number in the table. In fact, if we define the subscript range to be from 1 to 12, the month number used as a subscript can access the desired month name. Thus, we will create an array MonthName with components of type string[20], and the range 1..12 will be the *index-type*. The program will need to load the array with the month names as its first action. Then it can use the value of the month number entered by the user to gain direct access to the associated month name. A plan for this program is as follows:

PRELIMINARY PLAN FOR DATE-CONVERSION PROGRAM

1.0 Initialize table of month names

2.0 Get first month, day, and year

3.0 Process data and get next month, day, and year

Step 3.0 will require a loop to continue processing data. The loop will terminate when the user enters zero values for all variables. With this in mind, we can now complete the plan.

PLAN FOR DATE-CONVERSION (P9a)

1.0 Initialize table of month names

2.0 Get first month, day, and year

3.0 Process date and get next month, day, and year

    3.1 While not last Do

    3.2   OutputDate = converted date

    3.3   Write numeric date and OutputDate

    3.4   Get next month, day, and year

    3.5 End While

■ **Problem Solution.** It seems natural to implement step 1.0 of the plan as a procedure—say, LoadMonthNames. This procedure will initialize the array MonthName with the appropriate values. The conversion process can be implemented as a function ConvertDate, which will be a string-valued function that will import numeric values for month, day, and year and return the required character string equivalent as the value of the function. If the date is invalid because the month number is outside the range 1 to 12, the function will return 'Invalid date' as its value. A data-flow diagram showing the relationship among parts of the program is given in Figure 9.1.

    Program (9a) is shown in Figure 9.2. Note the declaration of type StringArrayType:

```
StringArrayType = array [1..12] of StringType;
```

This type is used in the declaration of MonthName:

```
MonthName : StringArrayType;
```

Integer subscript values in the range 1 to 12 will be valid; other values will be invalid. In the function ConvertDate, note that we are careful to make sure that the value of M is in

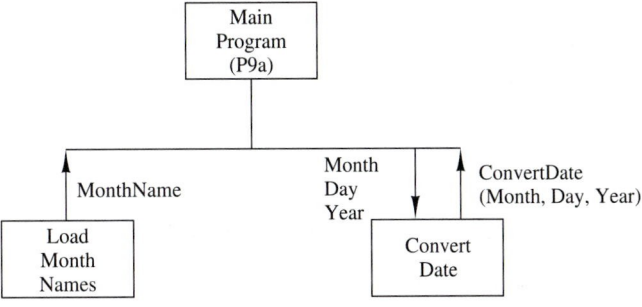

Figure 9.1 Data-flow diagram for date-conversion program (Program 9a).

```
program P9a (Input, Output);
{Program to convert dates from numeric to alphanumeric form}
type
      StringType = string[20];
      StringArrayType = array[1..12] of StringType;
const
      InputPrompt = 'Enter date in the form mm dd yy (0 0 0 to stop) ';
var
      Month, Day, Year: Integer;
      OutputDate : StringType;
      MonthName : StringArrayType;
{**********************************************************************}
      procedure LoadMonthNames(var MonthName : StringArrayType);
      {Procedure to initialize content of array MonthName}
      begin    {LoadMonthNames}
           MonthName[1]  := 'January ';
           MonthName[2]  := 'February ';
           MonthName[3]  := 'March  ';
           MonthName[4]  := 'April ';
           MonthName[5]  := 'May ';
           MonthName[6]  := 'June ';
           MonthName[7]  := 'July ';
           MonthName[8]  := 'August ';
           MonthName[9]  := 'September ';
           MonthName[10] := 'October ';
           MonthName[11] := 'November ';
           MonthName[12] := 'December '
      end;     {LoadMonthNames}
{----------------------------------------------------------------------}
      function ConvertDate (M, D, Y:Integer) : StringType;
      {Function to convert a date from numeric form to alphanumeric form}
      var
           Day, Year : StringType;
      begin   {ConvertDate}
           Str (D, Day);
           Str (Y:2, Year);
           if Year[1] = ' ' then
              Year[1] := '0';
           Year := '19'+Year;
           if (M >= 1) and (M <= 12) then
              ConvertDate := MonthName[M] + Day + ', '+Year
           else
              ConvertDate := 'Invalid date';
      end;   {ConvertDate}
{**********************************************************************}
```

Figure 9.2(a) Program 9a: Declaration part (part 1 of 2 parts).

the range 1 to 12 before using M to access an element of the array MonthName:

```
if (M >= 1) and (M <= 12) then
    ConvertDate := MonthName [M] + Day +', '+Year
else
    ConvertDate := 'Invalid date';
```

Note also the use of the Str procedure in the function ConvertDate. Recall that this procedure converts the value of a numeric variable into the string equivalent. The Str proce-

```
begin      {Main Program}

{1.0 Initialize table of month names}

     LoadMonthNames(MonthName);

{2.0 Get first month, day, and year}

     Write (InputPrompt);
     Readln (Month, Day, Year);

{3.0 Process date and get next month, day, and year}

     while Month * Day <> 0 do
           begin
                OutputDate := ConvertDate (Month, Day, Year);
                Writeln ('Numeric form of date :',Month:3,Day:3,Year:3);
                Writeln ('Alphanumeric form : ', OutputDate);
                Write (InputPrompt);
                Readln (Month, Day, Year)
           end;    {while}

end.   {Main Program}
```

Figure 9.2(b)   Program 9a: Statement part (part 2 of 2 parts).

dure is used once to convert the value of D to string form and store it in Day and a second time to convert the value of Y to string form and store it in Year as a two-character field. In order that values of Y in the range 0 to 9 do not show up in the final string as 19 *y*, the program checks the first character in Year. If that character is a space, then a '0' is inserted in its place. It is interesting to observe the similarity between the use of a subscript to access an element of an array and the use of a subscript to access a character in a string. Both the concept and the notation are the same in Turbo Pascal.

9.2.1   *Time Out*

1. Compile and execute Program 9a. Test the program with sample data.
2. Adapt the date-validation concepts used in Program 5b to Program 9a. How could you use an array showing the number of possible days in each month in the date-validation process?
3. Look up the codes used for each letter of the alphabet in communication systems. (The code for A is Alpha, B is Bravo, C is Charley, etc.) Write a program to allow the user to enter any sequence of alphabetic characters and have the program convert them into the communication code equivalent.
4. In Program 9a, the while loop that implements step 3 begins with

   ```
   while Month * Day <> 0 do
   ```

   Would it make the program more readable and self-documenting to write

   ```
   while (Month <> 0) and (Day <> 0) do ?
   ```

9.3 ARRAYS FOR COUNTING AND ACCUMULATION

Another potentially valuable application for an array is as a sequence of counters or accumulators. In these cases, the elements of the array are all initialized to an appropriate initial value (usually 0), and then the elements are selectively used to count occurrences of particular events or find the sum of specified data items. When all the data have been processed, the content of the array represents a summary of the results of the processing that has taken place.

For example, let us suppose that our hypothetical company (the one that makes the Widgets, Gidgets, and so forth) wishes to determine the total sales of each of the 10 products. The available data contain the product number (1 through 10) and the number of units sold as part of one transaction. Thus, a program to solve this problem will need to have 10 accumulators—1 for each product. As each transaction is processed, the appropriate accumulator will be increased by the number of units sold. One way to implement these accumulators is as an array of 10 elements. The first element of the array will be associated with product 1, the second element with product 2, and so forth. The following array declaration could be used:

```
var
    TotalSale : array[1..10] of Real;
```

The first task of the program will be to initialize these array elements to 0. The following code could be used:

```
for Index := 1 to 10 do
    TotalSale[Index] := 0;
```

Now as each sale transaction is read, the value of the product number can be used to pick out the appropriate accumulator:

```
if ProductNumber in [1..10] then
    TotalSale[ProductNumber] := TotalSale[ProductNumber]
                                    + SaleAmount;
```

Of course, if ProductNumber is not in the range 1 to 10, it is invalid and must not be used as a subscript value to access an element of TotalSale. Finally, when all the data has been processed, the program can produce a table showing total sales by product:

```
for Index := 1 to 10 do
    WriteIn (Index, TotalSales[Index]);
```

A similar concept can be used when the fundamental task of the program involves counting, as shown in the following completely solved problem.

■ **Problem Statement.**   Write a program to create a **frequency distribution** for a series of grades that range in value from 0 to 100. Write out only those frequencies that have a nonzero value.

■ **Problem Analysis.**   A frequency distribution shows the frequency of occurrence for a set of data items (that is, how many times each data item occurred). It is a very useful way of summarizing a large amount of data. If the data ranges from 0 to 100, we will need 101 counters—one for each possible value. As each item is processed, we will add 1 to the counter associated with the value of that particular item. When all the data has been processed, we can write out the list of counters; the list will represent the number of occurrences of the associated item in the actual data.

One way to implement the required counters is as an array. We can create an array Frequency with *component-type* Integer and use the subrange 0..100 as the *index-type*. In this way, Frequency[0] can be associated with the grades of value 0, Frequency[1] with grades of value 1, and so forth. Since these elements are counters, it will be necessary to initialize them to have the value 0 prior to processing the first data. After all the data has been read, the content of the array Frequency can be written and will represent the desired frequency distribution. With these considerations in mind, we can write the following plan for our program:

FREQUENCY DISTRIBUTION PROGRAM (P9b)

1.0 Initialize each element of Frequency to 0

2.0 Get first grade

3.0 While not end of grades process grade and get next grade

4.0 Write frequency distribution

5.0 Wait

Let us specify that a grade outside the range 0 to 100 will be used to terminate input.

■ **Problem Solution.**   A solution to this problem is shown in Figure 9.3 (Program 9b). The array Frequency is declared as an array with *index-type* 0..100 and *component-type* Integer:

```
Frequency : array[0..100] of Integer;
```

Step 1.0 of the procedure is accomplished using a for loop:

```
for Index := 0 to 100 do
    Frequency[Index] := 0;
```

In any program involving counting or accumulation, the initialization step is of critical importance. Unless you specify the value of a memory location, its content is unknown to you. The counting and accumulation processes depend on having the counters and accumulators set to 0.

```
program P9b (Input, Output);
{Program to create a frequency distribution for a set of grades}
uses
     Crt;
const
     InputPrompt = 'Enter a grade (negative value to stop) ';
var
     Frequency : array[0..100] of Integer;
     Grade, Index : Integer;
        .
        .
        .
begin        {Main Program}

{1.0 Initialize each element of Frequency to 0}

     for Index := 0 to 100 do
        Frequency[Index] := 0;

{2.0 Get first grade}

     Write (InputPrompt);
     Readln (Grade);

{3.0 While not end of grades process grade and read next grade}

     while (Grade >= 0) and (Grade <= 100) do
        begin
              Frequency[Grade] := Frequency[Grade] + 1;
              Write (InputPrompt);
              Readln (Grade)
        end;   {while}

{4.0 Write frequency distribution}

     ClrScr;
     Writeln ('Grade     Frequency');
     for Index := 0 to 100 do
        if Frequency[Index] <> 0 then
           Writeln (Index:4, Frequency[Index]:10);

{5.0 Wait}

     AlternateWait

end.    {Main Program}
```

Figure 9.3 Program 9b: Frequency distribution.

The actual calculation of the frequency is extremely easy because the value of Grade is used directly to pick out the appropriate element of Frequency to be incremented:

```
Frequency[Grade] := Frequency[Grade] + 1;
```

Finally, the production of the desired report is carried out using a for loop to "run through" all the elements of Frequency; only those that are not equal to 0 are printed:

```
for Index := 0 to 10 do
    if Frequency[Index] <> 0 then
        WriteIn (Index:4, Frequency[Index]:10);
```

9.3.1 Time Out

1. Compile and execute Program 9b. Test the program with sample data.
2. Modify the program to produce a horizontal bar graph as part of the frequency distribution output. *Hint:* Print a row of asterisks beside each frequency; the number of asterisks should be equal to the frequency.
3. Modify the program to produce a grouped frequency distribution, using the following intervals:

$$0–9$$
$$10–19$$
$$.$$
$$.$$
$$.$$
$$90–100$$

   Hint: There will be 10 intervals, so you will need 10 counters. Compute the interval number as a function of the grade.
4. Modify the program to allow the user to enter the number of groups desired. The program should produce the required grouped frequency distribution. For example, if the user enters 5 as the number of groups, the intervals would be

$$0–19$$
$$20–39$$
$$40–59$$
$$60–79$$
$$80–100$$

   If the number of elements in the range of data is not divisible by the number of groups, make the last interval contain the extra elements.
5. Write a program to compute the total sales, by product, for the company described earlier. Include the name of the product in the final report. (Make up 10 names of your choice.)

9.4 ARRAYS FOR DATA STORAGE

When there are multiple data items to be processed by a program, and there is a need to store all the items in memory at the same time, it is appropriate to use an array for storage of the data. A basic limitation to this technique is that there must be sufficient memory available to store the data; the memory of the computer is not infinite. When you create an array for **data storage**, you must know in advance the maximum number of elements to be accommodated. This number governs the number of array elements that you will create in the program. Not all of the array elements have to be used during any particular execution of the program. The program will need to count the number of data items as they are loaded into the array and use this number in subsequent access to the data.

When an array is used to store data, it is possible to divide the program into two distinct parts. In the first part, the data is read and stored in the array. In the second part, the data is processed, typically by beginning with the first data element and continuing to the end. If there is a need to perform further processing of the data, it is readily available in memory and can be accessed as many times as is necessary.

For example, let us consider the problem of reading and storing a list of customer names. We will assume that there are to be no more than 200 names, but their exact number will vary. We can create an array of *component-type* string[20] and *index-type* 1..200 to store this data; let us call the array CustomerNameList. It will be convenient to have a variable CustomerName of the same type as the components of CustomerNameList; this variable will be used to store the data entered by the user before it is placed in the array. We shall also need an Integer variable N to count the number of items in the list and another variable Index, which will be used to access elements of the array for processing. The required data declarations are as follows:

```
const
      Limit = 200;
type
      NameType = string[20];
      NameArrayType = array[1..Limit] of NameType;
var
      CustomerNameList : NameArrayType;
      CustomerName : NameType;
      N, Index : Integer;
```

The logic required to load data into an array can be summarized in the following:

PROCEDURE TO LOAD ARRAY FROM INPUT

1.0 N = 0

2.0 Read Data

3.0 While Data not = last item and N < limit of array Do

4.0   N = N + 1

5.0   Array[N] = Data

6.0   Read Data

7.0 End While

In the case of the customer-name data described, we must decide what value the user will enter to terminate data entry; let us use 'End' for this purpose. We will also need to have a prompt written each time a data item is entered. With these considerations in mind, we can now implement the load procedure as follows:

```
N := 0;
Write ('Enter customer name (End to stop) ');
Readln (CustomerName);
while (CustomerName <> 'End') and (N < Limit) do
     begin
          N := N + 1;
          CustomerNameList[N] := CustomerName;
          Write ('Enter customer name ');
          Readln (CustomerName)
     end; {while}
```

Although this procedure is very general and will work under all circumstances, there are other approaches you may want to consider that will accomplish the same basic task. One such approach is to use a Repeat/Until loop instead of a While loop to control the process. The procedure could then be rewritten as follows:

PROCEDURE TO LOAD ARRAY FROM INPUT (REPEAT/UNTIL ALTERNATIVE)

1.0 N = 0

2.0 Repeat

3.0   Read Data

4.0   If Data not = last item Then

5.0   N = N + 1

6.0   Array[N] = Data

7.0   End If

8.0 Until Data = last item or N = limit of array

In the case of the customer-name example, the Pascal procedure would be as follows:

```
N := 0;
repeat
     Write ('Enter customer name (End to stop) ');
     Readln (CustomerName);
     if CustomerName <> 'End' then
        begin
             N := N + 1;
             CustomerNameList[N] := CustomerName
        end {if}
until (CustomerName = 'End') or (N = Limit);
```

Another variation that can be used to accomplish this same task is to have the user enter the number of data items that the program will process (the value of N). It is then a simple matter for the program to read a data item and store it directly into the appropriate element of the array, using a For loop to generate the sequence of index values from 1 to N. In pseudocode form, this procedure would be as follows:

PROCEDURE TO LOAD ARRAY FROM INPUT (FOR LOOP VARIATION)

1.0 Read N

2.0 For Index = 1 to N Do

3.0   Read Array[Index]

4.0 End For

For the customer-name example, the procedure could be translated into Pascal as follows:

```
Write ('Enter number of customer names (Maximum of ',
        Limit,')');
Readln (N);
if N <= Limit then
   for Index := 1 to N do
      begin
          Write ('Enter customer name ');
          Readln (CustomerNameList[Index])
      end {for}
else
   Writeln ('Number of customer names is invalid');
```

Note that in the Pascal version, we have added a step to validate the value of N. This is important so that we do not generate an invalid subscript in case N is larger than Limit.

Once the data has been read and stored into an array, subsequent steps in the program can access that data many times and in any sequence. For example, the following program segment could be used to produce a list of the customer names both in the original sequence and in reverse sequence (from last name to first name):

```
{Customer name list in original sequence}
for Index := 1 to N do
    Writeln (CustomerNameList[Index]);
{Customer name list in reverse sequence}
for Index := N downto 1 do
    Writeln (CustomerNameList[Index]);
```

The use of an array to store and process data in the context of a complete program is illustrated in the solution to the following problem.

■ **Problem Statement.**   Write a program to process a maximum of 100 Real numbers. The output should consist of a list of the numbers, with the largest value in the list labeled with *****. It is possible that more than one element has the same largest value; all items having the largest value should be labeled.

■ **Problem Analysis.**   This is an example of a problem that requires at least two passes through the data to produce the required output. There is no way to know the largest value until all of the data has been entered; the required output cannot, therefore, be produced until this takes place. In such problems, it is convenient to store the data into an array to facilitate the multiple passes through the data that are required.

The problem can be conveniently divided into four smaller problems, as shown in the following preliminary plan:

PRELIMINARY PLAN FOR LARGEST VALUE PROGRAM

1.0 Load data into array

2.0 Find largest value in array

3.0 Print array and label largest value(s)

4.0 Wait

The task of loading data into an array has already been considered extensively; we will choose the While loop variation here. The program will need a Real variable Number, an array of *component-type* Real, which we will call Number-List, and a variable N, which will be used to count the items as they are stored into NumberList.

PLAN FOR LARGEST VALUE PROGRAM (FIRST REFINEMENT)

1.0 Load data into array

    1.1 N = 0

    1.2 Read Number

    1.3 While Number >= 0 and N < Limit Do

    1.4   N = N + 1

    1.5   NumberList[N] = Number

    1.6   Read Number

    1.7 End While

2.0 Find largest value in array

3.0 Print array and label largest value(s)

4.0 Wait

The task of finding the largest value in the array will require a variable LargestNumber. We can initialize this variable with the value of NumberList[1]. Then we must compare the current value of LargestNumber with each of the other elements in the array. If any one of them is larger than the current value of LargestNumber, we place that value into LargestNumber. This step is summarized in the following refinement of the program plan:

PLAN FOR LARGEST VALUE PROGRAM (SECOND REFINEMENT)

1.0 Load data into array

    1.1 N = 0

    1.2 Read Number

    1.3 While Number >= 0 and N < Limit Do

    1.4   N = N + 1

    1.5   NumberList[N] = Number

    1.6   Read Number

1.7 End While

2.0 Find largest value in array
  2.1 LargestNumber = NumberList[1]
  2.2 For Index = 1 to N Do
  2.3   If NumberList[Index] > LargestNumber Then
  2.4   LargestNumber = NumberList[Index]
  2.5   End If
  2.6 End For

3.0 Print array and label largest value(s)

4.0 Wait

The third major step in the program will entail processing all the elements of the array one more time. As each element is considered for output, we can check to see whether it is equal to LargestNumber. If it is, then the required label can be written; otherwise the value will be written without the label. This is summarized in the final plan for the program.

LARGEST VALUE PROGRAM (P9c)

1.0 Load data into array
  1.1 N = 0
  1.2 Read Number
  1.3 While Number >= 0 and N < Limit Do
  1.4   N = N + 1
  1.5   NumberList[N] = Number
  1.6   Read Number
  1.7 End While

2.0 Find largest value in array
  2.1 LargestNumber = NumberList[1]
  2.2 For Index = 1 to N Do
  2.3   If NumberList[Index] > LargestNumber Then
  2.4   LargestNumber = NumberList[Index]
  2.5   End If
  2.6 End For

3.0 Print array and label largest value(s)
  3.1 For Index = 1 to N Do
  3.2   If NumberList[Index] = LargestNumber Then
  3.3   Write NumberList[Index], '*****'
  3.4   Else
  3.5   Write NumberList[Index]
  3.6   End If
  3.7 End For

4.0 Wait

■ **Problem Solution.** A program to solve this problem is shown in Figure 9.4 as Program 9c. The program represents a very straightforward translation of the pseudocode just presented into Pascal.

```
program P9c (Input, Output);
{Program to list a series of positive numbers and label the largest}
uses
    Crt;
const
    InputPrompt = 'Enter positive number (negative value to stop) ';
    Limit = 100;
var
    NumberList : array[1..Limit] of Real;
    Number, LargestNumber : Real;
    Index, N : Integer;
    .
    .
    .
begin     {Main Program}

{1.0 Load data into array}

    ClrScr;
    N := 0;
    Write (InputPrompt);
    Readln (Number);
    while (Number >= 0) and (N < Limit) do
        begin
            N := N + 1;
            NumberList[N] := Number;
            Write (InputPrompt);
            Readln (Number)
        end;   {while}

{2.0 Find largest value in array}

    LargestNumber := NumberList[1];
    for Index := 1 to N do
        if NumberList[Index] > LargestNumber then
            LargestNumber := NumberList[Index];

{3.0 Print array and label the largest value(s)}

    ClrScr;
    for Index := 1 to N do
        if NumberList[Index] = LargestNumber then
            Writeln (NumberList[Index]:6:0, '*****')
        else
            Writeln (NumberList[Index]:6:0);

{4.0 Wait}

    AlternateWait

end.    {Main Program}
```

Figure 9.4 Program 9c: Largest value program.

9.4.1   *Time Out*

1. Compile and execute Program 9c. Test it with sample data, including data in which the largest value occurs more than once in the sequence.

2. Revise Program 9c, using the Repeat/Until technique to load the array.

3. Revise the array-loading portion of Program 9c, using the technique of asking the user to enter the number of elements in the data and then reading the data entered by the user directly into the array. Include an error message if the value of N is invalid.

4. Revise Program 9c to find the location of one of the largest values in the array instead of the value of the largest item. Modify the output procedure as needed so that all values equal to the largest are properly labeled.

5. Revise Program 9c to label the smallest value(s) in the list with ----.

6. Program 9c is written as a three-pass program; that is, three complete passes through the data are required: one to load the data, one to find the largest item, and one to produce the output. Actually, the problem could have been solved using just two passes. The value of the largest item could have been computed during the first pass (as the data is loaded into the array). When the number of items is small, the added time required to make the unneeded third pass may not be noticeable, but when the number of items is large, the extra time may be of great significance. Revise Program 9c so that only two passes are made through the data.

7. Program 9c makes the assumption that N ≠ 0. What would happen if N = 0? How could you modify the program to handle this problem?

9.5   USING AN ARRAY AS A PARAMETER FOR A SUBPROGRAM

It will often be necessary to pass an array as a parameter to a function or procedure. As with other types of parameters, the data types of the formal and actual parameters must be compatible. In the case of arrays, this means that the same type identifier must be used for both of them. This is true even though the actual underlying types might be identical. For example, consider the following program skeleton:

```
type
      ArrayType = array[1..10] of Integer;
var
      DataList : array[1..10] of Integer;
{***********************************************************}
      procedure Proc (A : ArrayType);
           .
           .
           .
{***********************************************************}
begin
           .
           .
           .
      Proc (DataList);  ◄─────────────────        Data-type mismatch error
           .                                      will occur.
           .
           .

end.
```

A data-type mismatch error will result in this program because the data type specified for DataList is not the same as the data type specified for the formal parameter A. (It does not matter that the underlying specifications of the two entities are identical; Pascal insists that the data-type identifier used for both the actual and formal parameters be the same.) The problem can be solved by changing the declaration of DataList to

```
var
    DataList : ArrayType;
```

When a value parameter of any type is passed to a function or procedure, a copy of the variable is made that is local to the subprogram. In this way, any change made to the value of the parameter within the subprogram has no effect on the value of the actual parameter. This characteristic of Turbo Pascal has presented no problems with the data types with which we have been concerned in the past. However, with arrays, a potential problem arises. Arrays may use large amounts of memory. A value parameter with an array type will automatically use up as much memory as is needed for the actual array. In a program with many arrays and several subprograms that process the arrays as value parameters, the utilization of extra memory for each array-type value parameter can become critical. In such cases, you may want to specify the array as a variable parameter in the subprogram, even though the subprogram makes no changes in the array that are to be passed back to the calling program. No local copy of variable parameters is made; therefore, a variable parameter of an array type uses up no extra memory. This practice is not without its dangers, however. The protection from inadvertent changes to the actual parameter afforded when a value parameter is declared is lost. It is imperative that the subprogram make no change in the value of the array elements that should not be passed back to the calling program. This places an added burden on the programmer to make sure that the logic of the subprograms is not only correct, but also consistent with this added restriction.

Let us illustrate the use of functions and procedures to process arrays by rewriting Program 9c. Recall that the plan for this program is as follows:

LARGEST VALUE PROGRAM (P9c)

1.0 Load data into array
2.0 Find largest value in array
3.0 Print array and label the largest
4.0 Wait

We could implement step 1.0 as a procedure that would export the array and the number of elements used in the array. A plan for this procedure could be as follows:

PROCEDURE LOADARRAY(EXPORT : DATA, N)

1.0 Initialize N
2.0 Read Number
3.0 While not end of data store Number and read next Number

The procedure declaration for LoadArray would appear as

```
procedure LoadArray (var Data : ArrayType; var N : Integer);
```

In this case, the formal parameter Data corresponds to the actual parameter NumberList. Data is declared as a variable parameter because the purpose of the procedure is to pass values contained in the array back to the main program. The complete procedure is shown in Figure 9.5, which contains the listing of Program 9d.

Module 2.0 of this procedure could be implemented as a function, since its purpose is to compute a single value based on the content of NumberList and N. Let us call the function Largest; it will return a Real value to the calling program. Since the parameters for this function are not to be modified, they could be declared as value parameters in the function declaration:

```
function Largest (Data : ArrayType; N : Integer) : Real;
```

The complete code for this function is shown in Figure 9.5(a). Remember, though, that by making the array parameter a value parameter, the system allocates memory for the variable, and when the function is invoked, the content of the actual parameter is copied into the local variable space. This action takes increased space in memory and some time, as the content of the actual variable is copied into the local variable locations. In order to maximize space utilization for the program, you could declare Data to be a variable parameter:

```
function Largest (var Data : ArrayType; N : Integer):Real;
```

The complete version of Program 9d is contained in Figure 9.5. A data-flow diagram for the program is shown in Figure 9.6.

9.5.1 Time Out

1. Compile and execute Program 9d.
2. Write a procedure for Module 3.0. Should the array parameter be a value parameter or a variable parameter?
3. Add a function to Program 9d to compute the average of the elements of the array. The average is computed by adding up the elements and dividing by the number of elements (N). Write out the average of the data.
4. Using the average function added in question 3, add a procedure to list the elements of the array that are less than or equal to the average and a procedure to list the elements that are greater than or equal to the average.

9.5.2 Array Elements as Parameters

You should make a clear distinction between the use of an **array subprogram parameter** and an array element as a parameter. In the first case, all elements of the array are being passed to the subprogram for processing; hence, the associated formal parameter

```
program P9d (Input, Output);
{Program to list a series of positive numbers and label the largest;
    program illustrates passing an array to a procedure and a function}
uses
    Crt;
const
    Limit = 100;
type
    ArrayType = array[1..Limit] of Real;
var
    NumberList : ArrayType;
    N, Index : Integer;
    LargestNumber : Real;
{*******************************************************************}
    function Largest (Data : ArrayType; N : Integer) : Real;
    {Function to find the largest value in an array}
    var
        Index : Integer;
        LargestNumber : Real;
    begin    {Largest}
        LargestNumber := Data[1];
        for Index := 1 to N do
            if Data[Index] > LargestNumber then
                LargestNumber := Data[Index];
        Largest := LargestNumber
    end;    {Largest}
{------------------------------------------------------------------}
    procedure LoadArray(var Data:ArrayType; var N : Integer);
    {Procedure to read values and store them into array A}
    const
        InputPrompt = 'Enter positive number (negative value to stop) ';
    var
        Number : Real;
    begin       {LoadArray}

    {1.0 Initialize N}

        N := 0;

    {2.0 Read Number}

        Write (InputPrompt);
        Readln (Number);

    {3.0 While not end of data store Number and Read next Number}

        while Number >= 0 do
            begin
                N := N + 1;
                Data[N] := Number;
                Write (InputPrompt);
                Readln (Number)
            end;   {while}

    end;   {LoadArray}
    .
    .
    .
{*******************************************************************}
```

Figure 9.5(a) Program 9d: Declaration part (part 1 of 2 parts).

```
begin   {Main Program}

{1.0 Load data into array}

    ClrScr;
    LoadArray (NumberList, N);

{2.0 Find largest value in array}

    LargestNumber := Largest (NumberList, N);

{3.0 Print data and label the largest value(s)}

    ClrScr;
    for Index := 1 to N do
        if NumberList[Index] = LargestNumber then
            Writeln (NumberList[Index]:6:0, '*****')
        else
            Writeln (NumberList[Index]:6:0);

{4.0 Wait}

    AlternateWait

end.   {Main Program}
```

Figure 9.5(b) Program 9d: Statement part (part 2 of 2 parts).

must be of the same array type as the actual parameter. In the second case, only one element of the array is being passed to the subprogram; thus, the associated formal parameter must be of the same type as the base type of the array. For example, suppose the following declarations are in place:

```
type
    ArrayType = array[1..100] of Real;
var
    X : ArrayType;
    Index : Integer;
```

Figure 9.6 Data-flow diagram for Program 9d.

Suppose further that we wish to compute the absolute value of each element in X. We can use the built-in function Abs as follows:

```
for Index := 1 to N do
    X[Index] := Abs(X[Index]);
```

In this case, the actual argument of the function Abs is an element of the array X, namely, X[Index]. Since the base type of the array X is Real, the function expects a Real argument, and everything is in order. It would *not* be valid to use X as an argument for the function Abs (as in Abs(X)), since X is an array-type variable and Abs is defined only for Real and Integer arguments.

9.6 PROCESSING WHOLE ARRAYS

In many instances, the processing steps that you will perform on data stored in an array will involve access to each individual element using subscripts. It is possible, however, to perform certain processing steps on an array without the overt use of subscripts. The primary example of this is simple assignment of the values contained in one array to corresponding locations in another array of the same type. The assignment statement is quite general in its use. The only requirement is that the data type of the variable on the left match the data type of the expression on the right. For example, suppose two variables have been declared as follows:

```
type
    ArrayType : array[1..100] of Integer;
var
    X, Y : ArrayType;
```

If we wish to copy all of the values contained in the array Y into the corresponding locations in the array X, the following assignment statement could be used:

```
X := Y;
```

After execution of this statement, the value of X[1] would be the same as that of Y[1], the value of X[2] would be the same as that of Y[2], and so forth.

The alternative to using the preceding statement would be a loop such as the following:

```
for Index := 1 to 100 do
    X[Index] := Y[Index];
```

It is obvious that the simple assignment statement is more convenient than the equivalent loop, which processes each element of the array using subscripts.

Unfortunately, Pascal provides no operators that can be used to create array-type expressions. It is possible, however, to write procedures that perform processing steps on arrays.[1] Using such procedures, you can effectively process entire arrays in one statement.

For example, suppose we wish to assign zero values to each element of an array. One way to do this is to write the loop

```
for Index := 1 to 100 do
    X[Index] := 0;
```

Another way to do the same task is to create a procedure with an array parameter. The procedure could be written as follows:

```
procedure Zero (var T : ArrayType);
{Procedure to create an array of zeros}
var
    Index : Integer;
begin {Zero}
    for Index := 1 to 100 do
        T[Index] := 0;
end; {Zero}
```

With this procedure in place, the program can reference it in statements such as the following, which will serve to initialize the ArrayType variables X and Y to zeros:

```
Zero (X);
Zero (Y);
```

As another example of this concept, consider the task of finding the sum of corresponding elements of two arrays and storing that result in a third array. One approach to this problem is to define a procedure (let us call it ArraySum) that imports three arguments—the two arrays and the number of elements in use (the variable we have called N in previous examples)—and exports an array having as its elements the required sums. The following program segment could be used to declare the required procedure:

```
procedure ArraySum (A, B : ArrayType; N : Integer;
                    var Sum : ArrayType);
{Procedure to compute sum of corresponding elements of
    N elements of arrays A and B}
var
    Index : Integer;
begin {ArraySum}
    for Index := 1 to N do
        Sum[Index] := A[Index] + B[Index]
end; {ArraySum}
```

---

[1]You cannot write a function that returns an array-type value. The value of a function must be either a scalar type, a string type, or a pointer type.

With this procedure in place, we could add the contents of corresponding elements of the ArrayType variables X and Y and store the result in the array X using the simple statement

```
ArraySum (X, Y, N, X);
```

9.6.1 Time Out

1. Using the concepts presented in this section, write an appropriate procedure to reverse the sequence of an array of data and store the result in a second array of the same type. (Remember that not all of the elements are in use.) The main program should read an array of Integer values of maximum length 100, using -1 to terminate the data-entry process. Use the procedure to reverse the sequence of the data and store the result in the original array. Write out the data in reverse sequence.

2. Write a procedure to place the following sequence into an array of 10 elements;

```
1, 2, 4, 8, 16, 32, 64, 128, 256, 512
```

(This sequence represents powers of 2, from 2^0 to 2^9.)

3. Write a procedure to replace all negative elements in an array with the value 0. Assume that the array is of length 100 and is of base type Real.

9.7 PARALLEL ARRAYS FOR DATA STORAGE

It is often necessary to store multiple data items for each entity in a set of elements. For example, in a program that processes a student's test grades, there might be several test grades for each student. In a program that could be used to balance a checkbook, each check would include a check number, a date, the payee, and the amount of the check. When this situation arises, it is necessary to use several arrays—one for each data element. The relationship between data elements can be maintained by using corresponding elements in each array for each distinct entity in the set—hence the description of this concept as **parallel arrays**.

For example, in the student test grade situation, we could use as many arrays as there were test grades. If there were three grades, then we could declare the three arrays as

```
const
    StudentLimit = 100;
type
    GradeArray = array[1..StudentLimit] of Real;
var
    TestGrade1, TestGrade2, TestGrade3 : GradeArray;
```

This structure could be visualized as follows:

TestGrade1[1]	☐	TestGrade2[1]	☐	TestGrade3[1]	☐
TestGrade1[2]	☐	TestGrade2[2]	☐	TestGrade3[2]	☐
.		.		.	
.		.		.	
.		.		.	
TestGrade1[100]	☐	TestGrade2[100]	☐	TestGrade3[100]	☐

In the program that processes these data, the content of TestGrade1[1], TestGrade2[1], TestGrade3[1] will be test grades for the first student. In general, the content of TestGrade1[I], TestGrade2[I], TestGrade3[I], will relate to the *I*th student.

In the checkbook-balancing example, the set of arrays that will be needed is somewhat more complex because the data elements associated with each check are of different data types. The check number is Integer, the amount is Real, and the payee is string. The date would actually consist of three distinct items: the month, day, and year, each of which would be Integer. The following program segment would create the variables required to store this data:

```
const
    CheckLimit = 200;
type
    CheckSubRange = 1..CheckLimit;
    IntegerArrayType = array[CheckSubRange] of Integer;
    StringArrayType = array[CheckSubRange] of string[20];
    RealArrayType = array[CheckSubRange] of Real;
var
    CheckNumber, CheckMonth, CheckDay, CheckYear:
                            IntegerArrayType;
    CheckPayee : StringArrayType;
    CheckAmount : RealArrayType;
```

In this program, the content of CheckNumber[1], CheckMonth[1], CheckDay[1], Check-Year[1], CheckPayee[1], and CheckAmount[1] will contain data from the first check.

The use of parallel arrays for data storage in the context of a complete program is illustrated in the solution to the following problem.

■ **Problem Statement.**   Write a program to analyze production and sales data for items in a company's inventory. Input data is contained in a Text file that consists of a description of the inventory item, the production quantity, and the sales amount for a specific period. The company wishes to pinpoint those items in which production has been greater than sales. Specifically, the program should produce a report (the Excess Production Report) with suitable headings showing those items in which the difference between production and sales is greater than zero and the amount of that difference.

■ **Problem Analysis.**   Let us assume that there are a maximum of 100 items in the company's inventory. For each item, we must store the description and the production and sales amounts. We will use parallel arrays—ItemDescription, ProductionData, and Sales-Data—each of which contains 100 elements. The first element of each array will relate to the first inventory item, the second element will relate to the second item, and so forth. Additionally, we will create an array of 100 elements called Difference to store the difference between the corresponding elements of ProductionData and SalesData. We will also need a variable N, which will contain the number of inventory items, and a variable Index to be used as a subscript in accessing the content of the arrays.

Since we will be using arrays to store and process the data, we can break the problem down into four distinct steps: loading the data, processing the data, producing the report, and waiting until the user is ready to proceed. The plan for the program is as follows:

PRODUCTION AND SALES ANALYSIS PROGRAM (P9e)

1.0 Load data

2.0 Compute difference between production and sales amounts

3.0 Print Excess Production Report

4.0 Wait

■ **Problem Solution.** In the implementation of the first step, let us have the user enter the number of inventory items (N) in advance of entering the data, using the for loop to control the data input. The calculation of the difference between the two arrays will make explicit use of the parallelism between the arrays. A for loop will be used to compute the difference between corresponding elements of ProductionData and SalesData and store the result in the corresponding element of Difference:

```
for Index := 1 to N do
    Difference[Index] := ProductionData[Index] -
                            SalesData[Index];
```

The final task for the program is to print the report. We must first print the heading, which consists of a title ("Excess Production Report") and descriptive headings for each column of data in the report. Then the content of the array Difference is accessed, using a for loop. For each positive element in Difference, the corresponding elements in all the arrays are printed in the report.

The complete program is shown in Figure 9.7 as Program 9e.

9.7.1 Time Out

1. Create a text file with data in the format required for Program 9e. Compile and execute Program 9e.
2. Note that it is possible that the report will contain no data. Write a line at the bottom of the report indicating the number of lines in it. This will reassure the reader that no program error has been made in case there are no lines in the report.

```pascal
program P9e (Input, Output, ProductionDataFile);
{Program to analyze production and sales data for inventory items}
uses
     Crt;
const
     ItemLimit = 100;
type
     StringType = string[20];
     ItemArrayType = array[1..ItemLimit] of StringType;
     RealArrayType = array[1..ItemLimit] of Real;
var
     ItemDescription : ItemArrayType;
     ProductionData, SalesData, Difference : RealArrayType;
     Index, N : Integer;
     ProductionDataFile : Text;
     .
     .
     .
begin      {Main Program}

{1.0 Load data}

     ClrScr;
     OpenInputFile (ProductionDataFile);
     N := 0;
     while not Eof (ProductionDataFile) do
           begin
                N := N + 1;
                Readln (ProductionDataFile,ItemDescription[N]);
                Readln (ProductionDataFile,
                     ProductionData[N], SalesData[N])
           end;   {while}
     Close (ProductionDataFile);

{2.0 Compute difference between production and sales amounts}

     for Index := 1 to N do
         Difference[Index] := ProductionData[Index] -
                              SalesData[Index];

{3.0 Print Excess Production Report}

     Writeln ('Excess Production Report':50);
     Writeln;
     Writeln ('Item':20,'Production':15,'Sales':15,'Difference':15);
     for Index := 1 to N do
         if Difference[Index] > 0 then
            Writeln (ItemDescription[Index]:20, ProductionData[Index]:15:0,
                 SalesData[Index]:15:0, Difference[Index]:15:0);

{4.0 Wait}

     AlternateWait

end.    {Main Program}
```

Figure 9.7 Program 9e: Excess Production Report.

3. If your system is equipped with a printer, add an option for the report to be produced on the printer, or on the screen, or to be sent to a text file, at the discretion of the program user.

4. Add a procedure to produce a second report, to be titled "Deficient Production Report," listing items in which the production amount is less than the sales amount.

9.8 TWO-DIMENSIONAL ARRAYS

So far, all the array structures with which we have been working have been linear lists accessed by one subscript. You can think of a **one-dimensional array** as a single column of items, all of the same type. Sometimes it is useful to create a more complex structure having two dimensions—rows as well as columns.[2] We could create a table such as the following for this purpose:

	Test 1	Test 2	Test 3
Student 1			
Student 2			
.			
.			
.			
Student 100			

We have seen how to use a series of three one-dimensional arrays to represent such data. Pascal also allows you to create a **two-dimensional array**. Each element of the array would represent a single grade for a student. You would use two subscripts to access the array elements. The first subscript would represent the student number, and the second subscript would represent the test number. If the name of the array was StudentGrade, then StudentGrade[1, 2], would contain the grade for the first student's second test. Student-Grade[3, 1] would contain the first test grade for student 3.

The structure just described can be declared by a number of essentially equivalent means in Pascal. The simplest and most direct method is as follows:

```
type
      RealTwoDimensionalArray = array[1..100, 1..3] of Real;
var
      StudentGrade : RealTwoDimensionalArray;
```

A general form for the declaration of a two-dimensional array is

```
array[index-type, index-type] of component-type
```

---

[2]The designation "rows" and "columns" to describe the two dimensions of a two-dimensional array is somewhat arbitrary, since we could use the opposite designations just as logically. The designation described here is conventional.

The first specification of *index-type* governs the number of rows in the structure and the range of allowable values for the first subscript in an array reference. The second specification of *index-type* governs the number of columns in the structure and the allowable range of values for the second subscript. In the preceding example, the array is composed of 100 rows and 3 columns. Thus, the first subscript can range from 1 to 100 and the second from 1 to 3.

Another way to define this structure is as a one-dimensional array, each of whose components is an array. Remember that *component-type* can be any type except file—a similar type such as Real or Integer or a structured type such as array. For example, the following coding segment could also be used to create StudentGrade:

```
type
    TwoDimensionalRealArray = array[1..100] of array[1..3] of Real;
```

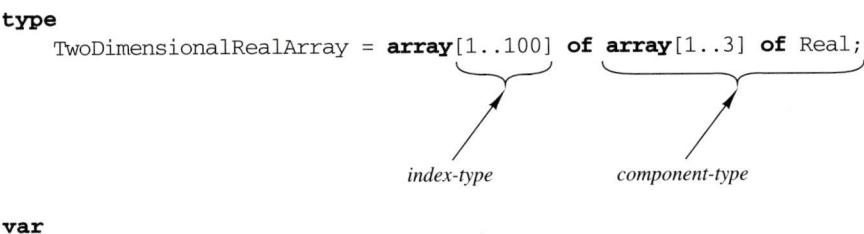

```
var
    StudentGrade : TwoDimensionalRealArray;
```

Whichever technique is used to create a two-dimensional array, the same types of subscript notation are used to access the components of the array. Again, two choices are available. One method is to use two subscripts separated by a comma and enclosed in brackets, as in StudentGrade[3, 2] or StudentGrade[Index, Test]. The second (and perhaps less desirable) method is to list the two subscripts separately, enclosing each in brackets. For example, StudentGrade[3] [2] is equivalent to StudentGrade[3, 2], and StudentGrade[Index] [Test] is equivalent to Student-Grade[Index, Test]. In this text, we shall use the first method exclusively, because it is more consistent with usual mathematical notation and the notation commonly used in other programming languages.

9.8.1 Time Out

1. Describe the structure created by each of the following coding segments:

(a) `type`
```
        RealArray = array[1..5] of Real;
        Real2DArray = array[1..3] of RealArray;
    var
        A : Real2DArray;
```

(b) `type`
```
            Integer2DArray = array[0..10, 5..9] of Integer;
        var
            B : Integer2DArray;
```

(c) type
```
        Char2DArray = array['a'..'z', 1..10] of Char;
    var
        C : Char2DArray;
```

2. Write Pascal coding segments to declare variables to be used in programs for each of
   the following:
   (a) A mileage table showing the mileage between 10 cities.
   (b) A table showing the allowable deduction for each of 10 tax brackets and the num-
      ber of dependents, ranging from 0 to 7.
   (c) An array to summarize sales by month for each of 20 stores.
   (d) A budget showing planned expenditures for each of 5 budget categories for a com-
      pany with 10 departments.

9.8.2   Processing Two-Dimensional Arrays

A program structure that is often useful in processing arrays of two dimensions is nested
for loops. We have already seen that to process a one-dimensional array, it is helpful to
use a for loop in which the index is used as the subscript for the array. Since two-
dimensional arrays have two subscripts, two for loops—one nested inside the other—can
be used to vary two indices, which can then be used as the two subscripts required to
access array elements.

   For example, suppose that you wish to create a two-dimensional array of a maximum size of 100 rows and 10 columns. In a particular instance, the user could elect to use
any number of rows (up to 100) and any number of columns (up to 10). This data structure could be created by the following program segment:

```
    const
        MaxRows = 100;
        MaxColumns = 10;
    type
        ArrayType = array[1..MaxRows, 1..MaxColumns] of Real;
    var
        A : ArrayType;
        N, M, {Number of used rows and columns respectively}
        RowIndex, ColumnIndex : Integer;
```

As indicated, it will be necessary to have two variables N and M to represent the number
of rows and columns that are to be used to store data.

   With this program segment in place, we can write the procedure to load the data into
the array. The user will first enter the values for N and M and then the entries in each of the
array positions, one at a time. The following program segment will accomplish this task:

```
    Write ('Enter number rows and columns ');
    Readln (N, M);
    {Row order data-entry procedure}
```

```
for RowIndex := 1 to N do
    for ColumnIndex := 1 to M do
        begin
            Write ('Enter value for element in row ',
                    RowIndex, ' column ',ColumnIndex);
            Readln (A[RowIndex, ColumnIndex])
        end; {for}
```

For each value of RowIndex, the value of ColumnIndex will vary from 1 to M. In all, there will be N × M repetitions of the data-entry operation.

In the preceding example, the data are entered in row order—first row 1, then row 2, and so forth. It is just as easy for the user to enter the data in column order—that is, all the elements of column 1, then all the elements of column 2, and so forth. To accomplish this task, the order of the two for statements is reversed:

```
{Column order data-entry procedure}
for ColumnIndex := 1 to M do
    for RowIndex := 1 to N do
        begin
            . . .
        end; {for}
```

When ColumnIndex is 1, the value of RowIndex will vary from 1 to N, thereby allowing the user to fill up the first column; when ColumnIndex is 2, the user will enter all elements of the second column, and so forth.

In general, there will always be two orders in which to process the elements of a two-dimensional array—row order and column order—as illustrated in the two preceding program segments. The choice of which order to use depends on the nature of the operations to be performed on the array. In the case of data input, the choice should be made on the basis of which order is most natural and convenient for the program user. In some cases the choice of order may be an arbitrary one, since the end result may be the same no matter which order is chosen. For example, suppose you wish to calculate the sum of the elements in the array. Using accumulation, you would add up all the elements, in either row order or column order to access the individual elements for processing. The following two program segments would have equivalent results (assume that Sum is a Real variable):

```
{Array Sum—row order}
 Sum := 0;
 for RowIndex := 1 to N do
     for ColumnIndex := 1 to M do
         Sum := Sum + A[RowIndex, ColumnIndex];
{Array Sum—column order}
 Sum := 0;
 for ColumnIndex := 1 to M do
     for Rowindex := 1 to N do
         Sum := Sum + A[RowIndex, ColumnIndex];
```

When writing out the content of a two-dimensional array, you would most commonly want to see the elements in row order. Usually, you would wish to have row 1 appear on the first line of the output, row 2 on the second line of the output, and so forth. For the example just presented, the following program segment would accomplish this task:

```
for RowIndex := 1 to N do
    begin
        for ColumnIndex := 1 to M do
            Write (A[RowIndex, ColumnIndex]:5:0);
        Writeln
    end; {for}
```

Note the importance of the Writeln statement: The inner for loop will cause the content of a row of the array to be printed in successive positions of a line. The Writeln statement with no parameters writes an end-of-line character, thereby forcing the next output to begin on a new line.

The use of a two-dimensional array for storing and processing data is illustrated in the solution to the following problem.

■ **Problem Statement.**   Write a program to analyze three test grades for up to 100 students. The desired output is a report showing the grades and the average of the three grades for each student.

■ **Problem Analysis.**   An appropriate structure for the data is a two-dimensional array of size 100 by 3, which we shall call StudentGrade. Each row will store three grades and correspond to one student. In order to store the averages, we will need a one-dimensional array (let us call it AverageGrade) of size 100. The first element of AverageGrade will correspond to the first row of StudentGrade, the second element will correspond to the second row, and so on. (We are using the concept of parallel arrays here.)

The program itself is relatively simple. We must first read and store the grades, then compute the averages, then write the report, and, finally, wait until the user is ready to proceed. This is summarized in the following program plan:

STUDENT GRADE-REPORT PROGRAM (P9f)

1.0 Load Data

2.0 Compute Averages

3.0 Write Report

4.0 Wait

■ **Problem Solution.**   Program 9f, which is a solution to this problem, is shown in Figure 9.8. An example of the appearance of the screen during the execution of the program is shown in Figure 9.9.

```
program P9f (Input, Output);
{Program to summarize student grades}
uses
     Crt;
const
     InputPrompt1 = 'Enter number of students ';
     InputPrompt2 = 'Grades for student #  ';
     InputPrompt3 = 'Enter test grade #  ';
     MaxNumberStudents = 100;
     ReportHead1 = '       Student Grade Summary Report';
     ReportHead2 = 'Student    Test      Test      Test  Average';
     ReportHead3 = 'Number      1         2         3';
     ReportFoot  = 'End of Report';
type
     Real2DArray = array[1..MaxNumberStudents, 1..3] of Real;
     Real1DArray = array[1..MaxNumberStudents] of Real;
var
     N,               {Actual number of students; Input Variable}
     StudentIndex, GradeIndex : Integer;
     StudentGrade : Real2DArray;   {Array for storage of the grades}
     AverageGrade : Real1DArray;   {Array for computation of  averages}
     .
     .
     .
```

Figure 9.8(a) Program 9f: Declaration part (part 1 of 2 parts).

The task of loading the data can be accomplished by having the user enter the number of students and then the grades for each student. Two methods are possible for the latter operation: Each entry could be on a new line with an appropriate prompt, or all values could be entered on a single line. The choice made in this case is to have the user enter each grade as a separate item, as shown in the implementation of Module 1.0 in Figure 9.8(b) and in the sample execution of the program (see Figure 9.9). The other approach, which would have been somewhat simpler to code, is as follows:

```
for StudentIndex := 1 to N do
     begin
          Writeln ('Enter test grades for student #',
                   StudentIndex);
          Readln (StudentGrade[StudentIndex, 1],
                  StudentGrade[StudentIndex, 2],
                  StudentGrade[StudentIndex, 3])
     end; {for}
```

The reason for choosing the more complicated approach is that it can be generalized readily to permit the number of grades to be a variable, whereas the simpler approach cannot.

```
begin      {Main Program}

{1.0 Load Data}

    ClrScr;
    Write(InputPrompt1);
    Readln(N);
    for StudentIndex := 1 to N do
        begin
            Writeln(InputPrompt2, StudentIndex, ' ');
            for GradeIndex := 1 to 3 do
                begin
                    Write (InputPrompt3, GradeIndex, ' ');
                    Readln(StudentGrade[StudentIndex, GradeIndex])
                end   {for}
        end;   {for}

{2.0 Compute Averages}

    for StudentIndex := 1 to N do
        begin
            AverageGrade [StudentIndex] := 0;
            for GradeIndex := 1 to 3 do
                AverageGrade [StudentIndex] :=
                    AverageGrade[StudentIndex] +
                    StudentGrade[StudentIndex, GradeIndex];
            AverageGrade[StudentIndex] :=
                AverageGrade[StudentIndex] / 3
        end;   {for}

{3.0 Write Report}

    ClrScr;
    Writeln (ReportHead1);
    Writeln (ReportHead2);
    Writeln (ReportHead3);
    for StudentIndex := 1 to N do
        begin
            Write (StudentIndex:4);
            for GradeIndex := 1 to 3 do
                Write(StudentGrade[StudentIndex, GradeIndex]:9:0);
            Writeln (AverageGrade[StudentIndex]:9:0)
        end;   {for}
    Writeln (ReportFoot);

{4.0 Wait}

    AlternateWait

end.      {Main Program}
```

Figure 9.8(b) Program 9f: Statement part (part 2 of 2 parts).

```
Enter number of students 3
Grades for student # 1
Enter test grade # 1 67
Enter test grade # 2 78
Enter test grade # 3 89
Grades for student # 2
Enter test grade # 1 90
Enter test grade # 2 98
Enter test grade # 3 100
Grades for student # 3
Enter test grade # 1 48
Enter test grade # 2 67
Enter test grade # 3 90




    Student Grade Summary Report
Student    Test      Test     Test   Average
Number      1         2        3
   1        67        78       89        78
   2        90        98      100        96
   3        45        67       90        67
End of Report
Press any key to continue
```

Figure 9.9 Sample execution of Program 9f.

The task of computing averages could be accomplished by the following very straightforward coding segment:

```
for StudentIndex := 1 to N do
    AverageGrade[StudentIndex] :=
                              (StudentGrade[StudentIndex, 1]
                         + StudentGrade[StudentIndex, 2]
                         + StudentGrade[StudentIndex, 3]) / 3;
```

Instead, we choose to use a more elaborate technique involving accumulation:

```
for StudentIndex := 1 to N do
    begin
        AverageGrade[StudentIndex] := 0;
        for GradeIndex := 1 to 3 do
            AverageGrade[StudentIndex] :=
                    AverageGrade[StudentIndex] +
                    StudentGrade[StudentIndex, GradeIndex];
        AverageGrade[StudentIndex] :=
                    AverageGrade[StudentIndex] / 3
    end; {for}
```

Again, the reason for the choice is that the latter technique can be readily adapted to process a variable number of grades, whereas the formula approach cannot.

9.8.3 Time Out

1. Compile and execute Program 9f. Test the program with sample data of your choosing.
2. Modify the program to locate the highest grade in the data. Include output similar to the following at the conclusion of the report:

```
The highest grade was earned by
            Student #_ on Test #_
```

Note that it is possible that several students tie for highest grade; include a separate line of output for each.
3. Generalize Program 9f to allow the user to process up to 10 grades for each student. Have the user enter both the number of students and the number of grades initially. Much of the program has already been designed to facilitate this generalization; however, a procedure will have to be designed to produce the second and third lines of the report heading, since they can no longer be included as constants.
4. Modify Program 9f to allow the user to enter student names along with the grades. Use a one-dimensional array to parallel the two-dimensional array StudentGrade.
5. Modify Program 9f to calculate and print the average for each test, as well as the average for each student. The test averages should be printed at the bottom of the report.

9.9 STRINGS VERSUS ARRAYS OF CHAR

The string data type in Turbo Pascal is actually a specialized array type with base type Char. In other versions of Pascal, which do not support the string data type, you would need to use a declaration such as the following to create the equivalent of a string-type variable:

```
var
     DataItem : array[1..20] of Char;
```

DataItem would consist of 20 elements, each of which could contain one character. Access to each element would be by a subscript, as with any other array element. For example, DataItem[1] would access the first character in the array, DataItem[2] would refer to the second character, and so forth.

Standard Pascal also allows you to use the packed option when declaring an array type. The word **packed** is inserted immediately to the left of the word array, as in the following example:

```
var
     DataItem : packed array[1..20] of Char;
```

The packed option is supposed to allow the compiler to generate code that optimizes the utilization of memory for the array. For example, if two memory locations (two bytes) are normally allocated for each element of an array of base type Char (to optimize the speed of execution of the program), then specifying the packed option would allow the compiler to allocate one memory location (one byte) for each element of the array. (This would be the minimum amount of storage required for a character.) The structure would occupy half as much memory, but the program might require longer to process each element (because the instructions required might be more complex). The packed option can be declared for an array of any base type (not just Char, although it is most often seen in this context).

Turbo Pascal allows you to use the packed option if you so desire, but the compiler ignores the option. Turbo Pascal always optimizes the allocation of memory for you.

There are some important differences between **arrays of Char** and strings. First, the value of a string variable can be read using Readln and written using Write or Writeln; a variable with an array type cannot. Second, a string variable contains information on the length of the string (remember, the zeroth element of the string contains the length); a variable of type array of Char contains the number of elements defined for it. Third, there are a number of built-in functions that process string data; there are none for arrays of characters.

9.10   ARRAYS OF STRINGS

As noted before, a string strongly resembles a one-dimensional array. It should not be surprising, then, that an array of base type string will resemble a two-dimensional array. For example, consider the following variable declaration:

```
var
     Data : array[1..10] of string[20];
```

The variable Data contains 10 elements of base type string[20]. You can visualize this structure as follows:

```
Data[1]    └┴┴┴┴┴┴┴┴┴┴┴┴┴┴┴┴┴┴┴┘
Data[2]    └┴┴┴┴┴┴┴┴┴┴┴┴┴┴┴┴┴┴┴┘
     .
     .
     .
Data[10]   └┴┴┴┴┴┴┴┴┴┴┴┴┴┴┴┴┴┴┴┘
```

The characters within each of the elements of Data can be accessed using the appropriate subscripts. As was the case with our previous discussion of two-dimensional arrays, the first subscript will designate the row (the major element of Data), and the second subscript will designate the column (a particular character within the major element of Data). For example, the second character of the first element of Data could be referenced as Data[1][2] or Data[1, 2]. We can expand the preceding diagram to show this concept:

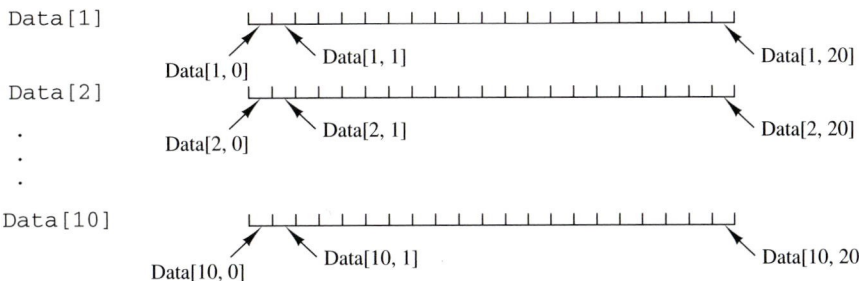

All the functions that you have been accustomed to using to process string variables continue to be available to process major elements of the variable Data. For example, Length(Data[1]) would return the length of the string stored in Data[1]. Moreover, operations that you are accustomed to performing on character data can be carried out on the individual characters of the string contained in Data. For example, Data[1, 1] + Data[1, 2] would be a string-valued expression consisting of the first two elements of Data[1].

Program 9a, which was used to convert dates from numeric to alphanumeric format, made use of an array of strings to store the month names (see Figure 9.2(a)). The output produced by the program contains the entire month name associated with the month number in the range 1 to 12 entered by the user. Suppose we desire to write out only the first three letters of the month name, instead of the entire name. We can access these characters by using a reference containing two subscripts—the first subscript will indicate the month and the second will indicate the character within the name of that month. In Program 9a, the following statement is used to assign a value to the function ConvertDate:

```
ConvertDate := MonthName[M] + Day + ', ' + Year
```

We can revise this statement to use only the first three characters of the month name as follows:

```
ConvertDate := MonthName[M, 1] + MonthName[M, 2] +
               MonthName[M, 3] + ' ' + Day + ', ' + Year
```

This version of the function ConvertDate is contained in Program 9g, which is shown in Figure 9.10. A sample of output produced by the revised version of the program is shown in Figure 9.11.

9.10.1 Time Out

1. Test Program 9g with sample data of your choosing.
2. In Program 9g, instead of using the concatenation operator to access the first three characters of each name, try using the Copy function.
3. If you haven't done so already, modify Program 9f to allow the user to enter the student's name along with the grades. In your output, print out the student's first two

```
program P9g (Input, Output);
{Program to convert dates from numeric to alphanumeric form;
     this version uses abbreviated month names}
     .
     .
     .
     function ConvertDate (M, D, Y:Integer) : StringType;
     {Function to convert a date from numeric form to alphanumeric form}
     var
          Day, Year : StringType;
     begin  {ConvertDate}
          Str (D, Day);
          Str (Y:2, Year);
          if Year[1] = ' ' then
               Year[1] := '0';
          Year := '19'+Year;
          if (M >= 1) and (M <= 12) then
               ConvertDate := MonthName[M, 1] + MonthName[M, 2] +
                    MonthName[M, 3] + ' ' + Day + ', '+Year
          else
               ConvertDate := 'Invalid date';
     end;  {ConvertDate}
     .
     .
     .
end.   {Main Program}
```

Figure 9.10 Program 9g: Revised version of procedure ConvertDate from Program 9a.

```
Enter date in the form mm dd yy (0 0 0 to stop) 9 9 9
Numeric form of date : 9 9 9
Alphanumeric form : Sep 9, 1909
Enter date in the form mm dd yy (0 0 0 to stop) 1 1 93
Numeric form of date : 1 1 93
Alphanumeric form : Jan 1, 1993
Enter date in the form mm dd yy (0 0 0 to stop) 12 25 94
Numeric form of date : 12 25 94
Alphanumeric form : Dec 25, 1994
Enter date in the form mm dd yy (0 0 0 to stop) 0 0 0
```

Figure 9.11 Sample execution of Program 9g.

initials instead of the full name. That is, if the user enters the name as Sam Jones, the output should contain only SJ, followed by the grades.

9.11 ARRAYS OF THREE OR MORE DIMENSIONS

Pascal allows you to create and process arrays of as many dimensions as you need. A general form for an array declaration is

array [*index-type-1, index-type-2 ...*] **of** *component-type* where you make one entry of *index-type* for each dimension. For example, suppose the following declaration is made:

```
var
     A : array[1..6, 1..3, 1..4] of Integer;
```

Then the array A is a **three-dimensional array**. Access to it requires three subscripts. You can visualize this array as a three-dimensional cube, as shown in Figure 9.12.

We can think of this structure as a series of six two-dimensional arrays, each of which has 3 rows and 4 columns. The first subscript is said to designate the *rank*, the second subscript designates the *row*, and the third subscript designates the *column*. For example, the element in the second rank, first row, and third column would be addressed as A[2, 1, 3], or A[2] [1] [3]. (The first form of address is preferred.) The same data structure could have been created in several different ways. For example, we could have created it as an array of two-dimensional arrays:

```
var
     A : array[1..6] of array[1..3, 1..4] of Integer;
```

Also, the structure could be created as an array of an array of arrays:

```
var
     A : array[1..6] of array[1..3] of array[1..4] of
Integer;
```

Or the structure could be declared as a two-dimensional array of arrays:

```
var
     A : array[1..6, 1..3] of array[1..4] of Integer;
```

All these alternatives would declare an identical structure and could be accessed by exactly the same means.

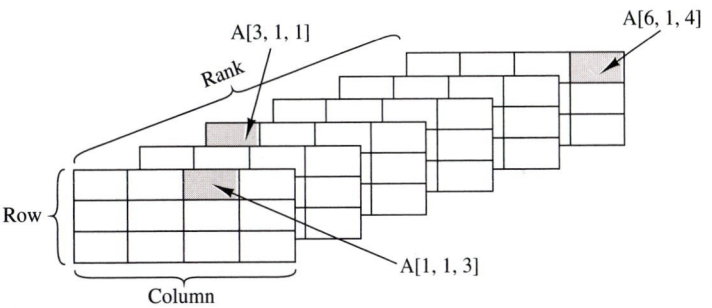

Figure 9.12 Visualization of a three-dimensional array.

For example, consider the problem of processing student grades that was solved in Program 9f. In this program, a two-dimensional array was used to store the data. The first subscript designates the student, and the second subscript designates the test. Suppose that we wish to expand the program to handle tests for the six grading periods in the academic year. In each period, the same set of students will take three tests. This added requirement can be met by creating six two-dimensional arrays (one for each grading period), but a much better approach would be a three-dimensional array. The first subscript (the one that designates the rank) can represent the grading period, the second subscript (the row designator) can represent the student, and the third (the column designator) can represent the test. The following declarations create this structure:

```
const
    MaxNumberStudents = 100;
type
    Real3DArray = array[1..6, 1..MaxNumberStudents, 1..3] of Real;
var
    StudentGrade : Real3DArray;
```

Any access to StudentGrade will require three subscripts, representing the grading period, student number, and test number, in that order.

You will often find that you need a program structure consisting of nested for loops in order to process a three-dimensional array. For example, suppose that the array StudentGrade is defined as described before, and we wish to write a program segment to compute the average of all the grades. Then we would need to compute the sum of all the elements and divide by the number of entries. The following program segment could be used (assume that GP, SN, and TN are integer variables, GradeSum and GradeAverage are Real variables, and N represents the number of students):

```
GradeSum := 0;
for GP := 1 to 6 do
    for SN := 1 to N do
        for TN := 1 to 3 do
            GradeSum := GradeSum + StudentGrade[GP, SN, TN];
GradeAverage := GradeSum / (6 * 3 * N);
```

The subscript GP designates the grading period (the rank), the subscript SN designates the student number (the row), and the subscript TN designates the test number (the column). In this case (since the entire array is to be processed), the ordering of the three for statements is immaterial. For the ordering given, all the grades from the first grading period will be processed first, then all the grades from the second period, and so forth.

In many cases, the ordering of the for loops must be chosen with care. For example, suppose you wish to produce a series of reports showing the test grades for each student for the year. For each student, the grading period would vary from 1 to 6, and within each grading period, the test number would vary from 1 to 3. The following program segment could be used:

```
for SN := 1 to N do
    begin
        Writeln ('Grade Report for Student Number ', SN);
        Writeln ('Period Test Grades');
        for GP := 1 to 6 do
            begin
                Write (GP:4);
                for TN := 1 to 3 do
                    Write (StudentGrade[GP, SN, TN]:6:0);
                Writeln
            end {for}
    end; {for}
```

In this program segment, the for loop controlling the student number (SN) is the outer loop because we wish to access all the grades for one student.

As was noted, the number of dimensions for an array in Pascal is unlimited. We can easily create a structure with four, five, or more dimensions if this type of structure would be an appropriate model for the data that needs to be processed. Unfortunately, the visualization of arrays of more than three dimensions becomes very difficult. A four-dimensional array can be thought of as a series of three-dimensional arrays, a five-dimensional array can be conceived of as a series of four-dimensional arrays, and so forth. Such conceptions become difficult to represent in a visual form. A four-dimensional array will require four subscripts; a five-dimensional array will require five subscripts, and so forth. The key to success in using these structures is to establish the meaning of each subscript and adhere to that meaning consistently within the program. Not being able to draw a picture of a structure should not inhibit our use of more elaborate array structures when they are appropriate for solving a particular problem.

For example, suppose we wish to expand the grade array to accommodate five different subjects that a student is taking. For each subject, there would be six grading periods. For each subject and grading period, there would be up to 100 students, each with three test grades. The structure could be declared as follows:

```
const
    MaxStudents = 100;
type
    Real4DArray = array[1..5, 1..6, 1..MaxStudents, 1..3] of Real;
var
    StudentGrade : Real4DArray;
```

In this structure, the first subscript represents the subject, the second represents the grading period, the third represents the student, and the fourth represents the test number. This array would take up $5 \times 6 \times 100 \times 3 = 9,000$ Real memory locations. Each Real location in Turbo Pascal takes 6 bytes; therefore, the structure consumes $9,000 \times 6 = 54,000$ bytes of memory. This is a fair amount of memory for a single variable. Arrays have a way of using up inordinately large amounts of memory. Your ability to use an array to solve a particular problem will to some extent depend on the amount of memory available on the particular machine on which the program is to be executed.

9.11.1   Time Out

1. Write a program segment to declare an array of Integers to store the daily sales for each of four divisions of a company for each day of a year. The program will need to summarize data by month.

2. Write alternative ways to make the following array declaration:

   ```
   array[1..4, 'a'..'e', 0..2] of Integer;
   ```

3. Revise Program 9f to summarize grades for up to six reporting periods. Write a separate grade report for each student.

9.12   Case Study: A Bar Graph

■ **Problem Statement.**   Write a program to create a bar graph for data entered by the user. The user should be able to enter a series of up to 10 values and associated identifiers. The program should list the data and print a bar graph. Each bar on the graph should be proportional in length to the related value of the series. The series values will be Integer values in the range 0 to 25.

■ **Problem Analysis.**   Although there are many approaches to this problem, let us adopt one that is quite general and can later be easily adapted to a variety of different requirements and circumstances. Our basic technique will be to create a two-dimensional array of base type Char (which we shall call Graph) to store the characters that will make up the graph. A row in the array will represent a bar in the graph. The number of columns in the array will be equal to the maximum length of a bar in the graph. In this case, the array Graph will need to have 10 rows and 25 columns, because there are a maximum of 10 bars, and each bar can be up to 25 characters in length. Once the graph is created in memory by storing appropriate characters into the array, it is a simple matter to print out the graph in a number of different variations. We will also need a one-dimensional array to store the series (let us call it Data) and another one-dimensional array to store the associated identifiers (let us call it Description). For example, suppose the user wished to graph the following information, which describes sales of widgets in each of three weeks:

Data	Description
10	Week 1
13	Week 2
5	Week 3

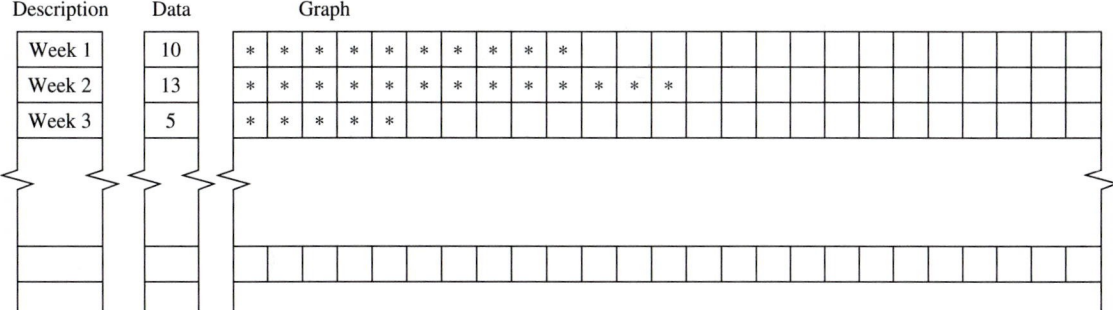

Figure 9.13 Relationship between the arrays Data, Description, and Graph.

The relationship between the arrays Data, Description, and Graph for this example is shown in Figure 9.13.

The solution to the problem can be broken down into four steps, as shown in the following program plan:

GRAPH PROGRAM (P9h)

1.0 Read data to be graphed

2.0 Initialize graph to spaces

3.0 Create graph for data

4.0 Write data and graph

5.0 Wait

■ **Problem Solution.**   Let us implement the program using four procedures that correspond to the four basic steps to be accomplished:

>   ReadData: Read values for the series and identifiers.
>   InitializeGraph: Place spaces in all the elements of Graph.
>   CreateGraph: "Draw" the bars that represent the data.
>   WriteGraph: Produce desired output, including the data and the graph.
>   AlternateWait: Wait until user presses a key.

We will need a variable N to represent a number of data elements to be graphed. The procedure ReadData will export values of Data, Description, and N to the main program. The procedure InitializeGraph performs a function akin to erasing a blackboard; it ensures that all the elements of Graph contain the space character. This procedure exports Graph to the main program with its new content in place. The procedure CreateGraph uses the content of Data to place the required number of graph characters in the respective rows of Graph. This procedure imports Data, N, and Graph and exports Graph with the bars in place. The procedure WriteGraph imports Data, Description, N,

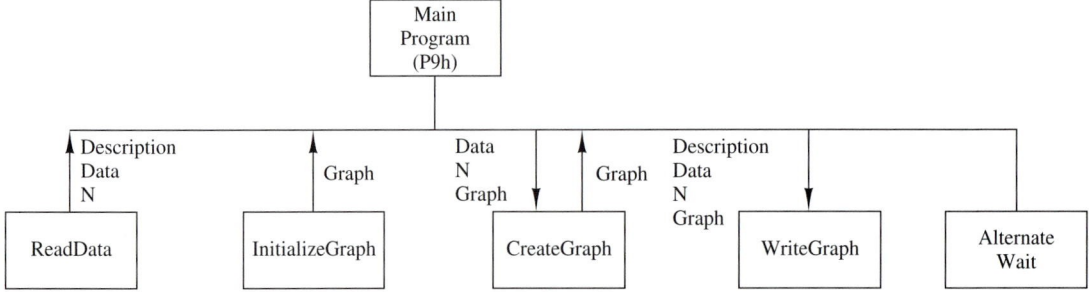

Figure 9.14 Data-flow diagram for bar graph program (9h).

and Graph and produces the required output. The relationship among the modules of the program is shown in the data-flow diagram of Figure 9.14.

The complete program is shown in Figure 9.15 (Program 9h), with a sample execution of the program shown in Figure 9.16.

A number of features of this program will make it easy to modify and extend. For example, note that the initial constants (SeriesLimit and DataLimit) control the size of all the arrays and the allowable ranges for all the related variables. In order to accommodate additional data items or make it possible to draw longer bars, the only modification that would be required is to change one or the other of these named constants. The constant GraphCharacter declared in the procedure CreateGraph controls the character used to draw the bars. This character could easily be chosen by the user rather than being a constant. Note that the output procedure is distinct from the procedure that creates the graph. This will facilitate producing output to different devices (e.g., the printer) and in alternative formats (bars of different widths and spacing or a different orientation, such as vertical instead of horizontal).

Note that in all the procedures, the array parameter is declared as a variable parameter whether the array is imported, exported, or both. Remember that this practice helps to avoid additional memory requirements that accompany the use of value parameters.

9.12.1   Time Out

1. Compile and execute Program 9h. Try out the program with sample data of your choosing.
2. You may have noted that the data does not get validated by the program. If a value is too large to represent in a bar (greater than 25), the program will not execute properly. Modify the program so that values larger than the maximum allowable data item are represented by a bar of maximum length. (This process is called *cropping*—data that cannot be represented are cropped at the maximum allowable value, much as a camera lens photographs only a part of a large building.)
3. Modify the procedure WriteData to make the bars two characters wide. The bars should be separated by at least one blank line.

```
program P9h (Input, Output);
{Program to produce a bar graph for data entered by the user}
{$R-}    {Range checking off}
uses
    Crt;
const
    SeriesLimit = 10;
    DataLimit = 25;
type
    SeriesSubSeq = 1..SeriesLimit;
    DataSubSeq = 1..DataLimit;
    Char2DArray = array[SeriesSubSeq, DataSubSeq] of Char;
    StringArray = array[SeriesSubSeq] of string[10];
    IntegerArray = array[SeriesSubSeq] of Integer;
var
    Description : StringArray;  {Stores description of each value}
    Data : IntegerArray;  {Stores series of values to be graphed}
    Graph : Char2DArray; {Stores the bar graph}
    N : SeriesSubSeq;  {Number of values in series}
{***********************************************************************}
    procedure ReadData(var L : StringArray;
                       var Series : IntegerArray;
                       var N : SeriesSubSeq);
    {Procedure to read and store data to be graphed}
    const
        InputPrompt1 = 'Enter number of data items in series ';
        InputPrompt2 = 'Enter label for data item number ';
        InputPrompt3 = 'Enter value for data item number ';
    var
        Index : SeriesSubSeq;
    begin      {ReadData}
        Write (InputPrompt1);
        Readln (N);
        for Index := 1 to N do
            begin
                Write (InputPrompt2, Index, ' ');
                Readln (L[Index]);
                Write (InputPrompt3, Index, ' ');
                Readln (Series[Index])
            end {for}
    end;    {ReadData}
{---------------------------------------------------------------------}
    procedure CreateGraph (var Series : IntegerArray;
                           N : SeriesSubSeq;
                           var Graph :Char2DArray);
    {Procedure to create graph of content of Series}
    const
        GraphCharacter = '*';
    var
        SI : SeriesSubSeq;
        RI, Limit : DataSubSeq;
    begin    {CreateGraph}
        for SI := 1 to N do
            for RI := 1 to Series[SI] do
                Graph[SI, RI] := GraphCharacter
    end;    {CreateGraph}
{---------------------------------------------------------------------}
```

Figure 9.15(a) Program 9h: Initial portion (part 1 of 2 parts).

```
        procedure InitializeGraph (var Graph : Char2DArray);
        {Procedure to place blanks in all of Graph}
        var
             SI : SeriesSubSeq;
             RI : DataSubSeq;
        begin    {InitializeGraph}
            for SI := 1 to SeriesLimit do
                for RI := 1 to DataLimit do
                    Graph[SI, RI] := ' '
        end;   {InitializeGraph}
{-------------------------------------------------------------------------}
        procedure WriteGraph (var L : StringArray;
                               var Series : IntegerArray;
                                  N : SeriesSubSeq;
                               var Graph : Char2DArray);
        {Procedure to write bar graph with labels and data}
        var
             SI : SeriesSubSeq;
             RI : DataSubSeq;
        begin    {WriteGraph}
            for SI := 1 to N do
                begin
                    Write (L[SI]:10, Series[SI]:3, ' ');
                    for RI := 1 to DataLimit do
                        Write (Graph[SI, RI]);
                    Writeln
                end    {for}
        end;    {WriteGraph}
        .
        .
        .
{***********************************************************************}
begin    {Main Program}

{1.0 Read data to be graphed}

    ClrScr;
    ReadData (Description, Data, N);

{2.0 Initialize graph to spaces}

    InitializeGraph (Graph);

{3.0 Create graph for data}

    CreateGraph (Data, N, Graph);

{4.0 Write data and graph}

    WriteGraph(Description, Data, N, Graph);

{5.0 Wait}

    AlternateWait

end.    {Main Program}
```

Figure 9.15(b) Program 9h: Final portion (part 2 of 2 parts).

```
Enter number of data items in series 3
Enter label for data item number 1 Week 1
Enter value for data item number 1 10
Enter label for data item number 2 Week 2
Enter value for data item number 2 13
Enter label for data item number 3 Week 3
Enter value for data item number 3 5
    Week 1 10 **********
    Week 2 13 *************
    Week 3  5 *****
Press any key to continue
```

Figure 9.16 Sample execution of Program 9h.

4. One feature that is missing from Program 9h is the capability to write a descriptive title for the graph. Modify the program to allow the user to enter a title and have the title printed along with the graph (for example, 'Widget Sales by Week').

5. Modify the procedure WriteData to create a vertical bar graph with the bar descriptors listed below the bars. Decide on a scheme to relate the series identifiers with the bars. One method is to write the identifiers for every other bar in one line of output and the other identifiers (offset by a few spaces) in the line below, as shown in Figure 9.17.

6. In Program 9h, the graphing scale is one to one; that is, one graph character represents one unit in a series value. In order to represent numbers of large (and small) magnitudes, it is necessary to use a different scale. For example, if the range of values to be graphed is from 0 to 200, you might use one graph character to represent 10 units in the series. (That is, values in the range 0 to 9 would be represented by 0 graph characters, values in the range 10 to 19 would be represented by 1 graph character, and so forth.) Modify Program 9h to allow the user to choose a scale factor for graphing the data.

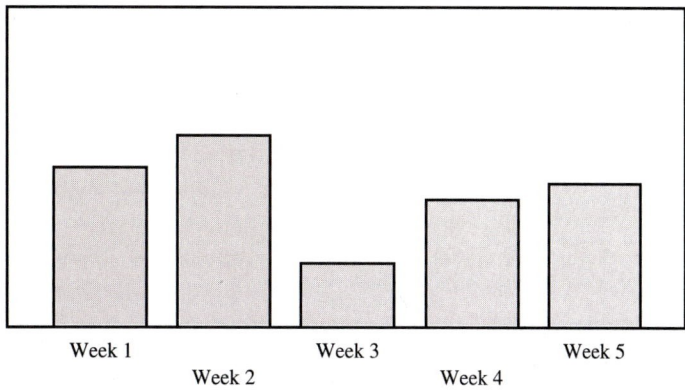

Figure 9.17 Example of a vertical bar graph.

9.13 PROGRAM DEBUGGING AND TESTING

One of the most insidious problems in developing and testing a program that involves arrays is the potential for the subscript value to be outside the range specified in the array declaration. Turbo Pascal will check for this condition for you. However, this checking slows down the execution of the program, so you may wish to turn the checking feature off. When subscript checking is not active and an out-of-range subscript is encountered, the program behaves in unpredictable ways. In general, a subscript value that is out of range causes an area of memory to be changed that may be outside the area allocated to the array. Needless to say, this event will cause the output produced by the program to be invalid.

By using the **R compiler directive**, we can institute range checking for subscripts and subranges. To activate range checking, use the directive {$R+}. By inserting the directive {$R−}, you are directing the compiler not to generate code within the program to check each subscript to see whether it is in range. If an out-of-range condition occurs, the usual execution-time error message will not be produced, nor will program execution be terminated.

One might ask why active range checking is not recommended for use in all programs making use of arrays. The trouble is that the extra code generated by its use will slow the execution speed of the program. It is recommended that you use the positive setting for the range-checking directive during the testing of a program and set it to passive for the version of the program that is placed in use. At any point in the program where a data item that has been entered by the program user is used as a subscript, the program should perform its own range check and print an appropriate error message. Ideally, the user should not experience a Turbo Pascal execution-time error message. By carefully validating data and performing range checking at critical points in the program, you can make sure that the program functions correctly and avoid the extra execution time overhead entailed by using the active range-checking option.

9.13.1 Time Out

1. Test the original version of Program 9h with the following data:

Description	Data
Widget	0
Gidget	40
Zidget	2

Observe that even though the value of Data[2] is out of range because it is greater than 25, there is no execution-time error. Rather, the 40 graph characters placed in row 2 of Graph actually spill over into row 3.

2. Now replace the compiler directive {$R−} in the program with {$R+} and test it with the same data. Observe the difference. If you inserted the code suggested in Time Out 9.11.1, Exercise 2, to crop the bar when the value to be graphed is too large, then you have effectively handled one of the potential problems of out-of-range subscripts for this program.

3. Add a validation procedure for the number of items to be graphed (the variable N) in Program 9h. This procedure, coupled with the cropping of the bar length, should ensure that no out-of-range subscript errors can occur in the program.

9.14 REVIEW QUESTIONS

1. How is the base type of an array declared?
2. The specification of *index-type* governs two important aspects of an array structure. What are they?
3. How might an array of constants be used in a program that would output the name of the day of a week based on a numeric date?
4. If an array of elements is to be used as a set of counters, what action must be performed on the array prior to processing data?
5. Explain why a grouped frequency distribution is often of more value than a frequency distribution based on individual values in the data.
6. In a program that uses an array for data storage, what fundamental limitation is imposed on the amount of data that can be processed?
7. How does a value parameter differ from a variable parameter with respect to allocation of memory? What implication does this difference have for programs that use arrays as parameters to subprograms?
8. Sometimes it would be useful to write a function that has an array as its type. Is this possible? What technique can be used as an alternative?
9. What is meant by the term *parallel arrays*? What basic limitation on arrays makes it necessary to use parallel arrays?
10. A two-dimensional array can be thought of as a set of one-dimensional arrays. What other conceptualization of a two-dimensional array is common?
11. What are two alternative formats for writing references to elements of two-dimensional arrays? Which format is recommended?
12. Processing a two-dimensional array is often accomplished by nested for loops. When processing an array in row order (all the elements in the first row, followed by all the elements in the second row, and so forth), which subscript would normally control the outer loop? Why?
13. What are some advantages to using a string data type as opposed to an array of Char? Are there any disadvantages?
14. When using an array of base type string, how does the program gain access to individual characters within a string?
15. What is the intended purpose of the *packed* option? Why is it ignored by Turbo Pascal?
16. What limitation is made on the number of dimensions that can be declared for an array?
17. What is the rank of a three-dimensional array? Which subscript denotes rank?
18. How should the R compiler option be used in developing a program?
19. Why is data validation particularly important when a data value entered by the user is used directly as a subscript in an array reference?

9.15 PROGRAMMING EXERCISES

1. Write a program to convert a positive integer entered by the user into any desired base N less than or equal to 10. Store each digit into an element of an array. Write out the number in base N. Recall that a method for converting from base 10 to base N is to divide the number by N using integer division. The remainder is a digit of the base N numeral. Successive repetitions of the division process yield additional digits. The process stops when the quotient is zero. For example, suppose we wish to convert 25 to base 2. Then the following calculations will generate the required binary digits:

$$
\begin{array}{rl}
 & 0\,r\,1 \\
2\,\overline{\big|} & 1\,r\,1 \\
2\,\overline{\big|} & 3\,r\,0 \\
2\,\overline{\big|} & 6\,r\,0 \\
2\,\overline{\big|} & 12\,r\,1 \\
2\,\overline{\big|} & 25
\end{array}
\quad\text{base 2 numeral}
$$

Check:

$$11001_2 = 1 \times 2^4 + 1 \times 2^3 + 0 \times 2^2 + 0 \times 2^1 + 1 \times 2^0 = 16 + 8 + 0 + 0 + 1 = 25$$

2. Write a program to convert a number in base N to base 10. A method that can be used can be derived from the following example: Suppose you wish to convert 11001_2 to base 10. The following calculation will yield the desired result and can be performed on successive digits of the binary numeral, proceeding from left to right:

$$1101_2 = (((1 \times 2 + 1) \times 2 + 0) \times 2 + 0) \times 2 + 1 = 25$$

Use an array to store the digits of the base N numeral.

3. Write a program to compute

$$\sqrt{x_1^2 + x_2^2 + \cdots + x_n^2} \cdot \sqrt{y_1^2 + y_2^2 + \cdots + y_n^2}$$

and

$$\sqrt{x_1 y_1 + x_2 y_2 + \cdots + x_n y_n}$$

for n values of x and y entered by the program user.

4. Write a program that will read, from a Text file, up to 100 temperature readings representing the day's high and low temperature and the location of the weather station reporting the data. Determine the highest and lowest temperatures. Write the data with appropriate labels for the high and low.

5. Write a program to read and store a series of N real values into an array. If the series is not in sequence (it is in sequence if each element is greater than or equal to its successor), then write an error message; otherwise, compute the median of the data. The median is the middle value. If N is odd, the median is the value at location $(N \text{ div } 2) + 1$; if N is even, the median is the average of the values at locations $N \text{ div } 2$ and $(N \text{ div } 2) + 1$. Following are

some examples:

Input	Output
$2, 4, 6, 9$	Median is $(4 + 6)/2 = 5$
$2, 4, 6, 9, 14$	Median is 6
$4, 6, 9, 2$	Error

6. Write a program to allow the use to enter an array of maximum length 100. Compute

$$S = a_1^2 + a_2^2 + \cdots + a_n^2$$
$$P = (1 - a_1)(1 - a_2) \cdots (1 - a_n)$$

7. Write a program to allow the use to enter N real data items. Compute the standard deviation using the formula

$$\sqrt{\frac{(X_1 - \overline{X})^2 + (X_2 - \overline{X})^2 + \cdots + (X_N - \overline{X})^2}{N - 1}}$$

where

$$N = \text{ the number of data items,}$$
$$\overline{X} = \text{ the mean (arithmetic average) of the data, and}$$
$$X_1, X_2, \ldots, X_N \text{ are the data items}$$

8. The geometric average of a series $X_1, X_2, \ldots, X_N$ is computed by

$$(X_1 X_2 X_3 \cdots x_N)^{1/N}$$

For example, the geometric average of 1, 2, and 4 is

$$(1 \times 2 \times 4)^{1/3} = 8^{1/3} = 2$$

Write a program to compute the geometric average of N Real values entered by the user.

9. Write a program to produce a frequency distribution of the word lengths of text read from a Text file. Assume that each word in the text is terminated by a space, period, or EOL. For example, for the text, "Now is the time for all good men to come to the aid of their country," the output should be as follows:

Word length	Frequency
2	4
3	7
4	3
5	1
7	1

10. The arithmetic average can be computed from a frequency distribution using the formula:

$$\frac{F_1 X_1 + F_2 X_2 + \cdots + F_N X_N}{F_1 + F_2 + \cdots + F_N}$$

where $F_1, F_2, \ldots, F_N$ represent the frequency of occurrence of the data items $X_1, X_2, \ldots, X_N$, respectively. Use this technique to compute the average length of the text in the program you wrote for Exercise 9.

11. Write a program to construct a frequency distribution showing the frequency of occurrence of each letter of the alphabet in a text string. Count uppercase and lowercase letters as equivalent.

12. In a business, it is often necessary to project revenues for future years based on past experience. Write a program to allow the user to input revenues for 10 years. Calculate the average growth rate. Use the rate to project revenues for 5 years. The average growth rate is computed by calculating the average of the percentage increases experienced for each of the years in the base data.

13. Write a program to translate a character string into Morse code. Use the following table:

A	. —	F	. . — .	K	— . —	P	. — — .	U	. . —
B	— . . .	G	— — .	L	. — . .	Q	— — . —	V	. . . —
C	— . — .	H	. . . .	M	— —	R	. — .	W	. — —
D	— . .	I	. .	N	— .	S	. . .	X	— . . —
E	.	J	. — — —	O	— — —	T	—	Y	— . — —
								Z	— — . .

Upper- and lowercase characters should be treated as equivalent.

14. Write a program to read a series of N elements into a real array A. Eliminate all zero elements, and write out the new array. *Hint:* If array element A[I] is equal to zero, then move the segment A[I + 1] . . . A[N] up one element each and reduce N by 1.

15. Write a program to allow a business to keep a running total of the amount left in each of nine expense accounts. The accounts are numbered 1 through 9. (All invoices to be posted to the accounts have the appropriate expense account number on them.) Current balances for the nine accounts are contained in a Text file. The program should allow the user to enter the account number and the dollar amount and should subtract the amount from the balance of the appropriate account. At any time, the program user should be able to request a display of the balance in all the accounts.

16. Write a procedure to place into array B the content of a 4 × 4 array *A* rotated 90° clockwise. For example:

$$A = \begin{array}{|c|c|c|c|} \hline 0 & -1 & 2 & 3 \\ \hline 4 & 7 & 0 & 1 \\ \hline -1 & 2 & 4 & 9 \\ \hline 1 & 0 & 5 & 7 \\ \hline \end{array} \qquad B = \begin{array}{|c|c|c|c|} \hline 1 & -1 & 4 & 0 \\ \hline 0 & 2 & 7 & -1 \\ \hline 5 & 4 & 0 & 2 \\ \hline 7 & 9 & 1 & 3 \\ \hline \end{array}$$

Write a program to allow the user to enter values for an array and then rotate the array 90°, 180°, or 270°, at the choice of the user. *Hint:* To rotate the array 180°, use the 90° rotation twice; a 270° rotation can be accomplished by using three 90° rotations.

17. Write a program to allow the user to enter the coordinates of up to 100 ships and determine which two ships are the closest to each other. If (X_i, X_i) are the coordinates of ship i and (X_j, Y_j)

are the coordinates of ship j, then the distance between ship i and j is

$$D_{ij} = \sqrt{(X_i - X_j)^2 + (Y_i - Y_j)^2}$$

18. Reconsider Exercise 10 from Chapter 8, Section 8.8. Suppose that the point A (the starting point) is moved to each of the interior points on the campus. (These constitute an array of size 4×6.) Associated with each of the points is a different probability of success. Write a program to create a two-dimensional matrix of probabilities. Intuitively, you would expect that the probability should be closer to 1 as the points get closer to point B. Is this confirmed by your data?

19. A magic square is a two-dimensional table in which the sums of the columns and of the rows are all equal. For example, the following is a magic square:

-2	2	3
6	1	-4
-1	0	4

Write a program to allow the user to enter a table and determine whether it is a magic square.

20. Write a program to tally the results of a survey in which there are 10 questions and five possible responses to each question. The responses are labeled a through e and are recorded in a Text file. When all the data has been entered, the program should present a two-dimensional frequency distribution of the responses, showing the number of occurrences of each response to each question.

21. Create a Text file that stores in its first line the correct answers to a multiple-choice test and in successive lines a student's name and the answers given by that student. Write a program to grade each test.

22. Create a Text file containing data collected in a population survey. Each line in the file should contain the following data: age, income, and sex ('M' or 'F'). Write a program to prepare the following summary of the data (each cell of the table should show the number of respondents in that category):

INCOME (IN $1,000)

AGE	Under 10		10–19		20–29		Over 30	
	Male	Female	Male	Female	Male	Female	Male	Female
Under 20								
20–29								
30–39								
40–49								
50–59								
60–69								
Over 69								

10

Records and Files

In this chapter, we consider two structured data types: records and files. A record is useful when you need to combine data items of different types and treat them as a single unit. A file is a mechanism for storing data. You have been using Text files in a variety of contexts. In this chapter, we will examine files of other types and additional statements designed to process files.

Some of you with knowledge of other programming languages may find it unusual that in Pascal we are able to define records that are unrelated to any file and define files that are unrelated to records. (In many programming languages, these two concepts are always used in conjunction with each other.) Do not worry. You will discover that the Pascal usage of the terms *record* and *file* is completely logical and consistent (and very useful). You will also discover that Pascal does enable you to relate the two in a natural way that is consistent with the usage of the terms in other contexts. (That is, a file can indeed be made up of records, but in Pascal a file can be made up of components of other types as well.)

10.1   RECORDS

The structure used to represent data in a program should reflect the relationships that exist in the actual data. This principle underlies all the structured data types available in Pascal. One situation that arises quite frequently is that several data items, all relating to the same entity, must be processed by a program. For example, a date is actually made up of three parts: month, day, and year. All three parts are necessary for a complete date. As another example, consider a program that processes inventory data. Each inventory item has associated with it an item number, description, number on hand, wholesale cost, retail price, and perhaps other data as well. In such situations, each item of data may have a different data type, but all items are logically related and should be treated by the program as one unit of information. Situations such as these motivate the inclusion of the structured type **record** in Pascal. A record can be made up of many related items; the group can be treated as a single unit for some purposes, but access to each part is also maintained.

A record is a structured data type that can be made up of a number of components of any type (except file and object). The components are called **fields**; each field is assigned an identifier, which is used to access that component. (Remember that one of the basic limitations on an array is that all elements must be of the same type—which is referred to as the base type of the array. Because a record is made up of components of different types (that is, records are heterogeneous), there is no such concept as the "base type" of a record.)

In declaring a record, you must specify an identifier for each field and the data type associated with each field. Because the number of fields is essentially unlimited, the language uses a variation of the familiar "begin . . . end;" notation to surround the list of field identifiers and associated data types; in this context, the language uses "record . . . end;". The general form for a **record declaration** is as follows:

```
record
        field-identifier-list-1 : type-1;
        field-identifier-list-2 : type-2;
                    .
                    .
                    .
        field-identifier-list-n : type-n
end;
```

where *field-identifier-list-1* . . . *field-identifier-list-n* are lists of Pascal identifiers and *type-1* . . . *type-n* are any data types except file and object. Field identifiers must be unique within a given record description. However, you can use the same identifier in another record description within the same program if desired. This is useful, since certain identifiers such as Name, Address, Number, and so forth are very descriptive and may be applicable to several different records in a program.

For example, suppose we wish to declare a record to represent a date made up of a Month, which is an integer in the range 1 to 12; a Day, which is an integer in the range 1 to 31; and a Year, which is an integer in the range 0 to 99. Let us use Month, Day, and Year as field identifiers. The record declaration would appear as follows:

```
record
      Month : 1..12;
      Day   : 1..31;
      Year  : 0..99
end;
```

This record declaration could be used to establish a named data type or used directly to declare the data type of a variable. The first option is, of course, more general, because by establishing a name for the data type, you can pass a variable of that type as a parameter to a function or procedure. The following program segment declares a data type DateRecordType and then declares two variables, DateOfPurchase and DateOfSale, to be of type DateRecordType:

```
type
      DateRecordType = record
                             Month : 1..12;
                             Day   : 1..31;
                             Year  : 0..99
                       end;
var
      DateOfPurchase, DateOfSale : DateRecordType;
```

You are probably wondering by now what operations can be performed on a variable that is assigned a record data type. Actually, there is only one statement that can process such a variable in its entirety: the assignment statement. You can assign the value of one variable to another with exactly the same record type. For example, you could write

```
DateOfPurchase := DateOfSale;
```

to place the content of DateOfSale into DateOfPurchase. Another way to use a variable that is assigned a record type is as a parameter for a function or procedure—provided, of course, that the associated formal parameter is declared with the same type identifier. You cannot use a variable with a record type in the list of items in a Readln, Write, or Writeln statement when the files being addressed are the usual Input, Output, and Lst files that we have been using up until now. (You are used to this restriction with other structured data types, such as set and enumerated data types.) We will see later in this chapter that it is possible to read and write entire records when a file of records is declared.

Most operations on record-type variables will take place on individual fields. To reference a field, you use the variable name followed by a period followed by the field identifier. The general form for a **field reference** is

```
record-identifier.field-identifier
```

For example, to reference the Month portion of the variable DateOfSale, you would write

```
DateOfSale.Month
```

and to refer to the Day part of DateOfPurchase, you would write

```
DateOfPurchase.Day
```

You may use such field references in the same way that you have used other variables: They can participate in input and output operations and calculations, just like a simple variable of the same type. For example, the following program segment would allow the user to enter DateOfPurchase:

```
Write ('Enter purchase date in form mm dd yy ');
Readln (DateOfPurchase.Month, DateOfPurchase.Day,
        DateOfPurchase.Year);
```

Note that you could not write

```
Readln (DateOfPurchase);
```

even though that would be simple and somewhat logical in this case. A record could be made up of an arbitrarily complex sequence of fields, of which some could be other structured types, such as sets, enumerated types, records, or arrays that are incompatible with Readln (and Write/Writeln).

Suppose we wish to create a structure to store information about the customers of a business. Each customer has a customer number (four digits long); a name, which is subdivided into last name, first name, and middle initial; the date of the last payment (month, day, and year); and the current account balance. The structure of this data can be visualized in the diagrams shown in Figure 10.1.

In this case, we might wish to refer to the entire customer name or to any part of the name. In a similar way, we might wish to refer to the entire payment date or parts of the date. To facilitate such access, each of these elements could be declared to be a record type. Then the following program segment could be used:

```
type
    NameType = record
                   Last, First : string[15];
                   MiddleInitial : Char
               end;
```

```
DateType = record
                Month : 1..12;
                Day   : 1..31;
                Year  : 0..99
          end;
CustomerRecordType = record
                        Number : Integer;
                        Name   : NameType;
                        PaymentDate : DateType;
                        AccountBalance : Real
            end;
var
    Customer : CustomerRecordType;
```

With these declarations in place, the following field references are possible:

Reference	Comment
`Customer.Number`	Type is Integer
`Customer.Name`	Type is NameType (a record type)
`Customer.PaymentDate`	Type is DateType (a record type)
`Customer.AccountBalance`	Type is Real

In order to gain access to the individual components of Customer.Name and Customer. PaymentDate, you use a further field reference by attaching a period and a field

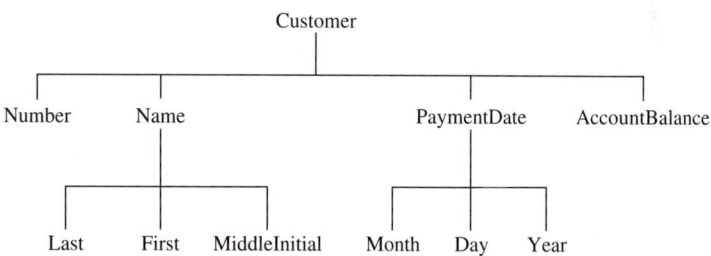

Figure 10.1 Alternative ways of visualizing the structure of the record type customer.

identifier to the field reference, yielding the following possible references:

Reference	Comment
Customer.Name.Last	Type is string[15]
Customer.Name.First	Type is string[15]
Customer.Name.MiddleInitial	Type is Char
Customer.PaymentDate.Month	Type is subrange 1..12
Customer.PaymentDate.Day	Type is subrange 1..31
Customer.PaymentDate.Year	Type is subrange 0..99

There are other interesting possibilities for the type of a field. When there is more than one occurrence of an element, the type can be an array. For example, suppose we wish to create a record to store information about a student that would include his or her name, three test grades, and the average grade. Then the following program segment could be used:

```
type
    StudentRecordType = record
                            Name : string[20];
                            Grade : array[1..3] of Real;
                            Average : Real
                        end;
var
    Student: StudentRecordType;
```

With these declarations in place, the following references would be possible:

Reference	Comment
Student.Name	Type is string[20]
Student.Grade	Type is array[1..3] of Real (an unnamed type; therefore, Student.Grade could not be used as a subprogram parameter or in an assignment statement)
Student.Grade[1]	Type is Real
Student.Grade[2]	Type is Real
Student.Grade[3]	Type is Real
Student.Average	Type is Real

10.1.1   Time Out

1. Consider the following declaration:

```
type
    VendorType = record
                    Name : string[20];
```

```
             Address : record
                          Street : string[20];
                          City : string[10];
                          State : string[2];
                          Zip : Integer
                       end;
             Discount : Boolean;
             AccountBalance : Real
          end;
   var
       Vendor : VendorType;
```

(a) Draw a data-structure diagram for this structure similar to one of those shown in Figure 10.1.

(b) List possible field references for this structure and the data type of each.

(c) The preceding program segment shows how record declarations can be nested. The disadvantage of this technique is that the nested item has an unnamed data type and therefore cannot be used in an assignment statement or as a subprogram parameter. Rewrite the segment to make a separate declaration for the type of Address.

2. Write a Pascal program segment to create a data structure for storage of inventory data for a business. Associated with each item is an inventory number, a description of the item, the wholesale cost, the retail price, the number on hand, the number on order, and the vendor from whom the item is ordered, identified by name and address (street, city, state and zip) and the date of the last order. Draw a diagram of the structure before you write the necessary Pascal declarations.

10.2 THE WITH STATEMENT

As we have seen, references to the components of a record are ordinarily made by writing the record name, a period, and the field identifier. In some instances, this practice results in identifiers that are quite lengthy and cumbersome. (This is particularly true when dealing with nested records.) Pascal allows you to use the with statement to shorten field references by omitting the name of the record variable. The **with statement** specifies the name of the record variable and begins a program block in which references to fields within that record can be made without specifying the record variable name. As with other similar statements in Pascal, the scope of the with statement is one statement, which is usually a compound statement (a "begin . . . end;" program segment).

The general form of the with statement is as follows:

```
with record-identifier-list do
     statement;
```

where *record-identifier-list* is a list of record-type identifiers, separated by commas. As noted before, the statement controlled by the with statement is usually a compound statement, so that the most usual pattern for the with statement is as follows:

```
with record-identifier-list do
      begin
            statement;
              .
              .
              .
      end;  {with}
```

For example, suppose a program has the following declarations in place:

```
type
    TimeRecord = record
                      Hours : 0..24;
                      Minutes, Seconds : 0..59
                 end;
    ExperimentRecord = record
                            ElapsedTime : TimeRecord;
                            Temperature : Integer
                       end;
var
    Control, Experimental : ExperimentRecord;
```

This program segment creates two record type variables (Control and Experimental) with the same form. In one part of a program we might wish to process the content of Control, and in another part of the program we might wish to process the content of Experimental. We might write Control.Temperature and Experimental.Temperature to process the two temperatures in the two parts of the program. Another option is to use the with statement to specify which record variable is to be assumed. The segment of the program that processes the content of Control would be enclosed by

```
with Control do
      begin
            .
            .
            .
      end;
```

Within this segment, the field Control.Temperature could be referred to more simply as Temperature. For example, the statements

```
Temperature := 50
```

and

```
Control.Temperature := 50
```

would be equivalent. The segment of the program that processes the record Experimental would be enclosed by

```
with Experimental do
     begin
             .
             .
             .
       end;
```

Within this program segment, a reference to Temperature would be the same as referring to Experimental.Temperature. For example, in this case, the statements

```
Temperature := 50
```

and

```
Experimental.Temperature := 50
```

would be equivalent.

As noted in the general form, the with statement can specify a list of record identifiers. For example, with the record declarations just described, you could specify either Control or Experimental and ElapsedTime to avoid field references such as Control.ElapsedTime.Hours and Experimental.ElapsedTime.Seconds. That is, within the program block enclosed by

```
with Experimental, ElapsedTime do
     begin
             .
             .
             .
       end;
```

a reference to Hours, as, for example, in the statement Readln(Hours), would be equivalent to the variable Experimental.ElapsedTime.Hours, as in the statement

```
Readln(Experimental.ElapsedTime.Hours)
```

The use of records and the with statement in the context of a complete program is shown in the revision of Program 9a contained in Figure 10.2. Recall that the purpose of this program was to convert a date in numeric form into an alphanumeric string form. The program declares a record type called DateRecordType:

```
DateRecordType = record
                       Month : 1..12;
                       Day   : 1..31;
                       Year  : 0..99
                 end;
```

```pascal
program P10a (Input, Output);
{Program to convert dates from numeric to alphanumeric form;
    this version illustrates the use of a record}
{$R-}
uses
    Crt;
type
    StringType = string[20];
    StringArrayType = array[1..12] of StringType;
    DateRecordType = record
                            Month : 1..12;
                            Day   : 1..31;
                            Year  : 0..99
                     end;
const
    InputPrompt = 'Enter date in the form mm dd yy (0 0 0 to stop) ';
var
    Date : DateRecordType;
    OutputDate : StringType;
    MonthName : StringArrayType;
{*********************************************************************}
    .
    .
    .
    function ConvertDate (CalendarDate : DateRecordType) : StringType;
    {Function to convert a date from numeric form to alphanumeric form}
    var
        D, Y : StringType;
    begin   {ConvertDate}
        with CalendarDate do
            begin
                Str (Day, D);
                Str (Year:2, Y);
                if Y[1] = ' ' then
                    Y[1] := '0';
                Y := '19'+Y;
                if (Month >= 1) and (Month <= 12) then
                    ConvertDate := MonthName[Month] + D + ', ' + Y
                else
                    ConvertDate := 'Invalid date'
            end {with}
    end;   {ConvertDate}
{*********************************************************************}
begin     {Main Program}
    .
    .
    .
{3.0 Process date and get next month, day and year}

    while Date.Month * Date.Day <> 0 do
        begin
            OutputDate := ConvertDate (Date);
            with Date do
                begin
                    Writeln ('Numeric form of date :',
                             Month:3,Day:3,Year:3);
                    Writeln ('Alphanumeric form : ', OutputDate);
                    Writeln;
                    Write (InputPrompt);
                    Readln (Month, Day, Year)
                end    {with}
        end;   {while}

end.   {Main Program}
```

Figure 10.2 Program 10a: Revision of Program 9a illustrating records.

This type is used for the variable Date, which will store the input data entered by the program user:

```
var
    Date : DateRecordType;
```

The statement part of the main program illustrates the syntax required to make field references in two ways—explicitly and under the control of a with statement. For example, the implementation of the while statement in Module 3.0 uses explicit references:

```
while Date.Month * Date.Day <> 0 do
```

Because Month, Day, and Year are field identifiers within the description of the record DateRecordType, they must always be used in conjunction with a variable of that type. We could rewrite this portion of the program using the with statement as follows:

```
with Date do
    while Month * Day <> 0 do
```

Because of the with statement, the references to Month, Day, and Year are now valid.

The function ConvertDate accepts a variable of type DateRecordType as a value parameter. The main program invokes this function using the statement

```
OutputDate := ConvertDate (Date);
```

The segment illustrates one of the most advantageous features of the record facility: You can pass many data items of a variety of types to a subprogram by specifying a single record-type variable name. Compare this version of the program to the original version shown in Figures 9.2(a) and (b). Note that in the statement part of the function, a with statement is used to simplify references to the fields within its parameter. The field identifiers Month, Day, and Year are global; that is, they are used to refer to fields within any variable assigned data type DateRecordType. Thus, in the function, the formal parameter is called CalendarDate. The with statement specifies this record variable name; within the scope of the with statement, the fields are referred to as Month, Day, and Year instead of CalendarDate.Month, CalendarDate.Day, and so forth. The with statement is also used in the main program to simplify a portion of the code within Module 3.0. Compare the Readln statement in this module with the Readln statement in Module 2.0. Instead of

```
Readln (Date.Month, Date.Day, Date.Year);
```

it is now possible to write

```
Readln (Month, Day, Year);
```

which is a significant simplification.

The main program shown in Figure 10.2 was written to illustrate the two forms of field reference. You could actually improve on this program by enclosing all the statements in a with-controlled program block.

10.2.1   Time Out

| Make the modifications just described to Program 10a. Test your revised program.

10.3   ARRAYS OF RECORDS

In previous examples, we have seen that a field within a record can be an array. When this occurs, the subscript follows the field identifier if a reference is made to an individual component of the array. Sometimes it will also be useful to create an array with a base type that is a record type. Each element of the array can then contain data items of a variety of types. This technique is often appropriate where parallel arrays would otherwise be used.

For example, suppose the following data must be stored for each student in a class of maximum size 100:

> Student name (maximum length 20)
>
> Three test grades (Integer)
>
> Average test grade (Integer)

It would be natural to create a record with the following description:

```
type
    StudentRecordType = record
                            Name : string[20];
                            Grade : array[1..3] of Integer;
                            Average : Integer
                      end;
```

With this type declaration in place, we could create an array of these records to store all the data for the students in the class:

```
var
     Student : array[1..100] of StudentRecordType;
```

This structure consists of 100 elements, each of which has five components, identified by the field identifiers Name, Grade[1], Grade[2], Grade[3], and Average, as illustrated in Figure 10.3.

The following references would access all the data for the first student:

```
Student[1].Name
Student[1].Grade[1]
Student[1].Grade[2]
Student[1].Grade[3]
Student[1].Average
```

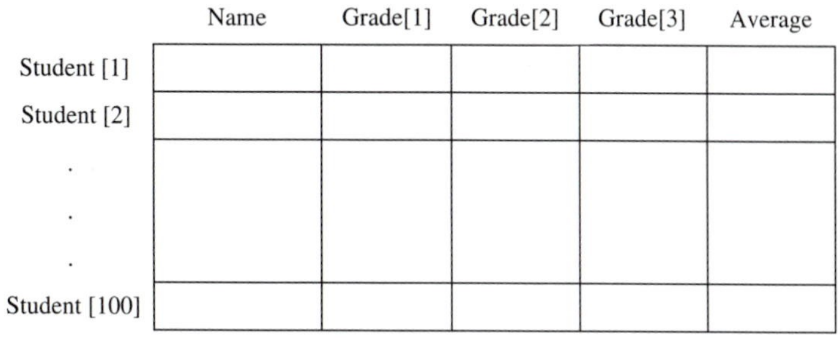

Figure 10.3 Structure of the array Student.

In this context, Student[1] is the record identifier, which is followed by a period and the field identifier (some of which also have attached subscripts). This data structure is much more descriptive of the relationships that exist in the actual data than the alternative structure based on parallel arrays (a one-dimensional array of names, a two-dimensional array of grades, and a one-dimensional array of averages).

It is important to note that when you create an array of records, the record variable must be followed by a subscript to gain access to a particular record in the structure. In a with statement, which you might wish to use to avoid complicated field references such as those just given, you would have to specify the subscript value (which, of course, might be a variable). For example, suppose N represents the number of students in a class, and suppose Index is an Integer variable. Then the following program segment could be used to compute the average test grade for each student:

```
for Index := 1 to N do
    with Student[Index] do
        Average = (Grade[1] + Grade[2] + Grade[3])/3;
```

Figure 10.4 illustrates the use of an array of records in a revision of Program 9e. Recall that that program produced an analysis of production and sales data for inventory items stocked by an imaginary company. For each item, the program needs to store the description, the production and sales amounts, and the difference between these amounts. In Program 9e, parallel arrays were used to store the data. In the revised version, an array of records is created:

```
type
    StringType = string[20];
    ItemRecordType = record
                         Description : StringType;
                         ProductionData,
                         SalesData,
                         Difference : Real
                     end;
    ItemArrayType = array[1..ItemLimit] of ItemRecordType;
var
    Item : ItemArrayType;
```

```pascal
program P10b (Input, Output, ProductionDataFile);
{Program to analyze production and sales data for inventory items;
    this version of the program illustrates the use of an array
    of records}
uses
    Crt;
const
    ItemLimit = 100;
type
    StringType = string[20];
    ItemRecordType = record
                            Description : StringType;
                            ProductionData,
                            SalesData,
                            Difference : Real
                    end;
    ItemArrayType = array[1..ItemLimit] of ItemRecordType;
var
    Item : ItemArrayType;
    Index, N : Integer;
    ProductionDataFile : Text;
    .
    .
    .
begin       {Main Program}

{1.0 Load data}

    ClrScr;
    OpenInputFile (ProductionDataFile);
    N := 0;
    while not Eof (ProductionDataFile) do
            begin
                N := N + 1;
                with Item[N] do
                    begin
                            Readln (ProductionDataFile,Description);
                            Readln (ProductionDataFile,
                                    ProductionData, SalesData)
                    end     {with}
            end;    {while}
    Close (ProductionDataFile);

{2.0 Compute difference between production and sales amounts}

    for Index := 1 to N do
        Item[Index].Difference := Item[Index].ProductionData -
                                    Item[Index].SalesData;

{3.0 Print Excess Production Report}

    Writeln ('Excess Production Report':50);
    Writeln;
    Writeln ('Item':20,'Production':15,'Sales':15,'Difference':15);
    for Index := 1 to N do
        with Item[Index] do
            if Difference > 0 then
                Writeln (Description:20, ProductionData:15:0,
                        SalesData:15:0, Difference:15:0);
    .
    .
    .
end.    {Main Program}
```

Figure 10.4 Program 10b: Revision Program 9e illustrating an array of records.

The statement portion of this program illustrates two forms for addressing elements of the structure. In the implementation of Module 2.0, explicit references (without the with statement) are used:

```
for Index := 1 to N do
    Item[Index].Difference := Item[Index].ProductionData -
                                 Item[Index].SalesData;
```

In other portions of the program, the with statement is used to simplify the code. For example, in the implementation of Module 1.0, we find the following:

```
with Item[N] do
    begin
        Readln (ProductionDataFile, Description);
        Readln (ProductionDataFile, ProductionData, SalesData)
    end     {with}
```

10.3.1   Time Out

As an exercise, revise Program 10b, writing the statement part of the program with explicit references completely. What can you say about the value of the with statement?

10.4   BINARY FILES

Thus far, we have been concerned with files of type Text, which is the only predefined file-type identifier available in Turbo Pascal. Although Text files are convenient and useful, they are not without some limitations. One such limitation is that data stored in a Text file must be translated from character form to the appropriate internal form each time it is read and must be translated from internal form to character form each time it is written. The Read, Readln, Write, and Writeln procedures take care of this translation automatically, but there is an element of time involved, which could be avoided by storing the data in their internal form in the file. A second problem with Text files is in the access techniques that are allowed. Because lines in a Text file are of varying lengths, there is no way to access these lines except by beginning at the first line and proceeding line by line until the end of the file. Both of these problems can be overcome by using files of a programmer-defined type; such files are called **binary files** because the data is stored in the file in internal (binary) format and thus does not need to be translated when read. Moreover, the components of a binary file all have the same length, making it possible to access (for either input or output) any file component on demand. This type of access is called *random access*. Both sequential (next-component access, which is similar to the technique used for Text files) and random access are available for a binary file. One of the disadvantages of a binary file is that you must write Pascal programs to create, list, and perform other processing of the files. The format of the file is not compatible with editors such as the Turbo Pascal text editor.

We know that every file must be declared with a file type. Text is a built-in file type. You can create your own file type using the file-type specification, which has the general form

```
file of type
```

where *type* can be any type (simple or structured) except file and object. The *type* specified in the type specification is called the *base type* of the file. Each component of the file has this type. For example, if you wished to store a large number of integers in a file, you could create a file with this base type by specifying

```
file of Integer
```

Each component in the file would be of type Integer; thus, Integer would be the base type of the file. Such a file could be declared by the program segment

```
var
      IntegerFile : file of Integer;
```

or by the more elaborate

```
type
      IntegerFileType = file of Integer;
var
      IntegerFile : IntegerFileType;
```

Very often, you will wish to have each component of a file contain related values of various types. In these cases, you can create a file of records. For example, suppose you wish to create a file to store the names and addresses of your business clients. Each client has a name, street address, city, state, and zip code. You would first create a type specification for the record and then declare the file to have that type:

```
type
      CustomerRecordType = record
                                  Name : string[20];
                                  Street, City : string[15];
                                  State : string[2];
                                  ZIP : string[5]
                           end;
var
      CustomerFile : file of CustomerRecordType;
```

You could also create a type identifier for the file type and use that identifier when declaring the file variable:

```
type
      ...;
      CustomerFileType = file of CustomerRecordType;
var
      CustomerFile : CustomerFileType;
```

The latter approach is necessary if the file is to be passed as a parameter to a procedure or function, since the formal parameter must be assigned a type using a type identifier. That is, if CustomerFile was the actual parameter, the corresponding formal parameter would be declared as follows:

```
procedure P (var FileVar : CustomerFileType);
```

In this text, we will follow the pattern of defining two type identifiers for any file with a record base type—one identifier for the record and a second for the file. (Although there are other valid alternatives, this approach is quite general and gives your program flexibility for future expansion.)

Binary files are processed using the procedures Read and Write. (Readln and Writeln are used only for Text files.) The general form of the Read procedure invocation for a binary file is

```
Read (file-variable, variable,...)
```

where *file-variable* is assigned to a binary file and each *variable* is of the same type as the base type of the file. For example, if IntegerFile is declared to have base type Integer, as illustrated, and Data is declared to be of type Integer, then the following statement would read one file component and store that value in Data:

```
Read (IntegerFile, Data);
```

Similarly, if CustomerRecord is a variable of type CustomerRecordType, then the following statement would read one record from the file CustomerFile and store the values in CustomerRecord:

```
Read (CustomerFile, CustomerRecord);
```

Recall that Turbo Pascal maintains the File-position pointer, which points to the next available component of a file. When the file is opened (using either Rewrite or Reset), the File-position pointer has the value zero, which is the location of the first file component. As components are read, the File-position pointer is updated to point to the next available component. For example, after component 0 is read, the File-position pointer would point to component 1; after component 1 has been read, the pointer would point to component 2; and so forth.

Data are written to a binary file using the Write procedure, which has the general form

```
Write (file-variable, variable,...)
```

where *file-variable* has been assigned to a binary file type and each *variable* is of the same type as the base type of the file. For example, assuming that Data is of type Integer, the following statement would write one component to the file IntegerFile:

```
Write (IntegerFile, Data);
```

Note that no format specifications are used when addressing a binary file. Format specifications are valid only for Text files. If CustomerRecord is defined as a variable of type CustomerRecordType (the same base type as the file CustomerFile), then the following statement would write one record to the file:

```
Write (CustomerFile, CustomerRecord);
```

The Write procedure advances the File-position pointer to point to the next component in the file.

10.4.1 Time Out

1. Write Pascal program segments to declare file variables for the following.
   (a) A file of Real numbers with identifier RealFile.
   (b) A file of records (PartsFile), where each record has the following fields:

   Part identifier (10 characters)
   Location code (3 characters)
   Number on hand (Integer)
   Number on order (Integer)

   The base type of the file should be PartRecordType.

2. Using the files defined in Exercise 1, write Pascal statements to perform each of the following tasks.
   (a) Write the content of the Real variable RealVar to RealFile.
   (b) Read a value from RealFile and store its content in a Real variable RealVar.
   (c) Suppose PartRecord is of type PartRecordType. Read a component of the file PartsFile and store it in PartRecord.
   (d) Again, suppose that PartRecord is of type PartRecordType. Write the content of PartRecord into PartsFile.

10.4.2 Creating a Binary File

As we noted earlier, one of the disadvantages of binary files is that you cannot create or perform other operations on the file outside the context of a Pascal program. You have been accustomed to being able to create Text files using the Turbo Pascal editor. This is not possible for a binary file; it will be necessary to write a program to create a binary file so that it can be available for other programs to process it.

The considerations involved in creating a binary file are essentially similar to those involved in creating a Text file as output from a program. The file must first be opened as an output file. As with a Text file, this is done in two steps: The Assign procedure assigns a name to the file, and the Rewrite procedure initializes the file for output and sets the File-position pointer to the first (zeroth) component. Then data are written to the file using the Write procedure. When all data have been entered and written, the file is closed using the Close procedure. These steps are illustrated in the program solution to the following problem.

■ **Problem Statement.** Write a program to allow the user to enter inventory data consisting of the following fields for each inventory item:

> Item description (10 characters)
> Sales data (Real)
> Production data (Real)

Create a binary file containing the data entered by the user.

■ **Problem Analysis.** Let us use the identifier InventoryFile for the required file. The steps required for this program can be summarized as follows:

INVENTORY FILE CREATION PROGRAM (P10c)

1.0 Clear the screen
2.0 Open InventoryFile for output
3.0 Get inventory data and write to InventoryFile
4.0 Close InventoryFile

The problem statement specifies that InventoryFile must be a binary file. Since each inventory item has three associated fields, it makes sense to create a file of records, where each record is defined as

```
record
      Description : string[10];
      SalesData, ProductionData : Real
end;
```

The user will enter successive values of these fields, and the program will write the entire record structure as one component of the file. To signal the end of the data-entry process, we can have the user enter a sentinel value (say, an asterisk) as the content of Description.

```
program P10c (Input, Output, InventoryFile);
{Program to create a binary file for inventory data}
uses
     Crt;
const
     InputPrompt2 = 'Enter item description (* to stop) ';
     InputPrompt3 = 'Enter sales and production amounts ';
     Sentinal = '*';
type
     InventoryRecordType = record
                                Description : string[10];
                                SalesData, ProductionData : Real
                           end;
     InventoryFileType = file of InventoryRecordType;
var
     InventoryFile : InventoryFileType;

     .
     .
     .
begin        {Main Program}

{1.0 Clear the screen}

     ClrScr;

{2.0 Open InventoryFile for output}

     OpenForOutput (InventoryFile);

{3.0 Get inventory data and write to InventoryFile}

     with InventoryRecord do
          begin
               Write (InputPrompt2);
               Readln (Description);
               while Description <> Sentinal do
                    begin
                         Write (InputPrompt3);
                         Readln (SalesData, ProductionData);
                         Write (InventoryFile, InventoryRecord);
                         Write (InputPrompt2);
                         Readln (Description)
                    end     {while}
          end;     {with}

{4.0 Close InventoryFile}

     Close (InventoryFile)

end.         {Main Program}
```

Figure 10.5 Program 10c: Inventory file creation.

■ **Problem Solution.** A solution to this problem is contained in Figure 10.5 (Program 10c). Note that the declaration of the file has three parts that we routinely use for any binary file. We first define a type identifier for the record (InventoryRecordType) and then define a type identifier for the file (InventoryFileType), which is defined as a file of InventoryRecordType. Then the file-type identifier is used in the declaration of the file variable:

```
var
     InventoryFile : InventoryFileType;
```

The open procedure for InventoryFile is identical to the open procedure for a Text file that will be created as output from a program. First, the user enters a file name, then the Assign procedure associates the file name with the file variable, and finally, the Rewrite procedure initializes the file for output.

Module 3.0 is enclosed in a with statement so that references to the fields within the record can be made without writing the cumbersome record variable followed by field-identifier notation. The user enters values for each of the fields, and when all the fields are filled, the Write procedure is invoked to write the completed record to the file:

```
Write (InventoryFile, InventoryRecord);
```

Note that the base type of InventoryFile and the type of InventoryRecord are identical—InventoryRecordType. This is an absolutely essential requirement imposed by Pascal.

When all the data has been entered, the file is closed using the close procedure:

```
Close (InventoryFile)
```

Remember that if a file is not closed, the directory entry that was begun when the file was opened is not completed, and the contents of the file are lost.

10.4.3 *Time Out*

1. Compile and execute Program 10c. Use the program to create a file with a name and several data records of your choice. It is a good idea to use the extension .DAT for data files. Remember the name of the file: You will need it when you execute a program that will process the file. This topic is covered in the next section.
2. Modify Program 10c to count the number of records placed in the file. Have the program inform the user of the number of records contained in the file when all the data has been entered.
3. Modify Program 10c to allow the user to edit the data that has been entered before it is written to the file. (Have the user confirm that the data is acceptable before writing to the file.)

10.4.4 **Reading a Binary File**

Once a binary file is in existence, it is necessary to write Pascal programs to process the file. (Remember that, because of the format of the file, it is not possible to process a binary file successfully using other software.) The processing program must contain a description of the file matching the description in the program that created the file. Identifiers may, of course, be different, but the component type of the file must be identically defined. If the file has base type Integer when it was created, it must have base type Integer in any program that seeks to process it. For files of record type, the field descriptions in the two programs must be identical in sequence, type, and (for string-type fields) length.

A file that exists and that will be processed as an input file by a program is opened using the Assign procedure, followed by an invocation of the Reset procedure. The Reset procedure positions the File-position pointer to point to the first component in the file that will be read by the first execution of a Read procedure. The processing of the file can proceed sequentially from component to component, since the Read procedure automatically updates the File-position pointer to point to the next component in the file. The Eof function is available for binary files and serves the same purpose used with Text files. The value of the Eof function will be False if the File-position pointer points to a component in the file; the value will be True if the File-position pointer points beyond the last component in the file. The process of reading a binary file is illustrated in the solution to the following problem.

■ **Problem Statement.** Write a program to produce a report showing the content of the inventory file that is created by Program 10c. Write appropriate headings on the report.

■ **Problem Analysis.** Let us call the inventory file InventoryFile. In order to give the program user maximum latitude in directing the output of the program, let us use a Text file (which we will call ReportFile) to contain the desired report. (The program will open InventoryFile as an input file and ReportFile as an output file. After the heading on the report is written, the content of InventoryFile will be read one record at a time, and the content of the record will be written onto ReportFile with proper formatting for readability. When InventoryFile has been processed, both files will be closed. This procedure is summarized in the following plan:

INVENTORY FILE LIST PROGRAM (P10d)

1.0 Clear the screen

2.0 Open InventoryFile and ReportFile

3.0 Write report heading

4.0 Process inventory items

5.0 Wait

6.0 Close files

■ **Problem Solution.** A solution to this problem is shown as Program 10d in Figure 10.6. The user enters the name of InventoryFile and the name of ReportFile. The latter file could be assigned to a file on disk or assigned to the screen using the file name CON. (Remember that CON is an operating system file name associated with the keyboard and the screen.)

Note again the use of the with statement, which encloses the program segment that reads and manipulates the content of InventoryFile. The with statement makes it possible

```pascal
program P10d (Input, Output, InventoryFile, ReportFile);
{Program to list content of binary inventory data file}
uses
     Crt;
const
     ReportHead = 'Description      Production     Sales';
type
     InventoryRecordType = record
                                      Description : string[10];
                                      SalesData, ProductionData : Real
                           end;
     InventoryFileType = file of InventoryRecordType;
var
     InventoryFile : InventoryFileType;
     InventoryRecord : InventoryRecordType;
     ReportFile : Text;
          .
          .
          .
begin     {Main Program}

{1.0 Clear the screen}

     ClrScr;

{2.0 Open InventoryFile and ReportFile}

     OpenForInput (InventoryFile);
     OpenForOutput (ReportFile);

{3.0 Write report heading}

     Writeln (ReportFile, ReportHead);

{4.0 Process inventory items}

     with InventoryRecord do
          begin
               while not Eof (InventoryFile) do
                    begin
                         Read (InventoryFile, InventoryRecord);
                         Writeln (ReportFile, Description:10,
                               ProductionData:12:0, SalesData:12:0)
                    end    {while}
          end;        {with}

{5.0 Wait}

     AlternateWait;

{6.0 Close files}

     Close (InventoryFile);
     Close (ReportFile)

end.       {Main Program}
```

Figure 10.6 Program 10d: Inventory file list program.

to use only the field identifiers to refer to the content of the record read from InventoryFile. The Eof function is used to control the loop, which processes all the data from InventoryFile.

10.4.5   Time Out

1. Compile and execute Program 10d. Use the file that you created by executing Program 10c as the data file for this program. Use the screen as the report file.
2. Repeat Exercise 1, but assign a disk file name to the report file. Use the Turbo Pascal editor to examine the content of the file you create.
3. Modify Program 9e to process the binary inventory file.

10.4.6   Random Access to Binary Files

When a binary file is opened for input using the Reset procedure, Pascal allows either sequential access (as was illustrated in the preceding section) or random access. To gain random access, the program must specify the component number for the component that is to be read from the file. The program then sets the File-position pointer to point to that component, and the next execution of the Read procedure will cause the desired component to be read. The **Seek procedure** performs the function of changing the File-position pointer. The general format for invocation of the Seek procedure is

```
Seek (file-variable, component-number)
```

where *file-variable* is assigned to a binary file, which has been opened using the Reset procedure, and *component-number* is an integer-valued expression. Execution of the Seek procedure will cause the File-position pointer to point to the component designated by *component-number*. Remember that components of a binary file are numbered 0, 1, 2, ... If the value of *component-number* does not correspond to a component in the file, an I/O error will result, and execution of the program will terminate. For example, if there are 25 components in the file, the value of *component-number* must be in the range 0 to 24.

Remember, the Seek procedure does not actually read a component from the file; it only changes the File-position pointer to point to the desired component. The Read procedure must be used to actually read the component. For example, suppose IntegerFile is declared as a file of Integer. Suppose further that we wish to read the third component in the file. Then the following program segment could be used:

```
Seek (IntegerFile, 2);
Read (IntegerFile, IntegerVar);
```

A somewhat more common occurrence is to use a variable to determine the desired component. (The value of this variable could be entered by the user or could be computed by some means.) In any case, if the Integer variable Position contains the position of the desired component in a binary file, then the Seek procedure would use *component-*

number Position − 1, as shown in the following example:

```
Write ('Enter position of desired component ');
Readln (Position);
Seek (IntegerFile, Position - 1);
Read (IntegerFile, IntegerVar);
Writeln ('The value at this position is ', IntegerVar);
```

If the value of *component-number* is invalid, an execution-time I/O error will result. It is a good idea to avoid this event if at all possible. One way to do this is to validate the value of *component-number* before execution of the Seek procedure. To do this, you must determine the number of components in the file. Fortunately, Turbo Pascal makes it easy to accomplish this task. Appended to the front of a binary file is information regarding the length of the file. This information is accessible to the program through the use of the **FileSize function**, which is an integer-valued function that returns the number of components in a binary file. The general form for invoking this function is

```
FileSize (file-variable)
```

where *file-variable* is assigned to a binary file. For example, if IntegerFile contains 25 components, the value of FileSize(IntegerFile) is 25. Using this function, we can revise the aforesaid program segment, which provides random access to IntegerFile, as follows:

```
Write ('Enter position of desired component ');
Readln (Position);
if (Position > FileSize (IntegerFile)) or (Position < 1) then
   Writeln ('Invalid Position Value')
else
   begin
         Seek (IntegerFile, Position - 1);
         Read (IntegerFile, IntegerVar);
         Write ('The value at this position is ', IntegerVar)
    end;   {if}
```

Random access to a binary file is further illustrated in the solution to the following problem.

■ **Problem Statement.** Write a program to allow the user to retrieve records randomly from the inventory file created by Program 10c.

■ **Problem Analysis.** As before, let us call the file InventoryFile. We will need to open the file using the Reset procedure, since it will be processed as an input file. It will be helpful to tell the user how many records are contained in the file before beginning the inquiry process. The user can then enter the number of the desired record, and the program will read that record from the file and display its contents. The user can enter record number 0 to terminate the session. If the record number entered by the user is invalid, the program should write an appropriate error message. The procedure is summarized in the following plan:

RANDOM ACCESS DATA-RETRIEVAL PROGRAM (P10e)

1.0 Clear the screen
2.0 Open InventoryFile for input
3.0 Write number of records in the file
4.0 Process user requests for data from the file
5.0 Close InventoryFile

■ **Problem Solution.** A solution to this problem is shown as Program 10e in Figure 10.7. Note the use of the FileSize function to determine the number of records in the file:

```
SizeOfFile := FileSize(InventoryFile);
```

Note also the use of the Seek procedure to locate the specified record prior to reading it:

```
Seek (InventoryFile, RecordNumber - 1);
```

Remember that the component number is always one less than the position of the component in the file, since the first component is component 0.

When a binary file is opened using the Reset procedure, you can process the file as either an input file (you can read components from the file) or an output file (you can write components to the file). (Remember that the Reset procedure is valid only for files that already exist.) If a program writes a component to the file, the current value of the File-position pointer determines which component will be written. If that component already exists in the file, then the old value will be replaced by a new value. For example, suppose IntegerFile is of base type Integer, and suppose we wish to add the value 1 to the third component of the file. We would first use the Seek procedure to locate the component and then read it. After computing the new value, we would again use the Seek procedure to reset the File-position pointer to the third component and then write the new value at that position. The required procedure would be as follows:

```
Seek (IntegerFile, 2);              {Locate third component}
Read (IntegerFile, IntegerVar);     {Read third component}
IntegerVar := IntegerVar + 1;       {Compute new value}
Seek (IntegerFile, 2);              {Locate third component}
Write (IntegerFile, IntegerVar);    {Write third component}
```

The important point with this procedure is that it is necessary to use the Seek procedure twice—once to locate the value and a second time to reposition the File-position pointer to that component. Remember that the Read procedure causes the File-position pointer to be automatically updated to point to the next component in the file. If the second Seek procedure invocation were not present, then the Write would change the next component (the fourth component in this case).

```pascal
program P10e (Input, Output, InventoryFile);
{Program to allow random access to InventoryFile by record number}
uses
     Crt;
const
     InputPrompt = 'Enter record number (0 to stop) ';
     ErrorMessage = 'Invalid record number ';
type
     InventoryRecordType = record
                                   Description : string[10];
                                   SalesData, ProductionData : Real
                            end;
     InventoryFileType = file of InventoryRecordType;
var
     InventoryFile : InventoryFileType;
     InventoryRecord : InventoryRecordType;
     RecordNumber, SizeOfFile : Integer;
  .
  .
  .

begin     {Main Program}

{1.0 Clear the screen}

     ClrScr;

{2.0 Open InventoryFile for input}

     OpenForInput (InventoryFile);

{3.0 Write number of records in the file}

     SizeOfFile := FileSize (InventoryFile);
     Writeln ('File contains ', SizeOfFile, ' records');

{4.0 Process user requests for data from the file}

     Write (InputPrompt);
     Readln (RecordNumber);
     while RecordNumber <> 0 do
          begin
              if (RecordNumber < 0) or (RecordNumber > SizeOfFile) then
                 Writeln (ErrorMessage)
              else
                 begin
                     Seek (InventoryFile, RecordNumber - 1);
                     Read (InventoryFile, InventoryRecord);
                     with InventoryRecord do
                         Writeln (Description:10, SalesData:10:0,
                                    ProductionData:10:0);
                 end;     {if}
              Write (InputPrompt);
              Readln (RecordNumber)
          end;     {while}

{5.0 Close InventoryFile}

     Close (InventoryFile)

  end.     {Main Program}
```

Figure 10.7 Program 10e: Random-access data retrieval program.

For example, suppose you wish to add 1 to each component of the file IntegerFile. Then the following program segment could be used (assume that the variables Position, Size, and IntegerVar are Integer variables):

```
Size := FileSize (IntegerFile);
for Position := 1 to Size do
    begin
         Seek (IntegerFile, Position - 1);
         Read (IntegerFile, IntegerVar);
         Seek (IntegerFile, Position - 1);
         Write (IntegerFIle, IntegerVar + 1)
    end; {for}
```

10.4.7 Time Out

1. Compile and execute Program 10e. Process the file that you created with Program 10c.
2. By a relatively simple modification of Program 10e, you can create a program that will allow the user not only to read the content of any record in the file, but also to change any record. After the record is read by the program and displayed, the program can ask the user whether any changes are needed. If so, the program can accept new values for all the fields (or, if you wish to get a little more sophisticated, any one or more of the fields). The program can then use the Seek procedure to reposition the File-position pointer and write the new content of the record. Make this modification to Program 10e.

10.4.8   Extending a Binary File

As we have seen, it is possible to process a binary file as both an input file and an output file if it is initialized using the Reset procedure. This enables a program to change existing components of the file. Sometimes it would be useful to be able to add new components to an existing file. It is not possible to insert new components directly between existing components, but it is quite easy to add new components to the end of the file. This is sometimes referred to as **extending a binary file**.

To extend a binary file, it must be initialized using the Reset procedure. (Remember that Rewrite would be inappropriate because you would automatically replace the existing file with a new file. Instead, we wish to leave the existing file alone and simply add on to it.) In order to add to the file, it is necessary to position the File-position pointer to point to the component beyond the last component in the file. This can be done by ascertaining the number of components in the file and then using this value as a parameter in the Seek procedure. If N is the number of components in the file, then $N - 1$ is the component number of the last component. (Remember, the first one is number 0, the second one is number 1, and so on.) Thus, as the Seek procedure positions the File-position pointer to point to component number N and a Write procedure is executed, a component will be added to the file one position beyond the (previously) last component. Successive executions of the Write procedure will add more components to the file. For example, if

IntegerFile is a binary file that has been initialized using Reset, then the following invocation of the Seek procedure would set the stage for adding components to the file:

```
Seek (IntegerFile, FileSize (IntegerFile));
```

Let us return to Program 10c, which is used to create a binary file with inventory data. We can modify the program to allow the user either to create a new file or to extend an existing file. After entering the file name, the user can choose to create the file (menu option 'C') or extend an existing file (menu option 'E'). If the create option is chosen, the file is initialized using Rewrite. If the extend option is chosen, the file is initialized using Reset, and then the Seek procedure is used to position the File-position pointer at the first component beyond the last record in the file. The relevant modification to the statement part of Program 10c is shown as Program 10f in Figure 10.8. Note that if the file exists and the user chooses the create option, the contents of the existing file will be lost. Also, if the user chooses to extend a file that does not exist, an I/O error will result because the Reset procedure must operate on an existing file.

10.4.9   *Time Out*

Test Program 10f by adding records to the sample inventory file that you created earlier.

10.5   *Case Study: Control Breaks*

When creating reports that summarize the content of a file, it is often necessary to include subtotals of various subsets of data within the file. For example, suppose a file contains data regarding sales at several retail stores owned by a company. Each sale is identified by the store number, the date of the sale (month, day, and year), and the amount of the sale. For purposes of this example, let us assume that the file is a Text file. Each line in the file contains data regarding one sale; a sample file is shown in Figure 10.9. All the data for each store are stored in contiguous lines in the file. (That is, all the data for store 12 occur in one group of lines, which is followed by all the data for store 13, and so forth.) The store number is called the *key data item* for this file, since the data are organized in sequence according to store number. The discussion that follows will assume that data has been placed into a sequence based on one or more key data items within each related group of items. We desire a report that shows the detail of all sales, subtotals for each store, and the total for all stores. The desired report for the sample data of Figure 10.9 is shown in Figure 10.10.

This type of problem occurs so frequently in data processing that standard terms have evolved regarding the data and the procedure required to produce the report. (The terminology derives from the days of unit record data-processing machines that processed data in punched-card form. Although the words have been around a long time, they remain useful because they are quite descriptive of the way in which data are often organized and processed.) The data item that serves as the basis for organizing the file is, as we have said, called the key item (or, more generally, the *key field*). Each sequence of related

```pascal
program P10f (Input, Output, InventoryFile);
{Program to extend a binary file for inventory data;
    if the file does not exist, it will be created;
    if the file exists, then the user can either re-create
        the file or add records to it.}
uses
    Crt;
const
    InputPrompt1 = 'Enter file name ';
    InputPrompt2 = 'Enter item description (* to stop) ';
    InputPrompt3 = 'Enter sales and production amounts ';
    Sentinal = '*';
    UsagePrompt = 'Do you wish to Create or Extend the file (C/E) ? ';
type
    InventoryRecordType = record
                                Description : string[10];
                                SalesData, ProductionData : Real
                          end;
    InventoryFileType = file of InventoryRecordType;
var
    InventoryFile : InventoryFileType;
    InventoryRecord : InventoryRecordType;
    Option : Char;
    FileName : string;
begin
    .

    .

    .
{2.0 Open InventoryFile}

    Write (InputPrompt1);
    Readln (FileName);
    Assign (InventoryFile, FileName);
    repeat
        Write (UsagePrompt);
        Readln (Option);
        Option := UpCase (Option);
        if Option = 'C' then
            Rewrite (InventoryFile)
        else if Option = 'E' then
                begin
                    Reset (InventoryFile);
                    Seek (InventoryFile, FileSize(InventoryFile))
                end;   {if}
    until Option in ['C', 'E'];
    Writeln ('File presently contains ',
            FileSize (InventoryFile), ' records');
    .

    .

    .
end.
```

Figure 10.8 Program 10f: Modification to Program 10c to allow extension of an existing file.

groups of data (or records with the same key-field value) is called a *control group*. There are three control groups in the sample file shown in Figure 10.9. When a program process-es a sequential file, it is necessary to detect when all the data from one control group has

Store	Date	Amount
12	02 03 92	45.67
12	03 04 92	9.34
12	03 04 92	34.89
13	05 06 92	6.00
13	05 06 92	4.56
14	04 15 92	7.90

Figure 10.9 Sample sales data.

Store	Date	Amount
12	2/ 3/92	45.67
12	3/ 4/92	9.34
12	3/ 3/92	34.89
Store Total		89.90*
13	5/ 6/92	6.00
13	5/ 6/92	4.56
Store Total		10.56*
14	4/15/92	7.90
Store Total		7.90*
Grand Total		108.36**

Figure 10.10 Sales report with subtotals for each store.

been read and processed and a new group has begun. Terminating one group and beginning a new one is called a **control break**. When the key item value for the group of items that has just been read by a program does not match the key item value for the previous group of items, a control break has occurred. The task of detecting control breaks will require that we read and store not only the current key data item, but also the key item from the previous group, so that the required comparison can be made.

Let us agree on some generic data names for the variables involved in this process. We refer to the key item as Key and the content of the previous key item as PreviousKey. The processing of a sequenced file with control-break detection can be summarized in the following procedure:

GENERAL CONTROL-BREAK PROCEDURE

1.0. Write report heading

2.0. Read group of related items from data file

3.0. PreviousKey = Key

4.0. Initialize accumulator(s)

5.0. Write first detail line in report

6.0. While not end of data file Do

7.0.   Read group of related items from data file

8.0.   If Key not = PreviousKey Then

9.0.   Write subtotal line in report

10.0.   Initialize accumulator for subtotal

11.0.   PreviousKey = Key

12.0.   End If

13.0. Write detail line in report

14.0. Add appropriate item(s) to accumulator(s)

15.0. End While

16.0. Write subtotal for last group

17.0. Write grand totals as appropriate

The first group of related items (or the first record in a binary file) must be processed outside the loop that is used to process the rest of the data in the file. After the first related group is read, the content of PreviousKey is replaced by Key. Next, the various variables that will be used to accumulate the required subtotals and grand totals are initialized. The first detail line in the report containing the first related group of data items is written at this time. Now the loop that will process the remaining data in the file can begin. The Eof function, which looks ahead at the next component in the file, can be used effectively to control this loop. If the next component exists, we process it; otherwise the entire file has been processed and the loop is terminated. After reading the next sequence of related items (the next record), it is time to determine whether a control break has occurred. This is done by comparing the contents of Key and PreviousKey. If they are equal, the data just read belong to the current group; if they are not equal, the data just read belong to a new group. In order to begin processing a new group, it is necessary to write the total line for the group just completed; to do so, we replace PreviousKey by the current value of Key and initialize the accumulators used for subtotals so that we can begin accumulating sums of the items for the new group. In any case, processing continues by writing a detail in the report and adding to the accumulators as needed. When all the data in the file has been processed, it is time to write the subtotal for the last group and write the grand total for the whole report. (Technically, the detection of end-of-file must be treated as a control break, which terminates the processing of the last group.) The use of this general procedure in a complete program is illustrated in the solution to the following problem.

■ **Problem Statement.** Write a program to process the sales file illustrated in Figure 10.9 to produce the report shown in Figure 10.10.

■ **Problem Analysis.** In this file, the key item is StoreNumber. We will need another variable, PreviousStoreNumber, to detect the control break, which will trigger the production of the required subtotals. We will also need two accumulators: StoreTotal for the subtotals for each store and GradeTotal for the total sales for all stores. A plan for the program that follows the general outline just presented is shown next.

CONTROL BREAK PROGRAM (P10g)

1.0. Clear the screen

2.0. Open SalesFile and ReportFile

3.0. Write report heading

4.0. Process first line in SalesFile

5.0. While not end of file, process remaining lines in SalesFile

6.0. Write subtotal for last store

7.0. Write grand total

8.0. Close files

9.0. Wait

■ **Problem Solution.** A solution to this problem is shown in Figure 10.11 as Program 10g. SalesFile is a Text file that is assumed to exist, so it is opened as an input file using the Reset procedure. As part of the processing of the first line of SalesFile, the accumulators StoreTotal and GrandTotal are both initialized with the value of SalesAmount, which is appropriate, since this is the total after having processed only one sale. The detection of control breaks occurs in Module 5.0. After the next line from SalesFile is read, the following if statement is used:

```
if StoreNumber <> PreviousStoreNumber then
    begin
        Writeln (ReportFile, 'Store Total', StoreTotal:12:2 '*');
        Writeln (ReportFile);
        PreviousStoreNumber := StoreNumber;
        StoreTotal := 0
    end; {if}
```

The first Writeln procedure invocation is used to write the value of StoreTotal on the report. Note that this is the total for the preceding control group, not the group that just began. The second Writeln invocation simply writes a blank line on the report to serve as a visual separator to improve the readability of the report. The content of PreviousStoreNumber is replaced by that of current StoreNumber in the next statement. (If this is not done, then only the first control group will be processed properly; each line thereafter will be treated as the beginning of a new group.) Finally, the accumulator StoreTotal is reset to 0. (Do not be tempted to place the value of SaleAmount into StoreTotal at this point; this will happen naturally during the routine processing of this line from the file.) When all data from the file have been processed, the subtotal for the last control group is written, which is followed by the grand total. Note that the control break produced by end-of-file does not require the reinitialization of the subtotal accumulator and PreviousKey. It would cause no harm to do the same things here that were done for control breaks detected during the processing of the file, but the additional actions are unnecessary at this point.

10.5.1   *Time Out*

1. Create a Text file in the format shown in Figure 10.9. Use the file to test Program 10g.

2. Modify Program 10g to produce a secondary control break based on date. That is, have the program produce a subtotal for each day's sales for each store. In this case, the store number is called the *primary key* and the date is called the *secondary key*. Note that a break in primary key values must automatically cause a secondary break.

3. Write a program to transform the Text file containing sales data into a binary file.

4. Revise Program 10g to process a binary sales file.

5. In Program 10g, there is an implicit assumption that the file has at least one line of data. What happens if the file is empty? How could you correct the problem?

```pascal
program P10g (Input, Output, SalesFile, ReportFile);
{Program to generate summary of SalesFile with subtotals
      by store; program illustrates control break logic.}
uses
    Crt;
const
    ReportHeading = ' Store    Date     Amount';
var
    StoreNumber, PreviousStoreNumber,
    SaleMonth, SaleDay, SaleYear : Integer;
    SaleAmount, StoreTotal, GrandTotal : Real;
    SalesFile, ReportFile : Text;
      .
      .
      .
begin    {Main Program}
      .
      .
      .
{4.0 Process first line in SalesFile}

    Readln (SalesFile, StoreNumber, SaleMonth, SaleDay, SaleYear,
                    SaleAmount);
    PreviousStoreNumber := StoreNumber;
    StoreTotal := SaleAmount;
    GrandTotal := SaleAmount;
    Writeln (ReportFile, StoreNumber:5, SaleMonth:4, '/',SaleDay:2,'/',
                    SaleYear:2, SaleAmount:8:2);

{5.0 While not end of file, process remaining lines in SalesFile}

    while not Eof (SalesFile) do
        begin
            Readln (SalesFile, StoreNumber, SaleMonth, SaleDay,
                            SaleYear, SaleAmount);
            if StoreNumber <> PreviousStoreNumber then
                begin
                    Writeln (ReportFile, 'Store Total',
                            StoreTotal:12:2,'*');
                    Writeln (ReportFile);
                    PreviousStoreNumber := StoreNumber;
                    StoreTotal := 0
                end;    {if}
            StoreTotal := StoreTotal + SaleAmount;
            GrandTotal := GrandTotal + SaleAmount;
            Writeln (ReportFile, StoreNumber:5,
                        SaleMonth:4, '/',SaleDay:2,'/',
                        SaleYear:2, SaleAmount:8:2);
        end;    {while}

{6.0 Write subtotal for last store}

    Writeln (ReportFile, 'Store Total', StoreTotal:12:2,'*');

{7.0 Write grand total}

    Writeln (ReportFile);
    Writeln (ReportFile, 'Grand Total', GrandTotal:12:2,'**');
      .
      .
      .
end.      {Main Program}
```

Figure 10.11 Program 10g: Control Break Program.

10.6   INPUT/OUTPUT ERROR HANDLING

We have made a number of references to input/output errors that can occur during the execution of a program. By now, you have probably encountered some of these errors during your attempts to write and run programs that manipulate files. One of the most common errors is error 2: File not found. This error occurs when you attempt to open a file using a Reset and the file cannot be found on the disk. You may also have encountered error 104, File not open for input, or error 105, File not open for output. These errors occur when there is a conflict between the way in which the file is opened and the type of procedure you are attempting to perform. Figure 10.12 contains a list of the I/O errors that you are most likely to encounter using the I/O procedures discussed in this chapter. A complete list of I/O errors is contained in the Turbo Pascal reference manual.

The normal action taken by the system when an I/O error occurs is to terminate the execution of the program. This may be acceptable if the user is a knowledgeable programmer and can interpret the standard error messages successfully. On the other hand, if the intended user of the program is not so knowledgeable, then encountering system error messages that may make little sense to him or her is not desirable. It would be better if the program could intercede when an I/O error occurs and write more appropriate error messages or even suggestions as to how the error might be corrected. If I/O errors do not automatically result in program termination, then it might be possible for the program to resume after the user takes corrective steps. Turbo Pascal makes it possible for the program to handle its own I/O error conditions by using the **I compiler directive**.

The default state of the I directive is positive—that is, {$I+}. In this state, I/O error program halts are enabled. If you set the option to negative using {$I-}, I/O program halts are disabled. In this state, the system places a number in a location that can be tested by the standard function IOresult. The value of this function indicates the outcome of the input/output operation just completed (including Reset, Rewrite, Read, Readln, Write, Writeln, and Seek). The value of IOresult corresponds to the I/O error number shown in Figure 10.12. If the value of IOresult is zero, the operation was executed normally; if the operation was not executed normally, an appropriate value is placed in IOresult. If an error is encountered, all further input/output operations are suspended until the value of the

Error number	Message
2	File not found
3	Path not found
4	Too many open files
5	File access denied
6	Invalid file handle
100	Disk read error
101	Disk write error
102	File not assigned
103	File not open
104	File not open for input
105	File not open for output
106	Invalid numeric format

Figure 10.12 Common I/O errors. *Note*: Refer to the Turbo Pascal reference manual for more information.

location storing the error number is cleared, that is, reset to 0. IOresult performs this task for you; the error number is set to zero by each execution of the **IOresult function**. (This is a very important point; the behavior of this function is unlike any other in Turbo Pascal. You cannot continually refer to IOresult after a given input/output operation; the first reference will reset the value to zero, and successive references will therefore return a value of zero.)

For example, suppose you wish to determine in a program whether or not a file exists after a Reset procedure attempts to open the file. (Ordinarily, the program will abort if the file doesn't exist.) You can perform this task in the following manner:

1. Suspend I/O error program halts using {$I−}.
2. Execute the Reset procedure.
3. Enable I/O error program halts using {I+}.
4. Test IOresult. If it is equal to zero, then the Reset operation was successful; if it is not equal to zero, then the Reset procedure was unable to locate the file.

The translation of this procedure to Pascal would appear as follows:

```
{$I-}
Reset (DataFIle);
{$I+}
if not (IOresult = 0) then
    Writeln ('File not found');
```

The trouble with this procedure is that the next statement could not repeat the test of IOresult, since the invocation of the function caused it to be set to zero. One way around this problem is to use a Boolean variable such as FileFound and assign its value using the statement

```
FileFound := IOresult = 0;
```

If the value of IOresult is zero, then the value assigned to FileFound will be True; otherwise the value will be False. Figure 10.13 shows this technique applied in Program 10h, which lists an existing Text file. The usual open procedure is expanded by using a repeat/until loop that will continue until the user has entered a file name that can be successfully Reset.

Another approach to the problem of referencing IOresult is to place its value in an Integer variable such as IOCode:

```
IOCode := IOresult;
```

Subsequent statements could test the value of IOCode and write appropriate error messages and suggestions as to what may have caused the error and how to correct the problem.

10.6.1 *Time Out*

1. Test Program 10h to list a file of your choice.
2. In Program 10e, the value of SizeOfFile was used to determine whether a user's request for a particular record was valid. Modify this program to use the I compiler directive to determine whether a record exists after a Seek procedure invocation. If the record does not exist, the error code will be error 100: Disk read error.

```
program P10h (DataFile, Input, Output);
{Program to read a text file and print content on the screen;
     this version includes logic to check for the existence of
     the file and gives the user the ability to pause at the end of
     each screen full of text.}
uses
     Crt;
var
     DataFile : Text;
     Data : string;
     LineCount : Integer;
{*********************************************************************}
     procedure OpenForInput (var InputFile : Text);
     {Procedure opens a Text file for input and includes error checking}
     const
          InputPrompt = 'Enter name of the file ';
          ErrorMessage = 'File cannot be found, try again';
     var
          FileName : string;
          FileFound : Boolean;
     begin    {OpenForInput}
          repeat
               Writeln (InputPrompt);
               Readln (FileName);
               Assign (InputFile, FileName);
               {$I-}   {Suspend I/O error program halts}
               Reset (InputFile);
               {$I+}   {Enable I/O error program halts}
               FileFound := IOresult = 0; {The logical expression
                                           IOresult = 0 is True if
                                           file is present and
                                           False otherwise}

               if not FileFound then
                    Writeln (ErrorMessage)
          until FileFound;
     end;    {OpenForInput}
          .
          .
          .
{*********************************************************************}
begin    {Main Program}

{1.0 Open DataFile}

     ClrScr;
     OpenForInput (DataFile);

{2.0 Process DataFile}

     while not Eof(DataFile) do
          begin
               ClrScr;
               LineCount := 1;
               while (LineCount <= 24) and (not Eof(DataFile)) do
                    begin
                         Readln (DataFile, Data);
                         Writeln (Data);
                         LineCount := LineCount + 1
                    end;    {while}
               AlternateWait;
          end;    {while}
     .
     .
     .
end.      {Main Program}
```

Figure 10.13 Program 10h: Text file list program illustrating I compiler directive.

10.7 RECORDS WITH VARIANT PARTS

In all record types with which we have dealt thus far, each record of a specific type has had exactly the same sequence of fields as all other records of that type. This restriction is not always convenient, because actual data do not always have such simple organization. For example, consider a situation in which we wish to maintain data regarding membership in a social club. Some members are married and some are not. For married members, we wish to store data regarding the spouse; for unmarried members, there would be no such data to store. Such situations can be handled in Pascal by creating records with variant parts. The variant part of the record will store different data, depending on some condition (such as whether or not the person is married).

A record with a variant part will be made up of a sequence of fields that will be the same in all records of this type. This sequence is called the *fixed part* of the record. The **variant part of a record** (if present) must follow the fixed part. The makeup of the variant part is dependent on the content of the field that is the last one in the fixed part of the record; this field is called the *tag field*. The tag field must be of an enumerated or a subsequence data type. For example, in the social club membership list example cited earlier, suppose a data type has been declared as follows:

```
type
    MaritalStatusType = (Married, Divorced, Single, Widow);
```

Then the tag field for this record could be of type MaritalStatusType. Another alternative is to declare a subsequence data type such as

```
type
    MaritalCodeType = ('M', 'D', 'S', 'W');
```

The tag field for this record could be of type MaritalCodeType.

In declaring a record with a variant part, the fixed part is declared first as a sequence of fields in the usual way. Then the variant part is declared using a structure that is a variation on the case statement. The general form of a record declaration with a variant part is as follows:

```
record-type = record
                  identifier-list-1 : type-1;
                         .
                         .
                         .
                  identifier-list-n : type-n;
                  case tag-field : tag-field-type of
                      constant-1 : (field-list-1);
                             .
                             .
                             .
                      constant-m : (field-list-m)
              end;
```

Fixed part

Variant part

The first sequence of identifier lists followed by type specifications describes the fixed part of the record. The *tag-field* specification is preceded by the reserved word "case" and followed by the reserved word **of** and then a list of constants (which represent potential values for the *tag-field*); each constant is followed by a colon and a description of the fields that will make up the record if the tag field has this value. The description (which is called a *field list*) must be enclosed in parentheses; all except the last of these must be terminated by a semicolon. A field list is made up of elements of the same format as the description of the fixed part of the record—that is, a list of field identifiers, followed by a colon, followed by a type specification and (if there are other specifications to follow) a semicolon. The syntax of this specification is perhaps the most complicated of any in Pascal, but a few examples will help you see the pattern.

Consider the example of the social club membership list. We wish to create a record that will have a fixed part containing the member's name, address, and marital status, the last of which will be the tag field for the variant part of the record. Let us assume that the marital status is of type MaritalStatusType declared before (an enumerated type). If the marital status has the value Married, the variant part of the record must contain the name of the spouse. If the value of the marital status is other than Married, then the record will have no fields in the variant part. The following program segment illustrates the declaration of this record:

```
type
    MaritalStatusType = (Married, Divorced, Single, Widow);
    MemberRecordType = record
                            MemberName :  string[20];
                            Street, City :  string[15];
                            State :  string[2];
                            Zip :  string[5];
                            case MaritalStatus :
                                MaritalStatusType  of
                            Married : (SpouseName :
                                            string[20]);
                            Divorced : ();
                            Single : ();
                            Widow : ()
                        end;
var
    MemberRecord : MemberRecordType;
```

Fixed part

Variant part

Notice that it is necessary to list all possible values of the tag field in declaring the variant part of the record. Also, note that if the record contains no fields for one or more values of the tag field, the associated constant must be followed by a colon and a pair of parentheses. In these cases, the associated field list is said to be null. One other point should be made with respect to this example: All field identifiers must be unique. For example, we could not have used the identifier Name for both the member name and the spouse name.

Consider another example. Suppose we wish to create a file to store personnel data. The file will be used to store basic identifying information about the employee (social security number, name), employment information (date hired, department number) and the year-to-date pay for each employee. Let us assume that the company pays all regular full-time employees a salary, but pays part-time employees at an hourly rate. Then each record in the file must store the employee's status and the related salary or hourly rate. In addition to employees who are currently employed, the file must store information on employees who have been terminated. For such an employee, we wish to store the date of termination and the reason (resigned, fired, laid off). The required record will have a fixed part containing basic information common to all employees: the social security number, name, date hired, department number, year-to-date pay, and employee's status (full time, part time, terminated). The employee status will be used as the tag field for the variant part of the record. For a full-time employee, we want to store his or her annual salary. For a part-time employee, we want to store the hourly rate. For a terminated employee, we want to store the date of termination and the termination status. The declarations for Program 10i, which uses this file, is shown in Figure 10.14.

In determining the actual length of a record with a variant part, TurboPascal adds the space required for the fixed part and the space required for the longest variant part. Each record will be allocated this number of bytes. You can think of the area allocated for the variant part as being defined in varying ways, depending on the value of the tag field.

```pascal
program P10i (Input, Output, PersonnelFile);
{Program to create or list PersonnelFile;
    program illustrates a record with a variant part.}
uses
    Crt;
type
    EmployeeStatusType = (FullTime, PartTime, Terminated);
    TerminateStatusType = (Resigned, Fired, LayOff);
    DateRecordType = record
                          Month, Day, Year : Integer
                     end;
    PersonnelRecordType =
        record
            SSN : string[9];
            Name : string[20];
            HireDate : DateRecordType;
            DepartmentNumber : Integer;
            YTDPay : Real;
            case EmployeeStatus : EmployeeStatusType of
                Fulltime : (Salary : Real);
                PartTime : (HourlyRate : Real);
                Terminated : (TerminateDate : DateRecordType;
                              TerminateStatus : TerminateStatusType)
        end;
    PersonnelFileType = file of PersonnelRecordType;
var
    PersonnelFile : PersonnelFileType;
    Choice : Char;
{*****************************************************************************}
```

Figure 10.14 Program 10i: Declaration part showing a record with a variant part.

For example, consider the following very simple (and quite arbitrary) example:

```
type
    TagFieldType = 1..3;
    RecType = record
                  FixedField1 : Integer;
                  FixedField2: Real:
                  case TagField : TagFieldType of
                  1 : (VarField1, VarField2 : Real);
                  2 : (VarField3 : Integer);
                  3 : ()
            end;
var
    DataRecord : RecType;
```

Fixed part — FixedField1, FixedField2, case TagField

Variant part — 1, 2, 3

The fixed part of DataRecord contains three fields: FixedField1, FixedField2, and Tag-Field. The variant part of the record has three different descriptions. If TagField = 1, the record contains two Real values (VarField1. VarField2). If TagField = 2, the record contains one Integer value (VarField3). If TagField = 3, the variant part of the record contains no data. The internal layout of this record can be visualized as shown in Figure 10.15. In this case, the field list associated with the first value of TagField is the longest and hence is used in governing the length of all of the records.

In a program that processes a record with a variant part, it is the responsibility of the program (and the programmer) to use the correct field identifiers for the variant part of the record. Typically, the program bases the processing of the data on the value of the tag field. For example, consider the task of creating the personnel field described previously. In the portion of Program 10i that reads data and places them into the record (before writing the record to the file), it is necessary to determine the employee's status based on a coded value entered by the program user. The required program segment is shown in Figure 10.16.

Once the value of the tag field EmployeeStatus is determined, the program can have the user enter the value of the relevant field(s). A case structure based on the value of EmployeeStatus would be appropriate, as shown in Figure 10.17. If EmployeeStatus is FullTime, then the user must enter the salary. If EmployeeStatus is PartTime, then the user must enter the hourly rate. If EmployeeStatus is Terminated, then the user must enter the termination date and reason. It is important to understand that it is the program's responsibility to choose which description of the variant part of the record to use. For example, Pascal would allow you to refer to the field TerminateDate, even though the value of EmployeeStatus was FullTime or PartTime! Such a reference would, of course, be a very

Fixed part of DataRecord			*Variant part of DataRecord*		
			VarField1		VarField2
FixedField1	FixedField2	TagField	VarField3		

Figure 10.15 Storage allocation for a record with a variant part.

```
procedure GetPersonnelData (var DataRecord : PersonnelRecordType);
const
      SSNPrompt = 'Social security number: ';
      NamePrompt = 'Employee name (last name first): ';
      DateHiredPrompt = 'Date hired (mm dd yy): ';
      DepartmentPrompt = 'Department number: ';
      StatusPrompt1 = 'Employee status';
      StatusPrompt2 = '  Full time/Part time/Terminated (F/P/T): ';
      RatePrompt = 'Hourly rate: ';
      SalaryPrompt = 'Yearly salary: ';
      TerminateDatePrompt = 'Date terminated (mm dd yy): ';
      TerminateStatusPrompt1 = 'Reason for termination';
      TerminateStatusPrompt2 = '  Resigned/Fired/Layoff (R/F/L): ';
var
      Status : Char;
begin     {GetPersonnelData}
      with DataRecord do
            begin
                  Write (SSNPrompt);
                  Readln (SSN);
                  Write (NamePrompt);
                  Readln (Name);
                  Write (DateHiredPrompt);
                  with HireDate do
                        Readln (Month, Day, Year);
                  Write (DepartmentPrompt);
                  Readln (DepartmentNumber);
                  repeat
                        Writeln (StatusPrompt1);
                        Write (StatusPrompt2);
                        Readln (Status);
                        Status := UpCase (Status);
                        if Status = 'F' then
                              EmployeeStatus := FullTime
                        else if Status = 'P' then
                              EmployeeStatus := PartTime
                        else if Status = 'T' then
                              EmployeeStatus := Terminated
                        else
                              Writeln ('Invalid Status Code');
                  until Status in ['F', 'P', 'T'];
```

Figure 10.16 Program 10i: Initial portion of the procedure GetPersonnelData.

grave error, but it is not one that Pascal would detect and warn you about with an error message—at least, not one that would specifically point out what had happened. The error would show up as an invalid value in one or more fields. It would be the programmer's responsibility to track down the cause. For this reason, you should use records with variant parts with great care; make sure that the processing of the record logically parallels the way in which the record was created.

10.7.1 Time Out

Program 10i is designed to allow a user to create or list the Personnel file described in this section. Many portions of the program are stubbed in. Complete the missing parts of the program.

```
case EmployeeStatus of
     FullTime : begin
                    Write (SalaryPrompt);
                    Readln (Salary)
                end;
     PartTime : begin
                    Write (RatePrompt);
                    Readln (HourlyRate)
                end;
     Terminated : begin
                    Write (TerminateDatePrompt);
                    with TerminateDate do
                        Readln (Month, Day, Year);
                    repeat
                    Writeln (TerminateStatusPrompt1);
                    Write (TerminateStatusPrompt2);
                    Readln (Status);
                    Status := UpCase(Status);
                    if Status = 'R' then
                        TerminateStatus := Resigned
                    else if Status = 'F' then
                        TerminateStatus := Fired
                    else if Status = 'L' then
                        TerminateStatus := LayOff
                    else
                        Writeln ('Invalid Status');
                    until Status in ['R', 'F', 'L'];
                end;
end;     {case}
```

Figure 10.17 Program 10i: Case statement used in the procedure GetPersonnel-
Data to assign a value to the variant part of the record.

10.8   THE DOS UNIT

The Dos unit contains functions and procedures designed to perform tasks directly related to the operating system. For example, the unit gives the program the ability to retrieve or set the system date and time, determine the version of DOS in use, determine the size of a disk and how much free space remains, and retrieve information contained in directories. In this section, we will examine the last of these features. You can read about other parts of the Dos unit in the *Turbo Pascal 7.0 Programmer's Reference* (or a similar manual if you are using an earlier version of Turbo Pascal.).

To access the features of the Dos unit, a program must include Dos in the list of units in the program's uses statement. For example, if only the Dos unit is needed, the uses statement would appear as

```
uses Dos;
```

If the unit Crt is also needed, the uses statement would appear as

```
uses Crt, Dos;
```

(As many units as are needed may be included in a single uses statement.)

Recall that in DOS, you can select which elements of a directory of files you wish to operate on by means of a mask. A *mask* is a sequence of characters that are matched against the names of files in the directory; all names that are matched are retrieved for processing. The mask can be made up of any sequence of characters, together with the wild cards * and ?. When used in a mask, * will match any sequence of characters. For example, a mask that will match all file names is *.*. This means any basic file name with any extension. The asterisk can be used before or after the period that separates the basic file name from the extension. For example, the mask *.PAS will match all files with the extension PAS. The mask DATA.* will match all files with the basic name DATA and any extension. The wild card ? will match any single character or the absence of a character. For example, the mask *.? will match any file with a single character extension or no extension at all. A mask can contain a complete path, including the drive and directory, or if these are omitted, the current drive and directory will be searched. For example, suppose that the current drive is drive C and the current directory is TURBO. Then any one of the following masks could be used to specify the files in this directory:

```
C:\TURBO\*.*        (a complete mask)
\TURBO\*.*          (drive C is used by default)
*.*                 (the current drive and directory are used)
```

All access to files through the Dos unit is controlled by a mask. The program must specify a mask; the procedures provided in the unit Dos will retrieve files obeying exactly the same conventions as used in the operating system itself. To secure a listing of a directory, two procedures are used. The first is called "FindFirst" and includes a mask as a parameter. This procedure locates the first file (if one exists, of course) that meets the criteria specified in the mask. After the first one is located, the procedure "FindNext" can be used to locate other file names that meet the criteria.

Both of these procedures require a variable of type SearchRec. This is the identifier for a record type defined in Dos. There are a number of fields in this type; they are used to return information about a file that has been located in a directory. Of specific interest here is the field Name of type string[12], which stores the name of the file. (Other fields store attributes of the file, the time the file was last modified, and the size of the file. More information is contained in the Turbo Pascal reference materials.)

The general form for invoking FindFirst is

```
FindFirst (path, attribute, search-variable)
```

where *path* is a string constant, variable, or expression specifying the mask, *attribute* is a value used to specify the attributes of special files to be selected (in addition to ordinary files), and *search-variable* is a variable of type SearchRec. For convenience in specifying the value of *attribute*, the Dos unit includes a number of predefined constants with self-documenting names. Following is a list of a few of these identifiers:

Identifier	*Specifies*
ReadOnly	Read-only files
Hidden	Hidden files
AnyFile	Files of all types

For example, suppose we have a variable of type SearchRec defined as follows:

```
var
    S : SearchRec;
```

Then the following statement would locate and retrieve information about the first file in the current directory;

```
FindFirst ('*.*', AnyFile, S);
```

In this invocation, the mask is specified as a constant; the two wild cards will match any file name. The path can also be specified as a variable. Suppose the following declarations are in place:

```
var
    S : SearchRec;
    Mask : string;
```

Then the following program segment would locate and retrieve information about the first file with the extension DAT:

```
Mask := '*.DAT';
FindFirst (Mask, AnyFile, S);
```

The procedures FindFirst and FindNext communicate the result of their execution by means of a variable DosError, which is defined in the unit Dos. If the value of DosError is 0 after the execution of either of these procedures, then the procedure was successful in locating a file. If the value of DosError is not zero, then the procedure was unable to locate a file. We use the value of this variable to continue processing, until all files matching a given mask have been located.

After the first file has been found, other files are located by the procedure FindNext, which has the general form

```
FindNext (search-variable)
```

where *search-variable* is a variable of type SearchRec. Notice that the execution of Find-First sets the mask for retrieval of files; FindNext uses the same mask. It is an error to execute FindNext without first successfully executing FindFirst.

For example, the following program segment will locate all files in the current directory:

```
FindFirst ('*.*', AnyFile, S);
while DosError = 0 do
    begin
        .
        .
        .
        FindNext (S)
    end;  {while}
```

Both FindFirst and FindNext retrieve information about the file that has been located and place this information in *search-variable*. The program can then use any of the fields in this variable. For example, to reference the name field, you would write

```
S.Name
```

This, as you remember from our work with fields, is a reference to the Name field in the variable S.

Program 10j, which is shown in Figure 10.18, makes use of the features of the Dos unit that we have just described to allow the user to enter a mask and then retrieve a directory listing. You will note that we use the mask *.* as a default. The variable Dir is declared as type SearchRec. Thus, after a file is successfully located, the statement

```
Write (Dir.Name:20);
```

```
program P10j (Input, Output);
{Program to display the directory of files corresponding
     to any desired mask.}
uses
     Dos;
const
     MaskPrompt = 'Enter mask (Press <Enter> for *.*) ';
     ContinuePrompt = 'List another directory (Y/N) ';
var
     Mask : string;
     Dir : SearchRec;     {SearchRec is a record type defined in Dos}
     NoFiles : Boolean;
     Answer : Char;
begin
     repeat
          Write (MaskPrompt);
          Readln (Mask);
          if Mask = '' then
             Mask := '*.*';
          FindFirst (Mask, AnyFile, Dir);
          NoFiles := True;
          while DosError = 0 do
               begin
                    NoFiles := False;
                    Write (Dir.Name:20);
                    FindNext (Dir)
               end;   {while}
          Writeln;
          if NoFiles then
               Writeln ('No files were found ');
          Write (ContinuePrompt);
          Readln (Answer)
     until UpCase(Answer) <> 'Y'
end.
```

Figure 10.18 Program 10j: Directory list program illustrating Dos unit facilities.

will write out the file name. Note that we have made provision through the Boolean variable NoFiles for the possibility that there are no files that match the particular mask in use. If the value of NoFiles remains True, then an appropriate message is produced.

10.8.1 Time Out

1. Test Program 10j with masks of your choosing.
2. Revise Program 10h to allow the program to list a directory if the user requests a file that is not found.

10.9 REVIEW QUESTIONS

1. Why is it not possible to define the base type of a record?
2. What is a field? What are the two parts of a complete field reference?
3. It is not necessary that field identifiers be unique. How does Pascal ensure that field references are unique?
4. Draw a data-structure diagram for the data described by the following Pascal program segment:

```
var
    Data : record
                Field1 : Integer;
                Field2, Field3 : Real;
                Field4 : record
                             Field5 : string[2];
                             Field6 : Real
                         end;
                Field7 : array [1..3] of Real
           end;
```

5. Is the with statement a convenience or a necessity? Explain.
6. What is an array of records? How is an array of records related to parallel arrays?
7. What Pascal statement(s) can be used to process a variable with a record type?
8. What is a file? How is a file unlike any other structured type in Pascal?
9. What is a binary file? What are the advantages and disadvantages of using binary files?
10. How is the component type of a file defined?
11. What is the purpose of the Seek procedure?
12. What is meant by random access to a file? Why is random access to a binary file possible, whereas random access to a Text file is not?
13. What is the purpose of the FileSize function? How is this function used to extend a binary file?
14. What is a control group? A control break? Why do these concepts make sense only for a sequenced file?
15. What is the purpose of the I compiler directive?
16. What is the variant part of a record? Why would a record need to have a variant part?
17. Draw a diagram similar to that in Figure 10.15 for the variant part of the record defined in the program segment shown in Figure 10.14.

18. Explain why the processing of a record with a variant part must closely parallel the way in which the record is defined.

19. What restriction is imposed on the placement of the variant part of a a record?

20. When a file is passed as a parameter to a procedure or function, why must the associated formal parameter be declared a variable parameter?

21. List some of the facilities provided by the Dos unit.

22. What purpose is served by the **path** parameter in the procedure FindFirst?

23. How are FindFirst and FindNext typically used to list a directory?

24. What purpose is served by the variable DosError? Where is it declared?

25. What purpose is served by the type SearchRec? Where is it declared?

10.10   PROGRAMMING EXERCISES

1. Add the following functions to Program 10i.
   (a) Random access (by record number) to the file's content.
   (b) An option to allow the user to extent the file.
   (c) An option to allow the user to edit (change any field) of any record in the file.

2. Create a system to allow the user to maintain checking-account information using a binary file to store the basic data for the account. Each record in the file will be in the following format: transaction date, transaction code (deposit or check), check number, amount, clearance code (cleared, outstanding). A program is needed that will allow the user to create the initial file and add transactions to the file. The program also needs to allow the user to post cleared transactions (based on the bank statement) and generate reports showing all cleared entries, all uncleared entries, or all entries.

3. Create a Text file showing the production records for five varieties of widgets at 10 different plants that produce the products. Each line in the file should contain the following data: plant number (1 through 10), widget model number (1 through 5), date, and quantity produced. The data should be in order by plant number. (All data for plant number 1 should precede data for plant number 2, and so forth.) For each plant, the data should be in sequence by widget number. Write a program to produce a report showing all of the input data, subtotals for each plant, and total widget production for all plants.

4. Modify the program written for Exercise 3 to show subtotals for each widget type, as well as plant totals and the grand total.

5. Create a text file with lines containing the following information about salespersons employed by XYZ, Inc:

   Name

   Social security number

   Date of sale

   Amount of sale

   Make sure that the data are in sequence by social security number; for each salesperson, the data should be sequenced by date. Write a program to create a report summarizing sales for each salesperson, no matter how many sales he or she makes.

6. Modify the program you wrote for Exercise 5 to include the percentage of total sales made by each salesperson.

7. Modify the program you wrote for Exercise 5 to include the total sales for each salesperson on each date, as well as the totals previously required. Write the salesperson's name as part of the first-day total only—do not list the name on subsequent lines of output for that salesperson.

8. Write a program to create a binary file containing data for salespeople employed by XYZ, Inc. Each record in the file should contain the salesperson's name, social security number, and classification—part time or full time. For part-time salespeople, the record should contain the commission rate; for full-time personnel, the record should contain the base salary amount and commission rate. The file should be sequenced by social security number.

9. Write a program to produce a report showing the content of the file created in Exercise 8. Allow the program user to specify whether the report should contain full-time, part-time, or all salespeople.

11
Searching and Sorting

In this chapter, we consider two fundamental problems of data processing: searching and sorting. Searching is required to look up specific information from a table when the exact location of the information is not known in advance. Sorting is required to place data into a desired sequence in preparation for generating a report or using the data in some other manner. Both tasks can be accomplished in a variety of ways. We shall examine alternative procedures for accomplishing these tasks and examine the various procedures from the standpoint of applicability and efficiency.

11.1 TABLE LOOKUP

Searching is always carried out with reference to an existing set of data stored in an organized fashion. We shall call the set of reference data a *table*. You use the basic ideas of searching when you look up information in a telephone directory or the meaning of a word in a dictionary. The telephone directory and the dictionary constitute tables in which the desired information is contained. Each entry in a table has two parts, which are called the **table argument** and the **table value**. In the case of the telephone directory, the table argument is the subscriber's name; the table value is the telephone number. In a dictionary the table argument is the word; the table value is the list of meanings and other information about the word. A search is initiated when a user wishes to access the content of an entry in a table corresponding to a particular argument value; we call this argument the **actual argument**; the associated table value is called the **actual value**. For example, when you use a telephone directory, the actual argument is the name of the person you wish to call; the person's telephone number is the actual value. In the dictionary example, the actual argument is the word the user wishes to look up in the dictionary; the associated information is the actual value.

The basic task of a **table lookup** procedure is to locate the table entry in which the table argument is equal to the actual argument. When the required entry is located, the associated table value becomes the actual value and can be processed as needed. For example, the telephone user searches the directory (the table) to locate the telephone number (a table value) for a specific person (the actual argument). The search is terminated when a subscriber (a table argument) is found whose name matches the person being sought (the actual argument); the associated telephone number (the actual value) is used to make the telephone call.

Of course, there are always two possible outcomes in a search: The required information may be located, or it may not. (It is possible that the person's telephone number is not in the telephone directory for any number of reasons; similarly, the required word may not be present in the dictionary.) In making use of a table lookup procedure, you must always allow for two possible outcomes; either the actual argument matches a table argument, or it does not. If the desired entry is found, the associated table value can be used; if the desired entry is not found, then some provision must be made for an alternative course of action.

11.2 SEQUENTIAL SEARCH PROCEDURES

Let us turn to a consideration of some specific search techniques. The simplest procedure involves a sequential comparison of the actual argument with successive table arguments until either a match is found or there are no more table entries. We will call this technique a **sequential search** because the table entries are examined in a sequential fashion from first to last. The elements involved are the table, which is made up of table arguments (TableArgument) and associated table values (TableValue); the actual argument (Actual-Argument); the actual value (ActualValue); the table limit (the number of elements in the table, TableLimit); and a variable, Index, which will enable us to advance from one element to another in the table. The procedure will also need some means of signifying whether or not the search was successful; the Boolean variable Found will be used for this purpose. When the procedure terminates, the value of Found will be True if the procedure was successful in locating a TableArgument equal to the ActualArgument and False otherwise. (We assume that the table is an array and therefore use subscript notation. A table may also take the form of a file; the concepts are the same, but the implementation is somewhat different.) The sequential search procedure can be summarized as follows:

SEQUENTIAL SEARCH PROCEDURE (IMPORT : TABLE, ACTUALARGUMENT; EXPORT : ACTUALVALUE, FOUND)

1.0 Index = 1

2.0 Found = False

3.0 While Index <= TableLimit and not Found Do

4.0   If TableArgument (Index) = ActualArgument Then

5.0   Found = True

6.0   ActualValue = TableValue (Index)

7.0   Else

8.0   Index = Index + 1

9.0   End If

10.0 End While

In this procedure, the initial value for Index is 1 and the initial value for Found is False. The While loop terminates when either a match is located (at which point Found is set to True and ActualValue is assigned the content of TableValue (Index)) or Index is advanced past the end of the table (in this event, the value of Found will remain False, signifying that no match was made). An example of the use of this procedure in the context of a complete program is found in the solution to the following problem.

■ **Problem Statement.** Write a program to allow users to enter the two-character abbreviations of U.S. state names and find out the full name of the state.

■ **Problem Analysis.** The program for solving this problem requires a table showing the state name abbreviations and the associated full state names. The program must first load the table with the abbreviations and associated names; then the user can access information from the table as desired. The basic plan for the program is as follows:

STATE NAME LOOKUP PROGRAM (P11a)

1.0 Load table

2.0 Process user requests for information from table

In this case, the table arguments will be the two-character abbreviations and the table values will be the full state names. The actual argument will be the abbreviation entered by the user. The actual value will be the state name associated with the actual argument. A Boolean variable, Found, will be used to communicate the result of the search procedure. After searching the table, if Found is True, the program will write the actual value. If Found is False, the program should write a message, such as "State not in Table."

We shall need to create a data structure to store the table. Several alternatives are available; we choose to use a record structure that is made up of three components: the number of states represented in the table (the table limit), an array of state abbreviations (the table arguments), and a parallel array of state names (the table values). This choice enables us to pass the entire table to a procedure or function using just one parameter and ensures that all relevant parts of the table are available to the subprogram.

There are two possible alternatives for loading data into a table: The values could be included as constants in the program, or they could be loaded from a file. Because these values are very stable, it makes sense to place them as constants in the program. (In another situation, where the table values were subject to change, it might make much more sense to place the values in a file that could be updated when needed to reflect changes as they occur. Choosing to put the values into the program as constants means that the program would have to be recompiled if changes occur.)

■ **Problem Solution.** A solution to this problem is shown in Figure 11.1 as Program 11a. Note that the table contains only 7 state names, although the arrays are set up for 50 elements. This was done to conserve space; the other state names could be added if desired. For reasons that will become evident shortly, the sequence of abbreviations in this representative table are in alphabetical order; however, the program does not require that the table arguments be in any particular sequence. You can extend the table with state names chosen at random, and the search procedure will continue to function correctly.

Note that the procedure Search declares Table to be a variable parameter, even though, technically, Table is imported into the procedure, not exported from it. The declaration of Table as a variable parameter was done to save memory; remember that a local copy of all value parameters is made at the time of invocation of a procedure. There is no real need to allocate the additional memory and take the time to make a local copy of the arrays that constitute Table each time the procedure Search is executed. In other respects, the implementation of Search follows the general sequential search procedure just presented.

11.2.1 Time Out

1. Compile and execute Program 11a. Test the program with states that are listed in the table and states that are not.
2. Extend the table by adding new entries. Remember that you must also change the table limit (NumberOfStates). Verify that the program does not require that the table arguments be in sequence to perform its function properly.
3. Create a Text file containing the data to be loaded into the table. (Each line of the file should contain the two-character abbreviation, followed by the state name.) Modify the procedure LoadStateTable to load the table with the content of the Text file. Verify that the program continues to function as before.

```
program P11a (Input, Output);
{Program to implement sequential search of an unsorted table}
const
     InputPrompt = 'Enter abbreviation for state (* to stop) ';
     Sentinal = '*';
type
     AbbreviationType = string[2];
     StateNameType = string[15];
     StateTableType =
          record
               NumberOfStates : Integer;
               Abbreviation : array[1..50] of AbbreviationType;
               StateName : array[1..50] of StateNameType
          end;
var
     StateTable          : StateTableType;
     AbbreviationOfName : AbbreviationType;
     ActualName          : StateNameType;
     Found               : Boolean;
{**********************************************************************}
     procedure LoadStateTable (var Table : StateTableType);
     {Procedure to load content of the state table; only a representative
          sample of data is included}
     begin {LoadStateTable}
          with Table do
               begin
                    Abbreviation[1] := 'AZ';
                    StateName[1]  := 'Arizona';
                    Abbreviation[2] := 'FL';
                    StateName[2]  := 'Florida';
                    Abbreviation[3] := 'NY';
                    StateName[3]  := 'New York';
                    Abbreviation[4] := 'TN';
                    StateName[4]  := 'Tennessee';
                    Abbreviation[5] := 'TX';
                    StateName[5]  := 'Texas';
                    Abbreviation[6] := 'VT';
                    StateName[6]  := 'Vermont';
                    Abbreviation[7] := 'WY';
                    StateName[7]  := 'Wyoming';
                    NumberOfStates := 7
               end;    {with}
     end;    {LoadStateTable}
{-----------------------------------------------------------------------}
```

Figure 11.1(a) Program 11a: Declaration part (part 1 of 2 parts).

4. Modify Program 11a to allow the user to add elements to the table during the execution of the program. When the actual argument is not found in the table, the program should give the user the option of adding the abbreviation and its associated state name to the table. (Simply increment NumberOfStates, and assign appropriate values to Abbreviation [NumberOfStates] and StateName[NumberOfStates].) If you have modified the program as suggested in Exercise 3, it will be necessary to write the new table to a file at the conclusion of the program in order for the system to "remember" the new data during the next execution of the program.

```
        procedure Search (var Table : StateTableType;
                              ActualArgument : AbbreviationType;
                         var ActualValue : StateNameType;
                         var Found : Boolean);
    {Sequential search of an unsorted table}
    var
        Index : Integer;
    begin    {Search}
        with Table do
            begin
                Found := False;
                Index := 1;
                while (Index <= NumberOfStates) and (not Found) do
                    if Abbreviation[Index] = ActualArgument then
                        begin
                            ActualValue := StateName[Index];
                            Found := True
                        end
                    else
                        Index := Index + 1;
            end    {with}
    end;    {Search}
{*********************************************************************}
begin    {Main Program}

{1.0 Load Table}

    LoadStateTable (StateTable);

{2.0 Process user requests for information from the table}

    Write (InputPrompt);
    Readln (AbbreviationOfName);
    while AbbreviationOfName <> Sentinal do
        begin
            Search (StateTable, AbbreviationOfName,
                ActualName, Found);
            if Found then
                Writeln ('Name of state is ', ActualName)
            else
                Writeln ('State not in table');
            Write (InputPrompt);
            Readln (AbbreviationOfName)
        end    {while}

end.    {Main Program}
```

Figure 11.1(b) Program 11a: Sequential search procedure and statement part (part 2 of 2 parts).

5. An alternative way to create the data type StateTableType for Program 11a is as follows:

```
StateType =
    record
            Abbreviation : AbbreviationType;
            StateName : StateNameType
    end;
```

```
StateTableType =
    record
            NumberOfStates : Integer;
            StateEntry : array[1..50] of StateType
    end;
```

Which structure seems most appropriate? How would the alternative declaration affect the program code?

11.2.2 Sequential Search of a Sorted Table

If the table arguments are sorted, then it is possible to make an improvement on the sequential search procedure of the preceding section. As before, the matching process will start with the first element of the table and proceed until a match is found. The improvement comes when an actual argument is not found. If the table arguments are in ascending sequence, then it is unnecessary to look beyond the first table argument that is greater than the actual argument to determine that the actual argument is not present in the table. For example, suppose we wish to search the following list of table arguments:

```
TableArgument[1]        2
TableArgument[2]        4
TableArgument[3]        7
TableArgument[4]       10
TableArgument[5]       14
```

Suppose further that ActualArgument has the value 5. ActualArgument is greater than TableArgument[1] and TableArgument[2], but ActualArgument is less than TableArgument[3]. Because the table arguments are sorted, we know that there could not be a match for ActualArgument in the sequence of table arguments following TableArgument[3]; hence, the search process could be terminated at this point. (If the table is not sorted, then we cannot make this assumption; it would be necessary to continue the search process through to the end of the table because there might be a match for ActualArgument anywhere in the sequence.) This improvement on the Sequential Search Procedure is detailed in the following general procedure:

**SEQUENTIAL SEARCH OF A SORTED TABLE PROCEDURE
(IMPORT : TABLE, ACTUALARGUMENT;
EXPORT : ACTUALVALUE, FOUND)**

1.0 Found = False

2.0 Index = 1

3.0 Continue = True

4.0 While Index <= TableLimit and Continue Do

5.0   If TableArgument (Index) = ActualArgument Then

6.0   ActualValue = TableValue (Index)

7.0   Found = True

8.0   Continue = False

9.0   Else If TableArgument (Index) > ActualArgument Then

10.0   Continue = False

11.0   Else

12.0   Index = Index + 1

13.0   End If

14.0 End While

Note that this procedure makes use of one additional control variable, Continue, not found in the previous procedure. Initially, Continue is True, signifying that the search procedure should continue. Continue is set to False when one of two events occurs: A match for ActualArgument is encountered or the current TableArgument is greater than ActualArgument. If neither of these events occurs during a particular pass through the While loop, then the value of Continue remains True, signifying the need to test the next TableArgument. The procedure makes the assumption that the table is in ascending sequence (smallest to largest). If the table is in descending sequence (largest to smallest), then the statement at step 9.0 would be revised as follows:

9.0 Else If TableArgument (Index) < ActualArgument Then

Note also that this procedure behaves exactly as does the preceding procedure when an actual argument is present in the table; the improvement comes when an actual argument is not present in the table. In the preceding procedure, it is necessary to search the entire table every time this occurs. In this procedure, the search can be cut short; on the average, only one-half of the table needs to be searched to determine that an actual argument cannot be found.

11.2.3   *Time Out*

1. An implementation of the revised search procedure is contained in Program 11b, shown in Figure 11.2. Test this program as you did Program 11a.
2. If you revised Program 11a to allow the user to enter new table entries, it will now be necessary to make sure that the new entries are inserted in such a way that the table remains sorted, in order to use this revised procedure. *Suggestion:* Locate the position in the table for the new entry. (This is the position of the first table argument greater than the new argument.) Then move all subsequent entries down one position, starting with the last one and working your way up to the position for the new entry. (You will have to do this operation on both arrays in the table.) Now you can place the new entry into the table, and the table will remain in sequence.

11.3   BINARY SEARCH

In the preceding section, we saw how to make part of the search process more efficient if the table is sorted. Unfortunately, the procedure we developed for a sequential search of a sorted table is more efficient only in the case where the actual argument is not present in the table; if the actual argument is present, then the revised procedure is no more efficient

```
program P11b (Input, Output);
{Program to implement sequential search of a sorted table}
        .
        .
        .
    procedure Search (var Table : StateTableType;
                            ActualArgument : AbbreviationType;
                      var ActualValue : StateNameType;
                      var Found : Boolean);
    {Sequential search of a sorted table}
    var
        Index : Integer;
        Continue : Boolean;
    begin    {Search}
        with Table do
            begin
                Found := False;
                Index := 1;
                Continue := True;
                while (Index <= NumberOfStates) and Continue do
                    if Abbreviation[Index] = ActualArgument then
                        begin
                            ActualValue := StateName[Index];
                            Found := True;
                            Continue := False
                        end
                    else if Abbreviation[Index] > ActualArgument then
                            Continue := False
                        else
                            Index := Index + 1;
            end    {with}
    end;    {Search}
        .
        .
        .
end.    {Main Program}
```

Figure 11.2 Program 11b: Sequential search of a sorted table.

than its predecessor, which makes no assumption about the organization of the table. Accordingly, let us examine another approach to the problem that will be more efficient in both cases—when the argument is present and when it is not present in the table.

Suppose someone said to you, "I am thinking of a number between 1 and 100. If you tell me a number, I will tell you if you guessed it or if you must guess higher or lower to find the number." What strategy should you use to guess the number in the fewest possible number of tries? It seems clear that starting with 1 and progressing by 1 until the number is found is not optimal. A better approach would be to begin dividing the possible range of values for the number into successively smaller sets until the value is known. The best strategy is to begin in the middle—50, in this case. If 50 is not the number, then the person will respond with either higher or lower, and you will immediately know that the target number is in the range 1 to 49 or 51 to 100. In either case, you have reduced the size of the range of possibilities by one-half. The strategy can be repeated; the next guess would be the midpoint of the new known range, thus yielding a still smaller range, and so forth, until you have either guessed the number or have made the range size equal to 1, at which point there are no more alternatives and the number has been found.

We can adapt this strategy to the task of searching a sorted table. The first step would be to compare the actual argument with the table argument in the middle of the table. If this is not the one for which we are searching, then we can rule out one-half of the table, based on the comparison of the actual argument and the middle table argument. If the actual argument is greater than the middle value, then we know that the target must be in the upper half of the table; if the actual argument is smaller than the middle element, then we know that the target must be in the lower half of the table. We can then adjust the limits of the table segment under consideration and repeat the procedure with a new (and smaller) table segment. The process can be repeated until either the desired element is found or the beginning and end of the segment are adjacent elements in the table (at which point we know that the actual argument is not present in the table). This strategy is called a **binary search** because the size of the table segment is reduced by one-half each time the process is repeated.

To implement a binary search, we shall need two variables that will point to the segment of the table under consideration. We may call these variables Low and High; Low will indicate the beginning of the segment and High the end of the segment. It is useful to initialize these variables to 0 and TableSize + 1, repectively, since initially the value may be found in positions 1, 2, . . . , TableSize. We shall need two Boolean variables: Found (which will be initialized to False and set to True if the required match is made) and Continue (which will be initialized to True and set to False when either a match is found or it is determined that the ActualArgument is not present in the table). We shall also need a variable Mid, which will be the index of the table argument in the middle of the table segment under consideration. The value of Mid will be computed by adding Low and High and dividing by 2, using integer arithmetic. During each pass through the procedure, the first step will be to compute the value of Mid based on the current values of Low and High. If TableArgument[Mid] is equal to ActualArgument, then the procedure terminates, since the desired value has been located. On the other hand, if this is not the element being sought, then we adjust the limits of the table segment. If TableArgument[Mid] is less than ActualArgument, then the target value lies in the upper part of the table segment, so we replace the value of Low by Mid; if TableArgument[Mid] is greater than ActualArgument, then the target value is in the lower part of the table, so we replace the value of High by Mid. After making the replacement, we can determine whether the beginning and end of the segment are adjacent elements (if High − Low = 1); if this is the case, then we can conclude that the ActualArgument is not present in the table. This procedure is more formally stated in the following plan:

**BINARY SEARCH PROCEDURE (IMPORT : TABLE, ACTUALARGUMENT;
EXPORT : ACTUALVALUE, FOUND)**

1.0 Found = False
2.0 Continue = True
3.0 Low = 0
4.0 High = TableSize + 1
5.0 While Continue Do
6.0   Mid = (Low + High)/ 2
7.0   If Table Argument[Mid] = ActualArgument Then
8.0   ActualValue = TableArgument[Mid]

9.0		Found = True
10.0		Continue = False
11.0	Else	
12.0		If TableArgument[Mid] < ActualArgument Then
13.0		Low = Mid
14.0		Else
15.0		High = Mid
16.0		End If
17.0		If High − Low = 1 Then
18.0		Continue = False
19.0		End If
20.0	End If	
21.0	End While	

At this point, it will probably be helpful to you to take a few minutes to trace the execution of the foregoing procedure with sample data, as shown in Figure 11.3. Experimenting with various actual arguments, some of which are present in the table and some of which are not, should convince you that the procedure is correct and provide you with a good intuitive feel for how the procedure works.

A revision of the Search procedure from Program 11a using the binary search method is shown in Figure 11.4. Note that the computation of Mid makes use of the Integer division operator div instead of the Real operator /. This is in keeping with the previous description of the procedure.

11.3.1 Time Out

1. Using tables similar to those shown in Figure 11.3, trace the execution of the binary search procedure for the following table and each of the following actual arguments:

TableArgument[1]	A
TableArgument[2]	C
TableArgument[3]	F
TableArgument[4]	J
TableArgument[5]	K
TableArgument[6]	N
TableArgument[7]	T
TableArgument[8]	Y

(a)	ActualArgument	C
(b)	ActualArgument	N
(c)	ActualArgument	E
(d)	ActualArgument	Z

TableArgument

[1]	2
[2]	4
[3]	7
[4]	10
[5]	14

ActualArgument

Low	High	Mid	Found	Continue	Comment
0	6	3	False	True	TableArgument[3] < 10
3		4	True	False	TableArgument[4] = 10

ActualArgument

4

Low	High	Mid	Found	Continue	Comment
0	6	3	False	True	TableArgument[3] > 4
	3	1			TableArgument[1] < 4
1		2	True	False	TableArgument[2] = 4

ActualArgument

12

Low	High	Mid	Found	Continue	Comment
0	6	3	False	True	TableArgument[3] < 12
3	6	4			TableArgument[4] < 12
4	6	5			TableArgument[5] > 12
	5			False	High − Low = 1

Figure 11.3　Sample executions of the binary search.

2. Test Program 11c. You may wish to add some output to the procedure to help you trace its execution for your sample data.

11.4　HASH TABLES

Even though a binary search is very efficient, there are times when it is desirable to have an even faster search procedure. The optimum search is one that requires only one operation to determine whether the actual argument is present. This can sometimes be accomplished when the table arguments coincide with the location of the table value. The actual argument can be used as a subscript to access the required table value. This is called *direct access*; it was the technique used in Program 9a, where we used a table of 12

```
program P11c (Input, Output);
{Program to implement binary search of a sorted table}
    .
    .
    .
    procedure Search (var Table : StateTableType;
                          ActualArgument : AbbreviationType;
                      var ActualValue : StateNameType;
                      var Found : Boolean);
    {Binary search of a sorted table}
    var
        Low, Mid, High : Integer;
        Continue : Boolean;
    begin    {Search}
        with Table do
            begin
                Found := False;
                Low := 0;
                High := NumberOfStates + 1;
                Continue := True;
                while Continue do
                  begin
                    Mid := (Low + High) div 2;
                    if Abbreviation[Mid] = ActualArgument then
                        begin
                            ActualValue := StateName[Mid];
                            Found := True;
                            Continue := False
                        end
                    else
                        begin
                            if Abbreviation[Mid] < ActualArgument then
                                Low := Mid
                            else
                                High := Mid;
                            if (High - Low) = 1 then
                                Continue := False
                        end    {if}
                  end    {while}
            end    {with}
    end;    {Search}
    .
    .
    .
end.    {Main Program}
```

Figure 11.4 Program 11c: Binary search.

elements to store the names of the months. The location of the name in the table corresponded to the number of the month. (The first element of the table stored 'January', the second element stored 'February', and so forth.) In this instance, direct access to the table by using the actual argument (a month number) as a subscript was possible. In other situations where table arguments are not so neatly arranged, we can construct a table that is almost as efficient by using a randomizing technique called a hash function.

The basic idea of a hash table is to scatter the table entries randomly throughout the table by using a function (called a *hash function*) to determine their locations. The same function is then used to search the table. In the table-loading process, the hash function accepts the table argument and returns a number in the range 1 to the table size. In general, this number is the expected location in the table for placement of the table argument and its associated value. In order to search the table, the same function is applied to the actual argument, and the resulting value is the expected location of the associated table entry (if it is present in the table). Unfortunately, hash functions that yield unique values for the entire range of possible table arguments are rarely available. That is, if the hash function value is used directly to place entries in the table, two entries could end up in the same location, which of course, is an impossible situation. Because of this possibility, the value of the hash function for a particular argument is actually used as the starting point for the search process. In creating a **hash table**, if the table element at the location specified by the hash function is already used, then a sequential search to locate an unused element for this table entry is employed. A similar strategy is used when searching the table to locate the element corresponding to some actual argument.

A great deal of research has been performed to determine optimum conditions for applying hash tables. It has been shown that the method works best if the hash table size is at least one-third larger than the number of active table entries. It has also been shown that the technique works best when the table size is chosen as a prime number (a number that is divisible only by 1 and itself). Almost any function that you could imagine has been proposed at one time or another for use as a hash function. In general, nothing has been shown to yield better results than computing the remainder after dividing the argument by the table size and then adding 1. For example, if the hash table contains 11 elements, the hash function would be

$$\text{Argument mod } 11 + 1$$

This function returns a value in the range 1 to 11, which corresponds to a location in a table with 11 elements.

An example will help you understand the table-loading and table-searching processes. For simplicity, let us ignore the table values and concentrate on the table arguments. Suppose you wish to create a hash table for the following arguments: 23, 20, 16, and 13. Let us use a table of size 7. The first task is to initialize the table entries so that all elements contain null values. A null value is some value that does not occur among the arguments to be stored in the table. (This is necessary in order to make it possible to determine whether a table element is available or has already been used.) Let us assume that the number 0 does not occur among the table arguments, so we can place this value in each table entry. At this point, the table will appear as follows:

TableArgument[1]   0

TableArgument[2]   0

TableArgument[3]   0

TableArgument[4]   0

TableArgument[5]   0

TableArgument[6]   0

TableArgument[7]   0

In this state, all table entries are available.

Now we will place the first entry in the table. The argument is 23 and the table size is 7, so we apply the hash function to obtain 23 mod $7 + 1 = 2 + 1 = 3$. The content of TableArgument[3] indicates that this entry is free, so we place 23 into the third table entry. The table now has one nonzero entry, as follows:

TableArgument[1]	0
TableArgument[2]	0
TableArgument[3]	23
TableArgument[4]	0
TableArgument[5]	0
TableArgument[6]	0
TableArgument[7]	0

The second argument is 20. Applying the hash function yields 20 mod $7 + 1 = 7$. The seventh table entry is free, so 20 is placed in this location:

TableArgument[1]	0
TableArgument[2]	0
TableArgument[3]	23
TableArgument[4]	0
TableArgument[5]	0
TableArgument[6]	0
TableArgument[7]	20

The next argument is 16. The hash function yields 16 mod $7 + 1 = 2 + 1 = 3$. Unfortunately, TableArgument[3] has already been used, since it does not contain the null value. (The arguments 16 and 23 are called *synonyms* because they yield the same value of the hash function.) When this occurs, we must search for some table entry that is free. Beginning with the entry following location 3, we seek an entry that is free. Fortunately, the fourth element is unused, so 16 will be placed in this location:

TableArgument[1]	0
TableArgument[2]	0
TableArgument[3]	23
TableArgument[4]	16
TableArgument[5]	0
TableArgument[6]	0
TableArgument[7]	20

The last argument we wish to place in the table is 13. The hash function yields 13 mod $7 + 1 = 6 + 1 = 7$. This table location is in use, so we must search for an unused table entry. When this occurred before, we looked at the next entry. This time we are already at the last entry. This problem is solved by treating the table as circular; that is, the element following the last element is the first one. The first entry is not in use, so 13 will be placed at this location. (If the first entry had been in use, we would have continued our search until the first free entry was located.) The table now appears as follows:

TableArgument[1]	13
TableArgument[2]	0
TableArgument[3]	23
TableArgument[4]	16
TableArgument[5]	0
TableArgument[6]	0
TableArgument[7]	20

Now let us consider the search process. Suppose the ActualArgument has the value 16. We apply the hash function to the ActualArgument, yielding 16 mod 7 + 1 = 3. If all goes well, we would expect TableArgument[3] to be equal to 16. Unfortunately it is not, so we must begin a sequential search. We find that TableArgument[4] is equal to 16, so the required table entry has been located. Now let us attempt to locate an ActualArgument, 12, that is not in the table. The hash function yields 12 mod 7 + 1 = 6. We find that TableArgument[6] is unused, so we conclude that 12 is not present in the table. (If it were present in the table, it would be found in this location.) Now suppose the ActualArgument has the value 6. Applying the hash function yields 6 mod 7 + 1 = 7. Although TableArgument[7] is not equal to 6, we *cannot* conclude that 6 is not in the table. (Six might have been a synonym for some other value.) Instead, we must conduct a search of successive elements of the table. The logical successor to the seventh element is the first element. The value of TableArgument[1] is not equal to 6, so we continue with the second element. TableArgument[2] is unused, so we can now conclude that 6 is not present in the table. Note that only when you encounter an unused table element can you determine that an ActualArgument is not present in the table.

Three procedures are required to manipulate a hash table: one procedure to place null values in the table entries (InitializeHashTable), a second procedure to load the table arguments and associated values into the table (LoadHashTable), and, finally, a procedure to search the table (Search). A plan for InitializeHashTable is as follows:

INITIALIZEHASHTABLE (EXPORT : HASHTABLE)

1.0 For Index = 1 to TableSize Do
2.0   TableArgument[Index] = NullValue
3.0 End For

The procedure LoadHashTable is more elaborate. It will import an Argument and its associated Value and export the hash table. Using the hash function and the searching procedure just outlined, it will place each Argument and the associated Value in the proper entry of HashTable. A plan for this procedure is as follows:

LOADHASHTABLE (IMPORT : ARGUMENT, VALUE; EXPORT : HASHTABLE)

1.0 Location = Hash (Argument)
2.0 While TableArgument[Location] not = NullValue Do
3.0   Location = Location + 1
4.0   If Location > TableSize Then
5.0   Location = 1
6.0   End If
7.0 End While
8.0 TableArgument[Location] = Argument
9.0 TableValue[Location] = Value

Finally, let us formalize the search procedure just presented informally. The Search procedure will import ActualArgument and HashTable; it will export ActualValue and a Boolean variable Found, which will indicate whether ActualArgument was present in the table or not:

SEARCH (IMPORT : HASHTABLE, ACTUALARGUMENT; EXPORT : ACTUALVALUE, FOUND)

1.0 Found = False
2.0 Index = Hash (ActualArgument)
3.0 Continue = True
4.0 While Continue Do
5.0   If TableArgument[Index] = ActualArgument Then
6.0   ActualValue = TableValue[Index]
7.0   Found = True
8.0   Continue = False
9.0   Else
10.0   If TableArgument[Index] = NullValue Then
11.0   Continue = False
12.0   Else
13.0   Index = Index + 1
14.0   If Index > TableSize Then
15.0   Index = 1
16.0   End If
17.0   End If
18.0   End If
19.0 End While

Pascal implementations of these procedures are shown in Program 11d, which is contained in Figure 11.5. This program is a revision of Program 11a using the hash table technique. The program retains the sequentially ordered StateTable, which is loaded with constant values in the procedure LoadStateTable. The contents of this table are then passed to the procedure LoadHashTable as the table arguments and values to be placed in the hash table. (Note that the procedure LoadHashTable used in the program differs a little from the general load procedure presented before. In the program, we pass the entire table of arguments and values (StateTable), instead of individual arguments and values, for placement into HashTable.) The hash table size is chosen to be 71. This is a somewhat arbitrary choice, but it meets the guidelines set forth earlier: It is at least one-third larger than the maximum number of elements that the table will need to hold, and it is a prime number.

In the examples presented previously, we assumed that the table arguments were integer values. In this program, the arguments are actually strings of length 2. It is necessary to convert the string value into a numeric value for use in the hash function. The Ord function is used for this purpose. The actual equation is as follows:

```
Hash := ((Ord (CharacterString[1]) +
         Ord (CharacterString[2])) mod HashTableSize) + 1
```

We choose to add the ordinal values of the characters; in fact, we could have chosen to multiply these values or subtract them. The important point is that both characters must be used in order to reduce the number of synonyms produced by the hash function. If we had chosen to use only the first character of the state name abbreviation, then all the states beginning with the same first letter would have been synonyms. The hash table technique works best when the hash function generates as few synonyms as possible.

Although the hash table technique results in more efficient search times than other techniques, it is not without its disadvantages. A primary problem is that, to be efficient, it requires more memory than is needed for the actual data to be stored in the table. For a large table or in a machine with limited available memory, this could be a primary consideration. A second disadvantage is that the order of the data is lost in the creation of the hash table. In some situations, you may wish to keep the data in its original sequence for some purpose unrelated to its use as a reference table. If this is a requirement, then the hash table technique is not appropriate.

11.4.1 Time Out

1. Create a hash table containing the following data:

Argument	Value
3	Widget
25	Gidget
21	Zidget
32	Digit

```pascal
program P11d (Input, Output);
{Program to implement hash table and related search procedure}
const
     InputPrompt = 'Enter abbreviation for state (* to stop) ';
     Sentinal = '*';
     HashTableSize = 71;
type
     AbbreviationType = string[2];
     StateNameType = string[15];
     StateTableType =
         record
               NumberOfStates : Integer;
               Abbreviation : array[1..50] of AbbreviationType;
               StateName : array[1..50] of StateNameType
         end;
     HashTableType =
         record
               Abbreviation : array[1..HashTableSize]
                                   of AbbreviationType;
               StateName : array[1..HashTableSize]
                                   of StateNameType;
         end;
var
     StateTable          : StateTableType;
     HashTable           : HashTableType;
     AbbreviationOfName  : AbbreviationType;
     ActualName          : StateNameType;
     Found               : Boolean;
{*************************************************************************}
     procedure LoadStateTable (var Table : StateTableType);
       .
       .
       .
     end;    {LoadStateTable}
{-----------------------------------------------------------------------}
     procedure InitializeHashTable (var HashTable : HashTableType);
        {Procedure to place null values into all elements of HashTable}
        var
              Index : Integer;
        begin     {InitializeHashTable}
              with HashTable do
                   for Index := 1 to HashTableSize do
                         Abbreviation[Index] := '';
        end;
{-----------------------------------------------------------------------}
     function Hash (CharacterString : AbbreviationType) : Integer;
        {Function to convert value of two character string into an Integer
          in the range 1 to HashTableSize}
        begin   {Hash}
              Hash := ((Ord(CharacterString[1]) +
                         Ord(CharacterString[2])) mod HashTableSize) + 1
        end;    {Hash}
{-----------------------------------------------------------------------}
```

Figure 11.5(a) Program 11d: Initial declarations (part 1 of 3 parts).

```
     procedure LoadHashTable (var HashTable : HashTableType;
                              var StateTable : StateTableType);
     {Procedure to place elements of StateTable into HashTable
          using hash function}
     var
          Index, Location : Integer;
     begin    {LoadHashTable}
          for Index := 1 to StateTable.NumberOfStates do
              begin
                    Location := Hash (StateTable.Abbreviation[Index]);
                    while HashTable.Abbreviation[Location] <> '' do
                        begin
                              Location := Location + 1;
                              if Location > HashTableSize then
                                 Location := 1;
                        end;    {while}
                    HashTable.Abbreviation[Location] :=
                          StateTable.Abbreviation[Index];
                    HashTable.StateName[Location] :=
                          StateTable.StateName[Index];
              end    {for}
     end;     {LoadHashTable}
{-------------------------------------------------------------------}
     procedure Search (var Table : HashTableType;
                           ActualArgument : AbbreviationType;
                       var ActualValue : StateNameType;
                       var Found : Boolean);
     {Search of a hash table}
     var
          Index : Integer;
          Continue : Boolean;
     begin    {Search}
          with Table do
              begin
                    Found := False;
                    Index := Hash (ActualArgument);
                    Continue := True;
                    while Continue do
                        if Abbreviation[Index] = ActualArgument then
                           begin
                                 ActualValue := StateName[Index];
                                 Found := True;
                                 Continue := False
                           end
                        else if Abbreviation[Index] = '' then
                                Continue := False
                        else
                            begin
                                 Index := Index + 1;
                                 if Index > HashTableSize then
                                    Index := 1
                            end;    {if}
              end    {with}
     end;     {Search}
{*******************************************************************}
```

Figure 11.5(b) Program 11d: Declarations of LoadHashTable and Search.

```
begin    {Main Program}

{1.0 Load Tables}

     LoadStateTable (StateTable);
     InitializeHashTable (HashTable);
     LoadHashTable (HashTable, StateTable);

{2.0 Process user requests for information from the table}

     Write (InputPrompt);
     Readln (AbbreviationOfName);
     while AbbreviationOfName <> Sentinal do
          begin
               Search (HashTable, AbbreviationOfName,
                    ActualName, Found);
               if Found then
                  Writeln ('Name of state is ', ActualName)
               else
                  Writeln ('State not in table');
               Write (InputPrompt);
               Readln (AbbreviationOfName)
          end   {while}

end.    {Main Program}
```

Figure 11.5(c) Statement part (part 3 of 3 parts).

The hash table should be of length 11. Place the entries in the table in the order given.

2. Compile and execute Program 11d. Add data to the table by modifying the procedure LoadStateTable and adjusting the value of NumberOfStates. Note that you can add data to the table without regard to order.

3. In Program 11d, reduce the HashTableSize to 17 by changing the value of the constant HashTableSize. Write out the content of HashTable after it is loaded. Compare the order of the data in the HashTable with the order of the data in StateTable.

4. Modify Program 11d to allow the user to add new abbreviations and names to the table during the execution of the program. You will have to write a procedure similar to LoadHashTable, but applicable to adding individual table entries.

5. Modify the hash function to use multiplication rather than addition of the ordinal values of the two characters in the abbreviation of the state name. As in Exercise 4, write out the content of the hash table after it has been loaded. Compare the output produced here with the output produced in Exercise 4. How do you account for the fact that, although the two tables are different, the program continues to work as before?

6. In the procedure that loads an element into a hash table, a problem occurs when the table is full. Modify the pseudocode version of the procedure LoadHashTable presented before to handle the problem.

11.5 ANALYSIS OF PROCEDURES

In our discussion of search procedures, we have alluded to the fact that some procedures are more efficient than others. Analyzing procedures in these terms forms a very important part of the discipline of computer science. One basis for analyzing a procedure is time: In general, if you have a choice between two procedures for carrying out a given task, the one that will take the least amount of time is the more desirable. Because the actual amount of elapsed time to execute a task is dependent on a great many variables (including the type of computer used, the skill of the programmer who wrote the program, and the type of program translator used, to mention just a few), an analysis of a procedure must be carried out in terms of the number of operations required. In general, a procedure that requires more operations will take longer to execute than one that takes fewer operations.

To simplify the analysis still further, we look only at the number of repetitions of the innermost loop in a procedure that is iterative in nature. For example, we say that the following procedure requires N operations:

    For Index = 1 to N Do

        ...

    End For

Notice that we do not care a great deal about the amount of work that is carried out in the body of the loop. The actual number of operations that must be carried out by the machine will be kN, where k is some constant. For purposes of analysis, we do not care very much about the value of k; we are more concerned with the relationship between the amount of time that will be required to execute the procedure and the value of N. In this case, the amount of time will be related directly to the value of N. That is, if N doubles in size, then we expect the execution time to double as well. This type of analysis gives us a rough method for comparing dissimilar procedures. Any procedure in which the execution time is directly proportional to the value of a single variable is said to be an **order** N (abbreviated **O**(N)) procedure.

The following procedure requires N^2 repetitions of its innermost loop:

    For Index-1 = 1 to N Do
        For Index-2 = 1 to N Do

            ...

        End For
    End For

We say that this procedure is an **O**(N^2) procedure; the time required for its execution is proportional to N^2. This means that if N doubles in size, then the time increases fourfold; if N is increased by a factor of 3, then the time is increased by a factor of 9; and so forth.

Let us use this technique to analyze the search procedures discussed in previous sections of this chapter. We are interested in two aspects of each procedure: its worst case behavior and its expected behavior. The worst case analysis assumes that the loop is executed to its logical completion. The expected behavior analysis focuses on what can be expected on average for a large number of executions based on an unbiased sampling of data. In analyzing search procedures, we must consider the two possible outcomes: Either an actual argument is found (if it is present in the table), or it is not found (if it is not present in the table). Thus, each procedure will be analyzed using the following matrix:

	Worst case	**Expected**
Find an argument		
Argument not present		

Let us begin with the sequential search of an unsorted table. Recall that in this technique we begin at the beginning of the table and proceed sequentially until we either locate the required table argument or exceed the limit of the table. Assuming that the table size is N, the worst case for finding an argument is to locate the entry in the Nth location, thereby requiring N repetitions of the loop. For randomly chosen arguments, however, we would expect roughly half of them to be located in the first half of the table and half of them in the second half of the table; in general, we would expect that an argument could be located in an average of $N/2$ repetitions of the loop. Now consider the behavior of this procedure when an argument is not present. The worst case behavior is the same as the expected behavior: The body of the loop must be executed N times to determine that the argument is not present, since the actual argument must be compared with each table argument to make this determination. This procedure is categorized as an $\mathbf{O}(N)$ procedure because there is a possibility that the procedure will take N repetitions to terminate.

Now consider the sequential search of a sorted table. Remember that in this procedure we are able to stop when we either locate the argument or find a table argument that is greater than the actual argument. The worst case and expected behaviors of this procedure are the same as in the sequential search of an unsorted table. The worst case behavior to determine that an argument is not present is also the same as for the unsorted table. The major difference in this procedure is in the expected behavior for determining that an argument is not present: We would expect that on average about half the table would need to be examined to determine that an element is not present, so the expected behavior in this case is $N/2$.

Analysis of the binary search is a bit more difficult than that required for the preceding two methods. Recall that the binary search involves successively dividing the table into smaller segments, each of which is half the size of the one that preceded it. The procedure will terminate when either the actual argument matches the table argument at the midpoint of a segment or the segment size is reduced to 1. The number of times that a table of size N can be divided into segments in this manner is based on the logarithm to the base 2 of N. (Recall that logarithms are powers of the base. Thus, $\log_2 8 = 3$ because $2^3 = 8$.) The actual number of repetitions of the binary search in the worst case to locate an element or determine that an element is not present is the smallest integer greater than $\log_2 N$. For simplicity, we say that the binary search is an $\mathbf{O}(\log_2 N)$ procedure. The expected behavior in locating an argument is, of course, somewhat less than $\log_2 N$ (we may encounter the desired element in one operation if it happens to be the midpoint of the table, or in two repetitions if it happens to lie at the midpoint of the second segment, and so forth). It is difficult to estimate the exact expected behavior; we will only note that it is less than $\log_2 N$.

The final search technique that we discussed was the hash table. Recall that this technique requires more space than is actually used to store data, but we gain efficiency in search time. The worst case behavior for either finding an argument or determining that one is not present occurs when the table is full; when this happens, it may take N repetitions of the body of the loop. When the table is not full, we expect to locate an entry or determine that an entry is not present on the first try most of the time; occasionally this task may require 2, 3, or more comparisons. The average number of repetitions for a large amount of data would be expected to be somewhat larger than 1; the exact value would be dependent on the specifics of the data, the table size, and the searches performed. (Experiments have shown that this value is primarily dependent on how full the table is; it tends to increase rapidly when the table is more than 66% full.) Because the worst case behavior of this technique requires N operations, it is classed as an **O**(N) procedure. However, the expected behavior makes the procedure almost as good as direct access (where the actual argument is used directly as a subscript). Direct access requires one operation to locate an entry or determine that one is not present; this technique is classed as an **O**(1) procedure. This means that the behavior of the procedure is not affected by the size of the table. In general, an **O**(1) procedure is the best choice of all if it is available to accomplish the task at hand.

Our analysis of search procedures is summarized in Figure 11.6. The expected behavior to determine that an element is not present forms the best basis for ranking the procedures in terms of desirability. The best procedure is direct access. The next best is the hash table, followed by binary search, sequential search of a sorted table, and sequential search of an unsorted table. The last of these procedures is the method of last resort.

11.5.1   Time Out

On a piece of graph paper, draw a graph of the expected behavior of each of the search procedures in the case that an argument is not present. Note the dramatic differences among the procedures as N increases.

Method	Category	Worst Case		Expected	
		Find an Argument	Argument not Present	Find an Argument	Argument not Present
Direct access	**O**(1)	1	1	1	1
Hash table	**O**(N)	N	N	> 1	> 1
Binary	**O**($\log_2 N$)	$\log_2 N$	$\log_2 N$	$< \log_2 N$	$\log_2 N$
Sequential search of a sorted table	**O**(N)	N	N	$N/2$	$N/2$
Sequential search of an unsorted table	**O**(N)	N	N	$N/2$	N

Figure 11.6 Summary of analysis of search procedures.

11.6   INTRODUCTION TO SORTING

One task that occurs time after time in processing data is that of resequencing data. The process of changing the sequence of a set of data items is called *sorting*. You have probably performed this task in different contexts many times. When you play a card game, it is often useful to arrange the cards in your hand into some sequence that is different from the random sequence in which they were dealt. In a filing system, it is almost imperative to maintain the files in some sequence (usually alphabetical) in order to reduce the amount of effort required to locate a particular file when it is needed. In these cases, you use some technique to rearrange the cards or the file folders into sequence—in data processing terminology, you perform a sort.

For example, consider the following data:

$$23$$
$$-5$$
$$2$$
$$80$$
$$16$$

It is possible to **sort** these data into two different sequences: ascending (from smallest largest) and descending (from largest to smallest). These two sequences are as follows:

Ascending sequence	Descending sequence
−5	80
2	23
16	16
23	2
80	−5

The most commonly required sequence is ascending; for this reason, we will concentrate on sorting for ascending sequence. Every technique for sorting can be modified slightly to obtain a descending sequence if this is needed.

Often, you will need to sort data that are organized either as an array of records or as parallel arrays. In either case, one field in the record or one of the arrays must be designated the *sort key*. The sort key is the data item to be used in resequencing the data. For example, consider the following data, which contain the social security number, name, and a sex code for a group of people:

111111111	Jones John	M
333333333	Smith Mary	F
222222222	Doe James	M
100000000	Brown James	M
200000000	Green Sue	F

You may need to sort this data into sequence by social security number for one purpose and into sequence by name for another purpose. If the social security number is designated the sort key, then the data would be sorted as follows:

100000000	Brown James	M
111111111	Jones John	M
200000000	Green Sue	F
222222222	Doe James	M
333333333	Smith Mary	F

If the name is the sort key, then the data would be sorted as follows:

100000000	Brown James	M
222222222	Doe James	M
200000000	Green Sue	F
111111111	Jones John	M
333333333	Smith Mary	F

Sometimes, more than one sort key may be required. For example, we may need to sort the data into sequence using the sex code as the primary key (all people with the same sex code value would be grouped together in the data sequence) and the name or social security number as the secondary key (for each value of the sex code, the data would be in sequence by name or social security number). Procedures that allow you to sort using multiple sort keys are outside the scope of this text. We shall focus on a variety of sort procedures that allow you to rearrange data based on a single sort key of your choosing.

As we discovered in our investigation of search procedures, there are considerations of efficiency that lead us to prefer some procedures over others. In the case of sorting, this is particularly true, since sort procedures tend to take a great deal of time to execute.

11.7 INSERTION SORT

Suppose you wish to create a sorted list of elements from data entered by the program user in random sequence. One approach that you could take would be to place the first item into the list in the first location and then, for each additional element, insert the new value into the list in such a way that the list is always in sequence. That is, you could search the existing list to determine the location for the new element, move all the elements from that position to the end of the list down one position, and insert the new value. After each value has been processed, the list will be in sequence.

For example, suppose the data to be placed in the list is as follows: 23, −5, 2, 80, 16. Then the initial value goes at the head of the list. After this value has been read, the list is as follows:

Data[1] | 23 |
Data[2] | |
Data[3] | |
Data[4] | |
Data[5] | |

Now let us process the next item, which is −5. The first task is to search the list to determine the location for the value. The location occupied by the first element in the list that is greater than the item to be inserted is the location for the new item. In this case Data[1] is greater than −5, so the new item must be placed in position 1. After making this determination, we move elements from this position to the end of the list down one and then place the new value into Data[1]. After this operation is performed, the list is as follows:

Data[1] | -5 |
Data[2] | 23 | ◄─── *This item moved down*
Data[3] | |
Data[4] | |
Data[5] | |

The next item is 2. Searching the list shows that this item should be placed in position 2; the new list is as follows:

Data[1] | -5 |
Data[2] | 2 |
Data[3] | 23 | ◄─── *This item moved down*
Data[4] | |
Data[5] | |

The next item is 80, which is greater than the last item in the current list. This item must, therefore, be placed in the location that follows the end of the current list. The new list is as follows:

Data[1] | -5 |
Data[2] | 2 |
Data[3] | 23 |
Data[4] | 80 | ◄─── *This item placed at end of list*
Data[5] | |

The last item is 16. Data[3] is the first element that is greater than 16, so 16 belongs in position 3. Accordingly, we move the segment of the list beginning at position 3 down one position (beginning with the last element and working up to position 3) and insert the new value in position 3. The final list is as follows:

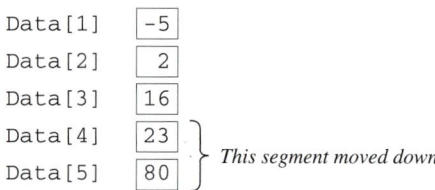

Let us design a program to perform this task for data entered by the user. We will process integer data, so let us call the list IntegerArray; we will assume that there is a maximum of 100 values to be placed in the list. A variable NumberOfItems will be needed to determine the actual length of the list. Let us also assume that none of the data items have value 0, so that the user can enter this value to terminate the data-entry process. The program should allow the user to enter the data and then write out the data in sequence. An initial plan for the program is as follows:

INSERTION SORT PROGRAM (PRELIMINARY PLAN)

1.0 Enter Data
2.0 List Data in sequence

Refining this plan using the scheme just described yields the following:

INSERTION SORT PROGRAM (P11e)

1.0 Enter Data
    1.1 Read DataItem
    1.2 NumberOfItems = 0
    1.3 While DataItem not = 0 Do
    1.4   NumberOfItems = NumberOfItems + 1
    1.5   Insert DataItem into IntegerArray
    1.6   Read DataItem
    1.7 End While
2.0 List Data in sequence
3.0 Wait

We will implement the insertion procedure in Module 1.5 as a procedure that will import the array, the new items, and the number of items and export the array with the new item in its proper place. A plan for this procedure is as follows:

**PROCEDURE INSERT (IMPORT: INTARRAY, NEWITEM,
            NUMBEROFELEMENTS; EXPORT:
            INTARRAY)**

1.0 If NumberOfElements $= 1$ Then
2.0   IntArray[1] = NewItem
3.0 Else
4.0   If NewItem $>$ last item in the existing list Then
5.0   IntArray[NumberOfItems] = NewItem
6.0   Else
7.0   Find first Location such that
                IntArray[Location] $>$ NewItem
8.0   Move segment of IntArray from end of the list
                to Location down one position
9.0   IntArray[Location] = NewItem
10.0   End If
11.0 End If

Program 11e, which is shown in Figure 11.7, is an implementation of the preceding program plan. Note that the task of listing the content of the array is coded as a procedure and used in the main program and the Insert procedure. By repeating the listing as each item is added to the list, you can watch the list grow and verify that it is indeed in sequence after each item is added to it.

How efficient is this sort procedure? To answer this question, we must determine how many operations must be performed to insert N elements in a list. Consider the following analysis: The first element requires 1 operation because the location into which it should be placed is known. The second item requires a maximum of 2 operations—one operation to determine where to place the item and one operation to place the item. In general, the jth item will require a maximum of j operations. On the average, we would expect to place the jth item in the middle of the list—in position $j/2$. Thus, it will take $j/2$ operations to determine where to put the item and another $j/2$ operations to move the upper segment of the list down to make room for the new item. Of course, a given item may have to be placed anywhere in the list—let us say at position k, where $k \leq N$. It will then take k operations to determine the location and $N - k$ operations to move the segment of the array above this location down to make room; the total number of operations in any case is N. (It is, of course, possible that a particular item will be placed at the end of the list, which requires only one operation; we are seeking to determine how the procedure behaves in the worst possible case.) Hence, to insert N elements in the list requires a maximum of $1 + 2 + \cdots + (N - 1) + N = N(N + 1)/2 = (N^2 + N)/2$ operations. This sort procedure is said to be an $\mathbf{O}(N^2)$ procedure.

```
program P11e (Input, Output);
{$R-}
{Program to sort an array of Integer values entered by the user;
     the insertion sort is used to maintain the list in sequence.}
uses
     Crt;
const
     InputPrompt = 'Enter a number (0 to stop) ';
type
     ArrayType = array[1..100] of Integer;
var
     IntegerArray : ArrayType;
     DataItem, NumberOfItems : Integer;
{**********************************************************************}
     procedure ListArray (var IntArray : ArrayType;
                                NumberOfElements : Integer);
     {Procedure to list current content of IntArray}
     var
          Index : Integer;
     begin   {ListArray}
          Write ('List contains ', NumberOfElements, ' item(s) : ');
          for Index := 1 to NumberOfElements do
               Write (IntArray[Index]:4);
          Writeln
     end;    {ListArray}
{----------------------------------------------------------------}
     procedure Insert (var IntArray : ArrayType;
                              NewItem, NumberOfElements : Integer);
     {Procedure to insert NewItem into IntArray, maintaining IntArray
          in ascending sequence}
     var
          Location, Index : Integer;
     begin
          if NumberOfElements = 1 then
               IntArray[1] := NewItem
          else if NewItem > IntArray[NumberOfElements - 1] then
               IntArray[NumberOfElements] := NewItem
          else
               begin
                    Location := 1;
                    while NewItem > IntArray[Location] do
                         Location := Location + 1;
                    for Index := NumberOfElements downto Location do
                         IntArray[Index] := IntArray[Index - 1];
                    IntArray[Location] := NewItem
               end;   {if}
          ListArray (IntArray, NumberOfElements)
     end;       {Insert}
     .
     .
     .
{**********************************************************************}
```

Figure 11.7(a) Program 11e: Insertion sort program. Declaration part (part 1 of 2 parts).

```
begin    {Main Program}

{1.0 Enter Data}

     ClrScr;
     Write (InputPrompt);
     Readln (DataItem);
     NumberOfItems := 0;
     while DataItem <> 0 do
          begin
               NumberOfItems := NumberOfItems + 1;
               Insert (IntegerArray, DataItem, NumberOfItems);
               Write (InputPrompt);
               Readln (DataItem)
          end;     {while}

{2.0 List Data in sequence}

     ListArray (IntegerArray, NumberOfItems);

{3.0 Wait}

     AlternateWait

end.    {Main Program}
```

Figure 11.7(b) Program 11e: Insertion sort program. Statement part (part 2 of 2 parts).

11.7.1   Time Out

1. Compile and execute Program 11e. Test the program with data of your choosing.
2. Modify the program to first load all the data into an array and then create a second array with the data in sequence.
3. In Program 11e, it is the responsibility of the Main Program to increment NumberOfItems before invoking Insert. Could this task be the responsibility of Insert? Modify the program accordingly, and test your new program. Comment on the advantages or disadvantages of the alternative approach.

11.8   SELECTION SORT

The **insertion sort** described in the preceding section is an appropriate technique for creating a sorted list one element at a time. It can be applied to sorting an existing list of elements as well, but the details are somewhat complicated.

Another fairly intuitive method that may be preferred for sorting an existing list is called the **selection sort.** This technique involves selecting the smallest element and placing it in the first location, selecting the next smallest element and placing it in the next location, and so forth. In placing an element in a particular location, the content of that location is interchanged with the content of the new element. Let us consider an example.

Suppose we wish to sort the following data using the selection sort method:

Data[1]	23
Data[2]	-5
Data[3]	2
Data[4]	80
Data[5]	16

Initially, we search the entire array and locate the smallest element, at location 2. Interchanging the content of Data[1] and Data[2] yields the following:

Data[1]	-5	← *This position now has the smallest value*
Data[2]	23	← *Contents of these two positions interchanged*
Data[3]	2	
Data[4]	80	
Data[5]	16	

At this point, we know that the first element of the list has the smallest value. We now locate the next smallest value by repeating the search process, this time beginning at position 2. We locate the next smallest value in position 3 and then interchange the contents of Data[2] and Data[3], yielding the following:

Data[1]	-5	
Data[2]	2	*These two positions are now sorted*
Data[3]	23	
Data[4]	80	
Data[5]	16	

Repeating the procedure, this time beginning at position 3, we locate the next smallest value at position 5. Interchanging Data[3] and Data[5] yields

Data[1]	-5	
Data[2]	2	
Data[3]	16	*These three positions are now sorted*
Data[4]	80	
Data[5]	23	

One further repetition of the procedure will result in the interchange of the contents of Data[4] and Data[5]; the entire list is then in sorted order:

Data[1]	-5	
Data[2]	2	
Data[3]	16	*All five elements are sorted after the fourth interchange*
Data[4]	23	
Data[5]	80	

Let us formalize this procedure by writing the pseudocode plan for a procedure that will import an array called IntArray containing NumberOfElements and export that array in ascending sequence. We shall need a variable Location to keep track of the beginning of the unsorted portion of the list. The value of Location will vary from 1 to Number-OfElements $-$ 1. For each value of Location, we will locate the smallest value in the list beginning at position Location and then interchange the content of this position with the content of IntArray[Location]. We will need a variable (Lowest) to point to the position of the smallest value. For each search, this variable will be initialized with the value of Location. Using a variable Index, which will vary from Location $+$ 1 to Number-OfElements, we compare the value of IntArray[Index] with that of IntArray[Lowest]. When IntArray[Index] is less than IntArray[Lowest], the value of Lowest is replaced by the value of Index. This procedure is summarized in the following pseudocode:

PROCEDURE SELECTION SORT (IMPORT: INTARRAY, NUMBEROFELEMENTS; EXPORT: INTARRAY)

1.0 For Location $=$ 1 to NumberOfElements $-$ 1 Do
2.0   Lowest $=$ Location
3.0   For Index $=$ Location $+$ 1 to NumberOfElements Do
4.0   If IntArray[Index] $<$ IntArray[Lowest] Then
5.0   Lowest $=$ Index
6.0   End If
7.0   Interchange IntArray[Location] and IntArray[Lowest]
8.0   End For
9.0 End For

To illustrate this procedure, let us write a program that will allow the user to enter a sequence of integer values. The program will then list the data in the original sequence, sort the data, and list the data in the new sequence. A plan for this program is as follows:

SORT PROGRAM (P11f)

1.0 Enter Data
2.0 List Data in original sequence
3.0 Sort Data into ascending sequence
4.0 List Data in ascending sequence
5.0 Wait

An implementation of this plan is shown in Figure 11.8 as Program 11f. The program makes use of a procedure ListArray, which imports IntArray and NumberOfElements and produces a listing of the content of IntArray. This procedure is invoked twice in the main program—once after the data has been entered and again after the data has been sorted. Another procedure, Swap, is included to perform the interchange required in procedure Sort.

```pascal
program P11f (Input, Output);
{Program to sort an existing list of Integers into ascending sequence;
     program uses selection sort.}
uses
     Crt;
const
     InputPrompt = 'Enter sequence of numbers separated by space';
type
     ArrayType = array[1..100] of Integer;
var
     IntegerArray : ArrayType;
     DataItem, NumberOfItems : Integer;
{********************************************************************}
     procedure ListArray (var IntArray : ArrayType;
                                  NumberOfElements : Integer);
     {Procedure to list current content of IntArray}
     var
          Index : Integer;
     begin   {ListArray}
          Write ('List contains ', NumberOfElements, ' item(s) : ');
          for Index := 1 to NumberOfElements do
              Write (IntArray[Index]:4);
          Writeln
     end;    {ListArray}
{--------------------------------------------------------------------}
     procedure Swap (var A, B : Integer);
     {Procedure to interchange content of A and B}
     var
          C : Integer;
     begin     {Swap}
          C := A;
          A := B;
          B := C
     end;        {Swap}
{--------------------------------------------------------------------}
     procedure Sort (var IntArray : ArrayType;
                         NumberOfElements : Integer);
     {Procedure to sort IntArray into ascending sequence.
         Selection sort procedure is used.}
     var
          Location, Index, Lowest : Integer;
     begin    {Sort}
         for Location := 1 to NumberOfElements - 1 do
             begin
                  Lowest := Location;
                  for Index := Location + 1 to NumberOfElements do
                      if IntArray[Index] < IntArray[Lowest] then
                          Lowest := Index;
                  Swap (IntArray[Location], IntArray[Lowest])
             end;  {for}
     end;       {Sort}
     .
     .
     .
{********************************************************************}
```

Figure 11.8(a) Program 11f: Selection sort program. Declaration part (part 1 of 2 parts).

```
begin      {Main Program}

{1.0 Enter Data}

     ClrScr;
     Writeln (InputPrompt);
     NumberOfItems := 0;
     while not Eoln do
          begin
               Read (DataItem);
               NumberOfItems := NumberOfItems + 1;
               IntegerArray[NumberOfItems] := DataItem;
          end;      {while}
     Readln;

{2.0 List Data in original sequence}

     Write ('Original ');
     ListArray (IntegerArray, NumberOfItems);

{3.0 Sort Data into ascending sequence}

     Sort (IntegerArray, NumberOfItems);

{4.0 List Data in ascending sequence}

     Write ('  Sorted ');
     ListArray (IntegerArray, NumberOfItems);

{5.0 Wait}

     AlternateWait

end.   {Main Program}
```

Figure 11.8(b) Program 11f: Selection sort program. Statement part (part 2 of 2 parts).

How efficient is the selection sort? For a list of N elements, $N - 1$ passes through the outer loop in the selection sort procedure will be required. The first pass requires $N - 1$ comparisons, the next pass requires $N - 2$ comparisons, and so forth. Thus, the number of repetitions of the innermost loop will be $(N - 1) + (N - 2) + \cdots + 2 + 1 = N(N - 1)/2 = (N^2 - N)/2$. This is somewhat better than the Insertion sort, but since the most significant term of the expression is N^2, both techniques are classified as $\mathbf{O}(N^2)$ procedures.

11.8.1   *Time Out*

1. Modify procedure Sort in Program 11f, to list the content of IntArray after each execution of the outer loop. Compile and test the program with sample data of your choosing. Note that you can observe the sorted portion of the list grow from left to right.
2. Test Program 11e with a list that is already in sequence. Does the fact that the data is in sequence have any affect on the number of passes through the data required for the procedure to terminate?

3. Modify Program 11e to allow the user to choose to sort the data into ascending or descending sequence. You will need a second sort procedure to accomplish the descending sort.

11.9   BUBBLE SORT

A second method for sorting data in place (that is, without creating a second list) is called the **bubble sort**. This method involves shifting the largest element to the bottom of the list on the first pass through the array by performing a comparison of successive elements and interchanging them when necessary. On the next pass, the largest value is shifted to the next-to-last position, and so forth, until the list is completely sorted. For example, let us sort the following data using this method:

Data[1]	23
Data[2]	-5
Data[3]	2
Data[4]	80
Data[5]	16

We begin by comparing the first two elements. Since Data[1] is greater than Data[2], we interchange Data[1] and Data[2], yielding the following list:

Data[1]	-5	
Data[2]	23	← *Data[2] is now greater than Data[1]*
Data[3]	2	
Data[4]	80	
Data[5]	16	

Now we compare the next two elements, Data[2] and Data[3]. Since Data[2] is greater than Data[3], they are interchanged:

Data[1]	-5	
Data[2]	2	
Data[3]	23	← *Data[3] is now greater than Data[1] and Data[2]*
Data[4]	80	
Data[5]	16	

Since Data[3] is less than Data[4] no interchange is required. At this stage, we know that Data[4] is greater than all the elements that precede it in the list. The first pass concludes by comparing Data[4] and Data[5]. Since Data[4] is greater than Data[5], they are interchanged, yielding the following list in which the largest value has now been shifted to the bottom:

Data[1]	-5
Data[2]	2
Data[3]	23
Data[4]	16
Data[5]	80 ← *Largest element is in last position after first pass*

Now the procedure is repeated, but this time we do not need to consider the last element, which is known to be in the correct position. The actions performed in the second pass are summarized as follows:

Data[1]	-5
Data[2]	2 ← *Data[1] and Data[2] are in sequence; no interchange*
Data[3]	23 ← *Data[2] and Data[3] are in sequence; no interchange*
Data[4]	16 ← *Data[3] and Data[4] are not in sequence; interchange*
Data[5]	80

After the interchange of Data[3] and Data[4], the list appears as follows:

Data[1]	-5
Data[2]	2
Data[3]	16
Data[4]	23
Data[5]	80

Last two elements are in sequence after second pass

At this point, the list is actually in sequence; however, one final pass will be required to verify that this is the case. The final pass would find that Data[1] < Data[2] and Data[2] < Data[3]. Since we know that Data[4] and Data[5] were already placed into proper sequence by previous passes through the loop, the procedure can now terminate. If the third pass had required one or more interchanges, then one more pass would be required to see whether the first two elements needed to be put into proper sequence. In general, the maximum number of passes required to sort N elements into sequence will be $N - 1$. The bubble sort has the advantage of terminating short of the maximum number of repetitions in some cases.

Let us design a procedure that will import an array (IntArray) and its length (NumberOfElements) and sort the array using the bubble sort method. We will need a variable (Last), which will point to the last element in the array to be compared during each pass through the array. This variable will vary from NumberOfElements -1 to 1. We will also need a Boolean variable (Finish) to determine when the loop can be terminated if the array becomes sorted prior to the maximum number of passes required. If one pass is made without performing an interchange, then the array is in sequence, and the value of Finish should be True; otherwise, Finish should be False. This procedure can be stated more formally in the following plan:

BUBBLE SORT PROCEDURE (IMPORT: INTARRAY,
NUMBEROFELEMENTS);
EXPORT: INTARRAY)

1.0 Last = NumberOfElements − 1

2.0 Finish = False

3.0 While not Finish and Last > 0 Do

4.0   Finish = True {Assume list is in sequence}

5.0   For Index = 1 to Last Do

6.0   If IntArray[Index] > IntArray[Index + 1] then

7.0   Interchange IntArray[Index] and IntArray[Index + 1]

8.0   Finish = False {Another pass may be needed}

9.0   End If

10.0   End For

11.0   Last = Last − 1

12.0 End While

Figure 11.9 shows an implementation of the bubble sort procedure in Program 11g. This program is the same as Program 11f, except for the sort procedure.

Let us now turn to the matter of the efficiency of the bubble sort procedure. As noted before, in the worst case, a list of N elements will require $N − 1$ repetitions of the outermost loop; in the sort procedure, each repetition constitutes a pass through the array. During the first pass through the array, $N − 1$ comparisons will be required; the second pass will require $N − 2$ comparisons; and so forth. In general, the number of comparisons will be $(N − 1) + (N − 2) + \cdots + 2 + 1 = N(N − 1)/2 = (N^2 − N)/2$. This is exactly the same expression derived for the selection sort procedure. The advantage to the bubble sort lies in its expected performance: If the data in the list are somewhat close to being in sequence at the outset, then the procedure can be expected to stop short of the maximum number of repetitions.

11.9.1   *Time Out*

Test Program 11g with data of your choice. Compare the behavior of Program 11f, which uses the selection sort, with this version using the bubble sort when the data are in sequence.

11.10   QUICKSORT

A sort method that is very efficient as regards its expected performance is the **QuickSort**. It was invented by a famous computer scientist, C. A. R. Hoare.[1] The basic idea behind the QuickSort is a simple observation: In a sorted list, all the elements above any element

---

[1]See *Computing Journal* Vol. 5 (1962): 10–15.

```
program P11g (Input, Output);
{Program to sort an existing list of Integers into ascending sequence;
    program uses bubble sort, with provision to terminate the
    procedure when the list is in sequence}
    .
    .
    .

    procedure Sort (var IntArray : ArrayType;
                        NumberOfElements : Integer);
    {Procedure to sort IntArray into ascending sequence;
        Bubble sort procedure with provision for termination
        is used.}
    var
        Last, Index : Integer;
        Finish : Boolean;
    begin     {Sort}
        Last := NumberOfElements - 1;
        Finish := False;
        while (not Finish) and (Last > 0) do
           begin
              Finish := True;   {Assume list is in sequence}
              for Index := 1 to Last do
                 if IntArray[Index] > IntArray[Index + 1] then
                    begin
                       Swap (IntArray[Index], IntArray[Index + 1]);
                       Finish := False   {Another pass may be needed}
                    end;   {if}
              Last := Last - 1
           end     {while}
    end;     {Sort}
    .
    .
    .
end.   {Main Program}
```

Figure 11.9 Program 11g: A bubble sort procedure.

are greater than that element, and all the elements below are less than that element. Thus, one way to sort would be to select an element (as close to the middle of the list as possible) and rearrange the list so that all the elements in the segment above are greater than it and all the elements in the segment below are less than it. This will parttion the list into two parts—one above and one below the middle value; each of those lists can then be sorted separately using the same approach. The process terminates when a list of length 1 is encountered. The QuickSort method is a classic example of the divide-and-conquer strategy of problem solving: To solve a difficult problem, we divide it into smaller problems, each of which can be approached independently.

The QuickSort procedure is most efficient when the median (middle) value is known. Unfortunately, this information is not usually available. (To find the middle value, the list would have to be sorted already.) Fortunately, the procedure will work (but not as efficiently) by using any value as the element that divides the two segments. If the chosen element is not close to the actual middle value (the median), then the lengths of the two segments will not be balanced, and the procedure will not be as efficient as it would otherwise be.

Let us illustrate the partition process using the following data:

```
Data[1]    23
Data[2]    -5
Data[3]    14
Data[4]    16
Data[5]    80
Data[6]     3
Data[7]     5
Data[8]     0
```

Our first task is to choose the element to be used to divide the list into two segments. As noted earlier, the process is most efficient if this value is the median. In an unsorted list, there is no reason to choose one element over another as an estimate for the median. Let us choose an element near the physical midpoint of the list.[2] In this case, the content of Data[4] is the estimated median. Our goal is to divide the list into two segments, with 16 as the dividing value. The lower set will all be less than or equal to 16, and the upper part will be greater than or equal to 16. (Of course, 16 can be a part of only one or the other of these segments.) We begin by placing the contents of Data[4] into a variable Middle-Value. MiddleValue will serve as a reference point in the partition process. (The content of Data[4] may change.)

We will partition the list in the following manner: Beginning at the first element of the list, we will search forward to find the first element that is greater than or equal to MiddleValue. We will use a variable Below to point to this element. Then, beginning with the last element in the list, we will search from the bottom up to find the first element that is less than or equal to MiddleValue. We will use the variable Above to point to this element. We now have one element that belongs in the upper segment and one element that belongs in the lower segment, so we interchange these two elements. With respect to the preceding sample data, we initially have the following:

```
Data[1]    23  ←─── Below
Data[2]    -5
Data[3]    14
Data[4]    16              MiddleValue    16
Data[5]    80
Data[6]     3
Data[7]     5
Data[8]     0  ←─── Above
```

---

[2]The rationale for choosing this point as the estimate for the median is to take advantage of the fact that, for a list that is sorted or nearly sorted, the middle value should be close to the median. In other implementations of the QuickSort, some other criterion may be chosen to estimate the median.

The content of Data[Below] is greater than MiddleValue, and the content of Data[Above] is less than MiddleValue, so we now interchange Data[1] and Data[8]. After interchanging, we must adjust the value of Below and Above so that they point to the next elements in the list. (Below is incremented and Above is decremented.) The list now appears as follows:

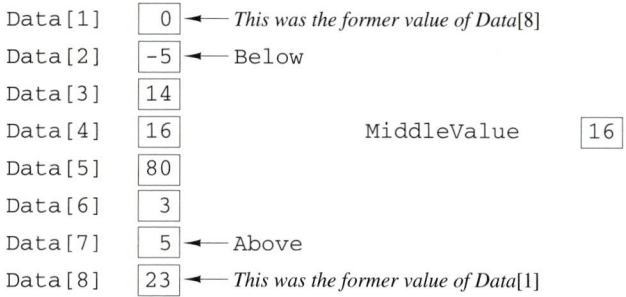

We now repeat the procedure. First we locate the next element in the list such that Data[Below] is greater than or equal to MiddleValue. This occurs when Below points to Data[4]. Then we locate the next element in the list such that Data[Above] is less than or equal to MiddleValue. This occurs when Above points to Data[7]. The situation is as follows:

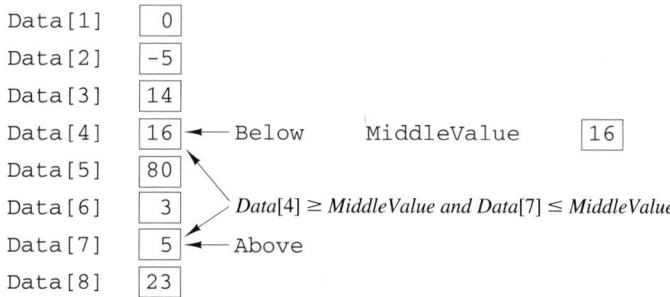

These two values are interchanged; Below is incremented and Above is decremented, yielding the following:

Data[1] 0
Data[2] -5
Data[3] 14
Data[4] 5   MiddleValue 16
Data[5] 80 ◄── Below
Data[6] 3 ◄── Above
Data[7] 16
Data[8] 23

Again, we search for the first element such that Data[Below] is greater than or equal to MiddleValue; this occurs at Data[5]. The first value such that Data[Above] is less than or equal to middle value occurs at Data[6]. After interchanging these two values, incrementing Below, and decrementing Above, we have the following:

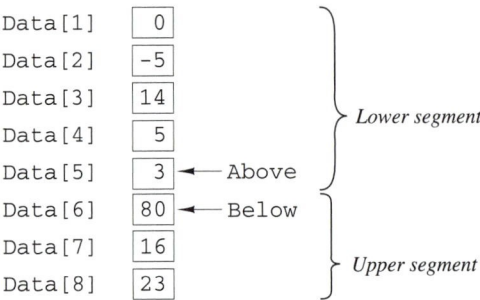

At this point, the partition process is concluded: The lower segment is from location 1 to Above, and the upper segment is from Below to 8. Note that neither of these segments is sorted. We have simply partitioned the list into two parts—the lower segment with all the elements that are less than or equal to MiddleValue and the upper segment with elements that are greater than or equal to MiddleValue. The procedure can detect when this occurs by comparing the values of Above and Below; the interchange process must continue until Below is greater than or equal to Above.

After the list is partitioned, the QuickSort procedure calls for the sorting of the two segments. Recursion is a valuable tool in the implementation of a QuickSort: The QuickSort procedure itself can be invoked to sort first the lower segment and then the upper segment. Remember that in any recursive procedure, there must be a stopping point. We will attempt to sort segments of length 2 or larger only. Eventually, the process divides the list into segments of length 1, at which point the data are in sequence. For example, consider the task of sorting the upper segment of the preceding list. It contains the following data:

```
80
16
23
```

The first task would be to partition the list as before. We use the middle element as our estimate for MiddleValue. Initially, Below points to 80 and Above points to 23, as shown:

The element at Below is greater than MiddleValue. The element at Above is also greater than MiddleValue, so we decrement Above so that Above points to 16:

The element pointed to by Above is now less than or equal to MiddleValue, so we perform an interchange, advance Below, and decrement Above, yielding the following situation:

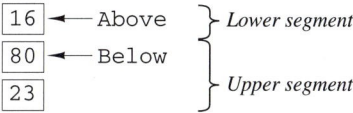

At this point, Below is greater than Above, so the partition process is completed. We have partitioned the list into two segments—the lower one from the first element to Above and the upper one from Below through the end of the list. The QuickSort procedure now calls for sorting each of these lists. In particular, the lower segment is of length 1. This means that there is no further work to be done on this segment, and the procedure would pass on to the sorting of the upper segment. Sorting this list would yield two segments, each of which would be of length 1. No further work would be required on either of these segments, and hence, the procedure would terminate; that is, there would be no further recursive calls.

Let us formalize our description of QuickSort by writing a plan for a procedure to sort an array that we shall call Array, between the limits of First and Last. (First and Last will point to the beginning and ending, respectively, of the segment of Array to be sorted.) We will need a variable MiddleValue, which will be used in the partition process, and variables Below and Above, which are used in the partition process and then to point out the limits of the two segments of the array. An initial version of the QuickStart procedure is as follows:

PROCEDURE QUICKSORT (IMPORT: ARRAY, FIRST, LAST; EXPORT: ARRAY)

1.0 Initialize variables

2.0 Repeat partition process until Array is partitioned into two segments based on MiddleValue

3.0 If Lower Segment is longer than 1, Then Sort Lower Segment

4.0 If Upper Segment is longer than 1, Then Sort Upper Segment

The value for MiddleValue can be computed as Array[(First + Last)/2] using integer division. The initial value of Below is First; the initial value of Above is Last. The interchange process involves three steps: First, we search from top to bottom to find an element of Array that is greater than or equal to MiddleValue (Below points to this value); second, we search from bottom to top to find the first element that is less than or equal to MiddleValue (Above points to this value); finally, if Below is less than Above, we interchange the two elements that have been located. This procedure is repeated until Below is greater than or equal to Above. At the end of the partition process, the lower segment is from First to Above and the upper segment is from Below to Last. This analysis is summarized in the following plan:

PROCEDURE QUICKSORT (IMPORT: ARRAY, FIRST, LAST; EXPORT: ARRAY)

1.0 Initialize variables
  1.1 MiddleValue = Array[(First + Last)/2]
  1.2 Below = First
  1.3 Above = Last
2.0 Repeat partition process until Array is partitioned into two segments based on MiddleValue
  2.1 Search list from top to bottom to find first element, which is $>=$ to MiddleValue; let Below point to the location of this element
  2.2 Search list from bottom to top to find first element, which is $<=$ to MiddleValue; let Above point to the location of this element
  2.3 If Below $<=$ Above interchange elements at these locations
3.0 If Lower Segment is longer than 1, Then Sort Lower Segment
4.0 If Upper Segment is longer than 1, Then Sort Upper Segment

Figure 11.10 shows an implementation of the QuickSort that is contained in Program 11h. The procedure would be invoked from the main program by a statement such as

```
Sort (IntegerArray, 1, NumberOfItems);
```

indicating that the entire array is to be sorted. The implementation of Module 3.0 uses the values of First and Above to determine the length of the lower segment. If First $<$ Above, then the segment is longer than one element in length. (If First = Above, then the segment is of length 1.) A similar comparison between Below and Last is used in the implementation of Module 4.0.

We noted earlier that the QuickSort procedure is expected to be a very efficient procedure (hence the name given to it). Assume that we are dealing with a list of length N. At each stage in the QuickSort, we divide the list into two halves and sort each half separately. If the division process results in sequences that are equal in length or nearly equal, then the number of such sublists is $\log_2 N$. For each subdivision, all the elements of the list must be compared, so the total number of such comparisons will be $N \log_2 N$. Although we expect the QuickSort procedure to be of order $N \log_2 N$, this expectation is based on the division of the list into nearly equal segments at each iteration. If by some unhappy coincidence we happen to choose the wrong estimate for MiddleValue each time, then it is possible that we would have to

```pascal
program P11h (Input, Output);
{Program to sort an existing list of Integers into ascending sequence;
    program uses QuickSort.}
    .
    .
    .

    procedure Sort (var IntArray : ArrayType;
                        First, Last : Integer);
    {Procedure to sort IntArray into ascending  sequence
        between limits of First and Last. QuickSort procedure is used.}
    var
        Below, Above,    {Indices for array segments}
        MiddleValue      {Estimate of median of the sequence}
            : Integer;
    begin   {Sort}

    {1.0 Initialize variables}

        MiddleValue := IntArray[(First + Last) div 2];
        Below := First;
        Above := Last;

    {2.0 Repeat interchange process until Array is partitioned
            into two parts based on MiddleValue}

        repeat

        {2.1 Search list from top to bottom to find first element
                that is >= to MiddleValue; let Below point to
                the location of this element}

                while IntArray[Below] < MiddleValue do
                    Below := Below + 1;

        {2.2 Search list from bottom to top to find first element
                that is <= MiddleValue; let Above point to
                the location of this element}

                while IntArray[Above] > MiddleValue do
                    Above := Above - 1;

        {2.3 If Below <= Above, interchange elements at these locations}

                if Below <= Above then
                    begin
                        Swap (IntArray[Below], IntArray[Above]);
                        Below := Below + 1;
                        Above := Above - 1
                    end;    {if}

        until Below >= Above;

    {3.0 If lower segment is longer than 1, then sort lower segment}

        if First < Above then
            Sort (IntArray, First, Above);

    {4.0 If upper segment is longer than 1, then sort upper segment}

        if Below < Last then
            Sort (IntArray, Below, Last);

    end;    {Sort}
    .
    .
    .

end.   {Main Program}
```

Figure 11.10 Program 11h: The QuickSort procedure

divide the list into N sequences, each of which is one shorter than the preceding one. Thus, in general, QuickSort is an $O(N^2)$ procedure, the same as other sort procedures we have examined. Experience with the procedure shows, however, that the observed behavior of the procedure closely approximates the expected optimal behavior. There is, however, one built-in disadvantage to the QuickSort: Because it is based on recursion, there is a need for local copies of value parameters. First and Last are value parameters; so for each invocation of the procedure, space must be found for copies of these variables. Fortunately, this restriction rarely is a serious problem, because the number of such local copies is equal to the number of recursive calls, which is expected to be $\log_2 N$.

11.10.1   Time Out

Test Program 11h. Include output from within the sort procedure to help you observe the action of the procedure as the sort is underway. How does it behave when data that is already in sequence is entered?

11.11   SELECTING AMONG SORT PROCEDURES

Each of the sort procedures has some advantages and disadvantages that should be considered in selecting among them for a particular programming task. These are summarized in Figure 11.11. In general, the insertion sort is useful when data must be sorted as it is entered. The bubble and selection sorts have the advantage of being simple and easy to implement; the bubble sort enables the procedure to terminate when a sorted list is derived, which is an advantage if the data being sorted has a high probability of being in sequence (or almost in sequence) when the sort is undertaken. The selection sort may have an advantage over the bubble sort when the ele-

Sort Procedure	Worst Case	Expected	Space	Comment
Insertion	N^2	N^2	N	May be useful for creating a sequenced table as data is read
Selection	N^2	N^2	N	No way to terminate when a sequenced list is derived at an intermediate step
Bubble	N^2	$< N^2$	N	Procedure terminates when a sequenced list is derived
Quick Sort	N^2	$N \log_2 N$	$> N$	Recursion requires some additional space; best expected behavior

Figure 11.11 Comparison of sort procedures.

ments being sorted are large (e.g., records with numerous fields). The reason for this is that, compared to the bubble sort, the selection sort requires less data movement (fewer interchanges between the elements being sorted). When the elements are large, the time required for an interchange may become significant. The QuickSort has the best expected behavior, making it the method of choice for large amounts of data; its disadvantages are that its simplest implementation requires recursion and that it does not terminate automatically if a sorted list is derived at some intermediate stage in the sorting process.

11.12   REVIEW QUESTIONS

1. Give an example of a table. Identify the table argument and table value(s).

2. Does the actual argument always have the same value as one of the table arguments? Explain.

3. There are two possible outcomes to any search procedure. What are they?

4. How does the sequential search of an unsorted table differ from the sequential search of a sorted table?

5. The name of the binary search derives from a fundamental property of the procedure. What is this property, and how does it affect the efficiency of the procedure?

6. Explain why the binary search is appropriate only for a sequenced table.

7. What is a hash function? How is the function used in creating a hash table?

8. What is a synonym? How does the existence of synonyms affect the creation and searching of a hash table?

9. What are the conditions for optimum expected efficiency when using a hash table?

10. Direct access is the most efficient search procedure. Under what circumstances can direct access be used?

11. If two procedures are both $O(N)$, would you expect the execution time for them to be equal? Why or why not?

12. Define the term *sort*.

13. Under what circumstances might an insertion sort be useful? What is the major disadvantage of the insertion sort, compared with other sort procedures?

14. What is the major advantage of the bubble sort, compared with the selection sort?

15. Which sort procedure has the best expected efficiency?

16. Occasionally, the QuickSort procedure divides the list into three segments: a lower segment, an upper segment, and a middle segment of length 1. Give an example showing how this occurs. Why is it unnecessary to take special note of this case in the procedure?

17. Under what circumstances might the expected benefits of the QuickSort not be realized?

18. In the pseudocode version of the QuickSort procedure presented in Section 11.10, Module 2.3 is as follows:

2.3 If Below $<=$ Above interchange elements at these locations

If Below is equal to Above, this step results in the interchange of an element with itself, which would seem to be an unnecessary action. Why is it necessary for the condition in this module to be less than or equal to rather than just less than?

11.13 PROGRAMMING EXERCISES

1. Write a program to allow the user to read a Text file containing up to 25 names and telephone numbers. The program should store this data in a table. The program should look up the telephone numbers for names entered by the user.

2. In Exercise 1, sort the table into sequence by name. Use a binary search to perform the lookup function.

3. In Exercise 1, allow the user to find out the telephone number by entering the name or find out the name by entering the telephone number.

4. Write a program to load the content of the inventory file processed by program 10b into a table. Sort the data into sequence with the description as the sort key. Create a binary file with the sorted data.

5. Write a program to look up information in the sorted binary inventory file created in Exercise 4. Allow the user to enter the description and have the program respond with the associated production and sales data. Instead of loading the content of the file into an array, use the random access capabilities of binary files to access the file. Use a binary search procedure adapted to processing the data from the file, rather than accessing the data from an array.

6. Write a program to transform the binary inventory file into a randomized file similar to a hash table. First create the randomized file with a suitable number of "dummy" records. Then use a hash function to write the content of the inventory file in appropriate locations in the randomized file. List the content of the file you have created and note the placement of the data records.

7. Write a program to look up data in the randomized inventory file created in Exercise 6. Do not load the content of the file into an array. Use the random access capabilities of binary files to access records in the file.

8. Write a program to examine the performance of the four sort procedures discussed in this chapter. The main program should generate lists of 25 random numbers. Each sort procedure should be modified to count the number of comparisons required to complete the sort process. (Add a variable parameter that will act as a counter.) Create a table showing the results obtained for each sort procedure for each of 10 different lists. Compute the average for each procedure. How do the values you computed compare to the expected values derived from an analysis of the procedure? (You may wish to write four different programs and correlate the results manually.)

9. Tables such as that shown in Figure 11.12 are often used in computing tax. Write a program to load this table from a Text file and then compute tax for income amounts entered by the program user.

10. Create a Text file (Salesperson Master File) containing the names and social security numbers for salespersons employed by XYZ, Inc. Create a second Text file (Sales Data File) containing the following information about each sale made by a salesperson: social security number, date of sale, amount of sale. Make sure that the data are in sequence by a social security number. Write a program to summarize sales for each salesperson. There should be one line of output for

each salesperson, showing social security number, name, and total sales. For this exercise, use an exhaustive search of the Salesperson Master File to match social security numbers with the associated names.

11. Modify the program you wrote for Exercise 10 to load the content of the Salesperson Master File into an array. Use an exhaustive search technique.

12. Modify the program you wrote for Exercise 11 to sort the content of the array containing the salesperson names and social security numbers. Then use the binary search technique to search for names.

Married Filing Joint Returns and Qualifying Widows and Widowers

Use this schedule if you checked **Filing Status Box 2 or 5** on Form 1040—

If the amount on Form 1040, line 36 is: Over—	But not over—	Enter on Form 1040, line 37	of the amount over—
$0	$3,000	.............11%	$0
3,000	28,000	$330 + 15%	3,000
28,000	45,000	4,080 + 28%	28,000
45,000	90,000	8,840 + 35%	45,000
90,000	....	24,590 + 38.5%	90,000

Figure 11.12 Sample tax table. (Source: 1987 Form 1040 Instructions, p. 43.)

12

Pointers and Abstract Data Structures

This chapter will cover the data type pointer. You will see how pointers work in conjunction with dynamic memory allocation—a technique that allows a program to make more efficient use of the computer's memory. We will also explore applications of pointers to create data structures that can be very useful in solving certain problems.

12.1   WHAT IS A POINTER?

In simplest possible terms, a **pointer** is an address for a data item. By using the pointer, we can gain access to the actual data. You have already used pointers of a sort in your work with arrays. The subscript that is used to access a particular element of an array is a pointer to that element. The subscript does not contain the data, but rather, it is the address within the array of the element that does contain the data. We have sometimes used the term *pointer* to refer to a variable that will be used as a subscript.

Pascal makes it possible to create variables that will be pointers to data of specified types. A pointer variable contains the address of the data in the memory of the computer. Pointers are used in conjunction with **dynamic memory allocation**. The allocation of space for all variables is static; that is, the compiler performs this task at the time the program is compiled. This means that memory locations are reserved for a variable and the address of that memory is used in the compiled program in place of the variable name. The data pointed to by a pointer variable is allocated dynamically—that is, during the execution of the program. This means that the program can create and destroy data items as needed.

Previously, we have used arrays to store large amounts of information. The problem with arrays is that their size is fixed at the time the program is compiled. We can choose not to use some part of an array for data storage (a common occurrence), but an array always has an upper limit on the amount of data that it can contain. By using pointers and dynamically allocated memory, the program can gain access to as much memory as may be needed. The program is limited only by the amount of available memory, not by some upper limit imposed at the time the program was compiled.

12.2   DECLARATION OF A POINTER VARIABLE

A pointer data type is specified using the caret symbol (^) followed by a type identifier; the general form is

```
^type-identifier
```

For example, the following program segment creates a pointer variable P that points to an Integer:

```
var
     P : ^Integer;
```

We can visualize the variable P as shown in the following diagram:

The data item pointed to by P is not assigned a separate variable name; the program gains access to that data by using the variable P to reference it. This is done using the notation P^, which literally means "the data pointed to by P." As we shall see, there will be a very limited number of operations that can be performed on the variable P—the one that contains the address—but the operations that can be performed on the data pointed to by P are limited only by the type of that data (which is Integer in this case).

It is quite useful to create a type identifier for pointer data types. For example, suppose we wish to store Real numbers using dynamic memory allocation. Then we could create a type identifier and, using that identifier, create pointer variables, as follows:

```
type
    RealPointer = ^Real;
var
    A, B : RealPointer;
```

The variables A and B are pointer variables; they can be made to point to Real data, as shown in the following diagram:

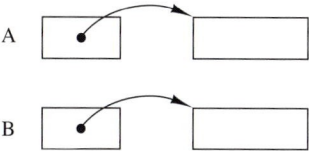

It is important to realize that declaring pointer variables does not automatically create the data items to which they point. As with any other Pascal variable, the content of a pointer variable is undefined when it is initially created. It will be up to the program to assign the variable an appropriate value. In order to create a data item of the appropriate type and assign the address of that item to a pointer variable, the procedure **New** is provided. The general form for invocation of this procedure is

```
New (pointer-variable)
```

For example, in order to create an Integer data item and associate with it the variable P, which has been declared as a pointer to data of type Integer, you would use

```
New (P);
```

Before execution of this procedure, the content of the pointer P is undefined:

P [?]

After execution of the procedure, P points to an Integer data item:

This item could then be assigned a value in any way consistent with its data type; for example, to assign it the value 2, the following statement would be used:

```
P^  := 2;
```

You could translate this statement as "assign the value 2 to the data item pointed to by the variable P." After execution of the statement, the content of the relevant portion of memory could be visualized as follows:

The following program statements would create two real data items associated with variables A and B, which have been declared as pointers to Real data:

```
New  (A);
New  (B);
```

The content of the relevant portion of memory can be visualized as follows:

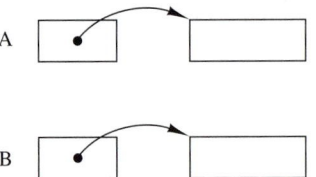

The program can then assign values to these two data items in any way desired by using the references A^ and B^. For example, the following statements would assign the value 2.0 to the item pointed to by A and add 1 to that value, storing the result in the data item pointed to by B:

```
A^  := 2.0;
B^  := A^  + 1.0;
```

The content of the relevant portion of memory could be visualized as follows:

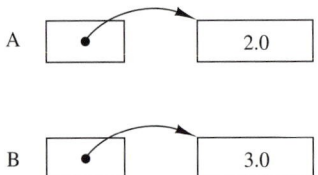

When dealing with pointer variables, it is important to keep clearly in mind the distinction between the content of the variable (which is an address) and the content of the data item pointed to by that variable. In the context of the previous example, the variables

A and B are references to addresses; A^ and B^ are references to the data stored at that address. Pointer variables can be manipulated by a program in only a very few ways. They can be used as the argument to the procedure New. They can be used in assignment statements, provided that both variables have the same type. Assume that A and B point to the data items, as shown in the previous example. Then the statement

```
B := A;
```

would cause A and B to point to the same data item, as shown:

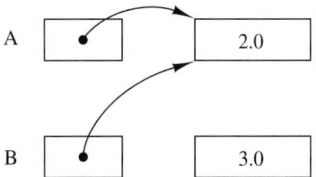

What has happened is that the content of B (an address) has been replaced by the value (also an address) that is contained in A. The data item that was previously pointed to by B still exists, but there is no way to gain access to its content. (Later, we shall see how to regain this space and make it available for other use.)

12.2.1   Time Out

1. Assume that the following declarations have been made in a program:

```
type
      NameType = string[10];
      NamePointer = ^NameType;
var
      NameA, NameB, NameC : NamePointer;
```

Draw diagrams similar to those in this section to show the content of the relevant portion of memory after each of the following program segments has been executed.

(a) New (NameA);
     New (NameB);
     NameA^ := 'Joe';
     NameB^ := 'Sue';
     NameC := NameA;

(b) New (NameA);
     NameA^ := 'Joe';
     New (NameC);
     NameC^ := 'Jim';
     NameA := NameC;
     NameB := NameC;

(c) `New (NameA);`
`NameA^ := 'Joe';`
`NameB := NameA;`
`New (NameA);`
`NameA^ := 'Jim';`

2. Explain why each of the following statements is invalid.
    (a) `NameA := 'Joe';`
    (b) `NameB := NameA^;`
    (c) `Writeln (NameA);`
    (d) `Readln (NameB);`

12.3 DYNAMIC STORAGE ALLOCATION

We have said that pointers make it possible to use memory that would otherwise be unavailable to a program. Moreover, this memory need not be allocated at the time the program is compiled, since the allocation is performed during the execution of the program. A quick look at how memory is allocated will help you understand how this is possible.

A compiled program is loaded into memory above the resident portion of the operating system and Turbo Pascal (if it is active), as shown in Figure 12.1. The program is divided into four parts: units, which contain routines required for the execution of the program; the code segment, which contains the executable program instructions; the data segment, which contains the memory that has been allocated for variables that have been created by the program; and a stack segment, which is used for temporary storage during the

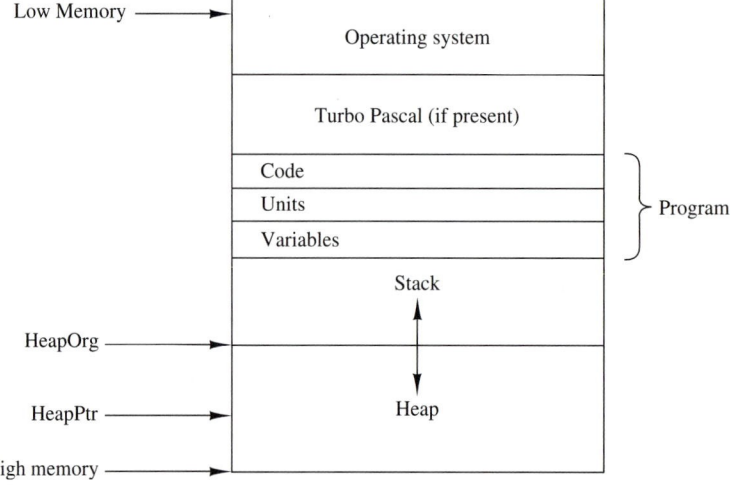

Figure 12.1 Memory map.

execution of the program. The remainder of the memory, from the end of the stack segment to the end of memory, is a free area known as the *heap*. A pointer to the heap (HeapPtr) is initialized at the beginning of the execution of the program. Generally, the heap begins at the first free byte above the stack area. When memory is allocated by the program (by using the New procedure), the setting of the heap pointer determines the part of the heap that will be allocated for the data item; allocating data causes the heap pointer to advance to the next available space.

12.4   PROCESSING POINTER VARIABLES

We have seen how to declare a pointer variable and how to initialize a pointer variable using the procedure New. Another way to initialize a pointer variable is to use the pointer constant **nil**. If a pointer variable is assigned a value nil, this means that it points nowhere; that is, it does not point to a data item. If P is a pointer variable, the statement

```
P := nil;
```

causes the value of P to be set to nil. The nil value for a pointer variable is symbolized in memory diagrams as follows:

P ▱

It is important to understand the difference between an undefined pointer variable and one that has an established value. The content of an undefined variable (one that is declared, but to which no value has yet been assigned) is an unknown. The procedure New creates a data item and establishes the value of the pointer variable. Assigning the value nil to a pointer variable also establishes its value, but it does so without allocating an associated data item. (The role of nil in dealing with pointers is somewhat analogous to the role of the empty set in dealing with sets. Both serve as a way of initializing a variable without assigning actual data to it.)

Earlier, we said that it is possible to reuse memory in the heap that may no longer be needed. This is done by using the procedure **Dispose**, which frees up the data item pointed to by its parameter. The general form for invocation of the Dispose procedure is

```
Dispose (pointer-variable)
```

For example, suppose PtrA and PtrB point to real data items, as shown:

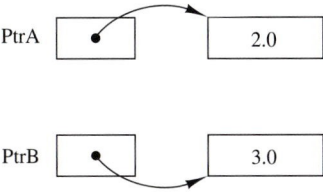

Then, after execution of the Dispose procedure for PtrA, as in

```
Dispose (PtrA);
```

the value of PtrA will be undefined, and the space that was allocated for this variable will be returned to the pool of usable space, to be allocated again if needed. At this point, the memory diagram is as follows:

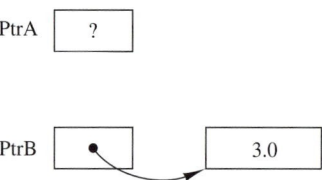

Note that this is quite different from simply assigning the value nil to PtrA. The action of assigning nil to PtrA would leave the data item that had formerly been allocated to PtrA still in use, but isolated, in the sense that there is no way for the program to gain access to its content, as shown in the following memory diagram:

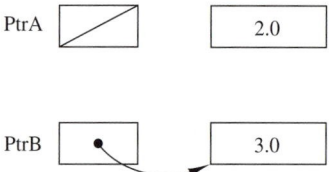

In programs that make heavy use of dynamic memory allocation, it is important to free up memory when it is no longer in use; otherwise, you may run out of memory in the heap.

Suppose you wish to have PtrA point to the same data item as PtrB and free up the data pointed to by PtrA. You would have to use the Dispose procedure first, as shown in the following program segment:

```
Dispose (PtrA);
PtrA := PtrB;
```

Suppose that, before executing this program segment, memory is arranged as follows:

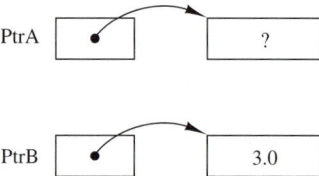

After execution of the Dispose procedure, memory would appear as follows:

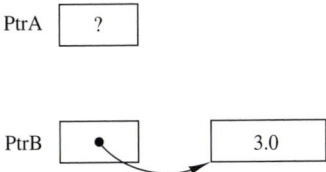

Then, after execution of the assignment statement, memory would appear thus:

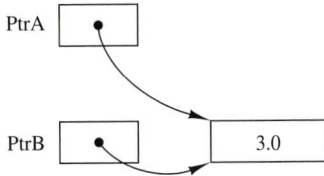

This is the desired state. Note that the result here is very different than with some other alternatives that you might try. For example, the statement

```
PtrA := PtrB;
```

without the statement Dispose (PtrA) would leave the data area previously associated with PtrA as allocated and therefore not reusable; moreover, since the path to the data area has been destroyed, there is no way to deallocate it.

12.4.1 Time Out

Assume that the following declarations have been made:

```
type
    NameType = string[10];
    NamePointerType = ^NameType;
var
    First, Second, Third : NamePointerType;
```

Draw a memory diagram showing the state of memory after execution of each of the following program segments:

1. ```
New (First);
First^ := 'Joe';
Second := nil;
New (Third);
Third^ := First^;
```
```

2.
```
First := nil;
New (Second);
Second^ := 'Jill';
Third := Second;
```

3.
```
New (First);
First^ := 'Joe';
New (Second);
Second^ := First^;
Dispose (First);
```

12.4.2 Comparing Pointers

Pointers can be used in replacement statements (provided that the types match), and they can be used as arguments in procedure and function invocations (again, provided that the actual argument and formal argument types match). Pointers can also be compared by using Boolean expressions. Testing for less than or greater than is not usually very meaningful, but it is useful on occasion to test for equality of two pointer variables. If two pointer variables are equal, then they point to the same data. For example, suppose PtrA and PtrB are the same pointer type. Then the expression PtrA = PtrB will be True if the two pointers point to the same data item, as shown in the following diagram:

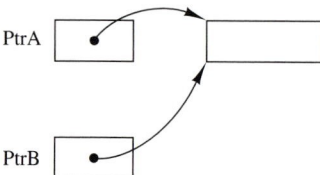

If the two pointers point to different data items (that is, items with different addresses), the expression PtrA = PtrB will be False.

Again, the distinction between the address of the item and the content of the item is very important. For example, suppose that PtrA and PtrB are suitably defined, and the memory diagram shows the following situation:

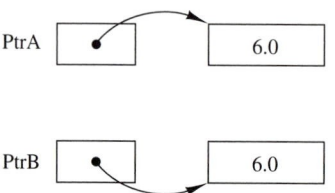

Then the value of PtrA = PtrB is False because the two pointers point to different memory locations, but PtrA^ = PtrB^ is True because the content of the data item pointed to by PtrA is equal to the content of the data item pointed to by PtrB.

Another way in which comparison of pointers is used is to test for the value nil. The expression PtrA = nil will be True if PtrA has been assigned a value nil and False otherwise.

12.4.3   *Time Out*

1. Suppose the following declarations are in place:

```
type
      DayOfWeek = (Mon, Tue, Wed, Thr, Fri, Sat, Sun);
      DayPointerType = ^DayOfWeek;
var
      A, B : DayPointerType;
```

Evaluate the expressions A = B and A^ = B^ after the execution of each of the following program segments:

(a) `New (A);`
`    New (B);`
`    A^ := Mon;`
`    B^ := Tue;`

(b) `New (A);`
`    New (B);`
`    A^ := Fri;`
`    B^ := A^;`

(c) `New (A);`
`    A^ := Sun;`
`    B := A;`

(d) `New (A);`
`    A^ := Sat;`
`    B := A;`
`    Dispose (A);`

2. Is it possible for the value of A = B to be True and the value of A^ = B^ to be False? Explain.

3. Is it possible for the value of A = B to be False and the value of A^ = B^ to be True? Explain.

4. Evaluate the expression A = nil after execution of each of the program segments in Exercise 1.

12.4.4   **Pointers to Records**

The type of data that can be the object of a pointer can be any type except a file. We have seen examples of pointers associated with simple data types (Integer, Real) and structured types (string and enumerated types). Often, it is useful to have a pointer associated with a record. For example, suppose we wish to create a record containing a name and address and have the space for this record allocated dynamically. The following declaration will perform this function:

```
type
    AddressRecordType = record
                            Name : string[15];
                            StreetAddr : string[15];
                            City : string[10];
                            State : string[2];
                            Zip : string [5]
                    end;
    AddressPointerType = ^AddressRecordType;
var
    AddressPtr : AddressPointerType;
```

Execution of New(AddressPtr) creates an address record. The individual fields within the record are addressed using the pointer variable notation that we have used previously, followed by a field specification. For example, to address the name field of the address record, you would write

```
AddressPtr^.Name
```

This reference may be interpreted as "the Name field of the data record pointed to by AddressPtr." In a program segment that processes all the fields, a with statement could simplify field references, as, for example:

```
with AddressPtr^ do
    begin
        . . .
    end; {with}
```

One very powerful feature of pointer data type is the ability to embed pointers into a record. This feature will be extremely important in implementing abstract data structures. For example, suppose we wish to create two records in such a way that one record points to the next one, as shown in the following diagram:

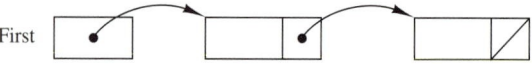

For simplicity, let us use records that contain only a name and the pointer to the next record. We might wish to create the structure in such a way that the names are alphabetized, as shown in the following diagram:

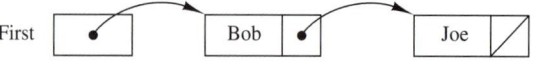

The declaration required to create this structure is as follows:

```
type
      NameType : string[10];
      NamePtr : ^NameRecordType;
      NameRecordType : record
                              Name : NameType;
                              Next : NamePtr
                  end;
var
      First, Temp : NamePtr;
```

If you study this program segment carefully, you will note that it violates one of the basic rules of Pascal: It contains a reference to an identifier that precedes the declaration of that identifier. Specifically, NamePtr is declared as a pointer to NameRecordType, but the identifier NameRecordType is not defined until the following line of code. This "violation" is permitted by Pascal; indeed, it would be impossible to create the preceding structure if this were not possible.

Now let us turn to a program segment that could be used to set up the structure just outlined. We shall see later that an iterative procedure will be much more useful than the approach taken here, but understanding the ideas presented here will help you understand the more sophisticated procedure later. There are an almost endless number of ways that we could create the required structure. One way would be to create the initial element by using

```
New (First);
First^.Name := 'Bob';
```

At this point, the state of the relevant portion of memory is as follows:

The content of First^.Name is defined, but the content of First^.Next (the pointer part of the record) is undefined at this stage. Now we can create another record for the next data by using the variable Temp:

```
New (Temp);
Temp^.Name := 'Joe';
```

The state of the relevant portion of memory is now

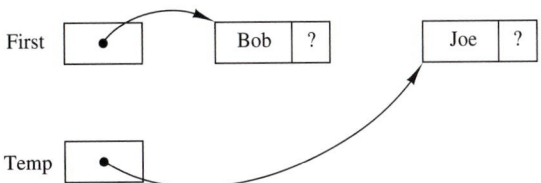

Now our job is to complete the linkage between the record containing 'Bob' and the record containing 'Joe'. The content of First^.Next needs to point to the data pointed to by Temp; we can make the connection very simply as follows:

```
First^.Next := Temp;
```

This is a very important (but somewhat subtle) step; the memory arrangement is now as follows:

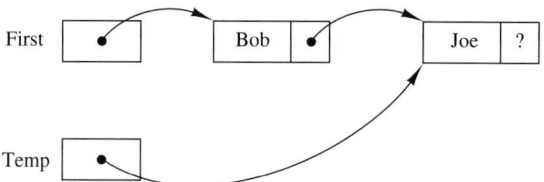

Finally, we can complete the structure by placing nil into the pointer portion of the last element:

```
Temp^.Next := nil;
```

The state of the relevant portion of memory at this point shows that the structure is complete:

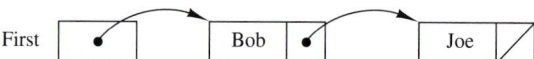

(We are no longer interested in the pointer variable Temp; it was merely an intermediate variable needed to create the structure.) The structure that we have just created is the initial portion of a list that could be extended almost indefinitely by using the pointer part of the second element to point to the next record, the pointer part of that record to point to the following record, and so on.

By now, you have probably realized the importance of the memory diagrams we have been drawing in understanding how pointers work. The diagrams will help you establish what needs to be accomplished in a particular procedure, and they will help you visualize what has happened after each statement is executed. Because you cannot write out the values of pointer variables, memory diagrams are a very valuable tool in debugging programs that use pointers.

12.4.5   Time Out

1. Given the preceding definition of AddressRecord, write a program segment to allow the program user to enter values for a name and address.
2. Assume that the definitions of First and Temp are as given before, and assume that the state of the relevant portion of memory is as follows:

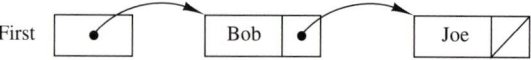

Now suppose the following program segment is executed:

```
New (Temp);
Temp^.Name := 'Abe';
Temp^.Next := First;
First := Temp;
```

Trace the execution of this program segment, and draw a diagram of the state of the relevant portion of memory at its completion.

12.5 LINKED LISTS

In the last section we presented (in an informal way) a structure that we called a *list*, which was composed of a pointer to the first element and elements that contained data and a pointer to the next element. This structure is called a **linked list**, the links being the pointers that tie the list together. The general form of a linked list may be visualized as shown in Figure 12.2. The pointer to the first element in the list is traditionally called the *head*, and the pointers within each element of the list are called *links*.

Linked lists are useful for maintaining information in sequence. Access to the list is gained by starting at the head and following the links from one element to the next until the final element is found. The link in the last element always has the value nil. An alternative technique for storing a list of data is to use an array. The array alternative, however, has two drawbacks:

1. Because an array has a fixed size, the list has an upper bound on its length, the value of which is determined at the time the program is written. (Linked lists do not require the program to allocate space, because they are implemented through pointers; therefore, the limitation on the length of the list is that imposed by the size of the memory of the machine.)

2. In order to insert new data into the midst of the array and maintain the list in sequence, elements of the array must be moved down to make room for the new element. (Inserting a new item in a linked list is a matter of adjusting the value of pointers; no data has to be moved. This can make the linked list approach significantly more efficient).

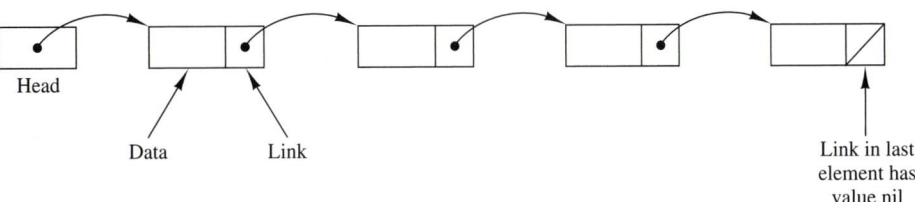

Figure 12.2 General form of a linked list.

Let us walk through the process of creating a linked list of data that maintains the order in which the data is entered. For simplicity, we will deal with letters of the alphabet. We will need a pointer for the head of the list; let us call this pointer Head. We will call the data portion of each element of the list Data and the pointer part of each element Link. Initially, the list is empty. The first element will be pointed to by the pointer Head. After creation of this element, we place the data into it and set the Link to nil. Let us assume that the first data item in the list is 'A'; then our list now appears as follows:

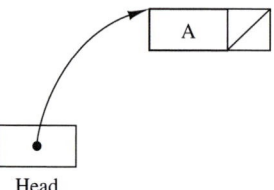

Once the initial element is in place, we can add additional elements to the list by an iterative procedure. We will need a pointer to point to the last element of the list; let us call the pointer Last. Initially, Last points to the first element, as shown:

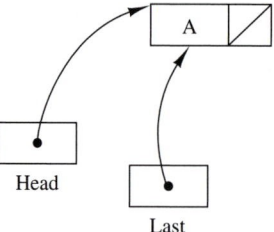

Now we insert the next data item (B) in the list. We must first create a space for the element. (Remember that we are using dynamic memory.) In order to create the space, we will need a temporary pointer (Temp), which will serve as a pointer to the new space. The new data will be placed in this element, as follows, and the link portion of the element will be initialized to nil:

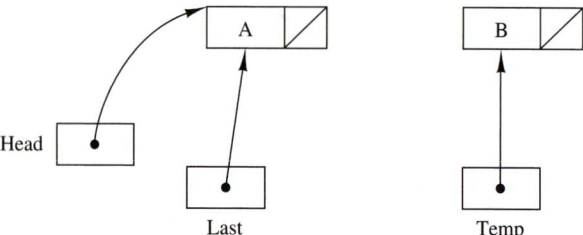

Next, we must adjust the pointers so that this new element is the last one in the list. This is accomplished in two steps:

1. The Link on the element containing A (previously the last element in the list) must point to the new element; this has the effect of adding the data to the list.

2. We change the content of Last so that it points to the new element; this shows where the next element is to be added.

After these adjustments, the list appears as follows:

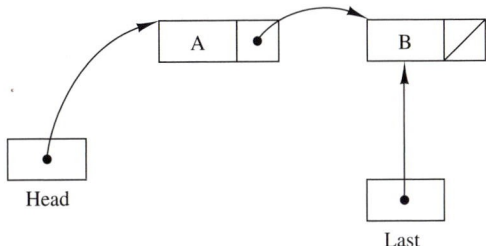

(For simplicity, we have omitted the pointer Temp, since its purpose has now been served.)

The procedure for inserting each data element (except the first one, which must be handled separately) can be summarized as follows:

PROCEDURE TO ADD AN ELEMENT TO A LINKED LIST

1.0 Create space for the element. (Use the pointer Temp to allocate the space; place the new data in this location and set the Link to nil)

2.0 Add the element to the list. (Adjust the Link in the element pointed to by Last)

3.0 Adjust Last to point to the new element.

This procedure must be repeated each time a data item is added to the list.

12.5.1   *Time Out*

Assume that the list contains data items 'A' and 'B', as shown before. Walk through the procedure for adding 'C' to the list. Show the status of memory after each step in the procedure.

12.5.2   Traversing a List

One of the advantages of a linked list is the ease with which you can write it out or search its content. The process of gaining access to elements in the list, beginning at the first and following the links to the end of the list, is called *traversing* the list.

Note that we are careful to make sure that the link on the last element always has the value nil. This makes sense because there are no data beyond the last element, so this link has nothing to point to. This fact is very important in a procedure for traversing a list. The location of the first element in the list is contained in the pointer Head, so this is where the process begins. We will need a pointer Temp to point to list elements, one at a time. The initial value of Temp is the content of Head. While the value of Temp is not equal to nil, we can use the data portion of this list element (use Temp^.Data) and then proceed to the next element by replacing Temp with the value of Temp^.Link—the content of the link portion of the current list element. The procedure is summarized in the following pseudocode.

PROCEDURE FOR TRAVERSING A LINKED LIST

1.0 Temp = Head
2.0 While Temp not = nil Do
3.0   Use data at element pointed to by Temp
4.0   Temp = value of Link at current element
5.0 End While

Let us walk through this procedure with a list. Assume the list is as follows:

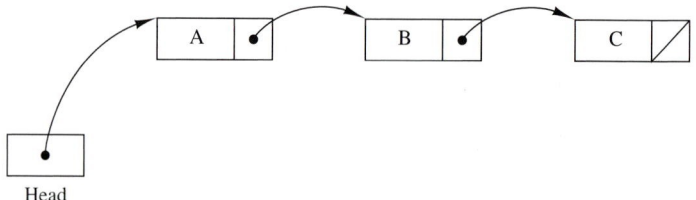

Initially, the value of Head is placed in Temp, yielding the following:

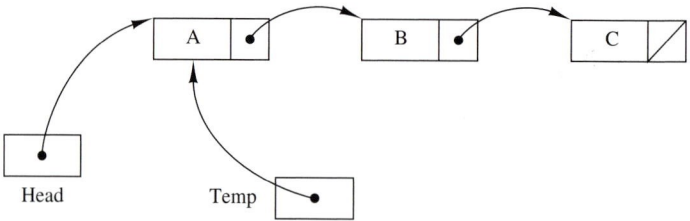

The value of Temp is not nil, so we use the content of the current element (A). (For example, we could write it out or compare it to some other value.) The Link portion of this element becomes the new value for Temp, so that Temp points to the next element as follows:

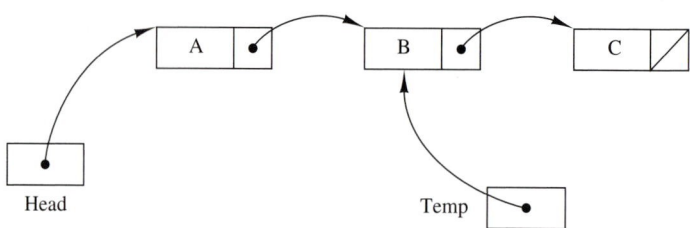

Since the value of Temp is not nil, we use the content of the element and adjust the value of Temp to point to the next element:

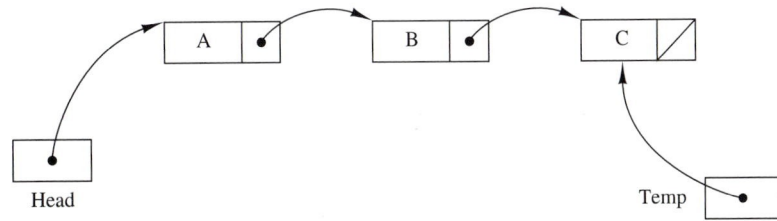

Again, the value of Temp is not nil, so the data in this element is used, and the link portion of the element becomes the new value of Temp:

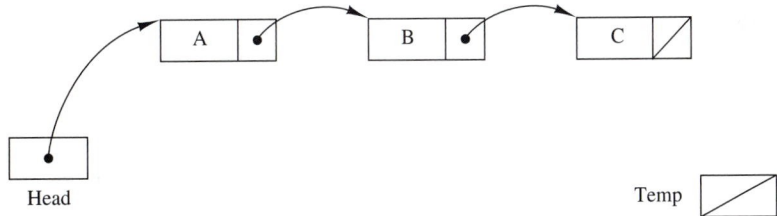

Now the value of Temp is nil, so the list has been completely traversed and the process terminates.

12.5.3 Time Out

Assume that in addition to the pointer Head that points to the first element in a list, you have available a pointer Last that points to the last element in the list. Devise a procedure to traverse the list that uses the fact that when Temp = Last, there are no more elements in the list.

12.5.4 Case Study: Creation of a Linked List

■ **Problem Statement.**   Write a program to allow the user to enter names (terminated by 'End'). The program should create a linked list structure containing the names. When all the data has been entered, the program should write the list in the order entered by the user.

■ **Problem Analysis.**   We shall need a record containing the name and a pointer to the next element in the list. We shall also need pointer variables for the first element in the list (Head) and the last element in the list (Last), as well as a temporary pointer for use in creating new list elements and in traversing the list. The required types and variables are as follows:

```
type
    NameType = string[10];
    PointerToData = ^Data;
    Data = record
                Name : NameType;
                Link : PointerToData
        end;
var
    Head, Last, Temp : PointerToData;
    InputName : NameType;
```

The variable InputName is used as an input variable to store the name, as entered by the user, prior to insertion of the item into the list.

Recall that the first element of a linked list must be treated separately from the others. After the first name is inserted, the pointer Last will point to the first element in the list. Then, Last will be updated each time a new element is inserted into the list. The data-entry process is terminated when the user enters 'End'. With these considerations in mind, we can design the required program:

LINKED LIST CREATION PROGRAM (P12a)

1.0 Read first name and insert at head of list

2.0 Initialize pointer to last element of list

3.0 Repeat read Name and insert in list until Name = 'End'
    3.1 Repeat
    3.2   Read a Name
    3.3   If Name <> 'End' Then
    3.4   Create space for Name
    3.5   Add Name to list
    3.6   Adjust pointer to last element
    3.7   End If
    3.8 Until Name = 'End'

4.0 Write the list of names

5.0 Wait

■ **Problem Solution.** The program to solve this problem is shown in Figure 12.3 as Program 12a. The implementations of the procedures to insert the first name in the list and add additional names are of primary interest. In order to insert the first name, we must create a list element, place the name in this element, and initialize the link portion of the element to nil, since it is (initially) the last element in the list. The required procedure is

```
New (Head);
Head^.Name := InputName;
Head^.Link := nil;
```

```pascal
program P12a (Input, Output);
{Program to create an unsorted list using a linked list structure}
uses
     Crt;
const
     InputPrompt = 'Enter Name (End to stop) ';
type
     NameType = string[10];
     PointerToData = ^Data;
     Data = record
                    Name : NameType;
                    Link : PointerToData
              end;
var
     Head, Last, Temp : PointerToData;
     InputName : NameType;
     .
     .
     .

begin     {Main Program}

{1.0 Read first name and insert at head of list}

     ClrScr;
     Write (InputPrompt);
     Readln (InputName);
     New (Head);
     Head^.Name := InputName;
     Head^.Link := nil;

{2.0 Initialize pointer to last element of the list}

     Last := Head;

{3.0 Repeat read name and insert in list until Name = 'End'}

     repeat
          Write (InputPrompt);
          Readln (InputName);
          if (InputName <> 'End') and (InputName <> 'end') then
               begin
                    New (Temp);              {Create space for Name}
                    Temp^.Name := InputName;
                    Temp^.Link := nil;
                    Last^.Link := Temp;   {Add name to list}
                    Last := Temp;         {Adjust pointer to last element}
               end;     {if}
     until (InputName = 'End') or (InputName = 'end');

{4.0 Write the list of names}

     Writeln ('---------');
     Temp := Head;
     while Temp <> nil do
          begin
               Writeln (Temp^.Name);
               Temp := Temp^.Link
          end;     {while}
     Writeln ('---------');

{5.0 Wait}

     AlternateWait

end.     {Main Program}
```

Figure 12.3 Program 12a: Creation of linked list (unsorted).

The procedure for adding a name to the list is divided into three parts. First a space is created for the name, which includes storing InputName in this location and setting the Link to nil. The pointer Temp is used to create the element, as shown next:

```
New (Temp);
Temp^Name := InputName;
Temp^.Link := nil;
```

Then the new element is added to the list by adjusting the Link on the last element in the list:

```
Last^Link := Temp;
```

Finally, we adjust the pointer Last so that it points to the new last element:

```
Last := Temp;
```

The procedure to list the elements uses the pointer Temp to proceed from the first element to the last, as shown next;

```
Temp := Head;
while Temp <> nil do
      begin
          Writeln (Temp^.Name);
          Temp := Temp^.Link
      end; {while}
```

12.5.5   Time Out

1. Compile and execute Program 12a.
2. Modify Program 12a to insert each new item at the beginning of the list rather than at the end. What effect does this have on the output produced by the program?
3. Program 12a makes the assumption that the list is not empty—that is, that there will always be at least one name in the list. Revise the program to take into consideration the possibility of an empty list.

12.5.6   Maintaining a Sorted List

Program 12a illustrates how to create a linked list, but its usefulness is somewhat limited because the list is in the same order as the data entered by the user. A much more useful program is one that would maintain the list in a given sequence. Such a procedure would be required first to search the existing list to locate the proper position for each new element and then to insert the element in that location. This task is much more efficient when a linked list is used than when an array is used for the list. An array requires that all the elements be moved down to make room for a new element. By contrast, a new element can be inserted into a linked list by a simple adjustment of pointers.

Let us examine the process of inserting a new element into the midst of a linked list. Suppose that we have the following simple linked list:

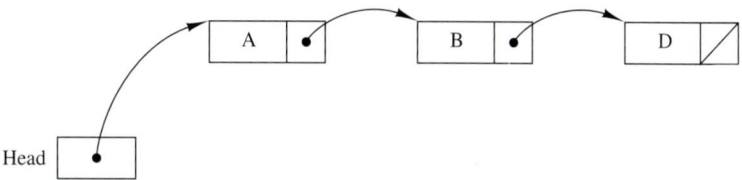

Now suppose we wish to insert the item C into the list and maintain the elements in proper sequence; that is, we wish to insert the element C between B and D. Our first task is to locate the element in the list that will immediately precede the new element. Let us assume that an appropriate search procedure has been devised and that we have a pointer, Loc, which points to the element immediately preceding the location for the new element. Also, let us assume that we have created a location for the new element at Temp, as shown in the following diagram:

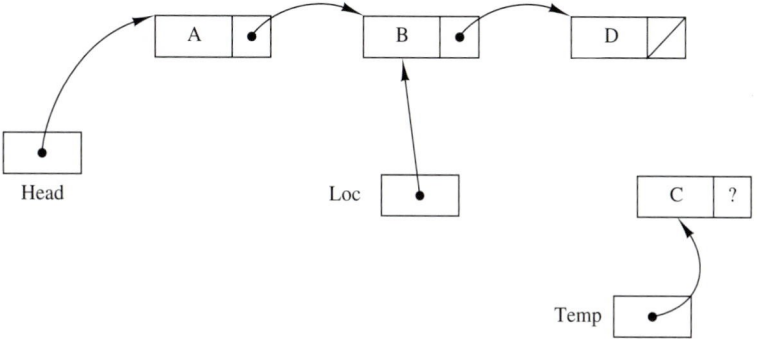

The task at hand is to insert the new element into the list. To do this, two links must be adjusted. The link at the new element must point to the element that previously followed the element pointed to by Loc. This can be accomplished by

```
Temp^.Link := Loc^.Link;
```

After execution of this statement, the memory diagram will be as follows:

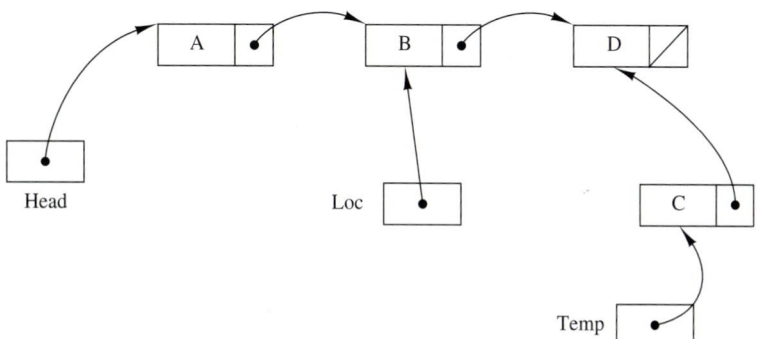

Now the link on the element pointed to by Loc must be changed so that this element points to the new element, which is at location Temp. This is done by

```
Loc^.Link := Temp;
```

After execution of this statement, the new item is completely inserted:

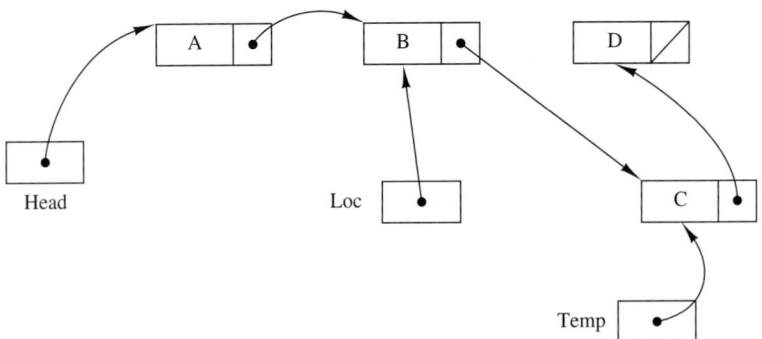

Note that it is imperative that these two statements be carried out in the sequence given: First adjust the link on the new element, and then adjust the link on the predecessor element. If the statements are executed in reverse sequence, the link at the new element will end up pointing to itself, which is a very undesirable situation indeed.

It will be necessary to take special action when the new element needs to be inserted at the beginning of the list. In this case, the pointer Head must be modified to point to the new element, and the link in the new element will point to what was previously the first element in the list.

It turns out that determining the proper value for Loc, which points to the predecessor of the new element, is somewhat more involved than adjusting the links to add an element to the list. Basically, our problem is to search the list and stop when the next item in the list is greater than the item to be inserted. It will be necessary to consider three cases: The new item may be inserted

1. At the beginning of the list
2. In the midst of the list
3. At the end of the list

The first case is relatively easy: If the first item in the list is greater than the one to be added, the new element must be inserted at the beginning. Let us assume that the first case does not hold. Then it will be necessary to traverse the list. We use the pointer Temp to point to the current item in the list and the pointer Loc to point to the previous element in the list. We must stop when either Temp^.Link is nil (we have reached the end of the list) or Temp^.Data has a value that is greater than the new item. If neither of these events occurs, then we will hold on to the current value of Temp by placing it into Loc; then we will replace Temp by Temp^.Link to proceed to the next element. Let us summarize this procedure in the following pseudocode.

PROCEDURE TO SEARCH A LINKED LIST

1.0 If new item is less than item at head of list Then

2.0   Loc = nil

3.0 Else

4.0   Temp = Head

5.0   Loc = Head

6.0   Continue = True

7.0   While Continue Do

8.0   Replace Temp by Link of current element

9.0   If Temp = nil Then

10.0   Continue = False

11.0   Else If data at current element is greater than or
              equal to new item Then

12.0   Continue = False

13.0   Else

14.0   Loc = Temp

15.0   End If

16.0   End While

17.0 End If

When this procedure terminates, the value of Loc will be nil if the new item should be inserted at the head of the list. Otherwise Loc will point to the largest item in the list that is less than or equal to the new item; this element becomes the immediate predecessor of the new item when it is added.

12.5.7   *Time Out*

Given the following linked list, trace the execution of the procedures outlined in this section to locate and add the element 'E' to the list.

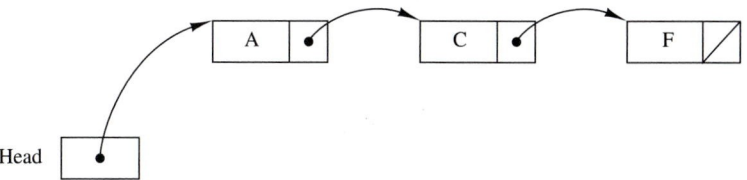

Draw diagrams of the relevant portions of memory to help you walk through the procedure.

12.5.8   *Case Study: Sorted List using a Linked List*

■ **Problem Statement.**   Write a program to create a sorted list of names entered by the user. Terminate the program when the user enters 'End'. The program should write the content of the list after all the data has been entered.

■ **Problem Analysis.** The task at hand can be described at a high level in the following program plan.

SORTED LIST CREATION PROGRAM (P12b)

1.0 Get first Name and place it in list
2.0 Repeat read Name and insert in list until Name = 'End'
    2.1 Repeat
    2.2   Read Name
    2.3   If Name <> 'End' Then
    2.4   Compute Loc = location of the
                      predecessor of Name
    2.5   If Loc = nil Then
    2.6   Insert Name at head of list
    2.7   Else
    2.8   Insert Name at location Loc
    2.9   End If
    2.10   End If
    2.11 Until Name = 'End'
3.0 Write the list of names
4.0 Wait

■ **Problem Solution.** Many operations on linked lists can be implemented as functions or procedures. There is no problem with passing pointer variables as parameters—either value parameters or variable parameters. It is, however, imperative that the programmer consider carefully whether a pointer should be a value or variable parameter. As with all value parameters, a local copy of the parameter is made by the subprogram, so that any change made to the variable within the subprogram is not reflected in the calling program. This fact can be used to advantage at times. If the parameter is a variable parameter, then changes made are reflected in the actual parameter value.

To implement the plan for Program 12b, let us write the following procedures and functions:

1. *Initialize:* Place the first name in the list; the procedure will need Head as a variable parameter and Name as a value parameter.

2. *Locate:* Function to determine the location of the predecessor for the new item; if the new item goes at the head of the list, the function returns nil. The function will need value parameters for Head and the new name; the function type will be pointer.

3. *Insert:* Procedure for inserting a new name in the list; the procedure will need value parameters for the location and the new name.

4. *NewHead:* Procedure for inserting a new name at the head of the list; the procedure must have a variable parameter for the Head and a value parameter for the new name.

5. *ListNames:* Procedure for writing the content of the list; the procedure will need Head as a value parameter.

```pascal
program P12b (Input, Output);
{Program to create a sorted list using a linked list data structure}
uses
    Crt;
const
    Prompt = 'Enter Name (End to stop) ';
type
    NameType = string[10];
    PointerToData = ^Data;
    Data = record
                Name : NameType;
                Link : PointerToData
           end;
var
    Loc, Head : PointerToData;
    NewName : NameType;
{*********************************************************************}
    procedure Initialize (var Head : PointerToData;
                              FirstName : NameType);
    {Procedure to place initial name on list}
    begin     {Initialize}
        New (Head);
        Head^.Name := FirstName;
        Head^.Link := nil
    end;        {Initialize}
{-------------------------------------------------------------------}
    function Locate (Head : PointerToData;
                     TargetName : NameType) : PointerToData;
    {Function to determine the location for insertion of TargetName to
        the list}
    var
        Continue : Boolean;
    begin     {Locate}
        if Head^.Name > TargetName then
            Locate := nil
        else
            begin
                Locate := Head;
                Continue := True;
                while Continue do
                    begin
                        Head := Head^.Link;
                        if Head = nil then
                            Continue := False
                        else if Head^.Name >= TargetName then
                            Continue := False
                        else
                            Locate := Head;
                    end;   {while}
            end;   {if}
    end;     {Locate}
{-------------------------------------------------------------------}
```

Figure 12.4(a) Program 12b: Initial declarations (part 1 of 3 parts).

Program 12b, which is shown in Figure 12.4, is an implementation of the plan just outlined. One minor difference exists in the implementation of the function Locate and the procedure outlined in Section 12.5.6. In the program, the pointer variable Head is used as

```
      procedure Insert (Location : PointerToData;
                        NewName : NameType);
      {Procedure to insert NewName at Location}
      var
          Temp : PointerToData;
      begin {Insert}
          New (Temp);
          Temp^.Name := NewName;
          Temp^.Link := Location^.Link;
          Location^.Link := Temp
      end;  {Insert}
{-----------------------------------------------------------------------}
      procedure NewHead (var Head : PointerToData;
                             NewName : NameType);
      {Procedure to insert NewName as the new head of the list}
      var
          Temp : PointerToData;
      begin     {NewHead}
          New (Temp);
          Temp^.Name := NewName;
          Temp^.Link := Head;
          Head := Temp
      end;     {NewHead}
{-----------------------------------------------------------------------}
      procedure ListNames (Head : PointerToData);
      {Procedure to print list of names}
      begin    {ListNames}
          Writeln ('----------');
          while Head <> nil do
              begin
                  Writeln (Head^.Name);
                  Head := Head^.Link
              end;    {while}
          Writeln ('----------')
      end;    {ListNames}
      .
      .
      .
{**********************************************************************}
```

Figure 12.4(b) Program 12b: Declarations of the procedures Insert, NewHead, and ListNames (part 2 of 3 parts).

the temporary pointer variable from the pseudocode version of the procedure. This is permissible because Head is a value parameter to this function, so that when it is changed by the statement

```
Head := Head^.Link;
```

only the local version of the variable is changed. The actual variable Head retains its proper value. (This is very important: If the value of Head is changed inappropriately, the only path to the first element in the list will be destroyed.)

```
begin     {Main Program}

{1.0 Get first Name and place it in list}

    ClrScr;
    Write (Prompt);
    Readln (NewName);
    Initialize (Head, NewName);

{2.0 Repeat read Name and insert in list until Name =  'End'}

    repeat
          Write (Prompt);
          Readln (NewName);
          if (NewName <> 'End') and (NewName <> 'end') then
             begin
                  Loc := Locate (Head, NewName);
                  if Loc = nil then
                     NewHead (Head, NewName)
                  else
                     Insert (Loc, NewName);
             end    {if}
    until (NewName = 'End') or (NewName = 'end');

{3.0 Write the list of names}

    ListNames (Head);

{4.0 Wait}

    AlternateWait

end.    {Main Program}
```

Figure 12.4(c)   Program 12b: Statement part (part 3 of 3 parts).

12.5.9   Time Out

1. Compile and execute Program 12b. Test the program with sample data of your choosing.

2. Modify Program 12b to create the list in descending sequence rather than ascending sequence.

3. Modify Program 12b to disallow the insertion of duplicate items. *Hint:* Remember that the name at Loc is the largest name, which is less than or equal to the new name.

12.5.10   Deleting Elements from a Linked List

In any general data-management program, it is necessary not only to add elements to a list, but also to delete elements that may no longer be needed. We have seen how to add elements at the head of a list or in the middle of a list. Let us turn to the related problem of deleting elements from a list. We need to consider two cases: deleting the first element of the list and deleting an element in the middle of the list.

To delete the first element in a list, it is necessary to make Head point to what was the second element in the list. We also need to dispose of the element that is no longer needed. To facilitate this, we will need a temporary pointer Temp, which will point to the element to be deleted. The link portion of this element becomes the new value for Head. Then we can use the Dispose procedure to eliminate the element pointed to by Temp. For example, suppose we wish to delete 'A' from the following simple linked list:

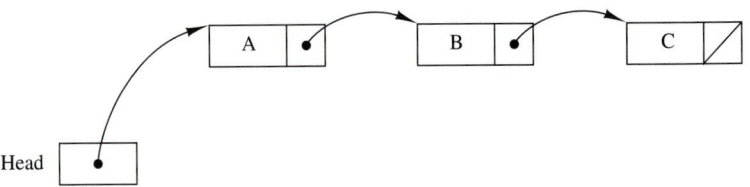

We first establish Temp to point to this element by

```
Temp := Head;
```

Now the memory diagram appears as follows:

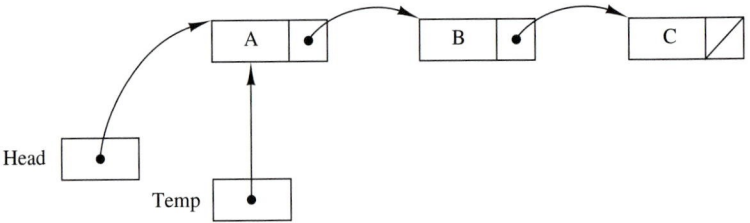

Next, we can establish the new value of Head so that it points to the element 'B':

```
Head := Head^.Link;
```

Memory now appears as

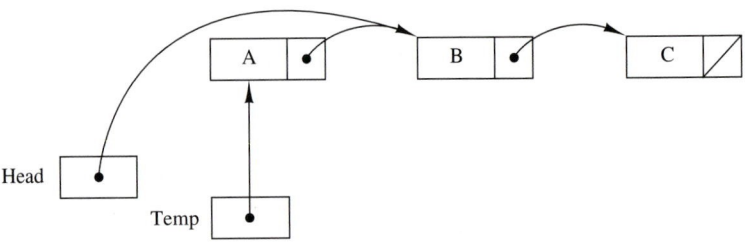

Finally, we can use Dispose to remove the element containing 'A':

```
Dispose (Temp);
```

Our memory is now cleaned up, and the list no longer contains the deleted element:

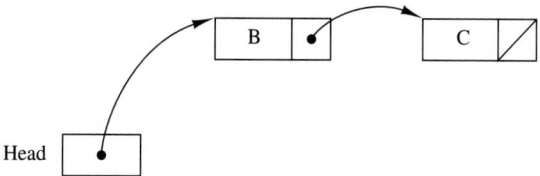

Program 12c, shown in Figure 12.5, contains a Pascal function to accomplish the deletion task for the data structure of Programs 12a and 12b. Note that it is imperative that the parameter Head be a variable parameter, because the change in the value must be communicated to the calling program.

Let us now consider the problem of deleting an element in the middle of a list. We assume that a pointer Loc points to the element that is the immediate predecessor of the element to be deleted. The link portion of this element needs to point to the successor of the element to be deleted, and we need to eliminate the deleted element. For example, suppose we need to eliminate the element 'B' from the following linked list, and suppose Loc points to its predecessor, the element containing 'A', as shown in the following diagram:

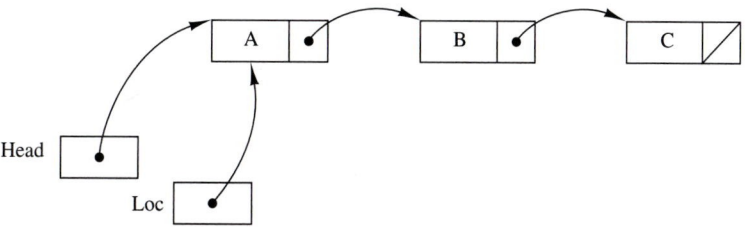

We first make Temp point to the element to be deleted by

```
Temp := Loc^.Link;
```

which yields the following memory layout:

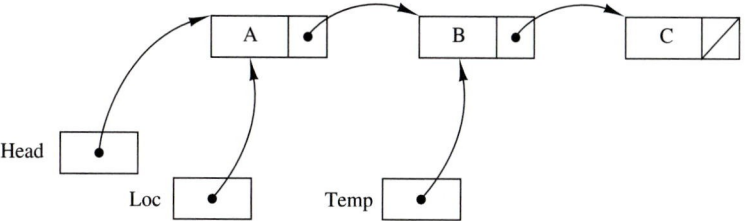

The element at Loc needs to point to the successor of the element at Temp. We accomplish this task by

```
Loc^.Link := Temp^.Link
```

```
program P12c (Input, Output);
{Program to create a sorted list and delete items from the list
    using a linked list data structure}
uses
    Crt;
const
    Prompt = 'Enter Name (End to stop) ';
    DeletePrompt = 'Enter Name to be deleted (End to stop) ';
type
    NameType = string[10];
    PointerToData = ^Data;
    Data = record
                Name : NameType;
                Link : PointerToData
           end;
var
    Temp, Loc, Head : PointerToData;
    NewName : NameType;
{*************************************************************************}
    .
    .
    .
    procedure DeleteHead (var Head : PointerToData);
    {Procedure to delete first element of the list}
    var
        Temp : PointerToData;
    begin    {DeleteHead}
        Temp := Head;
        Head := Head^.Link;
        Dispose (Temp)
    end;     {DeleteHead}
{----------------------------------------------------------------}
    procedure Delete (var Loc : PointerToData);
    {Procedure to delete item pointed to by Loc from  the list}
    var
        Temp : PointerToData;
    begin  {Delete}
        Temp := Loc^.Link;
        Loc^.Link := Temp^.Link;
        Dispose (Temp)
    end;     {Delete}
    .
    .
    .
{*************************************************************************}
```

Figure 12.5(a) Program 12c: Declaration part showing procedures Delete-Head and Delete (part 1 of 2 parts).

which yields the following layout:

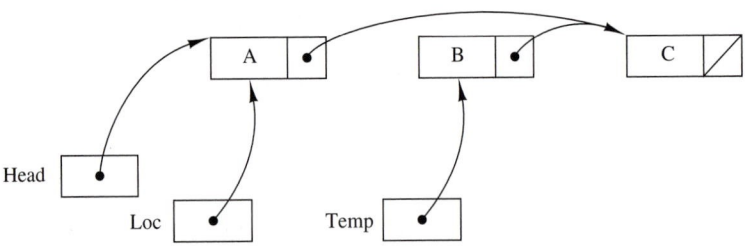

```
begin     {Main Program}
    .
    .
    .
{3.0 Repeat read Name and delete it from list until  Name = 'End'}

    Writeln;
    Writeln ('Begin deleting names from list');
    repeat
          Writeln ('Current List');
          ListNames (Head);
          Write (DeletePrompt);
          Readln (NewName);
          if (NewName <> 'End') and (NewName <> 'end') then
             begin
                  Loc := Locate (Head, NewName);
                  if (Loc = nil) then
                     Writeln ('Name not in list')
                  else if Head^.Name = NewName then
                       DeleteHead (Head)
                  else
                      begin
                           Temp := Loc^.Link;
                           if Temp^.Name <> NewName then
                                Writeln ('Name not in list ')
                           else
                                Delete (Loc)
                      end    {if}
             end      {if}
    until (NewName = 'End') or (NewName = 'end');
    .
    .
    .
end.    {Main Program}
```

Figure 12.5(b) Program 12c: Partial listing of the statement part (part 2 of 2 parts).

Now we can eliminate the element that is no longer needed by using the Dispose procedure:

```
Dispose (Temp);
```

After this is accomplished, the process of removing the unneeded item is complete:

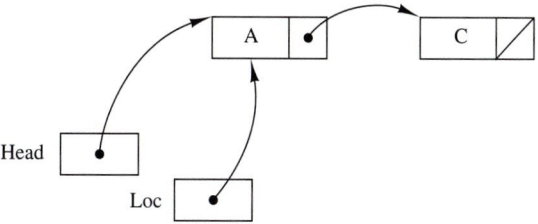

Note in Program 12c (Figure 12.5) that it is imperative that the parameter Loc be a variable parameter, since the change in its value must be communicated to the calling program.

12.5.11 Time Out

Test Program 12c with data of your choosing. Be sure to test the error message that is produced if the requested item is not present in the list.

12.6 STACKS

A **stack** is a type of list that is useful for some specialized applications, particularly in the area of computer science. A stack is formally described as a last-in, first-out queue; that is, the last element that is placed on the stack is the first element that is removed. You have seen such structures in other contexts. For example, in a cafeteria, you have probably seen stacks of plates in which clean plates are added to the top of the stack and plates that are used by customers are removed from the top of the stack. The last plate that is placed on the stack is the first one to be removed. Stacks arise naturally in the implementation of programming languages. For example, the easiest way to implement recursion is to maintain a stack of return addresses. When a procedure invokes itself, a return address is added to the stack. When the procedure terminates, the last address added to the stack is the first one to be removed and used as a return address.

There are four operations that are relevant to a stack:

1. Place an element on the stack. This is technically known as **pushing** an element.
2. Remove an element from the stack. This is called **popping** the stack.
3. Examine the value at the top of the stack.
4. List the content of the stack.

A linked list is an appropriate structure for implementing a stack.[1] A pointer Top always points to the first element in the list, which is called the top of the stack. Pushing a new element onto the stack involves creating a location for the element and adjusting pointers so that the new element is at the beginning of the list. Popping the stack involves adjusting pointers in order to unlink the first element in the list and then disposing of the element that has been removed. Listing the content of the stack involves traversing the list until the link portion of an element points to nil, indicating that the end of the list (also called the bottom of the stack) has been reached.

For example, suppose we have a stack containing the elements 'A' and 'B', as shown in the following diagram:

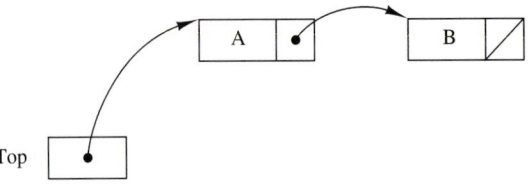

---

[1]An array can also be used to implement a stack, but it is limited to some predefined maximum size, whereas the linked list implementation is limited only by the amount of available memory.

Now suppose we wish to push the element 'C' onto the stack. The new element becomes the first element in the list. To add this element, we need a temporary pointer Temp. We create an element for the list and place the value in that element:

```
New (Temp);
Temp^.Data := 'C';
```

The results are:

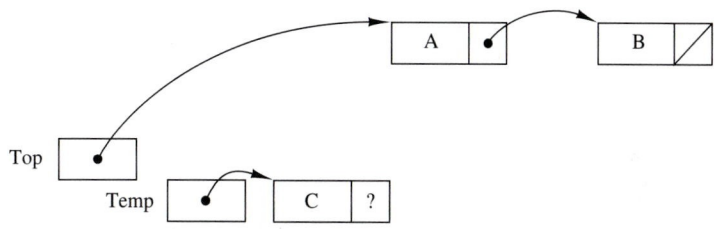

Now we insert the element into the list. The link portion of the new element must point to what was previously the first element in the list:

```
Temp^.Link := Top;
```

The results are as follows:

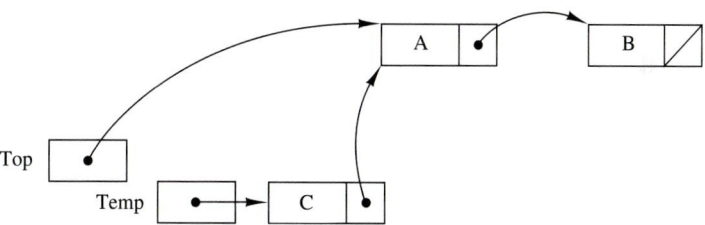

Now, Top must point to the new element:

```
Top := Temp;
```

The finished product shows the new item at the beginning of the list:

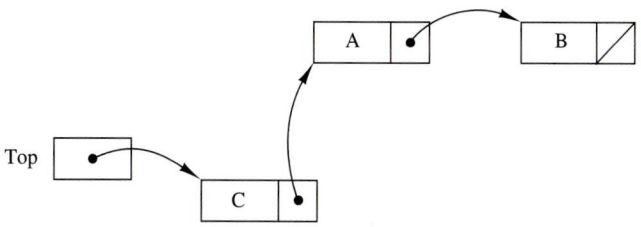

Popping the stack is accomplished by removing the first element from the list. If the list is empty, then the value of Top will be nil. Otherwise, we start by establishing a temporary pointer that points to the first element of the list:

```
Temp := Top;
```

The results are as follows:

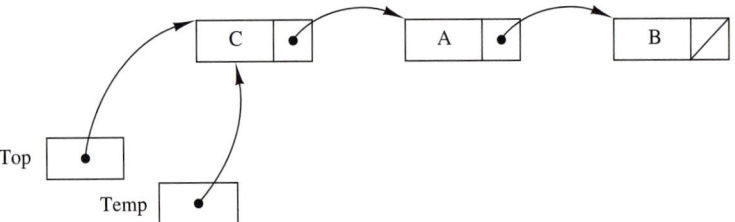

The new value of Top must be the link portion of the first element of the list—that is,

```
Top := Top^.Link
```

which yields

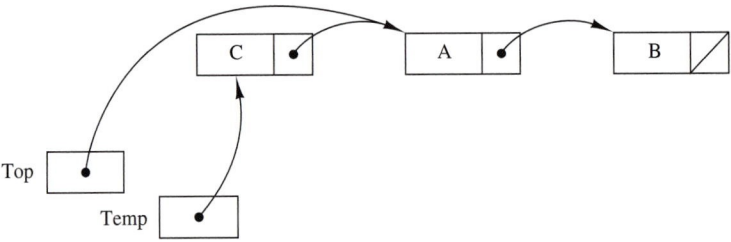

Now the location pointed to by Temp can be disposed of:

```
Dispose (Temp);
```

This done, the memory once occupied by that element is available for other use. The result is a list with the first element removed:

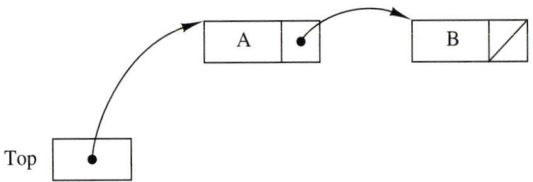

Program 12d, which is shown in Figure 12.6, illustrates the procedures required to maintain a stack in the context of a complete program. The data involved are names. The

```pascal
program P12d (Input, Output);
{Program to implement a stack}
uses
     Crt;
const
     MenuLine = 'Action (1 = Push, 2 = Pop, 3 = Quit) ? ';
     Prompt = 'Enter data item ';
type
     DataType = string[10];
     StackPointer = ^StackElement;
     StackElement = record
                              Data : DataType;
                              Link : StackPointer
                    end;
var
     Top : StackPointer;
     DataItem : DataType;
     Choice : Integer;
{**********************************************************************}
     procedure Push (var Top : StackPointer; DataItem : DataType);
     {Procedure to push DataItem onto Stack}
     var
          Temp : StackPointer;
     begin      {Push}
          New (Temp);
          Temp^.Data := DataItem;
          Temp^.Link := Top;
          Top := Temp
     end;     {Push}
{----------------------------------------------------------------------}
     procedure Pop (var Top : StackPointer);
     {Procedure to pop the stack}
     var
          Temp : StackPointer;
     begin    {Pop}
          if Top = nil then
             Writeln ('Stack is empty ')
          else
             begin
                  Temp := Top;
                  Top := Temp^.Link;
                  Writeln ('Item removed from stack is ', Temp^.Data);
                  Dispose (Temp)
             end     {if}
     end;   {Pop}
{----------------------------------------------------------------------}
     procedure ListStack (Top : StackPointer);
     {Procedure to list contents of the stack}
     begin    {ListStack}
          Writeln ('----------');
          while Top <> nil do
               begin
                    Writeln (Top^.Data);
                    Top := Top^.LInk
               end;      {while}
          Writeln ('----------')
     end;    {ListStack}
     .
     .
     .
{**********************************************************************}
```

Figure 12.6(a) Program 12d: Declaration part (part 1 of 2 parts).

```
begin    {Main Program}

{1.0 Initialize stack}

     Top := nil;

{2.0 Repeat get Choice and take action until Choice =   3}

     ClrScr;
     repeat
          Write (MenuLine);
          Readln (Choice);
          case Choice of
               1  :    begin
                            Write (Prompt);
                            Readln (DataItem);
                            Push (Top, DataItem);
                            ListStack (Top)
                       end;
               2  :    begin
                            Pop (Top);
                            ListStack (Top)
                       end;
               3  :    begin
                            Writeln ('Program terminated');
                            AlternateWait
                       end
               else
                            Writeln ('Invalid action ')
          end;    {case}
     until Choice = 3;

end.    {Main Program}
```

Figure 12.6(b)   Program 12d: Statement part (part 2 of 2 parts).

type declarations and variables required are very similar to those in other program examples in this chapter. (When implementing a stack, it is traditional to call the pointer to the first element Top rather than Head, which we have used up until now.) The user has three choices: to push an element onto the stack, to pop an element, or to quit. Each time an element is pushed, the program lists the content of the stack, using the procedure ListStack. When an element is popped from the stack, the program lists that element. Note that if the pop command is given and the list is empty (Top = nil), then an error message is produced. Note also that the procedures Push and Pop require the pointer Top as a variable parameter, since the content of Top is modified by either action. The procedure ListStack uses Top as a value parameter, so that it can be used as a temporary variable to follow the links from one element of the list to the next.

12.6.1   *Time Out*

1. Compile and execute Program 12d. Test the program with sample data of your choosing.

2. Why is there no need for the pointer Last to point to the last element of a stack?

3. What would happen if Top was listed as a variable parameter in the procedure ListStack?

12.7 BINARY TREES

One problem with a linked list is that the only available search strategy is a sequential search. We must begin at the head and proceed until the desired element is located. If the list is sorted, the search can conclude at the first entry that is greater than the desired element; otherwise, an exhaustive search is needed. We saw that when an array is used to implement a list, the random access capabilities of the array[2] permit a much more efficient search strategy for a sorted list—the binary search. Unfortunately, a linked list does not make random access to the data possible, so the binary search strategy is impossible. When an efficient search strategy is needed, and the benefits of a linked list structure implemented with pointers is desired, a structure called a **binary search tree** can be used.

A binary tree is made up of elements called *nodes* and links that connect the nodes. Each node can be connected to at most two other nodes, which are called the **descendants** of the node. One of the nodes is designated as the **root**—the beginning of the structure, which is analogous to the Head of a linked list or the Top of a stack. A typical binary tree structure is shown in Figure 12.7. As noted in this diagram, a node that is at the bottom of the structure (one that has no descendants) is called a **leaf**. The terminology used is obviously borrowed from botany; however, diagrams of trees are traditionally drawn with the root at the top of the structure and leaves at the bottom.

Each node in a tree can be treated as the root of a subtree that consists of the node and all its descendants. Because each node is the parent of two branches, two **subtrees**—a left subtree and a right subtree—are created at each node. One or the other of the subtrees may have no elements and are called empty subtrees. Both subtrees of a leaf are empty. The following tree illustrates the idea of subtrees:

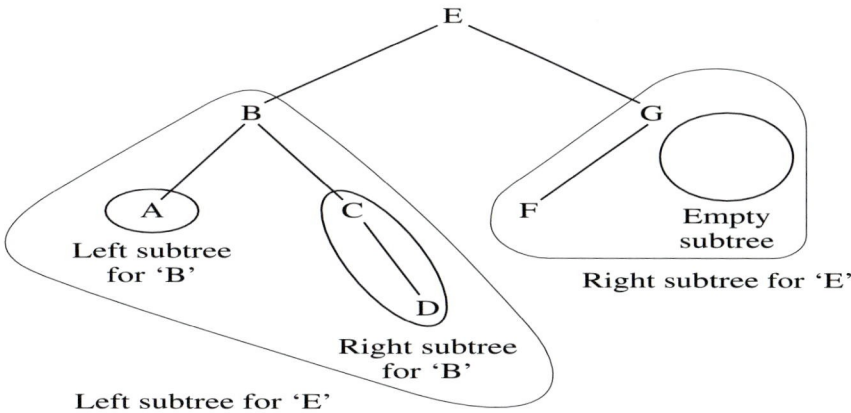

---

[2]Array are said to be random access structures because it takes the same amount of time to access any component of the array irrespective of the component's position in the array.

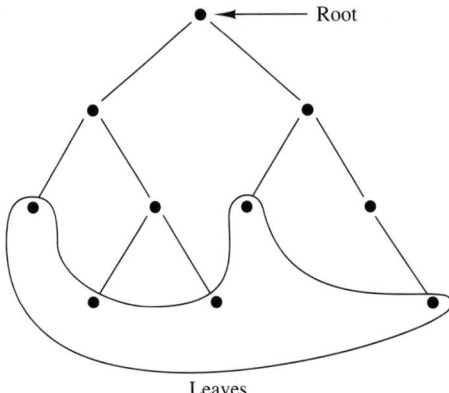

Figure 12.7 Typical binary tree.

This tree is a special type of binary tree called a **binary search tree**. In a binary search tree, all of the elements less than the element at a particular node are contained in the left subtree and all of the elements that have a larger value are contained in the right subtree.

In the preceding example, the root node, which contains 'E', is the parent of a left subtree, which in this case contains data that are less than 'E', and a right subtree, which contains data items that are greater than 'E'. Similarly, the node containing 'B' is the parent of two subtrees: The subtree on the left contains elements that are less than 'B' and the subtree on the right contains elements that are greater than 'B'. Consider the element at 'G'. The right subtree is empty; the left subtree has one element that is less than 'G'. This arrangement of data preserves the order of the data and also facilitates the search process.

Suppose we are given a binary search tree, such as the one just shown, in which each node is the parent of two subtrees—a left subtree containing all elements that are less than the data in the root node and a right subtree in which all items are greater than the data at the root. Let us consider the problem of searching for data in the tree. This is actually quite a simple task. We start with the root. If the data at this node is equal to the item being sought, then we stop. If the item is not found, then we continue our search with either the left subtree (if the item being sought is greater than the data at the root) or the right subtree (if the item being sought is greater than the data at the root). The search continues in the same manner until either the item is located or an empty subtree is encountered, at which point we conclude that the item is not present.

For example, given the preceding tree, let us trace the process of searching for an item with the value 'C'. Starting with the root of the tree, we note that 'C' < 'E'. Thus, we continue with the left subtree, which consists of

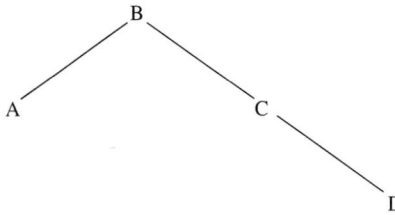

The root of this subtree contains 'B'. 'C' is greater than 'B', so we must look for the data in the right subtree, which contains

The data item at the root of this subtree is equal to 'C', so we have located the desired element.

Now consider the process of locating an element such as 'H', which is not present. Again, the process begins at the root node. 'H' > 'E', so we continue our search in the right subtree, which contains

Since 'H' > 'G', the search continues in the right subtree, which is empty; therefore, we conclude that 'H' is not present in the structure. (Note that if we desired to add 'H' to the tree, we have now located its proper place—as the right-hand descendant of 'G'.)

Let us turn to the somewhat more subtle problem of outputting the data in sequence. This process involves *traversing* the tree, which means following the links from node to node until an empty subtree is encountered. We begin at the root. Since all items less than the root are in the left subtree, we must traverse that tree, print the data contained at the root, and then traverse the right subtree, which contains all the items that are greater than the data at the root. This same process is followed for each subtree. We first traverse the left subtree, output the data at the root, and then traverse the right subtree. Each traversal is terminated when an empty subtree is encountered. The sequence for visiting the nodes in the tree we have used as an example is shown next:

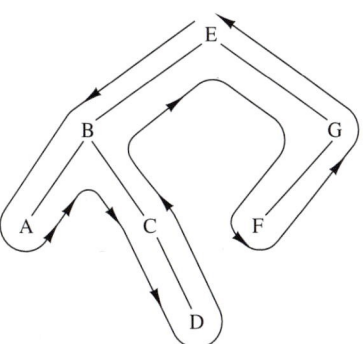

We begin at the root ('E') and traverse its left subtree. The left subtree has root 'B'; we traverse its left subtree, which has root 'A'. The left subtree of this node is empty, so we output the root 'A' and traverse its right subtree, which is also empty. Now we back up, output the content of the parent element 'B', and then follow the right subtree of this element. This subtree has 'C' as its root. We traverse its left subtree, which is empty, so we output 'C' and begin traversal of the right subtree of 'C'. This results in the output of 'D'. At this point, we have concluded the traversal of the left subtree with root at 'E', so we output 'E' and begin the traversal of its right subtree. This will result in the output of 'F' and, finally, 'G'.

The data structure required to represent a tree in Pascal requires a pointer to the root node. Each node is a record composed of data fields and two pointers—one to the left subtree and one to the right subtree. A Pascal program segment required to set up a structure for the tree to represent the data we have used as an example would be:

```
type
    NodePointerType = ^NodeType;
    NodeType = record
                    Data : Char;
                    LeftLink, RightLink : NodePointerType
              end;
var
    Root : NodePointerType;
```

A typical binary tree would be as follows:

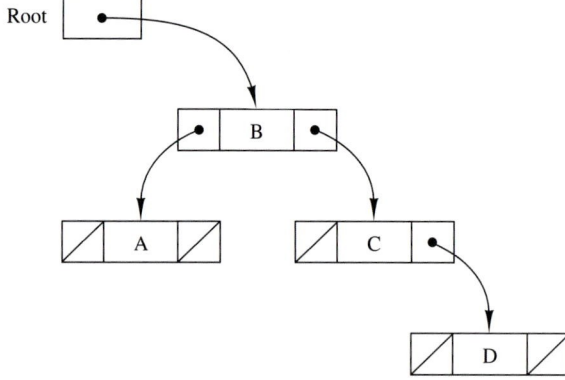

LeftLink and RightLink point to the root of the left subtree and the right subtree, respectively, of each node. Note that when the value of LeftLink or RightLink is nil; the left or right subtree is empty. When both links are nil, the node is a leaf.

Let us construct a procedure for building a binary search tree from data entered by the user. Initially, we set the value of Root to nil. Now we can insert elements into the tree. This essentially involves searching the tree to locate the node that is the logical predecessor or successor of each new item and linking the item as the root of a new subtree on the left or right of the parent node. If the new item is less than the item at the root of the tree, the new item must be inserted on the left subtree; if the new item is greater than the data at the root, then the new item must be inserted on the right subtree. The procedure is recursive. We repeat the same process until a node is found with an empty subtree; at this point, the new item is linked to the tree. For example, suppose we wish to build a tree with the data 'C', 'F', 'A', and 'B'. Initially, the value of Root is nil, so we have located the place for the first item:

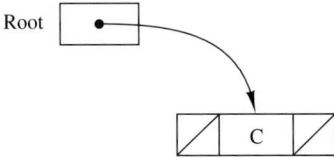

Now we proceed to the next item. Its value is greater than 'C', so the pointer to the root of the subtree to which it belongs is the right link of the element containing 'C'. The value of this pointer is nil, so we insert the item at this point:

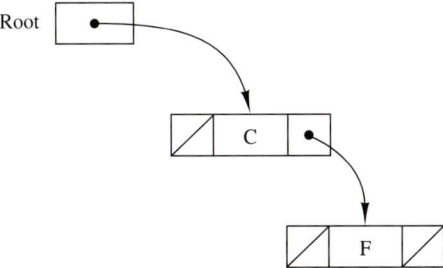

Now consider the element 'A'. 'A' is less than 'C', so the left link for the element containing 'C' points to the root of the subtree for this element. The value of this link is nil, so 'A' is inserted here:

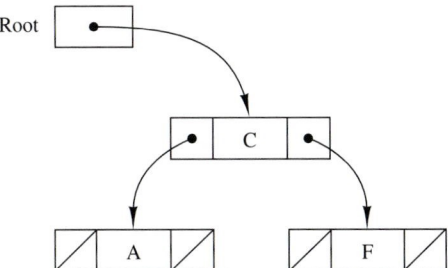

Now we wish to add the element 'B'. Since 'B' is less than 'C', it belongs in the left subtree. The left link for the element containing 'C' points to the root of the subtree in which 'B' belongs. This link points to the element containing 'A'. Since 'B' is greater than 'A', 'B' belongs in the right subtree of this element. Since the right link for the element containing 'A' is nil, we have found the proper location for this element, and we insert the element into the tree:

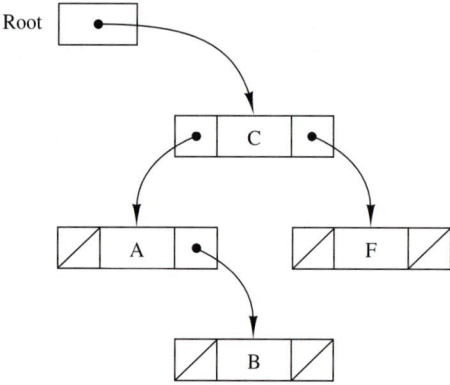

12.7.1 Time Out

1. Add elements 'E', 'G', and 'H' to the tree begun in this section. Draw an appropriate memory diagram to show the resulting tree.
2. Create a binary tree containing elements 'F', 'B', 'C', 'G', 'H', 'A', and 'E'. Comment on the difference between the tree created in this exercise and the tree that resulted from Exercise 1.
3. Perform traversals of the trees created in questions 1 and 2. Compare the output produced.

12.7.2 Case Study: Building a Binary Search Tree

■ **Problem Statement.** Write a program to build a binary search tree from data entered by the program user. Assume that the data consists of names of maximum length 10. After each insertion, print a list of the names in sequence.

■ **Problem Analysis.** The data structure required will be similar to that presented in the previous section. We need a node pointer type and a record for each node, which consists of a field for the name and two pointers—one for the left subtree and one for the right subtree. The required declarations are as follows:

```
type
    NameType = string[10];
    NodePointer = ^Node;
    Node = record
                Name : NameType;
                LeftLink, RightLink : NodePointer
            end;
var
    Root : NodePointer;
```

We have two basic tasks: to insert new data into the tree and to traverse the tree. Let us write separate procedures to accomplish these tasks.

The procedure to traverse the tree needs a value parameter for the root of the tree. It will execute itself recursively; first, it will traverse the left subtree by following the left links, and then, when an empty subtree is located, it will write out the contents of the root element and traverse the right subtree by following the right link of the current root element. A plan for this procedure is as follows:

PROCEDURE TRAVERSE (IMPORT: ROOT)

1.0 If Root not equal to nil Then

2.0   Execute Traverse using the value of the LeftLink at the Root location
            as the parameter

3.0   Write data at Root location

4.0   Execute Traverse using the value of the RightLink at the Root location
            as the parameter

5.0 End If

The procedure for inserting a new element into the tree is also recursive in nature. The procedure Insert needs a variable parameter for the pointer to the root of the tree and a value parameter for the new name. If the subtree in which the element belongs is empty, then the procedure must create a new location, place the new name in the data portion of the element, and link the element to the tree. If the subtree is not empty, then the procedure must compare the new name with the name at the current Root. If the new name is less than the current name, then the procedure executes itself using the left link as the pointer to the root of the subtree; otherwise, the procedure executes itself using the right link as the pointer to the root of the subtree. This is stated more formally as follows:

PROCEDURE INSERT (IMPORT: ROOT, NEWNAME; EXPORT: ROOT)

1.0 If Root = Nil Then

2.0   Create space for NewName

3.0   Link element to the tree by changing the value of Root to point to the
            new element

4.0 Else If NewName > name at Root Then

5.0   Execute Insert using RightLink of Root

6.0 Else

7.0   Execute Insert using LeftLink of Root

8.0 End If

■ **Problem Solution.**   A solution to this problem is shown in Figure 12.8 as Program 12e. Pay particular attention to the procedure used to insert an element into the tree. A

```
program P12e (Input, Output);
{Program to create and list a binary tree}
uses
     Crt;
const
     Prompt = 'Enter name (End to stop) ';
type
     NameType = string[20];
     NodePointer = ^Node;
     Node = record
                 Name : NameType;
                 LeftLink, RightLink : NodePointer
            end;
var
     Root : NodePointer;
     NewName : NameType;
{*****************************************************************}
     procedure Traverse (Root : NodePointer);
     {Procedure to perform an in-order traversal of a binary tree}
     begin    {Traverse}
          if Root <> nil then
             begin
                 Traverse (Root^.LeftLink);
                 Writeln (Root^.Name);
                 Traverse (Root^.RightLink)
             end;    {if}
     end;   {Traverse}
{---------------------------------------------------------------}
     procedure Insert (var Root : NodePointer; NewName : NameType);
     {Procedure to insert NewName into tree}
     var
          Temp, Curr : NodePointer;
     begin    {Insert}
          if Root = nil then
             begin
                 New (Temp);
                 Temp^.Name := NewName;
                 Temp^.LeftLink := nil;
                 Temp^.RightLink := nil;
                 Root := Temp
             end
          else if NewName > Root^.Name then
                 Insert (Root^.RightLink, NewName)
          else
                 Insert (Root^.LeftLink, NewName);
     end;   {Insert}
{*****************************************************************}
```

Figure 12.8(a) Program 12e: Declaration part (part 1 of 2 parts).

temporary pointer (Temp) of type NodePointer is needed. The first step is to create the node, using the procedure New:

```
New (Temp);
```

```
begin     {Main Program}

{1.0 Initialize Tree}

    Root := nil;

{2.0 Repeat read Name and insert in tree until Name = 'End'}

    ClrScr;
    repeat
        Write (Prompt);
        Readln (NewName);
        if (NewName <> 'End') and (NewName <> 'end') then
            begin
                Insert (Root, NewName);
                Writeln ('----------');
                Traverse (Root);
                Writeln ('----------')
            end    {if}
    until (NewName = 'End') or (NewName = 'end')

end.    {Main Program}
```

Figure 12.8(b) Program 12e: Statement part (part 2 of 2 parts).

Then NewName is placed in this location, and the links are initialized to nil:

```
Temp^.Name := NewName;
Temp^.LeftLink := nil;
Temp^.RightLink := nil;
```

Finally, the value of Root is changed to point to the new location:

```
Root := Temp
```

Because Root is a variable parameter, its new value will be incorporated into the data structure.

12.7.3   *Time Out*

1. Compile and execute Program 12e. Test the program with sample data of your choosing.
2. The procedure Traverse in Program 12e performs what is technically called an *in-order* traversal of the tree. Two other orders are possible: A *preorder* traversal is accomplished by writing the value of the data portion of the root node before traversing the right subtree and the left subtree; a *postorder* traversal is accomplished by writing the value of the data after traversing both the left subtree and the right subtree. Experiment with the procedure Traverse to produce a preorder and postorder transversal of the data. Compare the output with the tree structure of the data entered.
3. Modify Program 12e to allow the user to search the data after all names have been entered. Give the user the option of adding a name if it is not found.

12.7.4   A Final Word

The subject of abstract data structures is of great importance in computer science. In this text, we have covered only three of the best known and most widely used structures. If you pursue the field further, you will analyze these structures and others that are beyond the scope of the text. In most computer science curricula, the second-level course (which is taken after you have learned a programming language) includes a detailed discussion of data structures. We will return to this topic in our discussion of abstract data types presented in Chapter 15.

12.8   REVIEW QUESTIONS

1. Define the term *pointer*.
2. In what way can you think of a subscript used to address an array element as a pointer?
3. What restriction is made on the underlying data type of a pointer type in Pascal?
4. What is the purpose of the procedure New?
5. What is dynamic memory allocation? Compare it with static memory allocation.
6. How does the program gain access to the content of a data item that has been allocated dynamically?
7. What is the *heap*?
8. If a pointer variable has the value nil, what can be said about the data associated with that variable?
9. What is the purpose of the procedure Dispose? What value is placed in the argument used with this procedure?
10. If two pointers are equal, what can be said about the values of the data pointed to by the pointers?
11. What advantage does a linked list implemented with pointers have over an array for storing a list of data? Does the linked list have any disadvantages, compared with an array?
12. A stack is sometimes called a first-in, first-out queue. Comment on the appropriateness of this description of a stack.
13. Define the terms *push* and *pop* as they relate to stacks.
14. In most implementations of stacks, there is no separate pointer maintained to indicate the last element in the structure. Why?
15. If a stack is empty, what will be the value of the pointer Top?
16. What advantage does a binary tree have over a linked list for representing sorted data?
17. What is the root of a tree? Leaf of a tree?
18. What is a subtree?
19. What can be said about a node of a tree if both of its subtrees are empty?
20. Adding an element to a tree is very closely related to searching a tree. What is this relationship?
21. What does it mean to traverse a tree? What is an in-order traversal? What other orders are possible?

12.9 PROGRAMMING EXERCISES

1. Write a program to be used by a person to maintain a personal telephone list. For each person on the list, the user wishes to store the following information:

> Name (Last, First, Middle)
>
> Telephone Number (Area Code, Number)

The list should be sorted by name. Options that should be implemented in the program include the following:

> Load a list from a file
>
> Look up telephone number for a person
>
> Add names in the list
>
> Delete names from the list
>
> Change a telephone number for a person
>
> Store the current list on a file

Your program should create the list using a linked list implemented with pointers.

2. For some applications, a doubly linked list can be of value. In such a structure, each element has a pointer to its predecessor and successor. (The predecessor link for the first element has the value nil, as does the successor link for the last element.) The memory diagram for a representative doubly linked list is as follows:

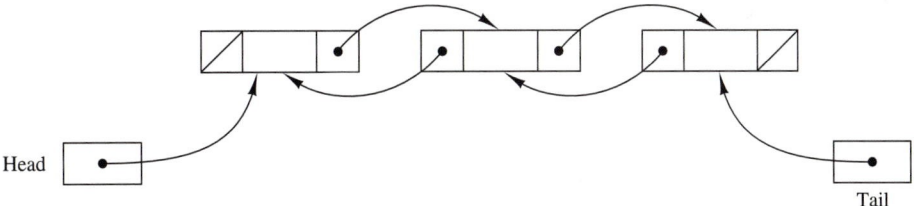

Write a program to create a doubly linked list containing names that are maintained in sequential order. As an option in the program, allow the user to list the elements in ascending or descending sequence.

3. Write a program similar to Program 12c to create a list of data entered by the program user with the following stipulations: When data is added to the list, the user may choose to add to the beginning of the list or the end of the list. Similarly, when data is deleted from the list, it can be deleted from the top or bottom of the list.

4. One method for representing an expression such as

$$4x^6 - 2x^3 + x - 1$$

is to use a linked list in which each element stores the coefficient and the exponent. This

example would be represented as

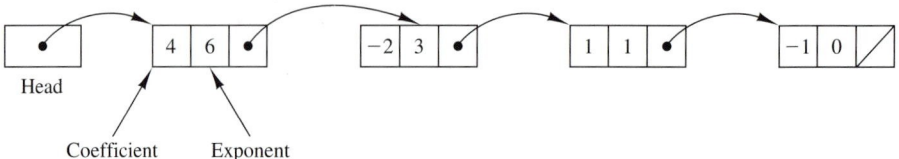

Head

Coefficient   Exponent

Write a program to allow the user to enter an expression ånd then have the program evaluate the function for appropriate arguments.

5. Widget Sales, Inc., employs 10 salespersons, identified as salesperson 1, 2, . . . , 10. Each salesperson submits sales reports on a periodic basis, depending on his or her sales activity; in other words, some salespersons submit reports daily, whereas others submit weekly, biweekly, or monthly reports. Write a program to allow the user to enter sales-report information for salespersons. When all the data has been entered, write a summary report showing detailed sales activity and total sales for each salesperson. Each sales report consists of a date and a total sale amount. *Hint:* Create an array of pointers, one array element for each salesperson. Consider each array element as the head of a separate list. When a sales report is entered, add that report to the appropriate linked list. The data structure could be visualized as follows:

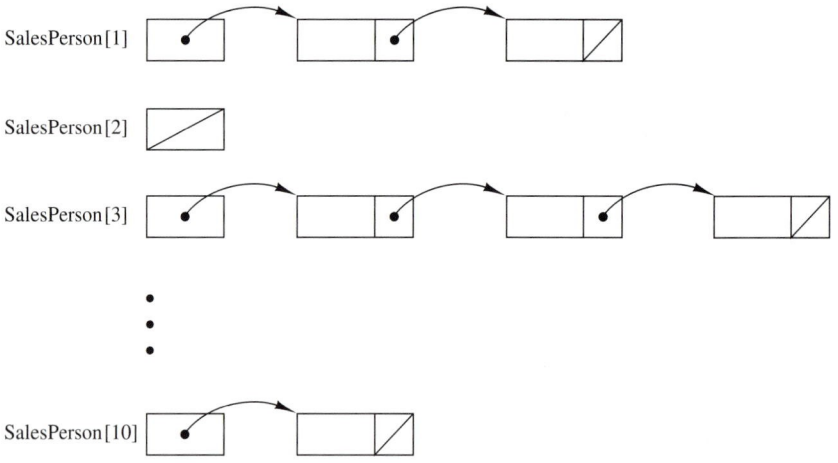

6. One very efficient way to sort data is to manipulate pointers to the data rather than manipulate the data itself. (This method is efficient because it eliminates the necessity of moving the data itself in the sorting process—only the pointers need be swapped.) Write a program to load data records containing the names and social security numbers of employees of XYZ, Inc., from a text file. Assume a maximum of 100 employees. Instead of using an array to store the data, use an array of pointers, with each element of the array pointing to one record in memory. Sort the data into sequence by social security number. When you are finished, the first pointer in the array should point to the first element in the list, the second element should point to the next element, and so forth. Have the program list the data in its original sequence and in its sorted sequence.

7. Modify the program you wrote for Exercise 6 to allow the user to request names associated with particular social security numbers. Use a binary search.

8. Use the concept of an array of pointers to implement a hash table to store the data contained in the data file described in Exercise 6. Allow the user to request names associated with particular social security numbers. *Note:* The advantage of this technique over an ordinary hash table is that memory is required only for table elements that are actually used.

9. Remember that a stack is a last-in, first-out queue. An alternative structure that is sometimes useful is a first-in, first-out queue. You experience such queues in supermarkets, banks, and so forth when people line up for service. In such situations, the first person in the line is the first one served. Write a program similar to Program 12d for a first-in, first-out queue.

13
Graphics

There is an element of truth in the old maxim that "a picture is worth a thousand words." Many times a picture or diagram may be a much more useful way to convey information than using words or numbers to represent the same meaning. In this chapter we explore ways that you can incorporate graphic output into your Turbo Pascal programs.

13.1 INTRODUCTION TO GRAPHICS

All of the output produced by the programs presented thus far has been character related.[1] The ANSI standard for Pascal supports only this type of output. However, most microcomputers are capable of graphic output, that is, diagrams, pictures, graphs, and so forth. Unfortunately, there is no universal standard for types of graphics adapters and monitors used with microcomputers. Each type has different capabilities and standards and hence requires different software (called a **driver**) to act as an interface between the program or user and the device itself. Turbo Pascal supplies such software for a wide variety of systems and enables your program to produce graphic output through an appropriate driver. Borland calls its system the **Borland Graphics Interface**, or **BGI**.

Ordinarily, output from a program is directed to the user's screen, which is sometimes called the text screen or DOS screen. This is the screen that you see when you display the user screen in Turbo Pascal. When a program makes use of Turbo Pascal's graphics system, output is directed to a **graphics screen**, which is quite distinct from the text screen. Only one of these screens can be displayed by the computer at any one time; the user (or the program) must choose to display the text screen or the graphics screen. When one screen is displayed, the other is invisible. It is not possible to display a portion of one screen along with a part of the other (although this might be a very useful feature and may be supported in the future.)

The text screen is divided into 80 columns and 25 rows; we say that the resolution of the text screen is 80×25. (**Resolution** is always expressed as number of columns $\times$ number of rows.) Each position on the screen can be addressed (by using the GoToXY procedure) and can contain a single character. In Section 9.12, you saw how the text screen could be used to display a fairly primitive bar graph. The very low resolution of the text screen limits its usefulness in displaying visual images. By contrast, the graphics screen has much higher resolution—from 320×200 to $1,024 \times 1,024$, with higher resolution systems promised in the future. Each position on a graphics screen is called a **pixel**—a term derived from "picture element." Just as each character position on a text screen can be addressed separately, a pixel, which is a rectangular area of the graphics screen, can also be addressed directly. If the screen is capable of displaying color, each pixel can be set to display any of the colors possible in the given system. The size of a pixel varies from system to system; the higher the resolution, the smaller is the size of each pixel. Higher resolution screens are very desirable, because they can display images that more closely approximate photographic quality.

13.2 OVERVIEW OF THE GRAPH UNIT

In Turbo Pascal, all of the procedures and functions required for a program to create graphics screens are contained in a unit called **Graph**. In order to make use of the content of this unit, a program must include Graph in the uses statement. With this in place, the

---

[1]Although your programs have dealt with a variety of data types (such as Integer, Real, Boolean, etc.), all output has been converted to character form before being sent to the screen or printer.

program is able to load the appropriate graphics driver, create and display graphics screens, and, if needed, alternate between graphics and text screens. In this section, we shall cover the details of how to set up a program to initiate and terminate graphic output and how to detect errors therein. In succeeding sections, we shall cover specific types of output (such as rectangles, characters, lines, ellipses, and so forth).

The first item of business in any program that will use the graphics screen is to load the driver appropriate for the particular configuration of the system in use. Turbo Pascal supports the most popular types of graphics adapters, including the Color Graphics Adapter (CGA), Extended Graphics Adapter (EGA), Video Graphics Array (VGA), and Hercules (a brand name) among others. Drivers are precompiled and are usually located in a subdirectory called BGI. It is possible to write programs that use the specific capabilities of any one of these systems; however such a program would not work if used on any other type of system. To overcome this difficulty, Turbo Pascal allows the program to detect the type of adapter in use and load the appropriate driver at the time the program is executed. We shall use this approach in all of the programs we present in this text. In this way, these programs should work properly on a great variety of different types of systems. All that is necessary to provide an appropriate driver—either one that was supplied with Turbo Pascal or one from some other source.

As shown in Figure 13.1, each driver may support several modes of operation for the display. For example, the CGA driver supports a low-resolution, 320×200 mode with four colors or a higher resolution 640×200 mode with only two colors. Similarly, the VGA driver supports three different modes of increasingly higher resolution, the lowest being 640×200 and the highest 640×480. To understand how this is possible, you need to know a little about the underlying technology behind graphics adapters. Each adapter has a quantity of memory called **screen memory** (sometimes also referred to as a frame buffer). Each pixel on the screen is represented in screen memory by one or more bits. In order to create an image on the screen, the driver manipulates screen memory, setting each pixel to its proper value. The adapter then transfers the content of screen memory to the

Driver number	Graphics driver	Constant name	Value	Resolution	Palette
1	CGA	CGAC0	0	320x200	C0
		CGAC1	1	320x200	C1
		CGAC2	2	320x200	C2
		CGAC3	3	320x200	C3
		CGAHi	4	640x200	2 colors
3	EGA	EGALo	0	640x200	16 colors
		EGALi	1	640x350	16 colors
6	IBM8514	IBM8514Lo	0	640x480	256 colors
9	VGA	VGALo	0	640x200	16 colors
		VGAMed	1	640x350	16 colors
		VGAHi	2	640x480	16 colors

Figure 13.1 Selected drivers and modes supported by Turbo Pascal 7.0.

actual screen, which produces the visual image. The mode of operation determines how the bits in screen memory are related to the pixels on the screen. For example, in a simple monochrome mode, only one bit in screen memory is needed for each pixel on the screen, since each pixel can display only black or white, which may be represented by 0 or 1, respectively, in the corresponding bit. To create color, the system requires multiple bits per pixel. For example, to handle 16 colors, at least four bits must be allocated to each pixel, since four bits can represent 16 numbers ranging from 0 to 15. In some cases, the drivers support two pages by dividing screen memory into two parts. While one page is being displayed, a second one can be built. By switching pages in rapid succession, a simple form of animation can be achieved.

13.2.1   The InitGraph Procedure

The first procedure from the unit Graph that you will need to use is called **InitGraph**. This procedure loads the appropriate graphics driver and sets the graphic mode. It is necessary to execute InitGraph before using any procedure to send output to the graphics screen. The general form for invoking InitGraph is

```
InitGraph (graph-driver, graph-mode, path-to-driver)
```

where **graph-driver** and **graph-mode** are Integer variables and **path-to-driver** is a string variable or constant. For example, suppose the following declarations are in place:

```
var
     GraphDriver, GraphMode : Integer;
```

Then an appropriate invocation of InitGraph might be

```
InitGraph (GraphDriver, GraphMode, 'C:\TP\BGI');
```

If the initial value of GraphDriver is not zero, then InitGraph will attempt to locate the driver associated with the value of GraphDriver in the path specified by *path-to-driver*—in this case, we assume that the drivers are to be found on drive C in subdirectory BGI, which is a part of the directory TP. The relationship between the value for GraphDriver and the associated driver is shown in Figure 13.1. For example, if the value of GraphDriver is 1, the CGA driver will be loaded; if the value of GraphDriver is 9, the VGA driver will be loaded. If InitGraph is successful in locating the specified driver, then the value of GraphMode will be set to a default value—the highest value available for the particular driver. For example, if the VGA driver is loaded, the value of GraphMode will be set to 2. (The programmer can reset this value using the procedure SetGraphMode, which is described later in this chapter.)

As mentioned earlier, trying to have a program specify a particular graphics driver makes the program unusable in a different system. To deal with this problem, the program can request that InitGraph determine what kind of graphics adapter is present in a machine and load the appropriate graphics driver. This is done by setting the initial value of the variable used to specify *graph-driver* to zero. In that case, InitGraph will execute a procedure that determines the graphics environment, resets the variable to an appropriate value, and then attempts to locate the related driver. (InitGraph cannot automatically recognize the IBM8514 adapter; if this adapter is present, the VGA driver will be loaded. The program will then execute, but without the increased resolution of the 8514 adapter.) As documentation regarding the relationship between the value in the *graph-driver* variable and the actual adapter, named constants have been provided in the unit Graph. These constants are listed in Figure 13.1 (CGA, EGA, etc.). Thus, the value of CGA is 1, the value of VGA is 9, and so forth. To facilitate automatic detection, a further named constant called **Detect** with value zero is provided. For example, assuming that the preceding variables have been defined, the following program segment could be used to automatically detect the graphics adapter and load the related driver:

```
GraphDriver := Detect;
InitGraph (GraphDriver, GraphMode, 'C:\TP\BGI');
```

If a VGA graphics adapter is detected, then, after execution of this program segment, the following will have been accomplished:

- the value of GraphDriver will be set to 9 (the number corresponding to VGA)
- the value of GraphMode will be set to 2 (the highest mode available for the VGA driver—640 × 480 with 16 colors)
- if the VGA driver is located, it will be loaded into memory, and the program will display a blank graphics screen.

Sometimes, you might wish to have the system look for the driver in the current path—the one used as the default by DOS during the execution of the program. If the value of *path-to-driver* is the null string, as in

```
InitGraph (GraphDriver, GraphMode, '');
```

then InitGraph will search the current path for the graph driver.

13.2.2 GraphResult and GraphErrorMsg

In all of the preceding discussion, we have been careful to point out that InitGraph must be able to locate the required driver in the specified path. If it cannot locate the driver, if the path is invalid, if there is no graphics adapter, if InitGraph cannot recognize the graphics adapter, or if any one of a number of other things goes wrong, then InitGraph will not place the system in graphics mode. A function called **GraphResult** is provided to communicate between graphics procedures, including InitGraph and the calling program. If the procedure is successful, the value returned for GraphResult will be zero. If the procedure is not successful, GraphResult will take on a value from −1 to −14, as shown in Figure 13.2, depending on what caused the error. (Most of the graphics procedures discussed in this chapter also set GraphResult.) For example, if InitGraph cannot locate a driver, the value of GraphResult will be -3. Corresponding to each of the possible settings of GraphResult is a named constant, shown in Figure 13.2, which can be used in place of the numeric value. For example, the constant grOK has the value zero, so we could write

```
InitGraph (...);
if GraphResult <> grOK then
    .
    .
    .
```

Note that the condition

```
GraphResult <> grOK
```

is equivalent to

```
GraphResult <> 0.
```

Observe that we called GraphResult a function instead of a constant. It is like the function IOResult in that it resets itself to zero after it is called. Because of this, it is recommended that a program place the value of GraphResult in a variable (such as ErrorCode), which can then be used as many times as necessary. The meaning of the code returned by a graphics procedure can be displayed using the function **GraphErrorMsg**, which has the general form

```
GraphErrorMsg (error-code)
```

Error code	Graphics error constant	Corresponding error message string
0	grOk	No error
-1	grNoInitGraph	(BGI) graphics not installed (use InitGraph)
-2	grNotDetected	Graphics hardware not detected
-3	grFileNotFound	Device driver file not found
-4	grInvalidDriver	Invalid device driver file
-5	grNoLoadMem	Not enough memory to load driver
-6	grNoScanMem	Out of memory in scan fill
-7	grNoFloodMem	Out of memory in flood fill
-8	grFontNotFound	Font file not found
-9	grNoFontMem	Not enough memory to load font
-10	grInvalidMode	Invalid graphics mode for selected driver
-11	grError	Graphics error
-12	grIOerror	Graphics I/O error
-13	grInvalidFont	Invalid font file
-14	grInvalidFontNum	Invalid font number

Figure 13.2 Possible values of GraphResult after execution of a graphics procedure such as InitGraph. Source: *Turbo Pascal Version 7.0 Programmer's Reference* (Copyright © Borland International, Inc. 1983, 1992. All rights reserved.)

This function returns a text string corresponding to the value contained in *error-code*, as shown in Figure 13.2. For example, if the value of *error-code* is −3, the value returned in GraphErrorMsg will be "Device driver file not found".

13.2.3   Halt and CloseGraph

Occasionally, it is worthwhile to use the **Halt** procedure to terminate execution of a program. The general form for the invocation of this procedure is

```
Halt (exit-code)
```

where *exit-code* is a value accessible to you through the operating system after termination of the program. (The Halt procedure is part of the standard unit and is essentially unrelated to graphics. We introduce the procedure at this point because it is a convenient way to handle program termination when system errors are encountered.) You might wish to use different values in each Halt statement in a program, so that after the program terminated, you could find out which of the Halt statements caused the termination. You can also use Halt with no parameter, which would result in an exit code value of zero. Consult the *Turbo Pascal Version 7.0 Programmer's Reference* for more details.

The procedure **CloseGraph** terminates the graphic output and restores the text screen. The general form to invoke this procedure is

```
CloseGraph
```

You typically use this statement as the last in a procedure or program that produces graphics output.

13.2.4   A Sample Program

Program 13a, shown in Figure 13.3, summarizes the foregoing discussion and provides a prototype for all graphics programs. Before proceeding, you should review the material in this section to make sure you understand each of the statements in the program and their relationship to one another.

13.2.5   Time Out

1. For the machine you will be using, determine

- the type of graphics adapter in use
- the path to the graphics drivers.

You may need to consult your instructor, computer lab assistant, or the documentation accompanying your system to determine this information. Record the path for use in the following exercise.

```
program P13a;
{Program illustrates setting up graphics screen}
uses Graph;
var
     GraphDriver, GraphMode, ErrorCode : Integer;
begin {Main Program}

{1.0 Initialize graphics screen}

     GraphDriver := Detect;
     InitGraph (GraphDriver, GraphMode, 'C:\TP\BGI');
     ErrorCode := GraphResult;
     if ErrorCode <> grOK then
        begin
             Writeln ('Graphics error : ', GraphErrorMsg(ErrorCode));
             Writeln ('Program aborted...');
             Halt(1)
        end;

{2.0 Statements to create graphic output will go here}

{3.0 Close graphics}

     CloseGraph
end.   {Main Program}
```

Figure 13.3 Program 13a: Basic setup for initialization of graphic output.

2. Compile and execute Program 13a, substituting your path for the *path-to-driver* used in the program. If you get an error message, modify the program accordingly. The most common errors result from an invalid path. If the program is working properly, you should see a momentary display of a blank screen. If it is not working properly, you will see an error message on the user screen.

13.3 DESIGN OF GRAPHIC OUTPUT

We have seen that there are many screen resolutions that may be encountered, depending on which graphic adapter and which mode is in use. Turbo Pascal allows you to address specific pixels on the screen by numeric location, or you can have the program compute a location for a particular graphic element. In this section, we shall discuss these two alternatives and describe how a program can draw rectangles on the graphics screen.

In all cases, locations on the graphics screen are addressed by two coordinates—an X-coordinate and a Y-coordinate, which are often written in the form (X, Y). The X-coordinate is the horizontal position and the Y-coordinate is the vertical position of the pixel on the screen. The pixel in the upper left-hand corner of the screen always has the address (0, 0). On a CGA screen with the mode that allows a resolution of 320 × 200, the address of the pixel in the lower right-hand corner of the screen is (319, 199). As shown in Figure 13.4, all other pixels have related addresses. For example, the address of the pixel in the middle of the screen is (160, 100).

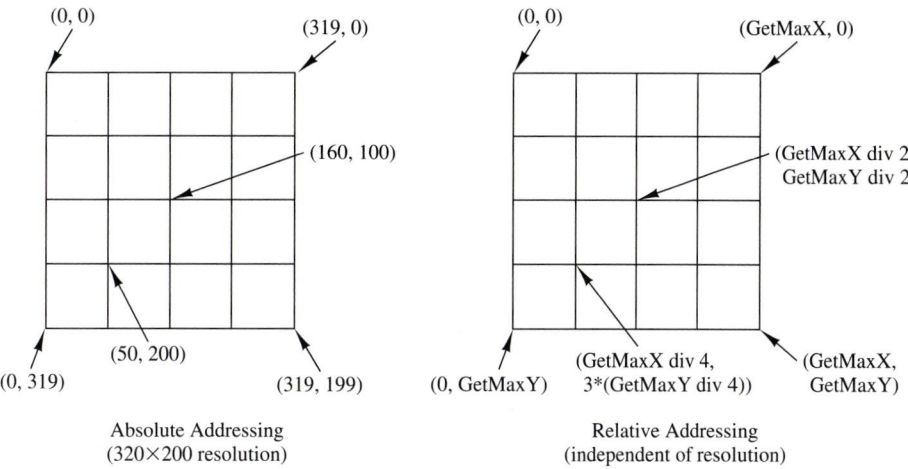

Figure 13.4 Comparison of absolute and relative addressing for selected graphics screen locations.

Because of the different resolutions available, the appearance of the output produced by a program that addresses screen locations by absolute addresses will be different, depending on the type of graphics adapter in use on the machine used to execute a program. For example, position (319, 199) is in the bottom right position on the CGA screen just described, but the same position is somewhat toward the middle of a VGA screen in 640 × 480 mode. To avoid having to have a different version of a program for each adapter and mode of operation, Turbo Pascal gives you the ability to have the program determine the maximum X- and Y-coordinates during its execution. These values are, of course, dependent on the particular adapter and mode of operation in use. The program can then address positions on the screen relative to the maximums in each direction.

GetMaxX and **GetMaxY** are functions provided in the Graph unit to return an Integer value representing the maximum X-coordinate and maximum Y-coordinate, respectively. The general form for invocation of these functions is

```
GetMaxX
GetMaxY
```

(There are no arguments for either function.) The functions can be used in any context to designate the maximum allowable X- and Y-coordinates. For example, as shown in Figure 13.4, the point (GetMaxX, GetMaxY) will always be in the lower right-hand corner of the screen, and the point (GetMaxX div 2, GetMaxY div 2) will always be in the exact center of the screen. This is essentially what we mean by proportional placement of points. When this technique is used, the appearance of a graphics screen will be relatively independent of the adapter and mode in use. (Of course, screens displayed using higher resolution tend to have a better appearance than the same screen displayed with lower resolution, but at least the objects will be in essentially the same location no matter what.)

Let us illustrate the concept of proportional placement of points by writing a program to display rectangles on the screen. The Graph unit contains a procedure called **Rectangle** to draw a rectangle on the screen. The program must specify the coordinates of the upper left corner and the lower right corner of the rectangle, and the system does the rest. The general form for invoking this procedure is:

```
Rectangle (x1, y1, x2, y2)
```

where $x1$, $y1$ are the coordinates of the upper left corner of the rectangle and $x2$, $y2$ are the coordinates of the lower right corner. For example, the following statement would draw a rectangle completely outlining a CGA graphics screen in 320 × 200 mode:

```
Rectangle (0, 0, 319, 199);
```

Of course, this same statement would draw rectangles of differing appearances when executed on machines with other resolutions. The only thing the rectangles would have in common is that they would all begin in the upper left-hand corner of the screen at the position (0, 0). By contrast, the following statement would always draw a rectangle around the boundary of the screen:

```
Rectangle (0, 0, GetMaxX, GetMaxY);
```

The functions GetMaxX and GetMaxY will always return the coordinates of the lower right-hand corner of the screen. Figure 13.5 shows some examples of the use of Rectangle with a diagram of the expected output.

Program 13a can be adapted to draw a rectangle bordering the screen by making the following modification:

```
{2.0 Statements to create graphic output will go here}
     Rectangle (0, 0, GetMaxX, GetMaxY);
     Readln;
```

Note the use of Readln in this program segment. The Readln statement causes the program to halt until the user presses the Enter key. Without this statement (or some similar mechanism, such as Delay), the graphics screen will flash by too quickly for anyone to see it.

13.3.1   *Time Out*

1. Make the preceding suggested modification to Program 13a, and test your program.
2. Try out each of the statements in Figure 13.5 by incorporating each one in turn into Program 13a.

```
Rectangle (0, 0, GetMaxX div 2, GetMaxY div 2);
```

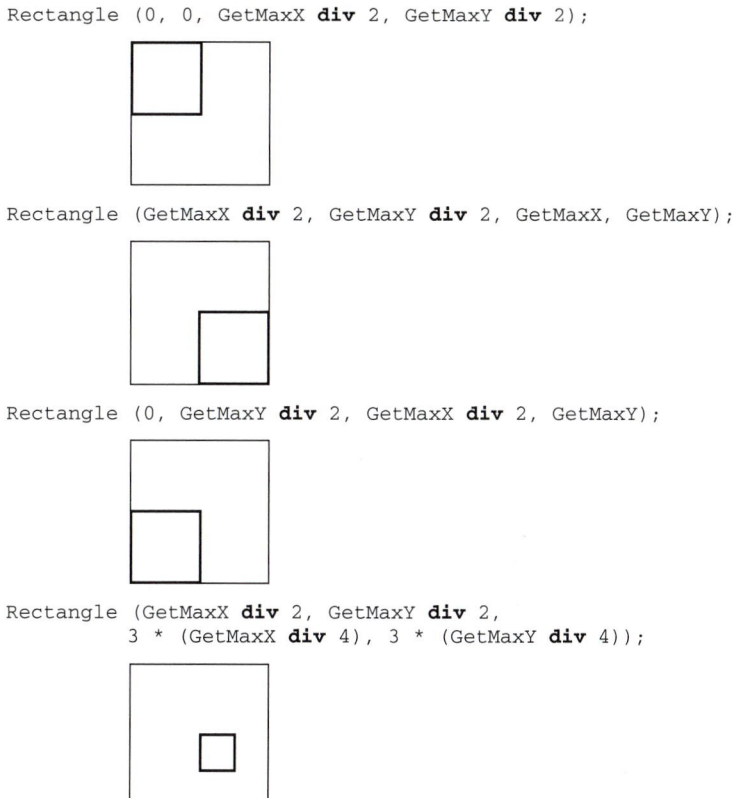

```
Rectangle (GetMaxX div 2, GetMaxY div 2, GetMaxX, GetMaxY);
```

```
Rectangle (0, GetMaxY div 2, GetMaxX div 2, GetMaxY);
```

```
Rectangle (GetMaxX div 2, GetMaxY div 2,
           3 * (GetMaxX div 4), 3 * (GetMaxY div 4));
```

Figure 13.5 Sample use of the Rectangle procedure.

3. Modify Program 13a to create the following four-by-four checkerboard:

Hint: Compute the coordinates for the upper left and lower right corners of each rectangle, based on GetMaxX and GetMaxY.

13.4 CHARACTERS

It will often be desirable to be able to write text (a sequence of characters) on the graphics screen. As we noted earlier, it is not possible to display the text screen and the graphics screen concurrently, so if character output on the graphics screen is needed (for example, as a label on a graph), it will be necessary to use alternatives to the usual Write and Writeln procedures that produce output on the text screen.

The Graphics unit contains a number of procedures related to character output, including SetTextJustify, which is used to specify the justification of character output, SetTextStyle, which is used to specify which of five alternative fonts is to be used and which direction (horizontal or vertical) will be used, and OutTextXY, which is used to specify the position and content of character output. Each of these procedures is described in detail in this section.

13.4.1 SetTextJustify

Justification refers to the vertical and horizontal positioning of text with respect to some fixed position. You specify the desired justification using the procedure **SetTextJustify**, which has the general form

```
SetTextJustify (horizontal, vertical)
```

where both arguments are Integer values in the range 0 to 2. To facilitate setting these parameters, and as an aid in helping programmers remember the meaning of the values, the Graph unit includes the following named constants intended for use in specifying a value for *horizontal*:

Identifier	Value
LeftText	0
CenterText	1
RightText	2

The following constants are included for use in specifying a value for *vertical*:

Identifier	Value
BottomText	0
CenterText	1
TopText	2

After invocation of the SetTextJustify procedure, all subsequent output produced by OutTextXY will be positioned as specified. For example, to produce text that is right justified and centered on a specific point, you would use

```
SetTextJustify (RightText, CenterText);
```

The positioning of text would be as follows:

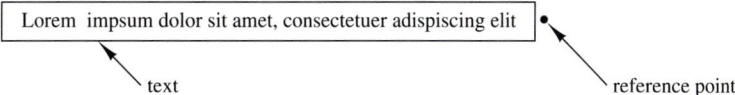

This example and the one that follows assumes that text is being displayed in a horizontal fashion. It is possible to display text in a vertical mode as well; this will be covered in conjunction with the discussion of SetTextStyle, which follows. If you wish to center the text both horizontally and vertically with respect to a point, you would use

```
SetTextJustify (CenterText, CenterText);
```

The positioning of text would now be as follows:

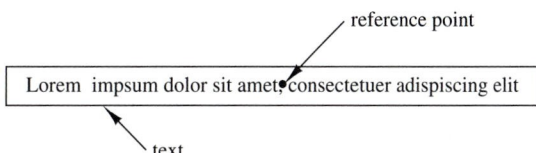

You can choose any combination of values for *horizontal* and *vertical* that you need to achieve the effect you desire.

13.4.2 Time Out

Assuming that text will be displayed in a horizontal mode, draw diagrams similar to the preceding to show how text would be displayed after invocation of each of the following:

1. `SetTextJustify (LeftText, BottomText);`
2. `SetTextJustify (CenterText, TopText);`
3. `SetTextJustify (RightText, BottomText);`

13.4.3 SetTextStyle

Turbo Pascal 7.0 supports five different fonts—styles of characters—that you can choose from. They are numbered from 0 to 4 and assigned named constants, as shown in the following table:

Identifier	Value	Type	Normal Size
DefaultFont	0	Bitmapped	1
TriplexFont	1	Stroked	4
SmallFont	2	Stroked	4
SansSerifFont	3	Stroked	4
GothicFont	4	Stroked	4

Font number 0, called DefaultFont, is a **bit-mapped font**. This means that each character is formed from an 8 × 8 square array of pixels. The other fonts are classed as **stroked fonts**. They are made up of line segments that roughly correspond to the strokes of a pen that would be used to create a given character. There are two essential differences between DefaultFont and the stroked fonts:

- When DefaultFont is displayed in larger sizes, the number of pixels used is increased, but the resolution is not. This means that in larger sizes, DefaultFont will appear jagged. By contrast, when stroked fonts are displayed in larger sizes, the strokes are all recomputed so that the characters retain their smooth appearance.
- If any part of a string of characters in DefaultFont would be displayed off the visible screen, none of the characters in the string will be displayed. When displaying any stroked font, if some portion of the string cannot be displayed on the visible screen, those parts are not shown, but other parts are shown.

Because of these considerations, the stroked fonts are usually more desirable than DefaultFont. The only disadvantages with stroked fonts is that they are loaded from disk (which takes time), and somewhat elaborate computations are performed to display each character (which also takes time). In other words, a program that uses DefaultFont will probably execute faster than a program that uses a stroked font.

Prior to writing text on the graphics screen, the program may set the font style and size using the procedure **SetTextStyle**, which has the general form

```
SetTextStyle (font, direction, character-size)
```

where *font* is an Integer value in the range 0 to 4 corresponding to the font type as shown in the table on page 659, *direction* is an Integer with the value 0 (for horizontal) or 1 (for vertical), and *character-size* is an Integer in the range 1 to 10 that determines the size of the characters to be displayed. To simplify the specification of *direction*, Turbo Pascal includes the following named constants:

Identifier	Value
HorizDir	0
VertDir	1

For example, the following statement would set the *font* to Defaultfont, the *direction* to horizontal, and the *character-size* to 4 (the standard size for this font):

```
SetTextStyle (DefaultFont, HorizDir, 4);
```

The following statement would be used to invoke the stroked font TriplexFont, displayed vertically in twice normal size:

```
SetTextStyle (TriplexFont, VertDir, 2);
```

Of course, this is equivalent to (but easier to read and understand than)

```
SetTextStyle (1, 1, 2);
```

Remember that you can use either the named constants or a numeric constant or a variable to specify any of the arguments in these procedures.

13.4.4   OutTextXY

Finally, the procedure **OutTextXY** sends the actual string of characters to the screen, using all of the settings that have been made in SetTextJustify and SetTextStyle. This procedure has general form

```
OutTextXY (x, y, text-string)
```

where x and y are Integers specifying the reference points for justification of the text and *text-string* is the string of characters to be displayed. All of these arguments can be specified by constants, variables, or expressions. The values of x and y must be in the range 0 to GetMaxX and 0 to GetMaxY, respectively.

For example, the following statement will display the characters "Turbo Pascal" on the screen:

```
OutTextXY (GetMaxX div 2, GetMaxY div 2, 'Turbo Pascal')
```

The exact position of this text will depend on the settings specified in SetTextJustify. The font, size, and direction of the text will depend on the settings made in SetTextStyle. For instance, the following program segment will display the characters horizontally, centered on the screen, in the font TriplexFont, and twice normal size:

```
SetTextJustify (CenterText, CenterText);
SetTextStyle (Triplexfont, HorizDir, 2);
OutTextXY (GetMaxX div 2, GetMaxY div 2, 'Turbo Pascal')
```

Note that the procedures SetTextJustify and SetTextStyle could have been invoked in any order prior to invoking OutTextXY.

13.4.5   *Time Out*

Modify Program 13a to print the characters "Turbo Pascal" in your choice of fonts, justifications, and positions on the screen. Experiment with several combinations, including some printed in vertical format.

13.4.6 Program Example

Program 13b, shown in Figure 13.6, illustrates how to display character data in all four stroked fonts in a variety of sizes. After each line of display, the user presses the Enter key to display the next line. Sample output from the program is shown in Figure 13.7.

The program divides the screen into eight logical lines, one for each line of output. Note how it computes the Y-coordinate for the output in the OutTextXY procedure invocation:

```
OutTextXY (GetMaxX div 2, I*(GetMaxY div 8), . . .)
```

```
program P13b (Output);
{Program illustrating output of stroked fonts}
uses Graph;
var
   GraphDriver, GraphMode, ErrorCode, I, TextStyle : Integer;
begin    {Main Program}

{1.0 Initialize graphics}

    GraphDriver := Detect;
    InitGraph (GraphDriver, GraphMode, 'C:\TP\BGI');
    ErrorCode := GraphResult;
    if ErrorCode <> grOK then
       begin
            Writeln ('Graphics error : ', GraphErrorMsg(ErrorCode));
            Writeln ('Program aborted...');
            Halt(1)
       end;   {if}

{2.0 Produce examples of character output in four stroked fonts}

    for TextStyle := 1 to 4 do
       begin
          SetGraphMode (GraphMode);
          Rectangle (0, 0, GetMaxX, GetMaxY);
          SetTextJustify (CenterText, BottomText);
          for I := 1 to 8 do
             begin
                  SetTextStyle(TextStyle, Horizdir, I);
                  OutTextXY(GetMaxX div 2, I*(GetMaxY div 8),
                     'Structured Programming in Turbo Pascal, 2nd Ed.');
                  Readln
             end;   {for}
       end; {for}

{3.0 Close graphic screen}

    CloseGraph

end.   {Main Program}
```

Figure 13.6 Program 13b: Illustrates how to invoke the four stroked fonts supported by Turbo Pascal.

TextStyle = 1
(TriplexFont)

TextStyle = 4
(GothicFont)

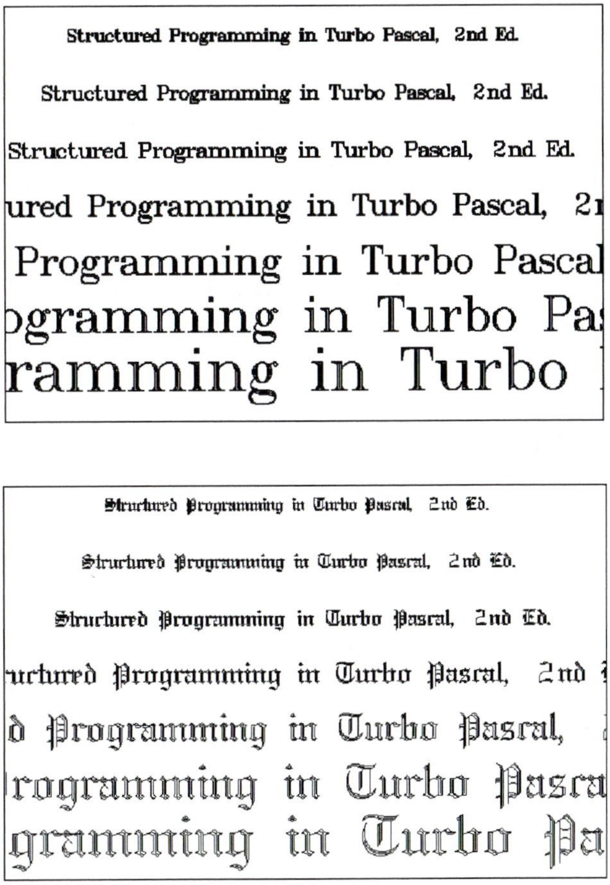

Figure 13.7 Sample output from Program 13b.

As the value of the variable I increases from 1 to 8, the vertical position of the line is changed by a distance of approximately one-eighth of the vertical size of the screen. This is an example of relative screen addressing, which is a very important technique in graphics programming.

13.4.7   *Time Out*

1. Compile and execute Program 13b, making sure that you substitute your *path-to-driver* for the one used in the program.
2. Substitute your name or the name of your school for the characters being displayed by Program 13b. Compile and test the program.

3. As written, Program 13b displays only stroked fonts. Modify the program to include DefaultFont. Remember that when any character being displayed in this mode falls off the screen, no characters are displayed. This means that several lines of text in the display will be blank. The user must still press Enter to advance to the next line.

13.4.8 Switching Between Graphics and Text Screens

The procedure **SetGraphMode** is used to set the graphics mode and clear the graphics screen. The general form for invoking this procedure is

```
SetGraphMode (graph-mode)
```

where *graph-mode* is an integer value ranging from zero to the maximum allowed for the current driver. For example, assuming that the variable GraphMode is defined as discussed previously, the statement

```
SetGraphMode (GraphMode)
```

would display a clear graphics screen. The current value of GraphMode would become the graphics mode. If this value is invalid for the operative driver, the value of GraphResult is set to -10 (grInvalidMode), as shown in Figure 13.2.

The procedure **RestoreCRTMode** changes the display to the text screen. The general form for invoking this procedure is

```
RestoreCRTMode
```

(The procedure requires no parameters.) When used in conjunction with SetGraphMode, RestoreCRTMode allows a program to switch between the text and graphic screens. You might wish to do this so that a user may enter data (which is normally done while viewing the text screen), followed by a graphic display based on that data. A typical program segment might be as follows:

```
begin
    RestoreCRTMode;
    {User enters data for processing}
    SetGraphMode (GraphMode);
    {Program creates graphic image}
end;
```

13.4.9 Time Out

Modify Program 13b to allow the program user to enter the desired string of characters and the value for TextStyle prior to displaying the screen full of data. Make sure that the value of TextStyle is in the range 0 to 4. Use RestoreCRTMode for the data entry and SetGraphMode to clear the graphics screen prior to displaying the output.

13.5 LINES

Lines are basic elements in many graphic images. Two of the procedures to draw lines on the graphics screen that are provided by Turbo Pascal are Line and LineTo. We will describe and illustrate the use of each of these procedures in this section and also introduce the concept of the Current Pointer and related procedures and functions.

13.5.1 The Line Procedure

The **Line** procedure is used to draw a line between two points that are specified as parameters. The general form for using this procedure is

```
Line (x1, y1, x2, y2)
```

where $x1$, $y1$ are the Integer coordinates of one end of the line and $x2$, $y2$ are the Integer coordinates of the other end of the line. For example, to draw a line between the points $(0, 0)$ and $(100, 100)$ we would use

```
Line (0, 0, 100, 100);
```

The following statement would draw a diagonal line across the screen:

```
Line (0, 0, GetMaxX, GetMaxY);
```

The following statements would draw a rectangle around the edge of the screen:

```
Line (0, 0, 0, GetMaxY);
Line (0, GetMaxY, GetMaxX, GetMaxY);
Line (GetMaxX, GetMaxY, GetMaxX, 0);
Line (GetMaxX, 0, 0, 0);
```

Of course, this coding segment is equivalent to

```
Rectangle (0, 0, GetMaxX, GetMaxY)
```

which is more convenient in this case.

The following program segment would draw 10 horizontal lines across the screen at equally spaced intervals (assume that I is declared as an Integer variable):

```
for I := 1 to 10 do
    Line (0, I * (GetMaxY div 10),
            GetMaxX, I * (GetMaxY div 10);
```

13.5.2 Time Out

1. Modify Program 13a to draw a rectangle around the outside of the graphics screen, using the Line procedure. Add lines forming an "X" by connecting opposite corners of the screen.
2. Using the Line procedure, modify Program 13a to draw the 4 × 4 checkerboard pattern illustrated in Problem 3 of Section 13.3.1.

13.5.3 SetWriteMode

The procedure **SetWriteMode** is useful to "erase" a line or rectangle from the screen. The general form for invoking this procedure is

```
SetWriteMode (write-mode)
```

where *write-mode* is an Integer with the value 0 or 1. If *write-mode* is 0, the line or rectangle[2] is written to the screen, as usual; we then say that the graphic figure is copied to the screen. This is the default mode if the SetWriteMode procedure is not used. If *write-mode* has the value 1, the figure is combined with the screen image, using the xor operation. This means that if a pixel in a particular location is turned off, it will be turned on, but if it is turned on, it will be turned off. We say that the figure is "XORed" to the screen. Two named constants are supplied for use with this procedure:

Identifier	Value
CopyPut	0
XORPut	1

The usual use of the procedure is to "erase" a figure from the screen. For example, consider the following program segment:

```
SetWriteMode (CopyPut);
Line (0, 0, 100, 100);
SetWriteMode (XORPut);
Line (0, 0, 100, 100);
```

As a result of the first two statements, a line is drawn between the locations (0, 0) and (100, 100). The second invocation of SetWriteMode specifies 1 as the value of *write-mode*, using the named constant XORPut. This sets the stage for "XORing" an image to the screen. The last statement, which appears to draw a line identical to the first one, actually now erases the line. Each pixel that was on is turned off, because the image is "XORed" rather than copied to the screen.

Program 13c, shown in Figure 13.8, is an example of the use of SetWriteMode to make lines appear and disappear on a graphics screen. The program sets a starting point

---

[2]The procedure SetWriteMode affects output produced only by the following procedures: DrawPoly, Line, Line-Rel, LineTo, and Rectangle. See *Turbo Pascal 7.0 Programmer's Reference* for more details.

```
program P13c (Output);
{Program displays lines at random locations on the screen;
     illustrates Line and SetWriteMode procedures}
uses Graph, CRT;
var
   GraphDriver, GraphMode, ErrorCode, Color, XB, YB, X, Y : Integer;
begin {Main Program}

{1.0 Initialize graphics screen}

     GraphDriver := Detect;
     InitGraph (GraphDriver, GraphMode, 'C:\TP\BGI');
     ErrorCode := GraphResult;
     if ErrorCode <> grOK then
        begin
            Writeln ('Graphics error : ', GraphErrorMsg(ErrorCode));
            Writeln ('Program aborted...');
            Halt(1)
        end;
     Rectangle(0, 0, GetMaxX, GetMaxY);

{2.0 Set starting point}

     Randomize;
     XB := Random (GetMaxX);
     YB := Random (GetMaxY);

{4.0 Set write mode to XORPut}

     SetWriteMode (XORPut);

{5.0 Display lines at random until user presses a key}

     repeat
            X := Random (GetMaxX);
            Y := Random (GetMaxY);
            Line (XB, YB, X, Y);
            Delay (500);
            Line (XB, YB, X, Y)
        until Keypressed;

{6.0 Close graphics screen}

     CloseGraph

end.   {Main Program}
```

Figure 13.8 Program 13c: Example of Line and SetWriteMode procedures.

by randomly selecting values for the variables XB and YB and specifies XORPut as the argument in its invocation of SetWriteMode. It then selects initial and terminal points using the variables X and Y (again at random) and draws a line. After delaying a suitable interval so that the user can see the line, the line is erased simply by rewriting it. Since SetWriteMode has been invoked using XORPut, the rewriting operation has the effect of turning each pixel off, thereby removing the line from the screen. A sample of the output produced by this program is shown in Figure 13.9, a simple line between two points. What

Figure 13.9 Sample output from Program 13c.

makes the program interesting is the appearance of movement achieved by rapidly writing and erasing lines anchored at a specific location.

13.5.4 Time Out

1. Try out Program 13c. Remember to substitute your character string for *path-to-driver* if necessary. You may wish to change the value used in the invocation of Delay to a larger or smaller value, depending on the speed of your machine.
2. Change the argument XORPut to CopyPut in step 3.0 of the program. How does this change the output?
3. Modify Program 13c to choose both endpoints of each line at random. Which version of the program do you prefer?
4. Modify Program 13c to use the Rectangle procedure to draw rectangles at random, making each one visible for a time before "erasing" it.

13.5.5   The Current Pointer and Related Procedures and Functions

The Turbo Pascal Graph unit maintains a pointer to the graphics screen called the **Current Pointer**, or **CP**. This pointer is composed of the X- and Y-coordinates of a position on the screen. The CP is similar to the position of the cursor on the text screen, except that there is no visible representation of it on the graphics screen. The SetGraphMode procedure resets the CP to (0, 0), which is its default value. Certain of the graphics procedures make use of and/or change the value of the CP. Among those procedures are MoveTo, which changes the value of the CP, and LineTo, which draws a line from the CP to a specified point and changes the CP. Each of these procedures is described in more detail in this section.

The **MoveTo** procedure changes the value of the CP. The general form for invoking this procedure is

```
MoveTo (x, y)
```

where *x* and *y* are Integer values that become the new values of the Current Pointer. For example, to set the CP to (100, 100), you would write

```
MoveTo (100, 100);
```

To set the CP to the middle of the screen, you would write

```
MoveTo (GetMaxX div 2, GetMaxY div 2);
```

The **LineTo** procedure draws a line from the position specified by the CP to a point specified in the argument of the procedure. A general form for invocation of this procedure is

```
LineTo (x, y)
```

where *x* and *y* are the coordinates of the endpoint of the line. In addition to drawing the line, LineTo updates the CP to the values specified for *x* and *y*. For example, the following two statements would draw a line between (0, 0) and (100, 100) and update the CP to (100, 100):

```
MoveTo (0, 0);
LineTo (100, 100);
```

Note that this program segment is equivalent to

```
Line (0, 0, 100, 100);
```

except that the Line statement will not update the CP.

The following program segment draws a rectangle around the edges of the graphics screen:

```
MoveTo (0, 0);
LineTo (0, GetMaxY);
LineTo (GetMaxX, GetMaxY);
LineTo (GetMaxX, 0);
LineTo (0, 0);
```

At the end of execution of this program segment, the CP will be set to (0, 0).

It is sometimes necessary to retrieve the content of the CP. This can be done by the functions **GetX** and **GetY**, which return the X- and Y-coordinates, respectively, of the CP. For example, consider the following program segment:

```
LineTo (GetMaxX, GetMaxY);
X := GetX;
Y := GetY;
```

After execution of this program, X and Y will have the values GetMaxX and GetMaxY, respectively.

In the program segments just presented as illustrations of LineTo, the same task could be accomplished more easily by other means. In fact, you can do everything with Line that can be done with LineTo. The LineTo procedure is very handy when the next line segment is to begin where the last one ended. This is the situation in Program 13d, which is shown in Figure 13.10. (The steps required to initialize the graphics screen are

```
program P13d (Output);
{Program creates a spiral pattern;
    illustrates MoveTo and LineTo procedures}
uses Graph, CRT;
const
    IncrementAmount = 10;
var
    GraphDriver, GraphMode, ErrorCode, XR, YR, Incr : Integer;
begin   {Main Program}

{1.0 Initialize graphics screen}
    .
    .
    .

{2.0 Set starting point}

    XR := GetMaxX div 2;
    YR := GetMaxY div 2;
    MoveTo (XR, YR);

{3.0 Initialize increment }

    Incr := 0;

{4.0 Produce pattern}

    repeat
        Lineto (XR + Incr, YR);
        XR := GetX;
        Incr := Incr + IncrementAmount;
        Lineto (XR, YR - Incr);
        YR := GetY;
        Incr := Incr + IncrementAmount;
        Lineto (XR - Incr, YR);
        XR := GetX;
        Incr := Incr + IncrementAmount;
        Lineto (XR, YR + Incr);
        Incr := Incr + IncrementAmount;
        YR := GetY;
        Delay (10);
    until KeyPressed;

{5.0 Close graphics screen}

    CloseGraph

end.    {Main Program}
```

Figure 13.10 Program 13d: Example of MoveTo and LineTo procedures.

the same as those in Program 13c and are omitted to save space.) This program creates a spiral maze, as shown in the sample output in Figure 13.11. We start the CP in the center of the screen at step 2.0 by using the MoveTo procedure. The pattern is produced by using the LineTo procedure to draw a line from the CP to locations that spiral outward to the left. As each line is drawn, the variable Incr is incremented by IncrementAmount. This variable is alternately added to and subtracted from the X- and Y-coordinate used in the LineTo procedure. After each line is drawn, the variable XR or YR is updated using GetX or GetY, so that these variables always reflect the endpoint of the line that has just been drawn.

13.5.6 *Time Out*

1. Try out Program 13d. Vary the value of IncrementAmount. What happens as this amount becomes larger? smaller?
2. Change Program 13d to choose a starting point for the spiral at random.
3. Change Program 13d so that IncrementAmount is chosen as a random value in the range 1 to some maximum for each repetition of the repeat loop. What effect does this have on the pattern produced?

Figure 13.11 Sample output from Program 13d.

4. Modify Program 13d so that the spiral opens to the right instead of the left. The result should be a mirror image of the original.

5. Revise Program 13d so that the spiral is drawn from some fixed external point toward the center instead of from the center outward.

13.6 COLORS AND PIXELS

The smallest unit of output that can be produced on the graphics screen is the pixel. As we have noted previously, each pixel can be one of a number of colors, depending on the current graph mode, as shown in Figure 13.1. Colors are assigned a number ranging from 0 (which is always black) to the largest available color (which is always white). For example, in VGA mode, 16 colors are available; they are numbered from 0 to 15. In this mode, 0 is black and 15 is white.

Because there are a different number of colors available, depending on the driver in use, Turbo Pascal provides the function **GetMaxColor**, which has general form

```
GetMaxColor
```

(There are no arguments.) This function returns a value in the range 0 to the maximum color number supported. For example, for VGA, the value of GetMaxColor will be 15; for CGA, the value of GetMaxColor will be 4. You can use GetMaxColor to determine the range of colors available for drawing on the graphics screen.

The procedure **PutPixel** can be used to write a pixel at a specific location on the graphics screen. The general form for invoking this procedure is

```
PutPixel (x, y, color)
```

where x and y are the coordinates of the desired pixel and *color* is a number in the range 0 to GetMaxColor. For example, to turn the pixel in the center of the screen to white, you could use

```
PutPixel (GetMaxX div 2, GetMaxY div 2, GetMaxColor);
```

To turn off the pixel at the middle of the screen (i.e., set the pixel to black), you could use

```
PutPixel (GetMaxX div 2, GetMaxY div 2, 0);
```

(Remember that 0 is always the color black, regardless of the driver and mode.)

Program 13e, which is shown in Figure 13.12, illustrates the use of PutPixel and GetMaxColor to display pixels at random in a variety of colors on the graphics screen. Execution of the program will show a screen rapidly filling up with points of different colors.

```
program P13e (Output);
{Program displays pixels at random;
    illustrates use of PutPixel}
uses Graph, CRT;
var
   GraphDriver, GraphMode, ErrorCode, Color, X, Y : Integer;
begin    {Main Program}

{1.0 Initialize graphics screen}

     .
     .
     .
{2.0 Display pixels at random until user presses a key}

     repeat
          X := Random(GetMaxX);
          Y := Random(GetMaxY);
          Color := Random (GetMaxColor);
          PutPixel (X, Y, Color)
     until Keypressed;

{3.0 Close graphics screen}

     CloseGraph

end.    {Main Program}
```

Figure 13.12   Program 13e: Illustrates use of PutPixel.

13.6.1   *Time Out*

1. Execute Program 13e and observe the results.

2. Modify Program 13e to delay a suitable period after displaying a pixel and then turn the pixel to black by using PutPixel with the same address, but with color 0.

3. Modify Program 13e to create a line that "crawls" across the screen. Start with a horizontal line created by turning on a series of adjacent pixels. Then turn a pixel off on the left of the line, and turn a pixel on at the right of the line, until the line disappears from the screen. Vary the color from 1 to GetMaxColor to observe the different colors available on your system.

13.7   FILL STYLE AND ELLIPSES

Turbo Pascal provides you with the ability to draw ellipses (and circles) with a single procedure call. These figures can be filled with the background color or with a variety of available fill patterns (such as solid colors, hatching, dots, and so forth). This section will discuss and illustrate the setting of the fill style and the drawing of ellipses.

The **SetFillStyle** procedure is used to specify the style and color of fill for several Turbo Pascal procedures that draw closed figures,[3] one of which is FillEllipse—the

---

[3]SetFillStyle affects the output from the procedures Bar, Bar3D, FillPoly, and PieSlice, as well as FillEllipse.

procedure that draws a filled ellipse. The general form for invoking SetFillStyle is

```
SetFillStyle (pattern, color)
```

where *pattern* is an Integer in the range 0 to 12 that specifies the geometrical pattern to be used and *color* is an Integer in the range 0 to GetMaxColor. The named constants shown in the following table are provided for use in specifying a value for *pattern*:

Identifier	Value	Fills With
EmptyFill	0	Background color
SolidFill	1	Solid fill color
LineFill	2	____
LtSlashFill	3	/ / /
SlashFill	4	/ / / (thick lines)
BkSlashFill	5	\ \ \ (thick lines)
LtBkSlashFill	6	\ \ \
HatchFill	7	Light hatch
XHatchFill	8	Heavy crosshatch
InterleaveFill	9	Interleaving lines
WideDotFill	10	Widely spaced dots
CloseDotFill	11	Closely spaced dots
UserFill	12	Fill pattern defined by user[4]

For example, in order to specify that a figure is to be drawn using white horizontal lines, you would use

```
SetFillStyle (LineFill, GetMaxColor);
```

The parameters set by invoking SetFillStyle remain in effect until changed by another call to the procedure. If the procedure is not invoked prior to using a drawing procedure, such as FillEllipse, the default fill pattern is SolidFill, and the default color is GetMaxColor.

The procedure **FillEllipse** can be used to draw an ellipse on the graphics screen, using the current fill style and color. The general form for executing this procedure is

```
FillEllipse (x, y, x-radius, y-radius)
```

where *x* and *y* are Integers specifying the center of the ellipse and *x-radius* and *y-radius* are Integers specifying the horizontal radius and vertical radius, respectively. For example, to draw an ellipse with center at the center of the screen and with a horizontal radius of 10 and a vertical radius of 20, you could use

```
FillEllipse (GetMaxX div 2, GetMaxY div 2, 10, 20);
```

---

[4]See *Turbo Pascal 7.0 Programmer's Reference* for more information.

If the value of *x-radius* is equal to the value of *y-radius*, then the ellipse will be a circle. For example, the following statement will draw a circle with radius of 10 pixels at the center of the screen:

```
FillEllipse (GetMaxX div 2, GetMaxY div 2, 10, 10);
```

Program 13f, shown in Figure 13.13, illustrates the use of SetFillStyle and FillEllipse to draw randomly placed circles on the screen with a solid fill and colors chosen at random. A sample of the output from this program is shown in Figure 13.14. The actual screens change rapidly with interesting patterns of circles in various colors.

13.7.1 Time Out

1. Compile and execute Program 13f.
2. Modify the invocation of SetFillStyle in Program 13f to choose a value for *pattern* by choosing a number at random in the range 0 to 11.
3. Modify Program 13f to draw ellipses rather than circles. Use randomly chosen values for both the *x-radius* and *y-radius*.

```
program P13f (Output);
{Program displays circles at random;
    illustrates use of SetFillStyle and FillElipse}
uses Graph, CRT;
var
   GraphDriver, GraphMode, ErrorCode, XR, YR : Integer;
begin   {Main Program}

{1.0 Initialize graphics screen}
   .
   .
   .
{2.0 Generate circles at random until key pressed}

   Randomize;
   repeat
         SetFillStyle(1, Random(GetMaxColor) + 1);
         XR := Random(300);
         FillEllipse(Random(GetMaxX), Random(GetMaxY), XR, XR);
         Delay(100)
   until KeyPressed;

{3.0 Close graphics screen}

   CloseGraph

end.    {Main Program}
```

Figure 13.13 Program 13f: Illustrates use of SetFillStyle and FillEllipse.

Figure 13.14 Sample output from Program 13f.

13.8 Case Study: Graph of a Function

■ **Problem Statement.**   Write a program to produce a graph of the function

$$f(x) = \cos x^2$$

for a range of values of x entered by the user.

■ **Problem Analysis.**   After the user enters the range of values of x (we will call these values LowerX and UpperX), the program will initialize the graphics screen and produce the desired output. This task can be divided into two parts: plotting the graph of the function and plotting the x- and y-axes. We will then wait until the user presses a key before closing the graphics screen. The plan is summarized as follows:

PLAN FOR FUNCTION-GRAPHING PROGRAM (P13g)

1.0 Get parameters for the graph
2.0 Initialize the graphics screen
3.0 Produce the graph of function

4.0 Plot axes

5.0 Wait until user presses a key

6.0 Close graphics screen

Initializing the graphics screen in this program is exactly the same as for all other programs in this chapter. We will implement the task using a procedure with no parameters.

Producing the graph of the function presents the biggest challenge. The basic problem that must be solved is how to map the set of points representing the function onto the screen; that is, we must decide which pixel on the screen will represent the (x, y) coordinates that will be computed by the program. We would also like to generate as many points for the function as is possible, given the number of pixels at our disposal, in order to create as smooth a curve as possible.

The values of x and y will need to be modified by some scaling factor to yield a graphics screen location expressed in pixels. It is unlikely that one pixel will represent 1 unit in the graph—that is, that the scaling factor will be 1. If the range of values to be represented is large, it will be necessary to divide the value to be plotted by a scaling factor greater than 1 to produce a pixel location that is in the allowable range. For example, if there are 200 pixels, and the values that must be represented range from 0 to 600, then the scaling factor could be 3: Dividing each actual value by 3 would yield a location in the range 0 to 200. In this situation, each pixel represents 3 units. On the other hand, if the values to be represented range from 0 to 2, then the scaling factor would be 0.01. Each pixel would then represent 0.01 unit; 100 pixels would represent 1 unit. In designing a program that produces a graph, you can choose to implement the scaling factor as a constant or a variable. Building the factor into the program as a constant makes the program quite inflexible, since a different function or a different range of values for the same function may require a different scaling factor for optimum results. Two other approaches are to allow the user to enter the scaling factor (this gives the user control over the appearance of the graph) and to have the program compute the factor for maximum utilization of the graphics screen (this gives the best possible graph, but the user has no control over its appearance). In this program we will take the approach of computing the scaling factor.

The problem of producing the largest number of points possible can be solved by computing the range of values of x (the difference between the largest and smallest values of x) and dividing by GetMaxX. We will call this quantity DX; it represents the incremental change in x for the purpose of generating points to be plotted, and it represents the scaling factor for computing the position of the pixel on the screen to represent the particular value of x.

We would like to choose a scaling factor for y that will enable us to represent all values of y that will be needed. This task can be accomplished by precomputing all values of y and choosing the one with the largest absolute value; we will call this LargeY. The scaling factor for y, which we will call DY, can then be computed as (2 * LargeY) / GetMaxY. The reason for doubling LargeY is to allow values of y in the range $-$LargeY to $+$LargeY to be represented.

We can summarize this discussion by refining step 3 of the foregoing plan as follows:

3.0 Produce graph of function
   3.1 DX = (UpperX − LowerX) / GetMaxX
   3.2 Compute LargeY
   3.3 DY = (2 * LargeY) / GetMaxY
   3.4 For each (x, y) coordinate pair, turn on corresponding pixel

We will plot the x-axis at the middle of the screen. The y-axis will be either on the left-hand border of the screen (if the smallest value in the x range is positive) or toward the middle of the screen (if the smallest value in the x range is negative). The intersection of the x- and y-axis forms the logical origin with coordinates (0, 0). The transformation of the computed (X, Y) coordinates to the screen location is given by

```
((X - LowerX) / DX, (LargeY - Y) / DY)
```

By subtracting LowerX from X, we transform the range of X values to begin at 0 (corresponding to pixel location 0 on the left edge of the screen). By subtracting the Y-coordinate from LargeY, we transform the range of Y values so that LargeY is represented by position 0 (corresponding to pixel position 0 at the top edge of the screen). By dividing by DX and DY, we scale the coordinates for placement on the screen.

■ **Problem Solution.**   A solution to this problem is Program 13g, shown in Figure 13.15. In this program, individual pixels are addressed to represent the graph of the function. (Note the use of the Round function to transform the Real values computed for pixel locations to the Integer form required to invoke PutPixel.) A sample of the output produced by the program is shown in Figure 13.16. You will note that some portions of the graph are represented by a nearly continuous line, but other portions are represented by a disconnected set of points. For this function, the mind can make the connection between adjacent points to visualize the curve as continuous, but for other functions doing so may present a problem.

An alternative to plotting pixels to represent the function is to draw line segments to connect adjacent points on the graph. This approach is illustrated in Program 13h, which is shown in Figure 13.17. In this program, the LineTo procedure is used to connect each point with its successor. We initialize the CP with the coordinates of the first point, using the MoveTo procedure, before entering the loop. Inside the loop, the LineTo procedure takes care of drawing the line segments and updating the CP for the beginning of the next segment. (Remember that LineTo updates the CP automatically.) A sample of the output from this program is shown in Figure 13.18. Compare it with the output produced by Program 13g. You will probably prefer the line plot of Program 13h to the pixel plot of Program 13g.

13.8.1   *Time Out*

1. Compile and execute Programs 13g and 13h. Experiment with different ranges of values for the function.

```pascal
program P13g (Input,Output);
{Program produces a plot of a function, using pixels}
uses Graph, CRT;
var
   LowerX, UpperX, LargeY, DX, DY, X, Y : Real;
   Color : Integer;

{***********************************************************************}

procedure OpenGraphWindow;
var
     GraphDriver, GraphMode, ErrorCode : Integer;
begin   {OpenGraphWindow}

     GraphDriver := Detect;
     InitGraph (GraphDriver, GraphMode, 'C:\TP\BGI');
     ErrorCode := GraphResult;
     if ErrorCode <> grOK then
        begin
             Writeln ('Graphics error : ', GraphErrorMsg(ErrorCode));
             Writeln ('Program aborted...');
             Halt(1)
        end;   {if}
     Rectangle (0, 0, GetMaxX, GetMaxY)

end;   {OpenGraphWindow}

{--------------------------------------------------------------------}

procedure GetGraphParameters (var LowX, UpX : Real);

begin   {GetGraphParameters}

     Write ('Enter lower and upper limits for X ');
     Readln (LowX, UpX)

end;   {GetGraphParameters}

{--------------------------------------------------------------------}

function F(X: Real) : Real;

begin   {F}

     F:= Cos(X*X)                         .

end;   {F}

{--------------------------------------------------------------------}
```

Figure 13.15(a) Program 13g: Plot of a function using pixels (part 1 of 3 parts).

2. Modify Program 13g to plot larger points by using FillEllipse to create small circles to represent the points. Experiment with circles with radii of sizes 1 and 2. Which type of point makes the graph easier to interpret?

```
function MaxY (LowX, UpX : Real) : Real;
var
      LY, X, Y : Real;
begin   {MaxY}

      X := LowX;
      LY := Abs(F(X));
      repeat
            Y := F(X);
            if Abs(Y) > LY then
                LY := Abs(Y);
            X := X + DX
      until X > UpX;
      MaxY := LY

end;   {MaxY}

{------------------------------------------------------------------}

procedure PlotAxes (BigY, DY, LowX, DX : Real);

begin   {PlotAxes}

{1.0 Plot X axis}

      Line (0, Round(BigY/DY), GetMaxX, Round(BigY/DY));

{2.0 Plot Y axis}

      if LowX < 0 then
          Line (Round(-LowX /DX), 0, Round(-LowX/DX),GetMaxY)
      else
          Line (0, 0, 0, GetMaxY)

end;   {PlotAxes}

{*********************************************************************}
```

Figure 13.15(b) (Part 2 of 3 parts).

3. Modify Program 13h to plot each of the following functions over suitable ranges of values:

(a) $f(x) = \dfrac{1}{e^x + e^{-x}}$

(b) $f(x) = ax^3 + bx^2 + cx + d$ for values of a, b, c, and d entered by the program user

(c) $f(x) = \sin^2 x$

13.9 BAR, BAR3D, AND PIESLICE

Two of the most common types of presentation graphs are the bar graph and the pie chart. Turbo Pascal provides procedures to draw bars in two styles that you can use to construct bar graphs. Also provided is a procedure to draw part of a complete circle called a "pie slice"; this procedure will be useful in constructing pie charts.

```
begin    {Main Program}

{1.0 Get parameters for the graph}

     GetGraphParameters (LowerX, UpperX);

{2.0 Initialize graphics screen}

     OpenGraphWindow;

{3.0 Produce graph of function}

     DX := (UpperX - LowerX) / GetMaxX;
     LargeY := MaxY (LowerX, UpperX);
     DY := 2 * LargeY / GetMaxY;
     X:= LowerX;
     Color := GetMaxColor;
     repeat
          Y := F(X);
          PutPixel(Round((X-LowerX)/DX), Round((LargeY-Y)/DY),Color);
          X := X + DX
     until X > UpperX;

{4.0 Plot axes}

     PlotAxes (LargeY, DY, LowerX, DX);

{5.0 Wait until user presses a key}

     repeat
     until KeyPressed;

{6.0 Close graphics screen}

     CloseGraph

end.    {Main Program}
```

Figure 13.15(c) (Part 3 of 3 parts).

The **Bar** procedure draws a rectangle filled with the current fill style and color. The general form for invoking this procedure is

```
Bar (x1, y1, x2, y2)
```

where $x1$ and $y1$ are Integer values representing the screen coordinates of the upper left-hand corner of the rectangle and $x2$ and $y2$ are screen coordinates of the lower right-hand corner of the rectangle. The procedure is essentially similar to Rectangle, except that no outline of the figure will be drawn, and the area will be filled with the current color and fill style as set by the last invocation of SetFillStyle. For example, to draw a bar along the left-hand border of the screen, you could use

```
Bar (0, 0, 10, GetMaxY);
```

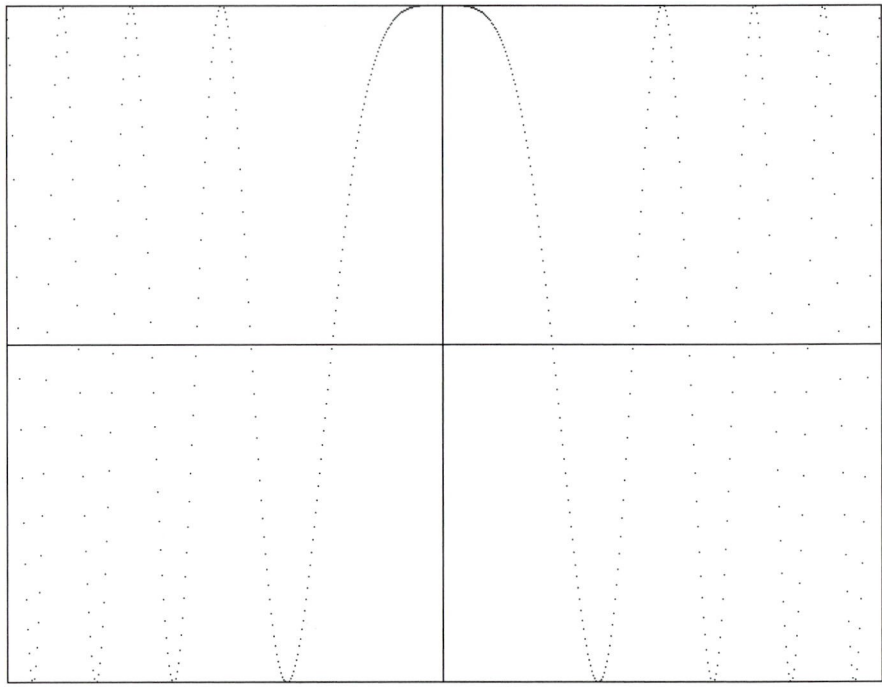

Figure 13.16 Output from Program 13g for $\cos x^2$ in the interval $|x| < 5$.

```
program P13h (Input, Output);
{Program produces a plot of a function, using lines}
      .
      .
      .
begin   {Main Program}
      .
      .
      .
{3.0 Produce graph of function}

      DX := (UpperX - LowerX) / GetMaxX;
      LargeY := MaxY (LowerX, UpperX);
      DY := 2 * LargeY / GetMaxY;
      X:= LowerX;
      Color := GetMaxColor;
      Y := F(X);
      MoveTo (Round((X-LowerX)/DX), Round((LargeY-Y)/DY));
      repeat
            X := X + DX;
            Y := F(X);
            LineTo (Round((X-LowerX)/DX), Round((LargeY-Y)/DY))
      until X >= UpperX;
      .
      .
      .
end.    {Main Program}
```

Figure 13.17 Program 13h: Plot of a function, using line segments. (Portions of the program not shown are the same as in Program 13g.)

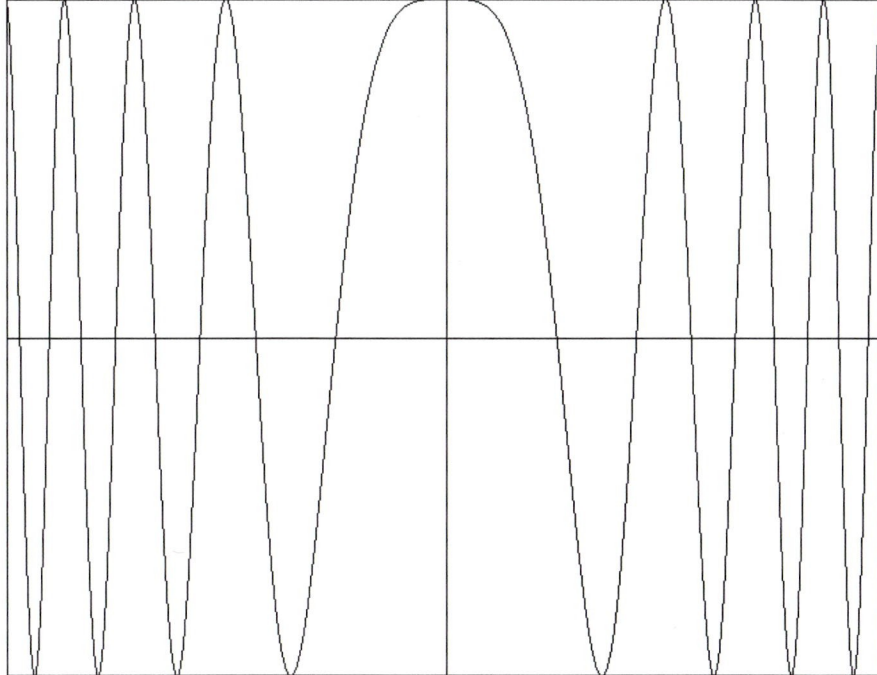

Figure 13.18 Output from Program 13h for cos x^2 in the interval $|x| < 5$.

The **Bar3D** procedure draws a three-dimensional bar, using the current style and color. The general form for invoking this procedure is

```
Bar3D (x1, y1, x2, y2, depth, top)
```

where $x1$, $y1$ are the Integer coordinates of the upper left-hand corner of the bar; $x2$, $y2$ are the coordinates of the lower right-hand corner of the bar; *depth* is the number of pixels representing the depth (the third dimension) of the bar; and *top* is a Boolean value that controls whether or not the top of the bar will be drawn. For convenience in specifying a value for *top*, the following named constants are defined:

Identifier	Value	Comment
TopOn	True	Top will be drawn
TopOff	False	Top will not be drawn

Unlike the Bar procedure, the Bar3D procedure will draw an outline around the bar. Examples of different types of bars that can be drawn using Bar3D are shown in Figure 13.19. The use of TopOff makes it easy to construct one bar on top of another to create a stacked bar chart. Note that it is possible to use this procedure to draw an outlined bar by using a *depth* of 0.

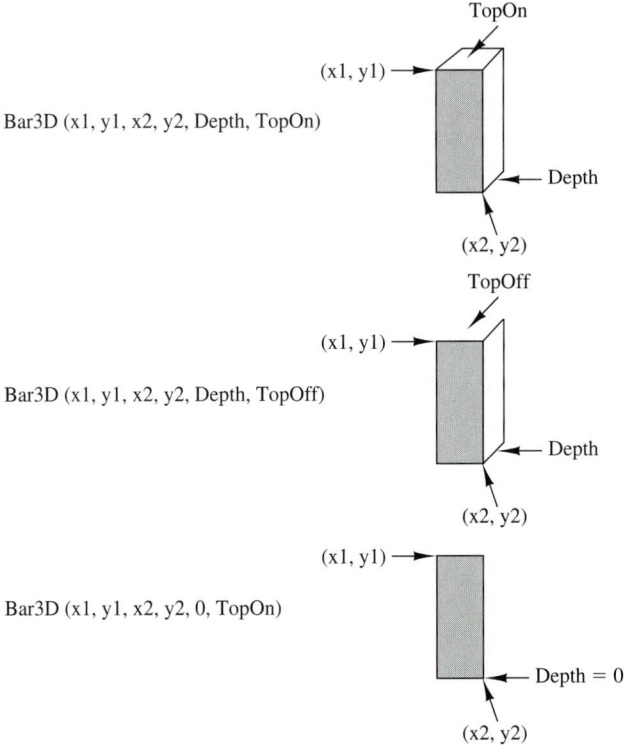

Figure 13.19 Examples of Bar3D.

The **PieSlice** procedure can be used to draw a sector of a circle in the form of a "slice of a pie." The general form for invoking this procedure is

```
PieSlice (x, y, start-angle, end-angle, radius)
```

where x and y are the coordinates of the center of the circle, *start-angle* is the angle to begin construction of the figure, *end-angle* is the angle to end the figure, and *radius* is the number of pixels to be used as the radius of the circle. All angles are expressed in Integer degrees. The angle 0° is at 3 o'clock, 90° is at 12 o'clock, and so forth, progressing in a counterclockwise direction around the circle, as shown in Figure 13.20. Figure 13.21 shows some examples of figures drawn using PieSlice.

13.9.1   Time Out

1. Modify Program 13f to draw randomly placed and randomly sized rectangles using the procedure Bar.
2. Modify Program 13f to draw three vertical three-dimensional bars, as shown in Figure 13.19.
3. Modify Program 13f to draw the three pie slices shown in Figure 13.21.

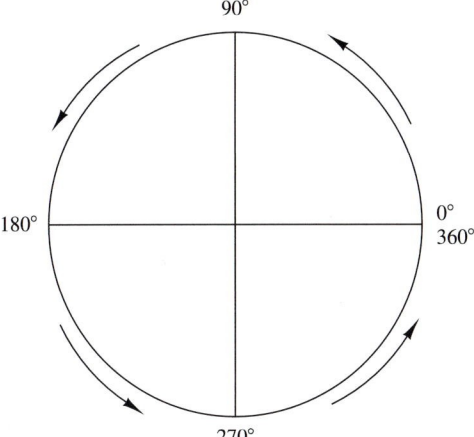

Figure 13.20 Angles used in specifying arguments for PieSlice.

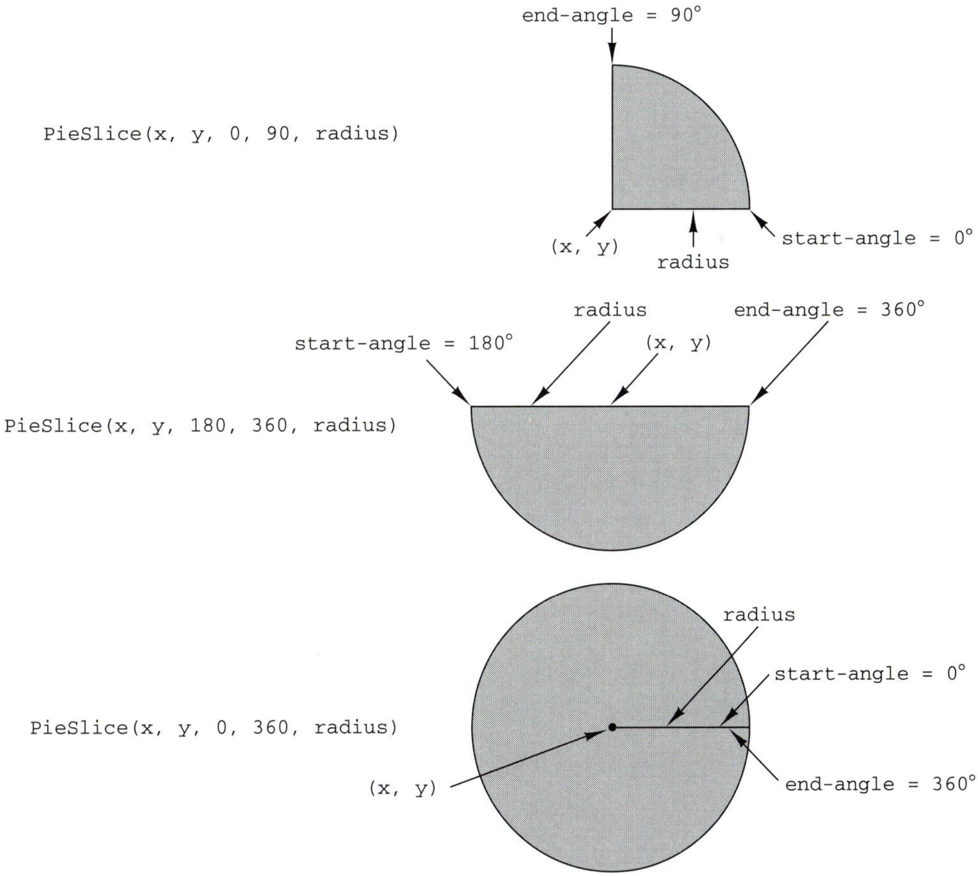

PieSlice(x, y, 0, 90, radius)

PieSlice(x, y, 180, 360, radius)

PieSlice(x, y, 0, 360, radius)

Figure 13.21 Examples of use of PieSlice.

13.10 Case Study: Presentation Graphics

■ **Problem Statement.** Write a program to construct a vertical bar graph and a pie chart from data entered by the program user.

■ **Problem Analysis.** This problem requires that the user enter data for the two graphs before the graphs are presented. A plan for the program is as follows:

PRESENTATION GRAPHICS PROGRAM (P13i)

1.0 Get data to be graphed
2.0 Draw bar graph
3.0 Draw pie chart

Analysis of a typical bar graph, shown in Figure 13.22, indicates that the user will need to enter the following data:

- The data to be graphed and their associated labels. We will use arrays to store these items: YValue will store the data points (such as profit amounts for each quarter for a corporation or sales amounts for each of several districts), and XLabel will store the associated descriptions (such as "First Quarter," "Second Quarter," etc., or "District 1," "District 2," etc.)

- The caption for the *x*- and *y*-axes (XCaption and YCaption). The *x* caption should describe the content of the graph (such as "Quarterly Profits for XYZ Corp." or "Monthly Sales by District." The *y* caption usually expresses the units, such as "Thousands" or "Millions."

- The scale value to be used on the *y*-axis. (This value could be computed from the range in YValues; however, allowing the user to enter the value gives him or her better control over the appearance of the graph.) Figure 13.22 has seven hash marks on the *y*-axis—an arbitrary choice, but one that creates a graph with pleasing proportions. For example, to represent data with a maximum value of 70, you could use a scale value of 10; this choice would create a graph in which the highest bar is aligned with the seventh hash mark.

The task of creating the bar graph can be broken down into the following smaller tasks:

2.0 Draw bar graph
    2.1 Initialize graphics window
    2.2 Compute relative X and Y coordinate increments
    2.3 Draw *x*- and *y*-axes
    2.4 Draw the bars
    2.5 Label the *x*-axis
    2.6 Label the *y*-axis
    2.7 Wait until user presses Enter
    2.8 Close graphics window

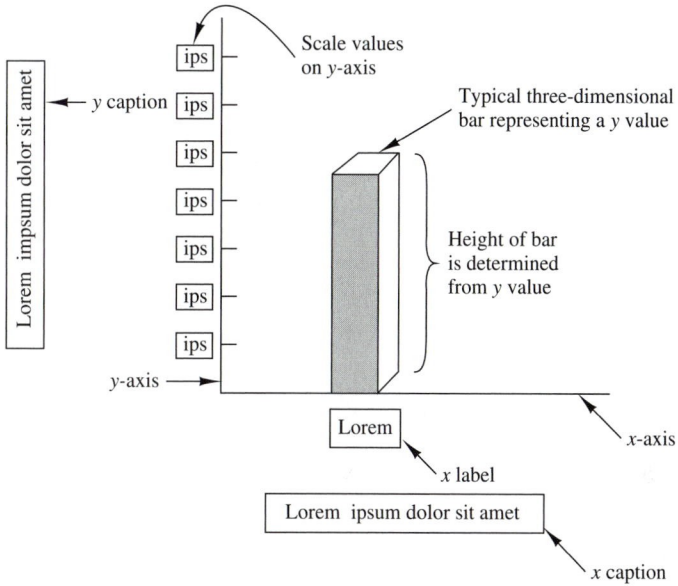

Figure 13.22 Layout of a typical vertical bar graph.

In order to make the program compatible with a variety of graphics environments, we will make extensive use of relative addressing for all elements of the graph. This will be accomplished by dividing the screen into an imaginary 10×10 grid. The distance between each line will be GetMaxX **div** 10 (for the x-coordinates) and GetMaxY **div** 10 (for the y-coordinates). The computation of these values (which we will call XIncr and YIncr) is carried out in step 2.2 of the procedure. The values will then be passed to each of the procedures that draw elements of the graph on the screen.

A layout of a typical pie chart is shown in Figure 13.23. Each slice of the circle represents a different YValue. A different fill is used for each slice to differentiate among

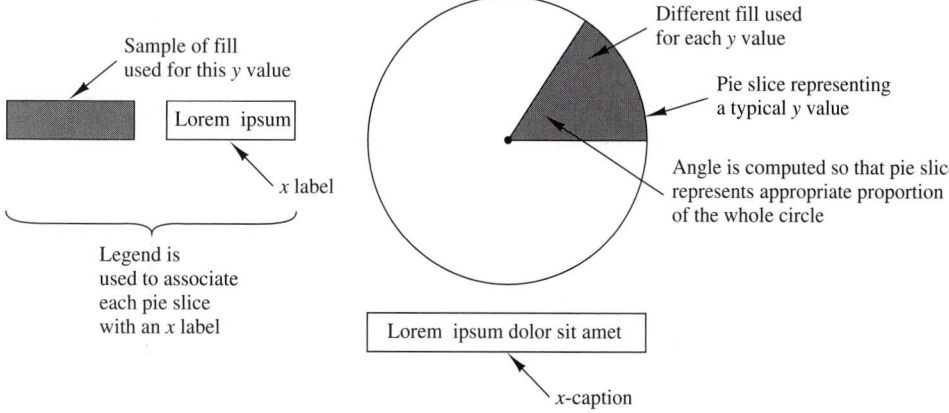

Figure 13.23 Layout of a typical pie chart.

them. A legend showing the fill and the related XLabel must also be created. XCaption will be listed across the bottom of the graph. Since a pie chart shows only the relationship of each YValue to the whole, there is no need for YCaption.

Drawing the pie chart can be summarized as follows:

DRAW PIE CHART

1.0 Compute sum of y values

2.0 Compute angles for pie slices

3.0 Draw pie slices

4.0 Write caption

As part of drawing the pie slices, the program will also need to create a legend showing a sample of the fill and the corresponding XLabel value.

■ **Problem Solution.** A solution to this problem is given in Program 13i, shown in Figure 13.24. The output for the sample data shown in Figure 13.25 is shown in Figure 13.26. For simplicity, we have constructed the program to use four y values. (A natural extension for the program would be to accommodate a variable number of data points.) Note the extensive use of relative addressing in the program. All items are placed on the screen based on the 10×10 grid concept described. For example, consider the procedure DrawAxes. Drawing the y-axis is carried out using the statement

```
Line (XIncr, 0, XIncr, 8*YIncr);
```

This will place a line beginning at the top of the screen and extending to grid position 8 (80 percent of the depth of the screen). The line will coincide with vertical grid line 1, which will be 1/10 of the total screen width from the left margin of the screen. Similar concepts are used throughout the program for all elements placed on the screen.

Drawing the pie chart is carried out in the procedure DrawPieChart. This procedure computes the angle for each pie slice as a proportion of the total represented by each y value times 360. (Remember that PieSlice needs to have its angle measures expressed in degrees.) As the circle is drawn, each pie slice is drawn with the beginning angle equal to the ending angle of the previous pie slice. The last pie slice uses an ending angle of $360°$ so that the last slice will end exactly on the beginning of the first slice.

13.10.1 Time Out

1. Compile and execute Program 13i with your own sample data.
2. Program 13i will produce somewhat unpredictable results if the maximum element in YValue exceeds 7*ScaleValue. Modify the program so that it computes a workable ScaleValue in this event.
3. Modify Program 13i to allow the user to select (via a menu) which type of graph is desired for a given data set.

```pascal
program P13i (Input, Output);
{Program produces bar graph and pie chart for data entered by user}
uses Graph, CRT;
type
    LabelType = array[1..4] of string[10];
    ValueType = array[1..4] of LongInt;
    CaptionType = string[30];
var
    XLabel : LabelType;
    YValue : ValueType;
    XIncr, YIncr : Integer;
    ScaleValue : Integer;
    XCaption, YCaption : CaptionType;

{**********************************************************************}

procedure OpenGraphWindow;
       .

       .

       .
{------------------------------------------------------------------}

procedure GetGraphData (var YValue : ValueType;
                        var XLabel : LabelType;
                        var XCaption, YCaption : CaptionType;
                        var ScaleValue : Integer);
var
    I : Integer;
begin   {GetGraphData}

    for I := 1 to 4 do
        begin
            Write ('Enter value # ', I, ' ');
            Readln (YValue[I]);
            Write ('Enter label # ', I, ' ');
            Readln (XLabel[I])
        end;   {for}
    Write ('Enter Y Scale value ');
    Readln (ScaleValue);
    Writeln ('Maximum value that can be graphed is ',7*ScaleValue);
    Write ('Enter caption for X (horizontal) axis ');
    Readln (XCaption);
    Write ('Enter caption for Y (vertical) axis ');
    Readln (YCaption)

end;   {GetGraphData}

{------------------------------------------------------------------}
```

Figure 13.24(a) Program 13i: Presentation graphics (part 1 of 5 parts).

4. Modify Program 13i to allow the user to enter a variable number of *y* values. (This will require you to analyze carefully how the program carries out relative addressing for the placement of graph elements and make suitable modifications to accommodate the new circumstances. Pay particular attention to the placement and width of bars in producing the bar graph.)

```
procedure DrawBars (XIncr, YIncr : Integer;
                    YValue : ValueType;
                    ScaleValue : Integer);
var
    I : Integer;
    PropHeight : array[1..4] of Integer;
begin    {DrawBars}

    for I := 1 to 4 do
        PropHeight[I] := Round(YValue[I] / ScaleValue);
    for I := 1 to 4 do
        begin
            SetFillStyle (Random(11)+1,Random(GetMaxColor));
            Bar3D ( (I*2+1)*XIncr-XIncr div 4, 8*YIncr,
                    (I*2+1)*XIncr+XIncr div 4,(8-PropHeight[I])*YIncr,
                      XIncr div 4, TopOn)
        end    {for}

end;    {DrawBars}

{-------------------------------------------------------------------}

procedure DrawAxes (XIncr, YIncr : Integer);
var
    I: Integer;
begin    {DrawAxes}

{1.0 Draw Y axis}

    Line (XIncr, 0, XIncr, 8 * YIncr);

{2.0 Draw X axis}

    Line (XIncr, 8*YIncr, 10 * XIncr, 8*YIncr);

{3.0 Draw hash marks on Y axis}

    for I := 1 to 7 do
        Line (XIncr - 2, YIncr * I, XIncr + 2, YIncr *I)

end;    {DrawAxes}

{-------------------------------------------------------------------}
```

Figure 13.24(b) (Part 2 of 5 parts).

5. Modify Program 13i to produce a horizontal bar graph instead of a vertical bar graph. Horizontal bar graphs usually make use of ordinary bars rather than three-dimensional bars.

13.11   REVIEW QUESTIONS

1. What is a driver? Why are different drivers necessary?
2. Compare the resolutions of the text screen and the graphics screen.
3. Define the term *pixel*.

```
procedure LabelYAxis (XIncr, YIncr : Integer;
                      YCaption : CaptionType;
                      ScaleValue : Integer);
var
    I : Integer ;
    YScale : string[4];
begin    {LabelYAxis}

    SetTextStyle (DefaultFont, HorizDir, 1);
    SetTextJustify (RightText, CenterText);
    for I := 1 to 7 do
        begin
            Str (I*ScaleValue, YScale);
            OutTextXY (XIncr - 3, YIncr * (8 - I), YScale)
        end;    {for}
    SetTextJustify (CenterText, CenterText);
    SetTextStyle (TriplexFont, VertDir, 1);
    OutTextXY (XIncr div 4, YIncr * 4, YCaption)

end;     {LabelYAxis}

{-------------------------------------------------------------------}

procedure LabelXAxis (XIncr, YIncr : Integer;
                      XLabel : LabelType;
                      XCaption : CaptionType);
var
    I : Integer;
begin    {LabelXAxis}

    SetTextStyle (DefaultFont, HorizDir, 1);
    SetTextJustify (CenterText, TopText);
    for I := 1 to 4 do
        OutTextXY ((I * 2 + 1)*XIncr,8*YIncr+10, XLabel[I]);
    SetTextStyle (TriplexFont, HorizDir, 4);
    OutTextXY (XIncr * 5, YIncr * 9, XCaption)

end;    {LabelXAxis}

{-------------------------------------------------------------------}
```

Figure 13.24(c) (Part 3 of 5 parts).

4. What is screen memory? Where is it located? Why does color require more screen memory than monochrome?

5. What purpose is served by the named constant Detect? With which procedure is it intended to be used?

6. Distinguish between absolute and relative addressing of positions on the graphics screen. Which type of addressing is preferred? Why?

7. What purpose is served by the functions GetMaxX and GetMaxY? What determines the value of these functions?

8. What are the basic differences between a bit-mapped font and a stroked font? Which type of font offers greater flexibility?

9. How is SetGraphMode used to erase the graphics screen? How can SetWriteMode be used to erase parts of the graphics screen?

10. What is the current pointer (CP)? How is it used?

```
procedure DrawPieChart (XIncr, YIncr : Integer;
                        YValue : ValueType;
                        XLabel : LabelType;
                        XCaption : CaptionType);
var
     XC, YC, Radius, Sum, I, StartAngle, EndAngle: Integer;
     Angle : array[1..4] of Integer;
begin   {DrawPieChart}

{1.0   Compute sum of Y values}

     Sum := 0;
     for I := 1 to 4 do
         Sum := Sum + YValue[I];

{2.0   Compute angles for pie slices}

     for I := 1 to 4 do
         Angle[I] :=  Round((YValue[I] / Sum) * 360);

{3.0   Draw pie slices}

     SetTextStyle (DefaultFont, HorizDir, 1);
     SetTextJustify (LeftText, CenterText);
     XC := GetMaxX div 2 + XIncr;
     YC := GetMaxY div 2;
     Radius := 2 *  XIncr;
     StartAngle := 0;
     for I := 1 to 4 do
         begin
             SetFillStyle (Random(11)+1,Random(GetMaxColor));
             if I < 4 then
                 EndAngle := StartAngle + Angle[I]
             else
                 EndAngle := 360;
             PieSlice (XC, YC, StartAngle, EndAngle, Radius);
             StartAngle := StartAngle + Angle[I];
             Bar (XIncr, (I+2)*YIncr-5,
                  XIncr + XIncr div 2, (I+2)*YIncr+5);
             OutTextXY (2*XIncr, (I+2)*YIncr, XLabel[I])
         end;   {for}

{4.0   Write caption}

     SetTextStyle (TriplexFont, HorizDir, 4);
     SetTextJustify (CenterText, CenterText);
     OutTextXY (XIncr * 5, YIncr * 9, XCaption)

end;   {DrawPieChart}

{*********************************************************************}
```

Figure 13.24(d) (Part 4 of 5 parts).

11. What purpose is served by the functions GetX and GetY?
12. What determines the value of the function GetMaxColor?
13. What are the two basic elements of fill style? How is the fill style set?
14. How can the procedure FillEllipse be used to draw a circle?

```
begin    {Main Program}

{1.0 Get data to be graphed}

     GetGraphData (YValue, XLabel, XCaption, YCaption, ScaleValue);

{2.0 Draw bar graph}

     OpenGraphWindow;
     XIncr := GetMaxX div 10;
     YIncr := GetMaxY div 10;
     DrawAxes (XIncr, YIncr);
     DrawBars (XIncr, YIncr, YValue, ScaleValue);
     LabelXAxis (XIncr, YIncr, XLabel, XCaption);
     LabelYAxis (XIncr, YIncr, YCaption, ScaleValue);
     Readln;
     CloseGraph;

{3.0 Draw pie chart}

     OpenGraphWindow;
     DrawPieChart (XIncr, YIncr, YValue, XLabel, XCaption);
     Readln;
     CloseGraph

end.     {Main Program}
```

Figure 13.24(e) (Part 5 of 5 parts).

15. What are the essential differences in the output produced by Rectangle, Bar, and Bar3D?

16. What is a pie slice? How is the procedure PieSlice used to create a pie chart?

17. What is meant by the justification of text? What options are available in Turbo Pascal?

18. What purpose is served by the function GraphResult? How is GraphResult similar to IOResult?

19. What are the basic differences between the procedures Line and LineTo?

20. What is the purpose of the function GraphErrorMsg? How is this function used?

```
Enter value # 1 20
Enter label # 1 North
Enter value # 2 30
Enter label # 2 South
Enter value # 3 60
Enter label # 3 East
Enter value # 4 45
Enter label # 4 West
Enter Y Scale value 10
Maximum value that can be graphed is 70
Enter caption for X (horizontal) axis Sales by Region
Enter caption for Y (vertical) axis Millions
```

Figure 13.25 Sample data entry screen for Program 13i.

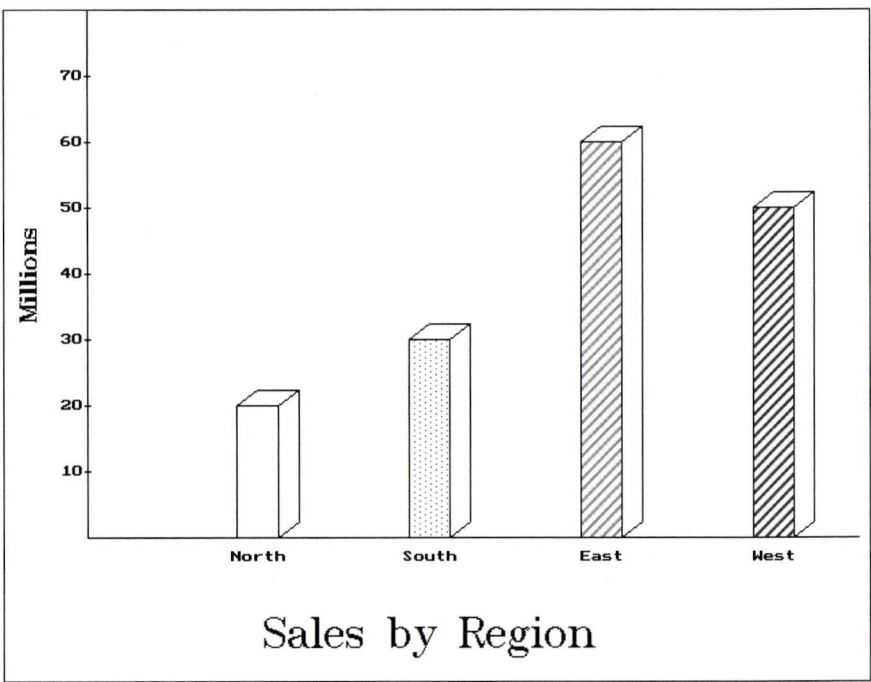

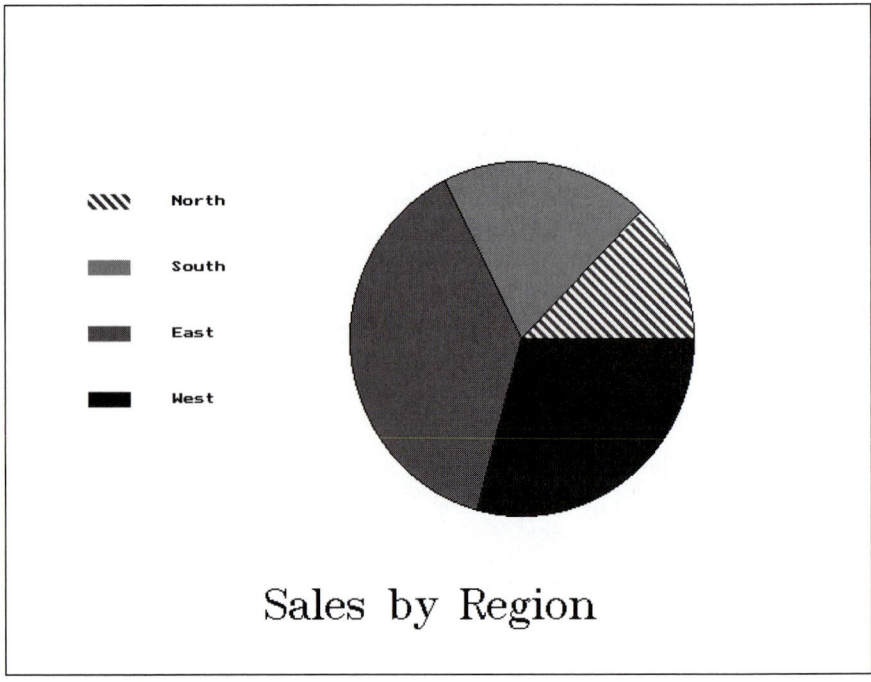

Figure 13.26 Output from Program 13i for sample data shown in Figure 13.25.

13.12   PROGRAMMING EXERCISES

1. Write a program to produce a series of rectangles, beginning with a small rectangle at the center of the screen and continuing with larger and larger ones until the screen is full of rectangles, one inside the other. As an alternative, you might wish to erase one rectangle before drawing the next, so that you get an animated effect. You may also wish to try this using squares, circles, and/or ellipses.

2. Write a program to create a stick person on the graphics screen. Create the design on graph paper before attempting to write the program. You might wish to attempt some simple animation by erasing and redrawing the person's arms or legs.

3. Another type of presentation graph is the line graph, illustrated in Figure 13.27. Write a program to allow the user to enter up to 10 data items with associated labels and produce the related line graph.

4. Write a program to produce a plot of (x, y) coordinates read from a data file.

5. Write a program to roll a die and display the result graphically as the image of the appropriate face of the die. You may wish to extend the program to roll two dice and display both results side by side.

6. Modify Program 13h by adding hash marks and a scale to both the x- and y-axes. The program should compute the scale value for each axis based on the range of x and y values to be graphed.

7. Modify Program 13h to graph two functions on the same screen.

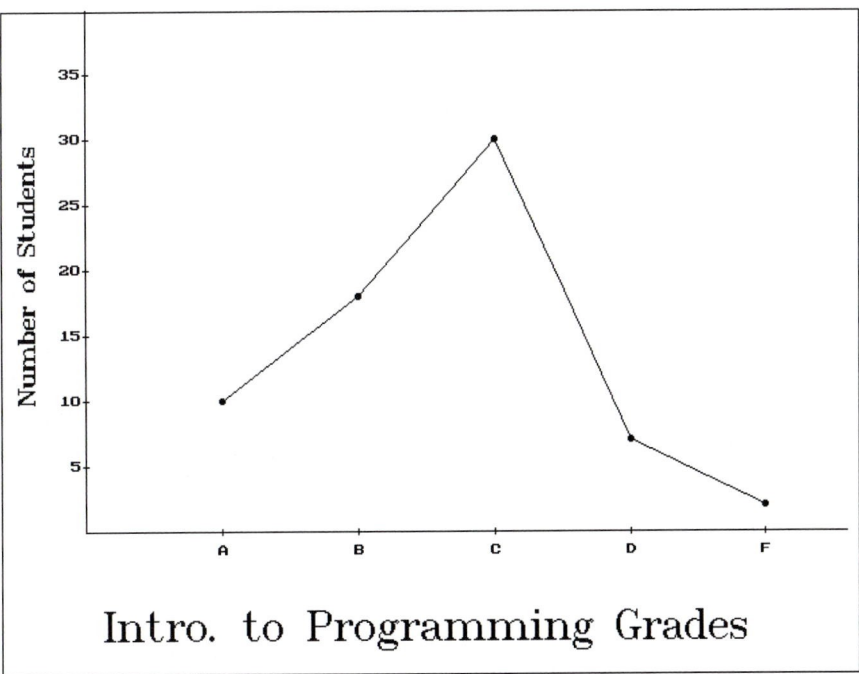

Figure 13.27 Sample line graph.

14

Units

By now, you may have discovered yourself writing certain procedures and functions repeatedly for different programs. You may have wondered whether there was a way for the programmer to make use of such program code without having to write and compile it repeatedly. After all, once a procedure or function is coded and tested, there should really be no reason to have to go through the process again. Turbo Pascal gives you this ability; the mechanism is called a unit. This chapter will review the units that you have already been using and describe how you can construct units of your own.

14.1 INTRODUCTION TO UNITS

A **unit** is a set of constants, types, variables, procedures, and functions that are compiled separately and linked to a program via the uses statement. Turbo Pascal provides a number of units as part of the program development package. You have used the Printer, Crt, and Graph units. You can also write your own units. The syntax is quite simple and entails only two additional reserved words—*interface* and *implementation*; the details are explained later in this chapter.

The most obvious benefit to using units is the ability to make use of code that has been previously written and tested. Since the unit is already compiled, there is also no need for the compiler to translate the code again; this can result in time saved during the program-development process. Units provide a convenient means for allowing multiple programmers to work on a large project independently from one another. The only thing that must be standardized and communicated is the code's interface, that is, those portions of the code that will be known to the program that uses the unit. The unit provides an effective means for hiding the details of implementation from the program that uses the unit's code. The programmer can focus on the facilities that are available in the unit without worrying about how these things are done. For example, when you use the Graph unit, you don't need to know how the procedure Rectangle draws a rectangle; you only know that it does its job, given the parameters that you pass to it. The benefit is that the program that uses one or more units is simpler and easier to read and understand when the person reading the program does not have to contend with excessive details.

Another benefit of using units is to provide for the construction of large programs. Although you probably have not had a problem yet with programs that are too large to fit into memory, Turbo Pascal restricts the size of each program or unit to 64K bytes. (The reasons for this are technical, but they derive from addressing restrictions imposed by early versions of the Intel family of microprocessors used in IBM PCs and compatible systems.) In order to write a program that will be larger than 64K bytes it is necessary to divide the tasks and data structures that are required into a series of units that can be linked by a coordinating program.

A third benefit of using units is in the area of memory management. Large programs often take up more memory than is available on the machine. For example, MS/PC DOS allows a program to address only the first 640K of memory. To create longer programs, it is necessary to use a system called **overlays**, by which portions of code reside on disk until they are needed. When the program comes to a point where the content of a particular overlay segment is required, it is placed in memory, overwriting some other portions of the program that are no longer needed. The smallest program segment that can be overlaid is the unit. Turbo Pascal provides a unit called Overlay that you can use to manage the overlay process.

14.2 THE STANDARD UNITS

Turbo Pascal provides a library of units containing code for specific purposes. There are eight units in all: System, Dos, Overlay, Crt, Printer, Graph, Turbo3, and Graph3. The first five of these (System, Dos, Overlay, Crt, and Printer) are contained in the file

TURBO.TPL. The remainder are contained in separate files: GRAPH.TPU, TURBO3.TPU, and GRAPH3.TPU. The extension **TPL** stands for "Turbo Pascal Library," and the extension **TPU** stands for "Turbo Pascal Unit." Both types of files contain compiled code. There can be only one TPL file, but there can be many TPU files. In fact, when you write your own unit and compile it, you get a TPU file.

The most basic unit is the **System unit**. This unit contains Turbo Pascal types, variables, functions, and procedures that are not part of standard Pascal. The System unit is automatically linked to every program.

The **Dos unit** provides the program with the ability to communicate with the operating system. This unit includes date and time procedures (such as GetDate, which returns the system date; GetTime, which returns the setting of the system clock; SetDate and SetTime, which allow the program to reset the system date and time, and so forth), file-handling procedures and functions (such as FindFirst and FindNext, which search a directory to locate files that meet a certain criterion), process-handling procedures (such as Exec, which allows a program to execute a specified program), and a variety of other procedures and functions of a somewhat technical nature.

The **Overlay unit** supports the overlay mechanism that allows a Pascal program to load program segments during program execution.

The **Crt unit** contains procedures and functions relating to reading the keyboard and writing the DOS text screen. Following is a list of the most often used procedures and functions in this unit:

KeyPressed	Returns True if a key is pressed and False otherwise
WhereX, WhereY	Returns the X (horizontal) and Y (vertical) position of the cursor
Delay	Delays execution of a program
GoToXY	Moves the cursor to a specified position on the screen
ClrScr	Clears the screen

Other facilities contained in CRT include support for windows, sound, and color for background and text.

The **Printer unit** contains the definition of the text file Lst and allows the program to direct output to a printer.

The **Graph unit** contains constants, procedures, and functions to allow the program to direct output to the graphics screen. The facilities of this unit have been described extensively in Chapter 13.

The **Turbo3 unit** and the **Graph3 unit** are provided to allow programs that were written in Turbo Pascal 3.0 to be compiled and executed using later versions of Turbo Pascal.

This list of standard units has been the same in versions 4.0, 5.0, 5.5, 6.0, and 7.0. (Version 3.0 did not support units.) Versions 6.0 and later have an additional suite of units called **Turbo Vision**. Turbo Vision allows you to develop programs using multiple windows, pull-down menus, mouse support, buttons, scroll bars, and much more. Using Turbo Vision requires a basic knowledge of object-oriented programming, which is discussed in Chapter 15.

14.3   THE STRUCTURE OF A UNIT

A unit is made up of four parts: the unit header, the interface part, the implementation part, and the initialization part. The first three are required in all units; the initialization part is optional.

The **unit header** specifies the name of the unit. It is similar to a program header, but the reserved word *unit* replaces the reserved word *program*. For example, to create a unit called MyUnit you would use the unit header

```
unit MyUnit;
```

The name of the unit must be the same as the file name used to store the source code for the unit. Thus, the unit MyUnit must be saved in a file MYUNIT.PAS. When Turbo Pascal compiles this code, it will generate a file, MYUNIT.TPU, to contain the object code. Because of this restriction, unit names must conform to the same rules that DOS file names do; that is, the maximum length is eight characters. (We have been using this convention for program names all along.)

The **interface part** of a unit lists the constants, types, variables, procedures, and functions that will be made available to a program that uses the unit. This part is preceded by the reserved word *interface*. Only the procedure and function headers are included in this part of the unit; the code required for their implementation is included in the implementation part of the unit. For example, to create a unit in which one constant, MyConstant, and one procedure, MyProcedure, would be made available to the using program, the following interface part could be written:

```
interface
    const
        MyConstant = 1;
    procedure MyProcedure (X : Integer);
```

Any program using MyUnit could now reference MyConstant (which would have the value 1) and execute MyProcedure, which would require an integer parameter. If any declarations in the interface part make reference to the content of some other unit, then a uses statement to specify the unit(s) required is required following the interface header. For example, if a unit requires access to the unit Graph, the following interface part could be written:

```
interface
    uses Graph;
    const
        MyConstant = CGA;
    procedure MyProcedure (X : Integer);
```

Recall that the constant CGA is defined in the unit Graph and has the value 1. Placing a uses statement in the interface part makes the content of the named unit available to all subsequent parts of the unit; it is not necessary to repeat the uses statement in the implementation part.

The **implementation part** of a unit contains the actual code required for the procedures and functions listed in the interface part. It consists of the reserved word *implementation* followed by an optional uses statement and then declarations of constants, types, variables, procedures, and functions. At a minimum, this part must include the actual code for all procedures and functions listed in the interface part, but it can contain any other code that may be required. The content of the implementation part is hidden from the using program, which may reference anything declared in the interface part, but nothing declared in the implementation part. The implementation part is intended to contain detail that is not needed by the using program. For example, an implementation part for the unit MyUnit could appear as follows:

```
implementation
    uses Printer;
    var
        MyVariable : Integer;
    procedure MyProcedure (X : Integer);
    begin
        MyVariable := MyVariable + 1;
        Writeln (Lst, MyVariable:4, X:4)
    end;
```

In this case, we have included a uses statement in the implementation part to give access to the unit Printer. The procedure header for MyProcedure is identical to the header contained in the interface part. Although this is good form, it is not actually required by Turbo Pascal syntax. You could use the abbreviated form

```
procedure MyProcedure;
```

which omits the list of formal parameters. Most authors advise against this, however, since it tends to separate the list of formal parameters from the body of the procedure, thereby making the program difficult to read and inviting careless errors. (In long programs, this is a particularly serious problem.) The preceding implementation part contains a declaration for MyVariable to illustrate an important point: While those things declared in the interface part are accessible to the using program, things declared in the implementation part are not visible to the using program. Thus, the using program may not refer to MyVariable because it is declared in the implementation part. However, any of the procedures or functions in the implementation part can use MyVariable as needed.

The last part of a unit is the optional **initialization part,** which typically contains code used to initialize variables specified as part of the unit. It corresponds to the statement part of an ordinary program. It consists of a compound statement of the usual form: the reserved word *begin*, followed by a sequence of statements and terminating with *end*. (As in ordinary programs, the period following the last *end* is required.) For example, the following initialization part could be written to initialize the value of

MyVariable to zero:

```
begin
    MyVariable := 0
end.
```

The program using a unit will cause the initialization part of the unit to be executed prior to beginning execution of its own statement part. If the statement part is omitted, then the unit is terminated simply by

```
end.
```

Figure 14.1 shows the sample unit MyUnit with its parts labeled. This unit illustrates the syntax required to construct a simple unit; it is not intended to be particularly useful. If however, a program did use the unit by including

```
uses MyUnit . . .
```

it could refer to MyConstant and execute MyProcedure.

MyProcedure would cause the value of its Integer argument to be printed on the printer, preceded by the number 1 the first time the procedure was executed, 2 the second time, and so forth.

14.3.1.   Example of a Unit

Let us illustrate the process of creating and using a unit with a unit that is potentially useful. When you write a program that produces a lot of output on the screen, you know that the output usually flashes by too fast for you to observe it. You need to halt the output when a full screen is created. This can, of course, be done by each program by counting the lines of output that have been produced, but it is a nuisance to have to repeat the process for each program. Let us create a unit containing two procedures—one simply to pause and a second that will pause when a full screen is detected.

Pausing can be accomplished very easily by writing a message such as

```
Press <Enter> to continue
```

and then executing a Readln statement. Once the user has pressed <Enter>, the procedure should clear the screen so that the next output begins on an uncluttered screen.

Pausing conditionally is a little more complex. We need to detect when the next output would go to the last line of the screen. If this occurs, we can execute the Pause procedure just described. To detect the position of the cursor on the text screen, we can use the WhereX and WhereY functions that are included in the Crt unit. These functions return the current position of the cursor. WhereX returns the X coordinate (the horizontal position), and WhereY returns the Y coordinate (the vertical position). The coordinates of the upper left-hand corner of the screen are (1, 1). The coordinates of the first position of the last line of the screen are (1, 25), (1, 43), or (1, 50), depending on whether the screen is in 25-line mode (the default) or 43- or 50-line mode. (You can change the screen to 43- or

```
unit MyUnit; ◀— unit name must match file name
```
unit header

```
interface

    uses Graph; ◀— optional

    const

        MyConstant = CGA;

    procedure MyProcedure (X : Integer);
```
interface part

```
implementation

    uses Printer; ◀— optional

    var

        MyVariable : Integer;

    procedure MyProcedure (X : Integer);

    begin                        argument list may be omitted

        MyVariable := MyVariable + 1;

        Writeln (Lst, MyVariable:4, X:4)

    end;
```
implementation part

```
begin                      may be omitted if not needed
        MyVariable := 0

end. ◀— statement required to terminate the unit
```
initialization part

Figure 14.1 Structure of a unit.

50-line mode by using the procedure TextMode, which is included in the Crt unit; consult Chapter 13 of the *Turbo Pascal 7.0 Language Guide* for details.) Since the number of lines on the screen may change, we do not want to build this number into the procedure as a constant. Rather, we should declare a variable (say, ScreenLines) that the using program could access if desired. To accomplish this, we need to declare ScreenLines to be part of the interface part of the unit. Of course, the usual screen mode is 25 lines, so the default value of ScreenLines should be 25. We can accomplish this by including an initialization part that establishes the initial value for ScreenLines.

The completed unit is called Unit P14a and is shown in Figure 14.2. The unit includes the variable ScreenLines and the procedures Pause and PauseIfScreenIsFull in its interface part. The implementation part provides the details of the two procedures. Note the use of comments in the listing of the unit. We have adopted the convention of using rows of asterisks and rows of dashes, as in programs.

Figure 14.3 shows a sample program that produces several screens of output. (It simply generates a list of the numbers from 1 to 100.) It includes the identifier P14a in its uses statement so that it can access the content of Unit P14a. After each line of output is

```pascal
unit P14a;
{Unit contains procedure to pause when a full screen is encountered}

interface
    uses Crt;
    var
        ScreenLines : Integer;
    procedure Pause;
    procedure PauseIfScreenIsFull;

implementation
{********************************************************************}
    procedure Pause;
    const
        PauseMessage = 'Press <Enter> to continue';
    begin   {Pause}
        Write (PauseMessage);
        Readln;
        ClrScr
    end;   {Pause}
{------------------------------------------------------------------}
    procedure PauseIfScreenIsFull;
    var
        Y : Integer;
    begin   {PauseIfScreenIsFull}
        Y := WhereY;
        if Y >= ScreenLines then
            Pause;
    end;      {PauseIfScreenIsFull}
{********************************************************************}

begin   {Initialization part}
    ScreenLines := 25
end.      {Initialization part}
```

Figure 14.2 Unit P14a: Pause procedure.

```pascal
program P14b (Output);
{Program tests unit P14a}
uses P14a;

var
    I : Integer;

begin
    Writeln ('Begin output of Program 14b');
    for I := 1 to 100 do
        begin
            Writeln (I);
            PauseIfScreenIsFull
        end;   {for}
    Writeln ('End output of Program 14b');
    Pause
end.
```

Figure 14.3 Program 14b, which tests Unit P14a.

```
Turbo Pascal Version 7.0 Copyright (c) 1983, 92 Borland International
Begin output of Program 14b
1
2
3
4
5
6
7
8
9
10
11
12
13
14
15
16
17
18
19
20
21
22
Press <Enter> to continue

95
96
97
98
99
100
End output of Program 14b
Press <Enter> to continue
```

Figure 14.4 Sample output from Program 14b.

produced, the program executes PauseIfScreenIsFull. If the cursor is positioned on line 25, execution will halt, and the program will wait for the user to press <Enter>. After all of the output is produced, the program uses the procedure Pause to halt execution so that the user can view the last screen produced by the program. A sample of the output of Program 14b is shown in Figure 14.4.

14.4 COMPILING AND TESTING UNITS

The process of compiling and testing a unit is somewhat different from that of compiling and testing a program. Remember that a unit cannot stand alone; it can be executed only by using a program. This means that when you compile a unit, you must store the resulting object code in an external file. Most likely, you have not previously compiled a program and created a separate file for the executable code. Usually, you will have used the "in-memory" compilation feature. This means that when a program is compiled, its object code is placed directly in memory and is ready for execution. This is usually faster than creating a separate file for the object code, but it also means that the program must be compiled before it can be executed—a somewhat wasteful process if there have been no changes to the program since the last time it was used. It also means that the program cannot be executed without the presence of the Turbo Pascal program-development system.

In order to compile a program or unit and store the resulting object code in a separate file, you must change the destination of the compilation. This is done by selecting Compile from the menu bar as shown in Figure 14.5 and highlighting Destination. The default direction is Memory. Pressing <Enter> after highlighting Destination will change the direction to Disk. Unfortunately, pressing <Enter> also causes the pull-down menu to disappear, so you might wish to select Compile a second time to verify that the destination of the compilation is indeed changed. But be careful: If you select Destination again, the destination will change back to Memory. To exit the menu without changing the destination, press <Escape>; this will leave the setting alone.

Once you have changed the destination, you can select Compile from the Compile menu to compile the program or unit in the currently active window. The name assigned to the compiled program or unit will be the same as the name assigned to the currently active window, and the resulting file will be placed in the current directory. If a program is compiled, the object file will be given the extension .EXE, indicating that this file contains an executable program. If a unit is compiled, the extension .TPU is given to the resulting file. An .EXE file can be loaded and executed directly from DOS. A program must include the name of the unit in a uses statement to be able to gain access to the content of a .TPU file.

Some words of caution are in order. When you are initially typing a program or unit, Turbo Pascal assumes a name such as NONAME00 as the name of the file. You should save the file prior to compiling it by using Save as . . . and specifying the appropriate name for the file. (Otherwise you will get a file NONAME00.TPU on disk.) Remember that the name of the file *must* match the name given in the unit header; there are no exceptions. Remember to change the default drive and directory using Change dir before saving a file. Otherwise you may end up storing your file on the hard disk. If you inadvertently compile a unit with the destination for the compilation set to memory, there is no warning. Rather, the compilation proceeds normally, and if no syntax errors are encountered, the message "compilation completed" is displayed. You may want to use

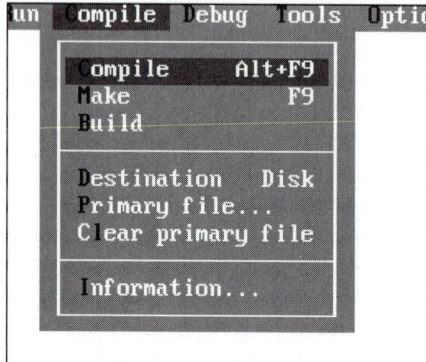

Figure 14.5 The Turbo Pascal 7.0 Compile submenu. Note that the destination for the compiled program has been changed to Disk.

in-memory compilation to verify that there are no syntax errors in a unit, but remember to change the direction of the compilation to disk and compile the unit again before going on to another task. In sum, you should use the following procedure when preparing a unit:

1. Use Change dir. . . to specify the disk drive and directory for the source and object files.
2. After typing the unit, use Save as. . . to save the source code and establish the file name. The file name for a unit must be the same as the unit name in the unit header.
3. Change the direction of the compilation to Disk by selecting Direction from the Compile menu. Remember that Direction toggles between Memory and Disk, so each time you select it, you will change its value.

14.4.1 *Time Out*

1. Compile Unit P14a. Create a .TPU file on disk by changing the direction of the compilation to Disk before compiling. Examine the current directory. You should see the file P14A.TPU listed. If you do not, you probably did not change the direction of the compilation to Disk before compiling Unit P14a.
2. Compile and execute Program 14b. Change the direction of compilation to Memory before compiling (or running) the program. If you leave the direction set to Disk, you will create an .EXE file—P14B.EXE. If you are unsuccessful in compiling the program, it is likely that the system cannot locate the TPU file containing the unit. Go back to exercise 1, and make sure that you change the direction of the compilation to Disk before compiling Unit P14a.
3. Modify Program 14b to set the value of ScreenLines to a smaller value—say, 20. (Remember that ScreenLines is in the interface part of Unit P14a, so the program using this unit can change the value of the variable.) How does this affect the output produced by the program?

14.4.2 Location of Units

When you carried out the exercises in Section 14.4.1, the unit that you created was placed in the current directory—that is, the directory in which the program that uses the unit is located. This is perfectly acceptable, but Turbo Pascal offers two other alternatives that allow you somewhat greater flexibility. Perhaps you would like to make the unit P14a available to other programs that you write. It would be very unmanageable if you had to copy the .TPU file into the directory of each program that needed access to the unit. Fortunately, there are two other options available to you: You can place the unit in a directory of your choosing and instruct Turbo Pascal to look in that directory, or you can merge your unit into TURBO.TPL. Let us examine each of these options in turn.

If you choose to place your unit in a directory other than the current directory, then you will need to instruct Turbo Pascal to look in that directory to locate the unit. This is done by adding the path to the directory in the Unit Directories input box, which is accessed by selecting Options from the menu bar and then selecting Directories. Once you enter a directory here, Turbo Pascal will attempt to locate .TPU files in that directory; it is no longer necessary to have a copy of the .TPU file in the current directory.

Another option for units that you plan on using very often is to merge them into TURBO.TPL. This is done using the utility program TPUMOVER.EXE. Consult the *Turbo Pascal 7.0 User's Guide* for more information on using this utility.

When the compiler encounters a unit in the uses statement, it searches for the object code associated with the unit in the following fashion: First, it looks into TURBO.TPL, which is loaded into memory at the beginning of each compilation. Second, if the unit is not located there, then the compiler looks at the current directory to locate the required .TPU file. Third, if the unit is still not found, the compiler looks at the directories listed in the Unit Directories dialog box.

14.4.3   Qualification of Identifiers

Occasionally, you may encounter conflicts between your program and a unit or conflicts among units; that is, you may find that the same identifier is defined in your program and a unit or in two different units that you are using. To resolve the conflict, you may use a qualified form in writing the identifier. The syntax is similar to that used in qualifying references to fields within records: You write the unit name, followed by a period and the identifier. For example, you could write a reference to the procedure MyProcedure located in MyUnit as

```
MyUnit.MyProcedure(...);
```

This would be necessary if your program had a procedure named MyProcedure or if two units that your program was using had procedures called MyProcedure.

14.4.4   Make vs. Build

You have probably noticed two fairly strange commands in the Compile menu: Make and Build. These commands are available to help you manage large projects that involve many units used by multiple programs. A problem arises when you make a change to a unit. In order to propagate that change, every program and every unit that uses the changed unit will have to be recompiled. This can be extremely tedious. Turbo Pascal offers the Make and Build commands to help you solve this problem. Instead of recompiling each unit after making a change, you only need to Make or Build the programs that use the unit. The **Make** command will cause units that need to be recompiled to be compiled automatically. This is accomplished by comparing the dates for the .PAS and associated .TPU files for the units referenced by the program. If the date on the .PAS file is more recent than that on the .TPU file, then the unit in the .PAS file will be recompiled to generate a new .TPU file. Also, if you made a change in the interface part of the unit, the Make command will recompile all of the units that use this unit. The **Build** command is similar, except it will automatically recompile all units referenced by the program, thus ensuring that everything is up to date. There is one catch, however:

The .PAS and associated .TPU must be located in the same directory. Therefore, it is a good idea never to separate the .PAS and its related .TPU file. Of course, neither Make nor Build will recompile units contained in TURBO.TPL.

14.5   *Case Study: Statistical Functions*

■ **Problem Statement.**   Write a unit to provide a variety of statistical functions, including computation of the mean (arithmetic average) and range (difference between the smallest and largest items in a set) for Integer data.

■ **Problem Analysis.**   Since statistical functions such as those outlined in the problem statement are used in a wide variety of circumstances, a unit containing these functions would be valuable. We will expand the scope of the problem statement a bit to compute the minimum and maximum of the data and use these functions to compute the range.

A problem involving data types occurs in passing any data other than simple types (such as Integer, Real, etc.) to a function or procedure defined within a unit. Structured types must be assigned a name, and that name must be used in declaring the variable that will be used for the actual parameter and the variable declared as the formal parameter in the function or procedure header. This means that we need to specify a named type in the unit and then use the identifier for this type when declaring the variable in the using program. Remember that Pascal requires that the type of the actual parameter and the type of the formal parameter be the same. It is not possible to use variables with an anonymous type as the actual parameter in invoking a procedure or function. In the case of this program, we will need to declare a named type for the array structure for the data to be passed to the various statistical functions. For a program to access these functions, it must specify the identifier for this data type in the declaration of the variables used as actual parameters in invoking the function.

■ **Problem Solution.**   Unit P14c, which is shown in Figure 14.6, is the required unit. Note that the interface part includes a definition of the type ArrayType. This type identifier is used in declaring the type of the formal parameters of the functions. Program 14d, which is shown in Figure 14.7, is a very simple program allowing the user to enter data and compute various statistics. This program uses unit P14c in a very straightforward fashion to produce its output. Note that the identifier ArrayType is used in the declaration of the variable Data in the program. If Data had been given any other type, the variable could not have been used as an actual parameter in invoking the various functions in Unit P14c. A sample execution of Program 14d is shown in Figure 14.8.

Note that the program uses both Unit P14a (the unit containing the Pause procedure) and Unit P14c. A program can use as many units as may be needed for it to perform its assigned task. Note also that the initialization part of Unit P14c is omitted, since it would serve no useful purpose.

```
unit P14c;
{Unit provides statistical functions}

interface
    const
        MaxSize = 100;
    type
        ArrayType = array[1..MaxSize] of Real;
    function Mean (A : ArrayType; N : Integer) : Real;
    function Max (A : ArrayType; N : Integer) : Real;
    function Min (A : ArrayType; N : Integer) : Real;
    function Range (A : ArrayType; N : Integer) : Real;

implementation
{***********************************************************************}
    function Mean (A : ArrayType; N : Integer): Real;
    {Function computes the arithmetic average of A}
    var
        I : Integer;
        Sum : Real;
    begin     {Mean}
        Sum := 0;
        for I := 1 to N do
            Sum := Sum + A[I];
        Mean := Sum / N
    end;     {Mean}
{----------------------------------------------------------------------}
    function  Max (A : ArrayType; N : Integer) : Real;
    {Function computes the maximum value in A}
    var
        I : Integer;
        MaxVal : Real;
    begin        {Max}
        MaxVal := A[1];
        for I := 1 to N do
            if A[I] > MaxVal then
                MaxVal := A[I];
        Max := MaxVal
    end;     {Max}
{----------------------------------------------------------------------}
    function Min (A : ArrayType; N : Integer) : Real;
    {Function computes the minimum value in A}
    var
        I : Integer;
        MinVal : Real;
    begin       {Min}
        MinVal := A[1];
        for I := 1 to N do
            if A[I] < MinVal then
                MinVal := A[I];
        Min := MinVal
    end;     {Min}
{----------------------------------------------------------------------}
```

Figure 14.6(a) Statistical functions unit (part 1 of 2 parts).

```
        function Range (A : ArrayType; N : Integer) : Real;
        {Function computes the range—difference between the
           maximum and minimum values in A}
        begin    {Range}
             Range := Max(A, N) - Min(A, N)
        end;     {Range}
{*********************************************************************}
end.
```

Figure 14.6(b) Statistical functions unit (part 2 of 2 parts).

```
program P14d (Input, Output);
{Program to test units P14c and P14a}
uses P14c, P14a;

var
     Data : ArrayType;
     I, N : Integer;

begin

{1.0 Get data for processing}

     Writeln ('Begin data input');
     Pause;
     Write ('Enter number of data elements ');
     Readln (N);
     for I := 1 to N do
         begin
                Write ('Enter data item ');
                Readln (Data[I])
         end;    {for}

{2.0 Write data}

     Pause;
     Writeln ('Following is a list of data you have entered');
     for I := 1 to N do
         begin
                Writeln (Data[I]:7:0);
                PauseIfScreenIsFull
         end;    {for}

{3.0 Compute statistics and write results}

     Writeln('-------------------');
     Writeln('Mean      :', Mean(Data, N):7:0);
     Writeln('Maximum :', Max(Data, N):7:0);
     Writeln('Minimum :', Min(Data, N):7:0);
     Writeln('Range     :', Range(Data, N):7:0);
     Writeln('-------------------');
     Pause
end.
```

Figure 14.7 Program 14d: Uses Program 14c.

```
Initial Screen
_____

Begin data input
Press <Enter> to continue

Data-Entry Screen
_____

Enter number of data elements 6
Enter data item 23
Enter data item 67
Enter data item 89
Enter data item 12
Enter data item -6
Enter data item -90
Press <Enter> to continue

Results Screen
_____

Following is a list of data you have entered
      23
      67
      89
      -6
     -90
----------------
Mean     :      16
Maximum  :      89
Minimum  :     -90
Range    :     179
----------------
Press <Enter> to continue
```

Figure 14.8 Sample execution of Program 14d.

14.5.1   Time Out

1. Compile Unit P14c. Compile and execute Program 14d. Test the program with data of your choosing.

2. Add a procedure to compute the median of the data to Unit P14c. Remember that if the number of data items is odd, the median is the middle value in the set, whereas if the number of data items is even, the median is the average of the two middle values. In order to compute this value, it will be necessary to sort the data. You may wish to add a sort procedure to the implementation part, but not the interface part, of Unit P14c.

14.6   Case Study: Presentation Graphics

■ **Problem Statement.**   Write a unit that contains procedures to create a bar graph and a pie chart for data supplied by the using program.

■ **Problem Analysis.**   Recall that Program 13i contains the code required to produce the two desired types of graphs. We will adapt the procedures contained in that program to create the required unit. As we noted in the previous section, the declaration of data types for arguments to be passed to a procedure or function contained in a unit must be in terms of type identifiers defined in the unit. Thus, we will need to begin the unit with suitable type declarations for the labels, values, and captions that form the basis for the graphs. The interface part will only need two procedures—one to produce bar graphs and the other to produce pie charts. In the implementation part, we will include all of the procedures contained in Program 14i, as well as the code for the two procedures declared in the interface part.

■ **Problem Solution.**   The required unit (P14e) is shown in Figure 14.9. In order to conserve space, those portions of the unit that are identical to Program 13i are not reproduced. Program 14f, which is shown in Figure 14.10, uses this unit to produce a bar graph and a pie chart from data entered by the program user. Compare the complexity of Programs 13i and 14f. Having the unit available hides most of the messy detail required to produce the graphs and contributes greatly to the readability of Program 14f. Now you can incorporate graphs of either type into any program of your choosing simply by using Unit P14e and invoking one of its procedures with appropriate data.

14.6.1 Time Out

1. Compile Unit P14e. Compile and test Program 14f with data of your choosing.
2. Revise Unit P14e to accommodate a variable number of values and labels. Test the unit with a revised version of Program 14f.

14.7 REVIEW QUESTIONS

1. What is a unit?
2. List the major benefits of using units as a software development tool.
3. What is an overlay? How are overlays related to units?
4. List the standard units supplied by Turbo Pascal, and explain briefly the purpose of each unit.
5. Explain the meaning of the file extensions TPL and TPU.
6. List the four parts of a unit. Explain briefly the purpose of each part.
7. What reserved words are used in writing units, but not in writing programs?
8. Where can the uses statement be placed in a unit?
9. When is the initialization part of a unit executed?
10. Explain the difference between the two destinations that are available for compiling a program or unit.
11. Explain how a .TPU file is produced.
12. When the compiler encounters a uses statement, it looks at a maximum of three locations in the system to locate the required unit. List these locations in the order in which the compiler seeks to locate the unit.
13. How can you modify the .TPL file supplied with Turbo Pascal?
14. Why might you need to use the unit name as a qualifier for identifiers defined within a unit?
15. Explain the difference between the Make and Build commands.

```
unit P14e;
{Unit for creating bar graph and pie chart for data entered by user}

interface
    uses Graph, Crt;
    type
        LabelType = array[1..4] of string[10];
        ValueType = array[1..4] of LongInt;
        CaptionType = string[30];
    procedure ProduceBarGraph (YValue : ValueType;
                               XLabel : LabelType;
                               XCaption, YCaption : CaptionType;
                               ScaleValue : Integer);
    procedure ProducePieChart (YValue : ValueType;
                               XLabel : LabelType;
                               XCaption : CaptionType);

implementation
{********************************************************************}
    procedure OpenGraphWindow;
      .
      .
      .
    end;   {OpenGraphWindow}

{-------------------------------------------------------------------}

    procedure DrawBars (XIncr, YIncr : Integer;
                        YValue : ValueType;
                        ScaleValue : Integer);
      .
      .
      .
    end;   {DrawBars}
{-------------------------------------------------------------------}

    procedure DrawAxes (XIncr, YIncr : Integer);
      .
      .
      .
    end;   {DrawAxes}

{-------------------------------------------------------------------}

    procedure LabelYAxis (XIncr, YIncr : Integer;
                          YCaption : CaptionType;
                          ScaleValue : Integer);
      .
      .
      .
    end;      {LabelYAxis}

{-------------------------------------------------------------------}
```

Figure 14.9(a) Presentation graphics unit (P14e) (part 1 of 2 parts).

```
    procedure LabelXAxis (XIncr, YIncr : Integer;
                          XLabel : LabelType;
                          XCaption : CaptionType);
        .
        .
        .
    end;   {LabelXAxis}

{---------------------------------------------------------------------}

    procedure DrawPieChart (XIncr, YIncr : Integer;
                            YValue : ValueType;
                            XLabel : LabelType;
                            XCaption : CaptionType);
        .
        .
        .
    end;   {DrawPieChart}
{---------------------------------------------------------------------}
    procedure ProduceBarGraph (YValue : ValueType;
                               XLabel : LabelType;
                               XCaption, YCaption : CaptionType;
                               ScaleValue : Integer);
    var
        XIncr, YIncr : Integer;
    begin  {ProduceBarGraph}
        OpenGraphWindow;
        XIncr := GetMaxX div 10;
        YIncr := GetMaxY div 10;
        DrawAxes (XIncr, YIncr);
        DrawBars (XIncr, YIncr, YValue, ScaleValue);
        LabelXAxis (XIncr, YIncr, XLabel, XCaption);
        LabelYAxis (XIncr, YIncr, YCaption, ScaleValue);
        Readln;
        CloseGraph
    end;   {ProduceBarGraph}
{---------------------------------------------------------------------}
    procedure ProducePieChart (YValue : ValueType;
                               XLabel : LabelType;
                               XCaption : CaptionType);
    var
        XIncr, YIncr : Integer;
    begin  {ProducePieChart}
        OpenGraphWindow;
        XIncr := GetMaxX div 10;
        YIncr := GetMaxY div 10;
        DrawPieChart (XIncr, YIncr, YValue, XLabel, XCaption);
        Readln;
        CloseGraph
    end;   {ProducePieChart}
{*********************************************************************}
 end.
```

Figure 14.9(b) Presentation graphics unit (P14e) (part 2 of 2 parts).

```
program P14f (Input, Output);
{Program produces bar graph and pie chart for data entered by user}
uses P14e;
var
    XLabel : LabelType;
    YValue : ValueType;
    ScaleValue : Integer;
    XCaption, YCaption : CaptionType;

{*********************************************************************}

procedure GetGraphData (var YValue : ValueType;
                        var XLabel : LabelType;
                        var XCaption, YCaption : CaptionType;
                        var ScaleValue : Integer);
  .
  .
  .
end;    {GetGraphData}

{*********************************************************************}

begin   {Main Program}

{1.0 Get data to be graphed}

    GetGraphData (YValue, XLabel, XCaption, YCaption, ScaleValue);

{2.0 Draw bar graph}

    ProduceBarGraph (YValue, XLabel, XCaption, YCaption, ScaleValue);

{3.0 Draw pie chart}

    ProducePieChart (YValue, Xlabel, XCaption);

end.    {Main Program}
```

Figure 14.10 Program 14f: Uses Unit P14e to produce a bar graph and a pie chart.

14.8   PROGRAMMING EXERCISES

1. Add a procedure to create line graphs, as described in Exercise 3 of Section 13.12, to Unit P14e. Write a menu-driven program to allow users to select the type of graph desired for a set of data.

2. Develop a unit containing functions and procedures that are useful in analyzing text. Your unit should compute the frequency of the occurrence of letters in the text (how many a's, b's, c's, etc.), count the number of words in the text, and compute the frequency of word lengths (how many words there are of one letter, two letters, three letters, and so forth). Test your unit with an appropriate program.

3. Create a unit of procedures that are useful for manipulating a linked list. Include provisions for creating the list, adding items to the list, deleting items from the list, and printing the content of the list. Test your unit with an appropriate interactive program.

4. Write a unit containing procedures related to manipulating matrices. Include provisions for adding, subtracting, and multiplying matrices. Test your unit with an appropriate program.

5. Add additional procedures and functions of your choice to the statistical unit P14c. Revise the test program accordingly.

15
Objects

Most of you have considerable experience in procedural programming—the programming model that we have used throughout this text. Procedural programming requires that you define data, procedures that act on the data, and then a logical structure that accomplishes the goals specified for the program. Throughout this text, we have stressed structured programming concepts, including top-down program design and implementation. These concepts and practices were developed in the 1970s and have become the de facto standard for software development.

In the software development world, there is considerable interest in an alternative way of thinking about the programming process. This model (which is professed to supplement or perhaps supplant the procedural model) is called **object-oriented programming**, or **OOP**. (Yes, this somewhat unfortunate acronym is pronounced just as it looks.) Despite the sound of the acronym, object-oriented programming is serious business. It has been the subject of a great deal of theoretical interest in the academic and software development communities for several years. This chapter will explore OOP concepts and the Turbo Pascal implementation of these ideas.

15.1   INTRODUCTION TO OBJECT-ORIENTED PROGRAMMING

The basic idea behind OOP is simple enough. We begin by defining **object classes** that consist of **attributes** (what we usually call data items) and **methods** that act on the objects (what we have been thinking of as procedures and functions). Programming then becomes a process of communicating with specific objects by **messages**—instructions that cause the object to take actions required to accomplish the objectives of the programming task at hand.

An analogy will help explain the idea behind OOP. Consider the process of directing a play. The director has at his or her disposal a set of individual actors on the stage. These actors are defined by attributes and methods. The attributes of an actor consist of the actor's height, weight, sex, name, and so forth. The methods associated with an actor include the ability to walk, run, talk, make gestures, and so forth. In OOP terminology, the list of these attributes and methods constitute an object class. Each individual actor is different (has different values for his or her attributes—different names, weights, and so on), but together they share the ability to use methods that are common to all actors. In OOP terminology, the individual actor is called an **instance** of the object class actor, or simply an **object**. Now consider the director. He or she gathers together a group of individual actors (objects) and puts on the play by giving them directions (messages). That is, the director tells Actor A to deliver a specific line, tells Actor B to walk to a specific place on the stage, and so forth. A message consists of two parts: the method to be used (such as speaking or walking) and the parameters of the method (the specific line to be spoken or the distance to be walked). In an OOP context, the process of solving a problem begins with defining one or more object classes—descriptions of attributes (data) and methods (procedures and functions) that carry out actions. Then, like the director of a play, the programmer defines suitable instances of the objects and performs the desired functions by sending messages to the objects—that is, by telling specific objects to take particular actions with specified parameters. In fact, this analogy is so appropriate that one of the widely available OOP languages is called Actor.[1]

By now you may be saying, "So what? It sounds like fancy new names for things that we have been using all along." To a certain extent this is true, but there are some additional concepts and extensions in the object-oriented approach that have considerable promise. Foremost among these concepts is the idea of **encapsulation**. The object class brings together as one entity (that is, it encapsulates) attributes (data) and methods (procedures and functions). In the traditional procedural approach, the data and procedures or functions are considered quite separately. The advantage of this is to hide the detail of how an action is performed from the program that needs to carry out the action. This helps the programmer to concentrate on the objectives of the task at hand without being burdened with superfluous detail that unnecessarily complicates the programming task; that is, it tends to make programs simpler and therefore easier to write, debug, and maintain.

---

[1]The original OOP language was Simula-67, which was a programming language developed for simulations. A second language that is still available is called Smalltalk. The concepts used in Smalltalk formed the basis of the graphical user interface developed for the first Macintosh computer. The language C++, which is based on the language C, incorporates OOP facilities. Beginning with Version 5.5, Borland has supported OOP in Turbo Pascal.

Using OOP techniques requires the programmer to make a considerable adjustment in the initial analysis of a problem. OOP seems to encourage a bottom-up approach rather than a top-down problem analysis technique. That is, the initial questions that must be confronted and answered relate to the objects (data and actions on the data) that will be needed. The programmer is encouraged to develop a library of method classes before beginning the work of solving the problem at hand. The advantage of this technique is that many of the routine details that often occupy an inordinate part of the programming effort and make a program difficult to debug and maintain will have been handled up front.

Object-oriented programming includes a very powerful concept called **inheritance** that allows new object classes to inherit (that is, to make use of) attributes and methods from previously developed object classes. We use this idea in other contexts quite frequently. Consider, for example, the techniques used by scientists to classify animals. An elaborate hierarchy has been developed to place each species (and subspecies) into a framework that describes attributes common to all members of each group. For example, consider the group called mammals. The members of this group all have attributes in common. As shown in Figure 15.1, mammals can be further classified as horses, cows, dogs, cats, and so forth. Because they are warm-blooded, all horses are mammals, but, of course, not all mammals are horses. The class of horses is a descendant of the class of mammals and therefore inherits all of the attributes of its ancestor class. In like manner, in an OOP environment, it is possible to construct an object class that is descended from another class and thus inherits its ancestor's attributes and methods. To use the actor analogy one more time, we can classify all actors as a larger class, people. Actors inherit many attributes (name, sex, and so forth) and methods (such as walking, talking, etc.) from their ancestor class, but there are certain additional attributes (such as education and experience) and methods (talking in a particular way required to deliver a line effectively) that are not shared with the class of people. We can envision other classes descended from people (for example, singer, dancer, and so forth) that, like the class of actors, share all of the attributes and methods from the class of persons but have additional unique attributes and methods that differ from the class of actors. These relationships are illustrated in Figure 15.1.

In a programming context, the advantage of the concept of inheritance is that it gives the programmer the ability to extend the work of previous programming efforts in a very powerful way. If we have a set of object classes related to the programming task at hand, we can create our own unique classes as descendents of existing classes. If we do

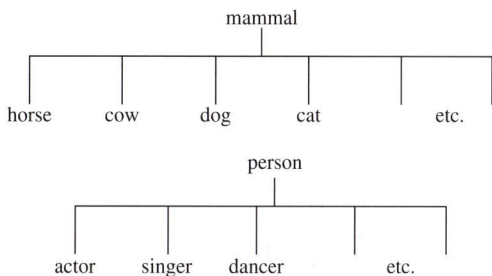

Figure 15.1 Examples of hierarchical relationships.

so, we can make use of all attributes (data) and methods (procedures and functions) that may have been declared for the ancestor class (or any class further up in the hierarchy of object class declarations). This means that we can effectively capitalize on previous work and, at the same time, customize it to do exactly what needs to be done to solve the problem at hand. But, you say, isn't that what units are all about? Indeed, we do use units to make available to the programmer sets of constants, types, variables, procedures, and functions that have been previously written and compiled. In the procedural mode, the content of a unit can be used (often to great advantage), but there is no obvious way to extend the underlying data structure or readily customize the code to meet specific needs unforeseen by whoever developed the unit. By contrast, in the object-oriented mode, we can extend either the data (the attributes), the procedures or functions (the methods), or both in a natural and very useful way. You can think of a traditional unit as a box with tools that the programmer is free to use at will. However, each tool is designed to perform a limited task. If this fits the needs of the problem at hand, the tool is useful; however, if it doesn't, the tool is essentially useless. A unit built in an OOP environment can be thought of as a box with tools that can *either* be used as is *or* be customized to work in a different environment—one that the originator of the unit never conceived of. This makes the reusability of code a real possibility, instead of a pipe dream of programming managers. Reusable code contributes to making the software development process less expensive because (in theory, at least) there is less code to write. As a corollary, software should also take less time to develop, because large portions of the code will have been previously written and tested.

There are more advantages to OOP that will become evident later. For the moment, the preceding discussion should serve to convince you that there is perhaps another approach to the programming task that could be useful and to set the stage for a detailed look at the Turbo Pascal implementation of this approach. You may not be convinced of the utility of these ideas just yet, but try to suspend judgment for a little while. OOP makes use of a provocative, but highly abstract, paradigm. It takes time and effort to shift mental gears to accommodate fundamentally new ideas. If you will make the effort, you will find the ideas intriguing. They just may give you a glimpse of the way software will be developed in the 21st century.

15.2 OBJECTS IN TURBO PASCAL

Turbo Pascal handles the concept of OOP by implementing a new data type called an object. An object consists of fields (attributes) and procedures and functions (methods). A variable that is assigned an object data type is assigned attributes as described in the object type declaration and has access to the methods appropriate to its type. Turbo Pascal treats an object type as an extension of the record data type. The primary difference is that a record consists entirely of fields, whereas an object has fields and procedures or functions associated with it.

The first step in working with objects is to declare an object type. The syntax of an object type declaration is similar to both the interface section of a unit and the declaration of a record type. The general form for declaring an object type is

```
type-identifier = object (heritage)
    field-declaration;
          .
          .
          .
    method-declaration;
          .
          .
          .

end;
```

where *type-identifier* is an identifier of the programmer's choosing, *heritage* is a type identifier for the ancestor of this object type, *field-declaration* has the same form as the usual variable declaration, and *method-declaration* is a procedure or function header. The entire heritage clause, including the parentheses, is omitted if the object is not a descendant of any other object type.

For example, suppose we wish to declare an object type called MyObjectType consisting of two fields (Field1 and Field2), a procedure (MyProcedure), and a function (MyFunction). The following program segment illustrates the syntax of the type declaration:

```
type
    MyObjectType = object
      Field1 : Integer;
      Field2 : Real;
      procedure MyProcedure;
      function MyFunction (FunctionArgument : Integer) : Integer;
    end; {MyObjectType}
```

This object is not a descendant of any other object type, so the heritage clause is omitted. If it were a descendant of some other object type, the heritage would be included as follows:

```
MyObjectType = object (AncestorObjectType)
```

(AncestorObjectType would have to be defined prior to the declaration of MyObjectType.) The comment used following the end of the list of method declarations is optional, but we will follow the same convention here as we have adopted throughout the text.

The actual declaration of the object's methods follows in the program's procedure declaration part. The only thing different from an ordinary procedure or function declaration is that the type identifier must precede the procedure or function identifier in the header. For example, the declaration of MyProcedure and MyFunction would appear as

```
procedure MyObjectType.MyProcedure;
                    .
                    .
                    .
            end; {MyObjectType.MyProcedure}
function MyObjectType.MyFunction (FunctionArgument : Integer)
            : Integer;
                    .
                    .
                    .
            end; {MyObjectType.MyFunction}
```

The dot notation is used here in the same sense as it is when used to specify a field within a record or a procedure, function, constant, or variable in a unit. In this example, MyProcedure has no parameters, while MyFunction has one parameter. The entire procedure or function header must be repeated from the *method-declaration* in the type declaration. If this is not done, Turbo Pascal will treat the header as containing a syntax error.

Remember that one of the basic ideas of OOP is that we create objects that are instances of object classes and then communicate with the objects via messages. In Turbo Pascal, you create an instance of an object class by declaring a variable to have an object type. For example, you could declare two variables to have type MyObjectType by

```
var
     MyObject1, MyObject2 : MyObjectType;
```

MyObject1 and MyObject2 have the same attributes (they have the same fields—Field1 and Field2), and they have access to the same methods (they can make use of MyProcedure and MyFunction). Just as the actual content of the fields in two variables with the same record type can be completely different, the content of the fields within these two objects can be (and usually will be) different. The declaration of two variables such as MyObject1 and MyObject2 creates two different areas of memory that store the values of each one's fields.

Declaring a variable with an object type handles the task of creating instances of object classes. How, then, does the program communicate with the objects it has created? This is done by invoking the methods associated with the object type. To tell the procedure or function which object it is expected to work on, we use the qualifying dot notation again. The general syntax is

```
object-variable.method-identifier
```

where *object-variable* is an identifier for a variable that has been assigned an object type and *method-identifier* is an identifier for a procedure or function that is part of the object type of that variable. For example, to invoke MyProcedure with MyObject1, we would write

```
MyObject1.MyProcedure;
```

We could also invoke MyProcedure with the other object variable as follows:

```
MyObject2.MyProcedure;
```

In a similar way, we could evaluate MyFunction with either MyObject1 or MyObject2. Think of this process as communicating with one of your objects: You are telling MyObject1 to carry out MyProcedure on itself or MyObject2 to carry out MyFunction on itself. Remember the actor analogy. The director (program) tells each actor (object) to carry out one of his or her methods. This is exactly the sense in which you must think of programming via messages.

Variables with an object type are similar to other Pascal variables in many respects. For example, it is permitted to use an object type variable in an assignment statement such as the following:

```
MyObject1 := MyObject2;
```

This statement will copy the values of all of the fields in MyObject2 into the corresponding fields in MyObject1. In using object type variables in assignment statements, the type of the variable on the right must be the same as the type of the variable on the left or a descendant of the type of the variable on the left. (It cannot be an ancestor of the type of the variable being replaced; we shall return to this point after discussing the concept of inheritance in more detail.)

Turbo Pascal is not a "pure" object-oriented language, so there are some things that are possible in the language that are not recommended in practice. One of these is the ability for a program to access fields within an object directly. The mechanism is exactly the same as when accessing a field in a record: You use the dot notation to qualify the variable name. For example, it is permitted to write a statement such as

```
MyObject1.Field1 := 1;
```

This would cause the content of Field1 in MyObject1 to be replaced with the value 1. Similar use could be made of the fields in both of the objects we have declared. However, even though this is possible, it should be avoided. One of the principles of OOP is that the only way to communicate with an object is through messages. We will see shortly that by constructing appropriate methods, it will not be necessary to manipulate the fields in an object directly.

Many authors in the field of OOP make use of **object diagrams** such as that shown in Figure 15.2 to illustrate relationships among object classes. The basic component of an object diagram is a rectangle (usually drawn with rounded corners) divided into three parts by horizontal lines. The top part contains the name of the object type (the object class). The middle part contains a list of fields (the attributes of the object class). The last part contains a list of the object type's procedures and functions (the methods of the object class). The diagram presents a synopsis of all of the relevant parts of an object class. It also serves as a visual reminder that all of these parts are contained within the class; that is, these things are encapsulated and can, therefore, be treated as one entity.

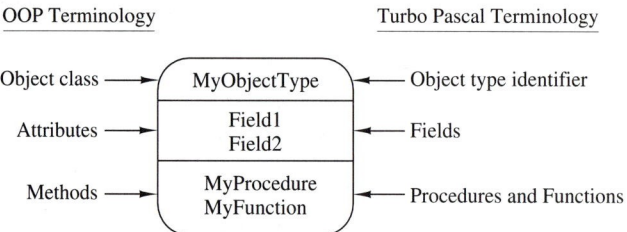

Figure 15.2 Object diagram for MyObjectType.

15.3   INHERITANCE

The focus of the preceding section was on the syntax used in Turbo Pascal to handle objects. The examples used were quite arbitrary and served only to help describe the syntax. Let us turn to a more meaningful example that will also serve to illustrate the concept of inheritance, which is one of the fundamental concepts of OOP.

Remember that analyzing a problem in an OOP context generally begins with the data and the fundamental procedures and functions that will be needed to process the data; we are able to defer decisions about how the data will be used in the context of a complete program until later. Let us use an example based on the sale of items in a retail store. The anticipated purpose of the ultimate program will be to allow the user to enter data about each transaction and receive a nicely formatted "invoice" showing all of the data and the total amount of the sale. Each sale constitutes a transaction—a good name for the object data type that we will construct to model the data and its attendant procedures and functions. So we begin by constructing an object data type named Transaction. The fields that will be needed are inherent in the application: We will need a field for an item description (a string field), a field for the quantity purchased (an Integer field), and a field for the price of each item (a Real field).

Let us now turn to the methods that will be required in our example. We mentioned earlier that it is poor practice for a program to reference a field within an object directly. Thus, we will need a procedure that places values in the object's fields. Since this requirement is common to all objects, one identifier that describes the desired action is usually used for all object types. Borland suggests using the identifier Init (which is an abbreviation of Initialize) for this purpose. There is nothing magical about this identifier; in fact, any identifier could be used instead. But because virtually everyone writing about OOP in a Turbo Pascal environment has adopted the same convention, we will choose to follow it as well. Thus, every object type must have (or inherit) a procedure Init, the purpose of which is to place values in the object's fields. We can get the data from any source—from Input (interactively), from a file, or through passing values to Init via parameters. For the purposes of our example here, we will assume that the program user will be entering the data at the keyboard, and we construct the Init procedure accordingly. A second type of procedure that will be needed in many object types is a procedure to make the fields of the object visible to the rest of the world—a kind of output procedure. For our example, we will wish to write the output on the screen, so we will call our procedure Display. Its purpose will be to write out the object's fields in an appropriate format.

We can summarize the discussion so far in the following coding segment:

```
type
    Transaction = object
        Description : string;
        Quantity : Integer;
        Price : Real;
        procedure Init;
        procedure Display;
    end;    {Transaction}
```

This program segment describes an object type Transaction that contains three fields and two procedures.

There are two types of transactions that normally occur in a retail environment: Some items are sold at list price (we will call this a regular transaction), and others are sold at a discount (we will call this a sale transaction). Thus, we will define two objects that are descendant from object type Transaction: object type Regular and object type Sale. Object type Regular will need a function to compute the Total amount of the transaction. It will also need the procedures Init and Display. Object type Sale will further need a field in addition to those it inherits from Transaction—say, Discount, to store the discount percentage. It will also need the procedures Init and Display and the function Total. We can summarize this discussion in the following code, which is patterned after the declaration of object type Transaction:

```
Regular = object (Transaction)
    procedure Init;
    procedure Display;
    function Total : Real;
end;    {Regular}
Sale = object (Transaction)
    Discount : Integer;
    procedure Init;
    procedure Display;
    function Total : Real;
end;    {Sale}
```

Note that in this coding segment, each of these object types is described as a descendant of the object type Transaction by using the heritage clause. This means that each of the object types inherits all of its ancestor's fields, procedures, and functions. An object diagram describing the relationships among these object types is shown in Figure 15.3. The arrows leading from Regular and Sale to Transaction denotes the ancestor-descendant relationship among these types.

We turn now to defining the procedures and functions required for the objects we have created. The full text of these is contained in Program 15a, which is shown in Figure 15.4. Figure 15.5 shows a sample execution of this program. Refer first to the definitions of the procedures Transaction.Init and Transaction.Display. There is nothing unusual in either of them. Transaction.Init is a straightforward data-entry module consisting of

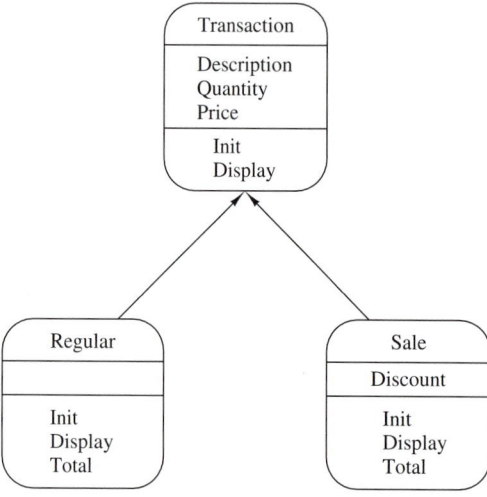

Figure 15.3 Object diagram for Program 15a. (See Figure 15.4.)

prompts followed by Readln statements for each of the fields in Transaction. Now consider Regular.Init. Remember that Regular inherits all of its fields from Transaction, so instead of writing a separate Init procedure for this, we simply execute the Init in its ancestor by using the statement

```
Transaction.Init;
```

The procedure Regular.Display needs to display all of the fields in the ancestor type, so it does this task with the statement

```
Transaction.Display;
```

Then the procedure computes and prints the total amount of the transaction by reference to the function Regular.Total. This function computes the total amount of the transaction by referring to the fields Quantity and Price. Note that it is not necessary to qualify these fields, since the procedure inherits all of the fields defined in the ancestor object type. Now turn to Sale.Init. Type Sale inherits all of the fields of its ancestor type Transaction, so it can invoke Transaction.Init to allow the user to enter values for the three fields defined in the ancestor type. Sale.Init concludes with code to allow the user to enter the value for Discount, the field defined in this object type, but not in Transaction. The procedure Sale.Display and the function Sale.Total are substantially similar to the corresponding elements of the type Regular, but include code for accommodating the discount to be applied to the transaction total.

Now examine the rest of the program. We begin by defining the following variables:

```
var
      RegularTransaction : Regular;
      DiscountTransaction : Sale;
      TransactionType : Char;
```

```pascal
program P15a (Input, Output);
{Program illustrates use of objects and inheritance}
type
    Transaction = object
                Description : string;
                Quantity : Integer;
                Price : Real;
                procedure Init;
                procedure Display;
    end;   {Transaction}
    Regular = object (Transaction)
                procedure Init;
                procedure Display;
                function Total : Real;
    end;   {Regular}
    Sale = object (Transaction)
                Discount : Integer;
                procedure Init;
                procedure Display;
                function Total : Real;
    end;   {Sale}
{*********************************************************************}
procedure Transaction.Init;
begin   {Transaction.Init}
    Write ('Enter item description ');
    Readln (Description);
    Write ('Enter quantity          ');
    Readln (Quantity);
    Write ('Enter price each        ');
    Readln (Price)
end;     {Transaction.Init}
{-----------------------------------------------------------------}
procedure Transaction.Display;
begin    {Transaction.Display}
    Writeln ('-------------------------------');
    Writeln ('Description':15, Description:8);
    Writeln ('Quantity':15, Quantity:8);
    Writeln ('Price':15, Price:8:2);
end;    {Transaction.Display}
{-----------------------------------------------------------------}
procedure Regular.Init;
begin   {Regular.Init}
    Transaction.Init;
end;    {Regular.Init}
{-----------------------------------------------------------------}
procedure Regular.Display;
begin  {Regular.Display}
    Transaction.Display;
    Writeln;
    Writeln ('Total $':15, Regular.Total:8:2);
    Writeln ('-------------------------------');
end;    {Regular.Display}
{-----------------------------------------------------------------}
```

Figure 15.4(a) Program 15a: Use of objects and inheritance (part 1 of 2 parts).

```
function Regular.Total : Real;
begin   {Regular.Total}
     Total := Quantity * Price
end;   {Regular.Total}
{-----------------------------------------------------------------------}
procedure Sale.Init;
begin   {Sale.Init}
     Transaction.Init;
     repeat
          Write ('Enter discount %         ');
          Readln (Discount);
          if (Discount > 99) or (Discount < 1) then
              Writeln ('Please enter discount in form dd');
       until (Discount > 0) and (Discount < 100)
end;   {Sale.Init}
{-----------------------------------------------------------------------}
procedure Sale.Display;
begin   {Sale.Display}
     Transaction.Display;
     Writeln ('Discount':15, Discount:8,'%');
     Writeln;
     Writeln ('Total $':15, Sale.Total:8:2);
     Writeln ('--------------------------------');
end;     {Sale.Display}
{-----------------------------------------------------------------------}
function Sale.Total : Real;
begin   {Sale.Total}
     Total := (100 - Discount)/100 * Quantity * Price
end;     {Sale.Total}
{*********************************************************************}
var
     RegularTransaction : Regular;
     DiscountTransaction : Sale;
     TransactionType : Char;
begin   {Main Program}
     repeat
          Write ('Enter type of transaction : (R)egular, (S)ale, (Q)uit ');
          Readln (TransactionType);
          case TransactionType of
               'R', 'r' : begin
                             RegularTransaction.Init;
                             RegularTransaction.Display;
                          end;
               'S', 's' : begin
                             DiscountTransaction.Init;
                             DiscountTransaction.Display
                          end;
          end; {case}
     until TransactionType in ['Q','q']
end.    {Main Program}
```

Figure 15.4(b) Program 15a (part 2 of 2 parts).

```
Enter type of transaction : (R)egular, (S)ale, (Q)uit  R
Enter item description  Shirts
Enter quantity            2
Enter price each          4.50
-------------------------------
    Description   Shirts
       Quantity       2
          Price    4.50

          Total $   9.00
-------------------------------
Enter type of transaction : (R)egular, (S)ale, (Q)uit  S
Enter item description  Shorts
Enter quantity            3
Enter price each          5
Enter discount %          20
-------------------------------
    Description   Shorts
       Quantity       3
          Price    5.00
       Discount      20%

          Total $  12.00
-------------------------------
Enter type of transaction : (R)egular, (S)ale, (Q)uit  Q
```

Figure 15.5 Sample execution of Program 15a.

The variable RegularTransaction is of type Regular, making it an object type variable, or, more simply, an object. Similarly, DiscountTransaction is of type Sale, making it also an object.[2] In the statement part of the program, we begin by asking the user to enter a code indicating the type of transaction. Based on the value of this code, the program executes

```
RegularTransaction.Init;
RegularTransaction.Display
```

or

```
DiscountTransaction.Init;
DiscountTransaction.Display
```

Remember the meaning of procedure invocations such as these: The statement

```
RegularTransaction.Init
```

quite literally means "RegularTransaction, initialize yourself," and the statement

```
RegularTransaction.Display
```

---

[2]You might wonder why this program declares variables after it declares procedures and functions. The only reason is to promote readability by placing the variable declarations closer to the statement part that makes direct reference to them. Standard Pascal requires that the declarations be placed in the prescribed order (const, type, var, procedures and functions); Turbo Pascal permits you to use any order that is convenient.

means "RegularTransaction, display yourself." In the statement part, we address actual objects—not the object type. This is a very fundamental distinction. The type is a sort of template describing what an object will look like. The variable with the object type is the actual object that must be manipulated in the program.

15.3.1   Time Out

1. Compile and execute Program 15a. Test the program with data of your choosing.
2. Modify Program 15a to include a type SpecialSale as a descendant of Transaction. This type is designed to accommodate a half-off sale that the store is having, so the user does not need to enter the percent of discount that would be built into the function Total defined for the type SpecialSale. Modify the statement part of the program to allow the user to choose between the three types of transactions.

15.3.2   Encapsulation with Units

One of the underlying themes in the theory of OOP is encapsulation, which, as we have seen, refers to the joining of data and the procedures and functions that act on the data into a single entity. We can further encapsulate the type declarations with their attendant procedure and function declarations by combining the entire package into a unit. The program that needs to make use of the object types declared in the unit includes the unit with a uses statement.

Figure 15.6 shows a unit, P15b, made up of the type and procedure and function declarations taken from Program 15a. (In this figure, we have omitted the coding details to conserve space.) Note that the type specification is placed in the interface part of the unit, while the procedures and functions are in the implementation part. Program 15c, which is shown in Figure 15.7, includes the uses statement to incorporate all of the content of the unit into the program. Program 15c is functionally equivalent to Program 15a.

The creation of a unit such as P15b in no way hampers the program from creating additional types that are descended from types declared in the unit. In fact, this is the way in which units are intended to be used in an OOP environment: The unit contains a library of types and methods that subsequent programs can use as is or modify as needed.

15.3.3   Time Out

1. Compile Unit P15b. Remember to set the destination of the compile to Disk. Now compile and execute Program 15c, and test it with your own data.
2. Modify Program 15c as directed in Exercise 2 of Section 15.3.1. Test your program. You do not need to modify the unit to make the required modifications, since Program 15c inherits all of the content of the unit.
3. Modify Program 15c to allow the user the choice of generating an invoice on the printer. (Add suitable objects to the structure defined in Unit P15b, and modify the logic of Program 15c.)

```
unit P15b;
interface
    type
        Transaction = object
                Description : string;
                Quantity : Integer;
                Price : Real;
                procedure Init;
                procedure Display;
        end;   {Transaction}
        Regular = object (Transaction)
                procedure Init;
                procedure Display;
                function Total : Real;
        end;   {Regular}
        Sale = object (Transaction)
                Discount : Integer;
                procedure Init;
                procedure Display;
                function Total : Real;
        end;   {Sale}
implementation
{***********************************************************************}
    procedure Transaction.Init;
    .
    .
    .
    end;     {Transaction.Init}
{----------------------------------------------------------------------}
    procedure Transaction.Display;
    .
    .
    .
    end;     {Transaction.Display}
{----------------------------------------------------------------------}
    procedure Regular.Init;
    .
    .
    .
    end;     {Regular.Init}
{----------------------------------------------------------------------}
    procedure Regular.Display;
    .
    .
    .
    end;     {Regular.Display}
{----------------------------------------------------------------------}
    function Regular.Total : Real;
    .
    .
    .
    end;     {Regular.Total}
{----------------------------------------------------------------------}
```

Figure 15.6(a) Unit P15b: Unit with object data types (part 1 of 2 parts).

```
        procedure Sale.Init;
            .
            .
            .
        end;    {Sale.Init}
{---------------------------------------------------------------------------}
        procedure Sale.Display;
            .
            .
            .
        end;       {Sale.Display}
{---------------------------------------------------------------------------}
        function Sale.Total : Real;
            .
            .
            .
        end;       {Sale.Total}
{*************************************************************************}
end.
```

Figure 15.6(b) Unit P15b (Part 2 of 2 parts).

```
program P15c (Input, Output);
{Program illustrates use of objects defined in a unit}
uses P15b;
var
        RegularTransaction : Regular;
        DiscountTransaction : Sale;
        TransactionType : char;
begin   {Main Program}
     repeat
            Write ('Enter type of transaction : (R)egular, (S)ale, (Q)uit ');
            Readln (TransactionType);
            case TransactionType of
                'R', 'r' : begin
                                RegularTransaction.Init;
                                RegularTransaction.Display;
                            end;
                'S', 's' : begin
                                DiscountTransaction.Init;
                                DiscountTransaction.Display
                            end;
            end; {case}
     until TransactionType in ['Q','q']
end.    {Main Program}
```

Figure 15.7 Program 15c: Use of objects defined in a unit.

15.4   POLYMORPHISM AND VIRTUAL METHODS

One of the major benefits of OOP is the ability of existing code to be adapted to solve problems not envisioned by its original designer. One way in which this is done is through the concept of **polymorphism**—literally, "many forms." With OOP techniques, it is possible to construct code that will take on different meanings, depending on the context in which it is used. Moreover, the original programmer does not have to know or foresee all of the possible uses in advance.

This concept is implemented in Turbo Pascal through a process of late binding of code to objects. Ordinarily, the compiler generates the address of a procedure reference at the time a program is compiled. This is called early binding. Late binding postpones the association of a specific address for a procedure reference to execution time. This makes it possible for an object that inherits a procedure from an ancestor effectively to redefine it to meet its own needs. The program waits until the time of execution to determine which of two or more procedures with the same name should be invoked.

A simple example will help illustrate the mechanics of the process. Consider the following program segment:

```
type
    MyObjectType = object
        procedure Init;
        procedure MyProcedure1;
        procedure MyProcedure2;
    end;
    MyDescendantType = object (MyObjectType)
        procedure Init;
        procedure MyProcedure2;
    end;
procedure MyObjectType.Init;

    .

    .

    .

end;
procedure MyObjectType.MyProcedure1;
begin
    MyProcedure2
end;
procedure MyObjectType.MyProcedure2;
begin
    Writeln ('Executing MyObjectType.MyProcedure2')
end;
procedure MyDescendantType.Init;

    .

    .

    .

end;
procedure MyDescendantType.MyProcedure2;
begin
    Writeln ('Executing MyDescendantType.MyProcedure2')
end;
var
    Object1 : MyObjectType;
    Object2 : MyDescendantType;
```

This program segment illustrates a situation in which Object2, which is of type My-DescendantType, inherits all of the procedures defined for MyObjectType. In the declaration of MyDescendantType, Init and MyProcedure2 are given different definitions, which are the ones that should be used for objects of this type. Thus, for objects of type MyObjectType, we wish to use one definition of MyProcedure2, and for objects of type MyDescendantType, we wish to use the other definition. (We have seen in the preceding section that there is generally no problem with redefining procedures in this way to accommodate the needs of descendant object types.) Consider now the output produced by each of the following procedure invocations:

Statement	Output
Object1.MyProcedure1	Executing MyObjectType.MyProcedure2
Object2.MyProcedure1	Executing MyObjectType.MyProcedure2

The first output is as expected, since Object1 is of type MyObjectType. The second statement presents a problem, since its output is definitely not as anticipated. Since Object2 is of type MyDescendantType, we would expect that the output would be

```
Executing MyDescendantType.Procedure2
```

Why did this problem occur? It happened because the compiler bound the address of MyProcedure2 to the program at the time of compilation, without allowing for the possibility that during execution, we might wish to use a different version of MyProcedure2. What is the solution? We can instruct the system to wait until execution of the program to determine which version of MyProcedure2 to use when executing MyProcedure1. If MyProcedure1 is invoked for an object of type MyObjectType, then the first definition is to be used; if MyProcedure1 is invoked for an object of type MyDescendantType, then the alternative definition should be used. This makes MyProcedure1 polymorphic; that is, it makes it possible for an invocation of MyProcedure1 to take on different meanings at the time the program is executed.

To accomplish this goal, it is necessary to introduce some additional Turbo Pascal syntax. A procedure or function that will be redefined must be declared to be **virtual**, using the general form

```
procedure-declaration; virtual;
function-declaration; virtual;
```

For example, to declare MyProcedure2 to be virtual, you could write

```
procedure MyProcedure2; virtual;
```

Furthermore, each object type that has a virtual procedure or function must have a **constructor procedure** which "constructs" the object's instance.[3] We have seen that it is

---

[3]The constructor procedure doesn't actually create the object, as might be implied in the word *construct*; rather, the object is created by declaring a variable having an object type. What the constructor procedure does is initialize pointers to virtual methods appropriate for the object.

advisable to have a procedure that we have called Init for each object type. When virtual procedures and functions are involved, the Init procedure header is preceded by the reserved word constructor instead of procedure. For example, a constructor header for type MyObjectType could be written as

```
constructor MyObjectType.Init;
```

Consider now the following revision of the program segment with which we began this section:

```
type
    MyObjectType = object
            constructor Init;
            procedure MyProcedure1;
            procedure MyProcedure2; virtual;
    end;
    MyDescendantType = object (MyObjectType)
            constructor Init;
            procedure MyProcedure2; virtual;
    end;
constructor MyObjectType.Init;
    .
    .
    .
end;
procedure MyObjectType.MyProcedure1;
begin
    MyProcedure2
end;
procedure MyObjectType.MyProcedure2; virtual;
begin
    Writeln ('Executing MyObjectType.MyProcedure2')
end;
constructor MyDescendantType.Init;
    .
    .
    .
end;
procedure MyDescendantType.MyProcedure2; virtual;
begin
    Writeln ('Executing MyDescendantType.MyProcedure2')
end;
var
    Object1 : MyObjectType;
    Object2 : MyDescendantType;
```

The differences between this version of the program and the original versions are screened. Now consider the output from the two statements presented previously:

Statement	Output
Object1.MyProcedure1	Executing MyObjectType.MyProcedure2
Object2.MyProcedure1	Executing MyDescendantType.MyProcedure2

The difference is immediately obvious: When MyProcedure1 is executed for an object of type MyObjectType, the output is produced by MyObjectType's version of MyProcedure2; when MyProcedure1 is executed for an object of type MyDescendantType, the output is produced by MyDescendantType's version of MyProcedure2.

One restriction exists that you must be aware of: Once a procedure or function is declared to be virtual in the specification of an object type, it must be declared to be virtual every time it is declared in any descendant object type. The rule is easy to remember: "Once virtual, always virtual."

15.4.1   An Application with Virtual Methods

One thing that is often true of OOP is that the first solution one arrives at is not necessarily the best or most desirable. Consider, for example, the object type Transaction and its descendants Regular and Sale described in the preceding section. Recall that the descendants of Transaction redefined each of its procedures: Init and Display. Moreover, there was some overlap between the procedures written for Sale.Display and Regular.Display. Let us rethink the organization of these object types with the ideas of polymorphism and virtual methods in mind.

To begin with, object type Regular does not differ in any respect from type Transaction, so, with the exception of an Init procedure, we could dispense with the remainder of Regular's procedures and functions, moving them to type Transaction. Type Transaction would then need procedure Init (a constructor) and a new procedure WriteData, which would write the content of the three fields that are part of Transaction and execute a procedure to write the total (DisplayTotal). It would then also need a procedure DisplayTotal to write out the total line and a function Total to compute the total amount of the transaction. Within object type Transaction, DisplayTotal and Total can contain the logic required for regular transactions. We will redefine DisplayTotal and Total for object type Sale, since these methods must take into account the discount to be applied to the total. An object diagram for these object types is shown in Figure 15.8.

An object of type Regular will inherit all of its methods (except Init) from its ancestor, Transaction. An object of type Sale will inherit the procedure WriteData, which invokes DisplayTotal, but in this case we must ensure that it is the procedure DisplayTotal defined within object type Sale that is executed, and not the procedure DisplayTotal defined within the ancestor, Transaction. This is the classic case for using virtual methods. We declare all procedures and functions that are duplicated between the ancestor and descendant object types to be virtual, so that the system will use the procedure or function that is appropriate for the object that invokes WriteData.

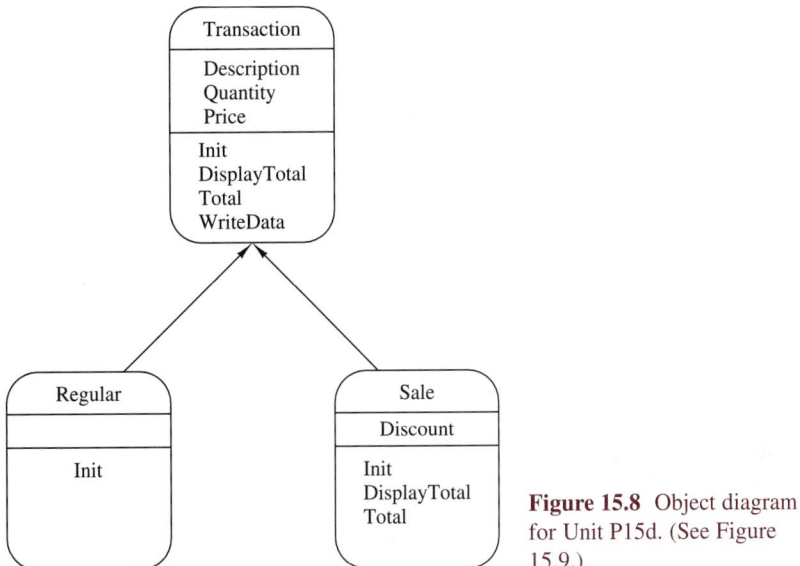

Figure 15.8 Object diagram for Unit P15d. (See Figure 15.9.)

The complete declaration of these object types and their methods is contained in Unit P15d, which is shown in Figure 15.9. Note that each object type has a constructor procedure Init. Remember that this is required for any objects using virtual methods. The program must invoke a constructor method for an object before using any of the virtual methods associated with it. The output from Program 15c would be identical whether it used Unit P15b or Unit P15d. Unit P15d represents a somewhat more sophisticated design because it allows other descendants of object type Transaction to inherit WriteData, but redefine DisplayTotal and Total.

15.4.2   Time Out

1. Compile Unit P15d. Then compile and execute Program 15e. This program (which is not reproduced in the text, but is contained in the accompanying software supplement) is quite similar to Program 14c, except that it uses Unit P15d and executes WriteData. Verify that the program continues to work as it did previously.
2. Modify Program 15e to contain an object type SpecialSale, as described in Exercise 2 of Section 15.3.1. Compare the modifications required to make this change for the two versions of the program.

15.4.3   Compatibility and Other Issues

Earlier, we discussed briefly the concept of type compatibility for assignment statements when variables have an object type. Remember that the type of the variable on the right must be either the same type as the variable on the left or a descendant type. The reason for this rule is quite straightforward. A replacement statement will cause the values of all of the fields in the variable on the right to replace the values of all of the fields of the

```pascal
unit P15d;
{Unit illustrates virtual methods, polymorphism, and inheritance}
interface
    type
        Transaction = object
                Description : string;
                Quantity : Integer;
                Price : Real;
                constructor Init;
                procedure DisplayTotal; virtual;
                function Total : Real ; virtual;
                procedure WriteData;
            end;   {Transaction}
        Regular = object (Transaction)
                constructor Init;
            end;   {Regular}
        Sale = object (Transaction)
                Discount : Integer;
                constructor Init;
                procedure DisplayTotal; virtual;
                function Total : Real; virtual;
            end;   {Sale}
implementation
{****************************************************************************}
    constructor Transaction.Init;
    begin   {Transaction.Init}
        Write ('Enter item description ');
        Readln (Description);
        Write ('Enter quantity          ');
        Readln (Quantity);
        Write ('Enter price each         ');
        Readln (Price)
    end;      {Transaction.Init}
{--------------------------------------------------------------------------}
    procedure Transaction.WriteData;
    begin   {Transaction.WriteData}
        Writeln ('-------------------------------');
        Writeln ('Description':15, Description:8);
        Writeln ('Quantity':15, Quantity:8);
        Writeln ('Price':15, Price:8:2);
        DisplayTotal;
        Writeln ('-------------------------------')
    end;     {Transaction.WriteData}
{--------------------------------------------------------------------------}
    procedure Transaction.DisplayTotal;
    begin   {Transaction.DisplayTotal}
        Writeln;
        Writeln ('Total $':15, Total:8:2);
    end;   {Transaction.DisplayTotal}
{--------------------------------------------------------------------------}
    function Transaction.Total : Real;
    begin   {Regular.Total}
        Total := Quantity * Price
    end;   {Regular.Total}
```

Figure 15.9(a) Unit P15d: Use of virtual methods, polymorphism, and inheritance (part 1 of 2 parts).

```
{----------------------------------------------------------------}
    constructor Regular.Init;
    begin   {Regular.Init}
        Transaction.Init;
    end;    {Regular.Init}
{----------------------------------------------------------------}
    constructor Sale.Init;
    begin   {Sale.Init}
        Transaction.Init;
        repeat
            Write ('Enter discount %       ');
            Readln (Discount);
            if (Discount > 99) or (Discount < 1) then
                Writeln ('Please enter discount in form dd');
        until (Discount > 0) and (Discount < 100)
    end;   {Sale.Init}
{----------------------------------------------------------------}
    procedure Sale.DisplayTotal;
    begin    {Sale.Display}
        Writeln ('Discount':15, Discount:8,'%');
        Writeln;
        Writeln ('Total $':15, Total:8:2);
    end;     {Sale.Display}
{----------------------------------------------------------------}
    function Sale.Total : Real;
    begin    {Sale.Total}
        Total := (100 - Discount)/100 * Quantity * Price
    end;     {Sale.Total}
{****************************************************************}
end.
```

Figure 15.9(b) Unit P15d (part 2 of 2 parts).

variable on the left. If the two variables have the same type, these fields match one to one. If the variable on the right is of a descendant type, then it must have at least the fields of the variable on the left, although it may have more. In any case, there is guaranteed to be a value for each of the fields in the receiving variable.

For example, in a program that uses Unit P15d, suppose we have the following declarations:

```
var
    R1 : Regular;
    S1, S2 : Sale;
    T1 : Transaction;
```

Then the following assignment statements would be valid:

```
S1 := S2; {Types are the same}
T1 := S1; {Type on right is descended from type on left}
T1 := R1; {Type on right is descended from type on left}
```

The following assignment statements would be invalid:

```
R1 := T1; {Type on right is ancestor of type on left}
S1 := R1: {Types are not the same, nor is the one on the
           right descended from the one on the left}
```

You might ask why we bothered with type Regular in the unit P15d, since it appears to be the same as type Transaction in all respects. In fact, we could make do without this type and simply use objects of type Transaction for transactions that were not sales. The reason for using the type Regular is somewhat philosophic. In situations such as this, the ancestor type is usually designed to be an abstract type; that is, it is designed to encompass all of the elements that are in common to its descendants, but it is not usually designed to be used as the type of an actual object. As an example, consider the hierarchy of animals descended from the type mammal. We can have instances of the type horse, dog, or cat, but it is nonsensical to talk about an instance of the type mammal, which is an abstract concept. In the same way, the design of types in an OOP environment proceeds from the abstract to the concrete. We generally only have instances of the bottommost descendants in the hierarchy of object classes.

One restriction imposed on a program that uses an object with virtual methods is that a program cannot invoke one of these methods without first executing the constructor method for the object. In addition to other tasks, the constructor initializes a table of pointers to the virtual methods relevant to the object. If a program does invoke a method without executing the constructor, the result is likely to be that the system will lock up, and the user will have to reboot the computer to regain control. Fortunately, Turbo Pascal provides a safety net to help keep this from happening. If range checking is active (set either by the {$R+} compiler directive or by the equivalent option under the main menu), then an execution-time error will result. Because running programs with range checking active takes extra time, the usual advice is to test a program with this option active, but turn it off for the final version of the program that will be put into use.

15.5   HIDING INFORMATION

We have seen that a program which declares an object type variable is able to access the methods appropriate for the object, as well as the fields associated with the object. For example, consider the following program segment:

```
type
    MyObjectType = object
        Field1 : Integer;
        procedure Init (FieldValue : Integer);
    end;
procedure MyObjectType.Init (FieldValue : Integer);
begin
    Field1 := FieldValue
end;
var
    Object1: MyObjectType;
```

The purpose of the Init procedure is to assign a value to the object's field. Thus, to assign the value 2 to the field associated with Object1, you would write

```
Object1.Init (2);
```

On the other hand, you could just as easily write

```
Object1.Field1 := 2;
```

since the results would be exactly the same. The practice of allowing a program direct access to an object's fields is discouraged in the theory of OOP. All communication with an object should be made through the object's methods. This keeps the program from taking shortcuts that could cause considerable difficulties if the structure of the object is ever changed. Notice that it is possible to redesign an object without modifying the program that uses the object if the methods and their parameter lists are not modified. (It would, of course, be necessary to recompile the program to make use of the new version of the object.) Allowing a program direct access to individual fields creates an undue dependency on a particular implementation of an object, which should be avoided.

Turbo Pascal provides a mechanism that allows certain information to be hidden from a program that makes use of an object type. This is done by including a private part in the declaration of the object type. The **private part** begins with the reserved word *private* and contains declaration of fields, procedures, and/or functions that will be available to the methods associated with the object, but not to the program that declares an instance of the object. For example, consider the following revision of MyObjectType defined earlier:

```
type
    MyObjectType = object
            procedure Init (FieldValue : Integer);
            private
                Field1 : Integer;
        end;
```

In this case, the field associated with the object is declared in the private part of the declaration. This makes the field available to the methods associated with the object, but not to the program declaring an object of type MyObjectType. Thus, the statement

```
Object1.Init (2);
```

would continue to be valid, but the statement

```
Object1.Field1 := 2;
```

would be treated as a syntax error by the compiler, since the identifier Field1 is no longer defined outside of the methods associated with the object.

In this example, the private part contained only the declaration of one field. In general, a private part may contain any desired number of fields and also procedures and functions that will not be available to the program that uses the object type.

15.5.1 Time Out

Revise the declarations of Transaction and Sale in Unit P15d to place all fields in private parts of the declarations. It would also be appropriate to place the function Total in the private parts, since this method is not intended to be invoked, except by the procedure DisplayTotal. Test your revised unit with Program 15e. There should be no change in the behavior of the program.

15.6 Case Study: An Abstract Data Type

We are by now used to dealing with the data types supplied with Turbo Pascal. They range from simple types such as Integer and Real to structured types such as string, array, set, record, and, of course, the most complex type of all: object. Associated with each type is a set of operations that can be performed on variables assigned that type. These are built into the language and form the basis for the construction of our programs. Often, it is useful to extend the standard data types to meet special needs. Such an extension is called an **abstract data type**, or **ADT**. Objects encapsulated in units offer a very useful way to implement an ADT in Turbo Pascal.

An abstract data type is defined to be a data structure, together with operations that can be performed on the structure. In Chapter 12, we dealt with lists, stacks, and trees, which are useful as ADTs. Associated with each of them is a data structure (a way of organizing data) and a set of operations that can be performed on the data organized in this fashion. For example, recall that associated with the stack we had the operations Push (place an element on the stack) and Pop (remove an element from the stack). ADTs such as these are useful in a wide variety of situations, so it is very helpful to compile the required code in a unit. Because programs often need multiple instances of a stack or list, it is useful to implement the ADT as an object type so that the program can declare as many instances of the object as may be needed.

■ **Problem Statement.** Construct a sorted list abstract data type. Data placed in such a list always preserves the order (from smallest to largest) of the list.

■ **Problem Analysis.** We will create a unit containing an object type SortedList. We have a choice of data structures to use. For simplicity (and to accommodate those who may not have read Chapter 12), we will choose an array, which we will call List, of base type string and a variable, Last, that will point to the last element in the list. These items become the fields for the object type SortedList. We will implement the operations that can be performed on the sorted list by means of procedures and functions (methods of the object).

We will need an initialization procedure to set up an empty list. We will use the procedure Init for this purpose; it will assign the value 0 to Last. A function Length will be useful to communicate the length of the list to the program. This function merely needs to report the value of the field Last. A procedure to output the current content of the list will be useful; we will implement this function with a procedure Display.

Finally, we come to the most complex procedure—the one that will add items to the list. We will call this procedure Add. It will need one string-type parameter, Item, that will contain the data to be added to the list. The mechanics of adding Item to the list depend on where it must be inserted. If the list is empty (Last = 0), then the item simply is placed in the first position in the array. If Item is greater than the last element in the list, then it is placed at position Last + 1 of the array. If neither of these is the case, then it is necessary to search the array to determine the location that should contain Item, move the segment of data beginning at this position through the end of the array down one position each, and then insert the Item in its proper position. In each case, when an element is added, the value of Last should be incremented by 1.

■ **Problem Solution.**   The required unit is shown as Unit P15f in Figure 15.10. Note that the fields List and Last are declared in the private part of the object declaration of SortedList. This prohibits a program from manipulating these fields directly, thereby ensuring the integrity of the data type. (If a program changed an element in List or changed the value of Last directly, then there would be no way to assure that the list would remain sorted and would have all of its data intact.) We have added a Halt to the procedure SortedList to terminate execution of the program if an attempt is ever made to add more than MaxLength elements to the list.

```
unit P15f;
{Unit illustrates abstract data type}
interface
     const
          MaxLength = 100;
     type
        SortedList = object
          function Length : Integer;
          procedure Init;
          procedure Add (Item : string);
          procedure Display;
          private
              List : array [1..MaxLength] of string;
              Last : Integer;
        end;   {SortedList}
implementation
{*********************************************************************}
     function SortedList.Length : Integer;
     begin   {SortedList.Length}
          Length := Last
     end;   {SortedList.Length}
{-------------------------------------------------------------------}
     procedure SortedList.Init;
     begin   {SortedList.Init}
          Last := 0
     end;   {SortedList.Init}
{-------------------------------------------------------------------}
```

Figure 15.10(a) Unit P15f: Illustrates abstract data type (part 1 of 2 parts).

```
    procedure SortedList.Add (Item : string);
    var
         I, L : Integer;
    begin   {SortedList.Add}
         if Last = 0 then
             begin
                   List [1] := Item;
                   Last := 1
             end
         else if Last = MaxLength then
                   begin
                         Writeln ('Error..list is full');
                         Halt (1)
                   end
         else if Item > List[Last] then
                   begin
                         Last := Last + 1;
                         List[Last] := Item
                   end
         else
                   begin
                         I := 1;
                         while Item > List[I] do
                               I := I + 1;
                         for L := Last downto I do
                               List[L+1] := List[L];
                         List[I] := Item;
                         Last := Last + 1
                   end;
         end;   {SortedList.Add}
{-----------------------------------------------------------------------}
    procedure SortedList.Display;
    var
         I : Integer;
    begin   {SortedList.Display}
         Writeln ('------------------------------');
         for I := 1 to Last do
             Writeln (List[I]);
         Writeln ('------------------------------')
    end;   {SortedList.Display}
{*********************************************************************}
end.
```

Figure 15.10(b)　Unit P15f (part 2 of 2 parts).

Program 15g, which is shown in Figure 15.11, gives a simple test program that uses the SortedList ADT. The program makes use of one object type variable, NameList. It begins by initializing the list, using the procedure invocation

```
NameList.Init;
```

Then it adds names to the list, using

```
NameList.Add (Name);
```

```
program P15g (Input, Output);
{Program illustrates use of ADT SortedList in unit P15f}
uses P15f;
var
     NameList : SortedList;
     Name : string;
     Answer : char;
begin    {Main Program}
     NameList.Init;
     repeat
          Write ('Enter name ');
          Readln (Name);
          NameList.Add (Name);
          NameList.Display;
          Writeln ('Items in list = ', NameList.Length);
          Write ('More data? (Y)es or (N)o ');
          Readln (Answer)
     until not (Answer in ['Y', 'y'])
end.     {Main Program}
```

Figure 15.11   Program 15g: Uses abstract data type SortedList.

and displays the content of the list, using

```
     NameList.Display;
```

(Remember that these statements can be read literally as "NameList, initialize yourself," "NameList, add Name to yourself," and "NameList, display yourself.") A sample execution of Program 15g is shown in Figure 15.12.

```
Enter name Jones
------------------------------------
Jones
------------------------------------
Items in list = 1
More data? (Y)es or (N)o Y
Enter name Smith
------------------------------------
Jones
Smith
------------------------------------
Items in list = 2
More data? (Y)es or (N)o Y
Enter name Kelly
------------------------------------
Jones
Kelly
Smith
------------------------------------
Items in list = 3
More data? (Y)es or (N)o Y
```

Figure 15.12   Sample execution of Program 15g.

15.6.1. Time Out

1. Compile Unit P15f. Then compile and execute Program 15g. Try enough data to verify that items are successfully added at the beginning, in the middle, and at the end of the list.
2. Modify Program 15g to create two lists—one of males and one of females.
3. Add a procedure to the definition of SortedList to allow a program to output the list in reverse sequence—from largest to smallest entry. Test the procedure by a suitable revision to Program 15g.
4. The base type of the data being added to the list, as written, is string. Add a descendant type that will enable the program to create sorted lists of Integer values. *Hint:* Use the functions Str and Val to change the type of the Integer item to string and from string back to Integer. The underlying data structure need not be altered.

15.7 THE BROWSER

Turbo Pascal 7.0 was released in two versions: TURBO, which runs on any IBM compatible computer, and TPX, which requires an 80286 or higher processor and two megabytes or more of memory. The purpose of the TPX version is to allow the development of longer programs that make use of the improved capabilities of 80286 and higher processors. In most respects, the user interfaces of these two versions are identical; however, there is one extension supported in the TPX version that the programmer will find very useful, particularly when working with units and objects: The Browser facility, which allows you to determine a variety of information about units, objects, and symbols through the use of convenient commands from the Search submenu.

The Search submenu for the TPX version of Turbo Pascal 7.0 is shown in Figure 15.13. (If your Search submenu does not look like this, then you are using the TURBO version of the software, which does not support browsing.) The bottom two parts of the submenu relate to the Browse facility. Essentially, Browser allows you to look up information about elements of your project that are spread out among various files. The only requirements are that all of the files be located in the current subdirectory and that all of them be compiled. For example, let us assume that Program 15a is in the active window and that it has been compiled. Then selecting Objects from the Search submenu will open a Browse screen such as that shown in Figure 15.14. This screen shows all objects defined in the program and the inheritance properties among them. Using the screen, we can select one of the objects and press Enter. This will display a second Browse window showing methods defined in the object. For example, if we select Regular from the screen shown in Figure 15.14, we receive the screen shown in Figure 15.15.

You will have noticed three characters that occur in the Browse window: S, I, and R. These act as buttons, allowing you to secure additional information about any highlighted entry in the window. In general, S indicates that the Symbol definition is displayed, I indicates that Inheritance information is displayed, and R indicates that Reference information is displayed. Note, for example, in the window shown in Figure 15.14 that only the I button is present, and it is highlighted. This means that this screen

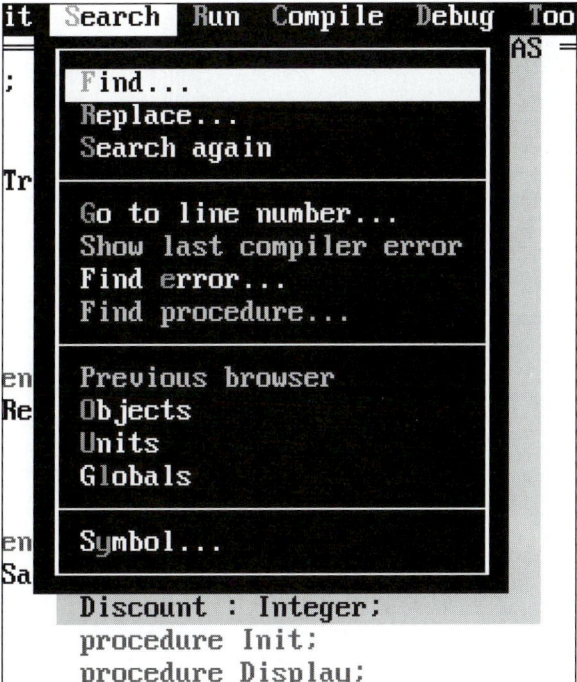

Figure 15.13 Search submenu in the TPX version of Turbo Pascal 7.0.

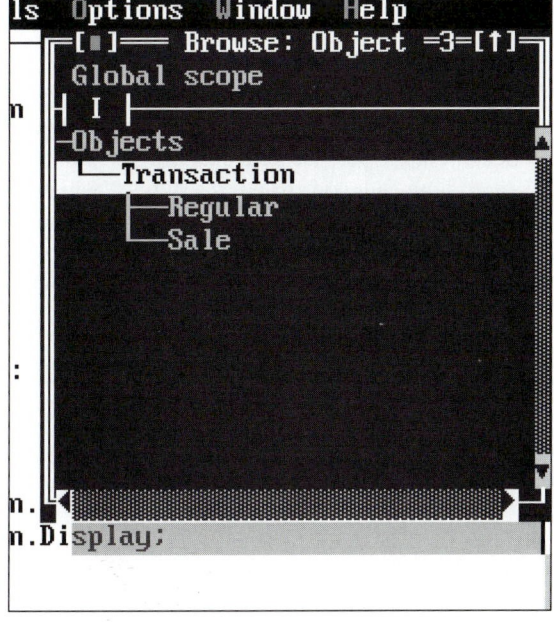

Figure 15.14 Browse screen showing inheritance properties of objects in Program 15a.

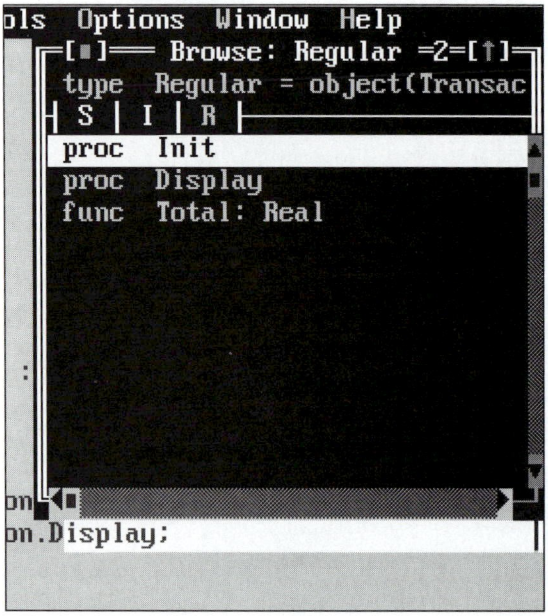

Figure 15.15 Methods defined within the object Regular.

shows Inheritance information, and no other options are immediately available. In the screen shown in Figure 15.15, all three buttons are available, with S highlighted. This means that the screen is now showing Symbol declaration information, but by highlighting one of the entries and clicking on I, you can receive Inheritance information, or by clicking on R, you can receive Reference information. An example of the latter type of screen is presented in Figure 15.16, which shows references to the variable Transaction-Type in lines 7, 11, 12, and 22 of Program 15c. (Remember that all relevant files must be compiled before they are accessible to the Browse facility.)

There are many other ways to use Browse. By selecting Units from the Search submenu, you can look at all units and select among them for further browsing. By selecting Globals from the Search submenu, you can examine all global symbols. By selecting Symbol from the Search submenu, you can enter a symbol, which the Browse facility will locate for you and then allow you to view its definition, inheritance properties, and references. You may find the Browse facility a little confusing at first, but with practice, you will see that it is useful for cross-referencing information from previously compiled units and programs.

15.8 REVIEW QUESTIONS

1. Define the following terms:
   (a) object-oriented programming (OOP)
   (b) object class
   (c) attribute
   (d) method

```
ebug   Tools   Options   Window   Help
15┌─[■]══ Browse: TraisactionType ═4═[↑]─┐
  │  var    TransactionType: Char        │
de┤ R ├──────────────────────────────────│
  │ P15C.PAS(7)                          │▲
  │ P15C.PAS(11)                         │
  │ P15C.PAS(12)                         │
  │ P15C.PAS(22)                         │
  │                                      │
ns│                                      │
  │                                      │
  │                                      │
  │                                      │
  │                                      │▼
ra└══ 1/4 ═══════════════════════════════┘
ransaction.Display;
```

Figure 15.16 References to TransactionType in Program 15c.

 (**e**) message

 (**f**) instance

 (**g**) object

2. Explain why the term *encapsulation* is closely associated with the concept of OOP.

3. Why is the idea of inheritance important in the concept and practice of OOP?

4. List some of the major advantages of OOP, compared with more traditional programming paradigms.

5. In Turbo Pascal, the declaration of an object type most closely resembles which other structured type?

6. In what case is a heritage clause required in the declaration of an object type?

7. Describe the Turbo Pascal implementation of each of the following OOP concepts:

 (**a**) object class

 (**b**) attribute

 (**c**) method

 (**d**) message

8. How is an instance of an object created in a Turbo Pascal program?

9. What is an object diagram?

10. What things are inherited by a descendant object class from its ancestor(s)?

11. How does a descendant object class override an inherited method?

12. Explain the concept of polymorphism. How is this concept implemented in Turbo Pascal?

13. What is a virtual method? In creating an object type, which methods should be declared to be virtual?

14. Define the term *binding*. What is the difference between early binding and late binding?

15. What system-related task is performed when a program invokes a constructor procedure for an object?

16. Explain the rule for type compatibility of assignment statements for object type variables.

17. What role does range checking play in debugging programs that use objects that have virtual methods?

18. What purpose is served by creating a private part in an object declaration?

19. What is an abstract data type?

15.9 PROGRAMMING EXERCISES

1. Add a method to the declaration of SortedList contained in Unit P15f to delete an item from the list. Test the revise version with a suitable modification to Program 15g. Now make the same modification by adding a descendant type either within the unit or in the declaration part of Program 15g. Compare the two methods of making the modification. (You might also wish to add a function that will return True if the specified item is deleted and False if the item was not found.)

2. Change the implementation of the sorted list in Unit P15f to use a linked list, as described in Chapter 12. Recompile Program 15g to use this revised implementation of the ADT. Note that you do not need to modify the program, even though a dramatic change was made to the implementation of the object type.

3. Create an ADT for a stack. Implement operations Push and Pop. Test your new type with a simple program similar to Program 15g.

4. Write a unit containing the object type declarations shown in Figure 15.17. The purpose of the object types declared is to create an environment for drawing circles and ellipses (and, of

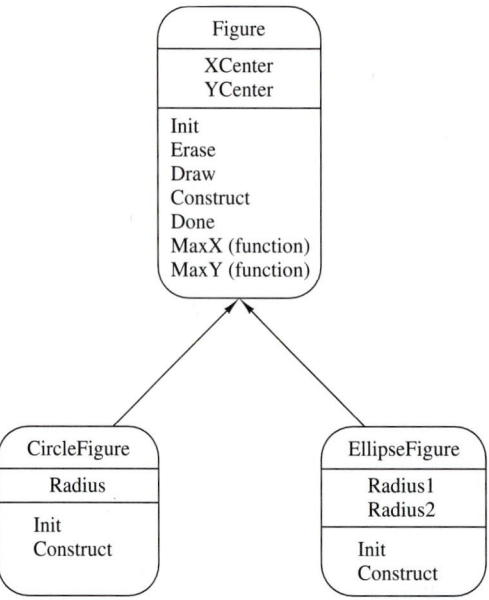

Figure 15.17 Object diagram for Programming Exercise 4.

course, by extension, other figures) on the graphics screen. Type Figure includes those things that will be in common to both figures, including fields for the coordinates of the center and the procedures Init (which must initialize the graphics screen), Erase (which clears the screen), Draw (which draws the figure, including a border around the edge of the screen), Construct (a dummy procedure that will be redefined for each descendant type), and Done (which closes the graphics screen and returns to text mode). Additionally, two functions—MaxX and MaxY—return the maximum (x, y) coordinates on the graphics screen. Type CircleFigure is a descendant of Figure. It includes a field Radius and methods Init and Construct (which actually draws a circle on the screen). Type EllipseFigure is also a descendant of Figure. It includes fields for the two radii of the ellipse and also methods Init and Construct. Note that Draw is inherited by each of the descendant types and is intended to be the technique for writing a circle or ellipse. This means that Draw should be polymorphic; that is, the selection of which version of Construct to execute must depend on the type of the object invoking the method. Test your unit with a suitable test program.

5. Write a unit containing the object type declarations shown in Figure 15.18. The purpose of the types declared is to create an environment for entering and displaying data about various classifications of people in a college. Test your unit with a suitable test program.

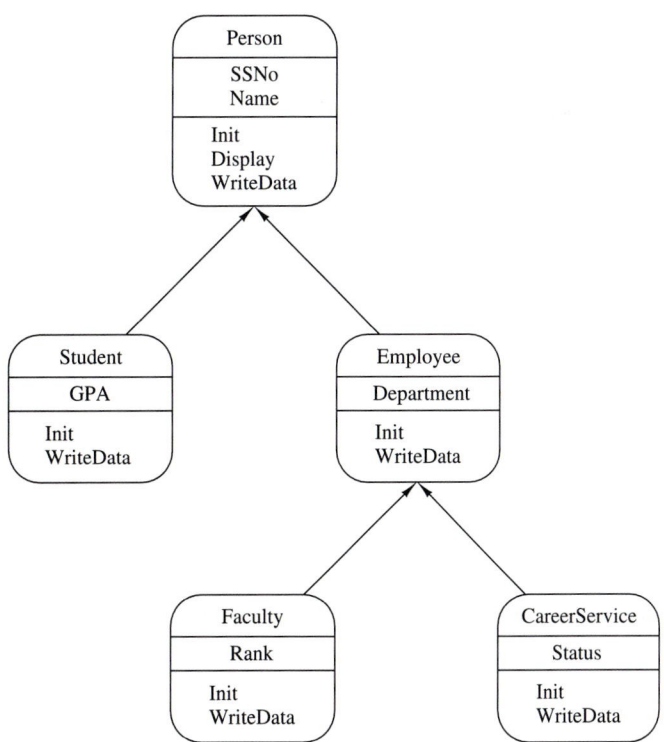

Figure 15.18 Object diagram for Programming Exercise 5.

6. Design and implement a unit containing object type declarations built around the hierarchical relationships shown in Figure 15.19. Consider the use that would likely be made of the object types declared. Test your design with a suitable test program.

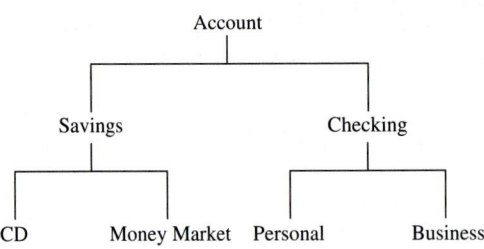

Figure 15.19 Hierarchical relationships among bank account types.

Appendix A

Turbo Pascal 7.0 Reserved Words, Standard Directives, Procedures, and Functions[1]

[1]*Turbo Pascal Version 7.0 Language Guide* and *Turbo Pascal Version 7.0 Programmer's Reference.* Copyright © Borland International, Inc. 1983, 1992. All rights reserved.

TABLE A.1 TURBO PASCAL RESERVED WORDS

and	end	mod	shl
array	file	nil	shr
asm	for	not	string
begin	function	object	then
case	goto	of	to
const	if	or	type
constructor	implementation	packed	unit
destructor	in	procedure	until
div	inherited	program	uses
do	inline	record	var
downto	interface	repeat	while
else	label	set	with
			xor

TABLE A.2 TURBO PASCAL STANDARD DIRECTIVES

absolute	far	near	resident
assembler	forward	private	virtual
external	interrupt	public	

TABLE A.3 FLOW-CONTROL PROCEDURES

Procedure	Description
Break	Terminates a **for**, **while**, or **repeat** statement.
Continue	Continues with the next iteration of a **for**, **while**, or **repeat** statement.
Exit	Exits immediately from the current block.
Halt	Stops program execution and returns to the operating system.
RunError	Stops program execution and generates a run-time error.

The transfer procedures Pack and Unpack, as defined in Standard Pascal, are not implemented by Turbo Pascal.

TABLE A.4 TRANSFER FUNCTIONS

Function	Description
Chr	Returns a character of a specified ordinal number.
Ord	Returns the ordinal number of an ordinal-type value.
Round	Rounds a real-type value to a type *Longint* value.
Trunc	Truncates a real-type value to a type *Longint* value.

TABLE A.5   ARITHMETIC FUNCTIONS

Function	Description
Abs	Returns the absolute value of the argument.
ArcTan	Returns the arctangent of the argument.
Cos	Returns the cosine of the argument.
Exp	Returns the exponential part of the argument.
Frac	Returns the fractional part of the argument.
Int	Returns the integer part of the argument.
Ln	Returns the natural logarithm of the argument.
Pi	Returns the value of *Pi* (3.1415926535897932385).
Sin	Returns the sine of the argument.
Sqr	Returns the square of the argument.
Sqrt	Returns the square root of the argument.

TABLE A.6   ORDINAL PROCEDURES AND FUNCTIONS

Procedure or function	Description
Dec	Decrements a variable.
Inc	Increments a variable.
High	Returns the highest value in the range of the argument.
Low	Returns the lowest value in the range of the argument.
Odd	Tests if the argument is an odd number.
Pred	Returns the predecessor of the argument.
Succ	Returns the successor of the argument.

TABLE A.7 STRING PROCEDURES AND FUNCTIONS

Procedure or function	Description
Concat	Concatenates a sequence of strings.
Copy	Returns a substring of a string.
Delete	Deletes a substring from a string.
Insert	Inserts a substring into a string.
Length	Returns the dynamic length of a string.
Pos	Searches for a substring in a string.
Str	Converts a numeric value to its string representation.
Val	Converts the string value to its numeric representation.

TABLE A.8   INPUT AND OUTPUT PROCEDURES AND FUNCTIONS

Procedure or function	Description
Append	Opens an existing text file for appending.
Assign	Assigns the name of an external file to a file variable.
BlockRead	Reads one or more records from an untyped file.
BlockWrite	Writes one or more records into an untyped file.
ChDir	Changes the current directory.
Close	Closes an open file.
Eof	Returns the end-of-file status of a file.
Eoln	Returns the end-of-line status of a text file.
Erase	Erases an external file.
FilePos	Returns the current file position of a typed or untyped file.
FileSize	Returns the current size of a file; not used for text files.
Flush	Flushes the buffer of an output text file.
GetDir	Returns the current directory of a specified drive.
IOResult	Returns an integer value that is the status of the last I/O function performed.
MkDir	Creates a subdirectory.
Read	Reads one or more values from a file into one or more variables.
Readln	Does what a *Read* does and then skips to the beginning of the next line in the text file.
Rename	Renames an external file.
Reset	Opens an existing file.
Rewrite	Creates and opens a new file.
RmDir	Removes an empty subdirectory.
Seek	Moves the current position of a typed or untyped file to a specified component. Not used with text files.
SeekEof	Returns the end-of-file status of a text file.
SeekEoln	Returns the end-of-line status of a text file.
SetTextBuf	Assigns an I/O buffer to a text file.
Truncate	Truncates a typed or untyped file at the current file position.
Write	Writes one or more values to a file.
Writeln	Does the same as a *Write*, and then writes an end-of-line marker to the text file.

TABLE A.9 DYNAMIC-ALLOCATION PROCEDURES AND FUNCTIONS

Procedure or function	Description
Dispose	Disposes of a dynamic variable.
FreeMem	Disposes of a dynamic variable of a given size.
GetMem	Creates a new dynamic variable of a given size and sets a pointer variable to point to it.
MaxAvail	Returns the size of the largest contiguous free block in the heap, indicating the size of the largest dynamic variable that can be allocated at the time of the call to *MaxAvail*.
MemAvail	Returns the number of free bytes of heap storage available.
New	Creates a new dynamic variable and sets a pointer variable to point to it.

TABLE A.10 POINTER AND ADDRESS FUNCTIONS

Function	Description
Addr	Returns the address of a specified object.
Assigned	Tests to determine if a pointer or procedural variable is **nil**.
CSeg	Returns the current value of the CS register.
DSeg	Returns the current value of the DS register.
Ofs	Returns the offset of a specified object.
Ptr	Converts a segment base and an offset address to a pointer-type value.
Seg	Returns the segment of a specified object.
SPtr	Returns the current value of the SP register.
SSeg	Returns the current value of the SS register.

TABLE A.11   MISCELLANEOUS PROCEDURES AND FUNCTIONS

Procedure or function	Description
Exclude	Excludes an element from a set.
FillChar	Fills a specified number of contiguous bytes with a specified value.
Hi	Returns the high-order byte of the argument.
Include	Includes an element in a set.
Lo	Returns the low-order byte of the argument.
Move	Copies a specified number of contiguous bytes from a source range to a destination range.
ParamCount	Returns the number of parameters passed to the program on the command line.
ParamStr	Returns a specified command-line parameter.
Random	Returns a random number.
Randomize	Initializes built-in random generator with a random value.
SizeOf	Returns number of bytes occupied by the argument.
Swap	Swaps the high- and low-order bytes of the argument.
TypeOf	Points to an object type's virtual method table.
UpCase	Converts a character to uppercase.

Appendix B

Turbo Pascal 7.0 Operator Summary[1]

[1]All tables in this appendix were reproduced from *Turbo Pascal Version 7.0 Language Guide*. Copyright ©
Borland International, Inc. 1983, 1992. All rights reserved.

TABLE B.1 PRECEDENCE OF OPERATORS

Operators	Precedence	Categories
@, **not**	first (high)	unary operators
*, /, **div**, **mod**, **and**, **shl**, **shr**	second	multiplying operators
+, −, **or**, **xor**	third	adding operators
=,<>, <, >, <=, >=, **in**	fourth (low)	relational operators

TABLE B.2 BINARY ARITHMETIC OPERATIONS

*The + operator is also used as a string or set operator, and the +, −, and * operators are also used as set operators.*

Operator	Operation	Operand types	Result type
+	addition	integer type real type	integer type real type
−	subtraction	integer type real type	integer type real type
*	multiplication	integer type real type	integer type real type
/	division	integer type real type	real type real type
div	integer division	integer type	integer type
mod	remainder	integer type	integer type

TABLE B.3 UNARY ARITHMETIC OPERATIONS

Operator	Operation	Operand types	Result type
+	sign identity	integer type real type	integer type real type
−	sign negation	integer type real type	integer type real type

TABLE B.4 LOGICAL OPERATIONS

*The **not** operator is a unary operator.*

Operator	Operation	Operand types	Result type
not	bitwise negation	integer type	*Boolean*
and	bitwise and	integer type	*Boolean*
or	bitwise or	integer type	*Boolean*
xor	bitwise xor	integer type	*Boolean*
shl	shift left	integer type	*Boolean*
shr	shift right	integer type	*Boolean*

TABLE B.5   BOOLEAN OPERATIONS

*The **not** operator is a unary operator.*

Operator	Operation	Operand types	Result type
not	negation	Boolean type	*Boolean*
and	logical and	Boolean type	*Boolean*
or	logical or	Boolean type	*Boolean*
xor	logical xor	Boolean type	*Boolean*

TABLE B.6   STRING OPERATION

Operator	Operation	Operand types	Result type
+	concatenation	string type, *Char* type, or packed string type	string type

TABLE B.7   SET OPERATIONS

Operator	Operation	Operand types
+	union	compatible set types
−	difference	compatible set types
*	intersection	compatible set types

TABLE B.8 RELATIONAL OPERATIONS

Operator	Operation	Operand types	Result type
=	equal	compatible simple, pointer, set, string, or packed string types	*Boolean*
<>	not equal	compatible simple, pointer, set, string, or packed string types	*Boolean*
<	less than	compatible simple, string, packed string types, or *PChar*	*Boolean*
>	greater than	compatible simple, string, packed string types, or *PChar*	*Boolean*
<=	less than or equal to	compatible simple, string, packed string types, or *PChar*	*Boolean*
>=	greater than or equal to	compatible simple, string, or packed string types, or *PChar*	*Boolean*
<=	subset of	compatible set types	*Boolean*
>=	superset of	compatible set types	*Boolean*
in	member of	left operand, any ordinal type T; right operand, set whose base is compatible with T	*Boolean*

Appendix C

Turbo Pascal 7.0 Syntax Diagrams[1]

Syntax diagrams are an alternate means for showing the general form for Pascal statements, constants, variables, and other entities which collectively are called constructions. For example, the following syntax diagram describes the construction "simple expression":

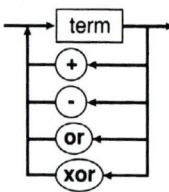

In order to read a syntax diagram you follow the arrows from left to right until you come to the end of the path. Sometimes, as in the above diagram, there may be multiple paths. In this example, a simple expression can be a term or a term followed by an operator ("+", "−", "or", or "xor") followed by a term, which in turn may be followed by an operator and another term and so forth. The elements in boxes are constructions that must be further defined; the elements in circles are the actual reserved word, operator, or mark of punctuation used in a program. In this example, "term" is a construction that will be further defined in a syntax diagram whereas "+", "−", "or", and "xor" are operators ("or" and "xor" also are reserved words).

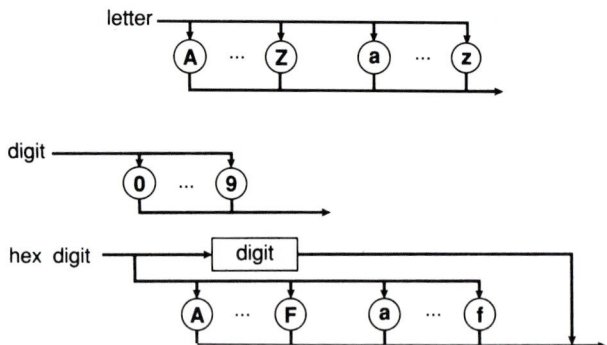

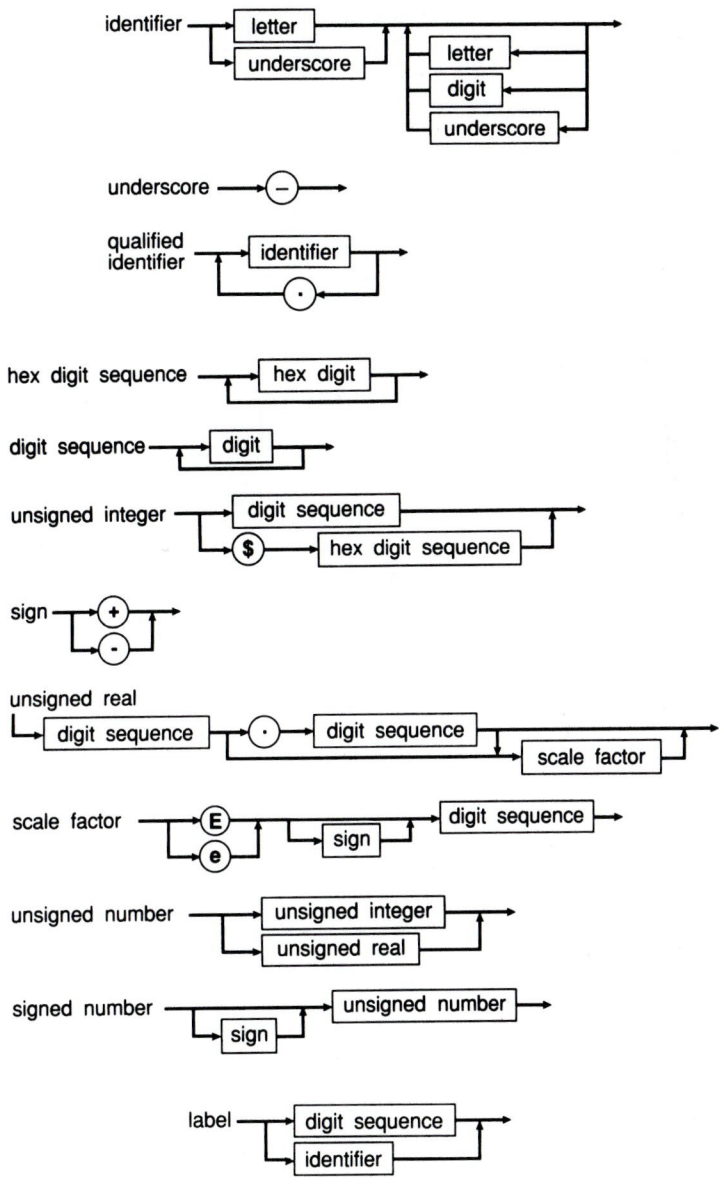

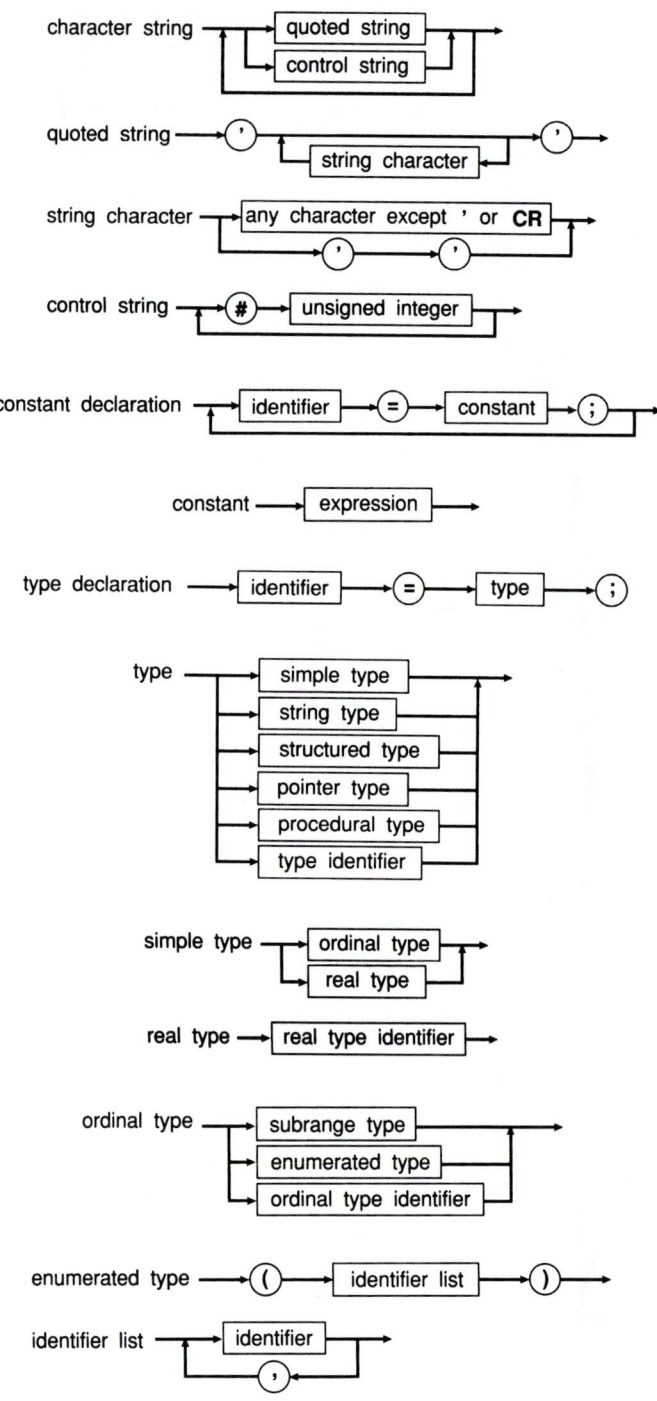

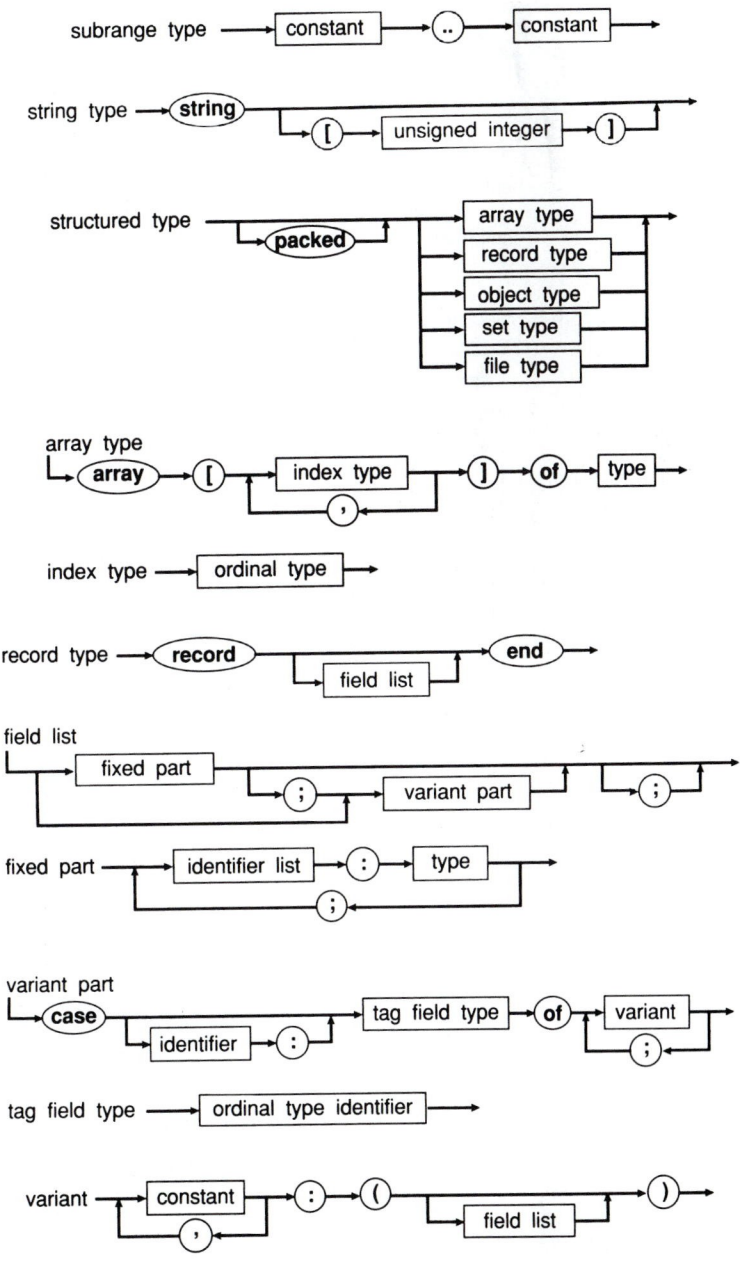

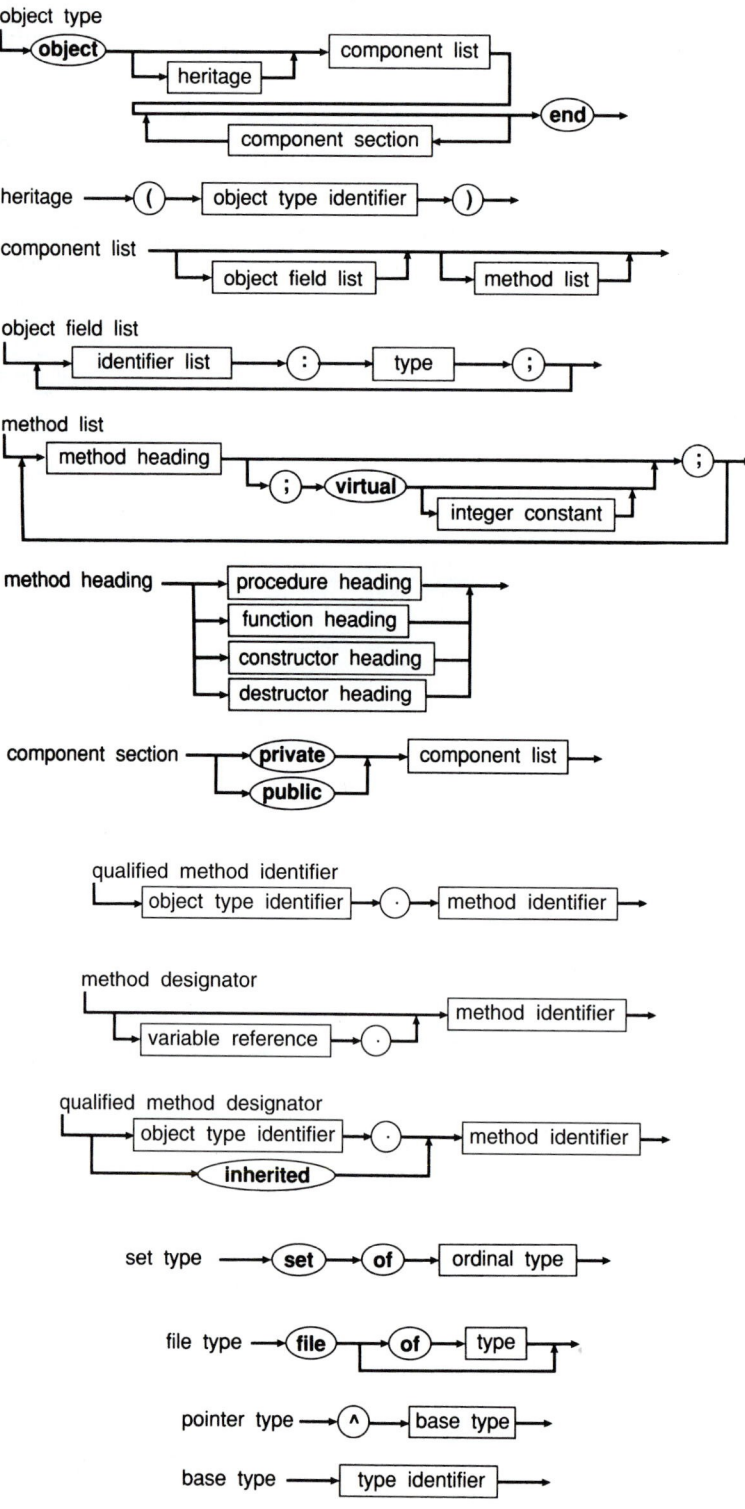

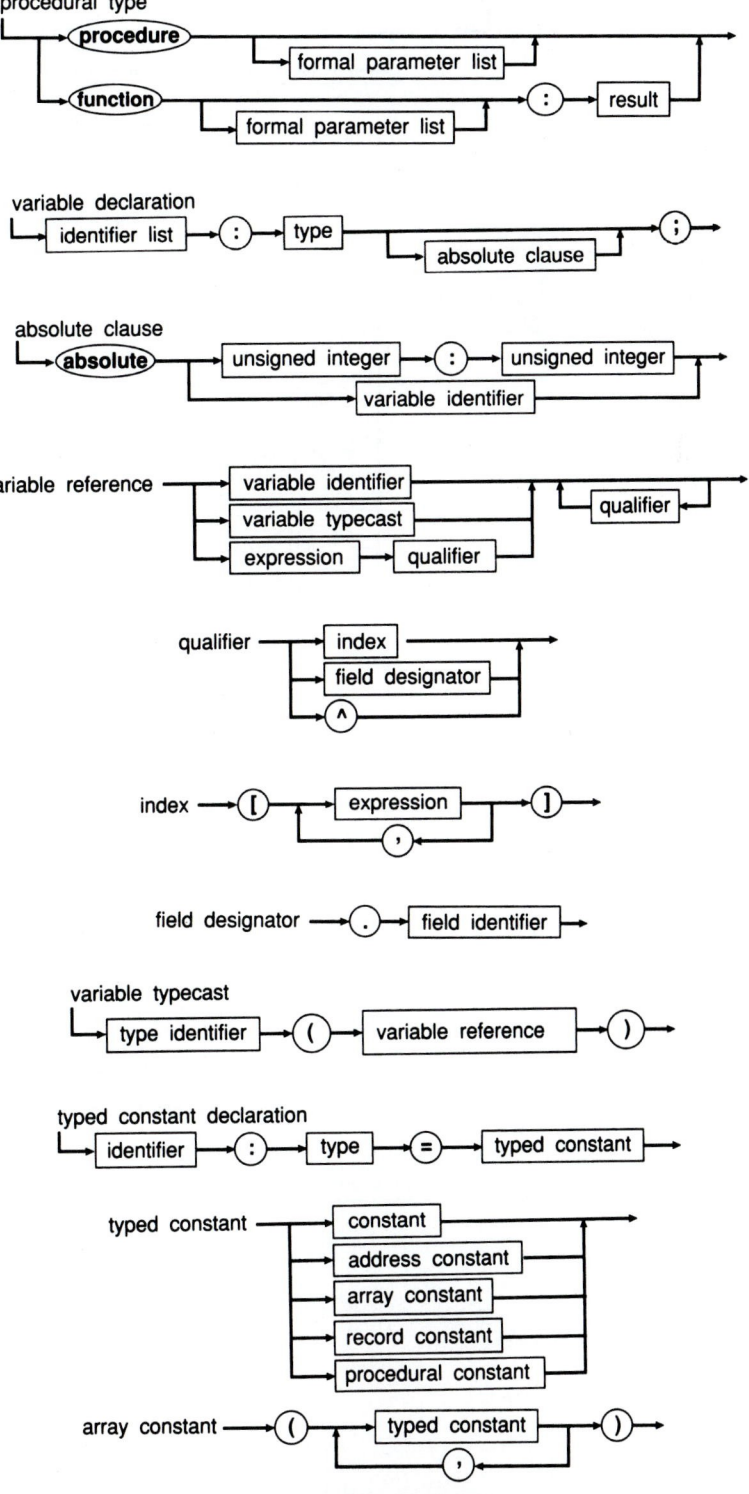

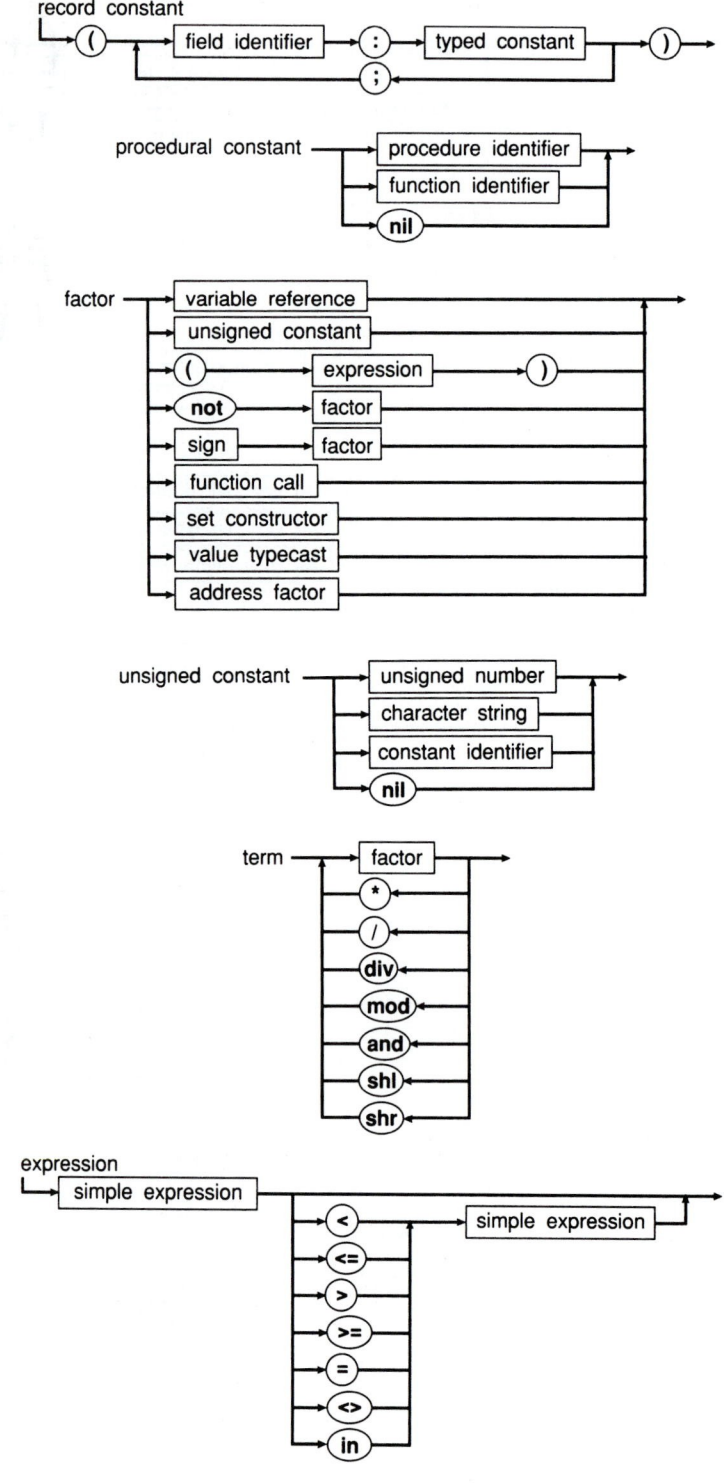

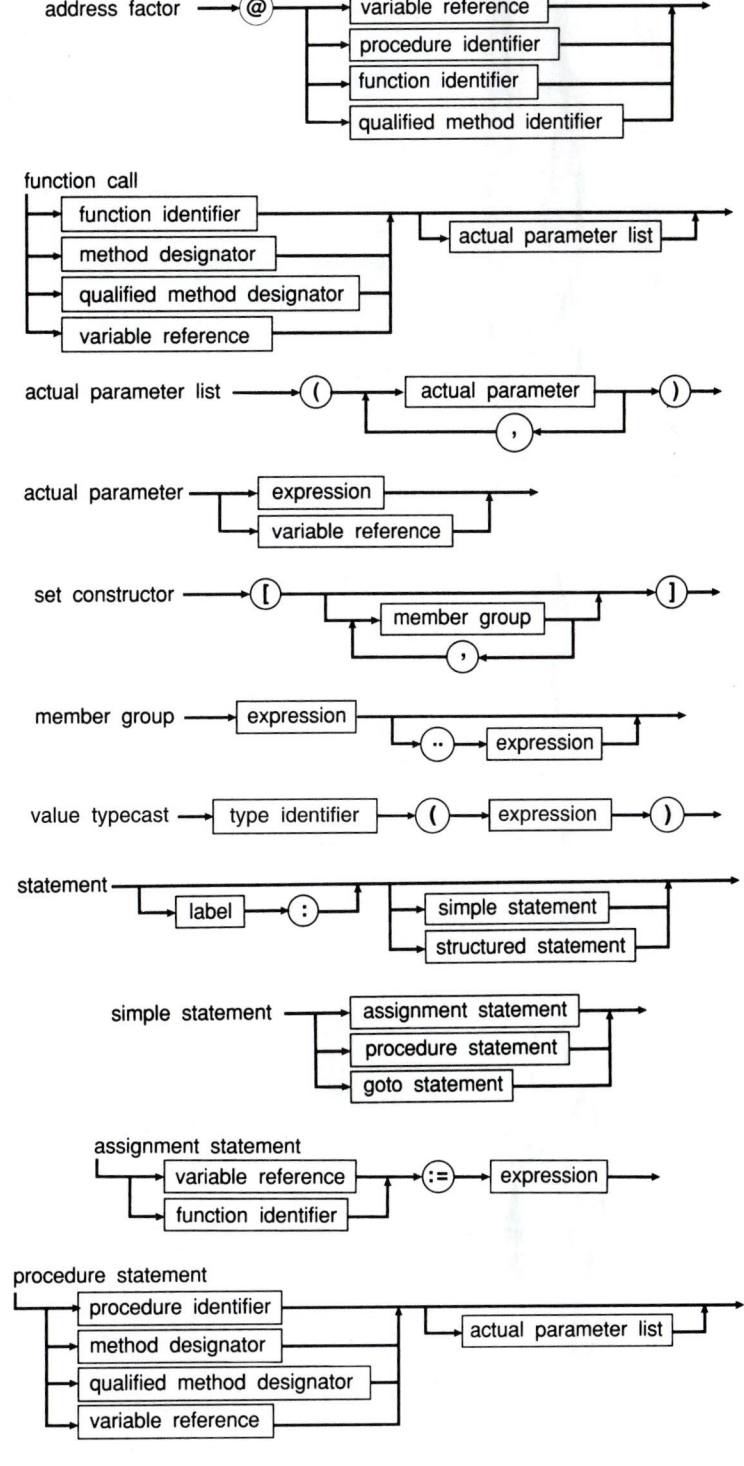

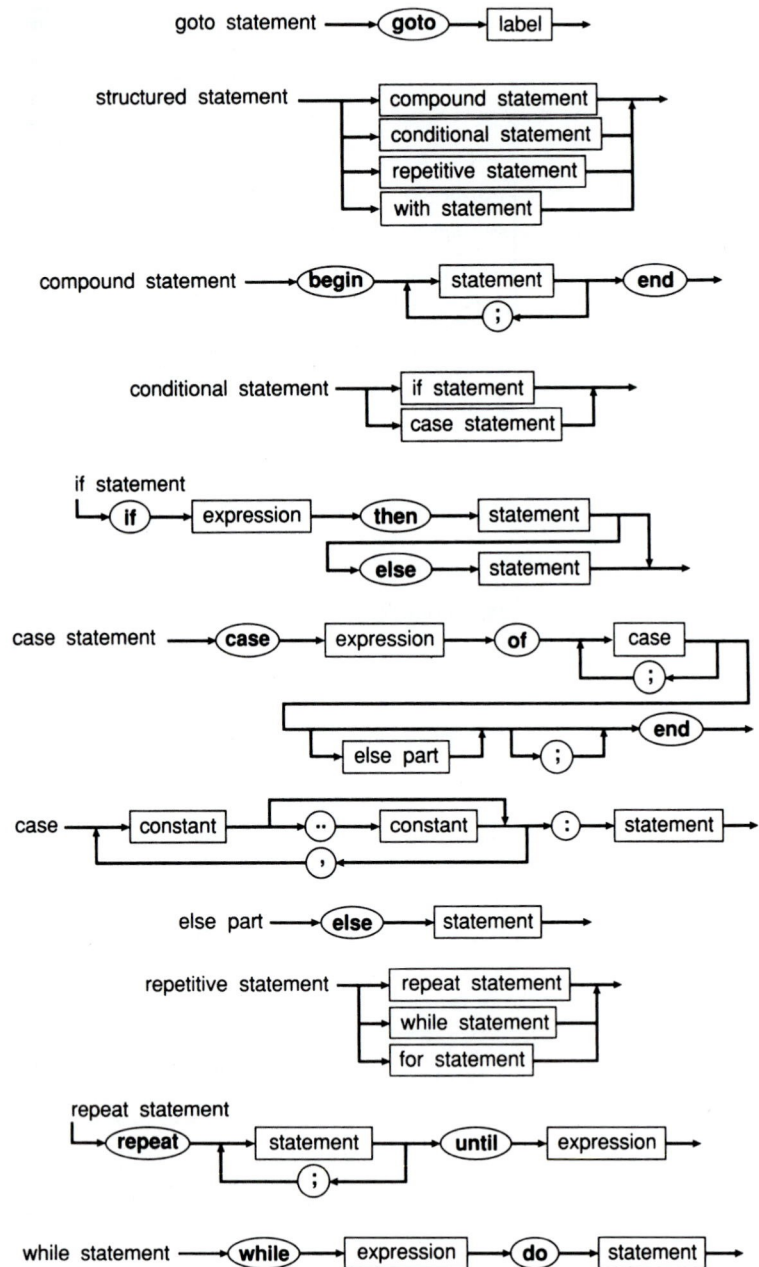

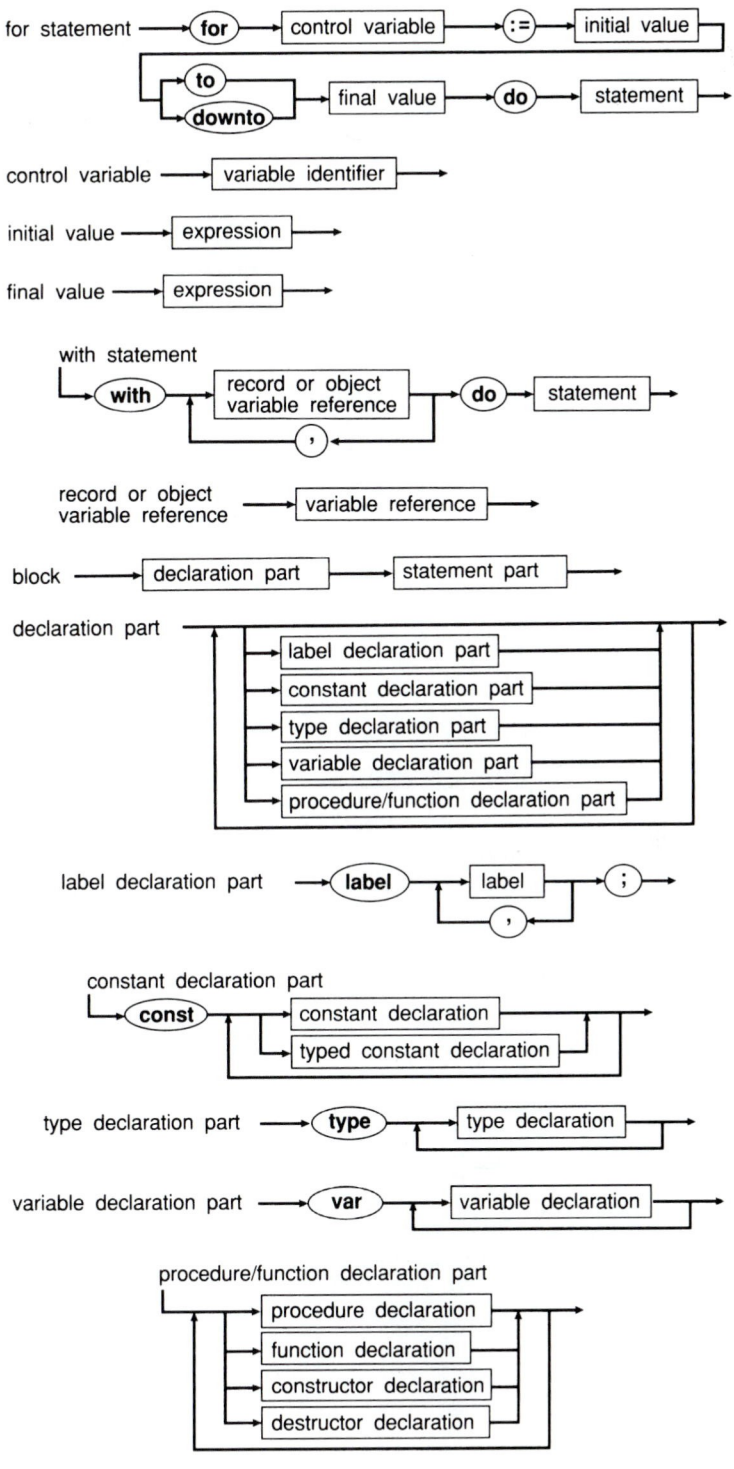

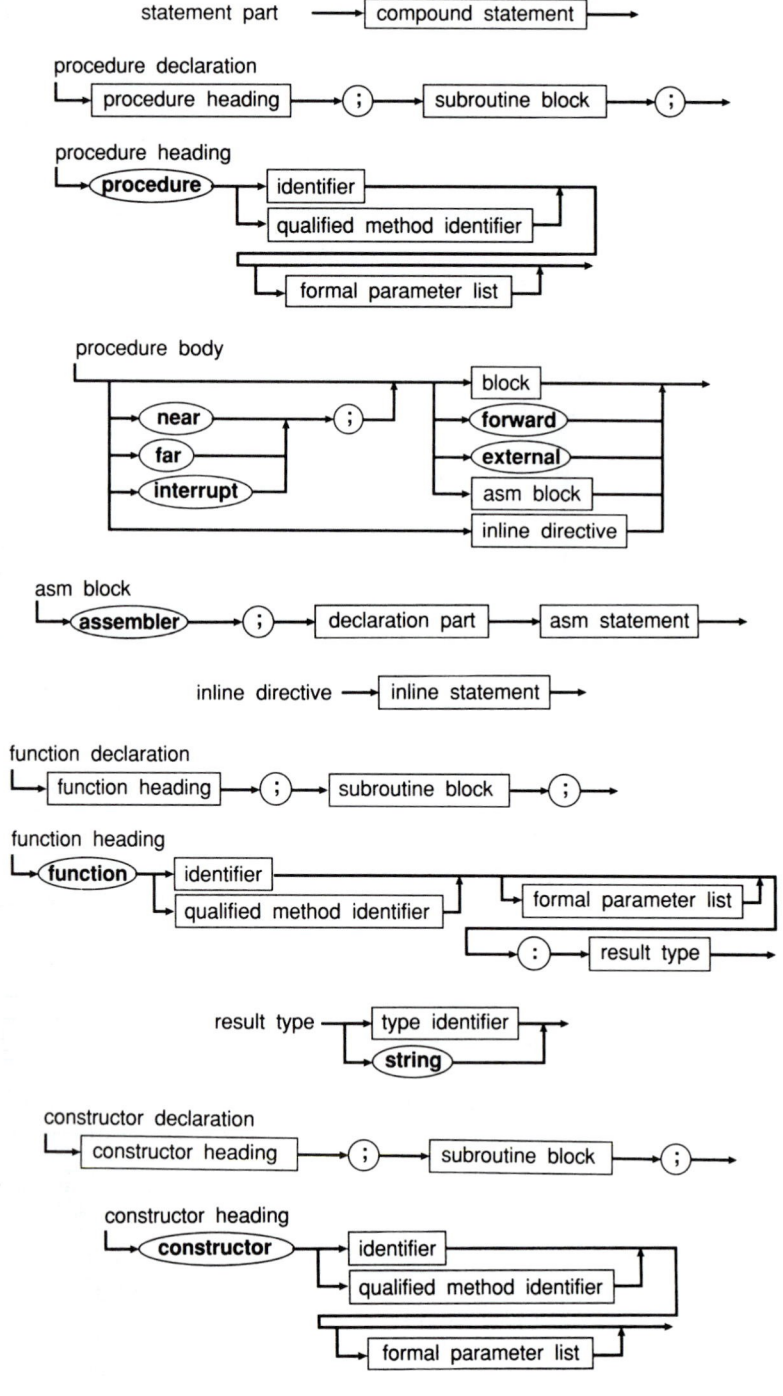

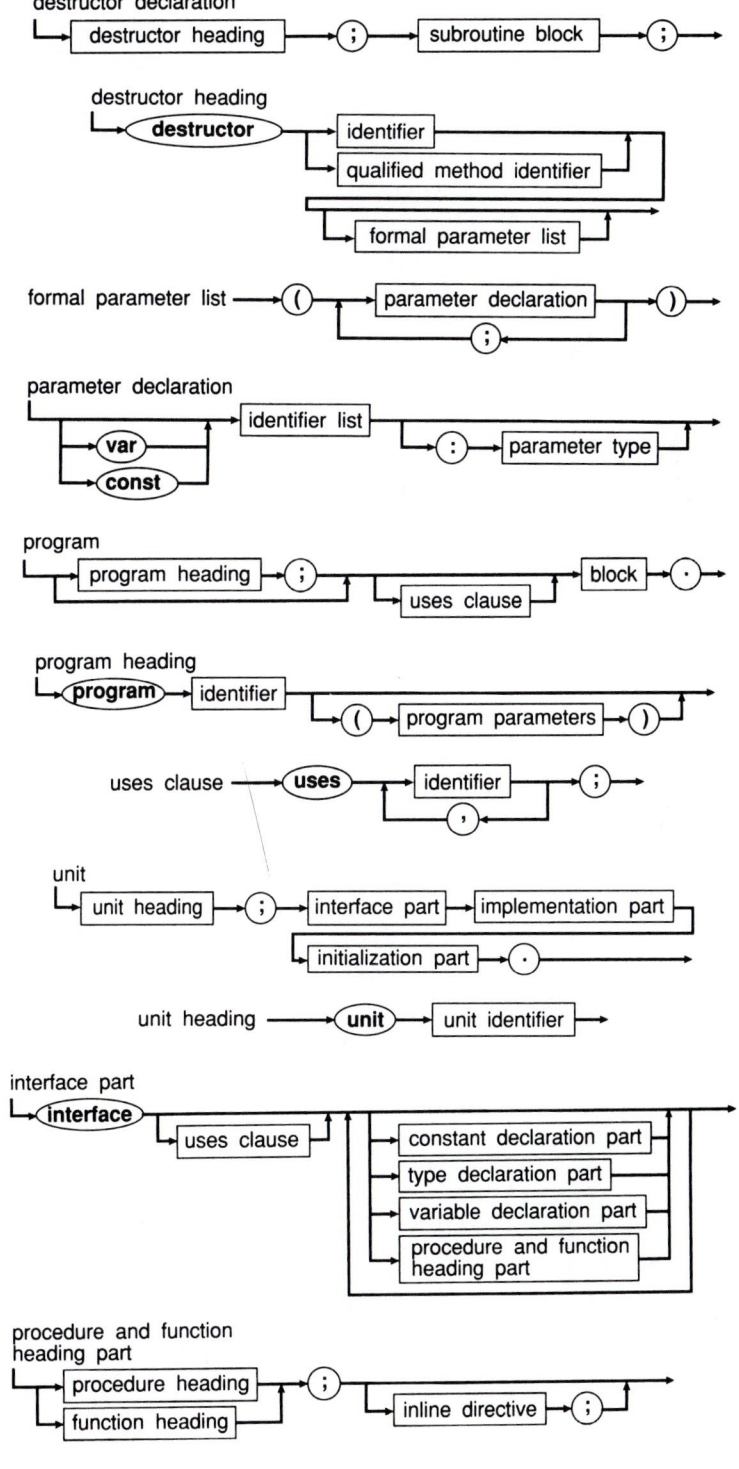

destructor declaration

destructor heading → ; → subroutine block → ;

destructor heading

destructor → identifier / qualified method identifier → formal parameter list

formal parameter list

(→ parameter declaration →)
;

parameter declaration

var / const → identifier list → : → parameter type

program

program heading → ; → uses clause → block → .

program heading

program → identifier → (→ program parameters →)

uses clause

uses → identifier → ;
,

unit

unit heading → ; → interface part → implementation part
initialization part → .

unit heading → **unit** → unit identifier

interface part

interface → uses clause → constant declaration part / type declaration part / variable declaration part / procedure and function heading part

procedure and function heading part

procedure heading / function heading → ; → inline directive → ;

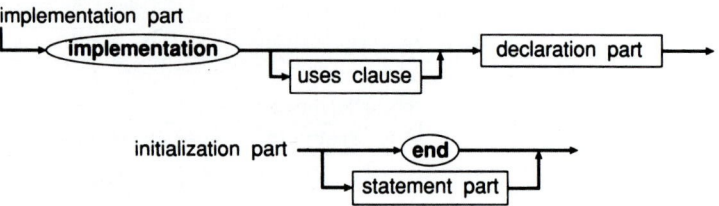

Appendix D

ASCII Codes[1]

[1]*Turbo Pascal Version 7.0 Programmer's Reference.* Copyright © Borland International, Inc. 1983, 1992. All rights reserved.

Dec	Hex	Char		Dec	Hex	Char	Dec	Hex	Char	Dec	Hex	Char
0	0	^@	NUL	32	20		64	40	@	96	60	'
1	1	☻	SOH	33	21	!	65	41	A	97	61	a
2	2	●	STX	34	22	"	66	42	B	98	62	b
3	3	♥	ETX	35	23	#	67	43	C	99	63	c
4	4	♦	EOT	36	24	$	68	44	D	100	64	d
5	5	♣	ENQ	37	25	%	69	45	E	101	65	e
6	6	♠	ACK	38	26	&	70	46	F	102	66	f
7	7	•	BEL	39	27	'	71	47	G	103	67	g
8	8	◘	BS	40	28	(	72	48	H	104	68	h
9	9	○	TAB	41	29	)	73	49	I	105	69	i
10	A	◙	LF	42	2A	*	74	4A	J	106	6A	j
11	B	♂	VT	43	2B	+	75	4B	K	107	6B	k
12	C	♀	FF	44	2C	,	76	4C	L	108	6C	l
13	D	♪	CR	45	2D	-	77	4D	M	109	6D	m
14	E	♫	SO	46	2E	.	78	4E	N	110	6E	n
15	F	☼	SI	47	2F	/	79	4F	O	111	6F	o
16	10	►	DLE	48	30	0	80	50	P	112	70	p
17	11	◄	DC1	49	31	1	81	51	Q	113	71	q
18	12	↕	DC2	50	32	2	82	52	R	114	72	r
19	13	‼	DC3	51	33	3	83	53	S	115	73	s
20	14	¶	DC4	52	34	4	84	54	T	116	74	t
21	15	§	NAK	53	35	5	85	55	U	117	75	u
22	16	▬	SYN	54	36	6	86	56	V	118	76	v
23	17	↨	ETB	55	37	7	87	57	W	119	77	w
24	18	↑	CAN	56	38	8	88	58	X	120	78	x
25	19	↓	EM	57	39	9	89	59	Y	121	79	y
26	1A	→	SUB	58	3A	:	90	5A	Z	122	7A	z
27	1B	←	ESC	59	3B	;	91	5B	[	123	7B	{
28	1C	∟	FS	60	3C	<	92	5C	\	124	7C	|
29	1D	↔	GS	61	3D	=	93	5D	]	125	7D	}
30	1E	▲	RS	62	3E	>	94	5E	^	126	7E	~
31	1F	▼	US	63	3F	?	95	5F	_	127	7F	

Dec	Hex	Char	Dec	Hex	Char	Dec	Hex	Char	Dec	Hex	Char
128	80	Ç	160	A0	á	192	C0	└	224	E0	α
129	81	ü	161	A1	í	193	C1	┴	225	E1	ß
130	82	é	162	A2	ó	194	C2	┬	226	E2	Γ
131	83	â	163	A3	ú	195	C3	├	227	E3	π
132	84	ä	164	A4	ñ	196	C4	─	228	E4	Σ
133	85	à	165	A5	Ñ	197	C5	┼	229	E5	σ
134	86	å	166	A6	ª	198	C6	╞	230	E6	µ
135	87	ç	167	A7	º	199	C7	╟	231	E7	τ
136	88	ê	168	A8	¿	200	C8	╚	232	E8	Φ
137	89	ë	169	A9	⌐	201	C9	╔	233	E9	θ
138	8A	è	170	AA	¬	202	CA	╩	234	EA	Ω
139	8B	ï	171	AB	½	203	CB	╦	235	EB	δ
140	8C	î	172	AC	¼	204	CC	╠	236	EC	∞
141	8D	ì	173	AD	¡	205	CD	=	237	ED	ϕ
142	8E	Ä	174	AE	«	206	CE	╬	238	EE	∈
143	8F	Å	175	AF	»	207	CF	╧	239	EF	∩
144	90	É	176	B0	░	208	D0	╨	240	F0	≡
145	91	æ	177	B1	▒	209	D1	╤	241	F1	±
146	92	Æ	178	B2	▓	210	D2	╥	242	F2	≥
147	93	ô	179	B3	│	211	D3	╙	243	F3	≤
148	94	ö	180	B4	┤	212	D4	╘	244	F4	⌠
149	95	ò	181	B5	╡	213	D5	╒	245	F5	⌡
150	96	û	182	B6	╢	214	D6	╓	246	F6	÷
151	97	ù	183	B7	╖	215	D7	╫	247	F7	≈
152	98	ÿ	184	B8	╕	216	D8	╪	248	F8	°
153	99	Ö	185	B9	╣	217	D9	┘	249	F9	•
154	9A	Ü	186	BA	║	218	DA	┌	250	FA	·
155	9B	¢	187	BB	╗	219	DB	█	251	FB	√
156	9C	£	188	BC	╝	220	DC	▄	252	FC	ⁿ
157	9D	¥	189	BD	╜	221	DD	▌	253	FD	²
158	9E	₧	190	BE	╛	222	DE	▐	254	FE	■
159	9F	ƒ	191	BF	┐	223	DF	▀	255	FF	

Appendix E

Using Turbo Pascal 5.0 and 5.5

E.1   OVERVIEW

Turbo Pascal Versions 5.0 and 5.5 are composed of an integrated program-development system and a program-debugging system. The user interfaces of the two versions are very similar; the major difference between the two is the addition of object data type (as described in Chapter 15) in Version 5.5. This appendix describes the program-development system, which is composed of the following elements:

- an editor used for creating files for programs and data
- a file manager used to store and retrieve files and execute programs
- a compiler used to translate the programs you write into machine language

The details of using the debugging system are similar to those of using the equivalent system in Version 7.0 which is described in Appendix G.

The first step in using Turbal Pascal 5.0 or 5.5 is to load it into the memory of your computer. The exact details of this operation vary greatly from one computer to another. Instructions are found in the Turbo Pascal reference manual; your instructor may also provide additional instructions. The screen that you will see when Turbo Pascal has been loaded will be similar to that shown in Figure E.1. (Your screen may differ slightly from the figure, depending on the way Turbal Pascal was installed.) If a copyright notice is present, it will disappear when you press any key.

Across the top of the screen, you see a menu bar (called the **Main Menu**) showing the seven basic commands that are available. In each case, to issue the command, you type

```
 File    Edit    Run    Compile    Options    Debug    Break/watch
══════════════════════════════════ Edit ══════════════════════════
      Line 1       Col 1    Insert Indent        Unindent    C:NONAME.PAS









































──────────────────────────────── Watch ───────────────────────────


 F1-Help  F5-Zoom  F6-Switch  F7-Trace  F8-Step  F9-Make  F10-Menu
```

Figure E.1 Initial Turbo Pascal Version 5.0 or 5.5 Screen.

the first letter of the command name. Or you can use the arrow key to highlight the desired command and then execute the command by pressing the Enter key. The File command is used to store and retrieve files and determine which files are present on a disk. This command can also be used to exit to the operating system and then return to Turbo Pascal. The Edit command activates the editor. This command is used to create a new program or modify an existing one. The Run command is used to execute a program and to view the user output screen. (If a program has not been compiled before the Run command is given, it is automatically compiled first.) The Compile command can be used to compile a program without automatically executing it. This command can also be used to perform other functions related to the compiler. The Options command is used to set various options relating to the way in which the system functions. Most of these options have predefined default values that are satisfactory to beginning students. The Debug command is used to gain access to the program-debugging system. The Break/watch command is used to set break points (points in the program at which execution will halt) and specify variables to be observed in the Watch window during program debugging. The Debug and Break/watch commands are part of the integrated program-debugging facility mentioned earlier. These commands are very similar to their counterparts in Version 7.0 (see Appendix G for details.)

The screen is divided into two windows labeled "Edit" and "Watch." The Edit window displays the text of the current program. The Watch window shows the values of specified variables during the debugging of a program. Until you begin using the debugging system, you can ignore the content of this window.

Along the bottom of the screen, you see a list of actions that you can perform with the function keys. By pressing F1, you can secure help; F5 will "zoom" the windows—that is, it will cause the Edit window to occupy the full screen (pressing F5 again will cause two windows to reappear); F6 will switch from one active window to another (for example, from the Edit window to the Watch window and back); F7 and F8 allow you to step through the execution of the program one line at a time (the difference between Trace and Step is covered in Appendix G); F9 performs a Make operation, which is a compilation of the program (the program is not automatically executed); and F10 will move you to the Main Menu. This key is used when you have finished using the Editor and wish to return to the Main Menu bar.

Note that at different times, the list of available function keys will change. Always examine the list of keys on the bottom of the screen to determine which keys are currently active. These keys are provided as an aid in using the system; there are always other ways to accomplish the functions performed by them.

Selecting one of the commands from the Main Menu will usually cause the system to display related menus called *submenus*. For example, if you issue the File command, the submenu shown in Figure E.2 is displayed. Selecting options from submenus is accomplished in the same way as selecting options from the Main Menu: either enter the first character of the command name, or used the arrow keys to highlight the desired command and then press the Enter key. The Load command is used to load a file. The Pick command is used to load a file that has recently been active. The New command erases the current program from the Edit window and enables you to start on a new program. The Save command allows you to save the current program, using a name of your choosing.

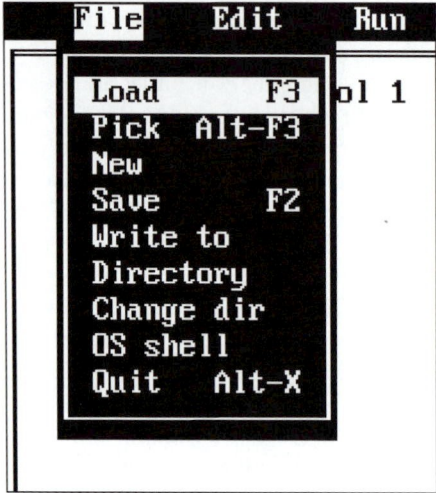

Figure E.2 File submenu in Turbo Pascal 5.0/5.5.

(Unless you assign a name to a file, the system uses the default file name NONAME.PAS.) The Write to command causes the system to write the current program to any file of your choosing. The Directory command allows you to secure a list of the files contained on a disk. The Change dir command allows you to change the current default directory. The OS shell command allows you to exit to the operating system. Turbo Pascal remains in memory; you type EXIT to return from the operating system to Turbo Pascal. Finally, the Quit commands terminates Turbo Pascal and returns you to the operating system. The submenus include a reference to *hot keys* beside some of the commands. A hot key is used to execute a command directly without entering the main menu. For example, F3 will execute the Load command, Alt-F3 (press both the Alt key and F3 simultaneously) will execute the Pick command, F2 will save a program, and Alt-X will terminate Turbo Pascal and return you to the operating system. Hot keys are provided as an aid to using the system for experienced users; you can always accomplish the same task through the menu system.

In all cases, you can return from the submenu to the Main Menu by pressing the Esc (Escape) key. In some cases, there will be other levels of submenus. the Esc key will return you from the current submenu to the next higher level in the menu structure. Figure E.3 contains a complete reference for the first five Main Menu commands. Complete details on all the commands are contained in the Turbo Pascal reference manuals supplied with the system.

In order to begin writing a program, you select Edit from the main menu. A **cursor** appears in the upper left-hand corner of the Edit window, and a **status line** is placed at the top of the window. Following is a sample status line:

```
    Line 1    Col 1     Insert  Indent     Unindent C:NONAME.PAS
```

The first two items on the line tell you where the cursor is placed in the file—in this case, line 1 column 1. As you move the cursor, these entries will change. The next two items

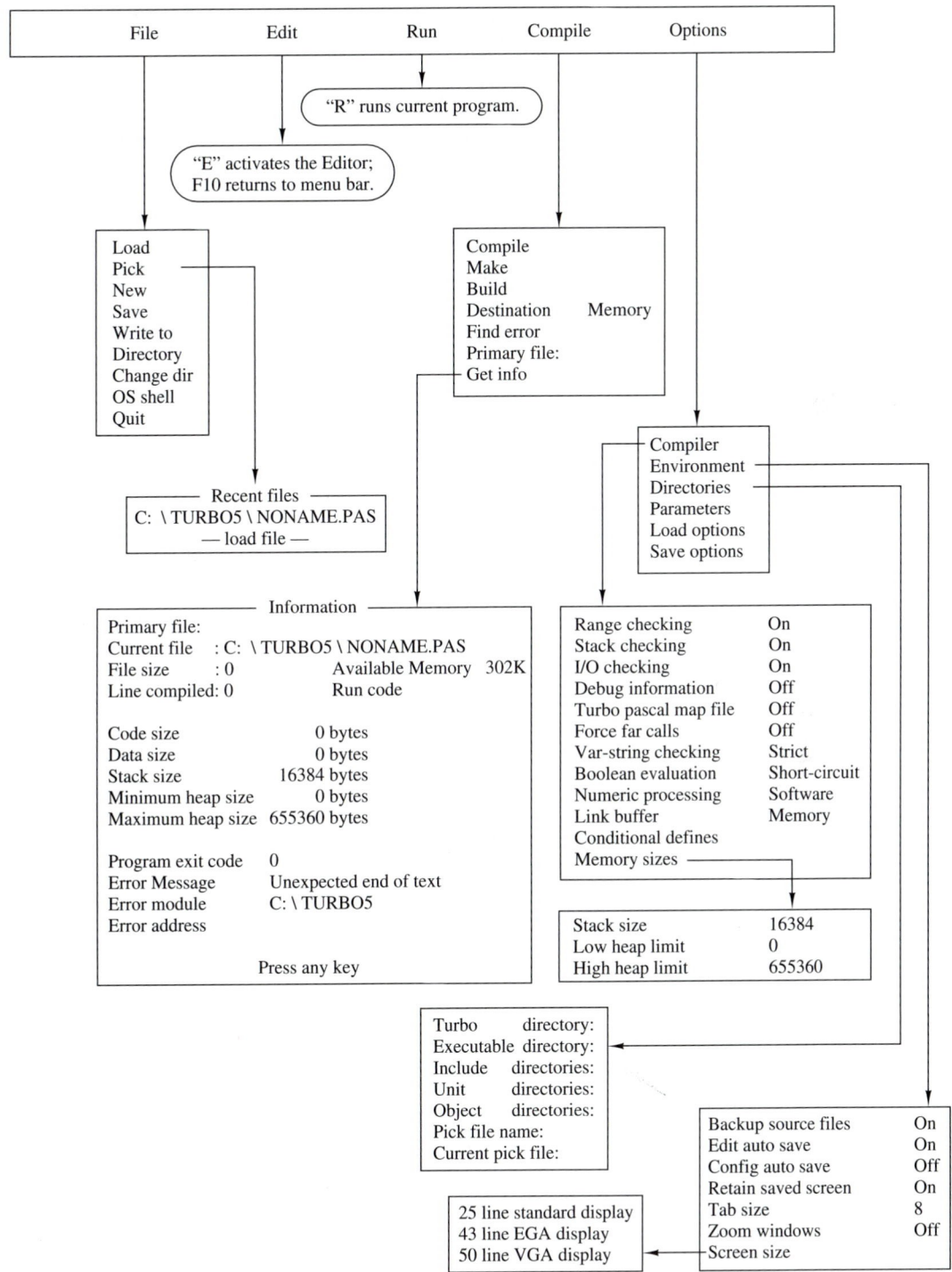

Figure E.3 General reference to the first five Main Menu commands in Turbo Pascal 5.0 and 5.5. Copyright ©
Borland International, Inc. 1983, 1988.

tell you that the editor is in Insert mode (which means that when you type, new characters will be inserted into the midst of any existing text) and that the Indent feature is on (which means that the Tab key will cause a new line of text to be indented to a position corresponding to the end of the first entry on the preceding line). The entry Unindent means that the backspace key used at the beginning of a line will move the entire line back to align with the beginning of the preceding line. All three options can be changed. (See the Turbo Pascal reference manual for details.) The last entry of the status line shows the file name of the current file. Initially, the "dummy" file name shown is used. You will want to change this to something meaningful; you do this when you save the file.

To enter a program, you type its content, as you would with most other word-processing software. The Turbo Pascal editor makes use of numerous **control key** sequence loosely borrowed from WordStar. These are summarized in Figure E.4. Don't be intimidated by this list of commands. You will be able to type simple programs without any of them. When you begin editing longer programs, you will find that these commands will save you much time and energy.

The appearance of the screen after entering Program 1a is as shown in Figure E.5. After typing a program and making any corrections that may be needed, press F10 to return to the Main Menu. Then select the Run command. At this point, the submenu shown in Figure E.6 will be displayed. At this time, only the first and last options will be of interest

Basic Movement Commands	
Character left	*Ctrl-S or Left arrow*
Character right	*Ctrl-D or Right arrow*
Word left	*Ctrl-A or Ctrl-Left arrow*
Word right	*Ctrl-F or Ctrl-Right arrow*
Line up	*Ctrl-E or Up arrow*
Line down	*Ctrl-X or Down arrow*
Scroll up	*Ctrl-W*
Scroll down	*Ctrl-Z*
Page up	*Ctrl-R or PgUp*
Page down	*Ctrl-C or PgDn*
Extended Movement Commands	
Beginning of line	*Ctrl-Q S or Home*
End of line	*Ctrl-Q D or End*
Top of window	*Ctrl-Q E or Ctrl-Home*
Bottom of window	*Ctrl-Q X or Ctrl-End*
Top of file	*Ctrl-Q R or Ctrl-PgUp*
End of file	*Ctrl-Q C or Ctrl-PgDn*
Beginning of block	*Ctrl-Q B*
End of block	*Ctrl-Q K*
Last cursor position	*Ctrl-Q P*
Last error position	*Ctrl-Q W*
Insert and Delete Commands	
Insert mode on/off	*Ctrl-V or Ins*
Insert line	*Ctrl-N*
Delete line	*Ctrl-Y*
Delete to end of line	*Ctrl-Q Y*
Delete character left of cursor	*Ctrl-H or Backspace*
Delete character under cursor	*Ctrl-G or Del*
Delete word right of cursor	*Ctrl-T*

Figure E.4(a) Turbo Pascal Editor commands (part 1 of 2 parts). Copyright © Borland International, Inc. 1983, 1988.

Block Commands

Mark block-begin	*Ctrl-K B or F7*
Mark block-end	*Ctrl-K K or F8*
Mark single word	*Ctrl-K T*
Print block	*Ctrl-K P*
Copy block	*Ctrl-K C*
Delete block	*Ctrl-K Y*
Hide/display block	*Ctrl-K H*
Move block	*Ctrl-K V*
Read block from disk	*Ctrl-K R*
Write block to disk	*Ctrl-K W*

Miscellaneous Commands

Abort operation	*Ctrl-U*
Autoindent on/off	*Ctrl-O I or Ctrl-Q I*
Control character prefix	*Ctrl-P*
Pair braces forward	*Ctrl-Q [*
Pair braces backward	*Ctrl-Q]*
Find	*Ctrl-Q F*
Find and replace	*Ctrl-Q A*
Find place marker	*Ctrl-Q n*
Invoke main menu	*F10*
Load file	*F3*
Exit editor, no save	*Ctrl-K D or Ctrl-K Q*
Repeat last find	*Ctrl-L*
Restore line	*Ctrl-Q L*
Save and edit	*Ctrl-K S or F2*
Set place marker	*Ctrl-K n*
Tab	*Ctrl-l or Tab*
Tab mode	*Ctrl-O T or Ctrl-Q T*
Language help	*Ctrl-F1*
Insert compiler directives	*Ctrl-F7*

Figure E.4(b) Turbo Pascal Editor commands (part 2 of 2 parts). Copyright © Borland International, Inc. 1983, 1988.

to you. (The other options relate to the debugging subsystem and are covered in Appendix G.) To execute a program, select the Run option from this submenu. The program is automatically compiled, and if there are no errors, it will be executed. In this case, the program produces two lines of output; this output is placed on a "user output screen," which is displayed momentarily before the system returns to Turbo Pascal. (You will notice the screen flicker momentarily—this signifies that the output is being produced.) In order to view the output, it is necessary to select the last option from the Run submenu–User screen. When this option is selected, the output screen is displayed and the system pauses. After reviewing your output, you return to Turbo Pascal by pressing any key.

Because you will need to perform these two actions (execute a program and view the user output screen) quite often, hot keys are provided for both operations. To execute a program, you can use Ctrl-F9; to view the user screen, you can use Alt-F5.

After successfully entering and executing a program, you will wish to secure a listing of the file on the printer (if your computer is so equipped). A simple technique is to use the command Ctrl-K P. This Editor command causes the printing of the current

```
 File     Edit     Run     Compile     Options     Debug     Break/watch
══════════════════════════════════════ Edit ═══════════════════════════
    Line 5     Col 5     Insert Indent          Unindent    A:P1A.PAS
program P1a (Output);
begin
    Writeln ('Hello');
    Writeln ('This is my first Turbo Pascal program')
end.




                              ─── Watch ───
 F1-Help  F5-Zoom  F6-Switch  F7-Trace  F8-Step  F9-Make  F10-Menu
```

Figure E.5 Program 1a in Turbo Pascal 5.0 or 5.5.

program. For a short program, this technique is acceptable; however, for a longer program, you will wish to use the program Lister. This program is provided with the Turbo Pascal system. Your instructor can provide a copy of the program for you.

To make your job a little easier, Turbo Pascal supports some "hot keys" that enable you to accomplish certain tasks by pressing one or two keys. Several of the "hot keys" supported by Turbo Pascal have already been described; some others are shown in Figure E.7. In all cases, it is necessary to press the specified keys simultaneously or press the first key and, while holding it down, press the second key.

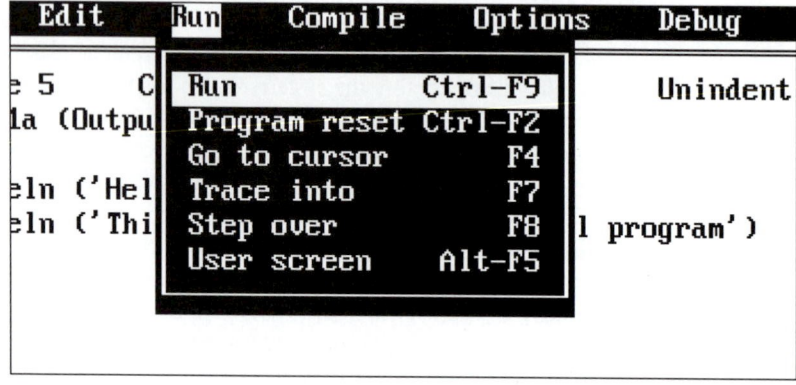

Figure E.6 Run command submenu in Turbo Pascal 5.5.

Key(s)	Function	Menu equivalent
F1	Calls up Help window with context-sensitive help	
F2	Saves the file currently in the editor	File/Save
F3	Lets you load a file (an input box will appear)	File/Load
F4	Executes to the cursor location	Run/Go to cursor
F5	Zooms and unzooms the active window	
F6	Switches the active window	
F7	Traces into subroutines	Run/Trace into
F8	Steps over subroutine calls	Run/Step over
F9	Performs a "Make"	Compile/Make
F10	Toggles between menus and active window	
Alt-F1	Calls up last Help screen you were reading	
Alt-F3	Lets you pick a file to load	File/Pick
Alt-F3	Takes you to the Execution screen	Run/User screen
Alt-F6	Switches the contents of the active window	
Alt-F9	Compiles your program	Compile/Compile
Alt-B	Takes you to the Break/Watch menu	
Alt-C	Takes you to the Compile menu	
Alt-D	Takes you to the Debug menu	
Alt-E	Puts you in the editor	
Alt-F	Takes you to the File menu	
Alt-O	Takes you to the Options menu	
Alt-R	Takes you to the Run menu	
Alt-X	Quits Turbo Pascal and takes you to DOS	File/Quit
Ctrl-F1	Gives language help while in the editor	
Ctrl-F2	Terminates a debugging session	Run/Program reset
Ctrl-F3	Displays call stack when debugging	Debug/Call stack
Ctrl-F4	Evaluates or modifies a variable	Debug/Evaluate
Ctrl-F7	Adds an expression to the Watch window	B/Add watch
Ctrl-F8	Toggles breakpoint	B/Toggle breakpoint
Ctrl-F9	Runs your program	Run/Run
Shift-F10	Displays the version screen	

Figure E.7 Turbo Pascal version 5.0/5.5 hot keys. Copyright © Borland International, Inc. 1983, 1988.

E.2   COPYING FILES

It is sometimes necessary to create different versions of a program during the debugging and testing process. For example, you may wish to keep the current version of a program and try out an alternative. Or you may wish to take an existing program and adapt it to different circumstances. In either case, what you need to do is copy an existing file into a file with a different name so that you can work on the new version of the program without disturbing a previous version.

There are three ways to accomplish this task. One way is to use the operating system's copy command. This means that you will need to leave the Pascal system momentarily, issue the appropriate command, and then reenter Turbo Pascal. The task is facilitated by using the OS shell option from the File menu. When this option is selected, a screen similar to that shown in Figure E.8 will appear. After issuing the appropriate DOS command, you then type EXIT to reenter Turbo Pascal. For example, the command to copy the file P2C.PAS, which is in the directory C02 on the disk in Drive A, onto a disk in Drive B is

        COPY A:\C02\P2C,PAS B:

If you wish to give the new file a different name, such as STU2C.PAS, the appropriate command is

        COPY A:\C02\P2C.PAS   B:STU2C.PAS

A second way to create a copy of a file is to use the Write to command from the File menu. This command will write the current file to the file whose name you specify. For example, if you wish to create a copy of the file P2C.PAS, you would first Load that file and then use the Write to command to place a copy of the file anywhere you desire. To place that copy on the disk in drive B, you could use the file name B:STU2C.PAS. The appearance of the screen would be as shown in Figure E.9.

If the computer system on which you are working does not have two disk drives, or if the second drive has a format different from the first one, the procedures just outlined will not be very useful. On a system with one disk drive, you will need to swap the disk containing the original program with another formatted disk. After you have loaded a program, remove the disk and replace it with another. Then you can simply save the file using the Save command from the File submenu (or press F2). This will save the file on the new disk without altering the name. As an alternative, you could use Write to the disk in Drive A and save a copy of the file there under a new name.

We recommend that you follow one of the procedures just outlined when you do exercises that relate to programs supplied with this text. That way, you will not change the content of the disk, and it will always be available in its original form when you want it later.

Turbo Pascal also supports a command that allows you to write blocks of text onto the disk without leaving the editor. This command is Ctrl-K W. To use it, you must first

```
Type EXIT to return to Turbo Pascal...

IBM DOS Version 5.00
            (C)Copyright International Business Machines Corp 1981-1991
            (C)Copyright Microsoft Corp 1981-1991

C:\TP5>copy A:\C02\P2C.PAS B:STU2C.PAS  ◄─────── Command to copy file
        1 file(s) copied

C:\TP5>EXIT  ◄─────── After pressing Enter, you will see Turbo Pascal reappear
```

Figure E.8 Example of using the OS shell command.

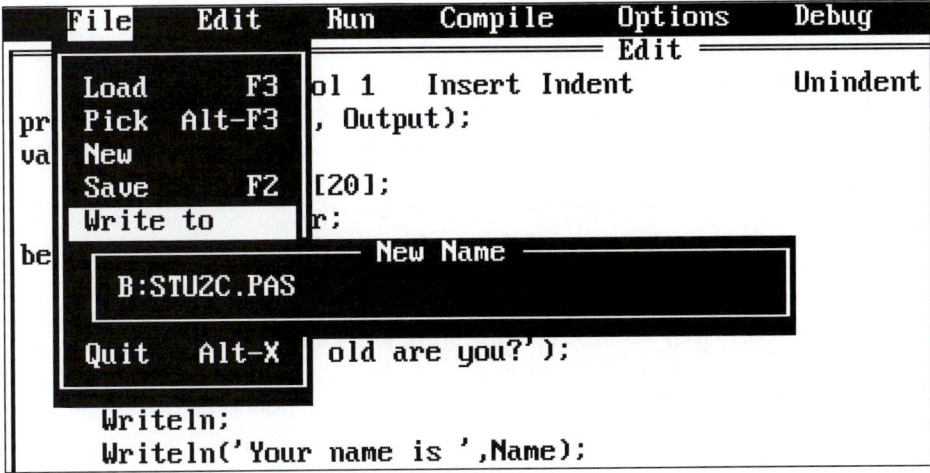

Figure E.9 Example of using the Write to command to create a copy of the current file.

mark the block of text that you wish to write. Use the following procedure:

1. Move the cursor to the beginning of the block of text. If you wish to write the entire program, move the cursor to the first character in the program.
2. Issue the command Ctrl-K B to begin a marked block.
3. Move the cursor to the end of the block to be written. If you wish to write the entire program, move the cursor to the position following the last character in the program.
4. Issue the command Ctrl-K K to mark the end of the block. The marked block will now be highlighted.
5. Issue the command Ctrl-K W to write the marked block to disk. You will be prompted for the name of the file. If you do not specify an extension, the extension .PAS will be supplied.
6. You can hide the marked block with the command Ctrl-K H.

The foregoing procedure is useful when you wish to use some portion of one program in another program. You write the part that is to be shared onto a disk file by marking it and using Ctrl-K W. Then, when you are editing another program and wish to import the code that is contained on the disk file, you use the Ctrl-K R command. You will be prompted for the name of the file to be read. The command causes the content of the file to be inserted in the program being edited, beginning at the position of the cursor.

E.3   ABOUT DIRECTORIES

Because of the number of files involved, the disk accompanying this text is organized into 15 directories corresponding to the 15 chapters in the text. The directories are named C01, C02, and so forth. All programs related to Chapter 1 are in the directory C01, all programs related to Chapter 2 are in the directory C02, etc.

In order to modify or execute one to these programs, you will need to use the Change dir command from the File submenu, as shown in Figure E.10. In the dialog box that appears when the Change dir command is issued, you will see the current path (which is composed of the drive designator followed by the directory name). Depending on how Turbo Pascal is installed in your system, the default path may be

```
C:\TURBO5
```

which indicates that the current directory is TURBO5 on drive C. To change this directory, you first press the Backspace key to erase the content of the dialog box and then type the new path as shown in Figure E.10. When you finish, you press Enter and the dialog box disappears. (Unfortunately, there is no indication on the screen of what the current default path is.)

Next, you use the Load command from the File submenu to load a file from the new directory. After selecting this command, a dialog box appears, as shown in Figure E.11. If you know the name of the file to be loaded, you press the Backspace key and type the file name. If you do not know the name of the file, you use the content of the dialog box as a mask to govern which files will be displayed in the directory that will follow. The default content of the box is

```
*.PAS
```

which indicates that all files with the extension .PAS are to be displayed. (The * is called a wild card and will match any sequence of characters in a file name. If you wished to look at all files in the directory, you could use the mask *.*, which would match any file name with any extension.)

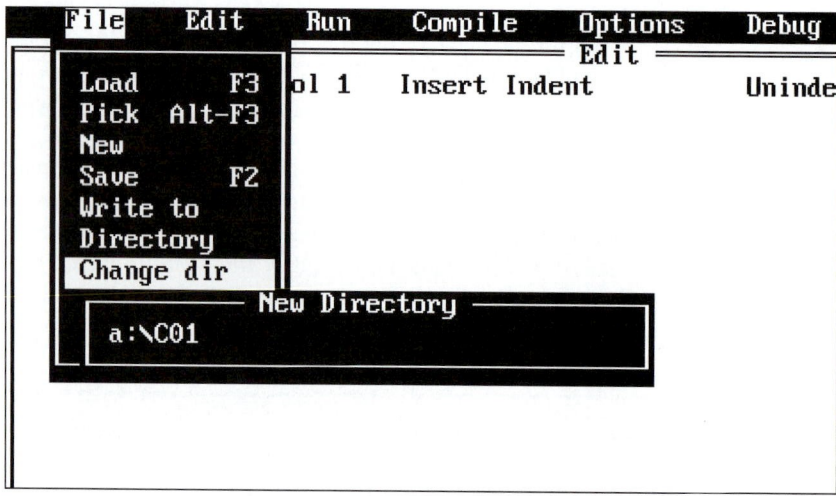

Figure E.10 Using the Change dir command to make A:\C01 the current directory.

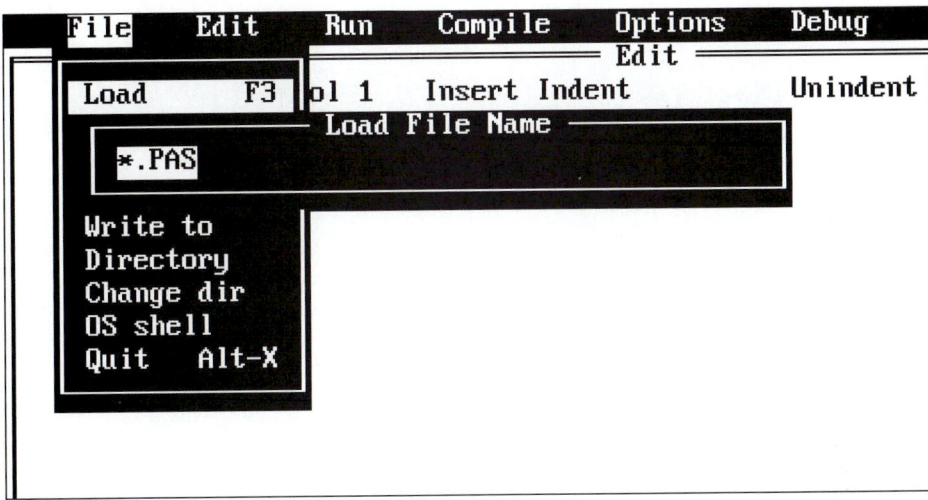

Figure E.11 Using the Load command to select among all files with the .PAS extension in the current directory.

When you press Enter with a mask in the dialog box, a directory such as that shown in Figure E.12 is displayed. You can now select the desired file by highlighting the file name. You do this by pressing the arrow key to move the selection bar. When you press Enter again, the file that is currently selected will be loaded.

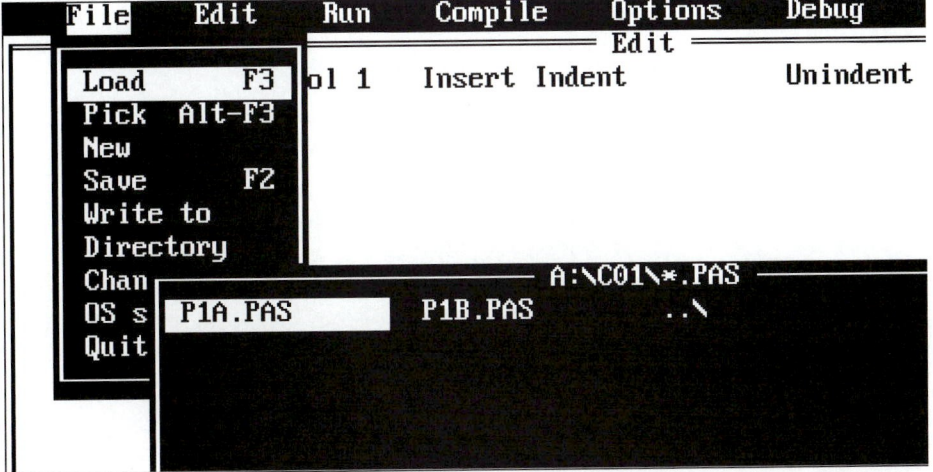

Figure E.12 Selecting among files in the current directory.

Appendix F

Miscellaneous Turbo Pascal Features

F.1   ADDITIONAL DATA TYPES

Turbo Pascal supports a variety of data types that are compatible with the standard data type Integer. A detailed list of these is shown in Figure F.1. All these types are operation and assignment compatible. When an arithmetic operation is performed, both values are converted to a common type before the operation is performed. The common type is a type that is sufficient to store all possible values of both types. For example, data-type Byte can store values in the range 0 to 255 and data-type Integer can store values in the range −32,768 to +32,767. The common type for Byte and Integer is therefore Integer—the smallest type sufficient to handle the entire range of both Byte and Integer. (Turbo Pascal chooses the data type with the shortest possible length as the common type in order to conserve space.)

One option that is available on IBM PC computers and compatibles is a numeric coprocessor (Intel 80x87, where x denotes a one-digit integer). In machines without this feature, floating-point operations (Real data-type operations) are performed through software routines. Because of the complexity of these operations (the routines often contain a fairly large number of machine instructions), they can have a considerable adverse affect on the speed of execution of a program that involves numerous floating-point arithmetic operations. The numeric coprocessor is capable of performing these operations by special circuits designed for the task, thereby making a significant improvement in execution speed for many programs. Turbo Pascal provides you several data types, as shown in Figure F.2, that are compatible with Real data, but are specifically designed for use in machines with a numeric coprocessor. In order to use these data types, you must

1. Compile and execute the program on a machine with a numeric coprocessor installed.
2. Use the compiler directive {$N+} in your program. This directive informs the compiler that it should recognize the additional Real data types and generate code appropriately. (The default setting for the N directive is {$N−}, which means that only Real data type is valid, and floating-point operations are to implemented via software.)

Type	Minimum	Maximum	Length	Signed	Standard
Integer	−32,768	32,767	16 bits	Yes	Yes
Byte	0	255	8 bits	No	No
Shortint	−128	127	8 bits	Yes	No
Word	0	65,535	16 bits	No	No
Longint	−2,147,483,648	2,147,483,647	32 bits	Yes	No

Figure F.1 Turbo Pascal data types compatible with Integer. Source: *Turbo Pascal Version 7.0 Language Guide.* Copyright © Borland International, Inc. 1983, 1992.

Type	Minimum	Maximum	Significant digits	Length	Makes use of numeric coprocessor
Real	$\pm 2.9 \times 10^{-39}$	$\pm 1.7 \times 10^{38}$	11–12	6 bytes	No
Single	$\pm 1.5 \times 10^{-45}$	$\pm 3.4 \times 10^{38}$	7–8	4 bytes	Yes
Double	$\pm 5.0 \times 10^{-324}$	$\pm 1.7 \times 10^{308}$	15–16	8 bytes	Yes
Extended	$\pm 3.4 \times 10^{-4932}$	$\pm 1.1 \times 10^{4932}$	19–20	10 bytes	Yes
Comp	$-2^{63} + 1$	$2^{63}-1$	19–20	8 bytes	Yes

Figure F.2 Summary of data types compatible with Real. Source: *Turbo Pascal Version 7.0 Language Guide.* Copyright © Borland International, Inc. 1983, 1992.

F.2   SHORT-CIRCUIT EVALUATION OF BOOLEAN EXPRESSIONS

Beginning with Version 4.0, Turbo Pascal introduced an interesting compiler option designed to speed the execution of programs. This feature is implemented through the B compiler option. When this option is positive {$B+}, the evaluation of Boolean expressions is completed in the mathematically "correct" fashion; that is, all parts of the expression are evaluated before assigning a value to the whole expression. When the option is negative {$B−} (which is the default setting), parts of Boolean expressions are evaluated only to the extent necessary to determine the value of the whole expression. This means that some parts of the expression may not be evaluated, thereby saving time during execution of the program.

An example will help you understand how this *short-circuit* method works. Suppose variable A has the value 2 and variable B has the value 0. Consider the Boolean expression

```
(A < 3) or (B = 1)
```

We know that any expression of the form *x* or *y* is true when either *x* or *y* or both are true. In this example, of the relation (A < 3) is true, and therefore, the whole expression is true, regardless of the value of the other part of the expression. Thus, it is unnecessary to evaluate the expression (B = 1) to determine that the whole expression is True. If the B compiler directive is positive, both parts of the expression will be evaluated before determining that the expression is True. It should be noted that if the first part of the expression had been False, it would still have been necessary for the system to evaluate the other part of the expression to determine the value of the entire expression. Thus, the short-circuit option saves execution time in the some instances, but not in all. It should be used with great care, since it is not a standard Pascal feature can cause programs that execute correctly in the Turbo environment to fail in another environment.

F.3 FORWARD REFERENCES

There will be times when it would be convenient or even logically necessary to be able to bypass the usual Pascal rule that specifies that an identifier must be declared before it can be referenced. For example, if you encounter a situation in which procedure X requires access to procedure Y and procedure Y requires access to procedure X, which should be declared first? If you declare X first, then the reference to Y in the statement part of X will be invalid because Y has not yet been defined; you run into a similar problem if you declare Y first. Pascal provides a solution to your problem by enabling you to declare procedures (and functions) as *forward*—that is, you specify that the actual declaration of the procedure will occur later in the program; in the meantime, references to the identifier for the procedure will be valid.

A **forward reference** is specified by writing the procedure header as usual and then writing the reserved word *forward*, as shown in the following general syntax:

```
procedure procedure-name (formal-parameter-section); forward;
```

Later in the program, the specified procedure is declared as usual, except that the procedure header is abbreviated by omitting the *formal-parameter-section*:

```
procedure procedure-name;
```

This header is followed by the usual procedure definition—declarations of constants, variables, other procedures, and statements.

For example, consider the following two program segments:

SEGMENT 1 (WITH FORWARD REFERENCE)

```
procedure X (A : Integer; var B : Char) ; forward;
procedure Y (C : Integer);
begin {Y}
   .
   .
   .
end; {Y}
procedure X;
begin {X}
   .
   .
   .
end; {X}
```

SEGMENT 2 (WITHOUT FORWARD REFERENCE)

```
procedure X (A : Integer; var B : Char);
begin {X}
```

```
        .
        .
        .
 end;  {X}
 procedure Y (C : Integer);
 begin  {Y}
        .
        .
        .
 end;  {Y}
```

If procedure X makes no reference to procedure to procedure Y, then the code in segment 2 is to be preferred. On the other hand, if procedure X makes a reference to procedure Y, then the code in segment 2 will not compile. You could either place the code for procedure Y in front of the code for procedure X or use the alternative shown as segment 1. In the unusual situation mentioned earlier (when X needs to refer to Y and Y needs to refer to X), then the only alternative is to use the forward reference, as shown in segment 1.

An example of forward references in the context of an actual program is shown in Figure F.3. The code is taken from Program 5d, which is shown in Figure 5.15. In this case, procedures ValidateMonth and ValidateDay have been declared as forward references and placed after the declaration of procedure ComputeJulianDate, which, of course, invokes both of them. The function of the program is not affected in any way by the use of forward references.

Insofar as the compiler is concerned, a forward reference causes information about the identifier for the procedure to be placed at the appropriate location in the symbol table. This makes it possible for the program units to refer to the identifier. When the actual procedure is declared, the compiler returns to the proper place in the symbol table to begin adding identifiers that may be declared as part of that procedure.

```
program PFa (Input, Output);
{Program to compute the difference between two dates  in the
     same year; this version illustrates forward  references}
     .
     .
     .
    procedure ValidateMonth (Month : Integer;
                          var ValidMonth : Boolean); forward;
{-----------------------------------------------------------------------}
    procedure ValidateDay (Month, Day : Integer;
                          var ValidDay : Boolean); forward;
{-----------------------------------------------------------------------}
    procedure ComputeJulianDate (CalendarMonth,
                                    CalendarDay : Integer;
                             var ValidDate  : Boolean;
                             var JulianDate  : Integer);
    {Procedure to compute the Julian Date}
    begin    {ComputeJulianDate}
         ValidateMonth (CalendarMonth, ValidDate);
         if ValidDate then
             ValidateDay (CalendarMonth, CalendarDay, ValidDate);
         if ValidDate then
            begin

               .
               .
               .
            end   {if}
    end;   {ComputeJulianDate}
{-----------------------------------------------------------------------}
    procedure ValidateMonth;
    {Procedure to determine if a Month is valid}
    begin    {ValidateMonth}
         ValidMonth := (Month >= 1) and (Month <= 12);
         if not ValidMonth then
             Writeln ('Invalid Month Number : ', Month)
    end;     {ValidateMonth}
{-----------------------------------------------------------------------}
    procedure ValidateDay;
    {Procedure to validate day of a month}
    var
         NumberDays : Integer;
    begin   {ValidateDay}
         case Month of
              2                   : NumberDays := 28;
              4,6,9,11            : NumberDays := 30;
              1,3,5,7,8,10,12  : NumberDays := 31
         end;     {case}
         ValidDay := (Day >= 1) and (Day <= NumberDays);
         if not ValidDay then
             Writeln ('Invalid Day Number : ', Day)
    end;   {ValidateDay}
     .
     .
     .
end.   {Main Program}
```

Figure F.3 Program Fa: Example of forward references.

Appendix G

Turbo Pascal Version 7.0 Debugging Facility

Beginning with Version 5.0, an integrated debugging facility was incorporated into Turbo Pascal. This appendix will introduce some of the most important and most useful features of this facility, as implemented in Version 7.0. For complete details, the reader is referred to the Turbo Pascal reference manuals.

There are two major components to the debugging facility:

1. *Execution path analysis:* the ability to follow the sequence of statements being executed. This is provided by the Step and Trace commands and the ability to set break points.
2. *Diagnostic output:* the ability to observe the values of variables and expressions during the execution of a program. This is provided through the Watch and Evaluation windows and related commands.

In early versions of Turbo Pascal, the user was forced to add output statements to a program to perform execution path analysis or to generate diagnostic output. Techniques for debugging using programmer-written statements are covered in the sections of this text labeled "Program Debugging and Testing." The major disadvantage of this approach is the time involved in coding the necessary statements and then removing them after the debugging analysis is complete. The interactive debugging facility makes programmer-written output statements obsolete, thereby greatly facilitating the program debugging and testing process.

G.1   TRACE INTO AND STEP OVER

Often, it is advantageous to be able to know the precise sequence in which the statements of a program are being executed. This ability is provided in the debugging facility by the Trace into and Step over commands. When you use these commands, the text of the program is displayed on the screen, and a highlighted bar (called an *execution bar*) is displayed over the lines of the program as the program statements are executed one at a time. After execution of one statement, the system advances the execution bar to the next line in the program and waits for you to issue the next Trace into or Step over command. Trace into and Step over serve similar purposes, but the two commands differ in one very important respect: Trace into will follow the execution of a procedure call (or function invocation) into the body of the procedure (or function), whereas Step over will not. That is, if the execution bar highlights a statement that invokes a procedure, and if you issue the Trace into command, the execution bar will next highlight the statement at the beginning of the procedure. In the same situation, if you issue the Step over command, the designated procedure will be executed, and the execution bar will advance to the next line in the program. *Note:* The Trace into command will follow only procedures and functions for which the source code is available to the editor. Trace into will not follow system-supplied procedures or functions, such as Readln or Writeln.

There are two techniques of issuing the Trace into and Step over commands. They can be issued by selecting the appropriate command from the Run submenu, as shown in

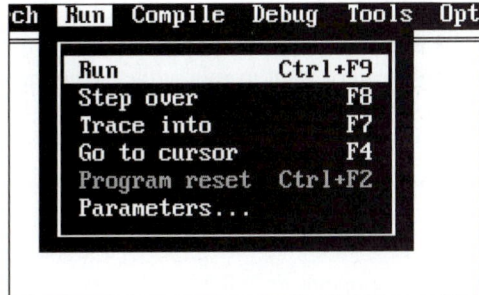

Figure G.1 The Run submenu.

Figure G.1, or they can be issued by using the equivalent function keys—F7 for Trace into and F8 for Step over.

The simplest way to examine the execution path of a program is to issue either the Trace into or Step over command to begin execution of the program. (If the program has been changed since it was last compiled, the system will automatically compile the program before execution begins.) Since the first statement to be executed is the begin statement in the Main Program, the line containing this statement will be the first one highlighted with the execution bar. When you then issue either the Trace into or Step over command, the system will advance one line at at a time through the program. If a Readln statement is executed, the user screen is displayed, and you will have to enter appropriate data in order to complete the execution of that statement and be able to proceed to the next statement in the program. This process can be repeated as long as desired or until the end of the Main Program is reached. If you desire to terminate the process early, you can use the command Program reset from the Run submenu (or use the hot key equivalent, Ctrl-F2). This command terminates the execution of the program, removes the execution bar, and returns you to the editor.

G.1.1   Time Out

1. Load any program with which you are familiar. (Program 3m is used in this appendix for illustrative purposes, but you can use any program that you want.) Now press F7, or select Trace into from the Run submenu. Observe the execution bar. Continue pressing F7 and observe the results. If you don't want to continue until the end of the program, select Program reset from the Run submenu or press Ctrl-F2.

2. To observe the difference between Trace into and Step over, you will need to work with a program that has at least one procedure or function. Program 3m has a simple procedure (ComputePayment), so it is a good one to use for this exercise, but any program containing at least one procedure will do. Load the program, and press F8 or select Step over from the Run submenu. Then continue pressing F8 and observe the result. Note that when the statement in the Main Program that executes a procedure is executed by the Step over command, the next statement to be selected by the execution bar is the next statement in the Main Program—not the first statement in the procedure.

3. Using the same program that you used in Exercise 2, experiment with using the Trace into and Step over commands alternately. You will observe a difference between the

commands only when the statement to be executed invokes a procedure or function. If you want to follow the execution path of that procedure or function, you select the Trace into command; if you don't want to follow the execution path of the procedure or function, use the Step over command.

G.2   BREAKPOINTS

The Step over and Trace into commands described in the preceding section can be used to examine the execution path of an entire program; however, for a very long program, this technique will prove to be very tedious. When debugging a program, the programmer usually has a fairly good idea of where in the program the problem is most likely to be. It would be very desirable to be able to execute the program in its normal automatic mode until the part of the program that is suspect is reached. At that time, the step-by-step execution could begin. This is exactly the facility provided by establishing breakpoints in a program.

A breakpoint is a program statement at which automatic execution of a program halts. The Turbo Pascal debugging facility provides two ways to create breakpoints in programs:

1. You can place the cursor at the point at which you desire execution to halt and use the Go to cursor command from the Run submenu (or the hot key equivalent, F4). Execution will halt at the line marked by the cursor.
2. You can mark a line as a breakpoint using the Add breakpoint command from the Debug submenu, as shown in Figure G.2, and then use the Run command from the Run submenu. When the breakpoint is reached during program execution, the program will halt.

Let us examine each of these alternatives in more detail. Using the cursor to mark the breakpoint is probably the easiest way to begin debugging a program at a point other than the beginning of the program. Simply move the cursor to the line at which you wish

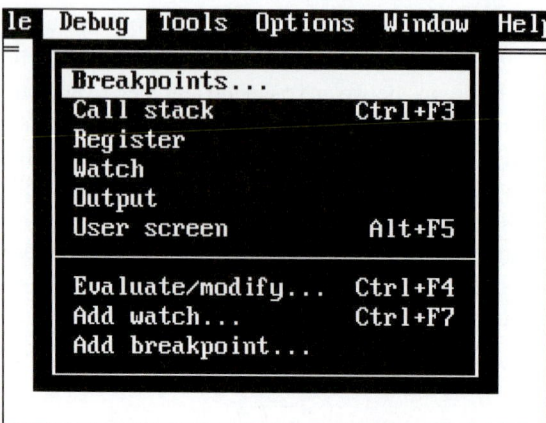

Figure G.2 The Debug submenu.

execution to halt. Then choose Go to cursor from the Run submenu (or press F4). Program execution will proceed in automatic mode until the line marked by the cursor is reached. At that point, execution will halt, the execution bar will highlight the designated line, and you can then use the Step over and Trace into commands as desired to execute the program one line at at time. Two other alternatives that may be useful are to use the Run command from the Run submenu to continue execution in the ordinary way and to move the cursor to another point in the program and use the Go to cursor command to continue execution of the program until the new line marked by the cursor is reached.

The trouble with using the cursor to mark the point at which execution is to halt is that there can be only one breakpoint at a time, and you must reset it every time you want to run the program for debugging. To solve these problems, Turbo Pascal allows you to set formally marked breakpoints using commands from the Debug submenu. To establish a marked breakpoint, you move the cursor to the desired line and issue the Add breakpoint command from the Debug submenu. The breakpoint line will be highlighted in the program. You can establish as many such lines as may be desired by repeating the procedure just described. Now when you use the Run command from the Run submenu, execution will proceed automatically until the first breakpoint is encountered, at which time execution will halt. The execution bar will be placed over the breakpoint line, and you can execute statements one at a time (using Trace into or Step over), or you can use the Run command to continue automatically until the next program statement marked as a breakpoint is encountered.

The Breakpoints command from the Debug submenu opens the window shown in Figure G.3. The Breakpoint list shows the line number of all breakpoints. The buttons in this window allow you to add or delete breakpoints as desired.

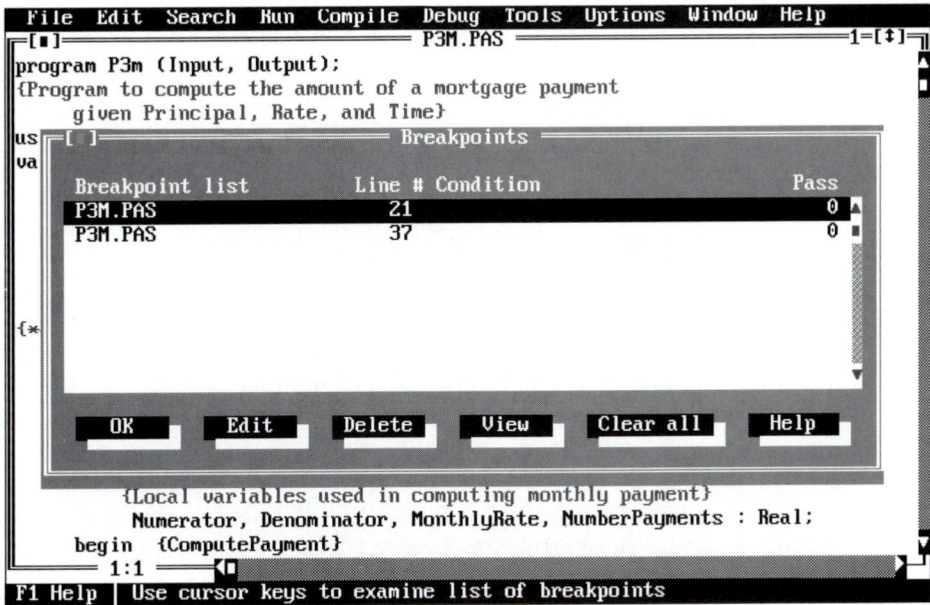

Figure G.3 The breakpoints window.

G.2.1   Time Out

1. Load a program with which you are familiar. Set the cursor somewhere in the statement part of the program, and issue the Go to cursor command. Observe the results. If the program did not halt at the desired point, it means that that statement was not executed. Try the exercise again by marking a different line.

2. Load a program with which you are familiar. Set a breakpoint. (Move the cursor to the desired line, and use Add breakpoint. Observe the highlighting used to mark the breakpoint. Now issue the Run command, and observe that execution will halt when the marked line is reached. Try setting other breakpoints and continuing execution. Try using the View button from the Breakpoints window to examine the breakpoints you have set up. When you are finished, use the Clear breakpoints command to remove the breakpoints. Remember to use the Program reset command if your debugging session did not continue to the the the end of the program.

G.3   THE WATCH WINDOW

With the Watch command from the Debug submenu, you can create a window (labeled "Watches" and sometimes referred to as a "Watch window") in which the values of variables will be displayed during the execution of the program. Using this facility makes it unnecessary for you to add diagnostic output to your program.

When you issue the Watch command, a window such as that shown in Figure G.4 is displayed. To add a variable to the watch window select the Add command (or press the Ins key). This command opens an Add Watch window, shown in Figure G.5. You can type the name of the variable you wish to examine in the Watch expression window. In the example shown in the figure, the variable Numerator has been added to the list of variables being "watched."

Figure G.4 shows the result of adding the variable Numerator to the Watch window during the execution of Program 3m. This variable is defined in the procedure ComputePayment so its value is displayed as "Unknown identifier." When the execution of the program proceeds into ComputePayment, the current value of the variable will be displayed in the Watch window.

You can add variables to the Watch window at any time during the execution of a program by repeating the steps just outlined. For example, Figure G.6 shows a Watch window listing five variables. The execution bar is on a statement in the procedure ComputePayment, so the values of all of the variables are defined and displayed in the window. The last item entered in the Watch window is highlighted and marked with a small bullet. The content of the Watch window can be controlled by using the commands from the Watch window (see Figure G.4). The Delete command will delete the highlighted item from the Watch window; Edit will allow you to modify the content of the window, and clicking on the Close button (upper left-hand corner of the box) will delete all items from the watch list.

```
  File  Edit  Search  Run  Compile  Debug  Tools  Options  Window  Help
 ┌──────────────────────────── P3M.PAS ──────────────────────────────1─┐
 │program P3m (Input, Output);                                          │
 │{Program to compute the amount of a mortgage payment                  │
 │      given Principal, Rate, and Time}                                │
 │uses Crt;                                                             │
 │var                                                                   │
 │      Principal, Rate : Real;            {Input variables}            │
 │      Time            : Integer;                                      │
 │      First, Last     : string[10];                                   │
 │      MiddleInitial   : Char;                                         │
 │      Payment         : Real;            {Output variable}            │
 │                                                                      │
 │{*********************************************************************}│
 │                                                                      │
 │      procedure ComputePayment;                                       │
 │      {Procedure to compute payment given Principal, Rate, and Time}  │
 ┌─[■]─────────────────────────── Watches ───────────────────────2=[↑]─┐
 │Numerator: Unknown identifier                                         │
 │                                                                      │
 │                                                                      │
 │                                                                      │
 │                                                                      │
 │                                                                      │
 └◄──────────────────────────────────────────────────────────────────►─┘
  F1 Help  F7 Trace  F8 Step  ← Edit  Ins Add  Del Delete  Alt+F10 Local menu
```

Figure G.4 The Watch window.

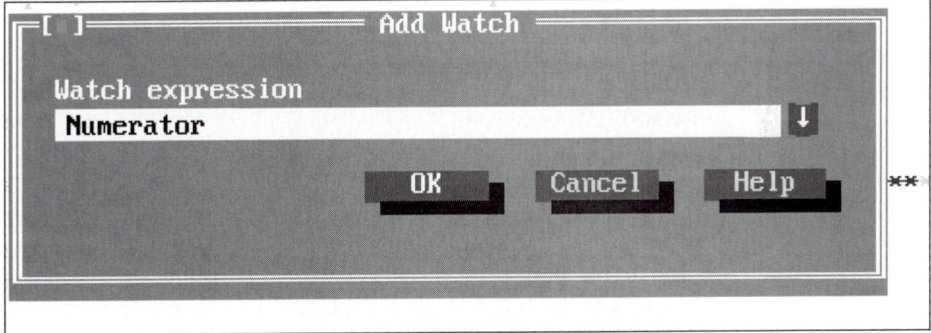

Figure G.5 The Add Watch window.

```
 ┌─[■]─────────────────────────── Watches ───────────────────────2=[↑]─┐
 │Numerator: 0.0072580751136                                           │
 │Time: 2                                                              │
 │Principal: 2000.0                                                    │
 │Denominator: 0.16129201817                                          │
 │Rate: 0.075                                                          │
 └◄──────────────────────────────────────────────────────────────────►─┘
  F1 Help  F7 Trace  F8 Step  ← Edit  Ins Add  Del Delete  Alt+F10 Local menu
```

Figure G.6 Example of multiple variables in a Watch window.

G.3.3   *Time Out*

Load any program of you choice. Select several variables and add them to the Watch window. Use Step over and/or Trace into to execute the program one statement at a time. Observe the content of the Watch window. When you are finished, use the Close button to remove the Watch window. Remember to use Program reset if you do not execute the program to its end.

G.4   EVALUATE/MODIFY

The Watch window is a very powerful tool, but it has two limitations:

1. The variables are displayed continuously during the execution of the program, whether or not you want them so displayed.

2. The content of the variables displayed in the Watch window cannot be changed by the programmer during the debugging session. (Changing their content can be very helpful at times.)

Both of these limitations are overcome when you use Evaluate/modify. This facility will let you display the content of variables that you select in the same way that you display variables in the Watch window, but the Evaluate and Modify window is not displayed continuously. (When you are finished, you can close the window.) However, the most significant difference between Watch and Evaluate/modify is that, by using Evaluate/modify, you can change the actual value of the variable during the execution of the program; the new value that you enter will replace the former value and will be used thereafter during the program's execution.

To use the facility, select Evaluate/modify from the Debug submenu (see Figure G.2), or use the hot key equivalent, Ctrl-F4. This will open an Evaluate and Modify window, shown in Figure G.7. in this example, Program 3m is being executed. We have entered the variable Payment in the Expression box. At this point, the current value of Expression will be displayed in the Result box. We have chosen to change the value of the variable Payment by typing the new value (100) in the the New value box. This becomes the new value of Payment and hence is also displayed in the Result box. When you close the Evaluate and Modify window (click on the close button or the Cancel button), the new value will continue as the value of Payment. You can verify this by examining the output produced by the program, shown in Figure G.8. Of course, the value of Payment is incorrect for the data entered by the user of the program. This points out a potential problem when using the Evaluate/modify facility: It allows the program to appear to produce incorrect results. The facility is useful primarily to test hypotheses about program bugs. That is, if you suspect that a program bug can be attributed to a mistake in the value of a particular variable, you can make

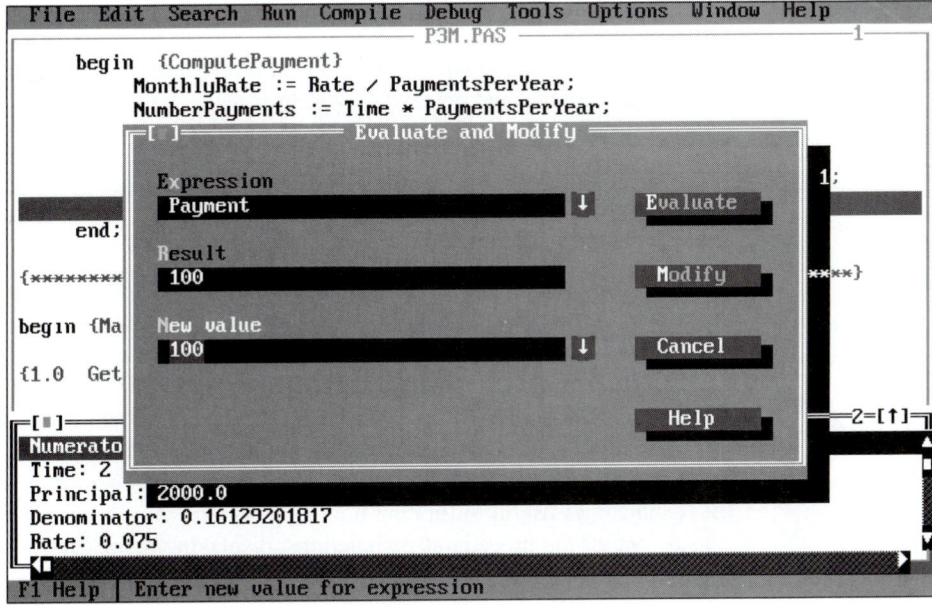

Figure G.7 Example of an Evaluate and Modify window.

the appropriate change in the value of the suspect variable during the debugging process and observe the results. If this change appears to solve the problem, then you should make the change in the program itself and test the program again.

```
Enter First Name Joe
Enter Middle Initial A
Enter Last Name Jones
Enter Loan Amount 2000
Enter Yearly Interest Rate in form 0.dddd .075
Enter Term of Loan in Years 2

Mortgage computation for Joe A. Jones
Principal =      2000.00
     Rate =         7.50%
    Years =            2
  Payment =       100.00
Press <Enter> to continue
```

Figure G.8 Sample output from Program 3m after using Evaluate/modify to change the value of the variable Payment. Note: the value of Payment is not correctly computed because of this action.

G.4.1 Time Out

Try out the Evaluate/modify command on a program of your choice. Try changing the value of a variable, and observe the results.

G.5 CALL STACK

One command from the Debug submenu that can be useful for tracing the execution path of a program is Call stack. This command causes the display of the current state of the execution stack of the program. When a program begins execution, the only entry on this stack is the name of the program itself. When a procedure or function is invoked, the name of that procedure or function is placed at the top of the stack. When a procedure or function terminates execution, its name is removed from the stack. When a program has numerous procedures and/or functions, and particularly when there is a degree of nesting, it is sometimes useful to find out how the program got to a certain point in its execution inside one of the procedures or functions; displaying the execution stack can reveal this information.

You can invoke Call stack from the Debug submenu or by using Ctrl-F3, which is the hot key equivalent. The command is available during a debugging session if the execution bar is highlighting a statement inside a procedure or function. For example, consider a debugging session for Program 3m. If we are currently executing a statement in the procedure ComputePayment and issue the Call stack command, the resulting screen is as shown in Figure G.9. The Call stack window indicates that the current procedure is ComputePayment—the procedure listed first—and that this procedure was called from the main program, P3m.

The Call stack command can be of great use in debugging programs that use recursion, such as Program 8f. This program includes a function, Factorial, that invokes itself. The value of the argument of the function is reduced by 1 each time it is invoked, until the argument is equal to 1. If the initial value for the argument is 5, the function is invoked five times with arguments 5, 4, 3, 2, and 1 in that sequence. Each time the function is invoked, the function (and its parameters) are added to the stack. Figure G.10 shows the state of the stack after the fifth invocation of the function Factorial. Note that the Call

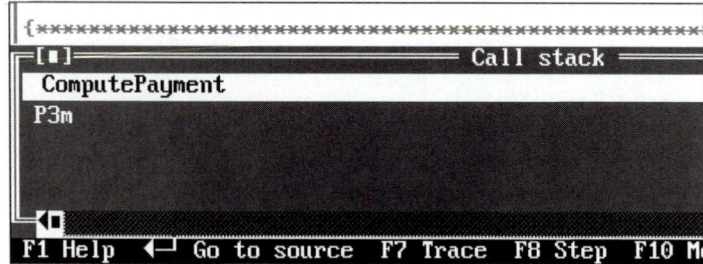

Figure G.9 Call stack window during execution of the procedure Compute-Payment in Program 3m.

stack window also displays the value of the parameter for the function—a very useful feature when you trace the execution path of a program that involves recursion.

G.5.1   Time Out

Load any program of your choice that includes one or more procedures or functions. Program 3m can be used if desired. Set a breakpoint in one of the procedures or functions. Use the Run command from the Run submenu to execute the program. When the program halts, select the Call stack command from the Windows submenu. Observe the content of the Call stack window.

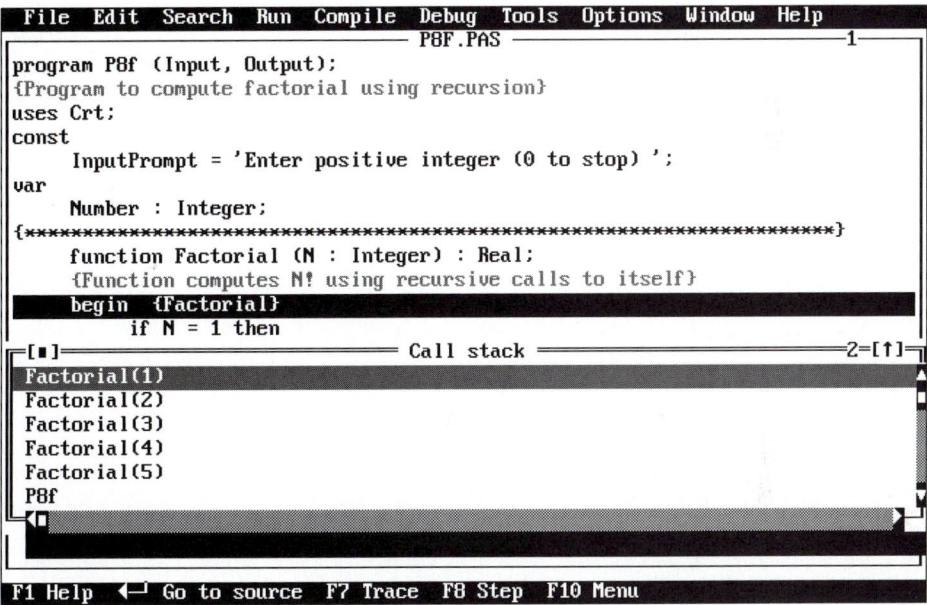

Figure G.10   Use of Call stack during the recursive execution of the function Factorial in Program 8f.

Appendix H

System-Related Exercises

This appendix contains a series of programming exercises that are related to specific systems typical of those found in business and other application areas. A brief description of each system is followed by programming exercises appropriate to each chapter of the text (beginning with Chapter 2).

H.1   INVENTORY SYSTEM

One type of system that is often required by businesses that manufacture or sell products is an inventory system. The purpose of such systems is to track the number of each item that is in stock and to provide related accounting information.

We will assume that you have been employed as a programmer at AAA Distributors, Inc. This company is a wholesaler of hardware products such as nails, screws, tools, pipe fittings, electrical supplies, and so forth—items that are typically found in local retail hardware stores. As you tackle each programming exercise, you will be building components of an inventory control system for the company.

H.1.1   Programming Exercises

Each of the following exercise numbers corresponds to the chapter for which the exercise is appropriate.

2. Write a program to allow the user to enter the following data about an inventory item:
   - Inventory number (five-digit numeric field)
   - Item description (up to 255 characters)
   - Number on hand
   - Number on order
   - Minimum order quantity
   - Vendor identification (five characters)
   - Date of order (month, day, and year)
   - Item cost (cost from manufacturer)
   - Item price (wholesale price to the retailer)

   The program should print the data in an appropriate format on screen (and on the printer if desired). The program should also compute and print the extended cost of the item (number on hand × item cost), the extended price (number on hand × item price), and the profit potential (difference between price and extended cost).

3. Modify the program you wrote for exercise 2 in the following ways:
   - The program should read its data from a file, with the user entering the name of the file interactively.
   - Format the output appropriately.
   - Create a separate procedure to perform the required computations.

   Use the Pascal editor to create sample files for use in testing this program.

4. Management needs to know how many items to order and when to order them. Generally, when the number on hand of a given item drops below the order quantity, it is time to order the item (if there is no outstanding order for this item). Write a program to process the file(s) described in exercise 3 to advise the user when to order items. Specifically, if the number on hand is less than the order quantity, and the number on order is zero, then print the inventory number, item description, number on hand, and minimum order quantity; otherwise print the inventory number, the item description, and a message indicating that no order is needed.

5. Using the data described in exercise 2, write a program to suggest changes in item pricing to management. The company would like to have a profit margin of at least 20%, but no more than 30%. If the difference between the item cost and the item price does not meet that criterion, the suggested price should be 120% of the item cost. If the difference between the item cost and the item price does meet that criterion, then no change in pricing is required. Structure your program, using procedures with parameters where appropriate.

6. **a.** Modify the program you wrote for exercise 5 to process data about multiple inventory items from the file. Create an appropriate Text file containing multiple series of data to test your program. (Hereafter, we will refer to this file as the AAA Inventory File.)

   b. Add summary output to the program you wrote for part a. Compute and print the following information:

   - Number of inventory items in the file
   - Number of items priced too low
   - Number of items priced too high
   - Total extended cost of all items
   - Total extended price of all items
   - Gross profit potential

7. Write a program to alert management when suppliers are not delivering goods in a timely manner. For each item in the AAA Inventory File that is on order, compute how long (in days) it has been since the order was placed. If the order is more than 60 days old, write a message alerting the user that there is a possible problem. You may wish to adapt the procedures for the computation of the Julian date found in Program 7a for use in this program. For purposes of this exercise, assume that the order date is in the current year.

8. **a.** Modify the program you wrote for exercise 7 to use a function to compute the required Julian date. Note that the same function can be used to compute the Julian date of the current date and the order date.

   b. The computation of the Julian date used in Chapter 7 takes into account only the day and month. When comparing dates in the same year, you will find that this is sufficient. However, in this application, it is likely that the current year may differ from the year in the order date. Modify the program you wrote for part a to take this difference into account.

9. **a.** Management would like to know how many items in its inventory fall into the following categories:

   - not on order
   - age of order $<= 10$
   - $10 <$ age of order $<= 20$
   - $20 <$ age of order $<= 30$
   - $30 <$ age of order $<= 40$
   - $40 <$ age of order $<= 50$
   - $50 <$ age of order $<= 60$
   - age of order > 60

   Modify the program you wrote for exercise 8 to include this report. Use an array to compute the required frequency distribution.

   b. Add a bar graph (horizontal or vertical) to the program you wrote for part a.

10. **a.** Write a program to transform the AAA Inventory File into a binary file. Modify the program you wrote for exercise 9 above to process the new file.

  b. Write a program to allow the user to extend the binary file created by the program you wrote for part a.

11. A second file (AAA Supplier Master File) is available to store information about suppliers of inventory items. For each supplier, the following data items are available:

- Supplier identifier (five characters)

- Supplier name

- Address (street, city, state, zip code)

Modify the program you wrote for exercise 4 to print the supplier's name and address for any items that need to be ordered. (*Hint:* Load the Supplier Master File into a table, sort it, and then use an appropriate search technique to look up the required information.)

12. Modify the program that you wrote for exercise 11 to load the Supplier Master File data into a binary search tree. Modify your search technique accordingly.

13. Using the graphics support provided by Turbo Pascal, modify the program you wrote for exercise 9b to produce a bar graph.

14. Using Unit P14c, write a program to perform statistical analysis of the data in the AAA Inventory File. Specifically, find the average number on hand of an item and the maximum time the item has been on order.

15. Create an ADT for the binary search tree. Modify the program you wrote for exercise 12 to make use of this ADT.

H.2 WEATHER SYSTEM

In this section, we will describe a system that stores and analyzes weather data. Similar (but more complex) systems are used by the National Weather Service and other organizations concerned about weather and climate.

We will assume that you have been hired as a programmer by the Climate Research Institute, a research organization under the auspices of a local university. As you carry out each programming exercise, you will be contributing to an overall system designed to understand fluctuations in weather and climate.

H.2.1 Programming Exercises

Each of the following exercise numbers corresponds to the chapter for which the exercise is appropriate.

2. Write a program to allow the user to enter the following data, which represent one observation at a particular weather station:

- Station identifier (5 characters)

- Name of person making report (20 characters)

- Date (month, day, and year)

- Time (assume a 24-hour clock; valid values are 600, 1200, 1800, 2400)

- Temperature (in degrees Fahrenheit)
- Humidity (in the range 0 to 100)
- Barometric pressure (in inches of mercury)
- Wind speed (in mph)
- Wind direction (as a compass point, e.g., N, NW, ESE)
- Six-hour rainfall amount (in inches)
- Six-hour snowfall amount (in inches)

The program should print the data in an appropriate format on screen (and on the printer if desired). The program should convert the Fahrenheit temperature to Celsius and display both temperatures. Recall that $C = 5/9 \, (F - 32)$. Also, compute the total precipitation assuming that one inch of snow is equivalent to .25 inch of rain.

3. Modify the program you wrote for exercise 2 in the following ways:

- The program should read its data from a file, with the user entering the name of the file interactively.
- Format the output appropriately.
- Create a separate procedure to perform the required computations.

Use the Pascal editor to create sample files for use in testing this program.

4. Write a program to validate the time and date in the file(s) you created for exercise 3. Valid times are 600, 1200, and 1400. In the date, the month must be in the range 1 to 12, and the day must be in the range 1 to 31. Display any items that contain invalid data with appropriate messages.

5. Modify the program you wrote for exercise 4 to make use of procedures with parameter lists where appropriate. Incorporate the data validation technique illustrated in Program 5b.

6. **a.** Modify the program you wrote for exercise 5 to process multiple data sets from a Text file containing multiple observations. Use the Pascal editor to create files to test your program. (Hereafter, we will refer to this file as the CRI Observation File.)

   b. Add summary output to the program you wrote for part a. Compute and print the following information:

   - Number of observations with invalid time or data
   - Number of valid observations
   - Average temperature, humidity, and barometric pressure for valid observations.

7. Write a program to categorize the observations in the CRI Observation File by season. (*Hint:* Compute the Julian date for each observation. Look up the Julian dates for the beginning of each season, and use these dates as the criterion. You may wish to adapt the procedures used in Program 7g to compute the Julian date.)

8. Modify the program you wrote for exercise 7 to compute the average Celsius and Fahrenheit temperatures for each season. Incorporate a function to convert from Fahrenheit to Celsius and a second function to compute the Julian date. You may also wish to implement portions of your data validation procedure using a Boolean-valued function.

9. Write a program to analyze temperature data for up to one year from a single reporting station. (*Hint:* Create a two-dimensional array with one row for each date, using the Julian date and one column for each temperature observation.) The program should compute and print the following:

- The highest and lowest temperatures
- The average temperature

- The number of days in which the average temperature was below freezing.

Have the user enter the station identifier for the desired reporting station.

10. **a.** Write a program to transform the CRI Observation File into a binary file. Revise the program that you wrote for exercise 9 to process this file.

   b. Write a program to allow the user to extend the binary file you created in part a.

11. A second file (Station Master File) is needed to store information about each reporting station. For each station, the following information is available:

   - Station identifier (five characters)

   - Name of person in charge of the station

   - Address of the station (street, city, state, zip code)

   Write a program to produce a notification to the responsible person for each invalid observation in the CRI Observation File. (*Hint:* Load the Station Master File into a table. Sort the table on the station identifier variable, and then use an appropriate search strategy to look up the required information.)

12. Modify the program you wrote for exercise 11 to load the Station Master File into a binary search a tree. Modify your search strategy accordingly.

13. Modify the program you wrote for exercise 9 to create a graph of the four temperature observations for any 30-day period selected by the user.

14. Using Unit P14c, write a program to perform statistical analysis on the data in the CRI Observation File. Compute high, low, and average temperatures, barometric pressures, humidity, and wind speed for each date, and then make similar computations for the year.

15. Create an ADT for the binary search tree. Modify the program you wrote for exercise 12 to make use of this ADT.

H.3   CHECKING ACCOUNT SYSTEM

One of the most familiar information systems is the personal checking account. The programming exercises in this section will focus on various aspects of checking account management and related accounting. In the system presented here, we assume that you have a personal checking account that you wish to manage with the help of the computer. We also assume that you wish to perform some simple accounting of the money coming in and going out of the account.

H.3.1   Programming Exercises

Each of the following exercise numbers corresponds to the chapter for which the exercise is appropriate.

2. Write a program to allow the user to enter the following information regarding a checking account transaction. (This information corresponds roughly to a check stub in a check book.)

   - Date (month, day, and year)

   - Current balance in the account

   - Type of transaction (C = check, D = deposit)

- Check number (0 for deposits)
- Transaction amount (For purposes of this exercise, checks will be entered as a negative amount, and deposits will be entered as a positive amount. We will make it possible to enter both as a positive amount later.)
- Tax-deductible flag (Y = Yes, N = No)
- Distribution account (three characters)

The following accounts are supported:

UND	Undistributed amount (not charged to any account)
INC	Income
SAV	Savings
INV	Investment
HOU	Household expense
PER	Personal expense
AUT	Automobile expense
ENT	Entertainment expense
INS	Insurance
TAX	Taxes
MED	Medical/dental expense
MIS	Miscellaneous expense

The program should display the data on screen (and on the printer if desired). The program should also compute and display the new account balance.

3. Modify the program you wrote for exercise 2 to write the transaction data to a Text file. (Do not write the new balance as part of the file.) Use appropriate formatting for both the file output and screen output. Create a separate procedure to perform the required computation.

4. **a.** Modify the program you wrote for exercise 3 to allow deposits and checks to be entered as positive amounts. The procedure that computes the new balance should subtract checks and add deposits to compute the new balance. (Note that the user might enter a check or deposit as a negative amount to correct an erroneous transaction.) Also, translate the account code into an account description when displaying the transaction on the screen.

   b. Write a program to validate the data contained in the file created by the program you wrote for part a.

   - The check number should be 0 for deposits
   - The month should be in the range 1 to 12; the day should be in the range 1 to 31
   - The distribution account should be one of the allowable three-character sequences
   - The tax-deductible flag would be Y or N

   Report all instances of invalid data to the user.

5. Revise the program that you wrote for exercise 4b to use procedures with parameters to perform the required computation and to validate each of the items in the data set.

6. **a**. Write a program to allow the user to enter data regarding multiple checking account transactions. The data for each transaction is similar to that described in exercise 2, except that you will omit the current balance and the transaction amount will normally be positive for both checks and deposits. Be sure to validate the data as described in exercise 4b. (We will refer to this file as the Checking Transaction File hereafter.)

b. Write a program to create a transaction register based on the Checking Transaction File created in part a. The user should enter the account balance at the beginning of the period and the name of the file to be processed. The program should create a report listing each transaction and the account balance as a result of each transaction. Include summary statistics, such as the number of checks and deposits and the total amount of the checks and deposits.

7. Write a program to summarize the transactions in a Checking Transaction File by distribution account. Use the following classification of accounts:

Income (Account INC)

Asset (Accounts SAV and INV)

Expense (Accounts HOU through MIS)

Undistributed (Account UND)

The program should produce an appropriately formatted report showing the total amounts of transactions for each account category. The report should also list the totals of all taxable and nontaxable transactions for each account category.

8. Modify the program you wrote for exercise 6a to make use of Boolean-valued functions in place of procedures to perform the data validation tasks.

9. Write a program to analyze the transactions in a Checking Transaction File by date and distribution account. The desired output is a report showing the total amount and number of transactions for each day in the year and similar information for each distribution account. (*Hint:* Convert the date to a Julian date. Convert each account code to an integer, and use arrays of counters and accumulators. Do not list dates for which the totals are zero on you report.)

10. a. Revise the program you wrote for exercise 6a to create a binary file. Add an option to allow the user to create a new file or extend an existing file.

b. Revise the program you wrote for exercise 6b to process the new version of the file.

11. a. A second file (Account Master File) is needed to store information about each account. For each account, the following information is available:

- Account identifier (three characters)
- Account description
- Balance (should be zero at the beginning of each year)

In addition to the distribution accounts, there is a record in this file for the checking account itself. The identifier for this account is CHE. Modify the program you wrote for exercise 6b or exercise 10b to look up the beginning checking account balance in the Account Master File, rather than having the user enter this amount interactively. Also, look up the account description for each account identifier. Include this description, rather than the account identifier, in the report. (*Hint:* Load the content of the Account Master File into a table, sort it on the account identifier, and then use an appropriate search technique.)

b. For each transaction processed by the program you wrote for part a, update the appropriate account balance. When all transactions have been processed, write the content of the table to a new Account Master File. (Give the file a different name so as not to overwrite the existing file. This file will be used as the basis for generating the next check register.)

12. Modify the program you wrote for exercise 11 to load the Account Master File into a linked list data structure. Modify you search accordingly.

13. Modify the program you wrote for exercise 9 to produce a bar graph showing the account balances.

14. Modify the procedures in Unit P14c to perform calculation with Real data. Use this modified unit to perform an appropriate statistical analysis of the transactions in a Checking Transaction File.

15. Modify the program you wrote for exercise 12 to make use of the sorted list ADT described in Chapter 15.

Time-Out Answers

Answer 2.1.1

1. **(a)** valid
   (b) invalid, apostrophe in identifier
   (c) valid
   (d) invalid, first character is numeric
   (e) valid
   (f) invalid, contains spaces
   (g) valid
   (h) valid
   (i) valid

2. **(a)** valid number
   (b) valid string
   (c) invalid string, missing quote
   (d) valid number
   (e) valid number (note use of − to indicate a negative value)
   (f) valid number (note use of + to indicate a positive value; this number is equal to 14 without the plus sign)
   (g) valid string
   (h) invalid string; use single quotes, not double quotes

3. **(a)** `NumberOfDays`
   (b) `Cost`
   (c) `RateOfPay`
   (d) `PayRate1` (Actually, this one is a matter of taste, but it seems more logical to call the variables `PayRate1`, `PayRate2`, etc., than `FirstPayRate`, `SecondPayRate`, and so forth.)

Answer 2.2.1

1. `const`

   ```
        HoursPerWeek = 40;
        MinimumRateOfPay = 3.35;
   ```

2. `const`

   ```
        SchoolName = '--------------------';
        SchoolLocation = '-------------------------';
   ```

3. `var`

   ```
        Length, Width     : Real;
        NumberOfRectangles :   Integer;
   ```

4. `var`

   ```
        CompanyName      :  string[15];
        StreetAddress    :  string[20];
        City             :  string[10];
        State            :  string[2];
        Zip              :  Integer;
   ```

Answer 2.3.1

1. **(a)** Integer
   (b) Real
   (c) Invalid, must have leading digit: −0.0056
   (d) Real
   (e) Invalid, embedded comma; and if the comma is removed, the number 98700 is too big for an Integer.
   (f) Real; an equivalent is 30000.0

(g) Invalid, must not have decimal point in exponent; a correct way to write this constant would be 2.3E3, which is equivalent to 2300.0.

(h) Invalid, no space allowed before the E; a correct way to write this constant would be 3E4, which is equivalent to 30000.0.

(i) Invalid, the largest Integer is 32767.

(j) Invalid, requires decimal digit.

(k) Invalid, the value is larger than 1E38.

(l) Valid, this is equivalent to 40000.0.

2. (a) Valid, length is 17.

(b) Valid, length is 6.

(c) Invalid, missing quote at end of string.

(d) Invalid, missing quote at beginning of string.

(e) Valid, this is the null string with length 0.

(f) Valid, this string contains one character—a space—and hence has length 1.

Answer 2.4.1

This program segment violates the fundamental law of identifiers because the definition of the constant Z refers to an identifier that has not yet been defined. The program could be corrected as follows:

```
const
    X = 12;
    Y = X;
    W = 2;
    Z = W;
```

Answer 2.5.1

1. The Readln statement is not advisable, because the user would have to type exactly 20 characters for Name before typing the Address. It would be better to use two Readln statements—one for reading Name and one for reading Address.

2. `Readln (PreviousMeterReading, PresentMeterReading)`

3. Some alternative ways are 0.03, 0.3E-1, 3E-2.

4. If you make an error in data entry before you press Enter, then use the backspace key to back up to the incorrect character, make the correction, and continue. If you discover the error after you have pressed Enter, you must rerun the program.

Answer 2.7.1 (Selected Exercises)

1. (a) D = 6.4, C = 2, E = 'Alpha'

(b) D = 23.5, E = ''(null string), statement C: = A is invalid because Real data (A) is not assignment compatible with Integer (C).

(c) E = ' '(string containing one space), C = 2, D = 2.0

2. (a) Use := instead of =.

(b) Incompatible data type; you cannot assign a string value to a numeric variable.

(c) No implied multiplication; correct statement is `C := 3 * (A + B);`

(d) Incompatible data types; you cannot assign a numeric value to a string variable.

(e) The variable must be placed on the left and the expression on the right; correct statement is `C := 2 - 3;`

3. (a) `Celsius := 5 / 9 * (Fahrenheit - 32);`

(b) `Area := 1 / 2 * Height * (Base1 + Base2);`

(c) `Circumference := Pi * Diameter;`

Answer 2.8.2 (Selected Exercises)

3. One acceptable answer is as follows (your answer may be considerably different, but still quite adequate):

    1.0 Get measurements of room
        1.1 Write prompt for Length and Width
        1.2 Read Length and Width
    2.0 Get price of carpet
        2.1 Write prompt for Price
        2.2 Read Price
    3.0 Compute cost of carpet for room
        3.1 Area $=$ Length $\times$ Width
        3.2 Cost $=$ Area $/\ 9 \times$ Price
    4.0 Write input values and computed cost
        4.1 Write Length, Width, Price
        4.2 Write Cost

Answer 2.9.6

1. **(a)** -1.0, Real
  (b) 7, Integer
  (c) 5.0, Real
  (d) 1.5, Real
  (e) 1, Integer
  (f) 1.5, Real
  (g) 1.5, Real
  (h) 6, Integer
  (i) 6.0, Real
  (j) 1, Integer
  (k) -1, Integer
  (l) -2, Integer
 (m) -0.4, Real
  (n) 0, Integer

2. **(a)** `X - Y - Z`
  (b) `2 * (X + Y)`
  (c) `X / Y`
  (d) `X * Y`
  (e) `X - (Y + Z + W)`

Answer 2.9.8

1. **(a)** 2.75
  (b) -10
  (c) 1.5
  (d) -2
  (e) 1
  (f) 2
  (g) 0
  (h) 2

2. **(a)** `A * B - (-3 / D)`
  (b) `2 * (A + B) / (-3)`

(c) ((A + B) / 2) * ((C - D) / 4)
(d) (X - 3) * (X + 4)
(e) (X + Y) / (X - Y)

Answer 3.2.6 (Selected Exercises)

1. (a) 3.6
 (b) 12.96
 (c) 5.0
 (d) 3.6
 (e) 3.0
 (f) −3.0
 (g) 0.6
 (h) 3
 (i) 4
 (j) 3.6
 (k) 3.6
2. (a) Abs (X - Y)
 (b) 3 * Sqr (X) + 4 * Sqr (Y)
 (c) Sqrt (Sqr (X) * Sqr (X) - Y * Sqr (Y))
 (d) Sin (X) - Cos (X)
 (e) Arctan (X)
 (f) Exp (X) - Exp (-X)
 (g) Ln (Sqr (X))
 (h) Sqr (Sin (X))
 (i) Round (X * 1000) / 1000
 (j) Round (X / 100) * 100

Answer 3.3.1

1. Exp (N * Ln (A)) - Exp (N * Ln (B))
2. $\sqrt[3]{x} = x^{1/3}$; Exp ((1 / 3) * Ln (X))
3. Exp ((A + B) * Ln (X))
4. Exp (A * Ln (X)) / Exp (B * Ln (Y))
5. A * Exp (B * Ln (X))
6. Exp ((2 * N) * Ln (X + Y))

Answer 3.5.4 (Selected Exercises)

1. (a) |_|_|_|A|B|C|

 (b) |A|B|C|_|

 (c) |_|_|_|−|1|2|3|

 (d) |−|1|2|3|

 (e) |2|.|3|5|E|+|0|1|

 (f) |_|_|_|2|3|.|4|9|0|

 (g) |_|_|_|_|2|3|.|4|9|

 (h) |−|1|0|0|

Answer 3.7.3

1. **(a)** False
   (b) True
   (c) False
   (d) True
   (e) True
   (f) True
   (g) True
   (h) True
   (i) False

2. **(a)** $\lfloor T_\lfloor R_\lfloor U_\lfloor E \rfloor$
   (b) $\lfloor T_\lfloor R_\lfloor U_\lfloor E \rfloor$
   (c) $\lfloor \_ \_ \_ T_\lfloor R_\lfloor U_\lfloor E \rfloor$
   (d) $\lfloor \_ \_ \_ A \rfloor$
   (e) $\lfloor T_\lfloor R_\lfloor U_\lfloor E \rfloor$
   (f) $\lfloor \_ \_ \_ F_\lfloor A_\lfloor L_\lfloor S_\lfloor E \rfloor$

Answer 3.12.1 (Selected Exercises)

1. $\lfloor 3_\lfloor 4 \rfloor \ \lfloor A_\lfloor B_\lfloor C_\lfloor EOL \rfloor -_\lfloor 3 \rfloor \ \lfloor 2_\lfloor EOL_\lfloor EOF \rfloor$

   File-position pointer

   X = 34, Y = 'ABC'

2. $\lfloor 3_\lfloor 4 \rfloor \ \lfloor A_\lfloor B_\lfloor C_\lfloor EOL \rfloor -_\lfloor 3 \rfloor \ \lfloor 2_\lfloor EOL_\lfloor EOF \rfloor$

   File-position pointer

   X = 34, Y = 'ABC', Z = −3.0

3. $\lfloor 3_\lfloor 4 \rfloor \ \lfloor A_\lfloor B_\lfloor C_\lfloor EOL \rfloor -_\lfloor 3 \rfloor \ \lfloor 2_\lfloor EOL_\lfloor EOF \rfloor$

   File-position pointer

   X = 34

4. $\lfloor 3_\lfloor 4 \rfloor \ \lfloor A_\lfloor B_\lfloor C_\lfloor EOL \rfloor -_\lfloor 3 \rfloor \ \lfloor 2_\lfloor EOL_\lfloor EOF \rfloor$

   File-position pointer

   X = 34, Z = −3.0

5.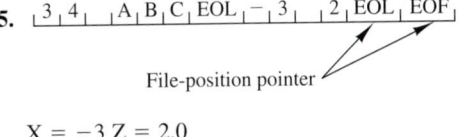

File-position pointer

$X = -3 \ Z = 2.0$

Answer 4.2.1

1. Version 1

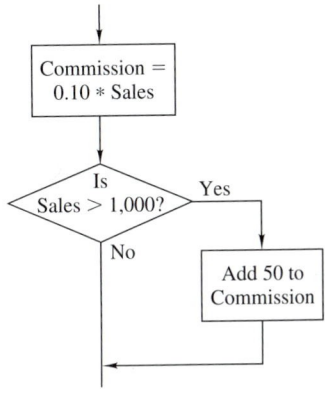

Version 2

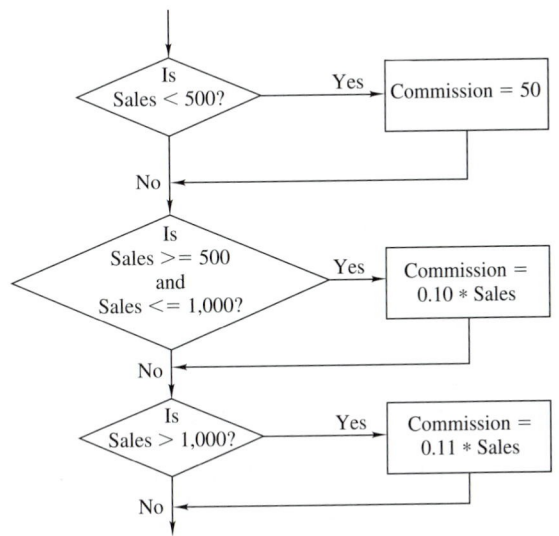

Version 3

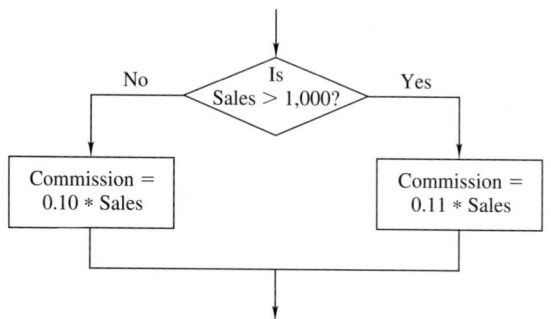

Version 4

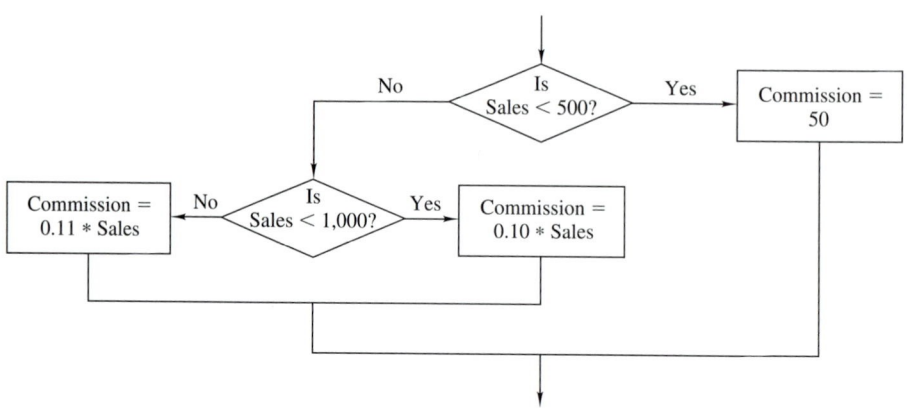

2. If $500 \le$ Sales $\le 1,000$, the execution path will be

                1.0,   2.1,   2.4,   2.5,   2.7,   3.0

If Sales $> 1,000$, the execution path will be

                1.0,   2.1,   2.4,   2.7,   2.8,   3.0

3.   **GRADE PROGRAM**

    1.0 Read TestGrade

    2.0 Assign Letter Grade

        2.1 If TestGrade $>= 90$ then

        2.2   LetterGrade $=$ 'A'

        2.3 End If

        2.4 If (TestGrade $>= 80$) and (TestGrade < 90) then

        2.5   LetterGrade $=$ 'B'

        2.6 End If

        2.7 If (TestGrade $>= 70$) and (TestGrade < 80) then

        2.8   LetterGrade $=$ 'C'

        2.9 End If

        2.10 If (TestGrade $>= 60$) and (TestGrade < 70) then

        2.11   LetterGrade $=$ 'D'

        2.12 End If

2.13 If TestGrade < 60 then
2.14   LetterGrade = 'F'
2.15 End If
3.0 Write TestGrade, LetterGrade

Note: This procedure makes use of a series of mutually exclusive conditions. There are many other ways to construct Module 2.0, including the use of nested If's. The method given here is preferred.

Answer 4.3.1

1. False
2. True
3. False
4. True
5. False
6. True
7. True
8. True
9. False
10. True

Answer 4.3.3

1. True
2. True
3. False (second string is longer than the first)
4. True (all alphabetic characters are greater than numeric characters)
5. False

Answers 4.4.1 (Selected Exercises)

1. (a) **if** SexCode = 'M' **then**
        Writeln ('Male')
    else
        Writeln ('Female');

   (b) **if** PayRate < 7.50 **then**
        Bonus := Bonus + 50;

   (c) **if** (SexCode = 'M') **or** (SexCode = 'm') **then**
        Writeln ('Male')
    else
        if (SexCode = 'F') **or** (SexCode = 'f') **then**
            Writeln ('Female')
        else
            Writeln ('Invalid Sex Code');

(d) if Sqr (A) + Sqr (B) = Sqr (C) **then**
       Writeln ('Right Triangle')
    else
       Writeln ('Not a Right Triangle');

Answer 4.5.1 (Selected Exercises)

1. (a) if A = B **then**
        begin
             C := C + 1;
             Writeln (C)
        end; {*if*}

(b) if A < B **then**
        begin
             C := C + 1;
             Writeln (A)
        end
     else
        begin
             C := C + 2;
             Writeln (B)
        end; {*if*}

(c) if TestGrade > 90 **then**
        begin
             LetterGrade := 'A'
             QualityPoints := 4
        end: {*if*}

2. 1, 2, 3, 4, 6: Yes, a statement follows;
    5, 7: No, statement is followed by end.

Answer 4.6.1 (Selected Exercises)

1. if   (Character >= '0') **and** (Character <= '9') **then**
             Writeln ('Numeric character')
   else if (Character >= 'A') **and** (Character <= 'Z') **then**
             Writeln ('Uppercase alphabetic character')
   else if (Character >= 'a') **and** (Character <= 'z') **then**
             Writeln ('Lowercase alphabetic character')
   else
             Writeln ('Character not alphabetic or numeric');

Implementation of this module with a series of simple if statements would be difficult because, although the three conditions are mutually exclusive, the last outcome represents all other conditions—that is, characters less than 0, characters between 9 and A, and so forth. The multiple selection structure is a natural way to implement this module.

2. if   (A >= B) **and** (B >= C) **then**
            Writeln (A, B, C)
    else if (A >= C) **and** (C >= B) **then**
            Writeln (A, C, B)
    else if   (B >= A) **and** (A >= C) **then**
            Writeln (B, A, C)
    else if (B >= C) **and** (C >= A) **then**
            Writeln (B, C, A)
    else if (C >= A) **and** (A >= B) **then**
            Writeln (C, A, B)
    else if (C >= B) **and** (B >= A) **then**
            Writeln (C, B, A);

This module will enable you to write out three values in descending sequences—from largest to smallest. The conditions are not mutually exclusive, because of the equal-to case. For example, if all three values are equal, all six conditions are true.

Answer 4.7.2 (Selected Exercises)

1. 1, 2, 4, 6: Yes; 3, 5, 7: No
2. (a) 1
   (b) 9
   (c) 10
   (d) 3

Answer 5.2.1 (Selected Exercises)

1. (a) Valid; all parameters specified by variables of the appropriate type.
   (b) Valid; the first and third parameters are value parameters that have values specified using appropriate constants, and the second parameter is a variable parameter that is specified by a variable of the appropriate type.
   (c) Invalid; the data type of the second argument does not match the data type of the second formal parameter.
   (d) Invalid; the second parameter is a variable parameter; its value cannot be specified by a constant.
   (e) Invalid; there must be three actual parameters.
   (f) Valid; the third parameter is of type Boolean; an appropriate way to specify a value for this parameter is a Boolean-valued expression such as the relation R <> 4.0.
   (g) Valid; an Integer expression can correspond to a Real value parameter.

Answer 5.3.2

1. The output produced by procedure Alpha is 4; the output produced by the main program is 3. The value of A is not changed in Alpha, because it is received into a value parameter.
2. The output produced by the program is the same as the input—3 4. Because First and Second are value parameters, changes in their values were not communicated to the main program variables C and D.
3. The value written for E will be 5. The procedure Beta receives the value of E into a value parameter that it does change, but the change has no effect on the main program.

Answer 5.3.4

1. The output produced by Alpha is 4. This procedure changes the value of the actual parameter H, so that the output produced by the main program is also 4. The difference between this program and the one in Exercise 1, Section 5.3.2, is that in this case Z is a variable parameter rather than a value parameter.

2. In this case, because First and Second are variable parameters, the corresponding actual parameters will be changed, resulting in the output 4 3.

3. The actual parameter corresponding to a value formal parameter can be a constant, as in the program in Exercise 3, Section 5.3.2. In the current case, the formal parameter is a variable parameter, which *must* be associated with an actual parameter that is a variable.

4. The output is   Line 1 0A

           Line 2 1Z

           Line 3 0A

Line 2 differs from Lines 1 and 3 because of the assignment statement in Sample6, but because Sample6 has value parameters, no change was made in the corresponding variables in the main program.

5. The output is   Line 1 0A

           Line 2 1Z

           Line 3 1Z

Line 2 and Line 3 are the same because Sample6 now has variable parameters; the changes made in Sample6 by the assignment statements change the values of the associated variables in the main program.

Answer 5.4.1

1.

2.

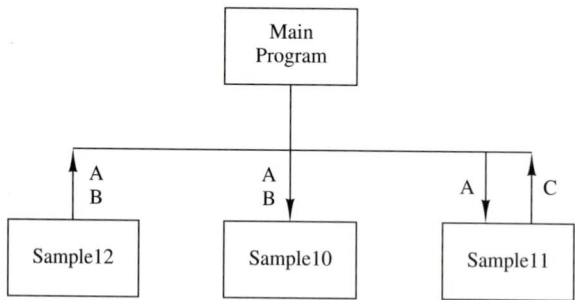

Answer 5.5.1 (Selected Exercises)

2. The procedure to determine whether a year is a leap year would import the year and export a Boolean variable, which might be True if the year is a leap year and False if it isn't. This procedure will be needed twice: once in the procedure ValidateDay and again in the procedure ComputeJulianDate. For this reason, an appropriate placement for the procedure would be as the first procedure declaration of the procedure ComputeJulianDate. In this way, it can be referenced by ValidateDay and by ComputeJulianDate. A possible data-flow diagram for ComputeJulianDate and its subordinate procedures is:

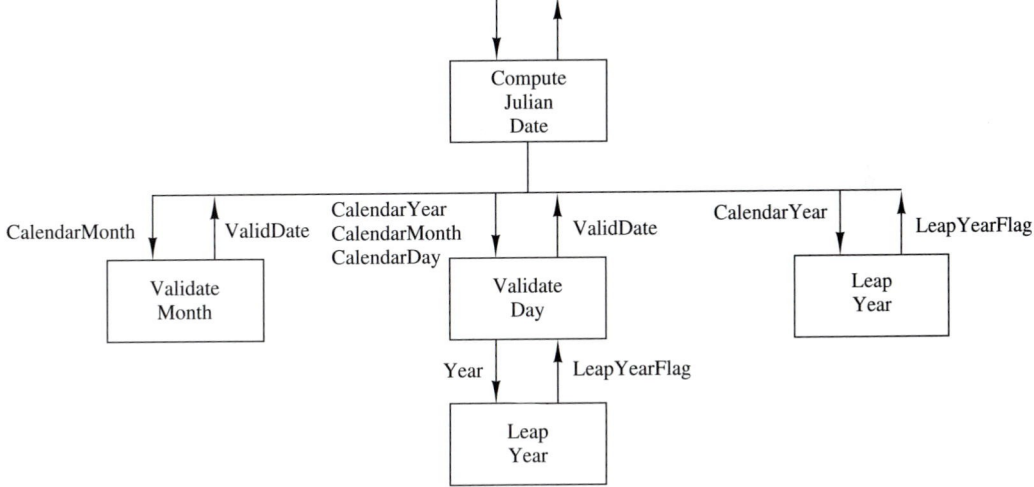

Answer 5.6.1 (Selected Exercises)

1. The data-flow diagram for Program 5c is:

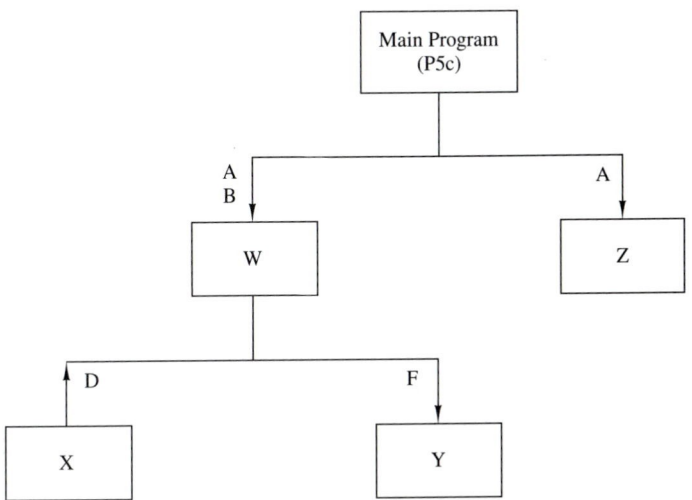

3. The structure of Program 5c in outline form is as follows:

MAIN PROGRAM (P5c)

> **1.0** W
> > **1.1** X
> > **1.2** Y
> **2.0** Z

Answer 5.6.3

1. The identifiers that are valid in each block are:
> Main Program: A, B, C, W, Z
> Block 1.0: A, B, C, D, E, F, G, W, X, Y
> Block 1.1: A, B, C, D, E, F, G, H, W, X
> Block 1.2: A, B, C, D, E, F, G, I, J, W, X, Y
> Block 2.0: A, B, C, K, W, Z

2. Procedure W could not invoke procedure Z because, although they are at the same level, Z is defined after W.

3. Procedure Z could invoke procedure W because they are at the same level in the definition of the main program block and Z is defined after W.

4. Procedure Y could not invoke procedure Z because, although procedure Z is at a higher level, it is defined after the definition of Y.

5. Procedure Z could not invoke procedure Y because Y is not defined as part of the block in which Z is defined. (Procedure Y is local to procedure W.)

6. Procedure X could reference constant F because F is defined in a block that contains X.

7. Constant J is local to Procedure Y. Since X is at the same level as Y, X could not reference constant J.

8. Procedure Z could not reference constant J, since J is defined in a block that does not contain Z.

Answer 5.9.1

1. ComputeJulianDate

Precondition:	CalendarMonth and CalendarDay have Integer values.
Postcondition:	If CalendarMonth and CalendarDay represent a valid date, then ValidDate will be True and JulianDate will be the equivalent date; otherwise ValidDate will be False, and the value of JulianDate will be unchanged.

ValidateMonth

Precondition:	Month contains an Integer value.
Postcondition:	ValidMonth will be True if Month is in the range 1 to 12 and False otherwise.

Wait

Precondition:	None.
Postcondition:	Control returns to next statement in program after user presses <Enter>.

2. ComputeCommission

Precondition:	Sales has a Real value.
Postcondition:	Value of Commission is computed based on value of Sales.

3. OpenInputFile

Precondition:	None.

Postcondition: If user enters the name of an existing file, then the file is opened for input and the variable InputFile is initialized; if user does not enter the name of an existing file, then program terminates.

ReadData

Precondition: GradeFile is open for input.

Postcondition: If file contains data, the values are read and returned to calling program in variables N, S, RT, T1, T2, and T3; if file does not contain sufficient data, program terminates.

Answer 6.2.2 (Selected Exercises)

1. **(a)** Final value of X will be 11.

(b) Values written for Y will be 10, 9, 8, 7, 6, 5, 4, 3, 2, 1, 0. When Y becomes -1, the loop is terminated.

(c) No output is produced, because this segment results in an infinite loop, since the value of X is not changed in the body of the loop.

(d) The output will be   5   5

3   8

1   9

(e) The values of X that will be printed will be 5, 3, 1, -1, -3, ... (The program will enter an infinite loop because the condition $X <> 0$ will always be True.)

(f) No output will be produced because the initial value of the condition $Y <> 0$ is True.

3. The program flowchart equivalent to the while statement is as follows:

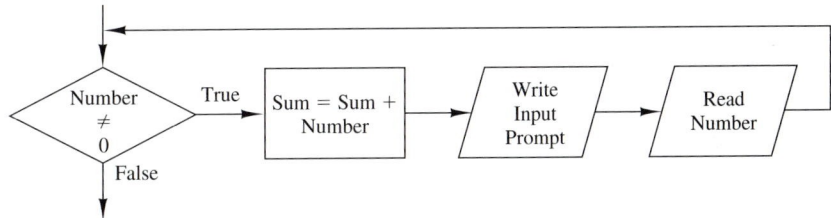

4. Suggested solution:

1.0 Initialize Sum to 0

2.0 Initialize Counter to 1

3.0 Compute sum of five Numbers

3.1 While Counter $<= 5$ Do

3.2   Read Number

3.3   Add Number to Sum

3.4   Add 1 to Counter

3.5 End While

4.0 Write Sum

5. Suggested solution:

1.0 Initialize Sum to 0

2.0 Initialize Counter to 0

3.0 Read Number

4.0 Accumulate sum of Numbers entered by user

4.1 While Number $<> 0$ Do

     4.2   Add Number to Sum
     4.3   Add 1 to Counter
     4.4   Read Number
     4.5 End While
  5.0 Compute and Write Average
     5.1 Average = Sum / Counter
     5.2 Write Average

Answer 6.2.4 (Selected Exercises)

3. A data-flow diagram of GetValidFigureOption is:

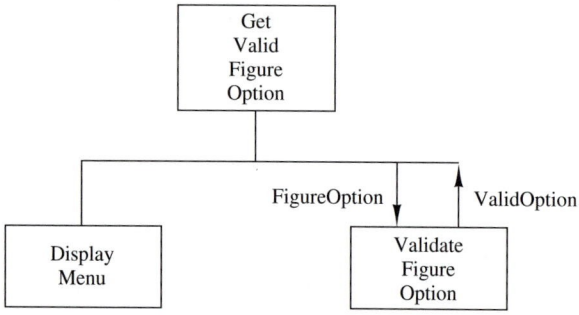

Answer 6.4.3 (Selected Exercises)

1. (a) A = 123, B = −3 Eoln (FileVar) = False

(b) A = 123, B = 89, C = 7, Eoln (FileVar) = True

(c) A = 123, B = −3, Eoln (FileVar) = False

(d) A = 123, B = −3, C = 89, Eoln (FileVar) = False

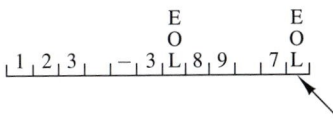

File-position pointer

(e) A = 123, B = 89, C = 7, Eoln (FileVar) = True

File-position pointer

Answer 6.5.2 (Selected Exercises)

1. (a) Output will be 1, 3, 5, 7, 9, 11, ... An infinite loop is created, since the condition will never be True.

(b) Output will be 15, 10, 5, 0. When Y becomes 0, the loop will terminate.

(c) Values assumed by X and Y are summarized in the following table:

X	Y
5	0
4	5
3	9
2	12
1	14
0	15
−1	15

When the loop terminates, the value of Y will be 15.

(d) No output will be produced, because this program segment will result in an infinite loop. The body of the loop does not affect the condition, which is False and will remain so.

Answer 6.6.2 (Selected Exercises)

1. (a) Values of X and Y are shown in the following table:

X	Y
0	
1	1
3	2
6	3
10	4
15	5

(b) Values assumed by X are 3, 2, 1, 0, -1, -2, -3.

(c) Values of X and Y are shown in the following table:

X	Y
1	1
2	2
3	6
4	24
5	120

(d) No output will be produced, because *initial-value* is greater than *final-value*.

(e) No output will be produced, because *initial-value* is less than *final-value*.

(f) The values of X will be 3, 4, 5, 6.

(g) The output will be A

B

C

D

E

(h) The output will be ZX. . . DCBA

Answer 6.10.1

1. Precondition: Value of Sum is 0; value for Number has been entered by the program user.

Postcondition: Value of Sum will be sum of all values entered by the user.

2. Precondition: Value of Number has been entered by the user; Factorial is 1 and I is 1.

Postcondition: Factorial contains the factorial of Number.

3. Precondition: Value of TableLimit is defined.

Postcondition: Required table is written.

Answer 7.3.1

1.
```
repeat
      Write ('Enter sex code (M)ale or (F)emale ');
      Readln (SexCode);
      case SexCode of
              'M', 'm' : SexOfClient := Male;
              'F', 'f' : SexOfClient := Female
           else
                 Writeln ('Invalid Sex Code ')
      end      {case}
until (SexCode = 'M') or (SexCode = 'm') or (SexCode = 'F') or
          (SexCode = 'f');
```

2. Club, Diamond, Heart, Spade

3. **(a)** Invalid; Suit is a data type, not a value to be assigned to Card.

(b) Invalid; Suit cannot have a value assigned to it.

(c) Valid; this statement assigns the value Diamond to the variable Card, which has the appropriate data type.

(d) Invalid; Card cannot store a string value.

(e) Invalid; arithmetic operations are not defined for an enumerated data type.

4. **(a)** True; Heart > Diamond

   (b) True; Heart ≤ Spade

   (c) True; False or True is True

5. **(a)** Club, Diamond, Heart

   (b) Spade, Heart, Diamond, Club

6. **type**

```
      Seasons = (Winter, Spring, Summer, Fall);
```

7. **repeat**

```
      Write ('Enter first character of name of',
                ' manufacturer of car ');
      Readln (CarCode);
      case CarCode of
            'G': Car := GeneralMotors;
            'F': Car := Ford;
            'C': Car := Chrysler;
            'T': Car := Toyota;
            'N': Car := Nissan;
            'B': Car := BMW;
            'V': Car := Volkswagen
            else
                      Writeln ('Unrecognized manufacturer')
      end  {case}
   until (CarCode = 'G') or (CarCode = 'F') or (CarCode = 'C') or
         (CarCode = 'T') or (CarCode = 'N') or (CarCode = 'B') or
         (CarCode = 'V');
```

8. **case** Car **of**

```
      GeneralMotors : Writeln ('General Motors');
      Ford          : Writeln ('Ford');
      Chrysler      : Writeln ('Chrysler');
      Toyota        : Writeln ('Toyota');
      Nissan        : Writeln ('Nissan');
      BMW           : Writeln ('BMW');
      Volkswagen    : Writeln ('Volkswagen')
   end; {case}
```

Answer 7.4.1 (Selected Exercises)

1. The base for IntegerRange is Integer; for FirstHalf it is Char.

2. Valid values for Language are Fortran, COBOL, Basic, and Pascal. Valid values for X are 5, 6, 7, 8, and 9. Valid values for Y are 'A', 'B', 'C', . . . , 'L', and 'M'.

3. This statement assigns an invalid value to the variable X. If range checking is in effect (that is, {$R+}), the program will terminate with an error message. If range checking is not in effect (that is, {$R−}), then the statement will be executed normally as if X were of type Integer.

Answer 7.5.1

1. 2
2. Basic
3. Pascal
4. 90
5. 'F'
6. 1
7. 1
8. 4

Answer 7.6.1

1. 6 (Integer)
2. 4 (Integer)
3. '0' (Char)
4. 48 (Integer)
5. Three (CardName)
6. 'a' (CharSeq)
7. '1' (Char)
8. 97 (Integer)
9. 1 (Integer)
10. 12 (Integer)
11. False (Boolean)

Answer 7.7.1

1. `[2, 4, 6, 8, 10, 12, 14, 16, 18, 20]`
2. `['a'..'z', 'A'..'Z']`
3. `[Dec, Jan, Feb]`
4. **(a)** True   **(b)** True   **(c)** True   **(d)** False
5. **(a)** `Y in [2, 4, 6]`
  (b) `Y in [5..10]`
  (c) `Month in [Mar, Apr, May]`
  (d) `Character in ['a'..'z', 'A'..'Z']`

Answer 7.7.3

1. X contains the empty set
2. Y contains the set `[1, 3, 4, 5]`
3. Z contains the set `['a', 'b', 'c', 'd', 'e']`
4. False
5. True
6. False
7. The value on the right side of the assignment statement is an integer, not a set; the statement X := [2] would be correct.
8. The in relation requires an element of the base type on the left and a set on the right; in this instance, we have a set on the left.

Answer 7.7.5

1. `Y = ['a'..'e', 'A'..'E']`
2. `Z = ['b', 'c', 'd', 'e']`
3. `W = ['a'..'e']`
4. `V = ['a']`
5. `Q = [1..5]`
6. `S = [1..10]`
7. `T = [ ]`
8. `U = [ ]`
9. True
10. False
11. True
12. True
13. True
14. True
15. The relation $<=$ requires that both operands be sets; you could write **if** `'a'` **in** X . . . ; or **if** `['a'] <= X` . . . ;
16. The operation union ($+$) requires that both operands be sets; you could write X := X + `['f']`;
17. Set operations must be performed on sets of the same type; without redefining the set R, there is no way to perform this operation.

Answer 8.1.3 (Selected Exercises)

1. **(a)** `'Turbo is great'`
   (b) `'Turbo Turbo'`
   (c) `'Turbo Pascal'`
   (d) `'Tur'`

Answer 8.1.8

1. `'AND'`
2. `'HN'`
3. `6`
4. `10`
5. `0`
6. `'MARY '`; this is an interesting way to extract the first word in a line of text.

Answer 8.1.10 (Selected Exercises)

1. **(a)** `'JN'`
   (b) `'MARY AND JO'`
   (c) `' JOHN'`
   (d) `'JOHN AND MARY AND JOHN'`
   (e) `'JOHN '`
   (f) `'JO'`

Answer 8.1.12

1. `'    456'`
2. `'  -45.68'`
3. `'    124'`
4. `'  -501.7'`
5. R = −2.789, C = 0
6. D = −12345, C = 0
7. D is undefined, C = 4 (sign as trailing character is invalid)
8. R is undefined, C = 1 (leading dollar sign is invalid)
9.
```
for Character := 'a' to 'z' do
    begin
        Position := Pos (Character, DataString);
        while Position <> 0 do
            begin
                Delete (DataString, Position, 1);
                Position := Pos (Character, DataString)
            end   {while}
    end   {for}
```

A similar procedure can be written to remove all uppercase alphabetic characters.

An alternative and somewhat more efficient routine to accomplish the same purpose could examine each character in the string using string indexing. If that character is not alphabetic, it could be concatenated to a new string, which would start off with a null string value. The following program segment uses this idea:

```
NewString := '';
for Index := 1 to Length (DataString) do
    if not (DataString[Index] in ['a'..'z', 'A'..'Z']) then
        NewString := NewString + DataString[Index];
```

10.
```
Str (RealData:8:2, DataString);
if Copy (DataString, 1, 2) = '  ' then
    Insert (' ' , DataString, 3)
else
    Insert (',', DataString, 3);
DataString := '$' + DataString;
```

Answer 8.4.1 (Selected Exercises)

1. The function header contains a syntax error because the function type is not specified. The logical error arises because the statement part never assigns a value to the function. A correct version of the program is as follows:

```
function Big (A, B : Real) : Real;
var
    Large : Real;
```

```
begin
    if A > B then
        Large := A
    else
        Large := B;
    Big := Large
end;
```

The variable Large in this program is actually not needed; the following program is equivalent:

```
function Big (A, B : Real) : Real;
begin
    if A > B then
        Big := A
    else
        Big := B
end;
```

2.
```
function SumOdd (Number : Integer) : Real;
var
    Sum : Real;
    I : Integer;
begin
    Sum := 0;
    I := 1;
    while I <= Number do
            begin
                Sum := Sum + I;
                I := I + 2
        end; {while}
    SumOdd := Sum
end;
```

3.
```
function Reverse (S : StringType) : StringType;
var
    R : StringType;
    I : Integer;
begin
    R := '';
    for I := 1 to Length(S) do
        R := S[I] + R;
    Reverse := R
end;
```

Answer 9.1.1

1. **(a)** ArrayA will consist of seven elements of component type Real. The subscripts must be Integers in the range −3 to 3. You would visualize this array as follows:

ArrayA[-3] ☐
ArrayA[-2] ☐
ArrayA[-1] ☐
ArrayA[0]   ☐
ArrayA[1]   ☐
ArrayA[2]   ☐
ArrayA[3]   ☐

   (b) ArrayB will consist of 5 elements of component type Integer. The subscripts will be of type Char and can range from 'a' to 'e'. You could visualize this array as follows:

ArrayB['a'] ☐
ArrayB['b'] ☐
ArrayB['c'] ☐
ArrayB['d'] ☐
ArrayB['e'] ☐

   (c) ArrayC will consist of 11 elements of component type Integer. Subscripts will be of type Integer and range from 10 to 20. You could visualize this array as follows:

ArrayC[10] ☐
ArrayC[11] ☐
    .   .
    .   .
    .   .
ArrayC[20] ☐

   (d) ArrayD will contain seven elements of type string[10]. The subscripts must be of type Day— an enumerated data type. You could visualize this array as follows:

ArrayD[Sun] ☐
ArrayD[Mon] ☐
    .   .
    .   .
    .   .
ArrayD[Sat] ☐

2. **(a)** The *component-type* for the array of temperature readings would be Real. Since the readings are hourly over a period of one day, there would need to be 24 elements. The subscript could

be an Integer value ranging from 1 to 24. The required program segment would be

```
type
    TemperatureArrayType = array[1..24] of Real;
var
    TemperatureReading : TemperatureArrayType;
```

(b) This array could have component type Char, since each element would consist of a single character. The index type could be Char as well, and the range would be from 'A' to 'z'. The required program segment would be

```
type
    CodeArray = array['A'..'z'] of Char;
var
    Substitute : CodeArray;
```

The program would then store into Substitute['A'] the appropriate character to be used to encode 'A' and would perform a similar action for each of the other characters in the alphabet.

(c) Two arrays are required, each containing 50 elements. The component type of the state name abbreviation array would be **string**[2], the component type of the state name array would be **string**[20]. The following coding segment could be used:

```
const
    NumberStates = 50;
type
    StateNumbers = 1..NumberStates;
    AbbreviationArrayType = array[StateNumbers] of string[2];
    NameArrayType = array[StateNumbers] of string[20];
```

Note in this case the use of the constant NumberStates in the definition of the *index-type* StateNumbers. In the somewhat unlikely case of more states being added, the program will be relatively easy to modify.

(d) A vector is a sequence of real numbers. Two vectors with a maximum of 10 components could be declared as follows:

```
type
    VectorType = array[1..10] of Real;
var
    Vector1, Vector2 : VectorType;
```

Answer 9.8.1

1. (a) The variable A can be visualized as an array of three rows, each of which contains five elements:

A[1, 1]	A[1, 2]	A[1, 3]	A[1, 4]	A[1, 5]
A[2, 1]	A[2, 2]	A[2, 3]	A[2, 4]	A[2, 5]
A[3, 1]	A[3, 2]	A[3, 3]	A[3, 4]	A[3, 5]

(b) The array B will consist of 11 rows of 5 elements each. In accessing the elements of B, the first subscript can range from 0 to 10; the second subscript can range from 5 to 9. You can visualize this structure as follows:

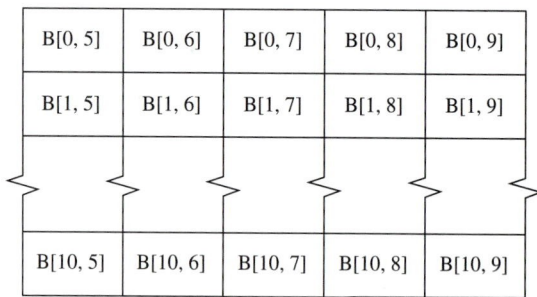

(c) The array C has 26 rows and 10 columns. Each component of the array is of type Char. The first subscript must be of type Char and be in the range 'a' to 'z'; the second subscript must be an Integer in the range 1 to 10. You can visualize this structure as follows:

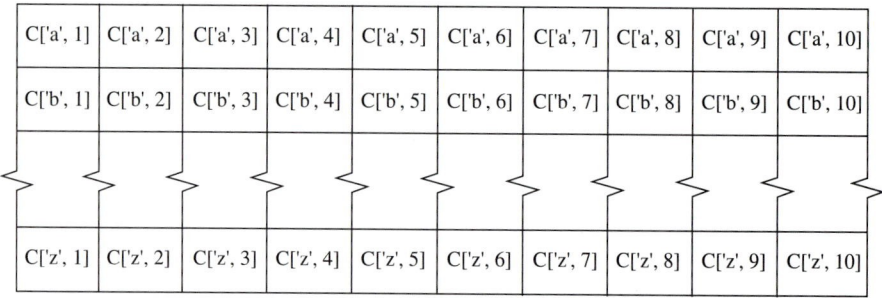

2. (a) `type`
      `Real2DArray = array[1..10, 1..10] of Real;`
   `var`
      `Mileage : Real2DArray;`

(b) `type`
      `Real2DArray = array[1..10, 0..7] of Real;`
   `var`
      `TaxTable : Real2DArray;`

The first subscript would represent the tax bracket, and the second would represent the number of dependents.

(c) `const`
      `NumberStores = 20;`
   `type`
      `Real2DArray = array[1..NumberStores, 1..12] of Real;`
   `var`
      `SalesSummary : Real2DArray;`

An alternative to this declaration could be the following:

const
```
    NumberStores = 20;
```
type
```
    Month = (Jan, Feb, Mar, Apr, May, Jun,
             Jul, Aug, Sept, Oct, Nov, Dec);
    Real2DArray = array[1..NumberStores, Month] of Real;
```
var
```
    SalesSummary : Real2DArray;
```

In this case, the first subscript would be of type Integer in the range 1 to 20; the second subscript would be of type Month. Thus, the sales for store 3 in October would be addressed by SalesSummary [3, Oct].

(d) **var**
```
    Budget : array[1..5, 1..10] of Real;
```

The first subscript would represent the budget category; the second would represent the department. An alternative would be as follows:

var
```
    Budget : array[1..10, 1..5] of Real;
```

In this case, the first subscript would represent the department; the second would represent the budget category.

Answer 9.11.1 (Selected Exercises)

1. **var**
```
    Sales : array [1..4, 1..12, 1..31] of Real;
```

With this declaration, the first subscript will represent the divisions of the company, the second will represent the month, and the third will represent the day of the month.

2. Some alternative ways to make this specification are:
```
    array[1..4] of array['a'..'e'] of array[0..2] of Integer;
    array[1..4] of array['a'..'e', 0..2] of Integer;
    array[1..4, 'a'..'e'] of array[0..2] of Integer;
```

Answer 10.1.1

1. (a) The diagram for this structure is as follows:

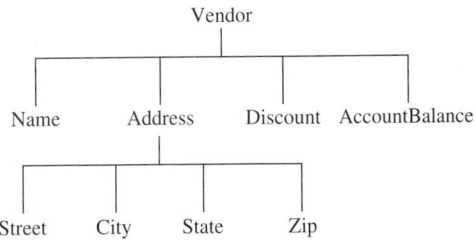

(b)

Reference	Type
Vendor.Name	**string**[20]
Vendor.Address	Unnamed record type
Vendor.Address.Street	**string**[20]
Vendor.Address.City	**string**[10]
Vendor.Address.State	**string**[2]
Vendor.Address.Zip	Integer
Vendor.Discount	Boolean
Vendor.AccountBalance	Real

(c) **type**
```
      AddressType = record
                        Street : string[20];
                        City : string[10];
                        State : string[2];
                        Zip : Integer
                 end;
      VendorType = record
                        Name : string[20];
                        Address : AddressType;
                        Discount : Boolean;
                        AccountBalance : Real
                 end;
   var
      Vendor : VendorType;
```

2. **type**
```
      AddressType =      record
                        Street : string[20];
                        City : string[10];
                        State : string[2];
                       Zip : Integer
                 end;
      VendorType = record
                        Name : string[20];
                        Address : AddressType
                 end;
      DateType =    record
                   Month : 1..12;
                   Day : 1..31;
                   Year : 0..99
                 end;
```

```
InventoryType = record
                    Number : Integer;
                    Description : string[20];
                    Cost, Price : Real;
                    OnHand : Integer;
                    Vendor : VendorType;
                    OrderDate : DateType
            end;
var
    Item : InventoryType;
```

A diagram of this structure is as follows:

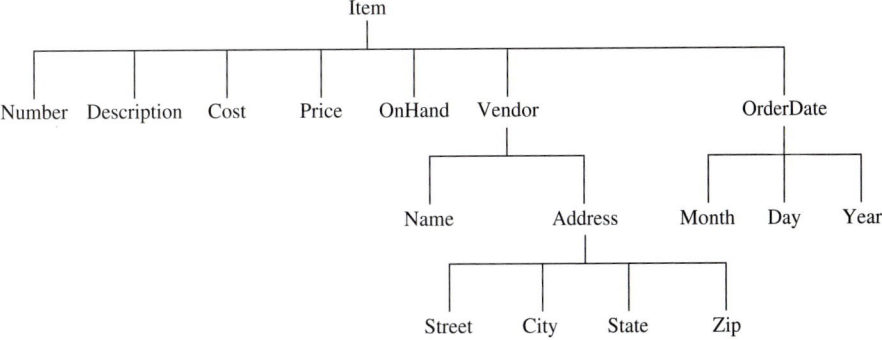

Answer 10.4.1

1. (a) **type**
    ```
    RealFileType = file of Real;
    var
        RealFile : RealFileType;
    ```

   (b) **type**
    ```
    PartRecordType = record
                        Identifier : string[10];
                        Location : string[3];
                        OnHand, OnOrder : Integer
                    end;
    PartsFileType = file of PartRecordType;
    var
        PartsFile : PartsFileType;
    ```

2. (a) Write (RealFile, RealVar);
   (b) Read (RealFile, RealVar);
   (c) Read (PartsFile, PartRecord);
   (d) Write (PartsFile, PartRecord);

Answer 11.4.1 (Selected Exercises)

1.

TableArgument[1]	32	TableValue[1]	Digit
TableArgument[2]		TableValue[2]	
TableArgument[3]		TableValue[3]	
TableArgument[4]	3	TableValue[4]	Widget
TableArgument[5]	25	TableValue[5]	Gidget
TableArgument[6]		TableValue[6]	
TableArgument[7]		TableValue[7]	
TableArgument[8]		TableValue[8]	
TableArgument[9]		TableValue[9]	
TableArgument[10]		TableValue[10]	
TableArgument[11]	21	TableValue[11]	Zidget

6. A technique for detecting a full table involves remembering the starting point at which the search for an unused entry began. If the search ever passes this point again, then we know that the table is full.

LOADHASHTABLE (IMPORT : ARGUMENT, VALUE;
EXPORT : HASHTABLE, FULLTABLE)

```
1.0   Location = Hash (Argument)
2.0   FullTable = False
3.0   BeginLocation = Location
4.0   While TableArgument[Location] not = NullValue and not FullTable Do
5.0       Location = Location + 1
6.0       If Location > TableSize Then
7.0           Location = 1
8.0       End If
9.0       If Location = BeginLocation Then
10.0          FullTable = True
11.0      End If
12.0  End While
13.0  If not FullTable Then
14.0      TableArgument[Location] = Argument
15.0      TableValue[Location] = Value
16.0  End If
```

Answer 12.2.1

1. (a)

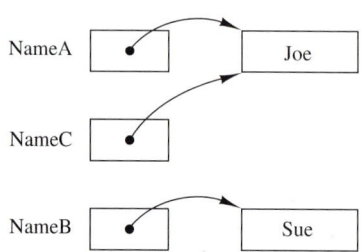

(b)

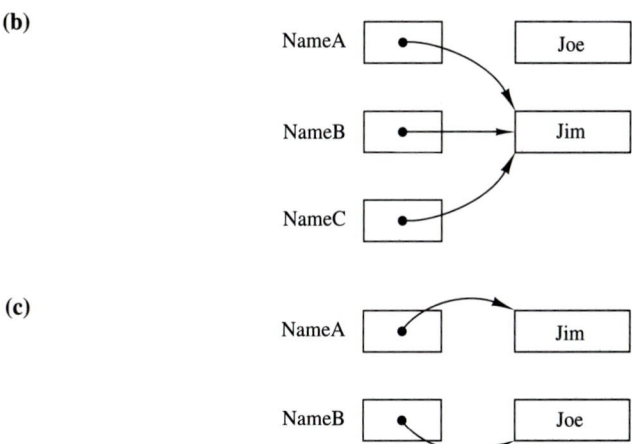

(c)

2. (a) This statement is invalid because the data type of NameA is a pointer and the data type of the expression on the right is string. Assuming that NameA has been defined using a call to New, a correct statement would be

```
NameA^ := 'Joe';
```

(b) This statement is invalid because NameA^ is of type string and NameB is of type pointer. Assuming that NameA is defined, then the following statement would be valid:

```
NameB := NameA;
```

As a result of this statement, NameB and NameA would point to the same data item; the memory diagram would be as follows:

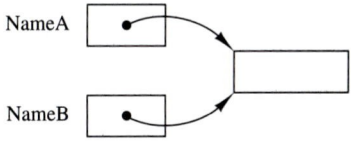

Assuming that both NameA and NameB are defined, then the statement

```
NameB^ := NameA^;
```

would be valid. This would cause the content of the data item pointed to by NameA to replace the content of the data item pointed to by NameB. The memory diagram would be as follows:

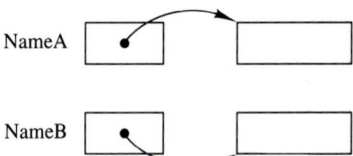

(c) The content of pointer variables cannot be read or written directly. To write the content of the data item pointed to by NameA, you could use

```
Writeln (NameA^);
```

(d) To read a value and store it into the data item pointed to by NameB, you could use

```
Readln (NameB^);
```

(This assumes that NameB has been defined using a call to New previously.)

Answer 12.4.1

1.

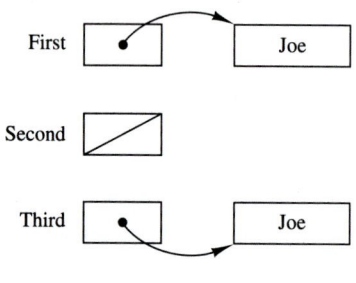

2.

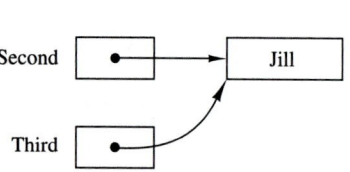

3.

Answer 12.4.3

1. (a)

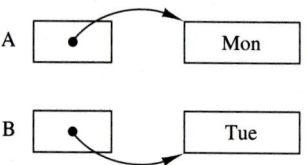

A = B is False, A^ = B^ is False.

(b)

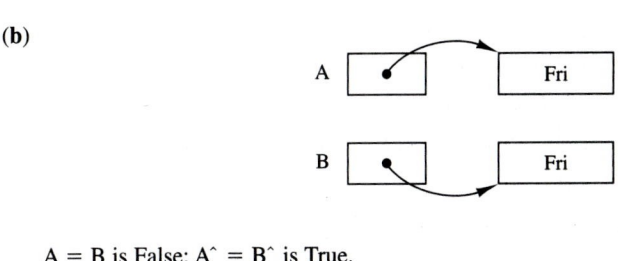

A = B is False; Aˆ = Bˆ is True.

(c)

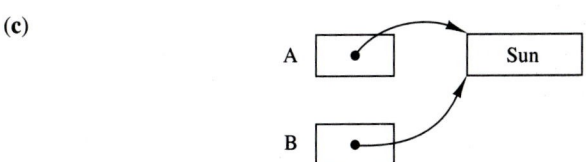

A = B is True; Aˆ = Bˆ is True.

(d)

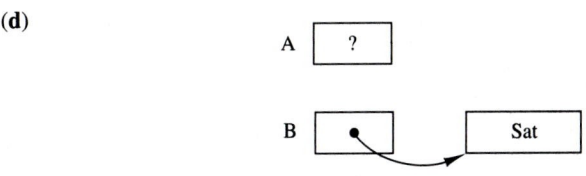

A = B is False.
Aˆ = Bˆ is False.

2. If A = B is True, then A and B point to the same location; therefore, Aˆ and Bˆ must have the same value.

3. If A = B is False, then A and B point to different locations; therefore, the contents of Aˆ and Bˆ may be the same, or they may be different.

4. The expression A = nil will be False after execution of all four segments.

Answer 12.4.5

1.
```
New (AddressPtr);
Write ('Enter Name ');
Readln (AddressPtr^.Name);
Write ('Enter Street Address ');
Readln (AddressPtr^.StreetAddr);
Write ('Enter City ');
Readln (AddressPtr^.City);
Write ('Enter State ');
Readln (AddressPtr^.State);
```

```
Write ('Enter Zip ');
Readln (AddressPtr^.Zip);
```

An alternative to this procedure using the with statement is as follows:

```
New (AdressPtr);
with AddressPtr^ do
    begin
        Write ('Enter Name ');
        Readln (Name);
        Write ('Enter Street Address ');
        Readln (StreetAddr);
        Write ('Enter City ');
        Readln (City);
        Write ('Enter State ');
        Readln (State);
        Write ('Enter Zip ');
        Readln (Zip)
    end; {with}
```

2. The program segment will insert a record containing 'Abe' at the beginning of the list. The memory diagram will be as follows:

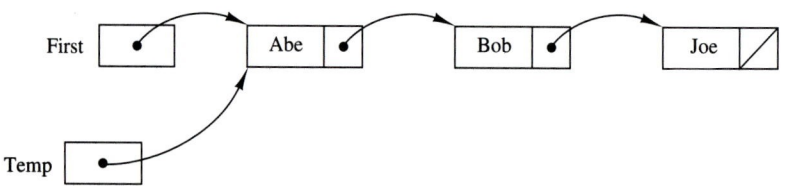

Answer 12.5.1

1. Create space for element.

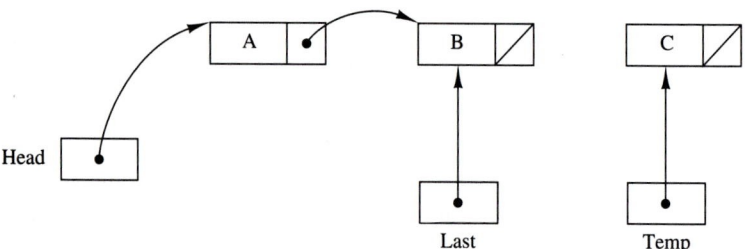

2. Add element to the list.

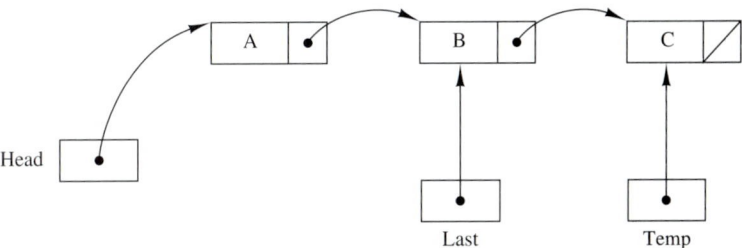

3. Adjust Last to point to the new element.

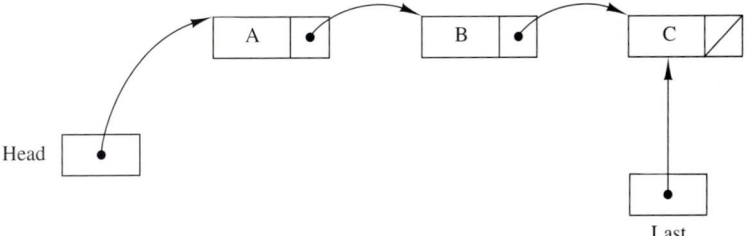

Answer 12.5.3

ALTERNATIVE LINKED LIST TRAVERSAL PROCEDURE

```
1.0   Temp = Head
2.0   If Temp = nil Then
3.0        Finished = True
4.0   Else
5.0        Finished = False
6.0   End If
7.0   While not Finished Do
8.0              Use data at element pointed to by Temp
9.0              If Temp = Last Then
10.0                Finished = True
11.0             Else
12.0                Temp = Temp≧.Link
13.0             End If
14.0  End While
```

Although this procedure is correct (try it with the sample list), it is somewhat more complex than the procedure that uses the fact that the link in the last element has the value nil.

Answer 12.6.1 (Selected Exercises)

2. A pointer Last is not needed because all actions in a stack affect the first element of the list.

3. Because ListStack changes the value of its parameter, the value of Top would end up being nil, thereby emptying the stack.

Answers 12.7.1

1.

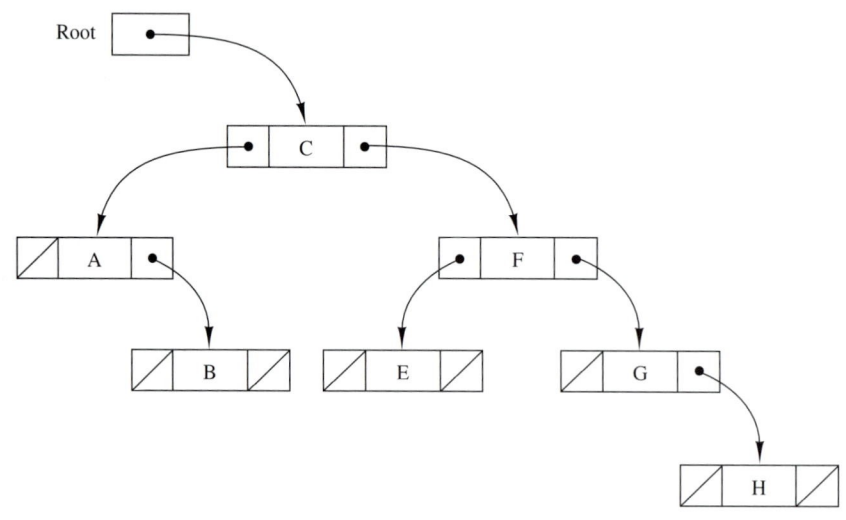

2.

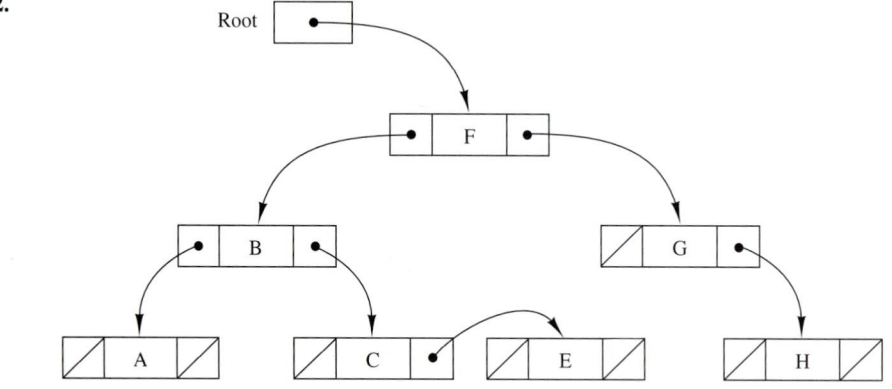

3. The output produced by a traversal of each structure is the same: 'A', 'B', 'C', 'E', 'F', 'G', 'H'.

Answer 13.4.2

1.

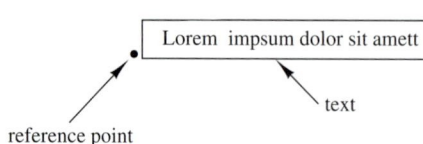

2.

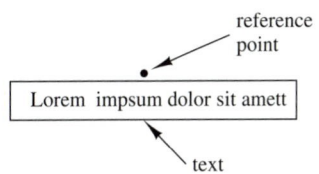

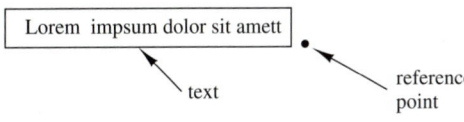

3.

Glossary

Abs Built-in function to compute the absolute value of a Real argument.

Abstract data type A data structure, together with operations that can be performed on the structure.

Accumulation Programming technique in which a variable amount is added to a variable in a loop; variations on accumulation involving other arithmetic operations may also be useful.

Actual argument Particular argument about which the user desires information.

Actual parameter Parameter specified when a procedure is executed.

Actual value Table value related to the actual argument.

Adding operators Addition ($+$) and subtraction ($-$); these operations have lowest precedence.

ADT abbreviation for abstract data type.

Algorithm A procedure that has the characteristics of precision, finiteness, effectiveness, input, and output.

Alpha testing Program testing performed by programmers or other data-processing professionals.

And Logical operation that computes the logical product of two Boolean values; if *expression-1* and *expression-2* are both true, the value of *expression-1* **and** *expression-2* is True; otherwise, the value is False.

Application software Software designed to perform specific tasks related to users' needs.

Arithmetic expression A constant, a variable, or a series of constants and/or variables linked by arithmetic operations and parentheses.

Arithmetic/logical unit Carries out arithmetic and logical operations.

Array Structured data type providing access to a sequence of data elements, all of which have the same type.

Array declaration General form of an array declaration is

```
array [index-type,. . . ] of component-type
```

where *index-type* can be any scalar type (except Real) and *component-type* can be any type (except file).

Array of Char A string is a specialized structure based on a one-dimensional array of Char; in standard Pascal, arrays of Char are used extensively to store alphanumeric data.

Arrays of more than three dimensions The number of dimensions that can be declared for an array in Pascal is unlimited; you can create arrays with four, five, or more dimensions.

Array subprogram parameters When an array is passed to a function or procedure as a value parameter, a copy of the structure is made for use within the subprogram. Because of the additional memory requirements entailed by this practice, arrays are often passed to subprograms as variable parameters, whether or not the subprogram will export values to the calling program via the array.

Assignment statement Statement that causes the replacement of the content of a variable by the value of an expression; the data type of the expression must be compatible with the data type of the variable.

Assign procedure Used to associate a file variable with an external file name; general form for invocation is

```
Assign (file-variable, file-name)
```

Attribute Data item associated with an object class; synonymous with Turbo Pascal *field* in an object data type.

Bar Procedure used to draw a filled rectangle; general form is

```
Bar (x1, y1, x2, y2)
```

Bar3D Procedure used to draw a filled and outlined rectangle with a third dimension; general form is

```
Bar3D (x1, y1, x2, y2, depth, top)
```

Base type The base type of a set, array, or file is the type of each element or component.

Basic units of a computer Input, output, memory, control, and arithmetic/logical.

Begin/end Reserved words used to signify the beginning point and ending point, respectively, of the statement part of a Pascal procedure or compound statement.

Beta testing Program testing performed by representative program users.

Binary file File with a programmer-defined type; general form for creating a binary file type is

```
file of type
```

where *type* can be any type except a file type; binary files are stored using internal binary codes rather than ASCII characters.

Binary search Procedure for searching a sequentially organized table; at each iteration, the size of the table segment that must be searched is halved.

Binary tree Data structure in which each element points to at most two other elements.

Bit-mapped font Characters formed from a square array of pixels.

Blocked access Occurs when a procedure has a local identifier that is identical to a global identifier; the local identifier takes precedence over the global identifier, thereby blocking access to the global identifier.

Body of a loop Program segment controlled by a loop-control statement.

Boolean Standard data type for a variable or constant that will have the value True or False.

Boolean constants True and False.

Boot Process of loading the operating system.

Borland Graphics Interface (BGI) Software supplied with Turbo Pascal to enable programs to produce output on the graphics screen.

Bubble sort Sort procedure in which the largest element is sifted to the bottom of the list by a series of interchanges of the values of successive elements of the list; then the next smallest value is sifted to the next-to-last location in the list, and so forth.

Build Command used to compile a program and all dependent units.

Byte A nonstandard Turbo Pascal data type; represents values in the range 0 to 255; compatible with Integer in assignment and arithmetic operations, but not in parameter lists.

Case list A list of values used in the case statement; if the expression is equal to one of the values in a case list, the corresponding statement is selected for execution.

Case statement Pascal statement that can be used to implement the multiple selection structure; general form is

```
case expression of
    case-list-1 : statement-1;
          .
          .
          .
    case-list-n : statement-n
    else
              statement-list
end
```

Central processing unit (CPU) Control and arithmetic/logical units.

Char A standard data type for a variable that will contain one character.

Character string Series of characters enclosed in single quotes, as in 'Hello'.

CloseGraph Procedure terminates the graphic output and restores the text screen.

Close procedure Terminates processing of a file; general form for invocation is

```
Close (file-variable)
```

ClrScr Standard procedure to erase the content of the screen.

Collating sequence Ordering of characters; the ASCII collating sequence for numeric and alphabetic characters is ' ' < '1' . . . < '9' < 'A' . . . < 'Z' < 'a' . . . < 'z'

Comment Information included in a program as documentation. Comments are enclosed in braces { and } or the character combinations (* and *). Comments may be placed anywhere in a program; they are ignored by the compiler.

Comparing character data Strings are compared from left to right; the first pair of characters found that are not equal to each other defines the relationship between the two strings.

Compiler Program translator that generates a complete, separate machine language program as the result of translating a high-level language program.

Compound condition A condition in which the expression involves one or more logical operators (and, or, not, xor).

Compound statement Pascal statement composed of other statements; general form is

```
begin
    statement-1;
        .
        .
        .
    statement-n
end
```

Computer Electronic device capable of processing data.

Computer hardware Physical components of the computer.

Computer software Programs that determine what the computer does.

Concat Function to perform string concatenation; general form is

```
Concat (string-1, string-2, . . . )
```

where *string-1*, *string-2*, and so forth are string-valued expressions.

Concatenation Literally means "a bringing together"; the concatenation operator for strings is +; forms a string from the two string operands.

Condition An expression with a Boolean value, used in an if statement as the basis for selection among alternative execution paths and in loop control statements (including repeat and while) to determine when to terminate the loop.

Constant Value that will not change during execution of a program.

Constructor procedure This procedure initializes the run-time pointers to virtual methods; usually, the Init procedure is declared as the constructor procedure.

Control break Detection of a break in the sequence of data in a sorted file; used to generate subtotals in a report.

Control commands Commands given by pressing the Control key and some other key simultaneously; numerous control commands are available when you use the Turbo Pascal editor.

Control structures Only the structures sequence, selection, and iteration are required for any programming task.

Control unit Executes program instructions one at a time.

Copy function Extracts a substring from a string; general form is

```
Copy (string, position, number)
```

where *string* is a string variable, *position* is the beginning of the substring, and *number* is the length of the substring.

Counting Programming technique in which a fixed amount is added to or subtracted from a variable in a loop.

Cr/Lf Stand for carriage return and line feed, respectively. These are control characters, which are included at the end of every output line produced by Writeln.

Crt unit One of the standard units; contains procedures and functions relating to reading the keyboard and writing the DOS text screen.

Current Pointer (CP) Pointer to the graphics screen maintained by Turbo Pascal; contains *x*- and *y*-coordinates.

Cursor Symbol on the screen that designates where the next character entered at the keyboard will be displayed on the screen.

Data flow diagram Diagram showing both the flow of control and the passing of data among procedures in a program.

Data storage Arrays and files are used for data storage. Usually, an array designed for this purpose is not completely filled up by the user's data. The size of the array determines the maximum number of data items that can be stored in the structure. The size of a file is limited only by the medium on which it is stored.

Data types Specifies ways of representing and manipulating data; four kinds of data types are simple, structured, pointer, and object.

Declaration of a pointer type Uses the general form

```
^type-identifier
```

where *type-identifier* can be of any type except a file type.

Declaration part Defines constants, variables, labels, types, procedures, and functions.

Delay Standard procedure that causes the program to pause during execution for an amount of time specified as a parameter.

Delete procedure Removes a substring from a string; general form is

```
Delete (string, position, number)
```

where *string* is a string variable, *position* is the position of the beginning of the substring, and *number* is the length of the substring.

DelLine Standard procedure that deletes the line on the screen at the current cursor position.

Descendants Elements pointed to by an element of a tree.

Detect Named constant with value zero; when detect is used as the initial value of the variable that specifies *graph-driver* when invoking InitGraph, the graphics environment will be detected and the appropriate driver will be loaded.

Diagnostic output Temporary output statements used to trace the source of a logical error in a program.

Directory List of files contained on a disk; a directory can be secured from the operating system using the command DIR *d:*, where *d* stands for the drive (A, B, or C), or from the Turbo Pascal Files command.

Disk or **floppy disk** Medium used for storage of programs and data; commonly used with microcomputers.

Disk drive Device used to read data stored on disks.

Dispose Procedure to deallocate data for the pointer variable specified as the parameter for the procedure; general form for invocation is

```
Dispose (pointer-variable)
```

After execution of the procedure, the value of *pointer-variable* is undefined, and the space that was allocated to the data element is freed up so that it can be reallocated as needed.

Dos unit One of the standard units; contains facilities to allow the program to communicate with the operating system.

Driver Software that acts as an interface between a program and a graphics card.

Dynamic memory allocation Memory-allocation technique that allows the program to allocate memory during the execution of the program; items allocated by this technique occupy an area of memory called the heap, which is above the memory allocated to the program by the compiler.

Editor Portion of the Pascal system that allows you to enter and manipulate Pascal programs.

Empty set Set containing no elements; denoted by [ ].

Empty subtree A subtree with no elements; the subtrees of leaf elements are empty.

Encapsulation The concept of bringing together attributes and methods into one entity—an object class.

End-of-line (EOL) Name for the Cr/Lf combination of control codes.

Enumerated data type A type defined by a sequence of identifiers that constitute the elements of the enumerated type; maximum number of elements in an enumerated type is 256.

EOF code End-of-file; signified by Ctrl-Z control code.

Eof function Function that returns True if the File-position pointer points to the end of the file and returns False otherwise; general form is

```
Eof (file-variable)
```

Eoln function Returns True if the File-position pointer points to the EOL code and False otherwise; general form is

```
Eoln (file-variable)
```

Execution path Sequence of statements executed in a program; programs that use the selection structure have multiple possible execution paths.

Exponential notation Method of expressing Real values in a form similar to scientific notation. The symbol E is used to separate the significant digits of the number from the integer representing a power of 10; e.g., the number 12.34 can be represented as 0.1234E2 or 1234E-2.

Exponentiation Can be implemented in Pascal in a variety of ways, but there is no exponentiation operator. A general form for computing x^a is Exp (A * Ln (X)), where X must be positive.

Export Values that are returned by a procedure to the calling program.

Extending a binary file Adding records to the end of an existing binary file.

Field One component of record.

Field reference General form is

```
record-identifier.field-identifier
```

File Structured data type used for storage and retrieval of data.

File extension An optional extension to the name of a file usually used to specify the file's type or usage; Turbo Pascal automatically assigns the extension .PAS to source program files if the user does not specify a file extension when the file is named.

File name Externally defined name used by the operating system to enable a program to access a file; MS DOS file names are made up of four parts: drive designator, path, basic file name, and extension. Only the basic file name is mandatory; default values will be supplied for all other parts of the name.

File-position pointer Internally maintained pointer that points to the next available component in a file.

FileSize function Returns an integer value representing the number of components in a binary file; general form is

```
FileSize (file-variable)
```

FillEllipse Procedure used to draw a filled ellipse; general form is

```
FillEllipse (x, y, x-radius, y-radius)
```

Font Style of characters used in character output to the graphics screen.

Formal parameter Parameter declared in the procedure declaration of a procedure.

Format A facility in Pascal that allows you to control the appearance of a value on an output line. Values of all data types can make use of a field width. Values that are Real can also have the number of decimal places to the right of the decimal point specified.

Format a disk Basic operation performed with the aid of the operating system to prepare a new disk for use.

For statement Loop-control statement that generates a sequence of values; two forms of the for statement are:

Form 1

```
for control-variable := initial-value to final-value do
    statement
```

Form 2

```
for control-variable := initial-value downto final-value do
    statement
```

Form 1 generates an ascending sequence; Form 2 generates a descending sequence.

Forward reference A facility for enabling reference to a procedure before it is actually declared in the program; the general form for declaring a forward reference is

```
procedure procedure-name (formal-parameter-section) ;
forward;
```

Later in the program, the procedure header used for the declaration of the procedure is

```
procedure procedure-name;
```

Frequency distribution Shows how many times each item in a set of data items occurs; an array of counters can be used to create a frequency distribution.

Function Procedure that performs a computation and returns a single value. The argument of the function is specified in the parameter list, which is enclosed in parentheses after the function name. Pascal includes a number of standard mathematical and other types of functions.

Function heading General forms are

```
function function-name: type;
```

and

```
function function-name (formal-parameter-section) : type;
```

where *type* is a type identifier that represents the type of the value to be returned by the function.

Fundamental law of identifiers An identifier must be defined before it can be referenced.

GetMaxColor Function that returns the maximum color number for the current graph mode.

GetMaxX Function returns the maximum x-coordinate.

GetMaxY Function returns the maximum y-coordinate.

GetX Function that returns the *x*-coordinate of the Current Pointer.

GetY Function that returns the *y*-coordinate of the Current Pointer.

Global identifier Identifier for a constant, variable, or other entity that is defined throughout the whole program.

GotoXY Standard procedure that positions the cursor at the X (column), Y (row) position, specified as parameters.

Graph Unit containing procedures and functions used for graphic output.

GraphErrorMsg Returns a description of the error specified in its argument; general form is

```
GraphErrorMsg (error-code)
```

Graphics screen Screen used to display graphic output, as opposed to the text screen, which is used to display character output.

GraphResult Function that returns a value between 0 and -14, according to the result of execution of graphics procedures.

Graph3 unit One of the standard units; allows programs that use the graphics facilities of Turbo Pascal 3.0 to be compiled under later versions of Turbo Pascal.

Graph unit One of the standard units; contains support for producing output on the graphics screen.

Halt Procedure terminates execution of a program; general form is

```
Halt (exit-code)
```

Hard disk Nonremovable disk with greater capacity and faster access speed than floppy disk.

Hash table Procedure for randomizing the placement of entries in a table using a hash function applied to the table argument.

High-level language Programming language related more directly to the way people think and solve problems than to the operations required by a machine.

I compiler directive Used to enable a program to handle input/output errors; in its default setting, {$I+}, an I/O error results in a standard Turbo Pascal error message and program termination; the programmer can set the option to negative using {$I−}, which will allow the program to continue if an I/O error occurs.

Identifier Symbolic name for a constant, variable, label, type, procedure, or function.

If statement Used in Pascal to implement the selection structure; two general forms are:

Form 1   *Form 2*

```
if condition then          if condition then
    statement                  statement-1
                           else
                               statement-2
```

Implementation part Contains the actual code for the procedures and functions described in the interface part, together with other required code; this part is preceded by the reserved word *implementation.*

Import Values that are brought into a procedure for processing.

In Relational operator used to test for set membership.

Inheritance OOP concept whereby descendants of an object class inherit all of the attributes and methods of the parent class.

InitGraph Procedure that loads the graphics driver and sets the graphics mode; general form is

```
InitGraph (graph-driver, graph-mode, path-to-driver)
```

Initialization part Follows the implementation part of a unit and has the same syntax as the statement part of a program; code will be executed before the statement part of a using program; often used to initialize variables defined in the unit.

In-memory compiler Compiler that places the object program in the memory of the computer rather than on disk.

Input unit Transfers data from the outside into the computer's memory.

Insertion sort Sort procedure in which elements are inserted into a new list in such a way that the new list is always kept in sequence.

Insert/overwrite Two basic modes of using the editor; when insert is active, characters are inserted into the midst of existing text; when overwrite is active, characters replace existing text.

Insert procedure Inserts a substring into the midst of a string; general form is

```
Insert (object, string, position)
```

where *object* is the substring to be inserted, *string* is a string variable, and *position* is the position for the insertion.

InsLine Standard procedure that inserts a line on the screen at the current cursor position.

Instance An individual object of a certain class is said to be an instance of the object class; in Turbo Pascal, instances are created when a program declares a variable with an object type.

Integer Data type for values that contain no decimal part; integer values may range from $-32,768$ to $+32,767$.

Integer division The symbol div denotes integer division for two Integer operands; the quotient is an Integer and therefore contains no decimal part.

Interface part Part of a unit that describes the constants, types, variables, procedures, and functions that will be available to the using program; this part is preceded by the reserved word *interface.*

Interpreter Program translator that translates and executes each high-level language instruction as it is encountered.

IOresult function Returns 0 if the preceding I/O procedure is executed normally; otherwise, IOresult returns the number of the error code; function resets the error code to 0, thereby enabling further I/O operations.

Iteration structure Controlled repetition of a program segment.

Justification Vertical and horizontal positioning of text with respect to a fixed position.

KeyPressed Boolean-valued function that returns False until a key on the keyboard is pressed, at which time the value of the function becomes True; usually used to wait until the user presses a key as shown in the following example:

```
repeat
until Keypressed;
```

Leaf Tree element with no descendants.

Length function Returns the actual length of a string; general form is

```
Length (string)
```

where *string* is a string variable.

Line Procedure used to draw a line between two points; general form is

```
Line (x1, y1, x2, y2)
```

LineTo Procedure that draws a line from location at Current Pointer to location specified as arguments for the procedure; general form is

```
LineTo (x, y)
```

Linked list List structure in which each element contains a pointer to its successor in the list; a pointer Head points to the first element in the list.

Local identifier Identifier for a constant, variable, or other entity that is defined for only a part of the program. Constants and variables defined as part of a programmer-written procedure declaration are defined only within that procedure (or any procedure subordinate to it).

Logical operations Operations defined on Boolean values. The logical operations are not, and, or, and xor.

Lst Pascal standard identifier for the printer; when Lst is included as the first parameter in the parameter-list for a Write or Writeln statement, the output is directed to the printer rather than the screen; Lst is defined in the unit Printer.

Machine language Low-level numeric language basic to the internal operation of all computers.

Main Menu Basic screen displaying Turbo Pascal commands.

Make Command used to compile a program and all dependent units that have been changed since they were last compiled.

Memory unit Also called main memory; used to store programs and data during execution of the program.

Menu List of functions and related codes displayed by a program; useful in multifunction programs.

Message Instructions that cause an object to take some action; implemented in Turbo Pascal by an invocation of an object's procedure or function.

Method Action that an object can perform; synonymous with *procedure* and *function,* declared as part of a Turbo Pascal object data type.

Microcomputer Computer based on a microprocessor; also called a personal computer.

Microprocessor Central processing unit on a single integrated circuit chip.

Modulus The operation mod denotes integer remainder after dividing the second operand into the first operand; it is defined only for two Integers.

MoveTo Procedure that changes the current value of the Current Pointer; general form is

```
MoveTo (x, y)
```

Multiple selection structure Program structure that allows the program to select from multiple alternatives; general form for this structure in Pascal is

```
if      condition-1 then
        statement-1
else if condition-2 then
        statement-2
```

```
         .
         .
         .
    else if condition-n then
            statement-n
    else
            statement-m
```

Multiplying operators Multiplication (∗), Real division (/), Integer division (div) and Modulus (mod); these operations have intermediate precedence.

New Procedure to allocate data for the pointer variable specified as the parameter for the procedure; general form for invocation is

```
    New (pointer-variable)
```

Nil Pointer constant used to initialize a pointer variable; the value means that the pointer variable does not point to a data item.

Not Logical operation that computes the negation of a Boolean value; not True is False, and not False is True.

Null string String with length 0; written as ' '.

Object An instance of an object class; synonymous with Turbo Pascal *object-typed variable*.

Object class Combination of attributes (fields) and methods (procedures and functions); synonymous with Turbo Pascal *object data type*.

Object diagram Schematic representation of object classes showing the name, attributes, and methods of each class and the hierarchy of ancestor-descendant relationships among the classes.

Object-oriented programming Programming paradigm in which data and methods for processing the data are combined into one entity called an object.

Object program Machine language version of a program originally written in another language; the original version of the program is called the source program.

One-dimensional array An array accessed by one subscript; a one-dimensional array can be visualized as a linear list of elements.

OOP Acronym for *object-oriented programming*.

Operating system Basic component of the system software that enables users to communicate with the computer and perform routine tasks such as loading and executing a program, formatting a disk, copying data from one place to another, displaying the directory of a disk, deleting and renaming files, and setting the time and date.

Or Logical operation that computes the logical sum of two Boolean values; if *expression-1* and *expression-2* are both False, the value of *expression-1* **or** *expression-2* is False; otherwise, the value is True.

Order of a procedure A measure of efficiency based on the most significant term derived from an analysis of the number of operations required to terminate a procedure; sometimes abbreviated as **O** (*N*), which is read as "Order *N*."

Ord function Returns an Integer value for any ordinal type argument; ordinal value of first element is 0.

Ordinal type A type in which a successor-predecessor relationship exists among elements; user-defined types and all standard scalar types except Real are ordinal.

Output unit Transfers information from the computer to the outside world.

OutTextXY Procedure that produces character output on the graphics screen; general form is

```
    OutTextXY (x, y, text-string)
```

Overlay Portion of a program that may reside on disk or in memory; when a program segment that is not in memory is required, it is copied into memory and replaces a segment that is no longer required.

Overlay unit One of the standard units; contains support for controlling the overlay process.

Packed Pascal allows you to insert the word *packed* before the word *array* in an array declaration, as in **packed array** [1..10] **of** Integer; the purpose is to allow the compiler to optimize use of memory. Turbo Pascal allows you to use the packed option, but it is ignored, since all array allocations are optimized automatically.

Parallel arrays Corresponding elements of two or more arrays are used to store data about a single entity. Parallel arrays are often required because the elements of a given array must be of the same type.

Parameter declaration Used in the *formal-parameter-section* of the procedure declaration of a procedure that will be invoked with parameters.

Pascal A high-level programming language originally designed by Nicklaus Wirth.

Period Delimiter used at the end of every Pascal program.

Pi Standard identifier for the constant 3.1415926536.

PieSlice Procedure used to draw a sector of a circle resembling the slice of a pie; general form is

```
PieSlice (x, y, start-angle, end-angle, radius)
```

Pixel Smallest element on a graphics screen; derived from "picture element."

Pointer Address of a data item; a structured data type in Pascal.

Pointer variable Variable that contains the address for a data item.

Polymorphism OOP concept in which a method is able to take on different meanings, depending on the context in which it is invoked.

Pop Operation of removing an element from a stack.

Pos function Locates instances of a substring within a string; general form is

```
Pos (object, string)
```

where *object* is the substring being sought and *string* is a string variable; function returns an integer value representing the position of the substring if it is found and returns 0 if the substring is not found.

Postcondition A condition that will hold after execution of a procedure if preconditions are true.

Posttest Program structure that tests a condition after execution of the body of a loop; repeat makes use of a posttest

Precedence Governs the order of evaluation of operations in an expression; operations with higher precedence are carried out before operations with lower precedence; operations with equal precedence are carried out from left to right.

Precedence of logical operations Highest precedence is assigned to not; and has intermediate precedence; or and xor have lowest precedence.

Precedence of relational operators Relational operators have lower precedence than all other operators; this makes it necessary to use parentheses in coding compound conditions based on two or more relations, such as

```
(A < B) and (B < C)
```

Precondition A condition that must be satisfied prior to execution of a procedure.

Pred function Returns the value of the predecessor of any ordinal type argument.

Pretest Program structure that tests a condition before execution of the body of a loop; while and for statements make use of a pretest.

Printer unit One of the standard units; contains support for direct output to the printer.

Private part Portion of the declaration of an object data type which contains fields and methods that will not be available to users of the type.

Procedural abstraction The use of procedures to hide the details of implementation (how a task is carried out) from a calling program.

Procedure Separate program segment that carries out some task.

Procedure declaration part Part of a program in which programmer-defined procedures are declared. Procedure declarations follow the declaration of constants and variables.

Program set of instructions specifying what a computer is to do and the order in which the operations are to be performed.

Program-development process Problem definition, program design, program coding, text entry, compilation and removal of syntax errors, program testing, program documentation and distribution, and program maintenance.

Program-development software Software designed to enable users to develop custom-designed programs.

Program flowchart Technique for drawing a diagram of a program; useful for visualizing the flow of control within a program or part of a program.

Program heading Defines program name and program parameters.

Program module Program segment with a clearly defined task and having a single entry and single exit; procedures are often used to implement program modules.

Program-parameters List of files referenced in the program; the standard output file is Output; the standard input file is Input.

Program statement First statement in every Pascal program; used to assign a name to the program and inform the compiler about input and output operations to be included in the program; general form is

```
program program-name (program-parameters);
```

Program testing Use of sample data to verify the correctness of a program.

Program translator Software that translates a program written in a high-level language into an equivalent machine language form.

Pseudocode Preliminary version of a program written in an informal language; used to verify that the program is correct and to serve as a guide for writing the source program.

Push Operation of placing an element on a stack.

PutPixel Procedure used to write a pixel at a specific location on the graphics screen; general form is

```
PutPixel (x, y, color)
```

QuickSort Sort procedure in which a list is partitioned into two parts based on an estimate of the median of the data and then each part of the list is sorted using a recursive call to the sort procedure.

Random function Returns a random number; general form for generating Real random numbers in the range 0 to 1 is

```
Random
```

(no argument); general form to generate Integer random numbers less than *number,* where *number* is an Integer expression, is

```
Random (number)
```

Random number A number that is unpredictable; Turbo Pascal provides the Random Function that generates pseudorandom numbers that have many of the same characteristics of randomness as true random numbers.

Range checking When this feature is active, any attempt to assign a value to a variable outside the range of values that are valid for the data type assigned to that variable will cause the program to terminate with an error message; range checking is activated by {$R+} and deactivated by {$R−}.

R compiler directive Controls automatic range checking during execution of a program. {$R+} means that range checking is to be performed; the option is set to negative by {$R−}. Programmers are encouraged to use the positive setting during program debugging and testing and the negative setting in a production program, because range checking slows the speed of execution of a program.

Readln Statement used to read values of variables from keyboard or other source.

Readln procedure Reads one or more lines from a Text file and leaves the File-position pointer pointing to the beginning of the next available line. When invoked with just the *file-variable,* Readln advances the File-position pointer past all remaining characters and the EOL to the beginning of a new line.

Read procedure Reads one or more components from a file and leaves the File-position pointer pointing to the next available component.

Real Data type for values that may contain a decimal part; Real data contains 11 significant digits and may range from 10^{-39} to 10^{38}.

Real division The symbol / denotes real division; it computes the real quotient for any combination of Integer and Real operands.

Record Structured data type made up of components of a variety of data types.

Record declaration General form is

```
record
      field-identifier-list-1 : type-1;
            .
            .
            .
      field-identifier-list-n : type-n
end;
```

Rectangle Procedure draws a rectangle on the screen; general form is

```
Rectangle (x1, y1, x2, y2,)
```

Recursion Programming technique in which a function or procedure invokes itself; may result in programs that are easy to understand, but always involves system overhead in the form of additional memory or execution time or both. If not done correctly, recursion can lead to an infinite loop during the execution of a program.

Relation A Boolean-valued expression of the general form

```
expression-1 relational-operator expression-2
```

Relational-operator One of the symbols = (equal to), < (less than), > (greater than), <= (less than or equal to), >= (greater than or equal to), <> (not equal to), and in (is an element of; used only in conjunction with sets).

Repeat Loop-control statement that continues execution of a loop until some condition becomes true; general form of the repeat statement is

```
repeat
      statement-1;
            .
            .
            .
   until condition
```

Repetitions of a for loop The number of repetitions of a for loop is | *final-value* − *initial-value* | + 1; this value is computed outside the loop, and the loop is repeated this many times regardless of the values taken on by *control-variable* inside the loop.

Representation of a string In Turbo Pascal, a string is represented as a sequence of bytes; the first byte in the sequence (which is referenced as **string**[0]) contains the length of the string.

Reserved word A word used in Pascal that has a predefined meaning and usage; we follow the convention of writing reserved words using lowercase letters.

Reset procedure Readies an existing file for processing by locating the file and setting the file-position pointer to point to the first component in the file; general form is

```
Reset (file-variable)
```

Resolution Size of a screen expressed as number of columns × number of rows.

RestoreCRTMode Procedure used to change from displaying the graphics screen to the text screen.

Rewrite procedure Readies a file for output; file is assumed not to exist and will be created by the program; general form is

```
Rewrite (file-variable)
```

Root Pointer to the first element of a tree.

Scalar type A type in which all data items are ordered; all standard types are scalar.

Scope of identifiers Identifiers are governed by these general rules:

1. An identifier must be declared before it can be referenced.
2. An identifier is defined only within the block of its declaration.
3. An identifier is defined in any block that is contained in the block where it is declared, but is undefined in an outer block.

Screen memory Memory on a graphics adapter; used to represent content of the graphics screen.

Secondary (auxiliary) memory Device used for permanent storage of programs and data in machine-readable form.

Seek procedure Used to position the file position pointer to any desired component of a binary file; general form is

```
Seek (file-variable, component-number)
```

Selection sort Sort procedure in which a list is searched for the smallest element; that element is then interchanged with the first element, and then the list is searched for the next smallest element, which is interchanged with the second element, and so forth.

Selection structure Fundamental program structure that enables the program to select from alternative actions.

Semicolon Delimiter used at the end of every Pascal statement when another statement will follow.

Sequential search Procedure that entails beginning at the first element of a table and proceeding until the required table argument is located or it can be determined that the argument is not present in the table.

Set A structured data type denoted by enclosing a list of elements in brackets; maximum number of elements in a set is 256; elements may be any ordinal type with value in the range 0 to 255.

Set difference Set of elements contained in one set that are not contained in a second set; denoted by the operator $-$.

SetFillStyle Procedure used to specify the style of fill used for several Turbo Pascal procedures; general form is

```
SetFillStyle (pattern, color)
```

SetGraphMode Procedure used to set the graphics mode and clear the graphics screen; general form is

```
SetGraphMode (graph-mode)
```

Set intersection Set of elements in common to two sets; denoted by the operator $*$.

SetTextJustify Procedure used to specify the justification of character output on the graphics screen; general form is

```
SetTextJustify (horizontal, vertical)
```

SetTextStyle Procedure used to set the font style and size; general form is

```
SetTextStyle (font, direction, character-size)
```

Set union Set of elements contained in either of two sets; denoted by the operator $+$.

SetWriteMode Procedure used to set a parameter that governs whether output from certain graphics procedures are copied or xored to the screen; general form is

```
SetWriteMode (write-mode)
```

Simple data types Basic types that may be used alone or to build more complex types; may be classified as either standard or user defined.

Sort To rearrange data into sequence; either ascending sequence (smallest to largest) or descending sequence (largest to smallest) is possible; ascending sequence is most common.

Stack Type of list in which elements are inserted and removed from the top; when implemented as a linked list a pointer Top points to the first element of a stack.

Standard data types Types supplied by Pascal; Byte, Integer, Char, Boolean, String, and Real are standard types supplied by Turbo Pascal.

Standard identifier Data and procedures provided by Pascal; we follow the convention of writing standard identifiers with the first letter of the word capitalized.

Standard procedures Turbo Pascal includes a variety of standard procedures for input and output, manipulation of strings and files, screen management, graphics, and other tasks.

Statement part Describes actions to be performed by the program.

Status line Line displayed by the editor showing the position of the cursor, the name of the file, and the options in effect.

Stepwise program development Technique for implementing a program a few modules at a time. This technique enables you to test the program one part at a time as each new module is added.

String Data type used for character data.

String data type Declared using the general form

```
string (length)
```

or

```
string
```

where *length* is an integer constant in the range 1 to 255. If *length* is omitted, the value of 255 is assumed.

String Indexing Allows reference to an individual character within a string using the general form

```
string [index]
```

where *string* is a string variable and *index* is an integer expression.

Stroked font Characters made up of line segments resembling strokes of a pen.

Str procedure Converts a numeric value into its string representation; general form is

```
Str (write-parameter, string)
```

where *write-parameter* is an Integer or Real expression that may be followed by format specifications and *string* is a string variable.

Structured data type A type made up of elements of another type or types; set, string, array, record, and file are structured types.

Structure diagram Block diagram showing the relationship among program modules; useful when a program is made up of multiple procedures.

Structured programming Programming technique based on concepts of program modularity, top-down program design, restriction on program structures, and readability standards.

Stub A dummy procedure often used in top-down implementation of a program.

Subrange A list element of the form

```
constant-1..constant-2
```

that can be used in case lists to include all the elements from *constant-1* to *constant-2* in the list; a subrange can be written for any scalar data type except Real.

Subrange type A type defined by specifying the beginning and ending values of a sequence; the base type of a subrange may be any ordinal data type; can contain a maximum of 256 elements.

Subscript Value used to specify a particular element of an array. Subscripts are always enclosed in square brackets [ ].

Substring A sequence of characters within a string.

Subtree Portion of a tree containing an element and all its descendants.

Succ function Returns the value of the successor of any ordinal type argument.

Symbol table Table of identifiers maintained by a compiler; the Pascal symbol table has a tree structure in which each branch corresponds to the identifiers declared in a program block.

Syntax error Error in constructing a Pascal statement; the compiler displays a message that is its best guess as to the cause of the problem and returns you to the editor so that you can correct your program.

System software Software designed to perform routine management functions required by computer users.

System unit One of the standard units; contains types, variables, functions, and procedures supplied with Turbo Pascal that are not part of standard Pascal and are not supplied in the other standard units.

Table argument Portion of a table entry that is used to organize the table and identify the data in each entry.

Table lookup Process of locating information in a table.

Table value Portion of a table entry that contains data related to the argument.

Text file Predefined file type in Turbo Pascal; a file made up of sequences of characters called lines separated by the carriage return (Cr) and line feed (Lf) codes.

Three-dimensional array An array accessed by three subscripts; a three-dimensional array can be visualized as a cube or as a series of two-dimensional arrays. The first subscript designates the rank (which of the two-dimensional arrays in the sequence), the second subscript designates the row, and the third subscript designates the column.

Top-down program design Program design technique in which the program is divided into a series of tasks, and each of these is subdivided into a series of still simpler tasks, and so forth, until the program is completely designed.

TPL File extension used on the Turbo Pascal Library file TURBO.TPL, which contains the units System, Dos, Overlay, Crt, and Printer.

TPU File extension used on the file created by compiling a unit; stands for *Turbo Pascal Unit*.

Traversing a tree Process of following the links of a tree from element to element in a systematic way.

Turbo Pascal Compiler for Pascal produced by Borland International.

Turbo3 unit One of the standard units; allows programs using features of Turbo Pascal 3.0 to be compiled under later versions of Turbo Pascal.

Turbo Vision A package of units first supplied with Turbo Pascal 6.0; provides support for windows, a mouse, a variety of types of menus, and so forth.

Two-dimensional array An array accessed by two subscripts; a two-dimensional array can be visualized as a table consisting of rows and columns. The first subscript designates the row and the second subscript designates the column.

Typecasting A nonstandard Turbo Pascal facility that allows the program to convert from one ordinal type to another; general form is

```
type (ordinal-value)
```

Typed constant Nonstandard feature of Turbo Pascal that allows a program to declare an initialized variable in the constant declaration section; general form is

```
identifier : type = value;
```

Type declaration Used to declare an identifier for a type; general form is

```
type identifier = type;
```

Unary minus The opposite of, as in $-A$; this operation has highest precedence.

Unit A set of constants, types, variables, procedures, and functions that are compiled separately and linked to a program via a uses statement. The term is also used to describe basic parts of a computer, such as the Input unit, Output unit, etc.

Unit header Specifies the name of a unit; general form is

```
unit unit-name;
```

where *unit-name* must be the same as the file name of the source code file.

Unnamed enumerated type An enumerated type specified in the variable declaration section is unnamed; such variables cannot be used in parameter lists.

UpCase Pascal function that converts lowercase alphabetic characters to their uppercase equivalents.

User-defined data types Types tailored to meet the needs of a particular program; subrange and enumerated are two kinds of user-defined types.

Uses Statement specifying that units are to be accessed in a program; general syntax is

```
uses unit-name-list;
```

Val procedure Converts a string representation of an Integer or Real value in internal form; general form is

```
Val (string, variable, error-code)
```

where *string* is a string expression, *variable* is an Integer or Real variable, and *error-code* is an Integer variable; if the value of *error-code* is 0, there was no error; otherwise the value of *error-code* points to the position within string where an error was encountered.

Value of a function Computed within a function using a replacement statement of the form

```
function-name := expression
```

Value parameter Parameter used to make the value of an actual parameter available to a procedure or function; general form of the parameter declaration for a value parameter is

```
identifier-list : type
```

If a procedure or function changes the content of a value parameter, the change is not reflected in the associated actual parameter.

Value typecasting See Typecasting.

Variable Value that may change during execution of a program.

Variable parameter Parameter used to provide a procedure or function with access to the variable specified in the actual parameter; general form of the parameter declaration for a variable parameter is

```
var identifier-list : type
```

If a procedure or function changes the content of a variable parameter, the change is reflected in the associated actual parameter.

Variant part of a record Portion of a record that has different makeup from the rest of the record, depending on the content of a field called a *tag-field*, which is the last field in the fixed part of the record; general form for declaring the variant part of a record is

```
case tag-field : tag-field-type of
    constant-1 : (field-list-1);
              .
              .
              .
    constant-m : (field-list-m)
```

V compiler directive When this feature is set as negative ({$V−}), compiler will accept corresponding formal and actual parameters of any type string-type; default is positive, which means that the compiler will accept only string-type parameters with exactly the same type specification.

Virtual Turbo Pascal reserved word used in declaring a procedure or function in an object type declaration; virtual procedures and functions may be redefined in descendant object types and result in the creation of an execution-time table of pointers to procedures and functions appropriate for each object.

Warm boot Command to load the operating system when the power to the system is on; on the IBM PC, the warm boot command is Alt-Ctrl-Del.

While Loop-control statement that continues execution of a loop while some condition remains True; general form of the while statement is

```
while condition do
        statement
```

With statement Used to simplify field references; general form is

```
with record-identifier-list do
        statement
```

Write A procedure that is similar to Writeln, except that the Cr/Lf control sequence is not included at the end of each output line.

Writeln Statement used to write a line of output on the screen or printer or other file; it can be used to write the values of constants (either string or numeric), variables, or expressions. General forms of the statement are

```
Writeln (parameter-list)
```

or

```
Writeln (file-variable, parameter-list)
```

Xor A Turbo Pascal logical operation that is not a part of standard Pascal; if *expression-1* and *expression-2* have the same value, the value of *expression-1* **xor** *expression-2* is False; otherwise, the value is True.

Index

A

Abs function, 91, 461
Absolute value function, 90–92
Abstract data structure. *See* Pointer(s)
Abstract data type (ADT), 744–48
Abstraction, procedural, 256
Access, blocked, 258–59
Accumulation, 267
  arrays for, 446–49
  programming example, 267–71
Accumulators, 386
Actual argument, 546
Actual parameters, 219
Actual value, 546
Adapters, graphics, 649
Addition (+), 61, 73–74, 77
Address functions, 759
Algorithms, 14–16
Alpha testing, 210
American Standard Code for
  Information Interchange.
  See ASCII (American Standard
  Code for Information
  Interchange)
and operator, 112
Anonymous (unnamed) enumerated data
  type, 344–45
ANSI (American National Standards
  Institute), 16
Application software, 6
Arctan function, 91
Arctangent function, 91, 92–93

Areas of circles, 303–7
Arguments, 220
  actual, 546
  table, 546
Arithmetic expressions, 61, 72–80
  addition and subtraction, 61, 73–74,
    77
  division, 61, 75, 77
  enumerated data types in, 338
  modulus, 75–76, 77
  multiplication, 40, 61, 74–75, 77
  precedence rules for, 77–79
  unary minus, 72, 77
Arithmetic functions, 757
Arithmetic/logical unit, 3
Array(s), 333, 435–39
  base type of, 435
  of char, 475–76
  for counting and accumulation,
    446–49
  for data storage, 449–56
    parallel arrays, 463–67
  debugging and testing, 488–89
  declaration of, 436–39
  initializing or loading, 441
  one-dimensional, 467
  packed, 110
  parallel, 463–67, 506, 569
  as parameter, 458–61
    for subprogram, 456–58
  processing, 461–63
  programming example, 482–87
  of records, 506–9, 569

  of strings, 476–78
  subscripts in, 436, 438
  for table lookup, 440–45
  of three or more dimensions, 478–82
  two-dimensional, 467–75
    processing of, 469–71
Arrow keys, 21
ASCII (American Standard Code for
  Information Interchange), 170
  codes, 781–83
  collating sequence, 170
  files in, 123
Assignment
  of files, 122
  set, 358–62
Assignment statement (:=), 10, 60–66
  fundamental limitation on, 62
  named constants in, 63–64
  string variable in, 63
Assign procedure, 122, 126, 128, 130,
  516
Attributes, 720

B

Bar3D procedure, 683–84
Bar graphs, 482–87, 680, 683–84, 687
Bar procedure, 681
Base type
  of array, 435
  of file, 123, 510
Begin statement, 18, 179
Beta testing, 210
BGI (Borland Graphics Interface), 648